DEVELOPMENT ECONOMICS AND POLICY

Also by David Sapsford

CURRENT ISSUES IN LABOUR ECONOMICS (*editor with Z. Tzannatos*)

THE ECONOMICS OF INTERNATIONAL INVESTMENT (*editor with V. N. Balasubramanyam*)

THE ECONOMICS OF THE LABOUR MARKET (*editor with Z. Tzannatos*)

THE ECONOMICS OF PRIMARY COMMODITIES (*editor with W. Morgan*)

PRIMARY COMMODITY PRICES, ECONOMIC MODELS AND POLICIES (*editor with L. A. Winters*)

Also by John-ren Chen

ECONOMIC EFFECTS OF REGIONAL INTEGRATION IN EUROPE AND NORTH AMERICA (*editor with C. Smekal*)

Development Economics and Policy

The Conference Volume to Celebrate the 85th Birthday of Professor Sir Hans Singer

Edited by

David Sapsford
Professor of Economics
Lancaster University
England

and

John-ren Chen
Professor of Economics
University of Innsbruck
Austria

First published by
MACMILLAN PRESS LTD
Houndmills, Basingstoke, Hampshire RG21 6XS
and London
Companies and representatives
throughout the world

ISBN 0–333–67898–2

A catalogue record for this book is available
from the British Library.

This book is printed on paper suitable for recycling and
made from fully managed and sustained forest sources.

Transferred to digital printing 2000

Printed in Great Britain by
Antony Rowe Ltd, Chippenham, Wiltshire

Contents

Acknowledgements

The papers collected together in this volume were presented at the Conference which was held between 1 and 5 May 1996 at the Grillhof Conference Centre, Vill, Innsbruck, Austria, to celebrate the 85th birthday of Professor Sir Hans Singer. We are indebted to the following bodies for their financial support which made this event possible:

Austrian Ministry of Foreign Affairs
Development Studies Association
United Kingdom Overseas Development Administration
Royal Economic Society
Universities of Lancaster and Innsbruck

In addition, we owe a great debt to many individuals for their help and support in organizing this surprise conference. Our special thanks go to John Shaw, John Toye, Richard Jolly and to Hans Singer's Secretary at the IDS, Caroline Pybus for their invaluable help and support at various crucial stages. Special thanks are also due to Herbert Stocker and Richard Hule for their outstanding help with the organization of the conference. Thanks are also due to Anne Stubbins and Helga Landauer for their help at all stages of the project and to Vidya Mahambare for compiling the index.

Lancaster, England
Innsbruck, Austria

DAVID SAPSFORD
JOHN-REN CHEN

Foreword

The University of Innsbruck is grateful and honoured to host this international conference on 'development economics and policies'. Therefore I would like to welcome you all as participants, speakers and discussants. You followed our invitation from almost all over the world and I hope that these four days in this quiet place surrounded by the Alps will contribute to make personal contacts closer and help to clarify some of the problems of economic development in our more and more globalizing world.

I am very happy that one important reason for this conference is to celebrate the Birthday and to give our high appreciation to the personality and the scientific work of Professor Singer. I remember very well the early sixties, when all the students of economics in Innsbruck had to read and study his 'little book' on *The Role of the Economist as Official Adviser*. From the beginning of his academic career Professor Singer has been concerned to combine in an optimal way theoretical analyses and practical applications. As consultant to many governments and international organizations, especially to the United Nations, he continued the tradition of two of our greatest economists in this century, Keynes and Schumpeter.

The topic of this conference meets Professor Singer's main field of interest, the studies of economic development. Whether within national areas or between countries or even continents, the aim of his studies was to find out how to reduce regional inequality and poverty with instruments of economic policy. In the last twenty years the liberalization and internationalization of national economies have made considerable progress towards a global world economy. Today differences in economic growth and income distribution show patterns of regional inequalities. Therefore more and more consideration has to be given to the determinants of economic growth, especially technical progress, labour qualification and productivity.

I do hope very much that the exchange of scientific knowhow and empirical experiences of this outstanding group of international economists will lead to solid results or at least to a better understanding of the causes of economic inequality and poverty in our world.

Before closing, please let me express my sincere thanks to Professor John-ren Chen, University of Innsbruck, and Professor David Sapsford,

University of Lancaster, who both organized and prepared this conference in an excellent way.

For you all I wish that you will be able to spend some interesting days in Innsbruck with a good combination of work and pleasure.

CHRISTIAN SMEKAL
Rector, University of Innsbruck

Notes on the Contributors

Sartai Aziz   Former Member of the Pakistan Senate

Ahalya Balasubramanyam   Researcher at Lancaster University, England

V.N. Balasubramanyam   Professor of Development Economics at Lancaster University, England

Harry Bloch   Professor of Economics, Curtin University, Perth, Western Australia

Sir Alec Cairncross   Formerly Master of St Peter's College, Oxford, England

John-ren Chen   Professor of Economics, University of Innsbruck, Austria

Trevor Crowe   Research Officer, Queen Elizabeth House, University of Oxford, England

Sam Daws   Formerly Research Assistant, Queen Elizabeth House, University of Oxford, England

Amitava Dutt   Professor of Economics, University of Notre Dame, Indiana, USA

David Greenaway   Professor of Economics, University of Nottingham, England

Hans Jürgen Jaksch   Professor of Economics, University of Heidelberg, Germany

Richard Jolly   Special Adviser to UNDP, New York, USA

Kwan Kim   Professor of Economics, University of Notre Dame, Indiana, USA

Andrew McKay Lecturer in Economics, University of Nottingham, England

Alfred Maizels Senior Associate of Queen Elizabeth House, University of Oxford, England

Chris Milner Professor of International Economics, University of Nottingham, England

Wyn Morgan Lecturer in Economics, University of Nottingham, England

Paul Mosley Professor of Economics, University of Reading, England

Theodosios Palaskas Senior Research Officer, Queen Elizabeth House, University of Oxford, England

Samir Radwan Director: Development and Technical Co-operation Department, International Labour Office, Geneva

Kunibert Raffer Associate Professor of Economics, University of Vienna, Austria

David Sapsford Professor of Economics, University of Lancaster, England

Prabirjit Sarkar Professor of Economics, Centre for Studies in Social Sciences, Calcutta, India

John Shaw Formerly Chief of the Policy Affairs Service of the World Food Programme, Rome, Italy

Christian Smekal Rector, University of Innsbruck, Austria

Nicholas Snowden Senior Lecturer in Economics, University of Lancaster, England

John Spraos Emeritus Professor of Economics, University College London, England

Frances Stewart   Director, International Development Centre, Queen Elizabeth House, University of Oxford, England

Herbert Stocker   Associate Professor of Economics, University of Innsbruck, Austria

Wolfgang F. Stolper   Professor of Economics, University of Michigan, USA

John Toye   Director, Institute of Development Studies, University of Sussex, England

Jon Wilmshurst   Formerly Chief Economist, Overseas Development Administration, London, England

Thomas Ziesemer   Professor of Economics, University of Maastricht, The Netherlands

1 Introduction and Overview

David Sapsford and John-ren Chen

It has been said that anybody who lives long can reach the age of 85. True, but what is important is what they do during this time. There are a few economists who can approach, let alone equal, the achievements of Hans Singer. Indeed, such are Hans Singer's achievements to date that this *Festschrift* is in fact the third such volume to be published in is honour! (See Cairncross and Puri, 1976; and Clay and Shaw, 1986.) Since the appearance of Hans Singer's first publication in 1935, the productivity of his pen has been formidable. This fact is clearly demonstrated by the length, breadth and depth of his list of publications (reproduced in the Appendix) which ran, at the time that this book went to press, to some 98 books and pamphlets, 244 articles and 82 reports to international bodies and governments. As observant readers will have already realized, the length of Hans' publication list exceeds the average length of the papers contained in this volume! While Gladstone supposedly continued to fell trees into his eighties and Bob Hope certainly continued to tell old jokes into his, it is clear that Singer is continuing to publish new papers embodying new ideas well into his eighties. However this list of publications – formidable as it is – fails to do justice to Hans Singer's contributions to international economic life. As Alec Cairncross remarks in Chapter 2 below, there 'are few of the developing countries that he has not visited and still fewer that he has not advised. He must have addressed a wider variety of academics in a wider variety of places about a wider range of subjects than any other economist, living or dead.'

The twenty-seven essays that make up this book were written by colleagues, friends and admirers of Hans Singer and were prepared for a conference convened jointly by the Economics Department at Lancaster University, England and the Institut für Wirtschaftstheorie und Witschaftspolitik at the University of Innsbruck in Austria to celebrate Hans Singer's eighty-fifty birthday. Each of these essays addresses a major topic in the area of trade and economic development on which Hans Singer has himself written and commented extensively.

The book begins with a chapter by Sir Alec Cairncross, who along with Hans Singer studied for his doctorate during the 1930s at Cambridge under the supervision of John Maynard Keynes. Cairncross's essay, which is based on the keynote address that he presented at the conference, begins with an overview of Hans' distinguished career; charting this through Hans's student days working initially under Joseph Schumpeter in Bonn and subsequently under Keynes at Cambridge, through the more than two decades that he spent with the United Nations Secretariat in New York, to his arrival at the Institute of Development Studies at the University of Sussex in 1969, an attachment that has remained to this day. The remainder of Chapter 2 provides an in-depth analysis of the influence of trade upon economic development. Beginning with an incisive analysis of the historical evidence regarding the link between trade and development, Alec Cairncross argues that the international division of labour between the industrial and developing countries can continue to develop to the mutual advantage of both country groups provided that trade between them in manufactures continues to expand. The nature and workings of the link between international trade and economic development has, in many ways, formed a central pillar to much of Hans Singer's work and it is therefore fitting that this volume should begin with a paper which addresses this issue in such a comprehensive manner.

It is by no means easy to classify under a small number of headings the many contributions that Hans Singer has made to scholarship and economic life. Nevertheless, it is convenient to group the papers presented at the Innsbruck Conference under five broad headings, each one of which constitutes an area in which Hans has researched and published extensively.

PART I: THE PREBISCH–SINGER TERMS OF TRADE HYPOTHESIS

One of, if not the, longest-standing hypotheses in the field of development economics is the so-called Prebisch–Singer hypothesis. According to this hypothesis, which was launched simultaneously by Hans Singer and Raul Prebisch in 1950, the net barter terms of trade between primary commodities and manufactured goods have been, and could be expected to continue to be, subject to a downward long-run trend. Over the decades, this hypothesis and the policy implications that follow from it have been challenged from time to time on various (typically, but not exclusively, statistical) grounds. However, in the ensuing debates, the hypothesis seems to have held its own to the extent that nowadays in many, if not most, quarters its validity seems established. There can be few other hypotheses in economics that can claim to have stood the test of time so well!

The Prebisch–Singer hypothesis has, over the half-century since its birth, generated a vast and still growing literature. The four papers contained Part I of this book provide a useful overview of some of the major dimensions of the debate surrounding the hypothesis, together with some fresh contributions. In Chapter 3, the first chapter in this section, David Sapsford and John ren-Chen provide a review of some crucial aspects of the recent statistical debate which has surrounded the hypothesis and present some new (and novel) evidence which they argue offers strong support for the thesis.

One set of issues which has received little systematic attention in the previous literature concerns the adequacy of the various hypotheses put forward by both Hans Singer and Raul Prebisch in order to explain the occurrence of the observed negative trend in the barter terms of trade. In Chapter 4 Harry Bloch and David Sapsford construct a model which is designed to allow one to test directly the arguments put forward by Prebisch and Singer in their seminal papers. The structural model that Bloch and Sapsford present is estimated as a system of simultaneous equations using price, wage and manufacturing mark-up data for the post-Second World War period. The results which emerge from this econometric analysis provide evidence to support the effects suggested by Prebisch and Singer as lying behind the downward trend. The results reported in this chapter suggest that these effects were sufficiently strong to more than offset positive effects on the terms of trade of primary producers arising from capital accumulation and growth in industrial production, thereby providing an explanation for the negative *net* trend in the terms of trade faced by primary producers over the post-war period.

In Chapter 5 Alfred Maizels, Theo Palaskas and Trevor Crowe revisit the Prebisch–Singer hypothesis, arguing that while the hypothesis was originally launched in the context of *vertical* (that is, commodities versus manufactures) terms of trade, the changes that have occurred in the structure of trade since the early 1980s require us to investigate the new issue of the direction of trend, if any, in terms of *horizontal* (that is, developing country manufactures versus developed country manufactures) trade. A recurring issue in the statistical debates which have surrounded the Prebisch–Singer thesis at various times during its life has been the adequacy, or otherwise, of the terms of trade data used for testing purposes, and in this chapter Maizels and his colleagues employ data from two previously underutilized sources: the UN COMTRADE database and that compiled by the Statistical Office of the European Community (EUROSTAT). Derived on the basis of a thorough analysis of these data, the results reported in this chapter indicate that in the context of the primary commodities versus manufactures terms of trade the deterioration faced by developing countries occurred at a substantially greater rate after 1980 than it did during the earlier decades of the post-war period, a conclusion which seems to be in large part borne out also by the manufactures versus manufactures barter terms of trade faced by developing countries.

As noted in Chapter 3, the Prebisch–Singer terms of trade hypothesis has, over the last decade or so, become something of a test-bed for the latest techniques of time-series econometrics. In this context, the particular data series which is invariably used is the aggregate index compiled by the World Bank to cover the period 1900 through to 1986, being derived by aggregating together separate price indices for twenty-four individual internationally traded primary commodities. This data set is analysed in Chapter 6 by John-ren Chen and Herbert Stocker, who present a detailed analysis of not only the behaviour of the aggregate World Bank series but also the behaviour of the twenty-four individual commodity price series that underlie it. In this chapter Chen and Stocker develop a new approach to the testing of the Prebisch–Singer hypothesis centring around a related commodities model. This approach allows the derivation of a set of reduced form equations which are estimated using the method of principal components. To the best of our knowledge, this is the first time that such an approach has been adopted in testing the Prebisch–Singer declining trend hypothesis and it is noteworthy that the results which emerge provide strong empirical support for the hypothesis.

PART II: TRADE STRATEGIES, GROWTH AND DEVELOPMENT

Part II of this volume consists of a collection of four chapters, each of which is concerned with the nature and functioning of the inter-relationships which exist between the character of a country's trade policy and its performance in terms of growth and the pace of its economic development. This is an area where Hans Singer has made very many major contributions, as is amply illustrated in the chapters which follow.

Chapter 7, by David Greenaway and Wyn Morgan, provides a detailed review of the theoretical arguments and empirical evidence relating to the nature and likely strength of the relationship between the orientation of trade policy and economic performance. The classification of any given country's trade policy as being *either* outwardly orientated *or* inwardly orientated is a process fraught with difficulty, as was amply illustrated by the controversy which surrounded the publication by the World Bank of its *1987 World Development Report*, not least because such a simplistic categorization ignores the fundamental fact that a country may be simultaneously operating outwardly-orientated policies in respect of some aspects of its economic relationships with the outside world, while at the same time operating inwardly-orientated policies with respect to others. The nature and operation of trade policies in Korea is often cited as a case in point. Greenaway and Morgan begin with a thorough review of the theoretical arguments which underlie the possible link between trade orientation and the pace of economic development and use this to inform their review of the empirical evidence. This part of their essay concentrates on three aspects of the link. First, there is the influence of exports upon growth, for which they find support, although they do express some reservations here regarding the question of the direction of causality. Second, there is the alleged positive relationship between trade liberalization and growth, and in this regard they are led to conclude that the evidence currently available is mixed and does not offer anything like the strength of support which seems to be assumed in the design and implementation of policy conditionality by the IMF and the World Bank. Lastly they explore the possible existence of a relationship between trade strategy and the pace of economic growth, and while they do recognize that more work needs to be done before firm conclusions regarding this link can be reached, they argue that there appears to be somewhat clearer evidence on an adverse effect of inward orientation than on the favourable impact of outward orientation.

The real world is considerably more complex than the $2 \times 2 \times 2$ world of the trade theorist and one area where this becomes apparent is the design and implementation of mixed and selective trade policy interventions. In Chapter 8 Andrew McKay and Chris Milner recognize this and develop a general equilibrium approach which allows them to shed new light on the trade policy intervention issue. In this chapter they explore the conditions under which the *ex post* outcome of such trade policy interventions might diverge from the *ex ante* strategic intent and investigate the possible role of externalities of the 'learning by doing' sort. McKay and Milner present convincing arguments to suggest that a proper appraisal of the welfare consequences of variations in trade policy necessarily requires a general equilibrium approach. Using such an approach, they demonstrate that the standard textbook conclusions regarding the supposed superiority of free-trade can, under certain circumstances, be reversed in situations where strong 'learning by doing effects' are present in the tradable goods sector of the economy. One implication of this analysis for policy formulation is the need to take proper account of the strength of such learning by doing effects in policy design, although as the authors do recognize, such information may be rather difficult to come by in practice.

In Chapter 9 John-ren Chen provides a detailed analysis of the roles of liberalization and privatization in Taiwan's spectacular growth performance over the post-war period. On many occasions, Hans Singer has argued that the classification of any particular economy as being *either* outwardly orientated or inwardly orientated is a misleading over-simplification because it ignores the fact that an economy can be *simultaneously* outwardly orientated in some spheres of its economic activity and inwardly orientated in others. As already noted, the policies adopted in the South Korean economy over the post-1960 period are often put forward as a case that illustrates this point. In many ways John-ren Chen's detailed analysis of the Taiwanese growth performance provides a further illustration of this point, in that he finds evidence to suggest that over the last thirty-five years Taiwan has adopted both import restricting and export promoting measures. In addition, Chen's analysis also highlights the importance of 'new growth theoretic' mechanisms in explaining Taiwan's spectacular growth performance, in the sense that he finds that the accumulation of knowledge with respect to the conduct of business activity was a crucial factor.

In Chapter 10, the final chapter in Part II of this book, Richard Jolly discusses the concept, pioneered by Hans Singer, of Redistribution with Growth. Richard Jolly traces the origins of this concept back to an ILO mission to Kenya in 1972 in which both he and Hans participated. This chapter documents with clarity how this concept quickly matured from a rather puzzling infant, to a fully-fledged adult (with associated empirical evidence as proof of maturity) through a chain of events which compelled policy-makers to begin to address the fundamental issue of how redistribution could be combined with growth in such a way as to ensure the continuation of that very growth.

PART III: THEORY AND PRACTICE OF DEVELOPMENT

The three chapters that make up Part III of this book address a set of issues that are close to Hans Singer's heart: international inequality, food-aid and the influence of technical progress upon the terms of trade between the north and the south.

In Chapter 11 Kwan Kim examines movements in the international distribution of income and explores the extent to which rapid growth alone can reduce income inequalities in the world economy, in general, and the extent of poverty in the developing countries in particular. In a number of ways this chapter develops the Redistribution with Growth issue introduced by Richard Jolly in the preceding chapter. On the basis of an extensive analysis of the international data, Kim argues that economic growth with equity is central to the achievement of political and social stability over the long term and moreover, that equity must be seen as a prerequisite to sustained economic growth.

Chapter 12, by Kunibert Raffer, explores Hans Singer's many contributions to the issue of food aid and demonstrates how these relate to questions concerning the terms on which trade between the countries of the developed and developing worlds take place, aspects of which are explored in Part I of this book. Raffer explores a range of possible improvements to the existing systems of food aid and argues that triangular food aid may be seen as optimal when seen from the Prebisch–Singer perspective since it has the potential to reduce structural disequilibra between importers and exporters.

In Chapter 13 Prabirjit Sarkar explores further the North–South terms of trade issue. Sarkar constructs a formal model, in the spirit of Kalecki and Kaldor, which illustrates the ways in which alternative mechanisms for the distribution of the fruits of technical progress as between the developed countries of the North and the developing ones of the South can account for the secular decline in terms of trade discussed by both Hans Singer and Raul Prebisch.

PART IV: THE DISTRIBUTION OF GAINS IN THE CONTEXT OF UNEVEN DEVELOPMENT

The six chapters in this part of the book address a range of topics associated with the twin issues of the distribution of gains between borrowing and investing countries and the phenomenon of uneven development, both of which feature prominently in the writings of Hans Singer.

In Chapter 14, the opening chapter of this part, Amitava Dutt considers the phenomenon of direct foreign investment (DFI) from the developed countries to the developing ones and explores the implications of such capital flows for the evenness, or otherwise, of global development. Hans Singer has long warned of the potential detrimental effects of such investment flows upon the developing countries and Dutt explores the implications of DFI for global development, using a simple North–South model. Dutt's analysis demonstrates that the effects of DFI depend crucially on which sectors of the South that Northern capital flows into. If flows occur into Southern sectors producing goods similar to those produced by the Southern domestic sector, the analysis suggests that uneven global development is likely to result. However, Dutt's model demonstrates that in cases where flows of foreign capital increase Southern production of goods that are *similar* to those produced in the North (reflecting recent trends towards the internationalization of production) the occurrence of beneficial effects in the South can not be ruled out.

The question of the distribution of gains between investing and borrowing countries is also central to the issues discussed in Chapter 15 by V.N. Balasubramanyam and Ahalya Balasubramanyam. In this chapter the authors revisit Singer's famous thesis regarding the distribution of gains in the context of trade in services. Given the growing importance of trade in services that has occurred over recent decades this is a welcome analytical development. On the basis of an investigation of the case of India's exports of computer software, they demonstrate how Singer's original thesis (grounded initially in the nature of commodities traded, but subsequently extended by Singer himself to the nature of the countries involved in trade) might be further extended to the case of trade in services.

Central to the issue of economic development in the third world is the question of debt. In Chapter 16 Thomas Ziesemer examines the relationship between debt and growth performance over the long run in the context of a model which, unlike many others currently available in the literature, abandons the small country assumption. Ziesemer's model is specified so as to capture what he sees as the Prebisch–Singer notions regarding the determinants of long-run growth. Central to this model from the viewpoint of long-run growth performance are the twin notions of imported capital and limited export demand. By introducing a spread function into the analysis Ziesemer is able to explore the implications of the 1982 debt crisis for the countries of the developing world.

The prevalence of small-scale agriculture is a fact of life in many of the world's poorest economies and in the following chapter (Chapter 17), taking Peru as a case-study, Hans Jürgen Jaksch develops a model that demonstrates clearly the central role that is played by uncertainty in such sectors.

The remaining two chapters in this section are concerned with primary commodity markets. In Chapter 18 John Spraos provides an elegant analysis of the interest costs associated with the stockpiling of a buffer stock scheme designed to compensate for supply shifts brought about by various natural causes, such as adverse weather conditions or pests. Spraos introduces a new dimension to the conventional analysis by recognizing producers in their capacity as consumers. The exposition of this chapter illustrates quite clearly how the failure of the existing literature to recognize this particular dimension of producer activity can be very misleading and lead to correspondingly misguided policy prescriptions.

In Chapter 19, John Toye provides a detailed critique of the workings of compensation schemes designed to deal with the temporary loss of export revenues experienced by primary commodity producers. Toye provides a detailed discussion of the structure and workings of both the European Union's *STABEX* scheme and the International Monetary Fund's *Compensatory and Contingency Financial Facility* (CFF) scheme. On the basis of this discussion he draws attention to a fundamental problem of such schemes, in that while both were designed to deal with *temporary* falls in the export revenues of developing countries caused by short-run interruptions in domestic supplies, the reality of the situation has been that many of the commodity supply problems experienced by eligible countries have turned out to be chronic rather than temporary, with export volumes in many cases declining continuously.

PART V: THE ROLE OF THE INTERNATIONAL AGENCIES

The importance to the international economy of a properly functioning set of international institutions is a central theme in much of Hans Singer's writings. The seven chapters that make up Part V of this book explore various dimensions of the working of the international agencies and offer an array of suggested reforms to improve their structure and performance.

In Chapter 20 Paul Mosley argues for a set of reforms to the World Bank that are akin to an expanded version of its present International Development Association, focused on poorer countries and softer in its financial terms. In Chapter 21 Frances Stewart and Sam Daws argue for the creation of an Economic and Social Security Council at the United Nations, while in Chapter 22 Nick Snowden provides a critical evaluation of the role of the International Monetary Fund as an international lender of last resort in the wake of Mexican peso crisis of 1994. The question of food aid is one close to Hans Singer's heart, and in Chapter 23 John Shaw provides a detailed analysis of the role of the World Food Programme in linking relief and development aid (and action) in a world characterized by an increasing frequency, duration and scale of emergencies. In Chapter 24, Samir Radwan charts Hans Singer's long-standing interest in the relationship between employment and development, beginning with his work in the 1930s on the conditions of 'men without work', through his contributions to the International Labour Office's World Employment

Programme to his recent writings on the issue of employment in a globalizing world economy. Chapter 25, by Sartaj Aziz, considers the problem of poverty, providing an assessment of the constraints faced by policymakers in practice when seeking to alleviate the problem of poverty and proposes a strategy which he argues will allow these barriers to be overcome.

Given the major influences which Hans Singer's work has had upon the formulation of economic policies at both the national and international levels it seems appropriate that such a volume as this should include a contribution reflecting the perspective of the government economist. Such a practitioner's perspective on Hans Singer's many contributions is provided in Chapter 26, by John Wilmshurst.

PART VI: HANS SINGER: STUDENT AND SCHOLAR

The final part of this volume is, perhaps somewhat unusually for a *Festschrift*, devoted to Hans himself; first as student and second as scholar. As already pointed out, Hans Singer began work on a dissertation under the supervision of Joseph Schumpeter at Bonn University in the early 1930s. However, events in that country were soon to overtake both Hans and Schumpeter and to send each on his separate road. In Chapter 27 Wolfgang Stolper, who studied under Schumpeter alongside Hans, provides a fascinating account of their period together in Bonn. This chapter goes far beyond a mere chronicle of events and experiences and provides a sensitive and detailed insight into the personality and life's work of Schumpeter, whose teaching, as both Hans Singer and Wolfgang Stolper freely acknowledge, was to exert such a profound influence upon both economists throughout their long and distinguished careers.

As described by Alec Cairncross in Chapter 2, the tide of events that overtook Europe during the 1930s propelled Hans Singer to Cambridge and Keynes's supervision. It is perhaps fitting therefore that this book concludes with a chapter by Hans himself which explores the modern relevance of his former teacher Keynes to the study of economic development. This chapter is based on the text of a public lecture delivered at the University of Innsbruck in May 1996 shortly before the Conference to honour his eighty-fifth birthday began. In it, Hans Singer argues forcefully that in a variety of ways Keynesian ideas and concepts, including the notion of disguised unemployment, continue to exert deep and lasting effects on development thinking and policy. Hans does not dismiss neo-classical ideas but argues instead that these become relevant only once full employment is achieved and secured. To quote Hans's own inimitable words 'the Keynesian principle of full-employment effective demand comes first. It is the dog which should be wagging the neo-classical tail'.

There can be no doubt that the conference which gave rise to this book was a unique occasion. To experience the simultaneous presence at one gathering of two economists who studied under Schumpeter and two who studied under Keynes, and to share their memories and reminiscences, was a very special experience indeed. As such we feel that the publication of this volume is an appropriate way to celebrate the eighty-fifth birthday of Hans Singer, friend and colleague.

References

Cairncross, A. and M. Puri (eds) (1976) *Employment, Income Distribution and Development Strategy: Problems of the Developing Countries. Essays in Honour of H.W. Singer* (London: Macmillan).

Clay, E. and J. Shaw (eds) (1987) *Poverty, Development and Food. Essays in Honour of H.W. Singer on his 75th Birthday* (London: Macmillan).

2 The Influence of Trade on Economic Development

Sir Alec Cairncross

INTRODUCTION

It is a great pleasure to me to take part in a conference in honour of my old friend Sir Hans Singer. I first met Hans early in 1934 when he was introduced to me by Richard Kahn with an admonition to help him to adjust to life in Cambridge. Two years previously he had embarked on a dissertation on the Kondratieff cycle under Schumpeter in Bonn; but first Schumpter had left to take up an appointment at Harvard and not long afterwards Hitler came to power. Hans abandoned his research and took refuge in Istanbul. There he was offered a scholarship to Cambridge provided by an unknown donor, possibly Keynes, and in due course arrived there, leaving all his books and other belongings behind in Istanbul.

Cambridge was for him, as it had been for me when I first arrived there from Glasgow, unfamiliar territory to which it took some time to get accustomed. In his first days, Hans was a little concerned to see the billboard reading 'Australia collapses'. He was much more deeply concerned when a day or two later a billboard read 'England collapses'. In his ignorance of test match cricket, he wondered if he had been a little rash to forsake the safety of Istanbul for the instability of England.

Gradually, Hans settled in, became a member of Keynes's Monday night discussion club, and began a new doctorate thesis on 'Urban House Rents'. This he brought to a successful conclusion in 1936 when he was awarded the fourth ever Cambridge PhD in economics; that is, it was a degree that had been awarded to only three others, of whom I was one. But while it took me eighteen years to publish the gist of my thesis, Hans has still to publish his.

After graduation, Hans joined Walter Oakeshott and David Owen on a Pilgrim Trust Enquiry into the condition of the long-term unemployed, taking part in the preparation of its Report, *Men Without Work*. I saw little of him in those years but I recall that when he came to see me in Scotland it was in an ancient motor car – inevitably a Singer – and that although it brought him safely up a steep hill to my house, the battery, if I remember correctly, had dropped off the running board.

In 1938 he was appointed to the staff of the University of Manchester and remained there (apart from a brief spell of internment) for much of the war. I remember that in the spring of 1941 he assured me, on the basis of pure logic, not inside information, that Hitler's next move would be to attack the USSR – as he did a couple of months later.

At the end of the war Hans worked for a time in the Ministry of Town and Country Planning (which he thought very ignorant of economic theory, particularly the theory of land values) and followed this with a year at the University of Glasgow. It was at this point that a message arrived from David Owen, by this time Assistant Secretary General of the United Nations, inviting me or alternatively Hans to join him in New York. I was otherwise engaged but Hans was delighted to accept the invitation.

It was a turning point in his career. Over the next fifty years, his life was devoted to the problems of the less developed countries, not as a matter of theoretical study but with a view to devising and urging measures of assistance to those countries. This he did during his twenty-two years on the UN Secretariat, where he became Chief of the Development Section and afterwards at the Institute of Development Studies at the University of Sussex of which he became a Fellow in 1969 and to which he remains attached twenty-seven years later.

In New York he held a bewildering number of posts both in the United Nations and in academic life. In addition to his many duties at the United Nations, he was a visiting professor at a number of universities and colleges. Books, papers, articles, reviews and reports poured out in an extraordinary variety of publications; and after he returned to Britain he continued to prepare a succession of reports to governments and international bodies, often in collaboration with others. He kept popping up (and still does) with some new idea or fresh comment. He is essentially an economic activist – perhaps one should say 'visionary' – full of what he thinks ought to be done, however improbable it may seem that sufficient support for it will ever be mobilized. After all, he did contribute powerfully to get the World Bank and the IMF to take a more elastic and imaginative view of the contribution they could make to helping the developing countries.

Hans's life has been anything but cloistered. He has made frequent journeys half around the world. There are few of the developing countries that he has not visited and still fewer that he has not advised. He must have addressed a wider variety of academics in a wider variety of places about a wider range of subjects than any other economist, living or dead. He has moved from continent to continent, expounding, advocating, and devising strategies of economic development. His influence has been felt as much by word of mouth in the succession of countries where he has lectured as through the pile of working documents and published papers that survive like a spoor from his travels.

There is a deceptive meekness about Hans, an even-tempered mildness of manner and modesty in debate, that tends to conceal the force of his intelligence and still more of his convictions. He gives the impression of a troubled, uncertain but reasonable man who is used to being contradicted but would not dare himself to contradict. In fact he rarely is contradicted and what he says very often implies a contradiction of somebody else even if he thinks it kinder not to say so. The voice is the voice of sweet reason and the words flow on imperturbably. Just because he expresses himself with such apparent moderation, one has to be on one's guard against an uncritical acceptance of his argument.

TRADE AND ECONOMIC DEVELOPMENT

I now turn to the topic which I should like the conference to consider: the influence of trade on economic development. When I first reviewed this topic in 1961 I found little enthusiasm for an increase in trade as a means of accelerating economic development. On the contrary, what economists have long regarded as one of the most powerful influences on economic development, the widening of markets, and one that interacts strongly with two other major influences – capital investment and technical innovation – was regarded with suspicion and distrust by writers on what were then called 'the less developed countries'. International trade at that time was not a popular engine of growth. Although no one looking back over the last century could doubt the conspicuous momentum that an expansion in exports had lent to the countries in process of industrialization, much of the literature on economic development looked in quite the opposite direction and was full of warnings of the dangers of relying on foreign demand. Let me remind you of some of the arguments which it took many pages even to outline.

First of all, reliance on foreign trade carried with it dependence on external forces not under the control of the indigenous authorities. In under-developed countries such dependence was particularly resented because it was associated with colonialism and the sense of inequality that always accompanies the dependence of the poor on the rich. Whatever the origin or justification of such attitudes, their very existence limited the scope for foreign trade.

Then there was the objection that foreign demand impinges on a limited sector of the economy. In 1953, in thirty of the less developed countries supplying 40 per cent of total exports from those countries, a single product accounted for at least half their export earnings. It looked then as if such a situation might well continue. Moreover in such economies the export sector was rarely the vehicle of rapid innovation in other sectors of the economy. If the export sector was in agriculture it was unlikely itself to be in the forefront of innovation; and if it was in mineral production any gains were likely to accrue to foreigners or be confined to an enclave within the economy.

To make matters worse, foreign demand for most forms of primary produce was inelastic and liable to fluctuate violently; and the average prices paid, according to one school of thought, seemed to be on a continuing downward trend in comparison with the prices paid for imported manufactures. There was also the risk that technology might permit the provision of substitutes for mineral and agricultural products that were capable of manufacture by industrial countries and would limit or reduce the demand for the natural product.

Even at the time, these arguments seemed to me far from convincing. I could see nothing that was necessarily regrettable about dependence on foreign trade. Without inviting foreign influences a country seeking development was unlikely to succeed. It needed foreign equipment, foreign capital and most of all, foreign ideas. As often as not, it seemed to me, it was trade that gave birth to the urge to develop, the knowledge and experience that made development possible and the means to accomplish it.

Whatever one made of the various arguments, the initial issue was whether the market for the exports of the less developed countries was so inelastic that it no longer provided a satisfactory engine of growth. Was their development being cramped by stagnation of the world demand for their traditional exports?

This was not a question to which it was possible to return a categorical answer valid in all circumstances. In the nineteenth century trade had grown fast; foreign markets undoubtedly grew faster than domestic markets. World trade had grown in the early years of the nineteenth century at 7 per cent per annum, in mid-century at 13 per cent per annum and at the end of the century at 7 per cent again. Most of the trade – probably two-thirds – was in primary produce and the great surge in the middle of the century reflected the opening up of countries in the American continent, in Australasia and elsewhere that had vast unexploited resources of land and minerals.

Twentieth-century experience has been very different. First there was a long period when trade showed no net growth at all while world production continued to expand. For example, between the late 1920s and the late 1940s the volume of trade both in primary produce and in manufactures contracted slightly, while world output of primary produce grew by a quarter and of manufactures by over two-thirds. But for the early post-war years growth in world trade regained the normal pre-1914 rate of growth of 7 per cent. The pattern of growth, however, had changed as the nineteenth-century 'countries of recent settlement' became industrialized. What has grown faster has not been the trade of industrial with non-industrial countries but the trade of the industrial countries with one another. Nevertheless the countries that remained under-developed could not complain that world trade was not expanding rapidly; it was expanding in the 1950s as fast as it had ever done except in the thirty years following the repeal of the Corn Laws in 1845.

I saw no reason in 1961 to think that the less developed countries in the 1950s were lagging badly in export performance. Each of the poorest continents of the world – Africa, Asia and Latin America – had a larger share of world exports in 1953 than in 1913. Indeed their total exports of primary produce, which in 1913 had been only half the corresponding total for the three richest continents – North America, Europe and Australia – had almost overhauled it by 1953. The big difference was in manufactures, exports of which from the poorer countries were almost negligible.

This was not because those countries were not producers of manufactures. According to GATT they produced two-thirds of the manufactures they consumed and this proportion was rising. Equally, foreign markets did not take a high proportion of their food and feeding-stuffs – only about one-tenth. But there could be no doubt that they were highly dependent on a very narrow range of exports in most of which they were in direct competition with the more advanced countries. There was everything to be said for exporting agricultural production but what if agriculture proved unresponsive? Might it not be wise to 'turn to a new model of this traditional engine of development and see what could be done through free trade in manufactured goods?' Through international trade it would be possible to remove the limits to the scale of operation that exclusive dependence on the domestic market imposed.

I went on to express my expectation that 'if there were complete confidence that the markets of the industrial countries would remain open, the supply of the simpler manufactured goods from underdeveloped countries would increase by leaps and bounds'. I confessed to some doubts.

I thought it right also to emphasize that the contribution that trade could make to economic development should not be exaggerated. Development, I argued, is not governed in any country by economic forces alone; and the more backward the country, the more this is true. The key to development lies in men's minds, in the institutions in which their thinking finds expression, and in the play of opportunity on ideas and institutions. It happens that the opportunities trade opens up in under-developed economies are in a sector where outlook and institutions are often highly conservative and in which external impulses tend to be dampened rather than amplified before they are transmitted to the rest of the economy. It is true also that the effort of grasping those opportunities may prove too great for a poor and backward country. But this does not justify us in minimizing the opportunities that trade affords or in pretending that they are losing an effectiveness they once possessed.

In the thirty-five years since 1961 exports of manufactures from what used to be called 'the less developed countries' have certainly increased by 'leaps and bounds': at first from a small group of countries in Asia, but in due course from a widening range of countries and in an expanding range of manufactures. My fears of a protectionist reaction in the industrial countries were not without substance and various restrictions aimed particularly at the trade of the developing countries persist. Nevertheless, their exports of manufactures have continued to expand rapidly even in the last twenty years when the industrial countries were left with a growing margin of unemployed resources.

Before I look more closely at the changes that have occurred, I must underline the growing difficulty of treating the developing countries as a single group, sharing common interests and characteristics. The experience of the oil-exporting countries has obviously been very different from that of the oil-importing countries. Even in mid-century petroleum and petroleum products were accounting for between half (in the years 1928–55) and two-thirds (in the later part of that period) of the growth in the total volume of exports from non-industrial areas. In the 1970s the two oil shocks dominated in the growth of world trade in primary produce and even more the growth in exports of primary produce from the developing countries, which increased in the seven years between 1973 and 1980 from $91 billion to $440 billion; that is, nearly fivefold in value terms.

There is a similar contrast between the countries now exporting a rapidly increasing volume of manufactures and those that are still almost entirely dependent on exports of primary produce. But even the latter group differ widely in their circumstances. Some writers single out a list of the *least* developed countries as if *they* formed a coherent group. The fact is that whatever they have in common by such measures as GNP per head or level of industrial production, every developing country is following a pattern of its own and faces the special problems of its peculiar circumstances.

None the less if I am to present to you a picture of the main changes in progress, I cannot avoid dealing in aggregates if only because country details on a comparable basis are very difficult to assemble, and would require a much longer paper.

Let me begin with the growth of world trade over the last forty years. Between 1953 and 1990 exports from the industrial countries grew at current prices by a factor of nearly fifty and the exports of developing countries by a factor of thirty. In volume terms the growth was much less although still extremely fast. In total the growth in those years was twelve-fold and even in the last decade (1980–90) it was close to 60 per cent. There was one and only one post-war decade in which the trade of the developing countries grew faster – in volume terms – than that of the industrial countries and this was the 1970s when, needless to say, the oil producers sold their exports at record prices.

If we go back to 1953 the exports of the developing countries consisted almost exclusively of primary produce; and trade in primary produce, except in the 1970s (and then only in value terms), grew much more slowly than trade in manufactures. The two had grown at much the same rate from 1870 (or earlier) until 1939, exports of primary produce forming 60–65 per cent of the total throughout. But after the Second World War the proportion was neither fixed nor stable. By 1973 it was down to 38 per cent; it rose after the oil shocks to a peak of 43 per cent but by the end of 1990 was down to 25 per cent. If fuels are left out, the proportion would fall to 15 per cent or no more than a third of the corresponding proportion in the early 1950s.

Not only have exports of primary produce grown much more slowly than exports of manufactures but the share of developing countries in the total has dropped over the post-war period. In the 1950s they accounted for 47 per cent of world trade in primary produce; by 1990 their share had fallen below 40 per cent. If we leave out fuels (including petroleum) and take a long-term view, looking at the exports of the developing countries in the form of primary produce as a proportion of total world trade, that proportion, which was above 20 per cent back in 1913 and 1953, had fallen by 1990 to under 5 per cent.

All this may leave you with the impression that there has been a fall in absolute terms in the volume of exports of primary produce over the last forty years. That is not so. The expansion in world trade has been so rapid that 5 per cent of the total in 1990 is three times as much in volume as 20 per cent of the total was in 1953. The conclusion to be drawn is rather that so long as the developing countries exported nothing but primary products they were failing to make use of a far more powerful engine of growth in the form of exports of manufactures.

As recently as 1959 Lamartine Yates (on whose work I have drawn heavily) could write that, apart from Japan, 'the underdeveloped world has not yet begun to export manufactures'. On his calculations their share in world trade in manufactures in 1953 was around 4 per cent. By 1990 it was over 14 per cent and still increasing. At constant prices, this meant an increase in less than forty years by a factor of seventy. In dollar terms, this increase was from about $1 billion in 1953 to $100 billion in 1980 and $350 billion in 1990. The rate of growth was not only accelerating but by the 1980s was twice as fast (at 10 per cent per annum) as the growth in the exports of manufactures from the industrial countries.

Of course, not all developing countries participated in this expansion in manufacturing. In 1990 half the total was accounted for by four countries alone, all of them in Asia: Korea, Taiwan, Hong Kong and Singapore. Other Asian countries – China, Malaysia, Thailand and Indonesia – accounted for nearly a quarter. So although the rate of change in the aggregate was remarkably high, the change was largely confined to a limited group of countries. Many other developing countries – in Africa particularly – have hardly begun to export manufactures. But since they are all producers of manufactures they are all *potentially* exporters.

Moreover if one looks at the mechanism of economic development, it is clear that an important part has been played by the efforts of industrial countries to find locations where costs – and particularly wage costs – are less burdensome and to which they can move production of some of their manufactures. The part played by Japan, for example, in the development of her Asian neighbours, through joint ventures or the provision of capital and management services or establishing branch factories is particularly notable. Nor is that the end of the matter. As wage costs rise in Korea and Taiwan they, too, begin to transfer some of their activities to other countries in Asia where labour is cheaper. The proliferation of modern methods of manufacturing may be slower in other continents but it is unmistakably the way of the future so long as world markets remain open.

The progress made by the developing countries in their trade in manufacturing can be illustrated by comparing their exports to industrial countries with the exports of manufactures from the industrial countries in the opposite direction, to the developing countries. Between 1960 and 1990 the ratio between the two fell from 8.3 to 3.5 and it was apparent that within a relatively few years exports of manufactures from the developing countries would overtake exports in the opposite direction.

The three largest markets for the developing countries are North America, Western Europe, and the developing countries themselves. The United States is much the largest single market, for exports not only from South America but also from Asian countries. Africa and the Middle East depend mainly on Western Europe. The industrial countries buy nearly three times as much from the developing countries as the latter do from one another.

It is not possible to say how this picture would be altered if the figures related exclusively to manufactures but it would seem that about the same proportion of exports of manufactures from the developing countries goes to other developing countries (25 per cent) as applies to total exports. It would be reasonable to expect this proportion to grow as the process of development proceeds.

What kind of manufactures do the developing countries export? I have comparable figures for 1973 and 1989 which show an astonishing change in those sixteen years. Total exports of manufactures rose from $23 billion in 1973 to $339 billion in 1989; that is, by a factor of nearly fifteen at current prices. In engineering products (of which about half consisted of household appliances and office and telecommunication equipment) the increase (also in current prices) was even greater – by a factor of twenty-three. In textiles, clothing and other consumer goods, it was rather less – a little over elevenfold. In iron and steel, chemicals and other semi-manufactures the increase was by a factor of thirteen. While a substantial part of the increase in each case reflected the rapid inflation of those years, the expansion in volume was undoubtedly very rapid. In the late 1980s, for example, the figures suggest a rise of about 80 per cent in the total volume of exports in four years.

One must, of course, remember that the flow of manufactures was far from being in one direction only. Exports of manufactures from the industrial countries to the developing countries grew very rapidly in the 1970s and continued to rise quite rapidly in the 1980s, although not at a rate comparable with the far more rapid increase in the opposite direction.

What are we to make of the trends that I have been describing? Are they likely to continue? Or are we approaching a limit to what markets in the importing countries can absorb? Is the success of Asian tigers limiting the chances of other developing countries following the same recipe? Was Paul Streeten right in arguing back in 1976 that 'if all developing countries had followed the strategy of Taiwan and Korea their exports would probably have fared less well?'

When Bela Balassa worked out the ratio between imports from the developing countries and total domestic sales in the importing countries for each of the leading groups of manufactures in 1978, he found no group with a ratio higher than 2 per cent, except textiles (4 per cent) and clothing (10 per cent). He then looked ahead to 1990, making what seemed plausible assumptions about the rate of expansion in demand and the rate of growth of imports from developing countries. He again found that the ratio between imports and demand was relatively modest on the average but much higher in the case of clothing, where it worked out at 15 per cent, and rising rapidly in the case of engineering products where it was just over 5 per cent.

This was, however, a hypothetical calculation. I have tried to repeat it, using the actual levels in 1990 of imports from developing countries and Balassa's forecast of consumption in industrial countries in that year. The result is a ratio of 3.5 which may have risen over the past five years to 4 per cent or a little more but does not look particularly alarming. Once again clothing is the big exception – on my figures just over 20 per cent. Most other groups work out between 3 and 4 per cent and the ratio for textiles at 3.3 per cent is slightly lower than the average of 3.5 per cent.

Looking back, the projections made at the beginning of the 1980s for the growth of trade proved to be a little too optimistic. Balassa expected exports of manufactures from the developing countries to grow at 12.5 per cent per annum over the decade while UNCTAD took over 13.5 per cent. In fact, growth was at 10 per cent – a remarkably high rate considering that in the 1980s 'the engine of growth was stuttering so noisily'.

Another way of forming a judgement about the sustainability of the growth in exports of manufactures from the developing countries is to look at the share they enjoy in total world exports. In 1973 the share was about 7 per cent and in 1989 had doubled to 14 per cent. But for such a large group of countries it was still relatively small. Where the share was already high in 1973, as in the case of clothing, textiles and other consumer goods, it rose least: in clothing from 30 to 45 per cent; in textiles from 17 to 31 per cent; and in other consumer goods from 13 to 20 per cent. The highest increases were in engineering products (from 3 to 12 per cent), in iron and steel (from 3 to 14 per cent) and in chemicals (from 4 to 10 per cent). These proportions are in striking contrast with the far higher proportions for primary products: 100 per cent for copra and over 90 per cent for rubber, coffee, bananas, palm oil and coconut oil. One cannot help contrasting the severe limits set by the inelasticity of demand for these products with the far greater scope for expansion in exports of a much wider and more easily enlarged range of manufactures. It is no doubt true that the more countries join in the game the tougher the going will become; but there still seems to be plenty of room for new entrants so long as the industrial countries do not begin to close their markets.

At the end of the day one has to ask what the developing countries have gained from international trade. Sometimes we are led to believe that an expanding level of trade is a sufficient and indispensable condition for economic development. At other times the net gains are made to seem very small indeed. I recall how in the early 1970s when Britain was trying to join the European Community those who favoured such a move laid stress on the gains from free trade. But when they came to do the sums they reached estimates of no more than a 1–2 per cent addition to GNP – about half the normal growth in a single year. If the sole gain took the form of cheaper imports and imports were about 20 per cent of GNP, an average reduction of 5–10 per cent in import costs would yield a net addition to GNP of 1–2 per cent. Would a similar calculation yielding an equally modest gain to the developing countries be reasonable?

I think not. It has always been true that the really major gains come from employing *more* resources through an increase in the level of economic activity rather than from an improved allocation in the use of resources. Impediments to trade that do no injury to employment are far less damaging than impediments that do. Conversely, the removal of impediments to trade is far less important than an increase in demand.

Thus the first advantage that increased sales of manufactures abroad bring to the developing countries is that they make an additional call on unskilled labour that might otherwise not be employed at all or find alternative employment of low net productivity. There are additional advantages in increasing returns and an elastic demand. Increased employment in manufacturing tends to raise productivity of the whole manufacturing sector where the opposite may occur if more labour is left to find employment on the land; and there is the prospect of an expanding demand as the world becomes more affluent whereas tropical produce may have to be disposed of in a far less (income) elastic market.

But it is not only the field of employment for labour that expands with trade in manufactures. Other resources are brought into play in ways that are difficult in primary production. There is scope for additional resources – some of them flowing in freely with trade – in knowledge, skill, enterprise and capital. Trade means new opportunities and new ideas and it is out of these that additional resources are generated. Moreover it is in the nature of these ideas and opportunities that they overflow beyond the immediate area of trade into other sectors of the economy so that there is a ramification and continuous growth that may in the long run be more important than the gain from exports. No doubt a country can borrow ideas and create opportunities for itself without engaging in trade, but progress in these respects and the modernization of a backward economy are likely to be faster when trade flows freely and permeates the economy with new knowledge, skill, enterprise and capital.

CONCLUSION

It seems to me, therefore, that the international division of labour between industrial countries like those of Western Europe and the developing countries in the three poorest continents of the world will continue to develop to the mutual advantage of both groups if trade between them in manufactures continues to expand. Such trade has so far provided an engine of growth for only a limited group of developing countries and has been heavily concentrated in an equally limited range of consumer goods. But as time goes on, a wider group of countries and additional categories of manufactures will be involved. It is important that this avenue of development should be kept open, that the industrial countries in Europe and elsewhere should be alive to the advantages that such trade brings them and that they should avoid blaming the developing countries for creating social problems to which these countries have contributed relatively little.

Part I
The Prebisch–Singer Terms of Trade Hypothesis

3 The Prebisch–Singer Terms of Trade Hypothesis: Some (Very) New Evidence

David Sapsford and John-ren Chen

3.1 INTRODUCTION

The chapters in this section of the book are concerned with various dimensions of an hypothesis which has become inextricably associated with the names Hans Singer and Raul Prebisch. According to this hypothesis, which was launched simultaneously by Singer (1950) and Prebisch (1950), the net barter terms of trade between primary products and manufactures have been, and could be expected to continue to be, subject to a downward long-run trend. Being in direct contradiction with the then prevailing orthodoxy, it is not surprising that the Prebisch–Singer hypothesis (P–S hereafter) attracted criticism from a number of quarters. The ensuing debate, which initially focused its attack on the basis of issues related to the treatment of transport costs and quality change, is well summarized by Spraos (1980), who showed that adjustments for shipping costs and changing quality left the hypothesis largely undented, in the sense that they failed to destroy its empirical validity. However, since the mid-1980s the debate surrounding the P–S hypothesis has shifted to the statistical arena. Indeed, such is the interest generated by the hypothesis amongst econometricians and time-series statisticians that it has established itself as one of the major test beds on which they routinely evaluate their latest methods of trend estimation!

The purpose of this chapter is to provide an overview and evaluation of the body of statistical evidence which surrounds the P–S thesis. The remainder of the chapter is organized as follows: section 3.2 provides an assessment of the weight of available statistical evidence, while section 3.3 reports some new evidence which we argue goes some way towards providing a final resolution of the debate. Section 3.4 offers some concluding comments and suggestion regarding fruitful directions for future research.

27

3.2   THE BALANCE OF THE EVIDENCE

The literature on the P–S hypothesis is large and growing ever larger. Scarcely a week passes by when another new study seeking to test the declining long-run trend hypothesis does not cross at least one of our desks. Table 3.1 provides a listing of what might reasonably be considered the major empirical works published in the field since 1950. Given the existence of such a vast literature, our selection of this particular array of studies as representative of the current state of the literature requires, perhaps, some justification. In order to be included in the table a study had to satisfy at least one of the following criteria: (1) to have been published in one of the World's leading scholarly journals; (2) to have been written by someone present at the Innsbruck Conference![1] Joking apart, we would argue that the studies listed in Table 3.1 are those which have been most influential and moreover, that the balance of evidence for and against the P–S hypothesis contained in this sample of studies is not appreciably different from that present in the wider literature as a whole (see Sapsford, 1990; Sapsford and Balasubramanyam, 1994 for reviews.

Table 3.1   Prebisch–Singer hypothesis: the statistical evidence

Author	Date	Trend
Singer	*American Economic Review*, 1950	Negative
Prebisch	*United Nations ECLA*, 1950	Negative
Spraos	*Economic Journal*, 1980	Negative
Sapsford	*Economic Journal*, 1985	Negative
Thirlwall and Bergevin	*World Development*, 1985	Negative
Grilli and Yang	*World Bank Economic Review*, 1988	Negative
Cuddington and Urzua	*Economic Journal*, 1989	None
Powell	*Economic Journal*, 1991	None
Ardeni and Wright	*Economic Journal*, 1992	Negative
Sapsford, Sarkar and Singer (SSS)	*Journal of International Development*, 1992	Negative
Bleaney and Greenaway	*Oxford Economic Papers*, 1993	Negative
Reinhart and Wickham	*IMF Staff Papers*, 1994	Negative

As may be seen from the entries in the final column, ten out of the *Top Twelve* studies listed in Table 3.1 provide support for the P–S hypothesis in that they reveal the presence of a negative and statistically significant trend in the net barter terms of trade between primary products and manufactured goods. This is a quite remarkable scorecard, especially so bearing in mind the differing time periods analysed, the differing data series studied and the widely differing array of statistical techniques employed, which range from the extremely simple (straightforward data inspection in the case of the original 1950 papers) through regression analysis in the 1980s contributions, to cointegration/error correction and structural time-series modelling approaches in the 1990s studies. There can be few hypotheses in economics which have stood the test of time, not to mention the onslaught of increasingly sophisticated statistical techniques, as well as the P–S hypothesis.

A particular milestone in the literature was the publication in 1988 by Grilli and Yang of the World Bank of an alternative, and arguably consistent, data series charting the behaviour of the net barter terms of trade between primary prices and those of manufactured goods over the period 1900 through to 1986. Although not without its difficulties (see Sapsford, Sarkar and Singer, 1992) this series has been adopted in the majority of post-1988 aggregate literature, as is reflected in the fact that six out of the seven *Top Twelve* studies summarized in Table 3.1 that were published since 1987 employed the Grilli–Yang data set.[3] In essence, then, the most recent literature has involved confronting the Grilli-Yang data set with increasingly sophisticated statistical weaponry. As is clear from Table 3.1, the P–S hypothesis has emerged virtually unscathed from this particular field of intellectual battle. In the next section we will present some evidence of a rather different character which, we will argue, provides what might be considered to be the crucial litmus test of the P–S thesis.

Given the nature of this volume and Hans Singer's background, it is appropriate also to recognise the evidence regarding the P–S thesis which may be found in the extensive German language literature that exists on the subject.[2]

3.3 SOME NEW EVIDENCE

In contrast to the most recent literature (which, as we have seen, consists primarily of applying new techniques of trend estimation to the same data set) the evidence reported in this section is obtained by the application of existing accepted techniques to a new and novel data set. The results that are obtained when a conventional semi-logarithmic trend model is fitted to this new terms of trade series for the period 1950 through to 1994 are summarized in Table 3.2 and plotted in Figure 3.1. As may be seen, these

Table 3.2   Regression estimates of trend in terms of trade, 1950–94

Variable	Coefficient	Std. Error	t-Statistic	Prob.
Constant	2.283107	0.062855	36.32338	0.0000
Trend	–0.016388	0.002460	–6.660723	0.0000
R-squared	0.507813	Mean dependent var		1.922580
Adjusted R-squared	0.496367	S.D. dependent var		0.302036
S.E. of regression	0.214346	Akaike info criterion		–3.036902
Sum squared resid.	1.975600	Schwarz criterion		–2.956605
Log likelihood	6.478053	F-statistic		44.36523
		Prob (F-statistic)		0.000000

Included observations: 45

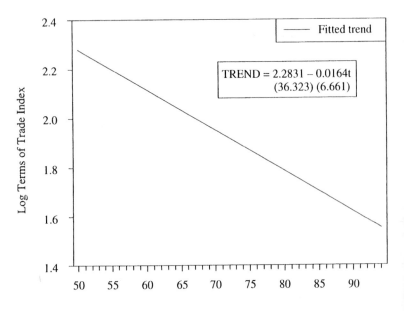

Figure 3.1   Trend in the terms of trade index, 1950–94 (1950 = 10)

results offer statistical support for the P–S hypothesis in that they reveal a negative trend (to the order of 1.64 percent per annum) which is statistically different from zero at better than the one per cent level.

Compared to the results reported elsewhere in the literature these results are fairly typical, in terms of *both* the estimated pace of the trend deterioration in the barter terms of trade and its statistical significance. What is remarkable, however, is the fact that such supportive results are obtained from the particular terms of trade series against which the model has been estimated. To appreciate the importance of this new evidence it is necessary to consider the nature of the data series employed. For want of a better title, we may term the data series which we analysed as the *knowledge-based terms of trade index (kbtt)*. This index is constructed on the assumption that knowledge – be it ultimately correct or incorrect – never dies. More specifically, our index was derived by taking 1950 as base (set arbitrarily equal to 10, just to be a little different) with the *t*th observation defined as follows:

$$kbtt_t = 10 + \sum_{i=1}^{12} d_{it} \qquad (t = 1950\ldots,1994)$$

where the subscript i ($i = 1, \ldots, 12$) refers to the ith study cited in Table 3.1 and the binary variable d_{it} is defined as follows:

$d_{it} =$ 0 for all time periods t prior to the date of publication

and

$d_{it} =$ *either* +1 for all subsequent periods if the ith study finds evidence of either trendlessness or the existence of a positive trend *or* –1 if the study finds evidence in favour of the P–S hypothesis.

In words, our index takes its initial base value and is thereafter increased by one unit for the remainder of the sample period each time a major study finds evidence which is not consistent with the P–S hypothesis and is decreased by one unit each time evidence consistent with the P–S hypothesis emerges from a major study. Accordingly, we might think of this particular terms of trade index as providing what amounts to an index of professional knowledge regarding the correctness, or otherwise, of the P–S thesis. If one accepts the validity of this particular index we would argue that the statistical evidence reported in this section provides strong (and novel) support indeed for the hypothesis advanced almost half a century ago by Hans Singer and Raul Prebisch. There can surely be very few hypotheses in economics that could pass this knowledge-based sort of test with such flying colours![4]

3.4   CONCLUDING REMARKS

This chapter has set the scene for the papers which follow in this section of the book, devoted to the Prebisch–Singer declining trend hypothesis. As we have seen, much of the recent literature in the field has concentrated on the application of new and increasingly sophisticated methods of trend estimation to the same long-run data set. The new evidence reported in this chapter has suggested that despite the fact that the declining trend hypothesis was launched almost half a century ago it has emerged from this process with what amounts to flying colours.

Interesting as the field of modern time-series analysis is, there are still important new fields of research to be explored in relation to the P–S deteriorating trend hypothesis. The Prebisch–Singer hypothesis is about much more than the sign and statistical significance of a time-trend term in a suitably specified time-series model. Reading the seminal contributions by both Prebisch (1950) and Singer (1950) one immediately sees that both authors provide a rich array of hypotheses regarding the *economic* behaviour that lies behind and generates the negative trend which has attracted so much statistical attention. We would argue that an important direction for further work on the long-run behaviour of the barter terms of trade is to devise approaches which enable us to test directly the economic hypotheses advanced by both Prebisch and Singer. To do so is not an easy matter. However, the prize of so doing, in terms of our understanding of the economic forces generating observed trends in the barter terms of trade, is a handsome one. Some first steps in this direction are provided in the following chapter in which Bloch and Sapsford specify and test what they term a structural model of the barter terms of trade. This theme of testing the hypotheses of the originators of the declining trend thesis is carried further forward in Chapter 15 below where Balasubramanyam and Balasubramanyam employ Hans Singer's (1950) *distribution of gains* model in an analysis of India's recently emerging software industry.

As research moves closer to the testing of hypotheses regarding the economic behaviour and forces that generate the observed long-run trend in the barter terms of trade, we would also argue that there is a need to move away from the almost exclusive attention on the same aggregate data set towards a greater emphasis on disaggregated tests. Such an approach is followed in the chapter by Chen and Stocker (Chapter 6) who analyse the time-series behaviour of the twenty-four separate indices which are combined together to form the aggregate Grilli–Yang series which, as we have seen, has figured so prominently in the recent literature.

Notes

1. Having a name beginning with S seems to help also!
2. Several important contributions to the P–S literature can also be found in the German literature. For example, Chen (1985) and (1992) reports evidence obtained, respectively, from UNCTAD and World Bank data sources that is consistent with the P–S hypothesis.
3. The single exception is the study by Reinhart and Wickham (1994) which analyses an alternative index compiled by the International Monetary Fund.
4. Professor Amitava Dutt suggested in discussion of this paper that our index might be further refined by weighting each d_{it} variable by either the estimated trend rate of growth of the terms of trade and/or the relevant Student's t' statistic reported in the *i*th study. Given that both of the studies cited in Table 3.1 that fail to find evidence in support of the P–S thesis report estimated trend growth rates which are insignificantly different from zero, the Dutt correction would lead to results even more supportive of the P–S thesis.

References

Ardeni, P.G. and B. Wright (1992) 'The Prebisch–Singer Hypothesis: A Reappraisal Independent of Stationarity Hypotheses', *Economic Journal*, vol. 102, no. 413 (1992) pp. 803–12.

Bleaney, M. and D. Greenaway (1993) 'Long-Run Trends in the Relative Price of Primary Commodities and in the Terms of Trade of Developing Countries', *Oxford Economic Papers*, vol. 45, no. 3 (Oct.) pp. 349–63.

Chen, J. (1985) *Terms of Trade und Außenhandelsbeziehungen der Entwicklungsländer – eine ökonometrische Studie; Schriften zur angewandten Ökonometrie*, Heft 14 (Frankfurt: Haag und Herchen Verlag).

—— (1992) 'Die Entwicklung der Weltmarktpreise für Rohstoffe von 1960/1 bis 1982/3', *Journal für Entwicklungspolitik*, pp. 387–411.

Cuddington, J. and C. Urzua (1989) 'Trends and Cycles in the Net Barter Terms of Trade: A New Approach', *Economic Journal*, vol. 99, no. 396, pp. 426–42.

Grilli, E. and M.C. Yang (1988) 'Primary Commodity Prices, Manufactured Goods Prices and the Terms of Trade of Developing Countries: What the Long-Run Shows', *World Bank Economic Review*, vol. 2, no. 1 (Jan.) pp. 1–47.

Powell, A. (1991) 'Commodity and Developing Country Terms of Trade: What Does the Long Run Show?', *Economic Journal*, vol. 101, no. 409, pp. 1485–96.

Prebisch, Raul (1950) 'The Economic Development of Latin America and its Principal Problem', UN ECLA; also published in *Economic Bulletin for Latin America*, vol. 7, no. 1 (1962) pp. 1–22.

Reinhart, C. and P. Wickham (1994) 'Commodity Prices: Cyclical Weakness or Secular Decline?', *IMF Staff Papers*, vol. 41, no. 2, pp. 175–213.

Sapsford, D. (1985) 'The Statistical Debate on the Net Barter Terms of Trade Between Primary Commodities and Manufactures: A Comment and Some Additional Evidence', *Economic Journal*, vol. 95, no. 379 (Sep.) pp. 781–8.

—— (1990) 'Primary Commodity Prices and the Terms of Trade', *Economic Record*, vol. 66, no. 195, pp. 342–56.

—— and V.N. Balasubramanyam (1994) 'The Long-Run Behavior of the Relative Price of Primary Commodities: Statistical Evidence and Policy Implications', *World Development*, vol. 22, no. 11, pp. 1737–45.

—— P. Sarkar and H. Singer (1992) 'The Prebisch-Singer Terms of Trade Controversy Revisited', *Journal of International Development*, vol. 4, no. 3 (May) pp. 315–32.

Singer, H. (1950) 'The Distribution of Gains Between Investing and Borrowing Countries', *American Economic Review, Papers and Proceedings*, vol. 40 (May) pp. 473–85.

Spraos, J. (1980) 'The Statistical Debate on the Net Barter Terms of Trade Between Primary Products and Manufactures', *Economic Journal*, vol. 90, no. 357 (Jan.) pp. 107–28.

Thirlwall, T. and J. Bergevin (1985) 'Trend, Cycles and Asymmetries in the Terms of Trade of Primary Commodities from Developed and Less Developed Countries', *World Development*, vol. 13, no. 7 (Jul.) pp. 805–17.

4 Prebisch and Singer Effects on the Terms of Trade between Primary Producers and Manufacturers

Harry Bloch and David Sapsford

4.1 INTRODUCTION

Papers by Prebisch (1950) and Singer (1950) argue that there is a secular decline in the terms of trade for developing countries in their dealings with the industrialized countries. Both Prebisch and Singer observe that exports from the developing countries are dominated by primary products, while imports are dominated by manufactured goods. They then associate the adverse change in terms of trade for developing countries with the decline in the price of primary products relative to the price of manufactures.

Statistical studies of the Prebisch–Singer hypothesis of a declining terms of trade for developing countries have focused on the time trend in the price of primary products relative to the price of manufactures in international trade. Sapsford and Balasubramanyam (1994) provide a useful survey. The issue generally addressed in these studies is whether a clear downward trend in the relative price of primary products can be established over the whole of the twentieth century or over substantial portions thereof.

Our objective in this paper is to provide a statistical study of movements in the price of primary products relative to the price of manufactured goods by estimating the coefficients of a structural model of price and wage determination in the world economy. Estimates from the structural model are then used to evaluate the contribution of various effects to the movement in the terms of trade for primary producers. In particular, we provide estimates of effects associated with arguments offered by Prebisch and Singer in explaining the downward trend in the terms of trade.

Price equations for both primary products and manufactured goods are derived in Section 4.2 below. As suggested by Prebisch (1950), primary-product prices are determined by setting the competitive supply from primary producers equal to the demand from manufacturers for primary product as raw material, assuming cost minimization by manufacturers. In contrast, prices for manufactured goods are set equal to a mark-up factor multiplied by the direct unit cost of the good. Singer's (1975) argument is incorporated by assuming that technical change in primary production is neutral in saving of factors of production, whereas technical change in manufacturing saves only raw material and labour inputs. The section concludes with a discussion of the determinants of the terms of trade between primary producers and manufacturers under the assumed conditions of technical change and pricing.

Our model of mark-up and wage determination is presented in Section 4.3. Prebisch argues for an impact of differential behaviour of wages in developing and industrialized countries, so we introduce separate variables for the wage of workers in primary production in developing countries and the wage of manufacturing workers in the industrialized countries. The wage rate for workers in primary production in the developing countries is assumed to equate the competitive demand for labour from primary producers with the supply of labour to primary production in these countries. We follow McDonald and Solow (1981) in treating the wage rate of manufacturing workers in the industrialized countries as the outcome of an efficient bargain between unions and employers.

Section 4.4 presents the results of estimating equations for product price and wage rate in both primary production and manufacturing as well as the manufacturing mark-up. These equations are estimated as a system using data from the post-Second World War period. Both the statistical properties of the estimates and the correspondence between the estimates and the predictions of our structural model are discussed therein. Implications of the estimation results for the trend in the terms of trade between primary producers and manufacturers are discussed in Section 4.5. In particular, we discuss the magnitude of the effects identified by Prebisch and Singer and their contribution to depressing the terms of trade for primary producers. These effects are then compared to the offsetting effects arising from diminishing returns to labour when there are fixed natural resources combined with expansion of output and manmade capital input.

4.2 PRICE DETERMINATION IN PRIMARY PRODUCTION AND MANUFACTURING

A competitive supply function for primary production is derived by assuming that primary producers choose output to maximize profit in a perfectly competitive market.[1] We assume that technical progress in primary production is neutral in saving factors of production and that production is subject to periodic disturbances due to influences such as droughts and wars. Otherwise, we assume a Cobb–Douglas production function without imposing constant returns to scale. The resulting production function is of the form

$$R = A e^{\alpha_0 t} L_R^{\alpha_1} K_R^{\alpha_2} \epsilon_R \qquad (4.1)$$

where R is the output of primary product, t is time in years, α_0 is the annual rate of factor-saving technical progress, L_R and K_R are, respectively, the quantity of labour and capital employed in producing the commodity and ϵ_R measures the impact of periodic disturbances on production.

We assume that primary producers are short-run cost-minimizers with labour being the only variable input to production in the short run.[2] Taking the derivative of the implied cost equation with respect to output gives the marginal cost of the product. Under the assumption of competitive market clearing, this gives the supply function for primary product as follows:

$$p_R = (1/\alpha_1) w_R [A e^{\alpha_0 t} K_R^{\alpha_2} \epsilon_R]^{-1/\alpha_1} R^{(1-\alpha_1)/\alpha_1} \qquad (4.2)$$

Where p_R is the commodity price and w_R is the wage for a unit of labour used in primary production.

Demand for primary product arises both from its use as a raw material in manufacturing and from direct consumption. We choose to model the demand for primary product as exclusively due to its use as a raw material in manufacturing. Our reasoning for this treatment is twofold: first, our treatment recognizes that the vast bulk of primary product is subject to a manufacturing process before reaching final consumers, notable exceptions being fresh fruit and vegetables; second, even where primary product is consumed without manufacturing, there is generally an intermediary between the primary producer and the final consumer. Our model incorporates the role of these intermediaries, often transnational corporations, in marking up the price of primary products (see Maizels, 1992, ch. 10).

We derive the demand for primary product as a raw material by assuming a Cobb–Douglas production function for manufacturing, allowing for factor-augmenting technical progress as well as periodic disturbances to production, such as those due to strikes and short-run fluctuations in the degree of capacity utilization. Following the arguments of Singer (1975), factor augmentation is allowed to occur only for labour and raw materials, with θ being the exponential annual rate of labour saving and Ψ being the corresponding rate of saving raw materials. Our manufacturing production function is then

$$X = B(e^{\theta t} L_x)^{\beta_1} (e^{\Psi t} R)^{\beta_2} K_x^{\beta_3} \epsilon_x \tag{4.3}$$

where X is the output of finished goods, L_x is the labour input to this output, K_x is the corresponding capital input and ϵ_x is the disturbance term. We assume that manufacturers utilize the cost-minimizing choice of labour and primary product input under conditions of given input prices. This yields a short-run derived demand for primary product as follows:

$$R = e^{-\Psi t} [X (B \epsilon_x)^{-1} K_x^{-\beta_3} e^{\beta_1(\theta - \Psi)t} ((w_x/p_R) \tag{4.4}$$
$$(\beta_2/\beta_1))^{\beta_1}]^{1/(\beta_1 + \beta_2)}$$

where w_x denotes the wage rate in manufacturing. The demand for primary products falls directly with technical progress that saves raw materials in manufacturing at the rate Ψ, but there is an offset with factor substitution if Ψ exceeds the rate of saving of labour in manufacturing, θ.

Substituting from equation (4.4) into the supply equation (4.2) provides a multiplicative equation for determining the market-clearing equilibrium price for primary product. Taking the derivative with respect to time of this equation and expressing the resulting equation in terms of time rates of change yields

$$\dot{p}_R = a_1 + a_2 \dot{X} + a_3 \dot{w}_R + a_4 \dot{w}_X + a_5 \dot{K}_R + a_6 \dot{K}_X + \dot{\mu}_R \tag{4.5}$$

where a dot over a variable indicates a time rate of change and

$$a_1 = -\gamma_R[(\beta_1 + \beta_2)\alpha_0 + [(1-\alpha_1)\beta_1]\theta + [(\beta_1 + \beta_2)\alpha_1$$
$$-(1-\alpha_1)\beta_1] \Psi],$$
$$a_2 = \gamma_R(1-\alpha_1),$$
$$a_3 = \gamma_R[\alpha_1(\beta_1 + \beta_2)],$$
$$a_4 = \gamma_R[\beta_1(1-\alpha_1)],$$
$$a_5 = -\gamma_R[\alpha_2(\beta_1 + \beta_2)],$$
$$a_6 = -\gamma_R[\beta_3(1-\alpha_1)],$$
$$\dot{\mu}_R = -\gamma_R[(\beta_1 + \beta_2)\dot{\epsilon}_R + (1-\alpha_1)\dot{\epsilon}_X], \text{ and}$$
$$\gamma_R = [\alpha_1\beta_2 + \beta_1]^{-1}$$

The standard restriction that all inputs have positive but diminishing marginal products implies that $1 > \alpha_1 > 0$, $1 > \alpha_2 > 0$, $1 > \beta_1 > 0$, $1 > \beta_2 > 0$ and $1 > \beta_3 > 0$. With this restriction, each of the parameters a_2, a_3 and a_4 in equation (4.5) has a positive value, while a_5 and a_6 each have a negative value. Furthermore, a_1 is almost certainly negative when there is no technical retrogression – that is, α_0, θ and Ψ are each non-negative. The only possible exception being when α_0, is small, Ψ exceeds θ, and the elasticity of manufacturing output with respect to labour, β_1, is very large relative to the elasticity of primary production with respect to labour, α_1. Thus, our simple model of competitive market clearing provides a predicted direction for the impact on the price of primary products for wage rates and capital stocks in both sectors, the output of manufactured goods and the pure time trend due to technical change. A further condition implied by the model is that the coefficients of the wage rate variables sum to one.

Industrial pricing studies generally find a relatively stable relationship between prices of manufactured goods and the combined unit cost of labour and materials (for example, Coutts, Godley and Nordhaus, 1978; Sawyer, 1983). These findings are explained by reference to a model in which prices in manufacturing are set by multiplying the sum of unit labour cost and unit materials cost by a mark-up factor. Combining this pricing assumption with the production function for manufacturing given in equation (4.3) yields the following equation for the price of manufactured goods, when it is further assumed that manufacturers use a cost-minimizing choice of labour and primary product inputs:

$$p_X = M[(B \epsilon_X)^{-1} X^{(1 - \beta_1 + \beta_2)} K_X^{\beta_3} ((\beta_1/\beta_2)^{\beta_2} + (\beta_2/\beta_1))^{\beta_1}) \qquad (4.6)$$
$$e^{-(\beta_1\theta + \beta_2\Psi)t} w_X^{\beta_1} p_R^{\beta_2})]^{1/(\beta_1 + \beta_2)}$$

where M is the mark-up factor and the other variables and parameters are as defined previously.[3] Taking the time rate of change of equation (4.6) then yields

$$\dot{p}_X = b_1 + b_2 \dot{X} + b_3 \dot{p}_R + b_4 \dot{w}_X + b_5 \dot{K}_X + b_6 \dot{M} + \dot{\mu}_X \qquad (4.7)$$

where

$$b_1 = -\gamma_X [\beta_1\theta + \beta_2\Psi],$$
$$b_2 = \gamma_X [1 - (\beta_1 + \beta_2)],$$
$$b_3 = \gamma_X \beta_2,$$
$$b_4 = \gamma_X \beta_1,$$

$$b_5 = -\gamma_X \beta_3,$$
$$b_6 = 1$$
$$\dot{\mu}_X = -\gamma_X \dot{\epsilon}_X, \text{ and}$$
$$\gamma_X = [\beta_1 + \beta_2]^{-1}$$

When all inputs to manufacturing production have positive but diminishing marginal products, β_1, β_2 and β_3 each has a positive value less than unity. This implies that b_3 and b_4 in equation (4.7) are each between zero and one, and that $b_3 + b_4$ equals unity. Also b_5 in equation (4.7) takes a negative value, while the value of b_1 is negative whenever there is factor-augmenting technical progress in manufacturing. Finally, b_2 takes a positive value whenever there are less than constant returns to the combination of labour and primary product, that is whenever $\beta_1 + \beta_2 < 1$.

Solving for the change in the terms of trade for primary producers from equations (4.5) and (4.7) and expressing the difference in terms of the structural parameters of the model yields

$$\dot{p}_R - \dot{p}_X = \gamma_R[(\alpha_1\beta_1)\theta + (\alpha_1(\beta_2 - \beta_1) + \beta_1(1 - \alpha_1))\Psi - \beta_1\alpha_0 \quad (4.8)$$
$$+ (\beta_1 - \alpha_1(1 - \beta_2))\dot{X} + (\alpha_1\beta_1)\dot{w}_R - (\alpha_1\beta_1)\dot{w}_X$$
$$- (\alpha_2\beta_1)\dot{K}_R + (\alpha_1\beta_3)\dot{K}_X - \dot{M} + \beta_3\dot{\mu}_R - \dot{\mu}_X]$$

A definite direction of impact on the rate of change of the terms of trade in equation (4.8) is predicted for each of the wage rate variables (positive for the primary sector wage and negative for the manufacturing sector wage) and capital stock variables (negative for the primary sector and positive for the manufacturing sector) as well as for the mark-up in manufacturing (negative impact). However, the pure time trend in the terms of trade, given by the first line of the RHS of (4.8), is ambiguous (labour-saving technical change in manufacturing has a positive effect, neutral factor augmentation in primary production has a negative effect and raw-material-saving technical change in manufacturing has an effect which is assured to be positive only in the unlikely event that the elasticity of manufacturing output with respect to raw materials is larger than the corresponding elasticity with respect to labour). Also, the direction of impact of output growth is assured to be positive only when restrictions are made on the structural parameters.

Coefficients of the wage variables and the manufacturing mark-up in equation (4.8) capture the Prebisch effect, in that the terms of trade for primary producers decline when the mark-up rises or when manufacturing wage growth exceeds primary sector wage growth (the coefficients of the wage growth variables in (4.8) are of equal magnitude, but opposite sign). The Singer effect of technical change putting downward pressure on the terms of trade is captured when the time trend as given by the first line of the RHS of (4.8) is negative.[4]

In addition to the Prebisch and Singer effects, the terms of trade in equation (4.8) depend on the rate of growth of manufacturing output and the rate of growth of capital input in both primary production and manufacturing. The impact of manufacturing output growth is positive whenever the elasticity of manufacturing output with respect to labour input is at least as large as the elasticity of primary production with respect to labour. This is the case assumed in Ricardo's classical analysis of economic growth with fixed natural resources in primary production. A positive output growth (Ricardo) effect can offset the downward impact of the Prebisch and Singer effects on the terms of trade of primary producers, leaving a net trend in the terms of trade that is ambiguous. This ambiguity is compounded by the fact that the rates of capital accumulation in the primary and manufacturing sectors exert negative and positive influences, respectively, on the rate of change of the terms of trade. Ambiguity remains even under the condition of balanced growth generally assumed in models of equilibrium growth (for example, Findlay, 1980), where industrial output grows at the same rate as capital stocks in both the primary and manufacturing sectors.

4.3 MARK-UP AND WAGE DETERMINATION

The terms of trade in equation (4.8) move in the opposite direction to changes in the mark-up factor, so that a trend increase in the market power of manufacturers contributes to long-run deterioration in the terms of trade. Changes in the mark-up factor may also affect the movement in the terms of trade over periods of time associated with the short or long business cycle and thereby may offset (enhance) the impact of the growth rate of industrial production on primary products in equation (4.8) if the mark-up changes are pro-cyclical (counter-cyclical). The following equation allows for trend and cyclical movement in one plus the manufacturing mark-up factor:

$$\dot{M} = c_1 + c_2 \dot{X} + \epsilon_M, \quad \text{where } E(\epsilon_M) = 0 \tag{4.9}$$

where ϵ_M is a disturbance term that captures the influence of factors other than trend and cycle on the rate of change of the mark-up factor in manufacturing. A positive value of c_1 is suggested by the arguments in Prebisch (1950) as contributing to the deterioration of the terms of trade for primary producers. The theoretical ambiguity of the value of c_2 is discussed by Bils (1987) and Rotemberg and Saloner (1986).

Prebisch (1950) argues that differences in wage behaviour between developing and industrialized economies also contribute to deterioration in the terms of trade for developing countries as exporters of primary products. He argues that a greater degree of organization among manufacturing workers in industrialized countries results in wage increases for these workers that persistently exceed the wage increases for workers in the primary sector of developing countries.[5] We treat workers engaged in primary production in the developing countries as unorganized in the sense that they take the wage rate for their labour as given and exert no market power over its level. Their supply of labour depends on the rate of growth of the underlying labour force and the returns to working in primary production relative to the returns from working elsewhere in the economy. We follow Lewis (1954) in treating wage labour as being drawn from traditional subsistence agriculture, so that it is the wage rate relative to the cost of living in the market economy that is compared to a subsistence real wage when deciding to enter waged employment.[6] A particular functional form for labour supply that captures these features in a multiplicative relationship is as follows:

$$L_R = L_{0,R} e^{\lambda t} [w_R / \omega_0 p_X]^\phi \qquad (4.10)$$

where $L_{0,R}$ is the initial labour force, λ is the rate of growth of the underlying labour force, ω_0 is the level of the subsistence real wage and the cost of living index (with a base value of one) depends solely on the price of manufactures.[7]

The demand for labour in primary production is given by solving for L_R in equation (4.1), substituting for R from the cost-minimizing condition for manufacturing production from equation (4.4) and substituting for the equilibrium price of primary production from equation (4.2). Equating this derived demand with the supply given in equation (4.10) and taking time rates of change for all remaining variables, gives the following market-clearing equilibrium condition for the rate of change of the nominal wage rate in primary production:

$$\dot{w}_R = d_1 + d_2 \dot{X} + d_3 \dot{w}_X + d_4 \dot{p}_X + d_5 \dot{K}_R + d_6 \dot{K}_X + \dot{\mu}_{w,R} \qquad (4.11)$$

where

$$d_1 = -\gamma_{w,R}[\beta_2\alpha_0 + \beta_1\theta + \beta_2\Psi + \lambda(\alpha_1\beta_2 + \beta_1)],$$

$$d_2 = \gamma_{w,R}$$

$$d_3 = \gamma_{w,R}\beta_1,$$

$$d_4 = \gamma_{w,R}\phi[(\alpha_1\beta_2 + \beta_1)],$$

$$d_5 = -\gamma_{w,R}\alpha_2\beta_2,$$

$$d_6 = -\gamma_{w,R}\beta_3,$$

$$\dot{\mu}_{wR} = -\gamma_{w,R}[\beta_2\dot{\epsilon}_R + \dot{\epsilon}_X], \text{ and}$$

$$\gamma_{w,R} = [\beta_1 + \phi(\alpha_1\beta_2 + \beta_1)]^{-1}$$

The standard assumption that all the exponential parameters in the production functions for primary product and manufactures are positive together with the restrictions in (4.10) imply that each of the coefficients, d_2 through d_4 is positive, while d_5 and d_6 are each negative. Furthermore, the pure trend coefficient, d_1, is negative as long as there is a positive rate of growth of the potential labour force for primary production. A final restriction on the coefficients is that the sum of d_3 and d_4 equals one, which means that (4.11) is homogeneous of degree zero in prices and nominal wages.

Manufacturing workers in the industrialized countries are organized in the sense that their wages and working conditions are generally collectively negotiated by labour unions. Employers also tend to be organized either formally into collective bargaining units or informally through the small number of dominant employers in any industry. McDonald and Solow (1981) analyse bargaining between a monopoly union and a monopoly employer, where the outcome is efficient in the sense that the wage–employment combination lies on a contract curve. They find that both product market conditions and the reservation wage of workers may influence the locus of wage rates and the levels of employment that represent the contract curve of efficient bargains. Further, they argue that labour productivity tends to positively influence the level of the wage rate under either historical considerations or formal bargaining outcomes.

We allow for a possible impact of output fluctuations on wage rates for manufacturing workers in the industrialized countries, but following the argument of McDonald and Solow place no expectation on the sign of the variable in our estimating equation.[8] The major expectation derived from the McDonald and Solow analysis is that there is trend growth in wage rates associated with the trend growth in labour productivity. We also allow for a possible positive effect of the lagged real wage rate on the current real wage rate operating through the reservation wage.[9] Finally, rather than impose the linear homogeneity of nominal wage rates in manufacturing prices suggested by the McDonald and Solow analysis, we introduce an unknown elasticity of nominal wages with respect to manufacturing prices to be estimated in our empirical results below.

Taking the time rates of change of an equation that allows for the above features in a multiplicative functional form yields

$$\dot{w}_X = f_1 + f_2 \dot{p}_X + f_3 \dot{X} + f_4 [\dot{w}_X(-1) - \dot{p}_X(-1)] + \dot{\varepsilon}_{w,X} \tag{4.12}$$

Our discussion of the McDonald and Solow model suggests that f_1 is directly related to the trend growth in labour productivity in manufacturing, so that it should be positive when our model is estimated over the post-Second World War period. Furthermore, f_2 is equal to one if nominal wages are linear homogeneous in manufacturing prices, the sign of f_3 is ambiguous, and f_4 is positive if lagged real wages increase the real value of the reservation wage for manufacturing workers.

4.4   EMPIRICAL EVIDENCE

The preceding sections specify a five-equation model consisting of equations describing the determination of the rates of change of the manufacturing mark-up, equation (4.9), of primary product prices, equation (4.5), of manufactured goods prices, equation (4.7), and of money wages in both the manufacturing sector of industrialized countries and the primary sector of developing countries, equations (4.12) and (4.11), respectively. This section reports the results obtained when this model is estimated against annual data spanning the period 1948 through to 1986.

The primary product and manufactured good price series employed in our empirical analysis are obtained from the World Bank data base. The primary price series is an index of the prices of twenty-four internationally traded non-fuel primary commodities (see Grilli and Yang, 1988), while the manufactured goods price series is an index of manufactured goods unit values. The manufacturing wage variable is obtained as an average of hourly manufacturing wage rates in five of the world's major industrialized countries, while the primary sector wage is obtained as a corresponding average of agricultural wage rates in a sample of third-world primary-producing countries. Manufacturing output is measured by the

International Monetary Fund Research Department's index of world industrial production. The mark-up in manufacturing is measured by the average of gross profit divided by direct production costs in the manufacturing sectors of the USA and the UK, where each of these individual series is constructed from manufacturing production census data of that country. The capital stock variables are each proxied in the usual way (for example Balassa, 1978; Feder, 1982). Investment share data are obtained from the Summers and Heston (1988) and (1991) data bases. All nominal values are expressed in US dollar terms and all growth rates are evaluated as the first difference in the natural logarithm of the variable in question. Further details regarding both the sources and definitions of these series are given in the data appendix to this chapter (pp. 61–2).

Testing the variables of a model for stationarity prior to regression estimation is now well established as an essential component of econometric practice. The results that are obtained when the augmented Dickey–Fuller unit-root tests are applied to the six variables of our model are summarized in Table 4.1. The results of these tests lead us to reject, for each variable expressed in growth rate form as a first difference of natural logarithms, the null-hypothesis of a unit root. In essence, what these results show is

Table 4.1   Unit root tests

Variable	Augmented Dickey–Fuller tests			
	Levels		First differences	
$\ln M$	−0.9338	(−2.9499)	−3.8467	(−2.9472)
$\ln p_R$	−0.3987	(−2.9472)	−5.4560	(−2.9446)
$\ln p_X$	0.5213	(−2.9499)	−3.8751	(−2.9472)
$\ln w_R$	−1.0198	(−2.9472)	−3.2705	(−2.9446)
$\ln w_X$	−0.3008	(−2.9472)	−3.9786	(−2.9446)
$\ln X$	−2.2446	(−2.9499)	−4.3122	(−2.9472)
$\ln K_R$			−2.9529	(−2.9472)
$\ln K_X$			−3.1665	(−2.9472)

Notes: In the normal way, the order of the lag polynomial for the ADF test is chosen in each case so that the residuals of the ADF regression appear as white noise. Figures in parentheses denote the relevant 95 per cent critical values.

that the levels of the logarithms of M, p_r, p_x, w_R, w_X, X, K_R and K_X are each $I(1)$ variables.[10]

For estimation purposes, the rate of growth of manufacturing output and the rates of growth of capital input in each sector are treated as exogenously determined. The remaining five variables of the model are treated as endogenous. The mark-up equation poses no particular estimation problems. As the right-hand side variable of equation (4.9) is exogenous, the parameters of this equation may be estimated by ordinary least-squares regression (OLS), or some suitable alternative single-equation procedure. The remaining four equations of the model make up a system of simultaneous equations and therefore require the application of appropriate simultaneous estimation techniques. In the empirical work reported below, the parameters of each of these four equations are estimated using the generalized instrumental variable (GIVE) method. Since the set of instruments employed in the estimation of these equations includes all the predetermined variables of the simultaneous equation model, the estimates obtained are equivalent to two-stage least-squares (2SLS) estimates. A listing of the instrument set is provided at the foot of Table 4.2.

The results obtained when the model is estimated using the data described above are summarized in Table 4.2. The results reported in equation number (T.2.1) indicate that the rate of growth of one plus the manufacturing mark-up is not significantly related to the rate of growth of manufacturing production. This suggests the absence, over the period under study, of cyclical movement in the rate of change of the mark-up factor in manufacturing.[11] Dropping the manufacturing production growth variable, we obtain the results reported in equation (T.2.2). The positive and significant estimated coefficient of the constant term in (T.2.2) provides evidence of a positive trend in the mark-up over direct cost in manufacturing over the 1948 to 1986 period, with the estimated trend being +0.368 percent per annum.[12]

Manufacturing production growth and the growth rates for both wages and capital stock in the manufacturing sector appear in the primary product price equation, equation (4.5), due to their potential influence on the derived demand for primary products as raw materials in manufacturing. The length of the production process and the time required for adjustment of input choices to relative input prices may result in a lagged response of the derived demand to the manufacturing variables. We allow for such lagged response by estimating equation (4.5) with various lag combinations for the manufacturing variables. This exercise confirms the presence of a one-period lag on the manufacturing wage variable, but no

Table 4.2 Estimates of model of manufacturing margin, price and wage growth, 1948–86

Part I Estimated coefficients of $\dot{M}$ equation

Equation no.	Dependent variable	Intercept	$\dot{X}$	R^2	D-W	LM_1	LM_R	LM_N	Estimation method
T.2.1	$\dot{M}$	0.00387 (1.52)	−0.00346 (0.10)	0.0003	1.726	0.085	0.801	2.246	OLS
T.2.2	$\dot{M}$	0.00368 (2.34)	—	0.0	1.719	0.078	—	2.304	OLS

Part II Estimated coefficients of primary product and finished goods price growth equations

Equation no.	Dependent variable	Intercept	$\dot{X}$	$\dot{w}_R$	$\dot{w}_X(-1)$	$\dot{K}_R(-1)$	$\dot{K}_X(-1)$	R^2	D-W	LM_1	LM_R	LM_N	Estimation method
T.2.3	$\dot{p}_R$	−0.16928 (0.51)	1.6138 (2.42)	0.30653 (0.55)	0.39614 (0.63)	0.70792 (0.66)	−0.24231 (0.13)	0.182	1.828	0.668	0.769	2.398	GIVE/2SLS

Equation no.	Dependent variable	Intercept	$\dot{X}$	$\dot{w}_X$	$\dot{p}_R(-1)$	$\dot{M}(-1)$	$\dot{K}_X(-1)$	R^2	D-W	LM_1	LM_R	LM_N	Estimation method
T.2.4	$\dot{p}_X$	−0.00617 (0.06)	0.2894 (1.15)	0.17613 (2.99)	0.57244 (3.64)	0.8453 (1.03)	−0.07413 (0.18)	0.718	1.52	—	—	—	GIVE/2SLS

Table 4.2 (Continued)

Part III Estimated coefficients of primary and manufacturing wage growth equations

Equation no.	Dependent variable	Intercept	$\dot{p}_X$	$\dot{X}$	$\dot{w}_X$	$\dot{K}_R(-1)$	$\dot{K}_X(-1)$	$[\dot{w}_x(-1) - \dot{p}_x(-1)]$	R^2	$D-W$	LM_1	LM_R	LM_N	Estimation method
T.2.5	$\dot{w}_R$	−0.3009 (0.98)	1.2549 (0.89)	−0.68764 (0.92)	0.06604 (0.04)	−1.0035 (0.71)	2.1562 (0.97)	—	0.24	1.903	0.232	4.06	1.553	GIVE/2SLS
T.2.6	$\dot{w}_X$	0.03356 (2.99)	0.90614 (5.48)	−0.147 (0.81)	—	—	—	0.28057 (1.27)	0.705	1.783	1.808	2.47	0.267	GIVE/2SLS

Notes:

(a) Figures in parentheses are absolute 't' ratios. LM_1 denotes the test statistic for the Lagrange multiplier test for first-order autocorrelation, which is distributed as χ^2 with 1 degree of freedom. LM_R denotes Ramsey's (1969) RESET test statistic of functional form, which is also distributed as χ^2 with 1 degree of freedom. LM_N is the Lagrange multiplier test of normality, which is distributed as χ^2 with 2 degrees of freedom. Equation (4.2.4) is adjusted for autocorrelation.

(b) As discussed in the text, equations (T.2.3) through (T.2.6) are estimated using the generalized instrument variable (GIVE) method. In each case the instrument set is as follows: intercept, $\dot{X}$, $\dot{p}_R(-1)$, $\dot{w}_x(-1)$, $M(-1)$, K_R, K_X and $\dot{p}_X(-1)$. Since this set of instruments is the full set of predetermined variables of the simultaneous equation model, this procedure yields 2SLS estimates. Notice that it is immaterial whether $w_X(-1)$ is used with $\dot{p}_X(-1)$ or $[\dot{w}_x(-1) - \dot{p}_x(-1)]$ in the instrument set as identical results are yielded.

(c) The rates of capital growth in each of the two sectors is proxied by the respective ratio of investment to income. To avoid any possibility of endogeneity problems, these ratios are used with a one-period lag. However, the results that are obtained when the model is estimated without such lags (available from the authors on request) are very little altered.

lag on the manufacturing production variable. The resulting specification of the primary-price equation is reported in (T.2.3).

The results set out in (T.2.3) provide an encouraging degree of support for our model of primary-product price determination. All variables other than the growth rate for primary-sector capital stock are correctly signed. However, the rate of output growth is the only variable that is statistically significant at the 5 per cent level in this particular equation. The regression diagnostics provide no evidence of serial-correlation problems of either first or higher order. In addition, they provide no evidence to throw into doubt either the functional form or the normality of errors.

Our analysis of industrial pricing suggests possible lags in the influence of the right-hand-side variables in the manufactured goods price equation. Examination of the results of regressions with a range of alternative lag specifications suggests that the most appropriate lag specification involves a one-period lag on both the primary-product price and the manufacturing mark-up, but no lag on the manufacturing wage rate. The results obtained when this specification is estimated by GIVE/2SLS are reported in equation (T.2.4).

The sign of each estimated coefficient in equation (T.2.4) is consistent with the predictions of our model of manufacturing price determination, and the primary-product price term and the manufacturing wage term are both statistically significant at the one percent level. Our model further implies the restriction that the coefficient of the growth rate of the manufacturing mark-up factor equals one. The estimated coefficient of this variable reported in (T.2.4) is 0.8453. Performing a 't' test on the null hypothesis that the coefficient of M is plus unity we obtain a value of 't', with 30 degrees of freedom, equal to –0.188, so that we are unable to reject the null-hypothesis. Another restriction implied by our model is that the coefficients of the primary price and manufacturing wages sum to one. The estimated coefficients reported in equation (T. 2.4) sum to 0.7485 and employing the conventional 't' test we obtain a 't' value of –1.80, which is such that we are unable to reject this restriction at the five per cent level on a two-tailed test. Finally, the estimated coefficient of the manufacturing output variable in equation (T. 2.4) is not significantly different from zero.[13]

As may be seen from equation (T. 2.5), none of the variables suggested by equation (4.11) as influencing wage movements in primary production shows up as significant. The weak results for this equation are perhaps not surprising given the poor quality of the available data on wage rates of primary sector workers in developing countries. The market for wage labour in developing countries is often not well developed, with much labour supplied through family and other traditional modes of economic organization.

The 2SLS results obtained by estimating equation (4.12) for wage growth in the manufacturing sector are set out in equation (T. 2.6). All variables in this equation are correctly signed. The estimated coefficient of the manufactured goods price term is highly significant and its value is such that we are unable to reject the restriction suggested by our model that its value is equal to plus one, the relevant 't' value being –0.57. Neither the coefficient of the lagged real wage growth term nor the coefficient of manufacturing output growth is significantly different from zero. It may be noted that this equation's diagnostic statistics provide no evidence of either serially-correlated or non-normally distributed errors or of a misspecification of functional form.

In overall terms, the simultaneous equation estimates summarized in Table 4.2 provide a degree of empirical support for our model. In particular, they offer confirmation of a number of hypotheses and parameters restrictions suggested by the model. However, one disappointing feature relates to the insignificance of the capital stock terms in equations (T. 2.3) to (T. 2.5). As noted above, in the absence of satisfactory capital stock data, we follow the standard and widely practised procedure of using the investment to output ratio as a proxy for capital stock growth. In the interest of providing a parsimonious and efficient set of parameter estimates, we omit capital stock variables and other variables with insignificant coefficients from the estimating equations.

Table 4.3 reports results that are obtained when the simultaneous equation of price and wage growth is re-estimated with variables omitted as explained above. The GIVE estimation procedure is again employed. Since the instrument set used in deriving the results set out in Table 4.3 includes all the retained variables that are predetermined, this procedure is equivalent to 2SLS.

All of the estimated coefficients reported in Table 4.3 are correctly signed. As with the results in Table 4.2, we are unable to reject the restrictions on coefficient values suggested by our model. The restriction that the coefficient of the manufacturing mark-up factor in equation (T. 3.4) is equal to one yields a 't' value of –0.22, while the same restriction on the coefficient of the manufactured goods price variable equation (T. 3.6) yields a 't' value of –1.33. Likewise, the results reported for equation (T. 3.4) are such that we are unable to reject the restriction that the coefficients of the primary product price and manufacturing wage terms sum to one, as the coefficients sum to 0.907 and the restriction yields a 't' value of –0.55. Another restriction implied by our model is that the

Table 4.3 Further estimates of model of price and wage growth, 1948–86

Part I Estimated coefficients of primary product and finished goods price growth equations

Equation no.	Dependent variable	Intercept	$\dot{X}$	$\dot{w}_R$	$\dot{w}_X(-1)$	R^2	D–W	LM_1	LM_R	LM_N	LM_S	Estimation method
T.3.3	$\dot{p}_R$	-0.08731 (2.14)	1.442 (2.81)	0.2164 (0.81)	0.45124 (1.66)	0.207	1.722	1.667	0.56	3.98	5.74 (2)	GIVE/2SLS

Equation no.	Dependent variable	Intercept	$\dot{X}$	$\dot{p}_R(-1)$	$\dot{w}_X$	$\dot{M}(-1)$	R^2	D–W	LM_1	LM_R	LM_N	LM_S	Estimation method
T.3.4	$\dot{p}_X$	-0.02589 (1.6642)	0.0814 (0.5873)	0.1279 (2.075)	0.7791 (3.8527)	0.83655 (1.1124)	0.774	1.537	2.437	4.43	4.6	0.198 (1)	GIVE/2SLS

Part II Estimated coefficients of primary and manufacturing wage growth equations

Equation no.	Dependent variable	Intercept	$\dot{p}_X$	$[\dot{w}_X(-1) - \dot{p}_X(-1)]$	R^2	D–W	LM_1	LM_R	LM_N	LM_S	Estimation method
T.3.5	$\dot{w}_R$	0.00430 (0.1473)	0.98826 (1.9461)	—	0.3	2.047	1.169	3.24	0.422	9.162 (4)	GIVE/2SLS
T.3.6	$\dot{w}_X$	0.03464 (4.939)	0.83639 (6.789)	0.10138 (1.1205)	0.751	1.786	0.57	2.364	3.421	3.48 (3)	GIVE/2SLS

Notes:
(a) Figures in parentheses are absolute 't' ratios. LM_1 denotes the test statistic for the Lagrange multiplier test for first-order autocorrelation, which is distributed as χ^2 with 1 degree of freedom. LMR denotes Ramsey's (1969) RESET test statistic of functional form, which is also distributed as χ^2 with 1 degree of freedom. LMN is the Lagrange multiplier test of normality, which is distributed as χ^2 with 2 degrees of freedom.
(b) The instrument set for all equations is intercept, $\dot{X}$, $\dot{p}_R(-1)$, $\dot{w}_X(-1)$, $\dot{M}(-1)$, $\dot{p}_X(-1)$.
(c) LM_S denotes Sargan's (1964) misspecification test for IV estimators. Under the null hypothesis that the regression is correctly specified and that the instrument set used is valid, it is distributed as χ^2 with degrees of freedom as indicated in parentheses under the test value.

coefficients of the two wage growth terms in the primary price equation, equation (T. 3.3), sum to unity. This restriction yields a 't' value of -1.05, so that we are unable to reject the restriction at the 5 per cent significance level.

The diagnostic statistics reported in Table 4.3 provide no evidence of serial correlation, non-normal errors or misspecification of functional form. Sargan's (1964) misspecification test statistic for instrumental variable estimation is denoted by LM_s. The values of this statistic as set out in Table 4.3 are such that in the case of each regression we are unable to reject the hypothesis that the regression is correctly specified and that the instrument set used is valid.

The weak performance of the primary-sector wage equation in Table 4.2 is noted above. The primary-sector wage equation is re-estimated with all but the manufacturing-sector price variable omitted and the results are reported as equation (T. 3.5). These results reveal that the rate of growth of prices in manufacturing exerts a positive and statistically significant influence upon the rate of wage growth in the primary sector. The diagnostic statistics indicate that this simple formulation does not suffer from either serial correlation or non-normality of errors. In addition, the results of Ramsey's (1969) RESET test provide no grounds to doubt the adequacy of the equation's functional form.[14]

4.5   PREBISCH AND SINGER EFFECTS ON TREND IN THE TERMS OF TRADE

Prebisch (1950) and Singer (1950) both find evidence of the existence of a downward trend to the terms of trade between primary producers and manufacturers using data covering the period up to the Second World War. The data used in our study for the period 1948 to 1986 also show a faster rate of increase for manufacturing prices than for primary product prices, such that there is an average decline in the terms of trade of primary producers of more than one per cent per annum in the post-war period.

Our structural model of prices and wages incorporates the effects that Prebisch and Singer identify as contributing to the downward trend. Differences in market structure identified by Prebisch are reflected in the labour and product markets for primary products being perfectly competitive, while markets for manufacturing labour and output are imperfectly competitive. Differences in technical change suggested by Singer are reflected in the assumption of neutral factor augmentation for primary product compared to only labour and raw material augmentation for manufacturing. We now use the regression estimates based on the structural model to examine the extent to which the Prebisch and Singer effects are responsible for a decline in the terms of trade of primary producers.

The rate of change in the terms of trade between primary producers and manufacturers is given by the rate of change of p_R/p_X and is approximated by the difference between the rates of change of primary prices and manufacturing prices. This difference can be expressed in terms of the estimated coefficients of our structural model by solving from the estimated coefficients of the pricing equations, taking account of the effect of primary product prices on manufacturing prices. For this purpose, we use solutions based on long-run constant growth rates, assuming that the current value of any variable is equal to its lagged value. The resulting solution using the regression coefficients for the pricing equations in the full model, equations (T. 2.3) and (T. 2.4), is given by:

$$\dot{p}_R - \dot{p}_X = -0.133 + 1.046\ \dot{X} + 0.301\dot{w}_R - 0.246\dot{w}_X \tag{4.13}$$
$$+ 0.583\ \dot{K}_R - 0.126\ \dot{K}_X - 0.845\ \dot{M}$$

The corresponding solution based on the reduced set of variables used in the regression estimates in equations (T. 3.3) and (T. 3.4) is given by

$$\dot{p}_R - \dot{p}_X = -0.050 + 1.176\dot{X} + 0.189\dot{w}_R \tag{4.14}$$
$$-0.385\dot{w}_X - 0.836\dot{M}$$

Equations (4.13) and (4.14) are used to decompose the trend in the terms of trade into components associated with each of the effects discussed in section 4.3 above. An estimate of the Singer effect, the impact of technological change on rate of change of the terms of trade of primary producers, is given by the constant term in either equation. The estimate from equation (4.13) is negative and large in magnitude at more than thirteen per cent per annum. However, it should be noted that the intercept terms in equations (T. 2.3) and (T. 2.4) are not statistically different from zero at the 10 per cent significance level using the two-tailed 't' test, so that the estimated effect on the terms of trade is lacking precision. The corresponding intercept terms in equations (T. 3.3) and (T. 3.4) are statistically less than zero at the 5 and 10 percent levels, respectively, suggesting greater precision for the implied estimate of the Singer effect from equation (4.14). However, this estimate of roughly −5 per cent per annum for the impact of technological change on the terms of trade suffers from potential bias due to absorbing the impact of a trend in any variable incorrectly excluded from the regressions in Table 4.3. Comparing the estimates from equations (4.13) and (4.14) suggests that the effect of this bias is to understate the negative impact of technical change on the terms of trade, leading to the conclusion that the true estimate is at least 5 per cent per annum.

Wage growth in manufacturing in our data sample exceeds that in the primary sector by approximately 3.5 per cent per annum (7 per cent growth in manufacturing versus 3.5 per cent growth in the primary sector). Using the coefficients from equation (4.13), this differential wage growth contributes somewhat more than 0.5 per cent to the downward trend in the terms of trade as part of the Prebisch effect. The other portion of the Prebisch effect is due to the upward trend in gross profit margins in manufacturing, which is approximately 0.4 per cent per annum over the period. Given the size of the mark-up coefficient in equation (4.13), the impact of this margin growth is to reduce the terms of trade of primary producers by approximately 0.3 per cent per annum. Hence, we estimate that the combined Prebisch effect lowers the terms of trade for primary producers by approximately 1 per cent per annum (the corresponding estimate of the Prebisch effect using equation (14) is that it lowers the terms of trade by approximately 2.5 per cent per annum).

Against the negative impacts of the Singer and Prebisch effects on the terms of trade for primary producers over the post-Second World War period, have been positive effects of capital accumulation and growth in industrial production (the Ricardo effect). As capital variables are excluded from the regressions reported in Table 4.3, only the Ricardo effect acts to offset the Singer and Prebisch effects calculated from equation (4.14). Manufacturing production has grown at historically high rates for most of the period since the war. Our measure of manufacturing output, the IMF index of world manufacturing output, grows at an average annual rate of 5.1 per cent from 1948 to 1986. This growth contributes almost 6 per cent per annum to the improvement in the terms of trade of primary producers using the coefficient of manufacturing output growth from equation (4.14), almost completely offsetting the Singer and Prebisch effects. The various components of the net trend in the terms of trade for primary producers are summarized in Table 4.4, leading to a net decline of almost 1.5 per cent per annum.

Using the coefficients for capital growth from Table 4.2 together with the mean values of capital growth for the manufacturing and primary sectors, we find that capital accumulation contributes almost 8 per cent toward an improvement in the terms of trade for primary producers. This adds to an estimated improvement due to the Ricardo effect of approximately 5.5 per

Table 4.4   Decomposition of trend in the terms of trade

Contribution to terms of trade due to:	Annual contribution calculated from:	
	Table 4.2 coefficients (%)	Table 4.3 coefficients (%)
Singer effect	−13.3	−5.0
Prebisch effect	−1.0	−2.4
Growth of manufacturing production (Ricardo effect)	+5.4	+6.0
Capital accumulation	+7.7	n.a.

cent per annum using the coefficients from Table 4.2. These two effects almost exactly offset the very large negative Singer effect in equation (4.13) to leave slightly more than the Prebisch effect of 1 per cent per annum as the estimate of the net decline in the terms of trade of primary producers.

The various influences on the terms of trade of primary producers identified in our post-war estimates may also help in explaining the negative trend found by Prebisch and Singer in the pre-war period. The index of manufacturing output growth used in this paper does not extend to the pre-war period, but other measures clearly suggest that the average annual rate of growth of manufacturing production was substantially lower in the earlier period. Data on manufacturing mark-up factors are even less readily comparable, but the large increases in concentration of production that occurred, particularly in the USA, in the late nineteenth century may have been associated with a more rapid increase in manufacturing mark-ups than that occurring in the post-Second World War period. Also, we have no reason to suspect that the difference in wage growth between workers in primary production and those in manufacturing contributed any less to deterioration in the terms of trade before the war than after the war. Thus, while we have no information on relative capital accumulation or the impact of technological change in the pre-war period, it is possible, although by no means proven, that it is differences in the rate of change of the variables in our structural model that account for a decline in the terms of trade of primary producers both before and after the Second World War. In particular, we have no reason to doubt the importance of Prebisch and Singer effects contributing to the adverse movement of the terms of trade of primary producers in either period.

The estimates from our structural model help to explain apparently conflicting findings in time-series analyses of trend in terms of trade between primary producers and manufacturers. There has been general support for the original finding of Prebisch and Singer of a downward trend in the terms of trade for primary producers in the period before the Second World War. However, differences emerge in the findings of various studies when the sample period is extended to include post-war years. A key element in reaching different conclusions is the inclusion of breaks or jumps in the data when estimating the trend relationship.[15] These breaks or jumps tend to occur at times of dramatic changes in the rate of growth of manufacturing output.[16] Equations (4.13) and (4.14) show that dramatic changes in the rate of growth of manufacturing output substantially alter the rate of change of the terms of trade. Thus, inclusion of breaks or jumps in the time-series analyses may simply disguise the influence of an omitted variable, namely manufacturing output growth.

Our analysis of the determination of prices of primary products and manufactured goods suggests that the trend in the terms of trade between primary producers and manufacturers is the net effect of separate and divergent influences. A full understanding of the movement in the terms of trade over any period requires examination of these influences. The estimates obtained from our five-equation model of price determination provide an illustration of how the various influences may be examined in the context of a relatively simple model over a relatively brief period.

Notes

An earlier version of this paper was presented to the Development Economics Policy Conference, celebrating Hans Singer's 85th birthday, hosted by the University of Innsbruck in May 1996. Comments from conference participants, particularly Hans Singer, are gratefully acknowledged. The usual disclaimer applies.

1. While elements of imperfect competition are found in at least some primary product markets, the extreme assumption of perfect competition allows us to draw a stark contrast between the general structure of commodity production and the general structure of manufacturing. We avoid having our empirical results influenced by the activities of the OPEC cartel by excluding fuels from our index of primary product prices used in the estimates presented in Section 4.4.
2. Long-run cost minimization in primary production requires a choice of capital and labour inputs that reflects the relative prices of these inputs. However, there are naturally determined constraints on the quantities of many capital inputs to primary production, for example, land, fish stocks and

mineral deposits. Even the quantity of man-made capital used in primary production is often difficult to vary except in the very long run, for example oil-drilling platforms, pipelines and irrigation systems. We therefore reject the idea that the quantity of capital employed in primary production will normally be at the cost-minimizing level. This corresponds to the type of assumption used by Darity (1990) in his analysis of long-period equilibrium in the trade between the developing and industrialized countries.

3. The relationship in (4.6) treats the transformation of primary products and labour into finished manufactured goods as occurring in a single instantaneous production process. In fact, there are generally several different firms operating at temporally separated stages of production. Primary product tends to enter at the first stage of production, so that it is reasonable to expect a lag in the effect of primary product prices on prices of finished goods. Likewise, the wage costs and mark-up factors of producers at early stages of production will have a lagged effect on prices of finished goods. Lag structures for the impact of wage rates, primary product prices and manufacturing mark-ups are empirically determined in the results presented below.

4. A negative time trend due to a high rate of neutral technical progress in primary production, need not harm primary producers as it also directly reduces the input required for production. However, a negative time trend due to raw material saving in manufacturing production lowers price to primary producers without the offsetting benefit of a direct reduction in inputs. Singer (1975) warns of the adverse consequence for primary producers of a bias in the research and development efforts of industrialized countries toward saving raw material, particularly in the development of synthetic materials. Singer also is aware that producers in developing countries may not be able to take advantage of technical change in either primary production or manufacturing, because they do not have access to information or to complementary capital and intermediate inputs.

5. The wage rates of manufacturing workers in developing countries and of primary sector workers in industrialized countries are not explicitly modelled in this analysis. Our purpose is to emphasize those wage rates that are most directly connected to the Prebisch–Singer hypothesis regarding deterioration in the terms of trade of those developing countries that are predominantly exporters of primary products and importers of manufactured goods. Thus, we measure the price of manufactured goods by a price index based exclusively on unit values of manufactured exports from industrialized countries, so that it is only the wage rates for manufacturing workers in the industrialized countries that properly enter into the determination of these prices. Likewise, it is the manufacturing wage rates in these countries that affect decisions on substitution between labour and primary product in the countries that account for the bulk of use of primary product as raw material in manufacturing, so that this wage rate properly enters equation (4.5), the price equation for primary products on world commodity markets. Wage rates for primary sector workers in either the developing countries or the industrialized countries could enter equation (4.5). However, if prices of primary products are equalized through arbitrage across countries and if there is competitive production in each country, market equilibrium requires a different rate of growth of capital stock in equation (4.5) depending on the wage

rate used. For the purpose of evaluating the Prebisch–Singer hypothesis, it is the growth rates of wage rates and capital stocks for developing countries that are included in estimating equation (4.5).

6. Our treatment of the wage rate in primary production as being competitively determined is consistent with the modelling of the agricultural wage rates in Harris and Todaro (1970). However, we do not allow for alternative employment in urbanized manufacturing. While some data on manufacturing wages in developing countries are available, there are no reliable corresponding data on unemployment rates for urban manufacturing workers. If it turns out that the expected wage rate for urban manufacturing, including allowance for expected periods of unemployment, is constant in real terms, then our model of labour supply to primary production fortuitously encompasses the alternative of urban manufacturing employment as well as the alternative of subsistence agriculture.

7. Lewis (1954) argues that unlimited supplies of labour in subsistence agriculture prevent real wage rates from rising with economic growth. This would occur in equation (4.11) if the value of ϕ approaches infinity. In contrast, a value of ϕ equal to zero implies a fixed supply of labour to primary production. The assumption that the cost of living depends only on the price of manufactures (and not the price of primary products) is consistent with our treatment of primary products as solely used as raw materials in manufacturing. When we estimate a primary wage equation that implicitly allows the price of primary products to enter the cost of living, we find that the estimated coefficient of the price of primary products is not statistically different from zero at the 5 per cent level.

8. McDonald and Solow argue that under plausible assumptions 'it would not be surprising to find large fluctuations in employment and small unsystematic fluctuations in real wages during business cycles' (1981, p. 896).

9. The reservation wage for workers in a particular manufacturing industry is primarily based on the current or lagged wage rates for workers in other industries. Aggregating over all of manufacturing leads to a reservation wage that is positively related to the aggregate level of current and lagged wage rates. As the wage rate outcome in the solutions to the bargaining problem in McDonald and Solow (1981) tend to increase with the reservation wage, there is a suggestion of positive feedback to the current wage rate from current and past wage rates.

10. Investment share is used as a proxy for the growth rate of each of the capital stock variables. Thus, there are no measures for the levels of the capital stock variables in our data set and no test value is shown for levels of the variables in Table 4.1. The test values shown for the first differences are actually for the levels of the investment share proxies.

11. We test for possible lagged cyclical responses by re-estimating equation (4.10) with a distributed lag term specified on the manufacturing production growth variable. The results obtained provide no evidence of significant cyclical responses.

12. Equation (T. 2.1) corresponds to the *difference–stationary* model due to Beveridge and Nelson (1981) and Nelson and Plosser (1982). As demonstrated by Cuddington and Urzua (1989), this is an appropriate procedure for trend-estimation in situations where it is not possible to reject the hypothesis

that the variable in question possesses a unit-root, as is indeed the case here with the level of log M.

13. A zero value for the coefficient of the manufacturing output growth variable in the manufacturing price equation, equation (4.7), occurs if there are constant returns to scale for the combination of labour and primary product as inputs to manufacturing. Such constant returns to scale are often imposed in applications of mark-up pricing to manufacturing. While the assumption of such constant returns is not required for our formulation of the manufacturing pricing equation, the insignificance of the estimated coefficient of the manufacturing output variable in equation (T. 2.4) suggests that the implication of the assumption cannot be rejected in any event.

14. Notice also that we are unable to reject the null hypothesis that the coefficient of the manufacturing price term in (T. 3.5) is unity, with the relevant 't' value being –0.02. This suggests that the nominal wage rate in the primary sector is linear homogeneous in manufacturing prices.

15. Spraos (1980) makes no allowance for breaks or jumps in the data and finds no evidence of trend when the sample period is extended to include data from the post-war period. More recently, Sapsford (1985) argues that once allowance is made for an upward break in the terms of trade in 1950, there is evidence of a downward trend to the terms of trade over a sample period including the post-war data. Finally, Powell (1991) finds no evidence of a trend in the terms of trade over the period 1900 to 1986 after allowing for downward jumps in the terms of trade in 1921, 1938 and 1975.

16. The break identified by Sapsford (1985) in 1950 occurs during a period of exceptionally high growth in manufacturing output, while the jumps identified by Powell (1991) each occur at points of sharp downturns in manufacturing output: 1921, 1938 and 1975. Bloch and Sapsford (1991–2) show clear evidence of procyclical movements of the terms of trade between primary producers and manufacturers in the post-war period, extending results found by Kalecki (1971) for the pre-war period.

References

Balassa, B. (1978) 'Exports and Economic Growth: Further Evidence', *Journal of Development Economics*, vol. 5, pp. 181–9.

Beveridge, S. and C. Nelson (1981) 'A New Approach to Decomposition of Economic Time Series into Permanent and Transitory Components with Particular Attention to Measurement of the Business Cycle', *Journal of Monetary Economics*, vol. 7, pp. 151–74.

Bils, M. (1987) 'The Cyclical Behaviour of Marginal Cost and Price', *American Economic Review*, vol. 77, pp. 838–55.

Bloch, H. and D. Sapsford (1991–2) 'Post-War Movements in Prices of Primary Products and Manufactured Goods', *Journal of Post Keynesian Economics*, vol. 14, pp. 249–67.

Cuddington, J.T. and C.M. Urzua (1989) 'Trends and Cycles in the Net Barter Terms of Trade: A New Approach' *Economic Journal*, vol. 99, pp. 426–42.

Coutts, K., W. Godley and W. Nordhaus (1978) *Industrial Pricing in the UK* (Cambridge University Press).

Darity, W. (1990) 'The Fundamental Determinants of the Terms of Trade Reconsidered: Long-Run and Long-Period Equilibrium', *American Economic Review*, vol. 80, pp. 816–27.

Feder, G. (1982) 'On Exports and Economic Growth,' *Journal of Development Economics*, vol. 12, pp. 59–73.

Findlay, R. (1980) 'The Terms of Trade and Equilibrium Growth in the World Economy', *American Economic Review*, vol. 70, pp. 291–9.

Grilli, E.R. and M.C. Yang (1988) 'Primary Commodity Prices, Manufactured Goods Prices, and Terms of Trade of Developing Countries', *World Bank Economic Review*, vol. 2, pp. 1–48.

Harris, J.R. and M.P. Todaro (1970) 'Migration, Unemployment and Development: A Two-Sector Analysis', *American Economic Review*, vol. 60, pp. 126–42.

Kalecki, M. (1971) 'Selected Essays on the Dynamics of the Capitalist Economy: 1933–1970', (Cambridge University Press).

Lewis, W.A. (1954), 'Economic Development with Unlimited Supplies of Labour', *Manchester School*, vol. 22, pp. 130–90.

McDonald, I.M. and R.M. Solow (1981), 'Wage Bargaining and Employment', *American Economic Review*, vol. 71, pp. 896–908.

Maizels, A. (1992) *Commodities in Crisis* (Oxford: Clarendon Press).

Nelson, C and G. Plosser (1982) 'Trends and Random Walks in Macroeconomic Time Series', *Journal of Monetary Economics*, vol. 10, pp. 139–62.

Powell, A. (1991), 'Commodity and Developing Country Terms of Trade: What Does the Long Run Show?', *Economic Journal*, vol. 101, pp. 1485–96.

Prebisch, R. (1950) 'The Economic Development of Latin America and its Principal Problems', UN ECLA; also published in *Economic Bulletin for Latin America*, vol. 7 (1962) pp. 1–22.

Ramsey, J.B. (1969) 'Tests for Specification Errors in Classical Linear Least Squares Regression Analysis', *Journal of the Royal Statistical Society* (Series B), vol. 31, pp. 350–71.

Rotemberg, J.J. and G. Saloner (1986) 'A Supergame-Theoretic Model of Business Cycles and Price Wars During Booms', *American Economic Review*, vol. 76, pp. 390–407.

Sapsford, D. (1985) 'The Statistical Debate on the Net Barter Terms of Trade Between Primary Commodities and Manufactures: A Comment and Some Additional Evidence', *Economic Journal*, vol. 95, pp. 781–8.

—— and V.N. Balasubramanyam (1994) 'The Long-Run Behaviour of the Relative Price of Primary Commodities: Statistical Evidence and Policy Implications', *World Development*, vol. 22, pp. 1737–45.

Sargan, J.D. (1964) 'Wages in Prices in the United Kingdom: A Study in Econometric Methodology,' in P.E. Hart, G. Mills and J.K. Whitaker (eds) *Econometric Analysis for National Economic Planning* (London: Butterworth) pp. 25–54.

Sawyer, M. (1983) *Business Pricing and Inflation* (London: Macmillan).

Singer, H. (1950) 'The Distribution of Gains Between Investing and Borrowing Countries', *American Economic Review, Papers and Proceedings*, vol. 40, pp. 473–85.

—— (1975) 'The Distribution of Gains Revisited', in H. Singer (ed.) *The Strategy of International Development* (London: Macmillan) pp. 58–66.

Spraos, J. (1980) 'The Statistical Debate on the Net Barter Terms of Trade Between Primary Products and Manufactures', *Economic Journal*, vol. 90, pp. 107–28.

Summers, R. and A. Heston (1988) 'A New Set of International Comparisons of Real Product and Price Levels: Estimates for 130 Countries, 1950–85', *Review of Income and Wealth*, vol. 34, pp. 1–25.

—— and —— (1991) 'The Penn World Table [Mark 5]: An Expanded Set of International Comparisons, 1950–1988,' *Quarterly Journal of Economics*, vol. 106, pp. 327–68.

DATA APPENDIX 4A.1

Primary product price (p_R)
World Bank index of the prices of twenty-four internationally traded non-fuel primary products.
Source: Grilli and Yang (1988).

Manufactured goods price (p_X)
World Bank index of unit values of manufactured exports from industrialized countries.
Source: Grilli and Yang (1988).

Manufacturing output (X)
International Monetary Fund index of world manufacturing output.
Source: International Monetary Fund Research Department (Commodities Division) database.

Primary sector wage (w_R)
Weighted average of agricultural wages (expressed in US$ terms) in the following sample of countries: Mexico, Sri Lanka, India, Chile and Turkey. Weights used are the shares of each country in world primary product exports.
Sources: wages – *International Labour Organisation Yearbook* and *United Nations Statistical Yearbook* (various edns); exchange rates – *International Financial Statistics* (International Monetary Fund, Washington DC) (various edns); weights – *Commodity Trade and Price Trends* (World Bank: Washington DC, 1980).

Manufacturing sector wage (w_X)
Unweighted average of manufacturing wages (expressed in US$ terms) in the following countries: UK, USA, France, Germany and Sweden.
Sources: wages – *International Labour Organisation Yearbook* and *United Nations Statistical Yearbook* (various editions) plus country-specific sources; exchange rates – as above.

Manufacturing mark-up factor (M)
One plus the average of US and UK ratios of gross profit (value added minus wage cost) to direct cost (cost of materials plus wage cost) for the manufacturing sector.

Sources: UK – *Historical Record of the Census of Production, 1900–1970* (HMSO, London) and annual censuses of production; USA – *Statistical Abstract of the US* (Bureau of Census, Washington) (various editions) and *The Statistical History of the US* (Basic Books; New York, 1976).

Capital stock growth ($\dot{K}_X$ and $\dot{K}_R$)

As noted in the text, the growth rates of capital stock are proxied by the share of investment in GDP. These proxies are constructed using the country-specific investment share data from the Summers and Heston (1988) database. The sample of countries and the pattern of weights for both sectors are the same as those noted above for use in the construction of the corresponding wage variables.

5 The Prebisch–Singer Hypothesis Revisited

Alfred Maizels, Theodosios B. Palaskas and Trevor Crowe

5.1 INTRODUCTION

Since the seminal contributions of Raúl Prebisch (1950) and Hans Singer (1950) on the tendency of the terms of trade of developing countries with developed countries to deteriorate over the long term, the ensuing debate on this issue has focused, until quite recently, on the evidence provided by the relative movements in the price of non-oil commodities and the unit value of manufactures exported by the developed countries. This was understandable and, indeed, entirely relevant since the greater part of the merchandise trade between these two groups of countries before the oil price increases of the 1970s had consisted of a 'vertical' exchange of non-oil primary commodities from developing countries for manufactured goods from developed countries.

The structure of the export trade of developing countries has, however, undergone a substantial transformation since the early 1980s, with a rapid growth in the exports of manufactures, which by the early 1990s had come to be the dominant flow of merchandise from developing to developed countries. By 1991, for example, manufactures exports to developed countries represented three times the value of non-oil commodities, whereas in 1980 exports of commodities had exceeded the value of manufactured exports (Table 5.1).

Over the past decade, the dominant exchange between developing and developed countries has thus become the 'horizontal' exchange of manufactures for other manufactures. This change in trade structure has led to the extension of the earlier debate – on the vertical commodities/manufactures terms of trade – to the new issue of the trend, if any, in the manufactures/manufactures terms of trade.

However, this new focus of the debate must not be taken to imply that the traditional concern with the commodities terms of trade can now be ignored. This is because the expansion in developing countries' exports of manufactures has been confined to relatively few countries. For example,

Table 5.1   Main trade flows between developing and developed countries: 1970, 1980 and 1991 ($ billion)

	Commodities	Fuels	Manufactures	Total
Exports from developing to developed countries				
1970	21	14	6	41
1980	74	265	63	401
1991	95	131	273	499
Exports from developed to developing countries				
1970	8	1	36	44
1980	54	7	254	315
1991	68	13	426	507

Notes:
1. 'Commodities' are all items in UN-SITC 0, 1, 2 and 4 plus 68; 'Fuels' relates to SITC 3 and 'Manufactures' to SITC 5 to 8 less 68.
2. 'Developed' countries are the developed market economies, while 'developing' includes China and Vietnam. Source: UNCTAD (1993), Appendix 5.1 tables.

the four Newly Industrializing Countries (NICs) of East Asia (Hong Kong, Singapore, South Korea and Taiwan) together with the ASEAN-4 (Indonesia, Malaysia, Philippines and Thailand) and China accounted for almost 80 per cent of the increase in the value of manufactures exported by all developing countries, including China, from 1980 to 1990. The proportion rises to almost 90 per cent if a further five countries (Brazil, India, Pakistan, Turkey and the former Yugoslavia) are included. This leaves well over 100 countries dependent, to a greater or lesser extent, on revenue from the export of primary (non-oil) commodities for the bulk of their export earnings. Thus, for the great majority of developing countries the commodity terms of trade remain a crucial element in their capacity to import essential goods for their economic development.

The present article reviews recent trends in both the commodity terms of trade and the manufactures terms of trade of developing countries *vis-à-vis* the developed countries using material both from the UN COMTRADE database, and from the data made available by the Statistical Office of the European Communities (EUROSTAT). Section 5.2 considers recent trends in the commodities/manufactures terms of trade, Section 5.3 is concerned with the manufacture/manufactures terms of trade, while Section 5.4 discusses terms of trade trends for certain developing areas. The final section of the present article brings together the main findings.

5.2 RECENT TRENDS IN THE COMMODITIES/MANUFACTURES TERMS OF TRADE

Real commodity prices had been on a downward trend in the 1950s, reflecting to a large extent the early post-war shortages of a wide range of foods and industrial raw materials (between the mid-1950s and the early 1960s the World Bank index of 33 commodities valued in constant prices showed an annual average deterioration of 4.0 per cent). From the early 1960s to the early 1970s, there appears to have been no significant trend in real commodity prices, while from the early 1970s to the end of that decade there was a small upward trend (see Table 5.2).

However, there was a dramatic change about 1980, with real commodity prices recording a fall so severe as to have been unprecedented since the Great Depression of the 1930s. By 1990, real commodity price had fallen to 45 per cent below the 1980 level, and continued to decline until mid-1993, with a temporary recovery from then to early 1995, when real commodity prices were little higher than 50 per cent of the 1980 level. The average annual deterioration in real commodity prices of over 5 per cent per annum has now been sustained for well over a decade

Table 5.2   Price trends of primary commodities and manufactures from 1960–2 to 1991–3 (per cent change per annum)

	1960–2 to 1970–2	1970–2 to 1979–81	1979–81 to 1983–5	1983–5 to 1991–3
Nominal prices:				
Commodities	2.2	11.8	−7.8	0.5
Manufactures	2.2	11.2	−2.2	5.8
Real commodity prices	0.0	0.6	−5.1	−5.2

Notes:
1. Prices in US dollars
2. Commodity price index from UNCTAD Monthly Commodity Price Bulletin (various issues), Geneva; Manufactures index is unit value of manufactures exported by developed market economy countries, in UN Monthly Bulletin of Statistics (various issues), New York.

(see Table 5.2). This major price shock for the commodity exporting countries has involved very large foreign exchange losses for them.

However, before using the commodity price index deflated by the manufactures unit value index as a measure of the 'commodity terms of trade', it is necessary to check whether in fact the former is a good proxy for commodity unit values (which would be the appropriate series to compare with manufactures unit values).

To do this, a commodity unit value series (UV) for the years 1970–88, which had been computed from UN COMTRADE data for an earlier study (Maizels, 1992, Table A.2) was updated to 1991, and also extended back to 1961. A comparison of this series with the UNCTAD commodity price index (PI) shows clearly that since 1980 the price index has not been a good proxy, while in earlier decades it was indeed acceptable. The regression $UV_t = a + bPI_t + u_t$ was run for the three samples 1961–91, 1961–79 and 1980–91. The (Chow test) F-statistic was then calculated to test the null hypothesis of no significant difference in the relationship between UV and PI in the two sub-periods (see Table 5.3). The F-statistic is highly significant and rejects the null hypothesis. Thus there does appear to be a break in the relationship at 1980, the unit value and price index diverging after that year. The large value for the constant in the sub-period 1980–91 may suggest the presence of a strong trend in the relationship in that period.

Probably a number of separate factors were involved in the smaller decline in commodity unit values than in the corresponding market prices since 1980. One factor was no doubt the well-known tendency of unit values to rise proportionately less than market prices during a price upswing, and to fall proportionately less than prices during a downswing.[1] However, a more important factor may have been the trend towards a

Table 5.3   Testing the relationship between UV and PI, 1961–91

	a	t-value (a)	b	t-value (b)	R-squared	Durbin–Watson statistic
1961–91	−1.872	−0.506	1.145	18.486	0.922	0.500
1961–79	−0.726	−0.411	1.037	29.002	0.980	1.202
1980–91	53.452	18.413	0.459	11.551	0.930	2.191

Chow test: $F_{(2,27)} = 198.68$.

higher proportion of processed goods in the total commodity exports of developing countries. A rough indicator of this trend is the increase in the proportion of commodity exports consisting of 'other food' (that is, other than tropical beverages and vegetable oilseeds and oils), the category containing most processed foods, which rose from 35 per cent in 1980 to 48 per cent in 1992. Processed foods are not included in the various published price indices, though they are in the unit value index. Price formation for most processed commodities is more akin to that for manufactures than to that for traditional commodities, so that their prices tend to be relatively 'sticky'. Their increasing share of total commodity exports of developing countries would thus appear to account for a significant part of the difference between the trends in prices and unit values since 1980.

A further contributory factor to this difference is that the price indices do not cover foods exported under preferential arrangements (for example, for sugar and bananas from ACP countries shipped to the European Community, or for sugar exported from Cuba to the former Soviet Union). Such exports, which are included in the unit value calculations, were effectively insulated from the sharp price declines suffered on the free market by comparable foods.

If the commodity unit value index is deflated by the UN index of unit value of manufactures exported by developed market economy countries, the deterioration in the deflated index (the 'commodity terms of trade') was 4.1 per cent per annum between the periods 1979–81 and 1989–91, as against 5.0 per cent per annum using the corresponding UNCTAD commodity price index. However, it seems likely that the UN unit value index for manufactured exports from developed countries has been subject to some significant downward bias since the mid-1980s, as a result of the sharp depreciation of the US dollar. This is an issue which requires further detailed examination.[2] Moreover, there exists the argument that a unit value index for manufactures might overstate the rise in manufactures prices because of the trend to quality improvement. With respect to commodity terms of trade, however, such an argument might well be defective because, as Hans Singer has argued, for many manufactures, quality has deteriorated over recent years, while, where technical quality has improved, the manufactures are often less appropriate for use in developing countries (for whom not all the technical changes incorporated are needed).

These results are still open to the criticism that both the commodity and manufactures unit value indices do not relate specifically to trade between developed and developing countries, so that there is a possibility that unit values for these flows of inter-regional trade may differ significantly from the corresponding unit values for total trade. Some insight into this problem can be had from the series of unit values of the trade between the European Community and developing countries calculated by EURO-STAT for the period from 1979 to 1994, which can usefully be compared with the corresponding unit value movement for the commodities and manufactures[3] intra-trade of the Community (note that all calculations involving EUROSTAT unit value series in this paper are in terms of the dollar, and as such might be influenced by dollar volatility, although such an influence would cancel out in terms of trade calculations).

Thus, with respect to the logarithms of unit value series for EU commodity exports to the developing countries (LUVEUXC) and EU commodity intra-trade (LUVEUIC), and EU manufactures exports to developing countries (LUVEUXM) and EU manufactures intra-trade (LUVEUIM), testing was performed to attempt to establish the relationship between the two. The order of integration of the series was established by Augmented Dickey–Fuller tests (see Table 5.4). A constant was included in the test regression as were two lags of the dependent variable in each case.

Evidently the four series in question are all non-stationary in levels. Further testing established them to be I(1). Given the problems associated with testing simple regressions of non-stationary variables, it was appropriate to test for a long-run equilibrium relationship (co-integration) between the two pairs of series. Co-integrating regressions and ADF statistics are given in Table 5.5.

No long-run stationary relationship was statistically established between the unit values for EU commodity exports to developing countries and EU intra-trade in commodities or between unit value series for EU manufactures exports to developing countries and EU intra-trade in manufactures. Nevertheless, and also bearing non-stationarity in mind, first differenced (Δ) regressions continually provided evidence of some relationship between the series, giving statistically significant coefficients (see Table 5.6).

Table 5.4 Testing series on EU/LDC trade and EU intra-trade for integration

Commodities	ADF-stat	Manufactures	ADF-stat
LUVEUXC	−1.226	LUVEUXM	−0.823
LUVEUIC	−1.303	LUVEUIM	−0.801

Table 5.5   Testing for co-integration between EU/LDC and EU intra-trade series

Co-integrating regression	ADF statistic
LUVEUXC = 1.146 + 0.746 LUVEUIC	−1.692 (2)
LUVEUXM = 0.054 + 0.989 LUVEUIM	−1.824 (2)

Note: The figures in brackets indicate the number of dependent variable lags used in the test regression to make the disturbance term white-noise.

Table 5.6   First differenced regressions of EU/LDC on EU intra-trade series

Dependent variable	Explanatory variable	Coefficient
ΔLUVEUXC	ΔLUVEUIC	0.669** (6.293)
ΔLUVEUXM	ΔLUVEUIM	0.900** (36.831)

Notes:
1. *t*-statistics in brackets.
2. ** indicates significance at a 99 per cent level.
3. one lag of the dependent variable was added to each regression to remove auto-correlation.

The close statistical relationship between the trends in unit values of EC exports of manufactures to developing countries and those of EC intra-trade in manufactures would indicate that the use of a unit value index for total manufactures exports from developed countries may well be a reasonable proxy for the corresponding unit value series for exports to developing countries. However, this conclusion needs to be verified by an analysis of export unit value trends for other developed countries, particularly the United States and Japan.

Further analysis of terms of trade, based on the annual EUROSTAT series for the period 1979–94 utilises the data for LUVEUMC (log of the unit value of EC imports of commodities from developing countries) and LUVEUXM (as defined above), together with LTTCMC2 (log of the NBTT facing developing countries in respect of the unit value of EC imports of commodities from them deflated by the unit value of EC exports of manufactures to them), and LITCMC2 (log of the income terms of trade of developing countries with respect to their manufactures trade with the EC).

The first part of the approach is in line with the methodology used by Sapsford, Sarkar and Singer (1992), and also by Cuddington (1992). The natural logarithms of the series (LY_t) were firstly tested for unit roots. The results of Said–Dickey (1984) tests are given in Table 5.7. In each case a constant was included in the test regression, but not a trend.

All the test statistics fail to reject the null hypothesis of non-stationary series at a 95 per cent level of significance. The series were all also tested for trend stationarity using the Said–Dickey (1984) approach presented in Cuddington (1992). In each case the hypothesis that the series are stationary around a trend was rejected. Further testing specifically established the series as I(1). Thus, it appears that all the series in question, according to our test results, contain unit roots, that is are I(1), integrated of order one.

As all the LY_t series are non-stationary in levels with and without a trend, and stationary in first differences, it is appropriate to use the difference stationary (D–S) model for the terms of trade.

$$LY_t - LY_{t-1} = (a-a) + b(t - (t-1)) + e_t$$

or

$$\Delta LY_t = b + e_t$$

(where $\Delta LY_t = LY_t - LY_{t-1}$, $A(L)e_t = B(L)u_t$, L is the lag operator, and b is the mean growth rate.

With respect to the difference stationary model, price shocks embodied in the innovations, u_t, may cause the growth rate temporarily to exceed or fall short of its mean rate. Provided the error process is stationary, the

Table 5.7　Estimated *t*-statistics for the unit root hypothesis

Series	t-statistic
LUVEUMC	–2.009 (2)
LUVEUXM	–0.823 (2)
LTTCMC2	–0.847 (1)
LITCMC2	–0.885 (2)

Note: figures in brackets following test statistics indicate the number of lags of the dependent variable used in the test regression to guarantee white noise residuals.

effect of the shock dies out over time, causing the growth rate to return to its historical mean rate.

Prebisch and Singer meant by secular deterioration a persistent, ongoing phenomenon (possibly obscured by strong cyclical movements). If shock effects die out over time, the trend (represented here by the constant) represents the long-run phenomenon. If ΔLy_t is stationary, then this constant represents the growth rate over time (interpreted as due to economic factors) after all cyclical movements (shocks) have been accounted for by the innovations term.

In the case of each of the series the D–S model was estimated by OLS. The results are given in Table 5.8. The series prefixed by Δ indicate the first difference series of the original logged series. In three cases the coefficient b (the time trend) was found to be statistically insignificant, thus providing no evidence for a trend in the series in question, while in one case (LTTCMC2, the logarithm of the commodities-manufactures terms of trade facing developing countries) the coefficient b was found to be statistically significant, providing evidence for a negative trend.

In each case the error process was also modelled. Box–Jenkins identification methods were used to identify the type of process from sample autocorrelations and partial autocorrelations, using up to 6 lags. The highest order moving average (MA) and autoregressive (AR) terms were noted. If MA and/or AR terms appeared to exist, Box–Jenkins estimation methods were used, bearing in mind the above information on the orders of AR and MA parts. If there appeared to be, or if estimation showed, no significant AR(ϕ) or MA(θ) terms, then the error process was modelled as well-behaved, that is $e_t = u_t$. If significant AR and/or MA terms were estimated then the error process was modelled as $A(L)e_t = B(L)u_t$, where L is the lag operator, noting only the significant ϕ and θ values. The resulting modelled error processes are shown in Table 5.9.

Table 5.8   OLS estimates of b from D–S model estimation (t-value in brackets)

Series	OLS estimate of b		Durbin–Watson statistic
ΔLUVEUMC	0.000	(0.004)	2.228
ΔLUVEUXM	0.042	(1.681)	1.580
ΔLTTCMC2	−0.042*	(−2.284)	1.517
ΔLITCMC2	−0.022	(−0.994)	1.491

Note: * represents significance at a 95 per cent level.

Table 5.9   Error processes

Series	Error process (t-values in brackets)
ΔLUVEUMC	$(1 + 0.923L^2)\,e_t = u_t$
	(2.761)
ΔLUVEUXM	$e_t = u_t$
ΔLTTCMC2	$e_t = u_t$
ΔLITCMC2	$(1 + 0.777L^2)\,e_t = u_t$
	(3.076)

Note: back forecasts used to generate starting values, etc. (BF) = 100.

Clearly, while some of the error processes are well-behaved, others follow AR processes. Innovations in the series not only affect any trend but also set in motion a cyclical movement in the series around the shifted trend. The nature of these cyclical deviations of actual series from their permanent level depends on the error process in question. In the two cases above in which it is not well-behaved, the error process contains AR components and thus shocks to the series are never fully dissipated; the series have long memory, allowing the anticipation of future movements in the series.

The second part of the approach follows the methodology introduced by Bleaney and Greenaway (1993). They observe that, if LY_t has a unit root it follows a random walk (possibly with drift) and does not in general revert to a trend, whilst if it has a less-than-unit root, it will tend to revert to trend. Thus they estimated the following specification:

$$\Delta LY_t = a + bt + \mu LY_{t-1} + e_t$$

If $\mu < 0$ it describes an error correction model in which the change in LY_t is negatively related to its current level. The error correction property arises from the fact that if LY_{t-1} is above its equilibrium value LY^*, then ΔLY_t will be lower than would otherwise be the case; and vice versa if $LY_{t-1} < LY^*$. If $\mu = 0$, LY_t describes a random walk with increasing variance over time. The closer μ is to -1, the faster LY_t will converge towards its long-run trend. The long-run equilibrium solution to the model is

$$\Delta LY_t = \beta, \text{ which gives } \beta = -b\mu^{-1} \text{ which is the implicit trend.}$$

The results of the estimated regressions are given in Table 5.10.

Evidently, the trend (time coefficient) is statistically significantly different from zero in every case. It is significantly negative for both terms

Table 5.10   Regression estimations

	constant (a)	time (b)	LY_{t-1} (μ)	dep. var. lags	ΔLY_{t-1}	imp. trend $(-b\mu^{-1})$	R^2	J–B stat. (normality)
ΔLUVEUMC	3.087** (3.221)	0.009** (2.584)	−0.697 (−3.289)	1	0.060 (0.271)	0.012	0.627	1.063
ΔLUVEUXM	2.050** (2.982)	0.037** (3.124)	−0.546 (−3.008)	1	0.390 (1.709)	0.068	0.517	0.393
ΔLTTCMC2	3.571* (2.416)	−0.036* (−2.265)	−0.677 (−2.447)	1	0.510 (1.726)	−0.053	0.400	0.416
ΔLITCMC2	5.582** (3.655)	−0.030** (−3.007)	−1.131* (−3.682)	1	0.758** (2.584)	−0.027	0.590	1.240

Notes
1. * and ** indicate significance at a 95 per cent and 99 per cent level respectively.
2. critical values for *t*-value of μ at 95 per cent and 99 per cent levels of significance respectively are −3.50 and −4.15.
3. *t*-values in brackets.

of trade series, *viz.* LTTCMC2 (the logarithm of the commodities-manufactures net barter terms of trade facing developing countries) and LITCMC2 (the logarithm of the commodities-manufactures income terms of trade facing developing countries). For all four series, the sign of the calculated implicit trend is the same as that of the time coefficient. In addition, the Jarques–Bera statistic is insignificant in each case, indicating the normality of residuals. Sufficient lags of the dependent variable were added in each case to remove any autocorrelation apparent after testing.

With respect to the nature of each of the series, Bleaney and Greenaway (1993) note that four distinct hypotheses exist, depending on the combination of the values of the estimated parameters b and μ. For $b = 0$ or $b \neq 0$ and $\mu = 0$ the generating process of LY_t is a random walk in both cases. When $b = 0$ it has zero mean and a short memory, while when $b \neq 0$ it has drift, so that its divergence from its equilibrium value depends on whether its sign is positive or negative. If $b = 0$ and $\mu < 0$, LY_t has no long-term trend but tends to be pulled back towards its historical mean, the speed of the adjustment depending on the proximity of μ to 1. If $b \neq 0$ and $\mu < 0$, LY_t reverts towards a non-zero long-run trend.

Thus, in terms of the nature of the series in question, it is evident that all of the series except one exhibit a random walk with drift. The one series which does exhibit a non-zero long-run trend is LITCMC2 (the logarithm of the commodities–manufactures income terms of trade facing developing countries) which shows a negative long-run trend. It should be noted that some of the series may not appear to exhibit a long-run trend due to the shortness of the sample.

Overall, both approaches provide supportive evidence for the Prebisch–Singer hypothesis. While the first approach identifies a downward time trend for the commodities–manufactures terms of trade facing developing countries, the second approach provides more information and identifies a significant negative trend for the commodities–manufactures net barter terms of trade facing developing countries, and a significant negative long-run trend for their commodities–manufactures income terms of trade.

The rate of deterioration in the commodities-manufactures NBTT of developing countries has worsened substantially since 1980. For the earlier post-war period, 1950–75, the careful analysis by Spraos (1983) found significant deterioration in the range of 1.1 per cent to 1.65 per cent per annum, depending on the series used, while the corresponding trend deterioration for earlier periods was estimated at 0.46 per cent or 0.64 per cent per annum from the 1870s to 1938, depending on the source used, and at 0.73 per cent per annum for 1900–38. However, for the longer period 1876 to 1970 he concluded that there had been no significant trend deterioration. Sapsford (1985) showed that, if the period is divided into two sub-periods, with a structural break for the Second World War, the deterioration for 1900–82 was 1.2 per cent per annum. A more recent study by Bleaney and Greenaway (1993) using a log-difference error correction model found a trend deterioration of 0.8 per cent per annum over the longer period 1901–91, with a structural break in 1980. A more detailed review of these and other relevant empirical studies concluded that 'seems little doubt that for the last thirty years, at least, the terms of trade of primary products of LDCs have deteriorated at roughly the average rate of decline estimated by Spraos for the period up to 1938' (Thirlwall, 1995).

This conclusion appears seriously to minimize the magnitude of the commodities–manufactures NBTT deterioration since 1980, at least as regards EC trade with developing countries (estimated at 4.2 per cent per annum in Table 5.8, or 3.6 per cent per annum in Table 5.10), and in the region of 4 per cent per annum for trade between all developed and developing countries. The deterioration in the commodities–manufactures NBTT of developing countries in their trade with the EC was, moreover, only partly offset by an expansion in the volume of commodities imported by the EC from developing countries (by some 2.2 per cent per annum). Consequently, the income terms of trade of developing countries in the exchange of commodities for manufactures was also on a negative trend from 1980.

5.3 RECENT TRENDS IN THE MANUFACTURES–MANUFACTURES TERMS OF TRADE

The original Prebisch–Singer thesis was supported essentially in terms of the much lower income-elasticity of demand for primary commodities than for manufactures, and an upward supply bias for commodities resulting from the existence of a pool of unemployed or underemployed labour in developing countries. In a later review of his original 1950 paper, Singer elaborated on the influence of scientific and technological capacities on the terms of trade of developing countries. Since, he argued, the developed countries have a near-monopoly of technological innovation, they can effectively determine not only the direction of technical progress in developing countries, but also of access to all the relevant information necessary for successful bargaining. This asymmetry results in a deterioration of the position of the developing countries in all their dealings with developed countries, including a deterioration in their terms of trade (Singer, 1971). This argument is especially relevant to the exchange of manufactures between developed and developing countries.

An important initial study of the trend in the terms of trade of developing countries (the periphery) in their exchange of manufactured goods with the developed countries (the centre) was carried out by Professors Sarkar and Singer (1991). They analysed the ratio of unit values of manufactured exports from the two regions over the period 1970–87 by means of time-series regressions. In addition, they used previously unpublished data to calculate the unit values of exports and imports of manufactures over the period 1965–85 for twenty-eight individual developing countries and one developing region.

The first part of their analysis, relating to the trend in the ratio of unit values of manufactured exports of the two regions, showed that the unit values of manufactured exports of the developing countries declined by about 1 per cent per annum in relation to those of the developed countries. However, allowing for the sharp expansion in the volume of manufactures exported by developing countries, there was an average annual increase of 10 per cent in their income terms of trade. The second part of the Sarkar–Singer analysis, however, did not reveal a clear unambiguous result, since the results for about half the countries studied were not significant, while there were both positive and negative manufacturing terms of trade trends among the other countries. However, the unweighted trend for all the countries taken together was negative (–0.65 per cent per annum) which, argued Sarkar and Singer, broadly confirmed the results of their aggregate analysis.

These results have been criticised on several grounds (mainly by Athukorala, 1993). First, they relate to the unit values of exports of manufactures to all countries, and not specifically to the trade between the centre and the periphery; since developing country markets account for only about 20 per cent of manufactured exports from developed countries, there is clearly a possibility that the trend in unit values of manufactures exported to the periphery will be significantly different from the corresponding unit value for total manufactures exported from the centre. While Sarkar and Singer agree that this problem exists, they argue that any bias may be against, rather than in favour of, their statistical results (Sarkar and Singer, 1993). The evidence of recent trends in the unit value of EC manufactures exports, discussed in the previous section, implies that there may well not be a significant bias, one way or the other, in the movements of the unit values of total manufactures exports from developed countries, if these are applied to their trade with developing countries. This conclusion depends, of course, on the assumption that the EC is a representative sample, in this respect, of the developed market-economy countries as a group.

A second limitation mentioned (Athukorala, 1993) is that the UN unit values of manufactures exports include non-ferrous metals, which are normally considered as primary commodities, and this is likely to distort the unit value trend for 'true' manufactures. Sarkar and Singer argue, on the contrary, that non-ferrous metals are more properly considered as manufactures, as are iron and steel, though this proposition is not necessarily convincing. However, in the consideration of trends over the more recent period covered by the EUROSTAT series, whether non-ferrous metals are treated as manufactures or not would appear most unlikely to influence the statistical results significantly. In 1980, non-ferrous metals accounted for just under 10 per cent of the total value of manufactures (including these metals) exported by developing countries, while by 1992 the corresponding proportion had fallen to only 3 per cent.

An additional limitation raised (Athukorala, 1993) is that unit values based on trade statistics necessarily have a bias, since they reflect not only 'genuine' changes in prices, but also changes in the product composition within each heading of the trade classification. However, as Sarkar and Singer point out, this criticism does not include a systematic bias of such unit value indices in any particular direction.

Further light on recent unit value trends for the exchange of manufactures for other manufactures is thrown by a further analysis of the relevant EUROSTAT series. Three series are analysed:

1. log of unit value of EC manufactures imports from developing countries (LUVECMM);
2. log of NBTT for EC manufactures imports from developing countries with respect to EC manufactures exports to developing countries (LTTMMC2); and
3. log of income terms of trade of developing countries with respect to trade in manufactures, defined as NBTT × volume of EC manufactures imports from developing countries (LITMMC2).

The approach follows that used in Section 5.2. First the natural logarithms of the terms of trade series were tested for unit roots. The results of Said–Dickey (1984) tests are given in Table 5.11. In each case a constant was included in the test regression, but not a trend. All the test statistics fail to reject the null hypothesis of non-stationarity at a 95 per cent level of significance. The series were all also tested for trend stationarity using the Said–Dickey (1984) approach presented in Cuddington (1992). In each case the hypothesis that the series are stationary around a trend was rejected. Further testing established the series as specifically I(1). Thus it appears that all the series in question, according to our test results, contain unit roots, that is are I(1), integrated of order one.

However, having established that the LY_t series need to be differenced once to be made stationary, and thus contain unit roots, they are estimated by OLS using the D–S model (see Table 5.12). The prefix Δ again indicates the first difference of the original logged series. In two cases the coefficient b (the time trend) was found to be statistically insignificant, thus providing no evidence for a trend in the series in question, while in one case, the logarithm of the income terms of trade for manufactures facing developing

Table 5.11   Estimated *t*-statistics for the unit root hypothesis

Series	*t-statistic*
LUVEUMM	−1.877 (3)
LTTMMC2	−0.936 (1)
LITMMC2	0.071 (1)

Note: figures in brackets following test statistics indicate the number of lags of the dependent variable used in the test regression to guarantee white noise residuals.

Table 5.12   OLS estimates of *b* from D–S model estimation (*t*-value in brackets)

Series	OLS estimate of b	Durbin–Watson statistic
ΔLUVEUMM	0.020 (1.147)	1.303
ΔLTTMMC2	−0.022 (1.571)	1.883
ΔLITMMC2	0.055** (3.038)	1.344

Note: ** represents significance at a 99 per cent level.

countries (LITMMC2), the coefficient *b* was found to be positive and statistically significant, providing evidence for positive trend.

In each case the error process was also modelled, Box–Jenkins identification methods being used to identify the type of process (see Table 5.13). Two of these error processes are evidently well-behaved, while the third follows an AR process. The implications of these processes as regards trend and cyclical deviations of terms of trade series from their permanent level are the same as those discussed for the commodities–manufactures series covered by Table 5.9.

Turning to the second part of the present approach, which follows the methodology introduced by Bleaney and Greenaway (1993), the results of the estimated regressions are given in Table 5.14. The results show that the trend (time coefficient) is statistically significant in every case. It is negative in the case of LTTMMC2 (the logarithm of the manufactures terms of trade facing developing countries with respect to the EU) and positive in the other cases. In addition the Jarques–Bera statistic is

Table 5.13   Error processes

Series	Error process (t-values in brackets)
ΔLUVEUMM	$e_t = u_t$
ΔLTTMMC2 (SEP.)	$(1 + 0.523L^2) e_t = u_t$
	(2.163)
ΔLITMMC2	$e_t = u_t$

Note: back forecasts (BF) = 100, SEP, indicates MA and AR parts estimated separately; the number of backward forecasts used to generate starting values etc. could be varied to avoid non-stationary errors, while in some cases AR and MA components were estimated separately to avoid the same problem.

Table 5.14   Regression estimations

	constant (a)	time (b)	LY_{t-1} (μ)	dep. var. lags	ΔLY_{t-1}	imp. trend ($-b\mu^{-1}$)	R^2	J–B stat. (normality)
ΔLUVEUMM	2.545** (4.055)	0.022** (3.663)	−0.618* (−4.038)	1,2	0.332* (1.964)	0.036	0.799	0.925
ΔLTTMMC2	4.231** (3.080)	−0.030** (2.834)	−1.000 (−3.058)	1	0.523 (1.905)	−0.030	0.487	0.434
ΔLITMMC2	2.144** (3.475)	0.041** (3.679)	−0.562 (−3.468)	1	0.500** (2.387)	0.073	0.617	1.333

Notes
1. * and ** indicate significance at a 95 per cent and 99 per cent level respectively.
2. critical values for *t*-value of μ at 95 per cent and 99 per cent levels of significance respectively are −3.50 and −4.15.
3. *t*-values in brackets.

insignificant in each case, indicating the normality of residuals. Sufficient lags of the dependent variable were added in each case to remove any autocorrelation apparent after testing.

With respect to the nature of each of the series, it is evident that all of the series except one exhibit a random walk with drift. However, one series does exhibit a non-zero long-run trend, LUVEUMM (the logarithm of the unit value series for EU manufactures imports from developing countries) which shows a positive long-run trend. It should again be noted that some of the series may not appear to exhibit a long-run trend due to the shortness of the sample.

Considering these results, the first approach identifies an upward time trend for the manufactures income terms of trade facing developing countries. The second approach provides more information and identifies significant trend coefficients using a differenced model for all the series in question, positive in each case except that of the logarithm of the manufacture terms of trade facing developing countries with respect to the EU.

5.4 TERMS OF TRADE TRENDS FOR MAJOR DEVELOPING REGIONS AND COUNTRIES

If, as Singer has argued, the level of scientific and technological development is indeed a general underlying influence on the terms of trade of developing countries, this should in principle apply also to different groups of developing countries at different stages of scientific and techno-logical development. An analysis of trends in the NBTT of the various developing regions in their trade with developed countries would thus provide an additional empirical test of the deterioration thesis.

An attempt at such a test is summarized in Table 5.15, based on EURO-STAT unit value and volume series for the period 1979–1994 for EC trade with major developing regions or groups of countries, and with two major developed countries – the the United States and Japan – included for comparative purposes.

Trends over this period in the commodities–commodities and commodi-ties–manufactures NBTT for the various regions or countries have been gen-erally negative in their trade with the EC. These results reflect, to a substantial degree, differences in the commodity patterns of trade of the various regions, and in price trends in the relevant commodity markets. However, for the manufactures–manufactures NBTT the trends do appear to be related to the general level of industrial development. For both the United States and Japan – the world leaders in a wide range of technology-intensive manufactures – their NBTT in their manufactures terms of trade with the EC had a marginally favourable trend, while for the NICs and Asean countries there was a deterioration but at a modest rate of little more than 1 per cent per annum. This is in sharp contrast with relatively high rates of deteriora-tion of the NBTT for the least developed and ACP countries, the two groups with almost certainly the lowest proportion of technology-intensive manu-factures and the greatest proportion of unskilled or semi-skilled labour inten-sive exports. The Latin American region and the countries of the Mediterranean Basin are intermediate between these two extremes as regards the rate of deterioration in their NBTT and very probably also as regards their general level of scientific and technological development. As far as it goes, then, this partial test does support Singer's line of argument.

5.5   THE MAIN FINDINGS

The commodities–manufactures terms of trade

1. For the period since 1980, the movement in commodity market prices is not an acceptable indicator of the movement in commodity export unit values.
2. The UN index of unit value of manufactures exported by developed market-economy countries appears to have a significant downward bias since the mid-1980s.

Table 5.15   Unit values, net barter terms of trade and income terms of trade between the EC and major trading partners, 1979–94, per cent change per annum

	Developing countries						Developed countries	
	Total	Least DCs	ACP	Latin America	Med. basin	E and SE Asia	USA	Japan
A. Commodities unit value								
EC imports	0.0	-0.9	-0.7	-0.0	1.8	0.7	2.0	2.0
EC exports	2.0	1.5	2.1	3.9	1.5	2.5	3.1	3.5
EC intra-trade								
(=1.8)								
B. Manufactures unit value								
EC imports	2.0	-1.3	-0.1	1.3	2.1	2.9	6.3	5.8
EC exports	4.2	4.4	4.6	4.9	4.4	4.1	5.9	5.4
EC intra-trade								
(=4.0)								
C. Region/country NBTT								
Commod./Commod.	-2.0	-2.3	-2.8	-3.9	0.3	-1.8	-1.2	-1.5
Commod./Manuf.	-4.2	-5.2	-5.4	-4.9	-2.6	-3.4	-3.9	-3.4
Manuf./Manuf.	-2.2	-5.7	-4.7	-3.6	-2.3	-1.2	0.4	0.5

Table 5.15 (Continued)

		Developing countries					Developed countries	
	Total	Least DCs	ACP	Latin America	Med. basin	E and SE Asia	USA	Japan
D. Region/country Income TT								
Commod./Commod.	-0.0	-3.0	-2.0	-0.7	-0.9	-1.0	-4.4	-3.4
Commod./Manuf.	-2.2	-5.9	-4.6	-1.7	-3.8	-2.6	-7.1	-5.3
Manuf./Manuf.	5.5	–	0.4	1.0	4.1	6.8	1.0	4.0

Notes

1. The regions or countries are shown broadly in order, from left to right, of their general level of industrial development.
2. 'E and SE Asia' includes the 4 NICs (Hong Kong, Singapore, South Korea and Taiwan) and the ASEAN-4 (Indonesia, Malaysia, Philippines and Thailand) as well as Brunei and Macao.
3. 'Least developed' economies includes 37 low income countries of which 27 are in sub-Saharan Africa. The manufactures-manufactures income terms of trade for this group is greatly inflated by a large expansion in the volume of diamond exports from Botswana. It should be noted that there is a considerable overlap between the ACP group and the least developed countries.
4. 'Mediterranean Basin' includes Israel, Turkey, and the former Yugoslavia, as well as Algeria, Cyprus, Egypt, Jordan, Lebanon, Malta, Morocco and Tunisia.
5. Percentage change from regression coefficients.

3. The deterioration in the commodities-manufactures NBTT of developing countries has been at a substantially greater rate since 1980 than in the earlier post-war decades.

The manufactures–manufactures terms of trade

1. The rate of deterioration in the manufactures–manufactures NBTT of developing countries has also been substantially greater since 1980 than in earlier post-war decades (though significantly lower than the corresponding rate of deterioration in the commodities-manufactures NBTT), if the trends in the NBTT between the EC and developing countries are reasonably representative of total trade in manufactures between developed and developing countries.
2. The deterioration in the manufactures–manufactures NBTT of developing countries was more than offset by the expansion in the volume of EC imports of manufactures from developing countries. In sharp contrast, the volume expansion in EC imports of commodities was insufficient to offset the deterioration in the commodities–manufactures NBTT of developing countries.
3. The NBTT deterioration since 1980 has been significantly less for the East Asian NICs and ASEAN near-NICs than for Latin America and other developing regions. This difference may well reflect, *inter alia*, the higher proportion of technology-intensive goods in manufactures exports from the NICs and near NICs than in exports from other regions.

Notes

1. Recent examples of differential movements in prices (p) and unit values (uv) during price upswings and price downswings are given in the following table:

Upswings (% change)			Downswings (% change)		
period	p	uv	period	p	uv
1972–4	+110	+98	1974–5	−20	−5
1978–80	+32	+21	1980–2	−35	−16
1987–89	+27	+8	1983–5	−15	−4
			1989–91	−12	−5

Testing has also shown that the relationship between price and unit values is asymmetrical over the period 1960–91.

2. The UN index of unit value of manufactures exported by developed market – economy countries utilises national unit value indices, many of which differ in methods of construction, while the weighting system reflects national exports of manufactures to all destinations. A sub-component of the UN index, for the unit value of manufactured exports from the European Community, shows an increase of 66 per cent from 1984–5 to 1992–4, whereas the corresponding EUROSTAT index shows an increase over this period of 100 per cent for exports to developing countries and 107 per cent for EC intra-trade in manufactures.

3. The EUROSTAT series is based on the UN classification, which includes non-ferrous metals (SITC 68) in 'manufactures'.

4. A crude indicator of the relative importance of technology-intensive goods in manufactured exports is the share of exports classified in SITC section 7 (Machinery and Transport Equipment). For E and SE Asia, this proportion rose from 20 per cent in 1980 to almost 40 per cent in 1991, while for Latin America the corresponding figures were 13 per cent and 20 per cent.

References

Athukorala, P. (1993) 'Manufactured Exports from Developing Countries and Their Terms of Trade: A Reexamination of the Sarkar–Singer Results', *World Development*, vol. 21, pp. 1607–13.

Bleaney, M. and D. Greenaway (1993) 'Long-Run Trends in the Relative Price of Primary Commodities and in the Terms of Trade of Developing Countries', *Oxford Economic Papers*, vol. 45, pp. 349–63.

Cuddington, J.T. (1992) 'Long-Run Trends in 26 Primary Commodity Prices: A Disaggregated Look at the Prebisch-Singer Hypothesis', *Journal of Development Economics*, vol. 39, pp. 207–27.

Maizels, A. (1992) *Commodities in Crisis* (Oxford: Clarendon Press).

Prebisch, R. (1950) '*The Economic Development of Latin America and its Principal Problems*' (New York: United Nations).

Said, S.E. and D.A. Dickey (1984) 'Testing for Unit Roots in Autoregressive Moving-Average Models with Unknown Order', *Biometrika*, vol. 71, pp. 599–607.

Sapsford, D. (1985) 'The Statistical Debate on the Net Barter Terms of Trade Between Primary Commodities and Manufactures: A Comment and Some Additional Evidence', *Economic Journal*, vol. 95, pp. 781–8.

Sapsford, D., P. Sarkar and H. Singer (1992) 'The Prebisch–Singer Terms of Trade Controversy Revisited', *Journal of International Development*, vol. 4, pp. 315–32.

Sarkar, P. and H. Singer (1991) 'Manufactured Exports of Developing Countries and Their Terms of Trade Since 1965', *World Development*, vol. 19, pp. 333–40.

—— and —— (1993) 'Manufacture-Manufacture Terms of Trade Deterioration: A Reply', *World Development*, vol. 21, pp. 1617–20.

Singer, H. (1950) 'The Distribution of Gains Between Investing and Borrowing Countries', *American Economic Review*, Papers and Proceedings, vol. 40, pp. 473–85.

—— (1971) 'The Distribution of Gains Revisited', Paper presented at IDS, Sussex, reprinted in A. Cairncross and M. Puri (eds) *The Strategy of International Development* (London; Macmillan, 1975).

Spraos, J. (1983) *Inequalising Trade? A Study of Traditional North-South Specialisation in the Context of Terms of Trade Concepts* (Oxford University Press).

Thirlwall, A.P. (1995) 'The Terms of Trade, Debt and Development: With Particular Reference to Africa', *African Development Review*, pp. 1–34.

UNCTAD (1993) *Handbook of International Trade and Development Statistics*, (New York and Geneva: United Nations).

6 A Contribution to Empirical Research on the Prebisch–Singer Thesis[1]

John-ren Chen and Herbert Stocker

6.1 INTRODUCTION

The Prebisch–Singer hypothesis has been subjected to numerous econometric tests over the past forty years. As pointed out by Sapsford and Balasubramanyam (1994) this thesis has become in recent years more and more a playground for time-series statisticians who have used this thesis to present their latest and most advanced techniques to amazed audiences. Usually, logarithmic relative prices (or terms of trade) are regressed on a time trend applying time-series methods.[2]

This discussion was mainly concerned with the time-series properties of the underlying stochastic process, for example, if it is trend-stationary or difference-stationary, and moreover, if and when structural breaks occurred. Although not unanimously, the majority of studies in this strain seems to be in favour of the Prebisch–Singer declining trend hypothesis. Trend-cycle decompositions (for example, Ardeni and Wright 1992, Reinhart and Wickham 1994) show similar results. Since this literature has been recently reviewed by Sapsford and Balasubramanyam (1994) we will not go into detail here.

Although the application of time-series methods has brought many interesting insights, such methods also have some shortcomings. There has been considerable dispute concerning the ambiguities of time-series properties and the general lack of power of unit root tests. It has also frequently turned out to be the case that the results emerging from such studies are very sensitive with respect to the occurrence of structural breaks.

However, what has often been neglected is the fact that the economic justification of these specifications often leaves much to be desired. As will be argued below, time series specifications frequently ignore relevant information and thereby have the potential to introduce specification errors that can result in biased and inconsistent estimators.

'Structural models' are certainly advantageous in this respect, but are also much more demanding in regard to the required data base. This is probably one reason why structural models are less commonly found in the literature (for notable exceptions see, for example, Bloch and Sapsford, 1991–2; Borensztein and Reinhart 1994; Bloch and Sapsford 1996). This drawback is especially serious if one is concerned with secular trends, since there are hardly any data available for variables that stand in the core of the Prebisch–Singer hypothesis – like demand and supply elasticities, mark-ups as a measure for market structure, technical progress in different sectors – that cover more than four decades.

Therefore, we will focus in the current chapter on a different approach. We refer to a model for 'related' commodities proposed by Chen (1992, 1994) to derive reduced form equations. This model is based on microeconomic theory and uses the results that follow from the theory in the specification of the equations to be estimated. However, since the reduced form equations are functions of many predetermined variables, the inclusion of the full set of such variables might not leave us enough degrees of freedom for estimation. Beside this, many predetermined variables are highly correlated and therefore could induce multicollinearity. To avoid these problems we will make use of principal component analysis (PCA). We will first apply this method in order to reveal how much of the variance of the relative prices series can be explained by common factors, and secondly, to incorporate important structural elements in a conventional regression analysis.

Summarizing, we consider this approach to be advantageous for at least three reasons:

1. it is theoretically founded in the microeconomic theory of commodity markets;
2. specification problems, such as omitted variables bias or multicollinearity, are likely to be considerably reduced, since principal components are uncorrelated with each other by construction;
3. the model can be applied for purposes of prediction as well as for structural analysis; a fact that may be relevant, for example, in the study of policy measures.

In what follows we are concerned with the behaviour of the ratio of primary commodity prices to those of manufactures, recognizing that primary commodities and manufactured products are input–output related. Section 6.2 introduces a partial equilibrium model for related goods. Section 6.3 reviews briefly the principal component analysis, discusses the data and reports some results which allow us to evaluate the usefulness of this approach. In Section 6.4 we re-examine the Prebisch–Singer hypothesis empirically using the data set of Grilli and Yang (1988). We first employ a principal component analysis in order to disentangle different components present in the original series. Subsequently we incorporate elements of a more fundamental analysis to overcome some of the specification problems that are often present in time-series models. Such an approach will also allow us to assess the 'robustness' of the results in respect to different specifications. Section 6.5 discusses the results and offers concluding remarks.

6.2　A PARTIAL EQUILIBRIUM MODEL FOR RELATED GOODS

As discussed in detail in Chen (1994), the supply and demand functions in the context of a connective model of related commodities can be written as

$$\mathbf{D} = D(\mathbf{P}, \mathbf{Y}, \mathbf{u}), \qquad \mathbf{S} = S(\mathbf{P}, \mathbf{W}, v)$$

where $\mathbf{D}$ is a matrix of demanded quantities, $\mathbf{S}$ a matrix of supplied quantities, $\mathbf{P}$ is a matrix of prices, $\mathbf{Y}$ consists of exogenous and predetermined variables that affect demand (for example, income), $\mathbf{W}$ is a matrix of exogenous and predetermined variables that affect supply (for example, factor prices); $\mathbf{u}$ and v are i.i.d. random variables. All matrices and vectors have appropriate dimensions.

The Jacobian matrices with all partial derivatives are given by

$$\mathbf{D}' = \frac{\partial D}{\partial P} \quad \text{and} \quad \mathbf{S}' = \frac{\partial S}{\partial P}$$

with

$\delta S^i / \delta P^i > 0$
$\delta D^i / \delta P^i < 0$ for non-Giffen goods,
$\delta D^i / \delta P^j > 0 \ (i \neq j)$ for substitutable goods,
$\delta D^i / \delta P^j < 0 \ (i \neq j)$ for complemetary goods,
$\delta D^i / \delta P^j = 0 \ (i \neq j)$ for non related goods,
$\delta D^i / \delta P^j < 0$ and $\delta S^i / \delta P^i > 0$ if good j is input related to good i,
$\delta S^i / \delta P^j > 0$ and $\delta S^j / \delta P^i > 0$ if good i and j are joint products,
$\delta S^i / \delta P^j < 0$ and $\delta S^j / \delta P^i < 0$ if good i and j are input competitive related goods.

Solving the model for the prices of primary commodities we derive following set of reduced form equations

$$\mathbf{P} = P(\mathbf{Y}, \mathbf{W}, \mathbf{u}, \mathbf{v})$$

In what follows we will refer only to the reduced form equations, since the statistical data available do not allow us to estimate the structural equations of the model. In the following estimations we use 'real' prices, that is commodity prices divided by an index for prices of manufactures. Because the reduced form equations are homogeneous of degree one, we also have to divide all predetermined and exogenous prices by the same index. This can be shown as follows:

$$D = D(\lambda P, \lambda Y, u) \quad \text{and} \quad S = S(\lambda P, \lambda W, v)$$

$$D(\lambda P, \lambda Y, u) = S(\lambda P, \lambda W, v)$$

$$\lambda P = (\lambda Y, \lambda W, u, v); \quad \lambda = \frac{1}{P_I}$$

where P_I is an index of prices of manufactures.

6.3   METHOD AND DATA

The method of Principal Component Analysis (PCA) serves essentially two purposes: first, to identify common factors which influence several variables simultaneously, and second, to reduce redundancy in the original data. As we have pointed out above, the second of these two points can be important if one wants to include additional variables in a statistical analysis when one is already running short of degrees of freedom. In this case principal components (PCs) can be used instead of the full set of variables (Kloeck and Mennes, 1960).

If K denotes the number of variables available, a PCA aims at the reduction of the K-dimensional vector space of variables to a V-dimensional vector space ($V < K$), spanned by V principal components (factors) f_i, $i = 1$, ..., V. The vector f_1 explains the maximum possible proportion of the variance of the original variables and is called the first principal component (PC(1), also termed the first factor). It gives the best linear description of the original variables in the least squares sense. The second principal component explains the maximum amount of the remaining variance that is possible subject to the condition that it is uncorrelated with the first PC, and so forth. The resulting PCs are orthogonal to each other (that is, they are uncorrelated) by construction and have unit-length. The principal components depend on the unit of measurement, with the consequence that they are influenced by a change in normalization. If variables are measured in different units and the numerical value of one variable dominates the other variables, the first principal component will reflect the behaviour of that variable rather closely. Consequently, normalization of the variables is a rather common practice.

Thus, principal component analysis can be used as a tool to uncover as yet unknown relations between the variables under examination, whereby the information contained in the original data is reproduced in summary form.

In what follows we use the annual real primary commodity price/terms of trade data set compiled by Grilli and Yang (1988). They computed a base-weighted \$US index of twenty-four internationally traded non-fuel primary commodity prices. For the basic version of their index they use 1977–9 values of world exports of each commodity as weights, and in these years the index covered 54 per cent of all non-fuel commodities traded in the world. (Grilli and Yang 1988, p. 3). Like previous studies we use the logarithm of the 'real' price of primary commodities in terms of manufactures, that is, $P^i = \ln (p^i / MUV)$, where MUV reflects the unit values of exports of manufactures of a number of industrial countries (see Grilli and Yang 1988).

Additionally, we use in the analysis that follows data on real aggregate output (expressed in log form) for the USA, UK, Germany, and France for the period 1900–86; these being obtained from Perron (1994).

The quality of the underlying data is of course always questionable. It is, for example, well known that measures of long-term trends in world export prices for manufactured goods, and in the terms of trade between manufactured goods and primary products, are sensitive to many choices in methods for weighting indexes, to the selection of base periods, as well as to changes in quality. Lipsey (1994), for example, estimates that adjusting the price index for exports of machinery and transport equipment for quality changes not otherwise accounted for reduces the rate of increase for those products by about one percentage point a year, and that adjustment for only those products reduces the estimated rate of increase in prices for all manufactures by about half a percentage point a year. This point certainly deserves attention, but we will dwell on it no longer.

To evaluate the potential improvement that can be achieved by the specification outlined above and the application to it of a PCA we form a data matrix consisting of all lagged relative prices (with lags 1 to 3) and of real aggregate output of the countries mentioned above, with lags 0 to 2.

Further, we distinguish between non-metals and metals. Thus, we have 66 variables for non-metals and 30 variables for metals. A PCA extracts 8 principal components for the non-metals and 5 principal components for the metals that account for 85.6 per cent of the variance for the non-metals and 89.3 per cent for metals.

Next we estimate ordinary least-squares regressions with the relative prices as dependent variables and the principal components as independent variables. To evaluate the contribution of the individual principal components we estimate first a regression of the relative price on an intercept and the first principal component, and subsequently add in each following regression one more principal component. For reasons of comparison we also report a simple regression on an intercept and a deterministic time trend, and another regression in which we add three lags of the dependent variable as additional right-hand side variables.

The complete set of results is reported in Table 6.A.4 in the Appendix. Comparisons of the corrected R^2 shows that the model with the trend and three lags of the dependent variable has the best fit for 19 out of 24 prices, whereas the simple trend model has the lowest $\bar{R}^2$. Also with respect to autocorrelation, the lag-model generally shows the best results as evidenced by the usual diagnostics, whereas the simple trend-model has the worst results.

There are several reasons for this result. Suppose that the error terms in the true model are autocorrelated. In this case the PCA might have a good fit for the systematic factors, but cannot account for the autocorrelated error terms. The influence of the error term can, of course, not be explained by the systematic factors in the regression equations.

6.4   A RE-EXAMINATION OF THE PREBISCH–SINGER HYPOTHESIS

One of the most controversial points concerning empirical tests of the Prebisch–Singer thesis is the question whether the trend found in the data can be attributed to a secular trend or whether it is rather a statistical artefact, brought about perhaps by singular historical events and/or structural breaks (see, for example, Sapsford 1985; Cuddington and Urzua 1989; Sapsford, Sarkar and Singer 1992). This calls for an adequate consideration of the volatility in the original data.

The idea is straightforward: in a PCA orthogonality ensures that each principal component obtained portrays a separate pattern of motion or relation between the variables. Thereby, a considerable simplification in the description of the structure of the interrelations between the variables is achieved. Since the first principal component explains most of the variance in the original price series its volatility certainly deserves attention.

A PCA on the twenty-four price series extracted five principal components. The first principal component alone explains almost half (49.3 per cent) of the total variance of the original variables, the second 14.6 per cent, and all five extracted factors together 84.9 per cent of total variance.

Figure 6.1 shows the first principal component PC(1) and the index of Grilli and Yang (GYCPI), both measured in deviations from their means (since all prices are measured in the same units we used deviations from the means as normalization in the PCA). It is quite remarkable that both series show rather similar patterns, although they were derived by completely different methods. What is even more important, is that the first principal component depicts the trend rather closely and much closer than does the Grilli–Yang index.

A simple (Cochrane–Orcutt) regression on an intercept and time trend shows that the standard error of estimate for the Grilli–Yang index

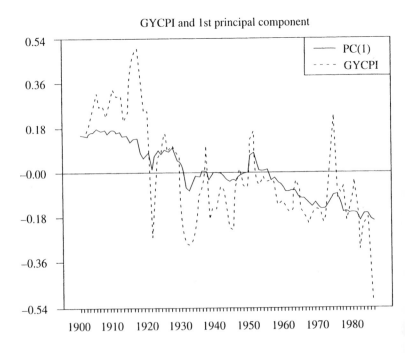

GYCPI and 1st principal component

Figure 6.1   First principal component and the GYPCI index by Grilli and Yang

(GYCPI in their notation) is more than five times as large than for PC(1) (0.11 vs. 0.02; while the coefficient of determination is 0.96 for PC(1) and 0.73 for GYPCI). Although not directly comparable, the annual average growth rate of GYCPI is approximately –0.6 per cent as compared to –0.4 per cent for PC(1). Both coefficients are highly significant.

One of the main problems of principal component analysis is that the economic interpretation of the derived factors is, in general, not straightforward. To ensure that the first factor really captures the trend we computed the correlations between each factor and the trend. These correlations for factors one to five are –0.943, 0.123, 0.256, 0.007, and –0.003 respectively.

Additionally, we regressed all factors on a constant and a time trend (again using a Cochrane–Orcutt procedure). Except for the first factor, none of the coefficients thus obtained was significant by any means.

Finally, in attempting to find an economic interpretation for the different principal components we used the stepwise regression method. We employed real income data for four countries (USA, UK, Germany, and France), the growth-rate of these incomes, and a set of dummy variables for wars and similar structural breaks. We then applied a stepwise regression procedure to decide for each factor which variables stay in the final regression.

The results of this exercise indicated that the trend appears as an explanatory variable for only the first factor. Although the marginal significance level for the trend is much higher than for any other variable in this regression, some evidence was found to suggest that (lagged) income and dummy variables also enter this equation, indicating that this factor captures more than just the trend.

The second factor, which explains 14.6 per cent of the variance, seems to capture external events, since only dummy variables appear as explanatory variables. The third factor explains less than 10 per cent of the variance and shows the most complex behaviour. It is correlated with four income variables (some lagged), four growth rates and six dummy variables. Factors four and five seem also to be related to external events captured by dummy variables. We might therefore conclude that the first principal component can be explained fairly well by a trend, whereas the other four principal components serve rather to depict structural breaks in the behaviour of the variables.

Summarizing, we could argue that there is a secular pattern of motion that governs the long-term behaviour of the relative prices of primary commodities, and that this pattern comes rather close to a trend. However, the point is somewhat more subtle. A declining index does not imply that

Table 6.1   Correlation with PC(1) and explained variances

	(1) $r_i f_1$	(2) C1	(3) C2	(4) C3	(5) C4	(6) C5	(7) Com. (%)
Coffee	−0.451	0.203	0.067	0.457	0.056	0.014	79.75
Cocoa	−0.039	0.001	0.665	0.140	0.081	0.000	88.71
Tea	0.168	0.028	0.077	0.184	0.010	0.331	63.00
Rice	0.671	0.450	0.006	0.037	0.003	0.002	49.79
Wheat	0.700	0.490	0.004	0.022	0.148	0.049	71.30
Maize	0.618	0.383	0.024	0.031	0.297	0.001	73.55
Sugar	0.550	0.302	0.124	0.014	0.138	0.335	91.27
Beef	−0.860	0.740	0.100	0.034	0.058	0.014	94.54
Lamb	−0.856	0.732	0.005	0.104	0.097	0.016	95.42
Bananas	−0.028	0.001	0.451	0.026	0.004	0.145	62.76
Palmoil	0.573	0.328	0.002	0.054	0.299	0.071	75.47
Cotton	0.656	0.430	0.053	0.233	0.100	0.009	82.52
Jute	0.166	0.027	0.003	0.371	0.098	0.188	68.73
Wool	0.727	0.528	0.203	0.033	0.109	0.007	88.09
Hide	0.722	0.522	0.008	0.009	0.109	0.010	65.75
Tobacco	−0.849	0.721	0.078	0.084	0.008	0.001	89.24
Rubber	0.911	0.830	0.092	0.008	0.001	0.018	95.01
Timber	−0.722	0.521	0.025	0.135	0.145	0.003	82.82
Copper	0.273	0.075	0.469	0.015	0.007	0.069	63.53
Aluminium	0.747	0.558	0.016	0.270	0.009	0.037	88.93
Tin	−0.634	0.402	0.292	0.032	0.024	0.028	77.85
Silver	−0.269	0.072	0.667	0.045	0.003	0.038	82.51
Lead	0.251	0.063	0.013	0.412	0.023	0.070	58.14
Zinc	0.139	0.019	0.314	0.059	0.084	0.043	51.95

all the prices of underlying commodities decreased. Hence we should have a closer look at the individual commodities.

Column (1) of Table 6.1 shows the sample correlations between the original variables and the first factor. As usual a negative sign indicates that a variable moves in opposite direction to the first factor, that is, it increases over time. Columns (2) to (6) report the share of variance that is explained by individual factors, and column (7) shows the share of variance that is explained by all five factors. For example, the correlation between the relative coffee price and the first factor is −0.45, indicating that the real coffee price was rising over the period. But this seems not to have been a very systematic tendency, since factor one explains only 20 per cent of the variance of the real coffee price, whereas the more volatile factor three explains 46 per cent. That more systematic increases in relative prices happened for particular commodities is demonstrated, for example, by the real prices of beef, lamb and tobacco. However, these cases seem to represent the exception rather than the rule.

After we have identified a secular pattern of motion in the long-run behaviour of the relative prices of primary commodities we next try to separate the trend more clearly. Many previous studies have tried to estimate the trend by univariate time series methods. It is, however, well known that the estimator of a coefficient in such models is biased and inconsistent if omitted variables are correlated with the variable under consideration. The sign of the bias depends on the correlation between the omitted variable and all included variables, as well as on the sign of the true trend coefficient.[3] Therefore, we should include all relevant variables that we suspect to be correlated with right-hand variables.

Moreover, most studies indicate the presence of autocorrelation. Autocorrelation is frequently an indicator of model misspecification, and could therefore be interpreted as a measure of our ignorance. The application of time series methods for consideration of autocorrelation is in this respect clearly second-best. It would be preferable to find an economic explanation for the underlying causes generating the autocorrelation. By taking into account the interrelations between the markets of primary commodities as pointed out in Section 6.2, we hope to improve the quality of our estimates.

Essentially, we distinguish three kinds of variables that we suppose to influence the long-run behaviour of the relative prices of primary commodities. These are: first, a trend component; second, changes in aggregate income as a proxy for common influences of demand (income itself is of course highly correlated with the trend); and third, the effects caused by the 'relatedness' of primary commodities. Regarding the latter, we are mainly interested in the correlations between prices that are caused by preferences and technologies, not by general trends or changes in demand, since these are already captured in the trend and income variables.

Since these variables are probably correlated and, therefore have the potential to introduce multicollinearity problems, we first try to disentangle the effects of these variables. We proceed in three steps: first, we remove the trend component from the data on real aggregate output. This, of course, raises objections regarding the stationarity of the underlying time-series processes. Fortunately, the time series on real aggregate output were extensively tested by Perron (1994, p. 145) who rejected the hypothesis of unit roots for these series when a structural break is allowed for. Incorporating Perron's estimate for the date of the structural break, we estimate the residuals around the trend and interpret these as a proxy for changes in the general level of demand.

The second step is somewhat more subtle, for in identifying the relevant interdependencies between markets for primary commodities we face two difficulties: first, there might be a considerable co-movement between prices caused by common trends, common changes in general demand, trade policies and the like. Secondly, even if we were able to disentangle these effects we would still be left with too many potentially important variables to be included in a regression. The first of these problems was handled as before, that is we removed these effects by estimating a regression of the following form:

$$P_t^i = \alpha^i + \beta^i T_t + \sum_{j=1}^{4}\sum_{l=0}^{2} \delta_{jl}^i RY_{t-l}^j + u_t^i$$

where RY_{t-l}^j denotes the residual income from the previous estimation for country with time-lag l. Again, this raises objections regarding the stationarity of the under-lying time-series processes. However, León and Soto (1994) tested these commodity price series extensively and found that all series except those relating to cocoa, banana, beef, and silver are trend stationary when structural breaks are allowed for. Given the general lack of power of these tests we simply assume that all underlying error processes are trend stationary. Therefore, we interpret the residuals of the above regressions as proxies which indicate the 'relatedness' of commodity markets. Since there is no reason why one should expect that the 'relatedness' is confined to one period we allow for three time lags, which gives us in total 72 series of residuals. Again, including them all in a regression is neither possible, since we would lack degrees of freedom, nor useful, since there is probably redundancy in these data.

Therefore, we again use a PCA to summarize the information contained in these variables. Because we have many more variables now, and because we have already extracted a part of the systematic movement in these series, we need 15 factors to explain 82.6 per cent of total variance, and the first factor alone explains only 25.8 per cent. Table 6.2 shows the correlations between the explanatory variables, where $PC(n)$ denotes the nth principal component, and $RYLx(y)$ denotes residual income with lag x of country y.

Evidently, no other variable captures the trend component and multicollinearity poses no problems. Therefore, we use these variables as independent variables to explain the behaviour of the individual relative

Table 6.2 Correlations between trend and PCs (1903–86)

	Trend	PC(1)	PC(2)	PC(3)
PC(1)	-0.035	1.000	-0.000	-0.000
PC(2)	-0.159	-0.000	1.000	0.000
PC(3)	-0.001	-0.000	0.000	1.000
PC(4)	-0.017	-0.000	-0.000	-0.000
PC(5)	0.072	-0.000	-0.000	-0.000
PC(6)	0.031	0.000	-0.000	0.000
PC(7)	0.056	0.000	-0.000	-0.000
PC(8)	0.081	0.000	-0.000	0.000
PC(9)	-0.014	-0.000	-0.000	0.000
PC(10)	0.029	-0.000	-0.000	-0.000
PC(11)	0.059	0.000	-0.000	0.000
PC(12)	-0.017	-0.000	0.000	-0.000
PC(13)	0.083	0.000	-0.000	-0.000
PC(14)	0.122	0.000	-0.000	-0.000
PC(15)	0.068	0.000	0.000	0.000
RYL0(USA)	-0.013	-0.101	-0.080	0.075
RYL0(UK)	0.023	0.165	-0.132	-0.033
RYL0(G)	0.012	-0.018	-0.059	0.117
RYL0(F)	-0.003	0.048	0.071	-0.025
RYL1(USA)	0.005	-0.046	-0.015	0.066
RYL1(UK)	0.013	0.091	-0.056	0.006
RYL1(G)	0.040	0.018	0.025	0.084
RYL1(F)	0.023	0.040	0.112	-0.009
RYL2(USA)	0.019	-0.007	0.039	0.027
RYL2(UK)	0.006	0.032	-0.017	0.009
RYL2(G)	0.067	0.030	0.095	0.029
RYL2(F)	0.053	0.030	0.120	-0.009

commodity prices. More specifically, we estimate four different models: first, we regress the individual prices on a trend only (model 1); second, on the trend and the residual income variables as proxies for common changes in general demand (model 2); third, on the trend and all principal components only (model 3); and finally, on all variables (model 4). This approach should allow us to assess the 'robustness' of the trend coefficient as well as the quality of the estimate. Since we are not interested in the individual coefficients of the residual income and factor variables we have only tested them jointly. The hypotheses that all principal components are equal to zero can be rejected in all cases, and the hypotheses that all income variables are zero can be rejected in all cases except sugar (at a significance level of 5 per cent). Table 6.3 reports the relevant summary statistics.

Column (1) in Table 6.3 gives the percentage growth rate of the real price of the commodity (that is, the coefficient of the trend times 100) and the second column gives the marginal significance level for a zero trend-coefficient. The remaining columns report summary statistics of the estimated equations. Column (3) shows the corrected R^2; column (4) the Durbin–Watson statistic; and column (5) the marginal significance level for the (Ljung–Box) Q-statistic (a test for higher order serial correlation). The final two columns give results for tests for heteroscedasticity, with column (6) showing the marginal significance level of a Breusch–Pagan test, and column (7) the marginal significance level of test for ARCH (Autoregressive Conditional Heteroscedasticity).

What comes as a surprise is that the estimated growth rate is quite 'robust' in respect to the different specifications. It does not change in sign in any of the cases, and there are only four cases where it is significant in the full model (model 4) and not significant in the other models (tea, banana, copper, and lead).

However, the specification is evidently quite important in respect of autocorrelation and heteroscedasticity. It is interesting to note that in most cases neither the deviations from trend–income nor the principal components alone could appreciably improve the estimate: however, both together reduced autocorrelation and heteroscedasticity drastically in most cases. Although the analysis is still rudimentary in many respects this result could be interpreted as an indication, that further research in this direction could prove fruitful.

6.5 CONCLUSIONS

In this paper we have re-examined the Prebisch–Singer thesis applying a principal components analysis and introducing additional economic structure to reduce potential misspecification errors. The results obtained from our analysis of the period 1900–86 are clearly in favour of the Prebisch–Singer thesis. Given the unconditional character of the Prebisch–Singer hypothesis, this finding is quite remarkable.

Another point we would like to stress concerns the methods applied. The majority of previous studies solely relied on time-series methods. However, these methods were mainly designed for short-term forecasts, not for measuring secular trends. Additionally, there is typically little, if any, economic reasoning behind these models. This can not only hide important interrelations between variables, but can also lead to serious

Table 6.3   Dependent variables: relative commodity prices (estimated by OLS)

	(1) β	(2) Sig. β	(3) R^2	(4) DW	(5) Sig. Q	(6) Sig. BP	(7) Sig. ARCH
Coffee							
Model 1 (T)	1.001	0.000	0.338	0.496	0.000	0.010	0.000
Model 2 (T, RY)	1.051	0.000	0.445	0.716	0.000	0.689	0.014
Model 3 (T, PC)	0.962	0.000	0.554	0.724	0.000	0.018	0.000
Model 4 (T, RY, PC)	1.011	0.000	0.792	1.604	0.581	0.150	0.658
Cocoa							
Model 1 (T)	0.611	0.007	0.075	0.324	0.000	0.048	0.000
Model 2 (T, RY)	0.632	0.006	0.038	0.388	0.000	0.003	0.000
Model 3 (T, PC)	0.588	0.000	0.664	0.998	0.004	0.330	0.169
Model 4 (T, RY, PC)	0.584	0.000	0.725	1.433	0.077	0.565	0.775
Tea							
Model 1 (T)	−0.053	0.648	−0.010	0.488	0.000	0.038	0.000
Model 2 (T, RY)	−0.046	0.602	0.441	1.080	0.017	0.012	0.085
Model 3 (T, PC)	−0.130	0.257	0.135	0.670	0.000	0.976	0.000
Model 4 (T, RY, PC)	−0.146	0.040	0.704	2.227	0.222	0.044	0.869
Rice							
Model 1 (T)	−0.767	0.000	0.351	0.601	0.000	0.105	0.000
Model 2 (T, RY)	−0.752	0.000	0.464	0.849	0.000	0.038	0.000
Model 3 (T, PC)	−0.829	0.000	0.679	1.116	0.003	0.506	0.066
Model 4 (T, RY, PC)	−0.827	0.000	0.777	1.942	0.400	0.713	0.780
Wheat							
Model 1 (T)	−0.764	0.000	0.423	0.630	0.000	0.188	0.000
Model 2 (T, RY)	−0.764	0.000	0.554	0.781	0.000	0.826	0.001
Model 3 (T, PC)	−0.796	0.000	0.557	1.001	0.000	0.048	0.156
Model 4 (T, RY, PC)	−0.836	0.000	0.781	1.791	0.075	0.031	0.545
Maize							
Model 1 (T)	−0.705	0.000	0.342	0.896	0.000	0.303	0.027
Model 2 (T, RY)	−0.714	0.000	0.467	1.022	0.236	0.140	0.017
Model 3 (T, PC)	−0.713	0.000	0.450	1.297	0.000	0.043	0.187
Model 4 (T, RY, PC)	−0.786	0.000	0.638	1.903	0.849	0.151	0.010
Sugar							
Model 1 (T)	−0.856	0.000	0.174	0.697	0.000	0.039	0.003
Model 2 (T, RY)	−0.849	0.000	0.170	0.791	0.000	0.006	0.008
Model 3 (T, PC)	−0.840	0.000	0.525	1.397	0.125	0.460	0.719
Model 4 (T, RY, PC)	−0.832	0.000	0.577	1.804	0.146	0.039	0.175
Beef							
Model 1 (T)	2.139	0.000	0.620	0.353	0.000	0.022	0.000
Model 2 (T, RY)	2.065	0.000	0.814	1.036	0.000	0.075	0.102
Model 3 (T, PC)	2.231	0.000	0.670	0.530	0.000	0.070	0.000
Model 4 (T, RY, PC)	2.089	0.000	0.862	1.750	0.212	0.188	0.899

Table 6.3 (Continued)

	(1) β	(2) Sig. β	(3) R^2	(4) DW	(5) Sig. Q	(6) Sig. BP	(7) Sig. ARCH
Lamb							
Model 1 (T)	1.896	0.000	0.511	0.322	0.000	0.001	0.000
Model 2 (T, RY)	1.820	0.000	0.744	0.833	0.000	0.106	0.212
Model 3 (T, PC)	1.968	0.000	0.545	0.531	0.000	0.005	0.000
Model 4 (T, RY, PC)	1.821	0.000	0.839	1.662	0.218	0.137	0.921
Bananas							
Model 1 (T)	−0.074	0.416	−0.004	0.227	0.000	0.341	0.000
Model 2 (T, RY)	−0.069	0.332	0.383	0.452	0.000	0.282	0.000
Model 3 (T, PC)	−0.086	0.268	0.330	0.446	0.000	0.175	0.000
Model 4 (T, RY, PC)	−0.106	0.022	0.794	1.715	0.233	0.262	0.476
Palmoil							
Model 1 (T)	−0.659	0.000	0.263	0.790	0.003	0.491	0.061
Model 2 (T, RY)	−0.656	0.000	0.444	1.043	0.272	0.070	0.838
Model 3 (T, PC)	−0.753	0.000	0.410	1.146	0.078	0.903	0.216
Model 4 (T, RY, PC)	−0.733	0.000	0.621	1.758	0.814	0.011	0.000
Cotton							
Model 1 (T)	−0.724	0.000	0.337	0.397	0.000	0.593	0.000
Model 2 (T, RY)	−0.702	0.000	0.500	0.522	0.000	0.006	0.000
Model 3 (T, PC)	−0.795	0.000	0.605	0.730	0.000	0.118	0.017
Model 4 (T, RY, PC)	−0.794	0.000	0.814	1.420	0.293	0.091	0.594
Jute							
Model 1 (T)	−0.097	0.480	−0.006	0.596	0.000	0.058	0.010
Model 2 (T, RY)	−0.083	0.477	0.279	1.171	0.134	0.036	0.918
Model 3 (T, PC)	−0.203	0.149	0.064	0.901	0.002	0.936	0.322
Model 4 (T, RY, PC)	−0.169	0.151	0.401	1.810	0.817	0.079	0.714
Wool							
Model 1 (T)	−1.282	0.000	0.547	0.585	0.000	0.136	0.012
Model 2 (T, RY)	−1.254	0.000	0.599	0.594	0.000	0.003	0.028
Model 3 (T, PC)	−1.395	0.000	0.772	1.312	0.634	0.592	0.728
Model 4 (T, RY, PC)	−1.388	0.000	0.877	1.957	0.004	0.764	0.243
Hide							
Model 1 (T)	−1.164	0.000	0.500	0.876	0.000	0.746	0.141
Model 2 (T, RY)	−1.155	0.000	0.572	0.955	0.000	0.458	0.075
Model 3 (T, PC)	−1.186	0.000	0.636	1.518	0.029	0.775	0.918
Model 4 (T, RY, PC)	−1.180	0.000	0.691	1.746	0.417	0.624	0.728
Tobacco							
Model 1 (T)	1.267	0.000	0.703	0.280	0.000	0.000	0.000
Model 2 (T, RY)	1.280	0.000	0.715	0.512	0.000	0.000	0.001
Model 3 (T, PC)	1.209	0.000	0.873	0.975	0.000	0.438	0.015
Model 4 (T, RY, PC)	1.203	0.000	0.895	1.678	0.613	0.714	0.840

Table 6.3   (Continued)

	(1) β	(2) Sig.β	(3) R²	(4) DW	(5) Sig. Q	(6) Sig. BP	(7) Sig. ARCH
Rubber							
Model 1 (T)	−2.782	0.000	0.656	0.372	0.000	0.007	0.000
Model 2 (T, RY)	−2.796	0.000	0.717	0.545	0.000	0.002	0.000
Model 3 (T, PC)	−2.847	0.000	0.811	0.858	0.000	0.081	0.028
Model 4 (T, RY, PC)	−2.809	0.000	0.910	2.098	0.287	0.400	0.757
Timber							
Model 1 (T)	1.072	0.000	0.618	0.448	0.000	0.070	0.000
Model 2 (T, RY)	1.074	0.000	0.786	0.636	0.000	0.121	0.003
Model 3 (T, PC)	1.042	0.000	0.768	0.95	0.000	0.085	0.001
Model 4 (T, RY, PC)	1.027	0.000	0.912	2.108	0.313	0.473	0.375
Copper							
Model 1 (T)	−0.129	0.343	−0.001	0.285	0.000	0.218	0.000
Model 2 (T, RY)	−0.153	0.197	0.249	0.697	0.000	0.078	0.002
Model 3 (T, PC)	−0.156	0.112	0.535	0.973	0.000	0.786	0.057
Model 4 (T, RY, PC)	−0.201	0.010	0.738	1.924	0.313	0.776	0.854
Autumn							
Model 1 (T)	−1.773	0.000	0.672	0.270	0.000	0.797	0.000
Model 2 (T, RY)	−1.803	0.000	0.774	0.598	0.000	0.040	0.055
Model 3 (T, PC)	−1.696	0.000	0.822	0.738	0.000	0.022	0.001
Model 4 (T, RY, PC)	−1.739	0.000	0.911	1.459	0.260	0.060	0.044
Tin							
Model 1 (T)	1.071	0.000	0.508	0.469	0.000	0.746	0.000
Model 2 (T, RY)	1.061	0.000	0.597	0.513	0.000	0.025	0.000
Model 3 (T, PC)	1.020	0.000	0.733	1.052	0.004	0.316	0.001
Model 4 (T, RY, PC)	0.976	0.000	0.873	1.930	0.599	0.048	0.254
Silver							
Model 1 (T)	0.600	0.002	0.105	0.226	0.000	0.019	0.000
Model 2 (T, RY)	0.576	0.002	0.196	0.296	0.000	0.042	0.000
Model 3 (T, PC)	0.604	0.000	0.673	0.710	0.000	0.561	0.028
Model 4 (T, RY, PC)	0.536	0.000	0.867	1.629	0.084	0.006	0.146
Lead							
Model 1 (T)	−0.089	0.413	−0.004	0.468	0.000	0.008	0.000
Model 2 (T, RY)	−0.064	0.463	0.356	0.799	0.000	0.000	0.000
Model 3 (T, PC)	−0.193	0.050	0.276	0.933	0.007	0.598	0.184
Model 4 (T, RY, PC)	−0.207	0.006	0.623	1.883	0.436	0.182	0.835
Zinc							
Model 1 (T)	0.033	0.750	−0.011	0.739	0.000	0.122	0.001
Model 2 (T, RY)	0.030	0.752	0.148	0.921	0.000	0.366	0.002
Model 3 (T, PC)	0.057	0.528	0.297	1.279	0.002	0.144	0.011
Model 4 (T, RY, PC)	0.040	0.608	0.511	2.017	0.147	0.203	0.641

specification problems. Therefore, we believe that future empirical research should focus on structural models, based on the determinants of supply and demand. Such models hold out the promise of enabling us to assess the magnitudes of the various different forces which drive the observed fluctuations in real commodity prices, an understanding of which we would see as being a necessary prerequisite for policy simulations in the commodity market context.

Notes

1. We gratefully acknowledge helpful comments by the participants of the Conference 'Development Economics and Policy' at the University of Innsbruck, Austria, in May 1996, celebrating Sir Hans Singer's 85th birthday. Special thanks due to David Sapsford, Harry Bloch and Richard Hule. The usual disclaimer applies.
2. For example $\ln P_t = \alpha + \beta T_t + ARMA(p, q)u_t$ for trend stationary and $\Delta \ln P_t = \beta' + ARMA(p', q')v_t$ for difference stationary processes.
3. If, on the other hand, irrelevant variables are included only efficiency is lost, but the result remains unbiased and consistent.

References

Ardeni, P.G. and B. Wright (1992) 'The Prebisch–Singer Hypothesis: A Reappraisal Independent of Stationary Hypothesis', *Economic Journal*, vol. 102, (July) pp. 803–12.

Bloch, H. and D. Sapsford (1991–2) 'Postwar Movements in Prices of Primary Products and Manufactured Goods', *Journal of Post Keynesian Economics*, vol. 14, no.2 (Winter) pp. 249–66.

—— and —— (1994) 'Trend in the International Terms of Trade Between Primary Producers and Manufactures', *Journal of International Development*, vol. 6(1) (August), pp. 53–67.

—— and —— (1996) 'Prebisch and Singer Effects on the Terms of Trade Between Primary Producers and Manufacturers', Paper presented at the Conference: 'Development Economics and Policy, A Conference to Celebrate the 85th Birthday of Profesor Sir Hans Singer', in this volume.

Borensztein, E. and C.M. Reinhart (1994) 'The Macroeconomic Determinants of Commodity Prices', *IMF Staff Papers*, vol. 41, no. 2 (June).

Chen, John-ren (1992) 'Die Entwicklung der Weltmarktpreise für Rohstoffe von 1960/61 bis 1982/83', *Journal für Entwicklungspolitik*, vol. viii, no. 4, pp. 387–411

—— (1994) 'Modelling of Related Commodities and Its Implications for Stabilization Policy of The World Market', *Journal of Agricultural Economics*, vol. 55, pp. 139–66.

Cuddington, J.T. and C.M. Urzua (1989) 'Trends and Cycles in the Net Barter Terms of Trade: A New Approach', *Economic Journal*, vol. 99, no. 396 (June) pp. 426–42.

Grilli, E.R. and M.C. Yang (1988) 'Primary Commodity Prices, Manufactured Good Prices, and the Terms of Trade of Developing Countries: What the Long Run Shows', *World Bank Economic Review*, vol. 2, no. 1 (January) pp. 1–47.

Kloeck, T. and L.B.M. Mennes (1960) 'Simultaneous Equations Estimation Based on Principal Components of Predetermined Variables', *Econometrica*, vol. 28, no. 1, pp. 45–61.

León, J. and R. Soto (1994) 'Structural Breaks and Long-Run Trends in Commodity Prices', mimeo.

Lipsey, R.E. (1994) Quality Change and Other Influences on Measures of Export Prices of Manufactured Goods, *World Bank Working Paper* (August).

Perron, P. (1994) 'Trend, Unit Root and Structural Change in Macroeconomic Time Series', in B. Bhaskara Rao (ed.) *Cointegration for the Applied Economist* (St Martin's press).

Reinhart, C. and P. Wickham (1994) 'Commodity Prices: Cyclical Weakness or Secular Decline?' *IMF Staff Papers*, vol. 41, no. 2 (June).

Sapsford, D. (1985) 'The Statistical Debate on the Net Barter Terms of Trade between Primary Commodities and Manufactures: A Comment and Some Additional Evidence', *Economic Journal*, vol. 95 (Sep.) pp. 781–8.

Balasubramanyam (1994) 'The Long-Run Behaviour of the Relative Price of Primary Commodities: Statistical Evidence and Policy Implications', *World Development*, vol. 22, no. 11, pp. 1737–45.

——, P. Sarkar and H.W. Singer (1992) 'The Prebisch–Singer Terms of Trade Controversy Revisited', *Journal of International Development*, vol. 4, no. 3, pp. 315–32.

Singer, H.W. (1950) 'The Distribution of Gains between Investing and Borrowing Countries', *American Economic Review, Papers & Proceedings*, vol. 5 (May) pp. 473–85.

Appendix

In Table 6A.1 Column (1) gives the corrected R^2 shows the Durbin–Watson statistic and for the lag-model the marginal significance level of a generalized LM-test for serial correlation. Column (3) gives the marginal significance level for the (Ljung–Box) Q-statistic (a test for higher order serial correlation). The final two columns give results for tests for heteroscedasticity: column (4) shows the marginal significance level of a Breusch–Pagan test, and column (5) the marginal significance level of test for ARCH (Autoregressive Conditional Heteroscedasticity).

Table 6A.1   Dependent variables: relative commodity prices (estimated by OLS)

	(1) R^2	(2) DW	(3) Sig. Q	(4) Sig. BP	(5) Sig. ARCH
Coffee					
Trend	0.376	0.496	0.000	0.007	0.000
Trend, P_{t-1}–P_{t-3}	0.713	0.767*	0.572	0.796	0.546
PC(1)	0.491	0.650	0.000	0.052	0.002
PC(1)–PC(2)	0.517	0.714	0.000	0.027	0.058
PC(1)–PC(3)	0.559	0.843	0.000	0.140	0.263
PC(1)–PC(4)	0.684	1.060	0.000	0.087	0.219
PC(1)–PC(5)	0.775	1.457	0.000	0.286	0.702
PC(1)–PC(6)	0.773	1.445	0.000	0.235	0.710
PC(1)–PC(7)	0.770	1.446	0.000	0.236	0.707
PC(1)–PC(8)	0.775	1.587	0.000	0.251	0.673
Cocoa					
Trend	0.036	0.301	0.000	0.094	0.000
Trend, P_{t-1}, P_{t-3}	0.745	0.850*	0.965	0.202	0.769
PC(1)	0.084	0.327	0.000	0.002	0.000
PC(1)–PC(2)	0.430	0.611	0.000	0.002	0.000
PC(1)–PC(3)	0.466	0.680	0.000	0.002	0.000
PC(1)–PC(4)	0.694	1.144	0.013	0.026	0.016
PC(1)–PC(5)	0.693	1.167	0.009	0.031	0.025
PC(1)–PC(6)	0.690	1.176	0.013	0.030	0.035
PC(1)–PC(7)	0.696	1.219	0.009	0.047	0.087
PC(1)–PC(8)	0.697	1.190	0.003	0.043	0.084
Tea					
Trend	−0.004	0.496	0.000	0.046	0.000
Trend, P_{t-1}, P_{t-3}	0.550	0.875*	0.597	0.017	0.009
PC(1)	0.080	0.566	0.000	0.403	0.000
PC(1)–PC(2)	0.394	0.885	0.003	0.674	0.046
PC(1)–PC(3)	0.406	0.969	0.026	0.494	0.102
PC(1)–PC(4)	0.583	1.234	0.020	0.069	0.267
PC(1)–PC(5)	0.616	1.269	0.094	0.137	0.378
PC(1)–PC(6)	0.622	1.354	0.088	0.088	0.306
PC(1)–PC(7)	0.617	1.358	0.099	0.083	0.292
PC(1)–PC(8)	0.623	1.382	0.047	0.084	0.362
Rice					
Trend	0.341	0.600	0.000	0.086	0.000
Trend, P_{t-1}, P_{t-3}	0.697	0.954*	0.935	0.076	0.878
PC(1)	0.366	0.633	0.000	0.157	0.000
PC(1)–PC(2)	0.359	0.637	0.000	0.143	0.000
PC(1)–PC(3)	0.354	0.642	0.000	0.182	0.000
PC(1)–PC(4)	0.389	0.686	0.000	0.030	0.000
PC(1)–PC(5)	0.392	0.698	0.000	0.015	0.000

Table 6A.1   (Continued)

	(1) R^2	(2) DW	(3) Sig. Q	(4) Sig. BP	(5) Sig. ARCH
PC(1)–PC(7)	0.532	1.070	0.000	0.018	0.004
PC(1)–PC(8)	0.605	1.110	0.000	0.014	0.023
Wheat					
Trend	0.380	0.591	0.000	0.240	0.000
Trend, P_{t-1}, P_{t-3}	0.714	0.041*	0.322	0.235	0.975
PC(1)	0.500	0.733	0.000	0.723	0.000
PC(1)–PC(2)	0.538	0.830	0.000	0.810	0.013
PC(1)–PC(3)	0.535	0.837	0.000	0.820	0.017
PC(1)–PC(4)	0.546	0.868	0.000	0.643	0.023
PC(1)–PC(5)	0.548	0.872	0.000	0.565	0.011
PC(1)–PC(6)	0.654	1.190	0.000	0.646	0.233
PC(1)–PC(7)	0.657	1.244	0.000	0.507	0.242
PC(1)–PC(8)	0.652	1.229	0.000	0.466	0.271
Maize					
Trend	0.301	0.880	0.001	0.236	0.026
Trend, P_{t-1}, P_{t-3}	0.520	0.173*	0.561	0.267	0.906
PC(1)	0.423	1.071	0.000	0.334	0.042
PC(1)–PC(2)	0.424	1.079	0.000	0.350	0.045
PC(1)–PC(3)	0.448	1.129	0.000	0.255	0.094
PC(1)–PC(4)	0.448	1.155	0.000	0.260	0.135
PC(1)–PC(5)	0.479	1.259	0.000	0.400	0.292
PC(1)–PC(6)	0.538	1.571	0.026	0.377	0.585
PC(1)–PC(7)	0.532	1.572	0.027	0.377	0.590
PC(1)–PC(8)	0.527	1.603	0.022	0.439	0.524
Sugar					
Trend	0.188	0.699	0.000	0.028	0.003
Trend, P_{t-1}, P_{t-3}	0.531	0.608*	0.688	0.170	0.838
PC(1)	0.179	0.718	0.000	0.023	0.003
PC(1)–PC(2)	0.387	1.007	0.006	0.001	0.033
PC(1)–PC(3)	0.379	1.006	0.007	0.001	0.033
PC(1)–PC(4)	0.388	1.035	0.026	0.001	0.021
PC(1)–PC(5)	0.390	1.036	0.022	0.001	0.026
PC(1)–PC(6)	0.431	1.170	0.016	0.001	0.190
PC(1)–PC(7)	0.425	1.184	0.013	0.001	0.145
PC(1)–PC(8)	0.461	1.172	0.000	0.003	0.115
Beef					
Trend	0.625	0.348	0.000	0.016	0.000
Trend, P_{t-1}, P_{t-3}	0.875	0.688*	0.798	0.806	0.988
PC(1)	0.751	0.573	0.000	0.337	0.001
PC(1)–PC(2)	0.752	0.585	0.000	0.546	0.006

Table 6A.1 (Continued)

	(1) R^2	(2) DW	(3) Sig. Q	(4) Sig. BP	(5) Sig. ARCH
PC(1)–PC(3)	0.777	0.659	0.000	0.166	0.047
PC(1)–PC(4)	0.798	0.750	0.000	0.253	0.020
PC(1)–PC(5)	0.860	1.136	0.053	0.540	0.697
PC(1)–PC(6)	0.860	1.181	0.073	0.546	0.628
PC(1)–PC(7)	0.869	1.255	0.011	0.670	0.927
PC(1)–PC(8)	0.869	1.272	0.031	0.585	0.890
Lamb					
Trend	0.537	0.322	0.000	0.001	0.000
Trend, P_{t-1}, P_{t-3}	0.853	0.011*	0.007	0.304	0.787
PC(1)	0.697	0.567	0.000	0.050	0.000
PC(1)–PC(2)	0.716	0.617	0.000	0.157	0.000
PC(1)–PC(3)	0.718	0.627	0.000	0.180	0.001
PC(1)–PC(4)	0.753	0.741	0.000	0.464	0.036
PC(1)–PC(5)	0.773	0.801	0.000	0.623	0.038
PC(1)–PC(6)	0.771	0.807	0.000	0.575	0.036
PC(1)–PC(7)	0.768	0.810	0.000	0.544	0.044
PC(1)–PC(8)	0.808	1.062	0.000	0.061	0.656
Bananas					
Trend	−0.012	0.210	0.000	0.579	0.000
Trend, P_{t-1}, P_{t-3}	0.783	0.887*	0.763	0.014	0.109
PC(1)	0.043	0.247	0.000	0.115	0.000
PC(1)–PC(2)	0.631	0.736	0.000	0.095	0.004
PC(1)–PC(3)	0.656	0.762	0.000	0.108	0.002
PC(1)–PC(4)	0.727	0.958	0.013	0.114	0.000
PC(1)–PC(5)	0.727	0.966	0.008	0.110	0.001
PC(1)–PC(6)	0.782	0.997	0.010	0.018	0.001
PC(1)–PC(7)	0.833	1.273	0.045	0.001	0.001
PC(1)–PC(8)	0.839	1.316	0.059	0.002	0.001
Palmoil					
Trend	0.239	0.765	0.000	0.604	0.031
Trend, P_{t-1}, P_{t-3}	0.534	0.745*	0.906	0.135	0.100
PC(1)	0.360	0.939	0.017	0.668	0.111
PC(1)–PC(2)	0.352	0.941	0.017	0.658	0.131
PC(1)–PC(3)	0.344	0.938	0.019	0.646	0.127
PC(1)–PC(4)	0.336	0.942	0.024	0.647	0.137
PC(1)–PC(5)	0.425	1.141	0.428	0.141	0.313
PC(1)–PC(6)	0.473	1.180	0.280	0.084	0.200
PC(1)–PC(7)	0.475	1.202	0.492	0.073	0.164
PC(1)–PC(8)	0.497	1.285	0.840	0.080	0.186
Cotton					
Trend	0.276	0.371	0.000	0.477	0.000
Trend, P_{t-1}, P_{t-3}	0.812	0.509*	0.983	0.001	0.021

Table 6A.1   (Continued)

	(1) R^2	(2) DW	(3) Sig. Q	(4) Sig. BP	(5) Sig. ARCH
PC(1)	0.552	0.743	0.003	0.519	0.001
PC(1)–PC(2)	0.547	0.743	0.002	0.525	0.001
PC(1)–PC(3)	0.541	0.743	0.002	0.527	0.001
PC(1)–PC(4)	0.538	0.762	0.003	0.586	0.003
PC(1)–PC(5)	0.565	0.784	0.001	0.541	0.013
PC(1)–PC(6)	0.580	0.860	0.001	0.511	0.109
PC(1)–PC(7)	0.596	0.979	0.005	0.211	0.103
PC(1)–PC(8)	0.639	1.039	0.000	0.031	0.411
Jute					
Trend	–0.012	0.566	0.000	0.032	0.008
Trend, P_{t-1}, P_{t-3}	0.510	0.155*	0.392	0.123	0.007
PC(1)	0.231	0.820	0.000	0.004	0.009
PC(1)–PC(2)	0.253	0.840	0.000	0.133	0.025
PC(1)–PC(3)	0.290	0.931	0.000	0.166	0.021
PC(1)–PC(4)	0.288	0.920	0.000	0.109	0.021
PC(1)–PC(5)	0.290	0.955	0.000	0.159	0.013
PC(1)–PC(6)	0.407	1.236	0.098	0.182	0.090
PC(1)–PC(7)	0.400	1.230	0.083	0.174	0.049
PC(1)–PC(8)	0.411	1.259	0.073	0.023	0.018
Wool					
Trend	0.483	0.516	0.000	0.036	0.001
Trend, P_{t-1}–P_{t-3}	0.786	0.492*	0.938	0.070	0.033
PC(1)	0.657	0.884	0.000	0.028	0.019
PC(1)–PC(2)	0.760	1.239	0.112	0.045	0.077
PC(1)–PC(3)	0.762	1.259	0.164	0.037	0.096
PC(1)–PC(4)	0.775	1.378	0.089	0.074	0.148
PC(1)–PC(5)	0.772	1.376	0.093	0.076	0.170
PC(1)–PC(6)	0.769	1.393	0.096	0.081	0.166
PC(1)–PC(7)	0.766	1.394	0.097	0.081	0.166
PC(1)–PC(8)	0.770	1.371	0.067	0.062	0.200
Hide					
Trend	0.478	0.835	0.000	0.668	0.024
Trend, P_{t-1}, P_{t-3}	0.653	0.326*	0.388	0.929	0.068
PC(1)	0.506	0.906	0.000	0.748	0.164
PC(1)–PC(2)	0.534	0.998	0.001	0.806	0.720
PC(1)–PC(3)	0.544	1.058	0.003	0.543	0.186
PC(1)–PC(4)	0.538	1.058	0.003	0.533	0.171
PC(1)–PC(5)	0.583	1.245	0.052	0.130	0.540
PC(1)–PC(6)	0.581	1.224	0.028	0.237	0.548
PC(1)–PC(7)	0.583	1.265	0.050	0.358	0.275
PC(1)–PC(8)	0.640	1.555	0.078	0.970	0.749

Table 6A.1   (Continued)

	(1) R^2	(2) DW	(3) Sig. Q	(4) Sig. BP	(5) Sig. ARCH
Tobacco					
Trend	0.731	0.262	0.0000	0.005	0.000
Trend, P_{t-1}, P_{t-3}	0.924	0.160*	0.630	0.009	0.085
PC(1)	0.712	0.293	0.000	0.001	0.000
PC(1)–PC(2)	0.802	0.461	0.000	0.006	0.000
PC(1)–PC(3)	0.802	0.457	0.000	0.007	0.000
PC(1)–PC(4)	0.866	0.674	0.000	0.321	0.001
PC(1)–PC(5)	0.912	0.966	0.000	0.206	0.005
PC(1)–PC(6)	0.911	0.957	0.000	0.186	0.008
PC(1)–PC(7)	0.912	0.988	0.000	0.116	0.011
PC(1)–PC(8)	0.912	1.002	0.000	0.085	0.017
Rubber					
Trend	0.682	0.376	0.000	0.012	0.000
Trend, P_{t-1}, P_{t-3}	0.880	0.792*	0.602	0.120	0.610
PC(1)	0.652	0.373	0.000	0.012	0.000
PC(1)–PC(2)	0.710	0.494	0.000	0.016	0.000
PC(1)–PC(3)	0.714	0.508	0.000	0.012	0.000
PC(1)–PC(4)	0.803	0.661	0.000	0.027	0.000
PC(1)–PC(5)	0.821	0.770	0.000	0.042	0.000
PC(1)–PC(6)	0.830	0.889	0.000	0.042	0.000
PC(1)–PC(7)	0.852	1.138	0.000	0.023	0.000
PC(1)–PC(8)	0.871	1.181	0.000	0.027	0.000
Timber					
Trend	0.652	0.444	0.000	0.196	0.000
Trend, P_{t-1}, P_{t-3}	0.844	0.180*	0.897	0.780	0.033
PC(1)	0.667	0.543	0.000	0.354	0.000
PC(1)–PC(2)	0.678	0.580	0.000	0.273	0.000
PC(1)–PC(3)	0.674	0.582	0.000	0.269	0.000
PC(1)–PC(4)	0.717	0.753	0.000	0.513	0.000
PC(1)–PC(5)	0.738	0.831	0.000	0.985	0.000
PC(1)–PC(6)	0.735	0.829	0.000	0.995	0.000
PC(1)–PC(7)	0.745	0.863	0.000	0.856	0.000
PC(1)–PC(8)	0.749	0.921	0.001	0.957	0.002
Copper					
Trend	0.012	0.298	0.000	0.159	0.000
Trend, P_{t-1}, P_{t-3}	0.722	0.544*	0.668	0.073	0.671
PC(1)	0.306	0.444	0.000	0.087	0.00
PC(1)–PC(2)	0.427	0.662	0.000	0.407	0.005
PC(1)–PC(3)	0.490	0.801	0.000	0.818	0.007
PC(1)–PC(4)	0.485	0.800	0.000	0.936	0.005
PC(1)–PC(5)	0.489	0.827	0.000	0.974	0.009
PC(1)–PC(5)	0.489	0.827	0.000	0.974	0.009

Table 6A.1 (Continued)

	(1) R^2	(2) DW	(3) Sig. Q	(4) Sig. BP	(5) Sig. ARCH
Aluminium					
Trend	0.702	0.268	0.000	0.824	0.000
Trend, P_{t-1}, P_{t-3}	0.929	0.575*	0.710	0.056	0.535
PC(1)	0.746	0.372	0.000	0.106	0.000
PC(1)–PC(2)	0.753	0.395	0.000	0.199	0.000
PC(1)–PC(3)	0.825	0.582	0.000	0.006	0.000
PC(1)–PC(4)	0.825	0.580	0.000	0.009	0.000
PC(1)–PC(5)	0.856	0.724	0.000	0.016	0.000
Tin					
Trend	0.536	0.547	0.000	0.716	0.000
Trend, P_{t-1}, P_{t-3}	0.807	0.898*	0.998	0.083	0.935
PC(1)	0.664	0.755	0.000	0.692	0.003
PC(1)–PC(2)	0.660	0.752	0.000	0.737	0.004
PC(1)–PC(3)	0.656	0.751	0.000	0.754	0.004
PC(1)–PC(4)	0.692	0.872	0.000	0.805	0.182
PC(1)–PC(5)	0.738	1.126	0.007	0.440	0.556
Silver					
Trend	0.077	0.218	0.000	0.010	0.000
Trend, P_{t-1}, P_{t-3}	0.821	0.979*	0.987	0.000	0.000
PC(1)	0.636	0.705	0.000	0.447	0.021
PC(1)–PC(2)	0.644	0.718	0.000	0.751	0.008
PC(1)–PC(3)	0.689	0.805	0.000	0.121	0.055
PC(1)–PC(4)	0.685	0.802	0.000	0.138	0.058
PC(1)–PC(5)	0.722	0.982	0.002	0.131	0.148
Lead					
Trend	−0.006	0.468	0.000	0.005	0.000
Trend, P_{t-1}, P_{t-3}	0.563	0.950*	0.996	0.396	0.041
PC(1)	0.018	0.479	0.000	0.009	0.000
PC(1)–PC(2)	0.037	0.515	0.000	0.010	0.000
PC(1)–PC(3)	0.442	0.994	0.000	0.456	0.030
PC(1)–PC(4)	0.494	1.119	0.023	0.397	0.008
PC(1)–PC(5)	0.554	1.386	0.444	0.073	0.624
Zinc					
Trend	−0.009	0.743	0.000	0.195	0.000
Trend, P_{t-1}, P_{t-3}	0.381	0.986*	0.799	0.453	0.880
PC(1)	0.134	0.887	0.000	0.319	0.001
PC(1)–PC(2)	0.123	0.885	0.000	0.322	0.001
PC(1)–PC(3)	0.175	0.981	0.000	0.385	0.001
PC(1)–PC(4)	0.291	1.407	0.183	0.507	0.260
PC(1)–PC(5)	0.284	1.400	0.149	0.498	0.251

* Generalized LM-test for serial correlation.

Part II
Trade Strategies, Growth and Development

7 Trade Orientation and Economic Development: Theory and Evidence[1]

David Greenaway and Wyn Morgan

7.1 INTRODUCTION

Should developing countries follow an inwardly or outwardly orientated trade policy? A simple question which only has a simple answer to the simple-minded! This is an issue which has taxed at least two generations of development economists. It is also an issue which has taxed the multi-lateral lending agencies for some time. The belief that outward-orientated policies 'work' has had a very considerable influence on the design and implementation of policy conditionality in the IMF and World Bank.

Hans Singer has been an active participant in the trade orientation debate both directly, in for example, his critique of the 1987 *World Development Report* (Singer, 1987) and indirectly via his seminal contributions to the Singer–Prebisch hypothesis (Singer, 1950). In the former he set out a scathing attack on a particular set of results used to show 'Why Outward Orientation Works'; in the latter he laid one of the cornerstones of the structuralist case for inward-orientated trade policies.

The paper is not an attempt to evaluate Hans' contribution to the trade orientation debate and its outcomes more generally. Hans has had a very considerable influence on the debate, and it is an issue he cares about deeply. Instead, what we aim to do is to stand back and evaluate the broader debate. A formidable amount of empirical work has now been completed, and this Festschrift offers a good opportunity for taking stock of it, especially the more recent evidence.

The remainder of the paper is organised as follows: in Section 7.2 we review the core theoretical canons on trade policy and economic development; Section 7.3 reviews the evidence. Finally, Section 7.3 sets out the agenda for further work, and concludes.

113

7.2   TRADE STRATEGY AND ECONOMIC PERFORMANCE: THEORY

The appropriate role of trade policy in economic development has been controversial for a very long time. Many of the arguments which underpin the case for inward or outward oriented policies are familiar.[2] None the less, it is instructive to remind ourselves of the broad thrust of the arguments involved.

Structuralism and the case for inward orientation

Structuralism is best thought of not as a school of thought, but a touchstone for the belief that the structural characteristics one finds in developing countries ensure that unfettered markets cannot be relied upon to allow full exploitation of the gains from trade. At the heart of the structuralist case is a belief in market failure on a widespread scale. This ensures that the vital signalling function performed by the market mechanism not only operates imperfectly, but may even emit misleading signals. Sources of market failure are manifold–capital market imperfections, production externalities, a complete absence of some markets. Moreover many of the imperfections are allegedly exogenous. Thus rather than giving the market a helping hand, policy should be directed at market replacement. The most influential imperfections alleged in the traded goods sector are terms of trade decline, export instability and infant industries.

Terms of trade decline

This is an issue with which the name of Hans Singer is inextricably connected. Singer (1950) and Prebisch (1950) independently identified the potential for an inherent tendency to a long-term decline in the terms of trade of primary producers. The combination of demand functions on the one hand for primary products which are relatively income inelastic, and are sold on markets that are very competitive and manufactures where demand is income elastic and markets less competitive on the other (allowing producers to capture the fruits of productivity improvement). This results in a secular tendency to relative price decline.

The argument is plausible and has been very influential. It has also been extensively researched in recent years with contribution from *inter alia* Spraos (1980), Sapsford (1985), Grilli and Yang (1988), Cuddington and Urzua (1989), Sarkar and Singer (1991), Bleaney and Greenaway (1993). Despite the fact that some results suggest that the best statistical explanation of the time series involved is one of a trendless series with one or more structural breaks, the bulk of this work does point to the presence of a trend decline of around half a per cent per annum. Although this is swamped by variations around the trend, it is nevertheless non-negligible. Quite what its policy significance is, and whether the optimal response is an inward-orientated trade strategy, is another matter. A significant decline through time in the relative price of primaries does not translate through to a terms of trade decline for all developing countries. It does of course for those heavily dependent on exports of primaries – typically the least developed. Even here the optimal policy response is clearly export diversification. The issue becomes one of how best to develop an industrial base – to which we return below.

Export instability

This also tends to be a feature of primary product markets. Elasticities are again at the heart of the problem, or to be more precise, price inelasticities in both demand and supply. This combined with a tendency to exogenous shocks triggered by weather conditions, pestilence and the like, results in large fluctuations in prices which translate through to large fluctuations in prices which translate through to large fluctuations in export earnings.

Recent evidence does point to greater variability in the price of primaries than that of manufactures. The evidence linking this variability to variations in growth is less conclusive, though this probably has something to do with the fact that most studies are cross-section rather than time-series. The recent 'trade shocks' literature, which is country specific/ time series does point up a close connection.[3] Again, one might ask what does this mean for trade policy? Is inward orientation the optimal response? Or should one be looking to forward markets for an answer? If the latter, and there is evidence even in the least developed countries of smoothing behaviour, then one is looking at a short-term response. In the longer term, the optimal response must again be diversification; which brings us back to the most appropriate policy for promoting industrialization.

Infant industry protection

Without doubt this has been the most pervasive and influential of all arguments for inward orientation. Even if diversification is the optimal policy response, with the prevalence of infant industries, how can it be expected to occur spontaneously? The crudest infant industry arguments are framed by reference to scale economies. The argument is quite simple. Established, mature producers benefit fully from scale economies. As a result they produce at the minimum efficient scale. So long as the scale curve is declining over the relevant range, developing countries are unable to compete. They do not have the market share required, nor are there any immediate prospects of acquiring that share. Thus temporary protection serves to raise the selling price of the mature competitor. This allows the new entrant to expand capacity, gain market share and move down the scale curve. In time the infant matures and the protection can be removed. However, as Johnson (1971), Baldwin (1969) and others have argued, scale economies *in themselves* do not constitute a defensible argument for infant industry protection. After all, they are a pervasive feature of manu-facturing activity in industrialized countries and the capital market has a mechanism for dealing with them: all 'infant' producers have to do is demonstrate that once scale economies are fully exploited, profits will be sufficient to offset initial losses and guarantee a rate of return at least equivalent to what could be earned elsewhere. However, in a developing country the capital market may not exist! Even if it exists it may operate imperfectly. For example, the inability to insure satisfactorily against pos-sible inappropriable returns to investment in physical and/or human capital can result in first-mover disadvantages. Alternatively private discount rates may be significantly in excess of social rates. In such circumstances it is argued that infant industry protection is required. Since manufacturing activity is a key element in the industrial sector, and since the entire manufacturing sector may potentially be in its infancy, it follows that widespread protection of manufacturing may be necessary.

Neo-classical analysis and the case for outward orientation

Like structuralists, neo-classical economists draw upon several model struc-tures in making a case for outward orientation, rather than framing the case in terms of a single paradigm. The basic case rests upon allowing markets to send out reliable and consistent signals, such that agents can react to these in appropriate ways to facilitate the exploitation of gains from trade.

- *Static gains from inter-industry exchange* are the standard deadweight gains associated with specialization and exchange. They derive from reallocating resources from activities in which a country enjoys a com-parative disadvantage into those where it has a comparative advan-tage. It is argued that these gains can only be maximized when markets are permitted to function.
- *Dynamic gains from inter-industry exchange* Empirical analysis sug-gests that static gains are of a modest order of magnitude. That does not mean they are not worth harvesting, of course. Rather it means

that the required gains from infant industry protection need not be that great to make inward orientation worthwhile. The dynamic gains from exchange are, however, likely to be much greater than static gains. These arise from X-inefficiency and a more rapid diffusion of technology. The former derive from the pro-competitive effects of trade; the latter from better information flows either directly, or indirectly through embodied technology. The potential losses from forgoing such benefits may be substantial.

- *Gains from intra-industry exchange* As the literature on intra-industry trade has demonstrated, there are both static and dynamic gains potentially available here also. Notwithstanding the documented growth in such trade in developing countries, this is really a phenomenon which is a dominant feature of North–North trade. However, if outward orientation is more conducive to industrialization, and if industrialization raises the propensity to intra-industry trade, then the present value of gains from trade will be lower with inward-orientated trade policies.

- *Rent-seeking and directly unproductive activity* The forgoing arguments are 'positive' reasons for pursuing an outward-orientated trade policy. In addition, a 'negative' argument against inward orientation is that it induces directly unproductive activity. In recent years neoclassical economists have deployed public choice analysis in assessing interest group behaviour in developing countries (see, for example, Bhagwati, Brecher and Srinivasan, 1984). From this it is argued that economies which rely heavily on direct controls create an incentive structure which generates rents. In turn the existence of rents gives rise to rent-seeking. Agents compete for the attention and favours of bureaucrats and politicians in an endeavour to secure the rents. As a result, much if not all of the rents are dissipated in the process of lobbying. This activity is unproductive in that it does not add anything to national output. Indeed, in so far as the resources invested have an alternative use, it may even deplete output. Thus this kind of activity is growth-inhibiting rather than growth-enhancing. It is argued that if a policy of free trade is followed, the kind of incentive structure which engenders directly unproductive activity cannot arise. As a result energies are diverted into productive activity and the level of rate of growth of national output are higher than they otherwise would be.

Summary

These, then, are the arguments. Our purpose in setting them out is not in some sense to weigh them up, but rather to remind ourselves of two things: first, the issue is a controversial one in the sense that arguments for both inward and outward orientation can be marshalled; second, the theoretical arguments are not wholly conclusive one way or the other. Does the empirical evidence help?

7.3   TRADE STRATEGY AND ECONOMIC PERFORMANCE: EMPIRICAL EVIDENCE

Empirical evidence on the relationship between trade strategy comes at the issue from several different angles. Some address the relationships between exports and economic growth on the assumption that more outward-orientated trade strategies are associated with higher exports. A second strand addresses the relationship between liberalization and exports. This is a narrower focus. However, in so far as liberalization means a move towards a more open trade strategy, it is a sensible question to ask. Third, there is a literature which attempts to use 'composite' indicators of trade strategy and link these to indicators of economic performance. Both multi-country and country specific studies abound. Given constraints on space, we concentrate on the former.

Exports and growth

There exists an extensive empirical literature on exports and growth. Table 7.1 presents a brief summary of the data, methodology and conclusions from a set of studies conducted between 1977 and 1993. Many find evidence of some association between exports or export growth and economic growth. Several find evidence of a difference in the effect of exports on growth between countries above and below some critical level of some variable, indicated in Table 7.1 as 'threshold effect'. A few brief comments are in order.

Michaely's (1977) study uses rank correlation methods while Balassa (1978) and Kavoussi (1984) use rank correlations and OLS regression analysis. Michaely is unusual in working with growth in the share of exports in GDP as his 'export' variable, arguing that since exports are part of the national product a positive correlation of the two variables is almost inevitable. The general conclusion from all the rank correlation studies is that high levels of economic growth are significantly associated with high levels of export growth.

The production function methodology originated in work by Michalopoulos and Jay (1973) and is used by Balassa (1978; 1984), Tyler

Table 7.1 A selection of empirical studies on the relationship between export growth and economic growth

Study	Data set	Methodology		Technique	Other variables	Conclusions
		Economic growth	Export growth			
Michaely (1977)	Cross-section 41 countries Average of 1950–73	Per capita GNP growth	Growth in export share	Rank correlation	None	Support of export growth hypothesis. Threshold effect
Balassa (1978)	Cross-section 10 countries Average of 1956–67 and 1967–73	GNP growth	Export growth or real export growth	Rank correlation OLS Production function	Labour force growth Domestic investment and foreign invest-ment/output	Support for growth hypothesis
Wiliamson (1978)	Cross-section 22 countries Average of 1960–74	Change in GDP	Lagged exports	OLS Linear models	Country dummies Direct investment Other foreign capital	Support for export growth hypothesis

Table 7.1 (Continued)

Study	Data set	Methodology		Technique	Other variables	Conclusions
		Economic growth	Export growth			
Fajana (1979)	Time series 1954–74 1 country	GDP growth	Export shares or export change/output	OLS	Trade balance Current account	Support for export growth hypothesis
Tyler (1981)	Cross-section 55 countries	GDP growth	Export growth	OLS Production function	Labour force growth Investment growth	Support for export growth hypothesis. Threshold effect
Feder (1983)	Cross-section 31 countries	GDP growth	Export growth or export change/output	OLS	Labour force growth Investment/output	Support for export growth hypothesis
Kavoussi (1984)	Cross-section 73 countries	GDP growth	Export growth	Rank correlation OLS Production function	Labour growth rate Capital growth rate	Support for export growth hypothesis. Threshold effect

Table 7.1 (Continued)

Study	Data set	Methodology			Conclusions	
		Economic growth	Export growth	Technique	Other variables	
Balassa (1984)[a]	Cross-section 10 countries	GNP growth	Export growth	OLS Production function	Labour force growth Ratio to output of domestic investment	Support for export growth hypothesis
Jung and Marshall (1985)	Time series 1950–81 37 countries	Real GNP (or GDP) growth	Lagged real export growth	Maximum likelihood Granger causality	Lagged GNP (GDP) growth	Little support for export growth causing economic growth
Moschos (1989)	Cross-section	Real GDP growth	Real export growth	OLS Production function	Labour force growth Real domestic investment growth	Support for export growth hypothesis. Threshold effect

Table 7.1 (Continued)

Study	Data set	Methodology			Other variables	Conclusions
		Economic growth	*Export growth*	*Technique*		
Salvatore and Hatcher (1991)	Time series 1963–73, 1973–85 26 countries in 4 groups by trade policy orientation	Real GDP growth	Real export growth	OLS Production function	Labour input growth Capital input growth Growth in industrial production	Support for export growth hypothesis
Ram (1985)	Cross-section 73 countries Average of 1960–70 and 1970–77	Real GDP growth	Real export growth	OLS tests for heteroskedasticity and specification bias	Labour force growth Investment growth	Support for export growth hypothesis Threshold effect
Darratt (1987)	Time series, 4 countries 1955–82	Real GDP growth	Real export growth and lagged real export growth	OLS, White test for causality	None	Rejection of export growth hypothesis in 3 out of 4 cases

Table 7.1 (Continued)

| Study | Data set | Methodology | | | Conclusions |
		Economic growth	Export growth	Technique	Other variables	
Greenaway and Sapsford (1994)	Cross section, 104 countries Average of 1960–73, 1973–90, 1980–88	Real (PPP) GDP growth	Growth in export ratio	OLS tests for heteroskedasticity	None	Support for export growth hypothesis Indirect evidence of threshold effect

Source: Jung and Marshall (1985) plus additions.
[a] Also includes summary of and comparison with Balassa (1978) study.

(1981), Kavoussi (1984), Moschos (1989) and Salvatore and Hatcher (1991). In all these studies the growth rate of GDP is regressed upon the growth rate of exports and a set of additional explanatory variables, usually related to the labour force and investment. All conclude that exports contribute significantly to the rate of growth of the developing countries studied.

Evidence on the existence of a 'threshold effect' is mixed. Michaely (1977) divided his sample of 41 countries on the basis of their per caput income levels, and found that while for the 23 countries in his higher-income group the rank correlation between economic growth and export growth was significant at the 1 per cent level, that for the low-income group was 'practically zero', and concluded that 'growth is affected by export performance only once countries achieve some minimum level of development' (p. 52). Tyler (1981), using the production function approach, concluded that 'a basic level of development is necessary for a country to most benefit from growth' (p. 124), and Kavoussi (1984), using the same approach, states that while 'in low income countries too export expansion tends to be associated with better economic performance' (p. 240), 'the contribution of exports ... is greater among the [more advanced developing countries]' (p. 242). Balassa (1984) however, comes to a different conclusion: 'for given increments of capital, labour and exports, the rate of economic growth will be higher the lower is the level of development'. Moschos (1989) searches for a critical switching-point in a cross-sectional production function analysis, and concludes that there is such a critical point, which may be best found from the data themselves rather than by reference to some arbitrary criterion, and that in the 'less advanced' group, output growth is influenced mainly by export growth and capital formation, while in the 'more advanced' group, labour growth is also important. Greenaway and Sapsford (1994) find that the strength of the export-growth relationship changes through time and interpret this as indirect evidence of a threshold effect.

Finally, we come to the question of causality – is there evidence that a higher rate of growth in exports causes a higher rate of growth in GDP? Jung and Marshall (1985) use Granger causality tests on a sample of 37 countries. They conclude that 'The time series results ... provide evidence in favour of export promotion in only 4 instances ... At the very least, it suggests that the statistical evidence in favour of export promotion is not as unanimous as was previously thought' (p. 11). A similar question mark has also been raised by Darrat (1987), albeit in a study of just four countries.

Overall, then, a substantial literature, using a range of methodologies supports some association between exports and growth. However, this association tends to be strongest in cross-section analyses, there being nothing like the same degree of agreement in time series work. Moreover, many of the results are the output of bivariate models or loosely specified aggregate production functions. Given the emphasis which is placed on the relationship, how robust is it? Levine and Renelt (1992) use extreme bounds analysis to investigate the robustness of a range of explanatory variables which are typically incorporated in growth models. Broadly speaking, they find that a relatively small number of variables appear to be robustly related to cross-country growth rates. Exports is one such variable. However, two interesting nuances are emphasized. First, imports or total trade substitute very well for exports. This is not a surprising finding, but it serves to emphasize that it is perhaps not exports *per se* which are important, but openness to trade, for which exports is acting as a proxy. Second, the relationship between exports and growth only robustly holds when investment is included, there being a robust and positive link between exports and investment. This suggests that the links between exports and growth may operate through improved resource accumulation rather than via improved resource allocation.

Liberalization and economic performance

There are some rather important complications associated with conducting an evaluation of liberalization. It is important to mention these, but only to mention them. Three stand out: first, what is the counterfactual? Should one just assume a continuation of pre-existing policies and performance. In practical terms this may be all one can do, although it has an important shortcoming: many of those liberalizations which are policy conditioned are initiated at a time of crisis when pre-existing policies are in fact unlikely to be sustainable. Second, and related to the above, how does one disentangle the effects of trade reforms from other effects? What is really important to note here is that it is not unusual to find both Structural Adjustment and Stabilization Loans put in place simultaneously. Third, supply responses will differ from economy to economy: how long should one wait before conducting an assessment?

Broadly speaking, two approaches to evaluating the economic effects of liberalization have been taken: cross-country and time series. The literature on the former falls into two genres, 'with–without' and 'before–after'. 'With–without' has been used by *inter alia* World Bank (1990) and Mosley *et al.* (1991). It involves taking a sample of countries subject to trade reforms, matching them with comparators which were not subject to reforms and ascribing any difference in performance to the reform programme. 'Before–after', which is again used by World Bank (1990) and Mosley *et al.* (1991) is similar in some respects but introduces a time dimension in that it compares the 'with–withouts' for a few years before and a few years after. In some cases, like Papageorgiou, Michaely and Choksi (1991), it is only the 'withs' that are examined, in that case for three years before and after.

Time series analysis is country specific and uses more or less sophisticated econometric methods. Examples include Harrigan and Mosley (1991), Papageorgiou, Michaely and Choksi (1991), Greenaway and Sapsford (1994), Greenaway, Leybourne and Sapsford (1995). Harrigan and Mosley (1991) focus on Structural Adjustment Loans (SALs) as one of a number of possible determinants of growth, export and investment performance. Greenaway and Sapsford (1994) use a structural break model to investigate whether or not liberalization appears to have a significant impact on growth. By contrast. Greenaway, Leybourne and Sapsford (1995) model growth as a smooth transition process then search for evidence of a coincidence of 'take off' and liberalization.

Despite the wide range of techniques used, the broad country coverage and the wide range of liberalization experiences examined, a degree of consensus exists, with one notable but very influential exception. That exception is the Papageorgiou, Michaely and Choksi (1991) study of 36 liberalization episodes in 19 countries. This can be read as very supportive of the view that liberalization is a panacea: it results in more rapid growth of exports, more rapid growth of real GDP and it accomplishes this without serious transitional costs in unemployment and without significant effects on the government's fiscal position. The veracity of these conclusions has been challenged by Greenaway (1993) and Collier (1993). The results are not convincing, partly for methodological reasons, partly for moral hazard reasons. Moreover, Greenaway, Leybourne and Sapsford (1997) look specifically at the timing of the PMC episodes and can find no systematic evidence of a connection between trade reforms and growth acceleration. In some cases there is a positive correlation, in some a negative correlation, in others no apparent correlation whatsoever.

The remaining evidence seems to suggest the following.

1. liberalizations, and reform programmes more generally, tend to be associated with an improvement in the current account of the balance of payments and with an improvement in the growth rate of real exports. The degree of improvement in the former typically outstrips the latter, indicating that some part of the change is operating through import compression. Since one of the objectives of Stabilization and

Structural Adjustment Programmes is to improve the current account, this is obviously a plus.

2. on balance, the impact on growth may be positive, in the sense that there are more cases of a positive growth impact than a negative growth impact. What this means of course is that in some cases growth performance does deteriorate: though of course it may not have deteriorated by as much as it would have done in the absence of reform! Since adjustment lending programmes are meant to improve growth, this would presumably score a plus.

3. a proportion of countries which have undergone adjustment show a subsequent improvement in investment. However, it is a minority; the majority appear to have experienced an investment slump. Since capital formation is crucially important to future growth, this clearly gives grounds for concern. Although Bleaney and Greenaway (1993) find other factors are more important in explaining investment slumps in the 1980s (terms of trade shocks, cost of capital) there are actually some plausible reasons for believing that adjustment programmes may be a contributory factor. In particular, deconfinement of the public sector may fail to crowd in private sector investment if there is a question-mark against the credibility of the reforms.

What can one say overall? There have certainly been some notable adjustment successes and some equally notable failures! Some adjustment programmes, where trade liberalization has figured prominently have resulted in rapid adjustment, a rapid supply side response and sustainable growth. In many other cases, especially in Sub-Saharan Africa, stabilization has turned out to be a false dawn as a significant supply response failed to materialize. One could particularize this to specific cases in order to identify specific ingredients of successful trade reforms. As always, the difficulty with that is the danger that country specific factors, which may not be generalisable, dominate. It is actually possible to distil more general lessons.

Trade strategy and growth

The recent literature on trade strategy and economic growth has tended to focus on categorizing countries into broad groupings based on a taxonomy of their trade policies. In many respects, this approach can be traced back to Greenaway (1986) and the World Development Report (WDR) (1987) which introduced the division of countries into policy blocks consisting of strongly outwardly-orientated (SOO), moderately outwardly-orientated (MOO), moderately inwardly-orientated (MIO) and strongly inwardly-orientated countries (SIO). While accepting that a strong emphasis was given to these results, the WDR has nevertheless provided a benchmark against which later work has been tested and it is interesting to note that the results it provided appear to be relatively robust.

This approach eschewed simply using effective and nominal rates of protection (ERP and NRP) as a means of classifying policies given the difficulties of data and issues surrounding the timing of policy shifts. Instead it employed a range of criteria, namely:

- ERP – the higher it is the greater the bias to import substitution
- Direct controls use (quotas, tariffs) – widespread use implies IO
- Use of export incentives
- Degree of exchange rate over-valuation – high value suggests IO.

Using 41 countries over the 1963–85 period, the paper suggests that outwardly-orientated countries have performed better than inwardly-orientated countries when looking at GDP per capita, inflation, savings ratios, incremental capital–output ratios and manufacturing exports. It suggests further that outward orientation aids the equitable distribution of income through the encouragement of employment and the removal of a bias towards capital intensive industries that inward orientation often encourages. Indeed outward orientation does not give rise to the lobbying inefficiencies associated with credit controls, licenses and foreign exchange which arise from inwardly-orientated policies.

Such a strong message, not surprisingly, elicited responses including that of Singer (1987). In a critique of the WDR, Singer questions the categorization used, especially as the SOO group included two city states (Hong Kong and Singapore) and suggested that all the WDR showed was that poorer nations grew more slowly than richer ones. While highlighting the Report's lack of consideration of third factors influencing the performance of economies, Singer suggests that what is important for developing nations is import revenue instability and that reducing this rather than realigning trade is the best policy for growth.

Greenaway and Nam (1988) provided a riposte to the structuralist viewpoint by re-emphasizing the relationship between outward orientation and growth. Indeed, acknowledging Singer's comments, the authors argue that outward orientation proponents often base their views on a neo-classical framework which *de facto* implies there must be no intervention in markets. It could not be claimed that Korea and Singapore meet this criteria and thus the authors conclude that while it is not easy to say what policies generate successful growth it is clear what policies, namely inwardly-orientated ones, do not.

More recent work has followed the lead given by these papers but has focused more specifically on the measurement of openness. In many respects this represents a new direction in the debate towards the generation of a consistent and robust methodology for measuring openness and its impact on growth in an attempt to establish a consensus in the literature. Highlighting this confusion is a key part of Harrison's (1991) work which demonstrates that the results from a selection of measures vary quite widely and in particular are sensitive to the time period chosen. Of most interest here are the discrepancies that arise between time-series models and cross-sectional models, perhaps suggesting that the 'snapshot' approach of the latter is not informative in this debate. Using time-series models Dollar (1991) measures openness by deviations in a price index away from an endowment based 'equilibrium' price. Using Greenaway and Nam categories, the evidence outlined suggests outward orientation has only been clearly influential in promoting growth in the last two decades and not in the 1950s and 1960s.

A new dimension to the argument was added by Ben-David (1993) who tried to establish a relationship between trade liberalization and economic convergence. While this focused on DMEs (namely the EU countries), it does furnish a general conclusion that convergence is a function of liberalization, based on a comparison of the EU against other nations and how the EU mirrors the experience of the USA. What is also interesting about this work is the fact that the data show a strong negative correlation between income level and growth as posited by neo-classical theory, something that does not appear in earlier empirical work based on LDC experiences.

The debate has been brought up to date in the comprehensive study by Sachs and Warner (1995) which not only gives a sound background of historical analysis but suggests that the way forward in researching the link between trade strategy and growth is to explore the timing of policy shifts and how these have impinged on growth performance. Amongst several pieces of empirical analysis, the authors show that open economies perform better than closed economies and that convergence can be achieved by poor countries as long as they are linked by trade to the richer ones. In fact they posit that there is no evidence to suggest liberalization has a downside – all economies which have liberalized have grown, and indeed open LDCs grew eight times faster than closed ones post-1970. What is significant, however, is their conclusion that 'poor' policies affect growth directly, even when controlling for other factors, and in particular they affect the accumulation of physical capital. It is this lack of physical (and human capital) which restricts poorer countries from developing and growing as rapidly as open economies which have a similar initial income level (Barro, 1991).

7.4   CONCLUDING COMMENTS

In this chapter we have reviewed both theory and evidence relating to the links between trade orientation and economic development. With respect to the former we rehearsed the key insights from structuralist and neo-classical perspectives. We devoted rather more time to the empirical evidence. There we reviewed work on three related issues: the links between exports and growth; the links between overall trade orientation and growth. As one would expect, this empirical work does not answer all of the questions conclusively. However, several points stand out. First there does appear to be a reasonably well established connection between export growth and output growth, though there are outstanding questions regarding causality. Second liberalization may or may not have a beneficial effect on growth, the evidence thus far is mixed. Third, although there does appear to be some connection between trade orientation and economic performance, the evidence is much clearer on the adverse impact of inward orientation on growth than on the favourable impact of outward orientation.

Notes

1.   This paper draws upon work underway in a Ford Foundation programme on 'Export Promotion and Economic Development in the New World Trading Order'. The authors acknowledge gratefully the Foundation's support. They also acknowledge helpful comments from Conference participants on an earlier draft.
2.   For a review see Toye (1991) and Greenaway and Milner (1993).
3.   See, for example, Bevan, Collier and Gunning (1993).

References

Balassa, B. (1978) 'Exports and Economic Growth', *Journal of Development Economic*, vol. 5, pp. 181–9.
——— (1984) 'Adjustment Policies in Developing Economies', *World Development*, vol. 12, pp. 23–38.
Baldwin, R.E. (1969) 'The Case Against Infant Industry Protection', *Journal of Political Economy*, vol. 77, pp. 295–305.

Barro, R. (1991) 'Economic Growth in a Cross-section of Countries', *Quarterly Journal of Economics*, vol. 106, pp. 407–43.

Ben-David, D. (1993) 'Equalising Exchange: Trade Liberalisation and Income Convergence', *Quarterly Journal of Economics*, vol. 108, pp. 653–79.

Bhagwati, J., R.A. Brecher and T.N. Srinivasan (1984) 'DUP Activities and Economic Theory', in D. Colander (ed.), *Neoclassical Political Economy*, (Cambridge, MA: MIT Press).

Bleaney, M.F. and D. Greenaway (1993) 'Adjustment to External Imbalance and Investment Slumps in Developing Countries'. *European Economic Review*, vol. 37, pp. 577–85.

Collier, P. (1993) 'Higgledy-Piggledy Liberalisation', *The World Economy*, vol. 16, pp. 503–12.

Cuddington, J.T. and C.M. Urzua (1989) 'Trends and Cycles in the Net Barter Terms of Trade: A New Approach', *Economic Journal*, vol. 99, pp. 426–42.

Darratt, A. (1987) 'Are Exports an Engine of Growth?', *Applied Economics*, vol. 19, pp. 277–83.

Dollar, D. (1991) 'Outward Orientation and Growth: an Empirical Study Using a Price-Based Measure of Openness'. mimeo.

Fajana, O. (1979) 'Trade and Growth: the Nigerian Experience', *World Development*, vol. 7(1), pp 73–8.

Feder, G. (1983) 'On Exports and Economic Growth', *Journal of Development Economics*, vol. 19, pp. 59–73.

Greenaway, D. (1986) 'Characteristics of Industrialisation and Economic Performance Under Alternative Development Strategies', *Background Paper to 1987 World Development Report*.

Greenaway, D. (1993) 'Liberalising Foreign Trade Through Rose Tinted Glasses', *Economic Journal*, vol. 103, pp. 208–23.

—— and C.R. Milner (1993) *Trade and Industrial Policy in Developing Countries* (London: Macmillan).

Greenaway, D. and C.H. Nam (1988) 'Industrialisation and Macroeconomic Performance in Developing Countries Under Alternative Development Strategies', *Kyklos*, vol. 41, pp. 419–35.

—— and D. Sapsford (1994) 'What Does Liberalisation Do for Exports and Growth?' *Weltwirtschaftliches Archiv*, vol. 130, pp. 152–74.

—— S.J. Leybourne and D. Sapsford (1997) 'Modelling Growth (and Liberalisation) Using Smooth Transitions Analysis', *Economic Inquiry*, Vol. 25, pp. 798–814.

Grilli, E.R. and M.C. Yang (1988) 'Primary Commodity Prices, Manufactured Goods Prices, and Terms of Trade of Developing Countries: What the Long-run Shows', *World Bank Economic Review*, vol. 2, pp. 1–47.

Harrigan, J. and P. Mosley (1991) 'Evaluating the Impact of World Bank Structural Adjustment Lending', *Journal of Development Studies*, vol. 27, pp. 63–94.

Harrison, A. (1991) 'Openness and Growth: A Time-Series, Cross-Country Analysis for Developing Countries', mimeo.

Johnson, H. (1971) *Aspects of the Theory of Tariffs* (London: George Allen & Unwin).

Jung, W. and P. Marshall (1985) 'Exports, Growth and Causality in Developing Countries', *Journal of Development Economics*, vol. 18, pp. 1–12.

Kavoussi, R. (1984) 'Export Expansion and Economic Growth: Further Empirical Evidence', *Journal of Development Economics*, vol. 14, pp. 241–50.

Levine, R and D. Renelt (1992) 'A Sensitivity Analysis of Cross Country Growth Regressions', *American Economic Review*, vol. 82, pp. 946–63.

Michaely, M. (1977) 'Export and Growth: An Empirical Investigation', *Journal of Development Economics*, vol. 4, pp. 49–54.

Michalopoulos, C. and J. Kay (1973), 'Growth of Exports and Income in the Developing World', AID *Discussion Paper*, vol. 28, Washington DC.

Moschos, D. (1989) 'Export Expansion, Growth and the Level of Economic Development', *Journal of Development Economics*, vol. 15, pp. 99–102.

Mosley, P., J. Harrigan and J. Toye (eds) (1991a) *Aid and Power: The World Bank and Policy-based Lending. vol. 1: Analysis and Policy Proposals*, (London: Routledge).

——, —— and —— (eds) (1991b) *Aid and Power: The World Bank and Policy-Based Lending. vol. 2: Case Studies* (London: Routledge).

Papageorgiou, D., M. Michaely and A. Choksi (eds) (1991) *Liberalising Foreign Trade* (Oxford: Blackwell).

Prebisch, R. (1950) *The Economic Development of Latin America and its Principal Problems* (New York: United Nations).

Ram, R. (1985) 'Exports and Economic Growth: Some Additional Evidence', *Economic Development and Cultural Change*, vol. 33, pp. 415–25.

Sachs, J.D. and A. Warner (1995) 'Economic Reform and the Process of Global Intergration', *Brookings Papers on Economic Activity*, vol. 1, pp. 1–118.

Salvatore, D. and R. Hatcher (1991) 'Inward and Outward Oriented Trade Strategies', *Journal of Development Studies*, vol. 27, pp. 7–25.

Sapsford, D.R. (1985) 'The Statistical Debate on the Net Barter Terms of Trade Between Primary Commodities and Manufactures: A Comment', *Economic Journal*, vol. 95, pp. 781–8.

Sarkar, P. and H.W. Singer (1991) 'Manufactured Exports of Developing Countries and their Terms of Trade Since 1965', *World Development*, vol. 19, pp. 333–40.

—— (1987) 'The World Development Report (1987) on the Blessings of Outward Orientation: A Necessary Correction', *Journal of Development Studies*, vol. 23, pp. 232–6.

Spraos, J. (1980) 'The Statistical Debate on the Net Barter Terms of Trade Between Primary Commodities and Manufactures', *Economic Journal*, vol. 90, pp. 107–28.

Toye, J. (1991) *Dilemmas for Development* (Oxford, Blackwell).

Tyler, W.G. (1981) 'Growth and Export Expansion in Developing Countries', *Journal of Development Economics*, vol. 9, pp. 121–30.

World Bank (1987a) *Annual Development Report* (Washington DC: World Bank).

World Bank (1987b) *World Development Report* (New York: Oxford University Press).

—— (1990) 'Report on Adjustment Lending II: Policies for the Recovery of Growth', Document R90–99 (Washington DC: The World Bank).

8 The Strategic Use of Trade Policies for Development: Some General Equilibrium Issues[1]

Andrew McKay and Chris Milner

8.1 INTRODUCTION

The neo-classical analysis of industrialization and trade strategy, especially in its 'strong' version, emphasizes neutrality across tradeables (with free trade the extreme version of this) and the avoidance of excessive selectivity of any factor or product market government interventions as the basis for success.[2] There is considerable merit to this analysis. It has, for instance, helped to shift the intellectual balance and policy-makers away from the belief in the importance of government intervention to try to correct market failure to a greater willingness to rely on market mechanisms and prices. But several commentators on the neo-classical perspective, including Hans Singer, point to the insufficient emphasis it places on market failure/inefficiency (see Evans, 1990; Lall, 1991). Singer (1989) in fact calls for the use of policies of efficient import substitution. The intention is that import-substituting industries should be encouraged to develop into export industries, where externality or learning-by-doing gains can be reaped. In order to avoid existing export industries (especially non-traditional ones) from being disadvantaged by this, compensating export subsidies may be required.[3] Thus the counter-case for selective or non-uniform interventions or strategic promotion of some import-substitute and export industries can be constructed around this 'alternative perspective'.[4]

This chapter does not seek to become embroiled in the debate about the pervasiveness or otherwise of market failure or about the actual incidence of trade-promoting interventions in developing countries. Rather, it is concerned with some first principles about the difficulties of designing mixed and selective trade policy interventions in a general equilibrium setting, and in particular with whether the *ex-post* outcome of such interventions may diverge from the *ex ante* strategic intent. It draws upon some more formal, earlier work in this area by the authors (Milner, 1995; Milner and McKay, 1996; and McKay and Milner, 1996, 1997).

The remainder of the chapter is organized as follows. In Section 8.2 we review the analytic issues surrounding the extensions to the traditional trade model required to investigate temporary and selective interventions in the presence of non-tradeables and learning effects. Section 8.3 concentrates on the implications of introducing non-tradeables, while Section 8.4 investigates the issue of selective intervention. Section 8.5 deals with temporary intervention in the presence of learning by doing externalities. Finally, Section 8.6 offers some summary conclusions.

8.2 SOME ANALYTICAL ISSUES

In the traditional two-sector trade model there is only one relative price; the price of one tradeable (importables, M) relative to the other (exportables, X). Non-uniform trade policy interventions will result in a bias in favour either of importables (import substitution, IS strategy) or of exportables (export promotion, EP). Alternatively, uniform trade interventions will not alter the relative price and a neutral trade regime can be achieved either by uniform trade policy interventions or by free trade. Other than for political economy reasons therefore, there would appear to be no motive for simultaneously trying to pursue (uniform) IS and EP, given that there is an inevitable negative relationship in this theoretical framework between the strategies in terms of the effect on relative prices; IS tending to induce an anti-export (pro-importables) bias and EP tending to induce an anti-importables (pro-exportables) bias.[5] This is the corollary of the famous Lerner-symmetry theorem. But how are the above arguments affected if we introduce a third good – non-tradeables – into the analytical framework? On the face of it a pro-tradeables (or anti-tradeables) bias can be induced by pursuing a mixed, uniform strategy to promote (or disprotect) all tradeables.[6] Certainly, in an *ex ante* sense it becomes feasible to think of pursuing trade policies to raise or lower the real exchange rate for tradeables as a whole and for each tradeable by raising the (nominal) price of tradeables. But we need to think about how the price of non-tradeables may endogenously adjust to disequilibrium-inducing changes in the price of tradeables.

If the scope for uniform promotion of all tradeables is constrained by the endogenous adjustment of the price of non-tradeables to commercial policy intervention (an issue we investigate further in Section 8.3), then the alternative may be non-uniform intervention or selective promotion of only some importables and exportables. Thus the aim of policy-makers may be to promote some importables (viewed by some criteria as more important for the economic strategy of the country) and perhaps non-traditional (as opposed to traditional) exportables. In order to investigate this option we need to increase the dimensions of the modelling framework further, so as to distinguish between (*ex-ante*) promoted and non-protected activities within both the importables and exportables sectors. Of course the rationale that is often used to specify selective intervention in the tradeables good sectors is that there are externalities or learning-by-doing benefits to be gained in some, but not all, sectors. Thus non-resource-intensive (non-traditional) and/or manufacturing sectors are seen as more likely to generate positive externalities; experience of new technologies or skills generating future and wider efficiency gains once learning by doing has occurred. Such a situation calls for interventions (trade policy measures as second best) which are *temporary*, giving the sector time to exploit the externalities and to be able to compete internationally.[7] This means not only that we need to incorporate inter-sectoral linkages into the analytical framework but also intertemporal effects. If interventions in the current time period may have output and welfare effects in a future time period, we need to be able to model the effects of (selective) temporary (that is, first time period) trade policy interventions.

The dimensions of the modelling framework need to be expanded therefore from the traditional two-sector–one-time-period model, to at least a multi-sector, two-period model in order to accommodate non-tradeability, selectivity and temporary interventions. In the ensuing discussion we consider the implications of increasing the dimensionality of the analysis in a piecemeal fashion so as to maintain tractability. At each stage, however, we do not seek a comprehensive discussion of all possibilities but rather to demonstrate the problems of successfully implementing strategic trade policy interventions.

8.3 TRADE POLICY IN THE PRESENCE OF NON-TRADEABLES

The simplest extension to the traditional two-sector (composite exportable (X) and importable (M)) trade model is the addition of a single, non-tradeable good (N), in the context of a small (distortionless) economy which produces and consumes all goods and where income equals expenditure (see for example, Connolly and Devereux, 1992). With the relative prices of tradeables (relative to non-tradeables) perfectly flexible so as to allow the market for non-tradeables to clear, the equilibrium condition for the economy can be represented following Walras's law by the market-clearing condition for non-tradeables (that is, zero excess demand (N_D) implies balanced trade). Following Dornbusch (1974) we can illustrate the equilibrium combinations of relative prices along zero excess demand schedules[8] using Figure 8.1; part (a) assumes substitutability in production and consumption and (b) complementarity in production between one of the tradeables and the non-tradeable good.[9] For simplicity we initially also hold real income constant along $N = 0$, assuming that any policy interventions will be small and be introduced from free trade.

The free trade relative price of tradeables or terms of trade is given by the ray OT, which intersects the $N = 0$ schedule at E. Import substitution measures (import tariffs or quotas and/or export taxes) tend to rotate the OT schedule rightwards towards OT' and export promotion measures (import subsidies and/or export subsidies) shift it leftwards towards OT'. Note here that the principle of Lerner symmetry is accepted, namely that a given change in the structure of domestic relative prices can be achieved by an import or export tax. But does the corollary of Lerner symmetry, namely that a uniform import tax and export subsidy results in the same equilibrium structure of domestic relative prices as under free trade conditions, hold in the presence of non-tradeables in the same way as it does in the standard two-sector model? The answer is that it may.

Let us illustrate this with the aid of Figure 8.1(a). Given substitutability in production and consumption including between tradeables and the non-traded good, any measure (IS or EP) seeking to promote some or all tradeables by raising their relative price tends to shift production (consumption) towards protected tradeables (non-tradeables) and away from non-tradeables (tradeables) and thereby generate positive excess demand for non-tradeables. The price of non-tradeables is therefore driven up by IS or EP measures. If IS (EP) is used then the price of non-tradeables rises until the excess demand is eliminated, and a policy-distorted equilibrium is reached at E' (E''); an IS (EP) strategy applies *ex post* at E' (E''). However, if uniform IS and EP measures are used simultaneously and the homogeneity properties of a general equilibrium model apply, then although relative prices of both tradeables may be initially raised (for example, shifting relative prices from E to D) the disequilibrium situation is not sustainable and the price of non-tradeables is driven up until excess demand for N is eliminated back at E. A long-term or equilibrium pro-tradeables bias in the structure of relative prices is not possible in this tradeables–non-tradeables model and the corollary of Lerner symmetry holds.

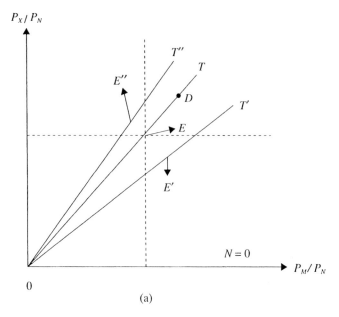

(a)

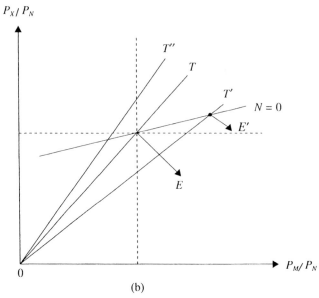

(b)

Figure 8.1

In fact the corollary of Lerner symmetry holds under a wider range of circumstances than the present simple model, in particular when income effects are allowed for. Indeed, in Figure 8.1(b), where a case of complementarity rather than substitutability is represented,[10] uniform IS and EP policies would tend to generate mutually offsetting positive and negative excess demand to drive equilibrium relative prices back towards E. The difference in this case is that an *ex post* or equilibrium structure of relative prices which is pro-tradeables in nature is possible, based on selective trade policy: take point E' at the intersect of the ray OT' and the $N = 0$ schedule. But this is achievable by (*ex ante*) IS measures only, that is by measures that shift OT to OT'. Thus even for the very simple extension of the basic model which incorporates a non-tradeable sector, it is easy to demonstrate that the *ex-post* outcome of trade policy intervention for the incentive structure may well diverge from the *ex ante* or intended one and that the *ex-post* outcome of a given, *ex ante* measure will vary substantially with the characteristics of the model. In particular, only in specific and selected circumstances is it possible to use trade policy to promote the tradeables sector as a whole; if possible at all this requires non-uniform rather than uniform intervention.

8.4　REAL EXCHANGE RATES AND SELECTIVE INTERVENTION

The relative prices shown in Figure 8.1 can be viewed as particular measures for the real exchange rate (e_i), that is, the price (P) of a type or of all tradeables (i) relative to non-tradeables

$$\left(\frac{P_i}{P_N}\right).$$

We established in the context of the analytical framework set out in the previous section that all e_i (aggregate or individual) are unaltered in the long-run equilibrium by uniform IS and EP measures. But with non-uniform interventions (that is, selective promotion of only some tradeables) it is obvious from Figure 8.1 that the real exchange rate for any aggregation of promoted and non-promoted sectors is generally ambiguous. Consider Figure 8.1(a) and the impact of IS (only or net) measures that shift OT to OT'. The real exchange rate for importables rises

$\left(\dfrac{P_M}{P_N} \uparrow\right)$, but that for exportables falls $\left(\dfrac{P_X}{P_N} \downarrow\right)$

in the move from E to E' structure of relative prices.[11] What happens to the aggregate real exchange rate for all tradeables is ambiguous and depends on the relative importance of the unpromoted and promoted sectors in tradeables overall and on the degree of substitutability between the promoted sector and non-tradeables; the greater the rise in the real exchange rate of the promoted sector (because of a small response of non-tradeables prices) and the more important the promoted sector in total tradeables, the greater the probability of raising the real exchange rate for the aggregate basket of tradeables.

The same principle applies if we consider selective interventions within the importables and exportables sectors. Selective promotion of some tradeables is possible, but the effect on any aggregate of promoted and unpromoted activities is ambiguous. Thus it may be possible to promote (that is, raise the specific real exchange rate for) non-traditional (for example, manufacturing) exportables and for particular importables, but the effect on the real exchange rate for all exportables or all importables or all tradeables will be ambiguous, if there is some substitutability (in production or consumption) between the promoted tradeables and non-tradeables. Since the price of non-tradeables can be expected to rise as a result, the real exchange rate for non-promoted activities in both the importables and exportables sectors will fall. Indeed with non-uniform intervention in the promoted sectors, it is not necessary that the real exchange rate actually increases for all the promoted sectors. Consider a case where the rate of nominal protection (that is, subsidization through tariff and non-tariff barriers) for some importables is 30 per cent (but is zero for other importables) and the rate of nominal export subsidization for non traditional exportables is 10 per cent (but zero or negative for traditional exportables). If the nature of substitution relationships is such that the price of non-tradeables rises by less than the protected importables but by more than promoted exportables, then only the real exchange rate for protected importables will rise. The real exchange rate falls will be greatest in the nominally unpromoted sectors, but in this case the real exchange rate also falls in the nominally promoted (non-traditional export) sector.

Again we have a result where the actual or *ex post* outcome of commercial policy intervention may diverge from the intended outcome, once we consider policy intervention in a general equilibrium setting. Alternatively, we might view the above analysis as drawing attention to the greater informational content or requirements of effective commercial policy intervention, that is to the need for information on the actual substitutional influences on the endogenous behaviour of the price of non-tradeables. The only way we could have eliminated this need for greater information would have been to set the rate of selective promotion at a uniform rate.[12] With a 30 per cent rate of import protection and export subsidisation for the selected sectors, the rise in the price of non-tradeables would tend to be less than 30 per cent and the real exchange rate would rise in both promoted sectors (albeit by less than the nominal rate of subsidization). But we know that there are political economy and budgetary pressures for higher rates of import protection than export subsidization, and that the uniform intervention solution to the information problem may not be available.

8.5 TEMPORARY TRADE INTERVENTIONS, INTER-TEMPORAL CONSIDERATIONS AND EXTERNALITIES

Thus far we have assumed that trade policy interventions are permanent. Many of the arguments about protection in a developing country context have implicitly or explicitly been concerned with temporary (or at least non-permanent) interventions. The infant-industry argument for intervention is concerned, however, with the application of support measures during a period of infancy, the need for which disappears after the achievement of certain learning-by-doing or externality gains. In other words interventions now, that is in the current time period, are aimed at achieving certain resource allocation or welfare effects in a future time period.

A number of authors (Edwards, 1989; Chen and Devereux, 1994) have in recent years sought to extend the one-period, tradeables–non-tradeables model of commercial policy to a two-period framework, in some cases also formally modelling specific externalities. They consider the case where trade policy interventions are temporary (that is, applied only in the first time period), where it is known for certain by agents that the measures will be removed in the second time period. In doing so such models are able to capture inter-temporal effects as well as the type of intra-temporal effects discussed in the earlier sections of this chapter.

Not surprisingly, there is greater complexity and ambiguity associated with the effects of temporary trade policy interventions in a two-period trade model. But for simplicity let us retain the assumption of substitutability, rather than complementarity between all goods. Temporary trade policy measures serve therefore to raise the price of non-tradeables in period one as a result of both intra-temporal and inter-temporal substitution effects. In other words, following nominal increases in the price of tradeables there is an incentive for production to be switched towards tradeables from non-tradeables in period one (the intra-temporal effect) and from production in period two (the inter-temporal effect) and for consumption to be switched away from tradeables towards non-tradeables in period one (intra-temporal effect) and towards period two (inter-temporal effect). Intuition might suggest that the incorporation of additional inter-temporal substitution possibilities serves to increase the magnitude of the total substitution effect, and to induce larger increases in the price of non-tradeables for given nominal trade policy interventions. But, the implication of homogeneity in the one-period model (namely that the increase in the price of non-tradeables is a weighted average of the (trade policy induced) increases in the prices of each tradeable) disappears. Now, rather than a uniform rate of nominal promotion of (all) IS and EP sectors resulting in an equal increase in the price of non-tradeables and, therefore, unaltered real exchange rates, the price of non-tradeables in period one may rise by more or less than the temporary, uniform rate of promotion of tradeables; the real exchange rate for importables or exportables may depreciate or appreciate.

The above ambiguity applies whether or not income effects are incorporated. Thus, although a pro-tradeables bias in the first time period might be induced by temporary (uniform) IS and EP policies, it is far from being the necessary outcome. Indeed McKay and Milner (1996) show that in the general case temporary uniform intervention can cause the real exchange rates for both importables and exportables to appreciate temporarily (that is, create a temporary anti-tradeables bias). Clearly this would be a perverse and undesirable outcome of a temporary intervention which was seeking to stimulate production in tradeable good sectors where externalities (future benefits) were believed to be available.

There are clearly many sources of complexity in the model, making the outcome ambiguous and intuition difficult. The situation, however, is clearer if we consider the introduction of trade policy measures about an initial free trade equilibrium. In these circumstances in the absence of learning-by-doing effects, the introduction of temporary trade policy measures has no welfare impact at the margin. However, once learning-by-doing effects are introduced, even marginal trade policy measures introduced about an initial free trade equilibrium will have welfare consequences.

This leads to the question of the circumstances under which trade policy measures may be welfare improving. Considering the most straightforward case of uniform intervention, the critical factor turns out to be the response of the real exchange rate in the first period. Where the trade policy measures generate a smaller proportionate increase in the price of non-tradeables so that the real exchange rate depreciates, this is welfare-improving. The consequent increased incentive to produce tradeables in the first period brings the learning-by-doing effect in the tradeables sector into play and so, by increasing the profitability of second period production, increases intertemporal welfare.

Unfortunately, however, even relative to an initial free trade equilibrium, it is not necessarily the case that the real exchange rate will depreciate in the first period: whether or not it does depends on the nature of the substitution relationships between the different goods and time periods. Clearly, if these are such that the real exchange rate appreciates, then the uniform trade policy measures will be counter-productive.

In reality, the interest may be more in selective, rather than uniform, trade policy interventions. Many of the above caveats still apply, however; selective protection or promotion of some tradeables may imply selective disprotection of others. Clearly if the trade policy interventions are to be potentially welfare-increasing, it is vitally important that they are focused on those sectors in which the learning-by-doing effects are strongest. Whether the externality or learning-by-doing effects are general to all tradeables or are possible only in specific activities within the tradeables sector, the bottom line is that the trade policy interventions need to raise the corresponding real exchange rate or rates at least temporarily if the potential gains are to be reaped. But again the effects of general or selective promotion of tradeables on aggregate or real exchange rates are ambiguous.

It is possible to design *ex-ante* policy interventions (that is, mixes of nominal IS and EP promotion) that result in the necessary temporary changes in real exchange rates; appropriate real exchange rate deprecations being welfare-raising. But the necessary real exchange rate depreciation(s) are not necessarily achieved by the apparent mix of nominal (*ex-ante*) interventions. Having correctly identified the relevant group of activities within the tradeable goods sectors where positive externalities are possible, it does not necessarily follow that nominal (IS and EP) promotion of these activities will induce the required changes in real exchange rates.

8.6 CONCLUSIONS

Irrespective of the initial state of the economy, changes in trade policy interventions will have general equilibrium consequences potentially affecting all goods as well as welfare. General equilibrium analysis is necessary, because trade policy measures affecting one good will inevitably have effects on other goods not directly affected. Indeed we demonstrate in this chapter that the desired or intended movement in relative prices (real exchange rates) may not actually be achieved under a fairly wide range of circumstances relating to the mix of trade policies and of model characteristics.

A consideration of the welfare consequences of trade policy change also requires that such general equilibrium effects are taken into account. Starting from an initial situation in which trade policy interventions are already present, changes in these trade policy interventions will inevitably have welfare consequences. However, even if trade policy becomes more protectionist on average, welfare need not necessarily fall; this is a standard second-best result. But in the absence of learning-by-doing effects, no equilibrium characterized by trade policy interventions will be welfare-superior to the free trade equilibrium. In short, in such a world free trade is a better strategy than pursuing active trade policy intervention.

The case may be different if there are learning-by-doing effects, however. Where these are present in the tradeable goods sector, then it is possible that an equilibrium characterized by trade policy interventions in favour of the sectors characterized by learning by doing will be superior in welfare terms to the free trade equilibrium (though not optimal). But this is by no means necessarily the case, because such interventions may in fact be welfare-lowering. Even in this world, trade policy interventions need to be very carefully designed, based on relatively detailed information about the economy, if they are not to lead to a reduction in welfare. The type of information which is likely to be required includes knowledge of the strength of the learning-by-doing effects in the different sectors, and knowledge of the nature and degree of substitution between different goods at a point in time and intertemporally. In practice, such information may be very difficult to come by and policy-makers should be wary that the actual outcomes may diverge from their strategic intentions.

Notes

1. The research on which this paper is based is supported by a Ford Foundation Programme on 'Export Promotion and Economic Development in the New World Trading Order'. The Foundation's support is gratefully acknowledged.
2. The 'strong' versions of the analysis do not see market failure as a major problem. In weaker versions, however, the possibility of market failure is admitted, but fearful of 'administrative failure' the recommendation is usually for low, uniform and temporary intervention in the tradeables good sector and for non-selective support of supply-side factors.

3. Duty-drawback can also offset some of the costs of protecting 'efficient' import substituting industries.
4. The implications of the instability of export prices is also a theme that has been central to Hans Singer's work on appropriate trade policies for developing countries.
5. In the case of selective intervention in favour of only certain, but not all, exportables and importables a higher dimensional framework would be required to investigate relative price outcomes. The present outcome might still apply, however, if protected and unprotected tradeables are substitutes in consumption and/or production.
6. This representation of commercial policy options is adopted by Liang (1992).
7. In this chapter we concentrate on the real exchange rate and welfare effects of trade policy interventions and make no attempt to compare them with alternative interventions. Optimal intervention analysis typically leads to the conclusion that trade policy interventions are not a first-best instrument.
8. The schedule is a blow-up of the neighbourhood of free trade equilibrium E, assuming small changes in policy variables.
9. Specifically in Figure 8.1(b) between the importable and non-tradeable.
10. The possibility of complementarities between tradeables and non-tradeables might be caused when domestic prices are supply determined. Edwards and van Wijnbergen (1987), for instance, model this possibility in the context of a Heckscher–Ohlin framework.
11. The larger the increase in the price of non-tradeables induced by selective intervention, the greater the share of the burden of protection that is borne by unprotected tradeables than by non-tradeables. For a discussion of the idea of shifting of the burden and incidence of protection see Sjaastad (1980) and Greenaway and Milner (1987).
12. Note also that the unambiguous outcome for the protected tradeables in the selective case may not apply if there are complementarities between non-tradeables and specific tradeables.

References

Chen, L.L. and J. Devereux (1994) 'Protection, export promotion and development', *Journal of Development Economics*, vol. 40, pp. 387–95.

Connolly, M. and J. Devereux (1992) 'Commercial policy, the terms of trade and real exchange rates', *Oxford Economic Papers*, vol. 44, pp. 507–12.

Dornbusch, R. (1974) 'Tariffs and non-traded goods', *Journal of International Economics*, vol. 4, pp. 177–85.

Edwards, S. (1989) *Real Exchange Rates, Devaluation and Adjustment: Exchange Rate Policy in Developing Countries* (MIT Press).

Edwards, S. and S. van Wijnbergen (1987) 'Tariffs, the real exchange rate and the terms of trade: on two popular propositions in international trade', *Oxford Economic Papers*, vol. 39, pp. 458–64.

Evans, D. (1990) 'Outward orientation: an assessment', in C. Milner (ed.) *Export Promotion Strategies: Theory and Evidence from Developing Countries* (Brighton: Wheatsheaf).

Greenaway, D. and C.R. Milner (1987) 'True protection concepts and their use in evaluating commercial policy in developing countries', *Journal of Development Studies*, vol. 23, pp. 200–19.

Lall, S. (1991) 'Explaining industrial success in the developing world', in V.N. Balasubramanyam and S. Lall (eds) *Current Issues in Development Economics* (London: Macmillan).

Liang, N. (1992) 'Beyond import substitution and export promotion: a new typology of trade strategies', *Journal of Development Studies*, vol. 28, pp. 447–72.

McKay, A.D. and C.R. Milner (1996) 'Trade orientation and protection in the presence of non-tradeables', mimeo.

—— and —— (1997) 'Defining and measuring trade strategy: theory and some evidence from the Caribbean', *Journal of Development Studies*, forthcoming.

Milner, C.R. (1995) 'Relative incentivies and trade strategies', *Economic Record*, vol. 71, pp. 217–26.

—— and A.D. McKay (1996) 'Neutrality and export promotion: issues, evidence and policy implications', in D. Greenaway and V.N. Balasubramanyam (eds) *Trade and Development: Essays in Honour of Jagdish Bhagwati* (London: Macmillan).

Singer, H.W. (1989) 'Industrialisation and world trade in the years after the Brandt Report', Paper prepared for the International Symposium 'The Crisis of the Global System: the World Ten Years after the Brandt Report'.

Sjaastad, K.A. (1980), 'Commercial policy, true tariffs and relative prices', in J. Black and B. Hindley (eds) *Current Issues in Commercial Policy and Diplomacy* (London: Macmillan).

9 Liberalization, Privatization and the Pace of Economic Development in Taiwan

John-ren Chen

9.1 INTRODUCTION: A HISTORICAL RETROSPECT

The economic development in Taiwan since the 1950s can be briefly characterized by privatization and liberalization. Liberalization is necessary for privatization, which was the result of the bad performance of public enterprises. In this paper we discuss the reasons for the success of the industrialization in Taiwan.

The performance of the economic development in Taiwan can be summarized by the brief statistics given in Table 9.1.

Taiwan had a totalitarian political system from 1945 to 1991. The first free election of Parliament was carried out in 1991, and in 1996 the first president of Taiwan was elected. Thus, Taiwanese economic development and the democratization of the political system have been successful.

What is the reason for the economic development in Taiwan?

We will discuss this question in Section 9.2.

Taiwan is an island with poor endowment of natural resources and a small domestic market. Therefore the world market is important for the Taiwanese economy. With this point of view Taiwan has tried to attend to the world market and has liberalized trade policy since the 1950s. What are the effects of trade liberalization? This is the main issue we consider in this chapter. Trade liberalization in Taiwan since the 1950s can be classified into two stages; 1958–80 and 1981–6. Trade liberalization has been smoothly implemented. The transition from the first stage to the second stage might have taken a period of several years.

In Section 9.3 we will summarize the effects of trade liberalization. In Section 9.4 we will construct a theoretical model to study the effects of trade liberalization. The model has been constructed with consideration of the special properties of the Taiwanese economy. In Section 9.5 we will

Table 9.1　Taiwan: a statistical overview

GNP per capita	1951	US$ 145
	1995	12 439
Share of agricultural production in GDP	1952	32.2
	1994	3.6
Share of industrial production in GDP (per cent)	1952	19.7
	1986 (Peak)	47.6
	1990	41.2
	1995	36.3
Share of exports in GNP (per cent)	1952	8.0
	1966	19.4
	1986 (Peak)	56.7
	1990	45.6
	1995	48.3
Average annual growth rate of GNP (per cent)	1950s	8
	1960s	10
	1970s	10
	1980s	8
	1991–5	6–7
Average annual growth rate of per capita GNP (per cent)	1950s	3.7
	1960s	7.3
	1970s	6.4
	1980s	7.4
Average unemployment rate (per cent)	1960s	3.3
	1970s	1.7
	1980s	2.0
Average inflation rate (per cent)	1950s	9.6
	1960s	4.9
	1970s	9.5
	1980s	4.6

give some empirical evidence for the theoretical propositions of the model. In Section 9.6 a short summary will be given.

9.2　PATTERN OF ECONOMIC DEVELOPMENT IN TAIWAN

The World Bank approach

In a World Bank policy research report (*World Bank, 1993*) the economic development of Taiwan since 1949 is divided according to development policy into five steps with different policies:

1. Land Reform and Reconstruction (1949–52)
2. Import-Substituting Industrialization (1953–7)
3. Export-Promotion (1958–72)
4. Industrial Consolidation and New Export Growth (1973–80)
5. High Technology and Modernization (1981 onwards).

To the above five stages the development period 1987–90 can be called liberalization of foreign exchange, and the period since 1991 can be termed the construction of an Asia–Pacific Regional Operation Centre. This way of classifying the stages of economic development seems to be critical, for the following reasons. First, there is often a discrepancy between announced policy and actual implementation. This is often true for developing countries and, as our short review of the events showed, it is also true for Taiwan. Thus the above classifications are based implicitly on the assumption that policy measures are effective and, therefore, may only show an official picture very different from reality. Second, it is not true that import substitution and export promotion were two separate phases. It seems more appropriate to characterize Taiwan's policy as outward-orientated including both import substitution and export promotion as part of an integrated trade policy from 1950 to 1986.

The pattern of activity of the Taiwanese private enterprises

There are other ways of classifying the pattern of Taiwanese economic development which may be relevant for development study. One way is to classify the stages according to the activity of Taiwanese private enterprises. In this way the pattern of the economic development in Taiwan can be classified in the following three stages.

1.   The domestic business activity stage (1946–67)

In this stage the main economic activities of the Taiwanese enterprises were activities focused on the domestic market. The share of foreign trade (ratio of exports and imports to GDP) was lower than 50 per cent. Taiwanese enterprises invested only domestically and the foreign economic relationship was mainly a trade relationship. Exports were carried out with the help of the Japanese trade houses.

2.   The international trade activity stage (1968–86)

In this stage the ratio of foreign trade was more than 50 per cent of GDP. The Taiwanese enterprises had become more and more international. A trade marketing net had been constructed. Joint ventures and technological transfers had become important international relationships of the Taiwanese enterprises as well as the trade relationship.

3. The global business activity stage (since 1987)

Since the beginning of this stage the Taiwanese enterprises have made their business activities global not only in the spatial sense but also in the sense of all business decisions such as trade, finance and investment. The Taiwanese enterprises consider the world as their field of activities. They are not only making international trade but are also seeking possibilities for finance and investment. To be able to make global business activity Taiwanese enterprises must have a free operational field. This has been enabled by the liberalization of foreign exchange controls and also by liberalization of international business (for example, liberalizing international trade and foreign investment).

First, Taiwanese private enterprises have been responsible for economic development in Taiwan. This great contribution to economic development can be shown by the fact that the non-agricultural private sector had a share of 39.6 per cent of GDP in 1951. This share has continually increased to 74.3 per cent (1994) for 44 years, while the share of the

Table 9.2   Gross Domestic Product

Period	Book value (at current prices)		Real product (at constant prices)	
	Amount (NT$)	Growth Rate (%)	Amount (NT$m.)	Growth rate (%)
1952	17 251	40.0	42 077	12.1
1955	30 091	19.3	53 758	8.2
1960	62 566	20.9	73 351	6.2
1965	113 196	10.6	115 990	11.7
1970	226 805	15.2	729 125	11.4
1975	589 651	7.3	1 117 169	4.4
1980	1 491 059	24.7	1 848 060	7.3
1985	2 473 786	5.6	2 557 447	5.6
1990	4 222 004	8.9	3 833 646	4.9
1993	5 874 513	10.0	5 514 104*	6.3

Note: NT$ indicates the New Taiwanese dollar.
Source: *Taiwan Statistical Data Book* (Taipei, 1992) p. 25.

agricultural sector reduced from 32.3 per cent in 1951 to 3.6 per cent in 1994 and the share of public enterprises decreased from 17.3 per cent in 1951 to 11.4 per cent in 1994

These data are calculated by the following definition:

$$\frac{Q_{na}}{GDP} = \frac{Q}{GDP} - \frac{Q_a}{GDP}$$

where Q = GDP of private enterprises
   Q_a = GDP of the agricultural sector
   Q_{na} = GDP of private non-agricultural enterprises (Figure 9.1).

The agricultural sector in Taiwan is represented by private farmers. The data given above clearly show the very fact that the private enterprises in the non-agricultural sector have been chiefly responsible for the so-called 'miracle' economic development in Taiwan since the 1950s.

Second, the private enterprises in the industrial sector have been outward-orientated and mainly responsible for the development of the foreign trade relationship in Taiwan since the 1960s. In the 1950s, sugar and rice were the most important export products of Taiwan with a share of more than 50 per cent of total exports. International business activities of private enterprises were insignificant because of a lack of know-how about doing international business and regulations both on export and import of private enterprises (see Figure 9.5).

The trade liberalization implemented in the 1960s and the expansion of private enterprises in the non-agricultural sector were mainly responsible for the fast increasing share of industrial products in exports. This share

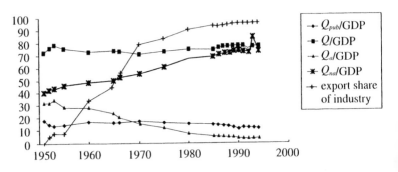

Figure 9.1

Source: Taiwan Statistical Data Book, 1996.

Table 9.3   Indices of industrial production

Period	General index	Mining	Manufacturing	Electricity, gas and water	Construction of buildings
1952	1.69	61.06	1.35	3.02	—
1955	2.53	65.82	2.13	3.95	1.39
1960	4.09	101.22	3.60	6.69	1.26
1965	7.86	151.83	6.88	11.05	6.13
1970	18.69	167.21	17.56	22.90	18.79
1975	34.00	149.32	31.95	39.57	46.99
1980	66.16	151.12	63.33	69.97	134.45
1985	87.83	106.99	86.87	89.86	110.38
1990	118.12	73.54	116.72	137.80	123.30

Source: *Taiwan Statistical Data Book* (Taipei, 1992) p. 82.

has overstepped 50 per cent since 1966 and 90 per cent since 1980 (see Table 9.3)

Third, the public enterprises in Taiwan have proved to be inefficient and their business mainly inward-orientated. The share of the public enterprises in GDP has declined from 17.3 per cent in 1951 to a share of 11.4 per cent in 1994.

Fourth, the policy-makers in Taiwan have been criticised for being passive. They have usually announced and implemented policy measures in reaction to pressure from private enterprises. For instance, the Taiwanese enterprises began global business activity while such investment abroad had to be approved, and investment in China as well as trade with China were not allowed. Even today trade with China has to be carried out indirectly through a third country. The financial settlement of trade and investment with respect to China is still restrictive and expensive. Even bilateral trade with China and the investment of Taiwanese firms in China have reached a significant share of the global activity of Taiwanese firms. For example, exports from Taiwan to China were $US 9.9 billion in 1995 and the direct investment of Taiwanese in China $US 3.2 billion (1992) and $US 1.1 billion (1995).

Fifth, the private enterprises not only need an institutional free field but also marketing know-how for doing business. Very restrictive measures like those in the 1950s had destroyed the activity of the private enterprises and, therefore, had a negative influence on the economic development in the earlier part of that decade. Trade liberalization in Taiwan since the late

1950s has not only given private enterprises a free field for business activities, but has also let them accumulate the special marketing know-how for doing international business. Taiwanese firms began their exports using the know-how and international network of the Japanese trading houses in the 1950s and have accumulated the marketing know-how and constructed their own international business network for more than 30 years. Trade liberalization and special liberalization of foreign exchange controls have enabled them to make global business activity.

The simple reason for inefficiency of economic policy is that stimulating measures can easily cause rent-seeking. Only firms which are willing to pay bribes are able to get the reward of stimulating measures. Measures of regulation are either effective or induce corruption because bribes are paid to avoid them and therefore they have a negative development effect.

The success of outward-looking development policy is due to privatization and liberalization. Allowing private enterprises to do international business and to import intermediates is the real story of economic development policy in Taiwan. The success of export performance since privatization in the 1950s encouraged the further privatization effort (Table 9.4). International business has been implemented and carried out by private enterprises. Privatization enforces economic development because resources can be used more efficiently, since the private enterprises are more efficient than the public ones.

Table 9.4   Distribution of industrial production by ownership (%)

Period	Total		Mining		Manufacturing	
	Private	Public	Private	Public	Private	Public
1952	43.4	56.6	71.7	28.3	43.8	56.2
1955	48.9	51.1	71.5	28.5	51.3	48.7
1960	52.1	47.9	75.8	24.2	56.2	43.8
1965	58.7	41.3	78.6	21.4	63.2	36.8
1970	72.3	27.7	71.00	29.0	79.4	20.6
1975	77.9	22.1	80.4	19.6	85.8	14.2
1980	79.1	20.9	52.0	48.0	85.5	14.5
1985	81.2	18.8	56.7	43.3	88.00	12.0
1990	81.3	18.7	34.7	65.3	89.3	10.7

Source: Taiwan Statistical Data Book (Taipei, 1992) p. 84.

Therefore, we consider *privatization* and *liberalization* to be the main driving forces for Taiwanese development. The main events since 1945 can be summarized as follows:

1945	Chinese takeover of Taiwan from Japan with more than 90 per cent of industrial capital owned by public enterprises.
1945–52	Regulation and restriction of private enterprises are carried out (Table 9.5).
1952	Privatization is implemented to finance the land reform with some liberalization to allow private enterprises to make business activity in some industries.
1951–7	A policy of over-valued currency, a multiple exchange rates system and foreign exchange controls is carried out.
1958	A uniform exchange rate with a depreciation of the New Taiwan dollar from NT \$24.78 to 36.38 for US\$ was implemented.
1960	The Kennedy administration stops US aid (Table 9.6) and gives Taiwan the status of a most favoured trading nation of the USA. Joint ventures and using 'the Japanese Trading House' international marketing know-how for exports of Taiwanese products introduces the era of international trade activity.
1965	With the construction of export processing zones (EPZ) special foreign trade relationships evolved, that is intermediates are imported and final products exported.
1962	Establishment of the Taiwan Stock Market where an enormous amount of shares of the public enterprises are a sold to the public.
1960–80	Using the special foreign trade relationship to export and joint ventures for the transfer of technology Taiwan had been expanding its world market share for several industrial products and realizing an export surplus since 1972.
1986	Start of appreciation to the US\$.
1986–91	56 per cent appreciation to the US\$
1987	Stop of foreign exchange control and forcing trade liberalization.

Foreign direct investment of the Taiwanese enterprises is allowed, as is investment in joint venture projects in China, Vietnam, and so on. Now Taiwan is the largest investor in Vietnam; the second-largest investor in China; the second-largest investor in Malaysia; the third-largest investor in Thailand; and the third-largest investor in Indonesia, implementing the above-mentioned special trade relationships.

Table 9.5   Restrictions on establishing new factories, 1951–65

Industry	Period	Kinds of restriction
Flour	1953–7	S_1
	1958–9	R_1
	1960–4	R_2
	1965–	S
Oil	1953–7	S_2
	1958–62	D
	1963–	S_2
Canned foods	1962–	R_1
Glutamate	1963–4	S_2
	1965	D
Textiles	1961–4	R_1
	1965–	D
Wool textiles	1951–62	S_1
Clothes	1951–3	S_1
	1954–62	D
Plywood	1962–64	X
	1965–	D
Cement	1963–	R_3
Aluminium products	1951–3	S_1
	1954–	D
Tractors	1961–	P
Motor machinery	1963–	G
Refrigerators	1963–	P
Air conditioning	1963–	P
Televisions	1963–	P
Automobiles	1961–	P
Motorcyles	1962–	S_2

Source: Ko-wei Chang, *Economic Development in Taiwan* (in Chinese) (Taipei, 1967), Tables 4–17 between pp. 276 and 277.

Notes:

S_1 Suspension for indefinite period
R_1 Requirements for establishment
X   Requirements for export
P   Progressive ratio for self-manufactured content
S_2 Temporary suspension
R_2 Requirements for assistance
G   Plant grading
D   Decontrol
R_3 expanded production only for export

Table 9.6   Distribution of US aid between public and private enterprises

	Public enterprises	Private enterprises	Mix
			27.2
Global	66.7	6.1	
Manufacturing	41	33	26

Source: Ko-wei Chang (ed.), *Economic Development in Taiwan* (in Chinese) (Taipei, 1967), p. 131.

Both privatization and liberalization have been implemented quite smoothly in Taiwan. From 1950 to 1986 trade policy measures have been implemented with the goal of promoting exports with a combination of import substitution. The development policy has obviously been outward looking since the 1950s.

Trade liberalization and the removal of foreign exchange controls in 1987 have helped the global business activity of Taiwanese enterprises since then.

Summarizing the above discussion we believe that *using policy measures to stimulate business activity is usually not effective but using policy measure to restrict business activity is painful.*

9.3   TRADE LIBERALIZATION

From the 1950s to the 1970s

Because of foreign exchange shortages many measures were implemented in the 1950s to regulate imports and stimulate exports. Among them high tariffs, import licences, an over-valued exchange rate, and a system of multiple exchange rates were the most important measures of trade regulations.

The first trade liberalization in Taiwan was implemented in 1958. A uniform exchange rate was introduced instead of the multiple exchange rates system. The New Taiwan Dollar was depreciated. To encourage export and foreign investment export processing zones (EPZ) was established in 1965.

The first trade liberalization and also the new US development policy of the Kennedy administration which recognized Taiwan as the most favoured trading nation of the USA have enabled the private enterprises in Taiwan to attain world market shares, especially in the US market.

Some tentative effects of the trade liberalization in this period can be summarized as follows:

1. *Rapid growth of industrial exports*: the share of industrial exports has increased from 8.1 per cent (1952) to 10.4 per cent (1955), 32.3 per cent (1960), 46 per cent (1965), 78.6 per cent (1970), 83.6 per cent (1975), 90.8 per cent (1980), 93.9 per cent (1985), etc.

2. *Export diversification in goods and area*: in the 1950s sugar and rice were the most important export goods of Taiwan with an export share of more than 50 per cent. This share has steadily been reduced since then and is now negligible (Figure 9.2). Foreign trade of Taiwan was very concentrated, Japan and USA being the most important trading partners of Taiwan with a more than 50 per cent, share of exports which has been reduced since then (Figures 9.3 and 9.4).

3. *Stabilization of export earnings*: to show this effect we calculate the normalized variances around a trend on export earnings for the periods 1951–60, 1961–80, and 1981–92, which are 0.0111, 0.019 and 0.0055 respectively. The variance in the last period is much smaller. The difference has a significance level of only about 10 per cent.

4. *Expansion of private enterprises*: the production share of non-agricultural private enterprises in GDP has increased from 39.6 per cent (1951), to 74.3 per cent in 1994 (Figure 9.5). Privatization, higher

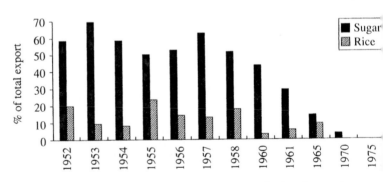

Figure 9.2   Diversification of commodity exports (as % of total export)

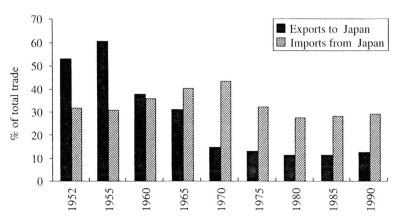

Figure 9.3   Foreign trade with Japan (as % of total trade)

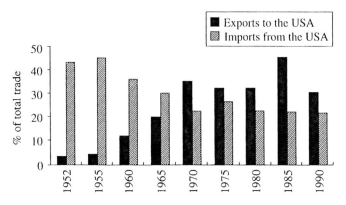

Figure 9.4   Foreign trade with the USA (as % of total trade)

efficiency and higher outward orientation of private enterprises due to trade liberalization might be the reason for this development.

5. *The effect of industrialization*: the production share of industry in GDP has increased from 19.7 per cent to 47.6 per cent (1986) since 1952. Also the employment share of industry has increased from 16.9 per cent in 1952 to 41.5 per cent (1986). Since private enterprises are outward-orientated, trade liberalization has enabled them to combine the inputs of foreign and domestic factors optimally and to improve their performance. Therefore, the first trade liberalization had an important industrialization effect for the Taiwanese economy.

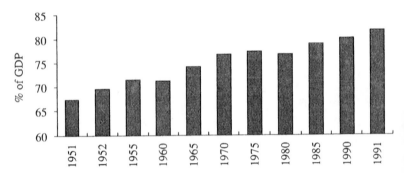

Figure 9.5   Share of private enterprises (as % of GDP)

Source: National Income in the Taiwan Area of the Republic of China 1995,
p. 78.

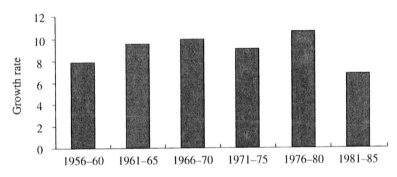

Figure 9.6   The average annual growth rate of real GDP

6. *The growth effect*: the growth rate has increased from 7.8 per cent
    (1956–60) and stabilized at this high level since the first trade
    liberalization.

Trade liberalization since 1980:

Preferential export credits, discrimination by tariffs against input for
domestic uses and foreign exchange controls were important foreign trade
measures up to 1986.

The export surplus, the appreciation pressure against the exchange rate
of the New Taiwan Dollar as well as the intention to participate in the
World Trade Organisation were the main reasons for the Taiwanese government carrying out a further trade liberalization in 1987. The trade regu-

lation measures mentioned above were all removed in that year. Also, trade with communist countries has been allowed, though trade with China can only be carried out through a third country. Another, maybe more important, measure of trade liberalization was implemented in 1987: the liberalization of trade and financial transactions. Taiwanese enterprises have been allowed to be involved in international business activities like foreign direct investment and joint international financial transactions. The main reason for this liberalization is to keep the roots of Taiwanese enterprises in Taiwan.

In the following section we will construct a simple model to study the effects of the second trade liberalization in Taiwan since 1987.

9.4 THE MODEL

Taiwan's foreign economic relationships can be described by some special properties as follows:

1. *Special trade relationships* Most export products from Taiwan are produced with imported intermediates. The value-added of these outputs has increased from a low level at the start of practising this special type of industrialization in the 1960s (see Chen 1976, 1978 and 1981).
2. *The Taiwanese economy is dominated by small and medium enterprises* This is the main difference between the Taiwanese and the Korean economies. While Korean industry is dominated by a few big companies, the main actors of the success story in Taiwan have been the small and medium enterprises which are usually price-takers in both the markets of their inputs and products.
3. *The connection between foreign trade and the foreign investment of the Taiwanese enterprises* Taiwanese investors usually export intermediates from Taiwan to the host countries. Thus the foreign direct investments have a trade creation effect for the Taiwanese economy with the host countries; and
4. *The high export incentive of the Taiwanese enterprises* Being able to sell their products on the world market has been used by the enterprises as a symbol of the high quality of their products and successful business activity.

To study the effects of trade liberalization a simple model which catches the special trade relationship of the Taiwanese economy will be constructed. Output both in the domestic and export sectors is produced by input of labour, capital and intermediates which are imported from abroad.

For simplicity, output in the domestic sector is assumed to be sold only on the domestic market, and output in the export sector is only to be supplied on the foreign market. This classification of domestic and export sector is artificial and due to different policy measures and different marketing costs for each sector, even if the technology used and the output of both sectors may be the same. The marketing cost of the export sector is usually much higher than the domestic sector due to the need for information about the foreign market, communication with foreign customers and also the administration procedures for exports, due to different languages, different preferences and more complicated administration procedures. Thus exports do not only need special know-how but are also much more expensive. The prohibitively high international marketing cost is a very severe barrier for carrying out the outward-looking development policy of a developing country at the beginning. An excellent example is the joint-venture between Chinese, Hong Kong's and Taiwanese enterprises. Another good example is the fact that the Taiwanese enterprises had to use the trading network of the Japanese 'trading houses' in the 1950s and the 1960s to get access to the world market. One of the main reasons that Japan was the most important market for Taiwanese exports in the 1950s was the lower international marketing since Taiwan was a Japanese colony and most of the persons responsible for business at that time in Taiwan were able to speak the Japanese language very well. Different policy measures and different marketing cost which are explicitly considered in this model are the reasons for specifying domestic and export sector in this model.

The technology of the model is assumed to be specified by the following neo-classical production function:

$$Q_1 = F(K_1, L_1, Z_1)$$
$$Q_2 = F(K_2, L_2, Z_2)$$

where Q_i = output of the i-th sector
K_i = Capital input of the i-th sector
L_i = Labour input of the i-th sector
Z_i = intermediates of the i-th sector
the subscript $i = 1$ for export and $i = 2$ for the domestic sector.
Assuming full employment:

$$L_1 + L_2 = L$$

where K_1 and L are the specific capital and labour endowment of the Taiwanese economy. We assume that there is no regulation other than a tariff on the import of intermediates.[1] Assuming the usual profit maximization behaviour of the enterprises in both sectors, their production decision can be described by the following optimization problem.

1. *The production decision for export*

$$Max\ P_1Q_1 - r_1K_1 - wL_1 - q_1Z_1 - C(Q_1,H) + \zeta P_1Q_1$$
$$s.t.\ Q_1 = F(K_1, L_1, Z_1)$$

where: P_1 = producer's price of the output for export

r_1 = interest rate for capital used in the export sector

w = wage rate

q_1 = price of intermediates paid by the producers in the export sector.

$C(Q_1, H)$ = cost of international marketing which is assumed to be an increasing function of exports and a decreasing function of accumulated export experiences H.

ζ = rate of export subsidy

2. *The production decision of the domestic sector*

$$Max\ P_2Q_2 - r_2K_2 - wL_2 - q_2Z_2$$
$$s.t.\ Q_2 = F(K_2, L_2, Z_2)$$

where P_2 = producer's price of the output of domestic sector

r_2 = interest rate for investment in the domestic sector

q_2 = price of intermediates used in the domestic sector

The model can be closed by the demand function of domestic product:

$$Q_2 = D\left(\frac{Y}{P_2}\right)$$

where

$$Y = r_1K_1 + r_2K_2 + wL + rqZ_2$$

The case of export subsidy and tariff discrimination

In the above formal description of the production decision we assume that the wage rate paid in both sectors is the same. But the interest rates can be different because of preferential credit for the export sector. The price of intermediates is different if different tariff rates are applied in each sector. The price of intermediates is lower in the export sector if its import is duty free only in the export sector.

Competitive behaviour is assumed both in the output and input markets in this model, since enterprises in Taiwan are dominated by small and medium enterprises. A decision of a single firm can therefore not influence the market of both domestic and foreign output as well as the input market. Thus all prices P_1, P_2, r_1, r_2, w, q_1 and q_2 are given for the production decision. Thus

$$P_1 = E\,\bar{P}_1, \quad q_1 = E\,\bar{q} \text{ and } q_2 = E\,\bar{q}(1 + \tau)$$

where E = price of US \$ in units of NT dollar.
$\bar{P}_1$ and $\bar{q}$ = world market price for output and intermediates in units of
US \$
τ = tariff rate for import of intermediates.

All prices with the exceptions of P_1 and q are given in units of the NT dollar.

If a preferential interest rate is given to the capital input of the export sector and the import of intermediates in the export sector is duty free, then

$$r_1 < r_2$$
$$q_1 < q_2$$

Now the behaviour of the production decision both in the export and domestic sector can be described by the following first order conditions for profit maximization:

1. *The export sector*

$$P_1 F_{11} = r_1$$
$$P_1 F_{12} = w$$
$$P_1 F_{13} = q_1 \text{ and}$$
$$P_1 Q_1 - r_1 K_1 - w L_1 - q_1 Z_1 - C(Q_1, H) \geq 0 \text{ and}$$

2. *The domestic sector*

$$P_2 F_{21} = r_2$$
$$P_2 F_{22} = w$$
$$P_2 F_{23} = q_2$$

with

F_{i1} = marginal product of capital in sector i
F_{i2} = marginal product of labour in sector i
F_{i3} = marginal product of intermediates in sector i for i = 1,2

Under the assumption that the input of the third factor does not influence the optimal input relationship of the other two factors (neutrality of technology) the input of capital and of intermediates per unit of labour in the export sector will be higher than in the domestic sector,

if $r_1 < r_2$ and $q_1 < q_2$, that is

$$\frac{F_{11}}{F_{12}} = \frac{r_1}{w} < \frac{r_2}{w} = \frac{F_{21}}{F_{22}} \quad \text{and}$$

$$\frac{F_{13}}{F_{12}} = \frac{q_1}{w} < \frac{q_2}{w} = \frac{F_{23}}{F_{22}}$$

The allocation of resources can be solved by using the first order conditions given above and the following restriction:

$$L_1 + L_2 = L$$

Thus a preferential credit for the export sector will induce a Pareto inefficiency in the economy and the production in the export sector will use more capital per unit of labour than in the domestic sector. A duty free import of intermediates in the export sector and a tariff for import of intermediates in the domestic sector (tariff discrimination against the domestic sector) will also cause Pareto inefficiency. The input of intermediates per unit of labour will be higher in the export sector than in the domestic sector.

A trade liberalization in the sense that no preferential credit is given to the investment in the export sector and no tariff discrimination is used against the domestic sector will induce Pareto-efficient resource allocations in the economy under consideration. This can very easily be shown.

In this case there is no difference for the producer between the foreign or domestic market. In this case the net price of both output for export and domestic market must be equal but the gross export price must be higher because of the international marketing cost.

The case of under-valued exchange rate policy

Now we study the case where the domestic currency is pegged and there exists an under-valued exchange rate policy. In this case the exchange rate will be kept at a level higher than the equilibrium exchange rate which is defined as the exchange rate for equalized balance of payment.

In using this policy the country under consideration will realize a balance of payment surplus. If no export subsidy and tariff discrimination are carried out the production decision can be described as follows:

1. *The export sector*

$$Max\ P_1Q_1 - rK_1 - wL_1 - qZ_1 - C(Q_1, H)$$
$$s.t.\ Q_1 = F(K_1, L_1, Z_1)$$

where

$$P_1 = E\bar{P}_1 \text{ and } q = E\bar{q}$$

2. *The domestic sector*

$$Max\ P_2Q_2 - rK_2 - wL_2 - qZ_2$$
$$s.t.\ Q_2 = F(K_2, L_2, Z_2)$$

The first order conditions for profit maximization are:

$$P_1F_{11} = r = P_2F_{21}$$
$$P_1F_{12} = w = P_2F_{22}$$
$$P_1F_{13} = q = P_2F_{23} \text{ and}$$
$$P_1Q_1 - rK_1 - wL_1 - qZ_1 - C(Q_1, H) \geq 0$$
$$\frac{F_{11}}{F_{12}} = \frac{r}{w} = \frac{F_{21}}{F_{22}} \text{ and}$$
$$\frac{F_{13}}{F_{12}} = \frac{q}{w} = \frac{F_{23}}{F_{22}}$$

'hus a policy of under-valued currency is Pareto efficient for the resource llocation. A policy of under-valued exchange rate has nevertheless differnt effects on the export and domestic sector. This can be shown by the input of intermediates whose world market price is given whereas the price in domestic currency will be higher in case of under-valued xchange rate policy.

$$P_1 F_{13} = q$$
$$P_2 F_{23} = q$$

where

$$P_1 = E \bar{P}_1 \text{ and } q = E \bar{q}$$

Thus the above first order conditions for profit maximization can be written in units of foreign currency as follows:

$$\bar{P}_1 F_{13} = \bar{q}$$

$$\frac{P_2}{E} F_{23} = \bar{q}$$

Therefore an under-valued currency policy will not directly influence the demand of the export sector for intermediates, since both the product of the sector and the intermediates are paid in foreign currency. But it is different from the domestic sector since its product is paid with the domestic currency and the intermediates have to be paid with foreign currency. Therefore an under-valued currency policy will immediately increase the real price of the intermediates. On the other side from the first order conditions for capital and labour input

$$E \bar{P}_1 F_{11} = r$$

$$E \bar{P}_1 F_{12} = w \quad \text{and}$$

$$P_2 F_{21} = r$$
$$P_2 F_{22} = w$$

ince r, w, and P_2 are prices given in units of domestic currency and $\bar{P}_1$ is given in units of foreign currency.

An under-valued currency policy will immediately reduce the price of domestic factor for the export sector but has no direct influence for the domestic sector.

Following these considerations of the effect of exchange rate policy an under-valued policy will influence the input share of domestic factors between the export and the domestic sector. An under-valued currency policy will increase the input share of domestic factors in the export sector and thus expand the export sector and meanwhile reduce the domestic sector.

9.5   EFFECTS OF TRADE LIBERALIZATION

Following the above discussion a trade liberalization can be interpreted as reducing or removing export subsidies, import tariffs or exchange rate intervention. In this section we are going to discuss the effects of trade liberalization only in these cases. The liberalization of the foreign exchange rate was discussed in the last section, and therefore we will only consider the following case.

Removing export subsidies, import tariffs and trade liberalization

If the preferential credit for the export sector and tariffs for import of intermediates in the domestic sector were to be removed then both sectors would have to pay the same price for the input of capital and intermediates. The resource allocation would be Pareto efficient, since no distortion occurs. But the domestic sector would now pay a lower price for the intermediates and the export sector would have to pay a higher price for the use of capital. Therefore the input share of the intermediates in the domestic sector would increase and the input of capital per labour would reduce and the input share of the domestic factors (capital and labour) would also decrease.

Since the case of sector-specific capital considered in the trade regulation above is due to the fact that only the input of capital in the export sector can get preferential credit, a distinction between the capital in the foreign and domestic sector is necessary. If the preferential credit for the export sector is removed, this distinction is not needed any more. Both domestic factors can now be transferred costlessly between these two sectors. Thus there is only one market for capital and labour respectively. There can also be only one price for every factor.

As a result of the above analysis the domestic sector will expand and the export sector shrink after a trade liberalization is carried out.

Liberalization of foreign trade and exchange rate regulation

An appreciation of the NT dollar will decrease the share of foreign trade and improve the terms of trade which can easily be shown with our model discussed above. Because of long-run surplus of balance of payments a liberalization of exchange rate regulation induced a high appreciation of the New Taiwan dollar, especially against the $US, which improved the terms of trade of the non-tradeable goods. The liberalization of exchange control has enabled private enterprises in Taiwan to invest abroad and the Taiwanese people to undertake travel in foreign countries. The statistical data given above has already shown the jump of Taiwanese foreign investment and travel spending since the liberalization of exchange regulation and exchange rate regulation. Both effects mentioned induce an increasing demand for foreign exchange and therefore reduce appreciation pressure on the New Taiwan Dollar.

9.6 SOME EMPIRICAL EVIDENCE

It is not easy to find empirical evidence for our theoretical findings by applying an econometric approach since we do not have the statistical data needed for making estimates, especially with respect to the effects of trade liberalization. The data for the import of intermediates are aggregated for the export and domestic sectors.

Despite these problems in getting empirical evidence for the effects of trade liberalization with respect to the reduction of import tariffs, export subsidies and other measures for 'import substitution' as well as 'export promotion' we can find strong empirical evidence with respect to the exchange rate policy.

In the 1950s the New Taiwan dollar was over-valued. In 1958 a depreciation was carried out combining with the change from a multiple to a unitary exchange rate system. Before the depreciation the share of exports to GDP was lower than 10 per cent. After the depreciation the export share increased annually without exception from 1958 to 1970 from 9.5 per cent up to 30.6 per cent. Though it is problematic to maintain that the depreciation of the New Taiwan dollar in 1958 was solely responsible for this development, there is not much doubt that the depreciation must have had a strong influence. In the 1950s the main export goods were sugar and rice. The development of exports was accompanied by strong volatility. In the 1960s industrial products became the most important export goods instead of sugar and rice and the volume of exports was now growing regularly.

Table 9.7 Liberalization and the exchange rate

Year	(US$) Exchange rate		Share of customs duties to import	Share of export to GNP	Net terms of trade	Income terms of trade
	Buying	Selling				
1952	15.7*	23.1**	21.3	8	100(+)	100(+)
1955	24.8*	40.2**	26.9	8.3	98(+)	146.9(+)
1960	36.4*	36.4**	13.8	11.5	95(+)	98.4(+)
1961	40	40.1	13.1	14	97.5(+)	125.6(+)
1962	40	40.1	13.1	13.6	97.2(+)	120.9(+)
1963	40	40.1	14.1	17.9	103.9(+)	149.3(+)
1964	40	40.1	14.3	20	92.2(+)	163.1(+)
1965	40	40.1	14.2	19.4	89.5(+)	149.2(+)
1966	40	40.1	15.2	21.9	85.2(+)	139.5(+)
1967	40	40.1	13	22.2	87.6(+)	147.5(+)
1968	40	40.1	12.4	24.4	87.1(+)	167.1(+)
1969	40	40.1	13.9	26.9	105.2(+)	250.0(+)
1970	40	40.1	12.8	30.4	111.0(+)	346.9(+)
1971	40	40.1	10.4	35.6	85(+)	436.7(+)
1972	40	40.1	9.6	42.2	111.4(††)	17.45(††)
1973	37.9	38.1	8.4	47.2	107.18(††)	22.56(††)
1974	37.95	38.05	5.9	43.9	95.3(††)	19.34(††)
1975	37.95	38.05	6.1	39.9	93.77(††)	18.92(††)
1976	37.95	38.05	5.8	47.8	98.48(††)	29.85(††)
1977	37.95	38.05	6.2	49.2	95.81(††)	31.68(††)
1978	35.95	36.05	6.7	52.5	92.52(††)	37.17(††)
1979	35.98	36.08	7.7	53.3	90.48(††)	38.86(††)
1980	35.96	36.06	7.6	52.6	83.22(††)	39.71(††)
1981	37.79	37.89	7.6	52.2	81.66(††)	41.84(††)
1982	39.86	39.96	7.5	50.1	82.85(††)	44.72(††)
1983	40.22	40.32	6.8	53	86.68(††)	55.62(††)
1984	39.42	39.52	7.3	55.6	87.59(††)	65.67(††)
1985	39.8	39.9	7.5	53.3	90.64(††)	72.1(††)
1986	35.45	35.55	5.9	56.7	100(††)	100(††)
1987	28.5	28.6	5.4	56.4	106.7(††)	124.19(††)
1988	28.12	28.22	4.6	53.4	105.34(††)	124.47(††)
1989	26.12	26.22	4.8	49.2	105.77(††)	129.35(††)
1990	27.1075	27.1075	4.3	46.5	109.02(††)	137.08(††)
1991	25.7475	25.7475	3.6	47.1	111.96(††)	157.32(††)

Notes:
(*) official rate
(**) market rate
(+) Basis year 1952 = 100
(††) Basis year 1986 = 100

Terms of trade deteriorated rapidly from 1957 to 1958 (more than 10 per cent). The improvement of the net terms of trade in 1963 and 1964 was due to the very high world market price for sugar. In both years more than 29 per cent of export revenues in Taiwan were due to sugar exports.

The exchange rate of the New Taiwan dollar to the US$ had been kept constant at about 40 NT$ to $US. Taiwan had pegged the exchange rate to the $US. Due to high export surpluses and pressure from the US government, a rapid appreciation of the New Taiwan dollar by more than 30 per cent occurred from 1986 to 1987.

Consequently Taiwan's export share reduced about 3 per cent after this appreciation from 1987 to 1988 and has decreased continuously from 56.4 per cent to 47.1 per cent from 1988 to 1991.

The barter term of trade have been improved since the appreciation of the NT$ against the $US in 1987.

The huge surplus of the Taiwanese bilateral balance of payments to the USA has reduced since the liberalization of exchange rate regulations, though Taiwan's global balance of payments has kept a high surplus. This can be explained by the expanding Taiwanese investment in China and its effects on Taiwanese exports. The last effects were not considered in our model presented in section 9.4.

9.7 CONCLUDING REMARKS

In this chapter we have discussed trade liberalization and the pace of economic development in Taiwan. After giving a brief account of economic development in Taiwan and the main policy measures carried out since the 1950s we critically discussed the World Bank pattern of economic development in Taiwan. According to this pattern the economic development in Taiwan is divided in to the following stages:

1. Land Reform and Reconstruction (1949–52);
2. Import-substituting Industrialization (1953–7);
3. Export Promotion (1958–72);
4. Industrial Consolidation and New Export Growth (1973–80);
5. High Technology and Modernization (1981–).

The World Bank uses the main policy measures to describe the pattern of economic development. This might be wrong because it assumes that economic policy is effective, which has not yet been proved.

The classification of development stages in Taiwan by the World Bank may also be criticised because both the import-restricting and export-promoting measures had been carried out for more than 35 years. It is not clear why the period 1952 to 1957 should be an import-substituting period and the period 1958 to 1971 an export-promoting period, since in both periods import-restricting and export-promoting measures were carried out.

Instead of this classification we suggest another way of classifying the pattern of economic development according to the business activity of private enterprises in Taiwan:

1.   the domestic business activity stage (1952–67);
2.   the international trade activity stage (1968–86; and
3.   the global business activity stage (since 1987).

This classification conforms to the new growth theory in the sense of accumulation of knowledge with respect to business activity. In the first stage the international marketing know-how of Taiwanese enterprises was very low. The know-how accumulated in the first stage gave Taiwanese enterprises a good basis for starting the second stage. Finally, in the third stage enough know-how of international business is accumulated to allow Taiwanese enterprises to make global business.

To study the effects of trade liberalization in Taiwan we have constructed a model which has considered explicitly the special international trade relationship of the Taiwanese economy. Following the results of theoretical analysis from our model, both preferential export credit and tariff discrimination would cause Pareto inefficient resource allocations and more capital as well as intermediate input in the export sector will be used than in the domestic sector. The construction of the EPZ and the undervalued exchange rate policy do not cause a Pareto inefficiency with respect to resource allocation in our model.

Thus trade liberalization has an effect on the terms of trade as well as on the share of foreign trade due to the special trade relationship, even if the economy considered is small or the enterprises in Taiwan apply the 'marginal cost equal to price rule' of decision.

Note

1. This was not the case in the 1950s in Taiwan.

References

Balasubramanyam, V.V. M. Salisu and D. Sapsford (1996) 'Foreign Investment and Growth in EP and IS Countries', *Economic Journal*, pp. 92–105.

Boycko, M.A. Schleifer and R.W. Vishny (1996) 'A Theory of Privatization', *Economic Journal*, pp. 309–19.

Chang, K. (ed.) (1967) *Economic Development in Taiwan* (in Chinese) vol. S1 and 2.

Chen, J. (1975) Abwertungs- und Aufwertungseffekte in einer Volkswirtschaft mit besonderen Außenhandelsverflechtungen, in O. Becker and R. Richter (eds) *Dynamische Wirtschaftsanalyse* (Tübingen: Mohr) pp. 39–65.

—— (1978) *Ein makroökonometrisches Modell für Taiwan* (Saarbrücken).

—— (1983) *Importrestriktionen der Industrieländer und ihre Auswirkungen auf die Ökonomie der Entwicklungsländer* (Göttingen).

—— (1987) 'Taiwan – ein Modell für ökonomische Entwicklung?', *Journal für Entwicklungspolitik*, pp. 13–39.

—— (1994) 'The Role of Government in Economic Development: A Case Study in Taiwan', Working Paper (Innsbruck: Institute für Wirtschaftstheorie und Wirtschaftspolitik).

—— and H. Stocker (1993) 'The Experience of the "Gang of Four"', S.M. Mushed and K. Raffer (eds) *Trade, Transfers and Development* (Cheltenham: E. Elgar) pp. 67–81.

World Bank, The (1993) *The East Asian Miracle* (London: Oxford University Press).

10 Redistribution without Growth

Richard Jolly

10.1 INTRODUCTION

Hans Singer, over his long and remarkable career, has played a leading and creative role in many areas of development thinking and practice, within the UN and outside it. This chapter describes one of Hans' less-publicized and less-well-known contributions – his creation of the concept of Redistribution with Growth. The chapter begins in section 10.1 with the origins of the concept during the ILO employment mission to Kenya in 1972 and, in Section 10.2, goes on to describe its subsequent development as the World Bank/IDS study, Redistribution with Growth. Section 10.3 looks back at the proposals in the light of experience of redistribution and growth since the study was published and ends, in Section 10.4, by drawing policy conclusions for the mid-1990s.

In the early 1970s, doubts began to emerge about the adequacy of accelerating economic growth as the central thrust of development and as the main mechanism for reducing poverty. Economic growth had indeed accelerated in the developing countries as a whole and widely, to rates faster than had been envisaged by the immediate post-Second World War development literature. Indeed, the rates achieved over the 1960s were more rapid, on average, than the goal set in 1961 by the General Assembly for the Development Decade – that the developing countries as a whole should approach a rate of growth of 5 per cent per annum by the end of the decade.

Hans Singer, as one of the leading economists within the UN, had played an important part in all these developments. It was Hans Singer who was the main draftsman of the 'blue document', which set out the plan of action for the decade. The goal was thought to be ambitious, but in the event, an average of 5 per cent *over the decade* was achieved, encouraging the establishment of a 6 per cent target for the 1970s. This also *on average* was almost achieved, but with increasing disparities between developing countries – and with a build-up of debt, deficits (foreign and domestic) and other imbalances, which set the stage for the lost decade of the 1980s and the still losing decade, in many cases, of the 1990s.

Notwithstanding the successes in the 1960s and the positive ambitions for more growth in the early 1970s, the mood towards development was pessimistic. (Perhaps it always is!) Unemployment was a rising problem in most regions of the Third World, and with it poverty and rapid rates of urbanization and population growth. Partly in response, the ILO announced in 1969 a World Employment Programme, as a measure to celebrate its 50th anniversary. It was far from clear what the WEP would comparise, let alone what impact it would have – but in those simpler and less-critical days, the UN was allowed more creativity and room for manoeuvre. So Hans Singer was appointed (with Walter Galenson) as one of the two advisers on the WEP to David Morse, the ILO's Director General. With Hans as a creative shadow behind the throne, WEP began to take shape – and within five years had achieved great success, sufficient for it to be treated at the time and with hindsight, as one of the formative influences on development thinking and policy in the 1970s.

Three key steps determined in my view the enormous and most positive influence of WEP:

1. the establishment of WEP as special and independent unit within ILO, with strong, free-thinking leadership in the form of Louis Emmerij[1];
2. the decision to emphasize support for individual country strategies, as the central thrust of the programme. This minimized bland, over-generalization and gave specificity and immediacy to the reports;
3. the decision to turn to leading but unorthodox economists to organize and direct employment missions to work with countries in producing the first few country reports. Dudley Seers was chosen as the mission leader of the first two missions to Colombia and Sri Lanka and Hans Singer as the leader of the third to Kenya. On the insistence of Dudley Seers, the team leader, not the ILO or any other international organization, was given final responsibility for the content of the report – also a strategic decision.

It was within this frame that Hans (with myself as co-leader) led the team which produced the ILO Kenya Mission Report, 'Employment, Incomes and Equality'. The team was large, some 45 members, about half were Kenyan or others with at least two or three years of experience working and living in Kenya. Most were economists – but not all. And we were blessed by the solid professional assistance and friendship of the late Philip Ndegwa, then Permanent Secretary of the Ministry of Finance and Economic Planning, who recognized the need for a frank and professional analysis and ensured that the team had the support to achieve this. Philip also made sure that after the mission the Government of Kenya produced a formal response to the report, indicating the places where the government agreed or disagreed with the team's analysis and specifying specific proposals for action.

The report focused on three major types of 'employment problem' rather than on unemployment as such: first, the problems of poverty and the working poor, mostly of households with very low incomes; second, the problems of frustrated job-seekers, unemployed in some cases but mostly people working in the informal sector or in other employment, and including many school leavers; and thirdly, the problems of low productivity among many in employment, rural and urban. In this three-fold analysis of the 'employment problem', the report followed the approach of the earlier two missions.

But there were several important areas of innovation, which I believe account for the special character and impact of the Kenya report. The Kenya report gave major emphasis and, for the time, original treatment to the informal sector, This drew heavily on the work of John Weeks and was a first for an international report at the time, both for its analysis, its recognition of the positive side of the informal sector and its recommendations on ways in which the contribution of the informal sector could be made more effective and less constrained. Indeed, I think it was the first time that the informal sector was mentioned as such in an international report.

Secondly, the report identified seven categories of households, rural and urban, including three in poverty – employees rural and urban with very low incomes, informal sector workers, again rural as well as urban; and smallholders, including pastoralists in the semi-arid and arid zones. All this laid the basis for a treatment of what needed to be done to raise the incomes and meet the needs of these diverse groups – the forerunner of approaches later developed further as the Basic Needs Approach.

Finally, the report put strong emphasis on inequality. Again, the need for measures to achieve greater equality was unusual for international reports of the time – though this was an area on which the earlier report on Colombia had placed considerable emphasis.

It was the challenge of how to achieve greater equality which gave rise to the strategy of Redistribution from Growth, and which in turn was made the integrating core of the Kenya Report. Later this became the theme of a major World Bank/IDS Sussex study, published in 1974 as Redistribution with Growth, and revisited in the World Bank's annual conference last year. Since Hans Singer was very clearly the originator of the concept and its basic idea, it is an appropriate theme for a *Festschrift* in honour of Hans.[2]

The right starting point is probably the evening towards the end of the mission, when Hans Singer first sketched out his idea. I remember the occasion well. It was after dinner, in one of the small lounges of the Fairview Hotel, with a group of about eight of us talking about the report – Dudley Seers, Louis Emmerij, Frances Stewart, myself and several others. Hans announced that he had an idea, which might serve as an integrating theme for the report, which by then had begun to take shape, with many chapters already in draft. Hans said that the challenge was to achieve a rapid increase in the incomes of the poorest, more rapid than could be achieved if one relied on growth alone. With population growing at about 3 per cent per annum,[3] even a 6 per cent per annum growth rate would take 25 years to double the incomes of the poorest. Suppose, therefore, said Hans, that the Kenya economy were to grow at a future rate of 6 per cent, but with the increments of growth channelled into forms of investment directed towards increasing the incomes and production of the poorest. The incomes of the poorest would rise much more rapidly – but the process of redistribution from the increment of growth would mean that one would be adding to the income and assets of the poor without having to take away from anyone else's income, thereby avoiding both economic disruption and political opposition.

Hans sketched out his idea with numbers scribbled on a back of an envelope. He assumed a growth rate, he estimated the shares of income of the poorest, he guessed at a capital output ratio – for illustration, he assumed it to be one – and he showed that it would be possible for the poor to advance very rapidly. I remember it well. Far from being impressed with the approach, all the rest of us rocked and roared with laughter! Dudley Seers, in particular, threw his head back, grinned and guffawed, egging us all on with his deep-throated and wheezy laugh, whenever merriment appeared to be about to die out. We all thought we had scarce heard such a crazy notion. Such is the recognition accorded to new ideas by fellow professionals at their moment of birth!

But by the next morning, after we had all slept on it, we came downstairs, one by one, in a totally different frame of mind. We were all convinced. I think of this moment of creation many times when I hear RWG referred to!

The rest, as they say, is history. The Kenya Report was delivered to the Government and published for more general consumption. It became the most cited of all the ILO country mission reports. At least 20 000 copies were distributed, many in Kenya, many beyond. And unlike many UN documents, more were sold, I understand, than were given away.

10.2 REDISTRIBUTION WITH GROWTH

It was clear from all three employment missions that a stronger analytical frame was needed for modelling the employment strategies proposed. The RWG strategy of the Kenya mission was one example. The strategy of the Colombia mission was another. Dudley Seers, the leader in Colombia, had made a great point of starting with employment objectives, not with growth. So the mission analysed the issues, sector by sector, and reached its policy conclusions, without even calculating the growth rate of GNP implied in the proposals and in the totality of the strategy. This was a point of pride for Dudley – to have produced a major economic report without, he claimed, any mention of an economic growth rate. But there was to be a sting in the tail for Dudley. When others later reviewed the report,[4] they calculated the implicit growth rate – and it turned out to be about 8 per cent per annum, too high to be credible.

So IDS turned to the World Bank and suggested a collaborative effort with Hollis Chenery, then Vice President for Research, to explore more analytically the relationships between growth, employment and income distribution. A working group was established and a conference held in Bellagio, to discuss first drafts and to develop a more coherent argument. Later, the papers were reviewed at a larger, more representative conference in IDS. By then, the major theme had been generalized to become redistribution *with* growth', not just redistribution *from* growth. And debate in the conference took on a particular sense of *real politik* and immediacy, as news arrived from Chile during the final session that Pinochet had seized power in a *coup d'état*, with Allende overthrown and killed.

The joint IDS–World Bank study was published in 1974 as 'Redistribution with Growth'. The volume analysed empirically the relationships between growth and redistribution, heavily influenced by the data of the time, which appeared to confirm the Kuznet's finding that there was an inverted U-shaped relationship, in which inequality tended to increase in the early stages of economic growth and then declined again as higher levels of income were reached. This finding was based on cross sectional data and on the assumption that the essence of economic development consisted in the transfer of labour from the rural areas to the urban, with the urban sector typified by a level and structure of income that was both higher and more unequal than in the rural sector.[5] It followed that as the process of labour transfer proceeded, income inequality would at first increase but then, later, decrease again as most of the labour became absorbed into the urban sector.

Notwithstanding this somewhat determinist finding, RWG generalized the Kenya strategy to suggest various options in which redistribution could be combined with growth: growth with the some share of the increment channelled into asset creation for the poorest – with asset creation including both investment in human assets through education and investment in material assets; growth with the incremental share channelled into consumption transfers; and growth without redistribution but with the increment channelled into an increase of savings so as to create growth at a more rapid rate, and thus for the poor to gain from an extra amount of trickle down.

All three options were quantitatively modelled and their results compared over a twenty-five-year period. Not surprisingly, in the first few years the poor would gain most in consumption from the direct transfer strategy. But after a few years this result would be outweighed by the much larger impact of an approach based on distribution channelled into asset creation, with increases in the incomes of the poorest resulting from the increases in their assets. Trickle down came out worst, although with different technical assumptions, it would seem possible for trickle down to perform best over some middle-range period.[6]

10.3   REDISTRIBUTION WITHOUT GROWTH

What has happened in the twenty years since RWG was published? It may be useful to begin with a summary of recent findings on income distribution, drawing heavily on the excellent World Bank Policy Research Working Paper, prepared by Michael Bruno, Martin Ravallion and Lyn Squire (1996). Using data from 63 surveys spanning 1981–92 and covering 44 countries, Bruno and his colleagues show that neither the time-series nor the cross-sectional data reveal any evidence of the Kuznets inverted U-shaped relationship. In addition, they probe additional evidence from a panel of 45 developed and developing countries covering the period 1947 to 1993. Of these 45 countries, less than a third showed any significant trend in inequality – and of these, in only 6 or 7 cases was the trend substantial (UK, China, Germany, Thailand showing substantial *increases* in inequality from the 1980s to the 1990s and Norway and France showing substantial *decreases*, respectively, from the 1970s to the 1980s and from the 1960s to the 1980s, with no data available for the 1990s). Over an earlier period, the 1960s to the 1970s, Mexico also apparently showed some diminution in income inequality.

When seeking explanations for changes in income distribution, Bruno and his colleagues put much of the emphasis on increasing access to primary and secondary education. A one per cent increase in the percentage of the labour force that has at least secondary education increases the share of income received by the bottom 40 or 60 per cent by between 6 and 15 per cent. Evidence is also reported to suggest that primary and secondary school enrolment has a quantitatively important effect on the income share received by the poorest 40 per cent – but is of low importance in reducing inequality as measured by the Gini index.

But the main conclusion of Bruno and his colleagues is that growth is by far and away the largest influence on reducing poverty:

> We have surveyed past and new evidence on [the belief that growth would be inequitable in poor countries] and rejected it as a generalization ... There does not appear to be any systematic tendency for distribution to improve or worsen with growth. On average then absolute poverty will fall [with growth].[7]

This leads on to their calculation of the elasticities between poverty and growth, which they find to be about 2 for a group of 20 countries for the period 1984 to 93 and about 1.3 for India over the last 40 years.

In summarizing this extensive statistical exploration of most of the latest data, Bruno and his colleagues reached a carefully measured conclusion. They stress that

> It is not correct to say that growth *always* benefits the poor, or that none of the poor lost from pro-growth policy reforms ... The point is not that distribution is irrelevant, or that it never changes, but rather that its changes are roughly orthogonal to economic growth.[8]

The significant element omitted so far is the record of growth – or rather of non-growth, which has occurred over much of the period since the mid 1970s when RWG was first published. The 'lost decade' has been much emphasized in which 68 countries recorded a decline in real per capita income over the 1980s as a whole. However startling this experience, its full significance has, I believe, been understated by the tendency to concentrate on averages for the decade and averages for regions as a whole rather than to consider the number of individual countries recording a decline in per caput income, the period over which this has occurred – or is still occurring – and the number of years since the country first reached its present level of real per caput income. Looked at with this perspective the situation appears even more serious.

Some 100 countries were still in 1993 at a lower level of real per capita GNP in 1993 (the latest year for which time-series GNP data is generally available) than the level they had reached five or more years earlier. And of these, 69 were at or below a level they had first reached some time in the 1970s, 35 at a level first reached in the 1960s and 19 at a level they had reached in 1960, 35 or more years ago. This is hardly a record of sustained growth.

A diversity of patterns lies behind this extraordinary and under-emphasized record of failed or unsustained economic growth. About two-thirds of the cases show a pattern of reasonably steady growth over the 1960s and 1970s, with a sudden and severe decline beginning around 1980 for the non-CIS countries and around 1990 for the CIS countries. The other third show more fluctuations. But the common element for most of the countries, is a major decline over much of the last 15 to 20 years – with the decline usually longer in duration and often greater in depth than anything experienced during the Great Depression by most of the now industrial countries.[9]

In the light of this experience, the challenge for poverty reduction is the majority of these countries is the challenge of restoring growth – albeit growth of a quality and structure in which the poor will benefit.

There are two brighter sides to this experience. In terms of the original argument for redistribution from growth, to increase more rapidly the incomes of the poorest, one should note that the developing countries now growing rapidly include about two-thirds of the population of developing countries. Secondly, notwithstanding the failures of economic growth, basic indicators of human development have advanced in almost all countries of the world.

Over the last 35 years, education enrolments have continued to expand, with the proportion of children enrolled in primary school rising from less than half to more than three-quarters, with faster growth of enrolments at secondary and higher levels, and in most cases, with female enrolments expanding faster still. Child malnutrition has decreased by about a third and child mortality rates have more than halved. Life expectancy has increased by about a third. All this has contributed significantly to human asset creation – of the sort called for in RWG. In the phrase of the Amartya Sen and of the Human Development report, it is a strengthening of human capabilities. And at least in this respect, redistribution without sustained growth has proved possible.

Given the economic setbacks and failures to sustain economic growth over such long periods, it is interesting to ask how the maintenance of education, health and central elements of human development has proved possible, especially since the record is more positive than had seemed likely in the early 1980s. There are several parts to the answer. In part, the positive achievement reflects some priorities for these sectors, notwithstanding many pressures to the contrary; it also reflects the ability to make economies and to maintain advances in health and even education at lower cost than was often envisaged (relying in large part on the willingness of teachers and health workers to carry on working at greatly reduced salaries); and finally, popular support for these sectors has often mobilized additional resources and contributions in voluntary effort. Thus advances in human development and human asset creation have proved possible, even in the absence of economic growth.

Nevertheless, the real picture is probably less positive than many of the figures would suggest. There is much evidence to suggest that the quality of education, especially basic education, has fallen in many countries, with very severe cutbacks in expenditure on books and equipment, as well as teachers salaries. In 20 countries of Africa, enrolment ratios have actually fallen over the 1980s and 1990s. And though infant mortality has fallen, the quality of routine health services has often also slipped, with desperate shortages of basic medical supplies, especially in the rural areas. Again, communities have shown remarkable initiative and community solidarity in mobilizing resources of their own, but nevertheless the overall quality of health services has mostly fallen severely.

Most worrying of all, are the questions of what next to expect in the absence of strong resumed growth. An analysis of the relationships between economic growth and human development over time, shows that a lop-sided relationship is possible to maintain for a period, but difficult to sustain after a decade or so. Thus even though human development has been maintained in the absence of growth in a number of countries over the last decade, unless strong growth is soon resumed the advances in human development may begin to peter out. This holds major implications for national and international policy.

10.4   CONCLUSIONS FOR POLICY

Redistribution from growth grew out of a direct concern for policy and a strong commitment to poverty reduction in developing countries. Nearly 25 years after the basic idea was first conceived by Hans Singer, more evidence is available on which to rest its basic conclusions for action.

Combining redistribution with growth will increase the speed and the extent to which the poor will benefit from growth and accelerate the reduction in the numbers and proportions of people in poverty in the country concerned.

There is no evidence to suggest that measures of redistribution will have any deleterious effect on the rate of economic growth.

On the contrary, 'countries which give priority to basic human capabilities in schooling, health and nutrition not only directly enhance well-being, but are more likely to see improving income distributions and higher average incomes over the longer term.'[10]

Other forms of redistribution are also important. Creation of physical assets owned by the poorest, including by households headed by women, and other initiatives of redistribution are all important means to ensure not only a more equitable pattern of growth but also faster growth rates and thus more rapid reductions in poverty. Even though more difficult to implement, land reform should remain high on the agenda, both for redistribution and for increasing agricultural production.

The need to sustain and to restore growth is a major challenge of the time. Redistribution without growth may have proved to be possible for a short period, at least in the areas of investing in human capabilities. But restoration of growth now needs to be a priority, especially in the poorest and least developed countries. Those with levels of per capita income below levels earlier achieved, especially need accelerated growth. The case for combining this with measures of redistribution is as strong as when Hans Singer first proposed it.

Notes

1. Some may think of this identification of individuals as mere name-dropping or, more forgivable, name-dropping of friends. Far from it. It is my considered opinion, based on experience both within and outside the United Nations, that individual leadership is a much more important factor for effectiveness and impact than it is usually recognized to be. Given this, it is important to identify the specific examples when they occur.

2. One of my deep regrets is that the originating contribution of Hans Singer was never properly acknowledged in the World Bank/IDS volume, for reasons that are not entirely clear. The point was made at the time and Hollis Chenery agreed that Hans' contribution should be acknowledged in the preface. Somehow the volume went to press without this having been done.

3. Later it appeared that Kenya's population was growing at about 4 per cent per annum at the end of the 1970s.

4. It was Graham Pyatt, I think, who made the calculations.

5. As in the Arthur Lewis model of development with unlimited supplies of labour.

6. Keith Griffin, in a critique of the whole approach, commented that the impact of RWG was not very significant. He made a good point about the

calculations as given in the book, in which the increment of growth channelled to redistribution was kept at 25 per cent. Had a larger fraction been
chosen, the impact of RWG would of course have been larger. Moreover,
one must always ask – what is the alternative?

7. Bruno *et al.* (1996) p. 10.
8. Ibid., pp. 21–2.
9. It is interesting to speculate on why this remarkable experience has received
so little attention. I venture four reasons. First, the experience is overwhelm-
ingly that of the smaller developing countries. Almost all of the richer OECD
countries have experienced nothing like this, so the issue has not been high
on the G-7 agenda. Secondly, most of the larger developing countries have
recently experienced continuing growth or restored and often accelerating
growth – not only China and India, but also Korea, Indonesia, Malaysia,
Thailand, Pakistan and Bangladesh. Thus the spectacular growth of the tigers
has tended to dominate the scene. Third, much of the failed growth relates to
the situations of stabilization and adjustment, in which the Bretton Woods
institutions have a strong stake in arguing that many countries are successfully adjusting and that those that are adjusting are just about to turn the
corner and resume strong growth. The record speaks for itself. This said, it
deserves to be noted that the countries which have shown strong or resumed
growth include about two thirds of the population of developing countries.
Thus in terms of the population of developing countries, most live in countries where the growth experience has been more positive.
10. Bruno *et al.* (1996) p. 23.

Reference

Bruno, M., M. Ravallion and L. Squire (1996) 'Equity and Growth in Developing
Countries: Old and New Perspectives on the Policy Issues', *Policy Research
Working Paper*, no. 1563 (Washington DC: The World Bank).

Part III
Theory and Practice of Development

11 Distributional Inequity in International Comparative Perspective: Causes and Consequences[1]

Kwan S. Kim

Although many conventional economists continue to believe that economic growth, particularly when sufficiently rapid, will improve the distribution of income, an increasing number of them argue that inequality follows growth, which can in turn hamper further growth.[2] Professor Hans Singer was among the earlier critics who pointed out that rapid growth alone cannot be relied on to reduce income inequality or to reduce poverty in developing countries. A growth strategy is seen possibly to increase the extent of poverty. Therefore, there is a need for a strategy for redistribution from growth during the process of economic growth in developing countries.

Recent critics of the conventional wisdom also argue that income disparities, especially when accompanied by continued increases in poverty, as is the case in the United States, will lead to high economic costs. Since low-income households spend a larger proportion of their income, growing inequality not only leads to less aggregate demand but also to increased costs of social programmes and lost productivity due to reduced access of the impoverished to health care and training. Moreover, real costs in a highly inequitable society may come with increased political instability and social conflicts between the 'haves' and the 'have-nots.'

This chapter re-evaluates from an international comparative perspective the relationship of distributional equity to growth. While economists mostly look at the measurement, nature, and causes of equality or inequality, the question that is given special attention here concerns the social and political consequences of income distribution. This study surveys cross-country experiences to compare the factors contributing to, and the broad implications of, recent changes in income distribution for the economy and society, and collects insights for policy that can be gleaned from the regional comparisons. More specifically, different regions of the global economy are compared in terms of the levels of and changes in distribution, causes of inequality, the relationship of equity to growth, and the social and political consequences of inequality. The concluding section highlights the policy implications.

11.1 DISTRIBUTION EQUITY: A GLOBAL PERSPECTIVE

Over the past fifty years since the end of the Second World War, world income in real GDP rose sevenfold, and threefold in terms of per capita real GDP. But the fruits of economic growth have not been shared evenly. Between 1950 and 1990, the gap between the industrialized countries (OECD nations) and the rest of the world widened by 60 per cent (World Bank, 1992, pp. 218–19). In recent calculations using Theil's inequality indices, Stocker (1994) concludes that international inequality in the sample of 89 countries has unequivocally worsened over the past three decades. The increased inequality has largely been accounted for by a widening gap between North and South, which he defines as inequality between the OECD group and the rest of the world. Indeed, the richest quintile of the global population now earns income on a per capita basis about 50 times that of the poorest quintile and accounts for well over four-fifths of global income. One of our greatest contemporary paradoxes is that although current worldwide production of grain, for instance, could provide every person on earth with more than sufficient calories and protein for a healthy daily life, one person in five still lives in hunger and is malnourished (Harvard School of Public Health, 1988). The global prospects for the rest of this century are not encouraging; according to a recent International Labour Organization global job survey (ILO, 1995), some 2.5 billion people accounting for 30 per cent of the world's labour force will remain either unemployed or underemployed.

Growing inequality among nations is accompanied by that within national boundaries. Many developing nations – more recently, several developed nations as well – are experiencing a widening gap in income as well as wealth holdings between their rich and poor citizens. In terms of asset distribution, De Garcia and Johnson (1988) calculated that in the 83 poorest countries of the world, a meagre 3 per cent of their people control more than 80 per cent of their land. Severity in inequality and its consequences have varied from region to region of the global economy. Income inequality is on the whole relatively less severe in the industrialized west, which is a common heritage of political democracy. Recently, diverging trends in levels of inequality within the industrialized group have emerged: beginning in the 1980s, inequality in the United States has steadily increased, accompanied by more than its share of poverty-related social violence and instability. In the case of emerging democracies in Asia, Africa, Latin America, and the former Easternbloc, increased income inequalities caused by abrupt market reform threaten the very process of transition to democracy. Distribution inequity in these countries has frequently deepened social crisis by heightening the tensions and conflicts between classes, which has retarded sustained economic development. In what follows, the trends in distribution and its sociopolitical consequences will be examined in different regions of the global economy.

Industrial democracies

Trends in growth and distribution

Rich, industrialized countries are generally known to have more equal income distribution than low-income, developing countries. Begining in the early 1980s, however, some diverging trends in income equality have appeared among industrialized democracies of Europe and the United States (Tables 11.1). Growth in trade with and investment in the developing countries, coupled with rapid technological advance, has reduced demand for unskilled workers, thereby depressing wages in much of the

Table 11.1   Income distribution in selected OECD countries during the 1980s (%)

Country	(1) Income share of bottom 20%	(2) Income share of top 20%	The ratio of (1) to (2)
France	6.3	40.8	6.48
Great Britain	5.8	39.5	6.81
Italy	6.8	41.0	6.03
Germany	6.8	38.7	5.69
Japan	8.7	37.5	4.31
USA	4.7	41.9	8.91
Average	6.5	39.9	6.14

Source: World Bank, *World Development Report* (1989, 1990). Also cited by Lechner (1992) p. 8.

industrialized world (Wood, 1994), and structural unemployment among less-skilled workers has risen as a discernible trend in a number of the OECD countries (Bloom and Brender, 1993). The ILO's assessment of the job situation in the industrialized world reveals substantially elevated unemployment rates[3] and an 'endemic feature' in joblessness for most industrialized nations, with the possible exceptions of Switzerland, the United States,[4] and rapidly industrialized nations of East Asia (Table 11.2). The double-digit unemployment rates are projected to prevail at least until the end of this century in France, Germany, Italy, Canada, Australia and several other industrialized nations, including Spain, whose official unemployment rate tops 20 per cent.

Among the OECD nations, the United States – economically the most powerful country in the world – has recently emerged as the least equal country (Atkins, Rainwater, and Smeeding; 1995; see also Table 11.3). Japan, the other of the two most powerful countries, provides a sharp contrast in terms of income equality: post-war Japan had an equitably shared economic growth, which paved the way for its social and political stability.

During the 1970s, the Japanese economy expanded at an average annual rate of close to 10 per cent and had perhaps the most even distribution of income among industrialized countries. In 1975 the income share of the

Table 11.2   Unemployment rates in OECD countries: 1995 and projections for 2000 (%)

Country	1995	2000
Spain	24.4	23.7
France	12.2	14.0
Italy	11.9	13.2
Belgium	12.7	11.8
Australia	9.5	11.7
Canada	10.2	11.5
UK	8.2	9.4
Sweden	7.8	8.3
Germany	10.0	8.2
Netherlands	9.5	6.8
USA	5.8	5.8
Japan	2.8	2.8
Switzerland	3.8	1.3

Source: International Labour Organization (1995).

lowest income class in Japan exceeded that of the welfare-orientated Nordic and other Western European countries and was about twice that of the United States. As for the United States, the 1960s and 1970s saw greater equality of incomes; in terms of the Gini index, it fell steadily from a high of 0.364 in 1960, to 0.356 in 1980. The trend then reversed throughout the 1980s, with the Gini coefficient rising to 0.401 in 1989 and to 0.426 in 1990. During the 1980s, supply-side policies were introduced in the United States, which turned out to reward the well-to-do and extract heavier tolls from more vulnerable groups of society. The US reversal is reflected by the widening of the inequality gap between the US and Japan (Figure 11.1).[5]

In the United States, the experiment of Reaganomics moved the country steadily toward a two-tiered distributional structure of the haves and have-nots. In 1990 the gap between rich and poor reached an all-time high since

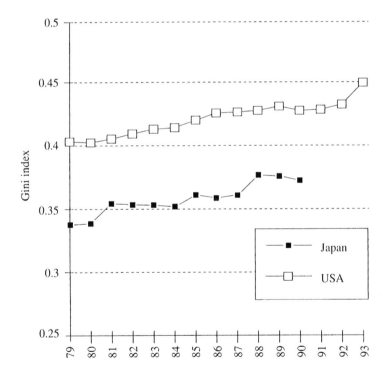

Figure 11.1   Trends in income distribution: USA and Japan

Sources: For US data, Bureau of the Census; for Japanese data, see Mizoguchi (1992).

family income statistics were first published in 1947. According to government estimates,[6] between 1980 and 1990 the richest fifth of American families were the only ones whose income share increased while the share received by the other 80 per cent declined. Among the well-to-do, the top 5 per cent received 17.4 per cent of all family income, earning more income than the poorest 40 per cent combined.[7] The wealthiest one per cent received an astounding 60 per cent of the growth in after-tax income between 1977 and 1990.[8] On the other hand, the families at the median of income distribution saw their income go up only 4 per cent, to $36 000. The bottom 40 per cent of families experienced actual declines in income. In particular, the lowest 20 per cent group's income fell by as much as 9 per cent during the period between 1977 and 1990.[9]

In Japan the land reform initiated by the Allied Occupation Forces at the end of the Second World War and subsequent improvements in the agricultural terms of trade gradually eliminated rural poverty.[10] Japan's central and local governments quickly enforced a universal education system at the basic and secondary levels. The economic success of the earlier postwar era made it possible for governments to implement comprehensive social security and national health programs. Japan is now considered to be one of the most developed countries in these fields. Over 90 per cent of the population consider themselves to belong to the middle class.

Causes of inequality: theoretical considerations

There is really no single, definitive explanation for the growing inequality in the industrialized world. The causes of inquality in America are complex in nature as they involve the intricate dynamics of interactions among various social, economic and political factors. Based on the recent literature on this issue, however, an argument can be made from the perspectives of changing labour and capital markets within the domestic economy, which in turn are inextricably interlinked to the global economy in technology, trade, and capital flows.

First of all, there is the argument that globalization widens the income gap between capital and labour. Increased global competition induces domestic corporations to seek access to low-wage labour pools in other countries, which eventually forces down the domestic wages, especially for unskilled workers (Bluestone, 1990). Many firms, in attempts to reverse declining profits in the face of global competition, adop new technologies which make highly skilled workers more productive, farm out production to foreign sources, leaving only management and financial jobs in the home country (Bluestone and Harrison, 1982; Kosters and Ross,

1988). As transnational capital mobility eases, a process of de-industrial-ization in the economy sets in through outsourcing to escape from union agreements and a shift toward technologies that substitute physical capital and highly-skilled workers for less-skilled production personnel (Murphy and Welch, 1992). What is left would be the rise in profits relative to wage income and a growing concentration of employment in both higher wage professional occupations and lower wage service industries.

As already discussed, the widening wage gap among workers is another consequence of globalization. Recent studies (Wood 1995, and Batra 1993) indicate that in the industrialized world not only have the employ-ment shares of less-skilled production workers fallen in favour of skilled workers burt structural unemployment in the former category has also increased. They argue that expansion of trade with developing countries is the main cause of the decline in low-skilled wages and income inequality. This is more conspicuous for the de-industrialized countries with cumula-tive trade deficits as in the case of the United States. Import penetration from the newly industrializing developing countries has displaced the tra-ditional industries producing standardized products, thereby laying-off workers with fewer skills.

Capital and factory outflow from the developed to the developing countries in globalized capital markets is an additional cause of the deter-iorating situation of unskilled workers. Thus, trade and capital move-ments coupled with technological change inducing the automation process in production and marketing have accelerated a pre-existing downward trend in the relative demand for low-skilled workers while raising the skilled-worker demand in high value-added, technology-based industries as industrialized countries' comparative advantage shifts to those sectors.

As already mentioned, the global economy is also linked to the domes-tic labour market, as the wage gap between skilled and unskilled has widened due to the adoption of labour-saving technologies and the shift in consumer demand towards technology-intensive products away from stan-dardized products. Figure 11.2 shows the effects of the global economy on labour markets. The labour market is divided into two sectors producing output using skilled labour and those relying on unskilled labour. For instance, we may think of all the knowledge-intensive and high-tech industries as belonging to the skilled sector; and the traditional manufac-turing branches producing standardized products as belonging to the unskilled sector. The supply of workers in the short run is fixed at OL, with the numbers of skilled workers shown by distance OE and that of unskilled by EL.

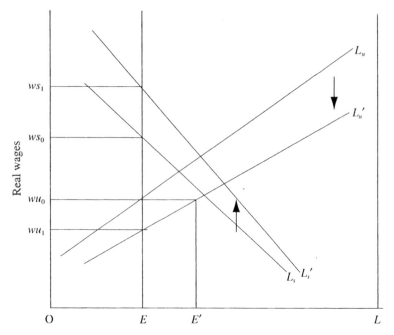

Figure 11.2   Effects of the new global environment on domestic labour markets

The curves, L_s and L_u, indicate labour demand in the skilled and unskilled sectors, respectively, with the vertical axis measuring the real wage earnings in terms of unskilled goods. Given the assumption of rigidity in occupational mobility in the short run, the initial wage gap is shown by the difference between skilled wages, $O\ ws_0$, and unskilled wages, Owu_0. The rise in the demand for knowledge-intensive products causes a shift to the right of the curve L_s to that L_s'. Since the demand curve reflects labour productivity, technology that improves the efficiency of skilled workers will cause a similar upward shift of the curve. On the other hand, the decline in consumer demands for standardized industrial products – reflecting the impact of import penetration of global competitors – causes a downward shift in the unskilled labour demand curve. The effect of the shift is shown by the curve L_D'. As a result, skilled wages rise to ws_1 from ws_0. As for the unskilled sector, if the unskilled real wage rate is rigid, there will be increased unemployment by quantities EE'. If the wage rate is assumed to be flexible, it will fall to wu_1 from wu_0. This will further widen the initial wage gap between skilled and unskilled.

Evidence for the decline of unskilled labour demand in the industrialized world is reflected by the diminished role of organized labour unions as management shifts – and sometimes threatens to shift – production to low-wage countries and sets up non-union operations in the country. As companies are able to undermine the union's wage-and-benefit packages, the union membership has declined in many industrialized countries. Unions have also become more amenable to settle strikes under pressure from companies, as evidenced by the plummeting in the frequency of strikes in Europe, Japan, and the United States over the past two decades (Table 11.3).

Political and social consequences of inequality

The recent deterioration in income distribution in the midst of economic slow-down in a number of countries of the industrialized West prompted damaging changes in each nation's economic and social fabric, frequently threatening changes in political regime. In the United States the deterioration in the distribution was accompanied by the rise in the incidence of poverty.[11] The proportion of the nation's population officially counted as poor rose from 11.7 per cent in 1980 to 13.1 per cent in 1988 and to 14.2 per cent in 1991.[12] Racial minorities, in particular, blacks and Hispanics, have been especially hard-hit by economic changes.[13] The uneven impacts of economic changes have not been confined to the working poor. The burden of the recession in the late 1980s, for instance, fell heavily on

Table 11.3 Working days lost to strikes in selected industrialized countries, 1975–94

Country	Hourly wages and benefits ($) 1994	Work days lost[a]		
		1975	*1990*	*1994*
USA	17.10	226	55	45
Canada	15.68	1303	296	62
Germany	27.31	3	15	3
France	17.04	227	36	21
Japan	21.42	221	3	2

[a] Calculated per 1000 employees.
Source: US Bureau of Labor Statistics, reported in *Wall Street Journal*, 25 March 1996.

middle America as well: job displacement became prevalent among blue and white-collar occupations, which was then reflected in the rapid increase in the number of the homeless on city streets.

Neo-liberal economic policies have had grave sociopolitical implications in the United States. According to the UN-developed Human Development Index (HDI), which provides a broader measure of social well-being in addition to income,[14] the United States which ranked second in per caput income in 1987 fell to nineteenth place, or last among the OECD nations in 1990 (UN Development Programme, 1990). Japan was the best in the overall rating, followed by Sweden, Switzerland, the Netherlands, Canada, and so forth.

A serious issue in the United States, which is not considered in the HDI, is the problem of social unrest and violence. Past failures of US government policies to safeguard an equitable sharing of the benefits from growth are a major cause behind the rise crimes and social unrest related to economic incentives. The racial riots that have scarred American cities in the recent past may have been fuelled by race-related issues, but their root cause can invariably be traced to economic inequality and deprivation. In terms of social violence, over the period from 1983 to 1992 the crime rate per population rose by 19.2 per cent with the violent types of crime[15] increasing by 40.9 per cent (Federal Bureau of Investigation, 1992). Property crimes, which account for more than 85 per cent of crimes in the American community, also increased over the period, though at a somewhat slower rate of 5.7 per cent. The majority of violent crimes included robberies which can be considered as related to economic incentives for criminality.

Many state and local governments in the United States have been rapidly increasing expenditures on the upkeep and construction of prisons. As of 1993, the number incarcerated reached 1.9 per cent of the male work force, and 8.8 per cent of the black male work force (Freeman, 1994). Massive imprisonment of criminals has not deterred violence, as the victims of growing inequality and economic deprivation continue to seek redress through violent means. In tandem with rising trends in incarceration, the propensity to commit crime among the non-institutionalized population has persistently risen.

The contemporary American experience contrasts with Japan's. From a historical perspective, Japan's industrialization strategies in the pre-Second World War era led to a concentration of wealth with consequent widespread poverty. Estimates of the Gini coefficient for pre-war Japan have ranged from a high of 0.62 in 1923 to 0.49 in 1937 (Minami, Kim and Yuzawa, 1994, p. 360). During the 1920s and the first half of the

1930s the rural–urban income gap in Japan widened, accompanied by frequent disputes between urban landowners and tenant farmers. The government, which was allied with the conglemerates of family-owned businesses, *zaibatsu*, largely failed to resolve the disputes. This climate triggered interventions by Japan's young military faction in sympathy with the distressed farmers. Though two mutinies by young officers – one in May of 1932 and the other in February of 1936 – failed, a large segment of the Japanese population began to sympathize with the rebels, paving the path to the rise in Japan's militarism. Thus, Minami (1986, pp. 149–50) points out that behind the move toward militarism in pre-war Japan were increasing income inequality and growing dissatisfaction among the working population.

Post-Second World War Japan, after successfully implementing policies for the redistribution of assets, has been relatively free from the epidemic rise in criminality that has accompanied industrialization and urbanization in other industrialized democracies, having had one of the lowest crime rates in the industrialized world. The earlier comparisons, as shown in Table 11.4, are particularly striking. Although different country definitions of crimes and accuracy of crime reports render international comparisons less meaningful, the contrast in magnitude and the trends in crimes rates as reported in the table is none the less striking. More recent data shows similar trends: the average number of offences committed per 100 000 inhabitants in 1986–8 was 1.3 in Japan, as against 5.7 in the United Kingdom and 8.4 in the United States. The corresponding figure for crimes against property is 1135 per 100 000 as against 4432 in West Germany, 5634 in the United Kingdom, and 4943 in the United States.

There are certainly social and cultural factors contributing to low crime rate in Japanese society: the cultural and ethnic homogeneity in Japanese society leads to fewer internal conflicts than in societies with diverse ethnic origins. In Asian societies, traditional institutions like family, school and local community are able to exert social control over the behavior of community members with reasonable effectiveness. Nonetheless, the fact that crime rates, particularly economic-related crimes, declined during the period of rapid growth with sustained equitable distribution in the 1970s reveals that Japanese were generally satisfied with economic conditions.[16]

The developing world

Income distribution varies distinctly by regions in the developing world; East Asian Newly Industrialized Countries (NICs) have attained rapid

Table 11.4   Crimes on police records in selected countries, 1975
(rate per 100 000 population)

Country	Total	Murder	Rape	Robbery	Theft
USA	5282	9.6	2.6	218	4800
	(+233)[a]	(+125)	(+226)	(+331)	(+230)
England	4278	2.3	2.1	2.3	2483
	(+193)	(+100)	(+102)	(+462)	(+151)
West Germany	4721	4.8	11	33	3111
	(+44)	(+143)	(+6)	(+252)	(+123)
Japan	1101	1.9	3	2.1	927
	(−11)	(−21)	(−42)	(−56)	0

[a] Figures in the parentheses show percentage changes from 1960 to 1975. For the
United States, the total crime rate in 1992 was 5600.2 (Federal Bureau of
Investigation, 1992), which shows an additional increase of 60 per cent over the
period from 1975 to 1992.
Source: Japanese Ministry of Justice, *Hanzai hakusho* (August, 1977).

economic growth with equity. In most of Latin American and African
countries the distribution of income has worsened, coupled with increased
impoverishment of more vulnerable classes in society. Distributional
inequity in these countries has been an important cause of heightened
social tensions and conflicts among economic classes, frequently resulting
in social unrest and political instabilities. In a number of emerging democracies in Asia, Africa, East Europe and Latin America, increased inequality exacerbated by recent market reforms threatens the very process of
democratization.

Sub-Sahel Africa

Trends in growth and distribution   No region is poorer than Sub-Sahel
Africa. In the recent past, many African governments have embraced
market realities and embarked on market reform measures. Although
several countries experienced market gains in economic growth, those
adjustment polices have not successfully reduced poverty. Poverty in
Africa is largely a rural phenomenon, since most of the poor (about 60 per
cent of the continent's population) depend on agriculture for jobs and
income. According to a recent UN estimate,[17] the self-sufficiency rate in
cereals for Sub-Saharan African fell from a high of 97 per cent during

1969–71 to 86 per cent in 1988–90 in comparison to the self-sufficiency rate of 91 per cent for all developing countries in 1988–90. The UN data also show that during 1988–90 some 175 million Africans went hungry and in the absence of viable alternatives to drastically boost production of food crops and livestock products, by 2010 some 300 million people, one-third of the continent's population, would suffer the 'scourge of chronic undernutrition'.

African poverty is shaped by social forces reflecting imbalances in resource allocation. Progress in redistributive land reform is limited by political constraints; the rural poor have limited access to credit, land, and extension services; lack of both genuine political commitment and strong public sector support for rural producers is another major factor exacerbating rural poverty. In this context, the impacts of structural adjustment policies which typically focus on macroeconomics financial problems have often failed to reach the rural poor, and are in some instances blamed for the exacerbation of poverty. The World Bank acknowledges that after a decade of implementing structural adjustment programmes, not many African countries have succeeded in a sound macroeconomic policy.[18] The Bank considers Ghana to have the most effective adjustment policies, but predicts that the poor in Ghana will not cross the poverty line for another 50 years.

African countries will face a further deterioration in their economies as trade liberalization on a global scale unfolds. The new General Agreement on Trade and Tariffs (GATT) will probably diminish African export revenues as existing tariff preferences for Africa are eroded under multilateral trade liberalization. In particular, food-importing countries in Africa will be hit hard by higher world food prices brought on by reductions in agricultural subsidies in European countries. Furthermore, because of the failure to bring the Multi-Fibre Agreement under GATT discipline many African countries are likely to experience reductions in growth rates of textile exports. Recent OECD calculations, as shown in Figure 11.3, show that net annual losses for Africa could reach $2.6 billion in the period to 2002. In contrast, the industrialized countries reap $135 billion or 64 per cent of total annual gains in world income from the new GATT (Goldin *et al.*, 1993).

Political and social consequences of inequality   The gravest concern in Africa over the past two decades has been the biological survival of humanity. According to a recent (1993–4) United Nations study, undernutrition and disease is more widespread today in Sub-Sahel Africa than it was 30 years ago and could remain 'rampant' in the absence of a

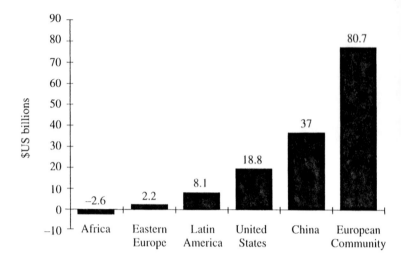

Figure 11.3   GATT winners and losers (projections to year 2002)

Source: UN Department of Public Information. *Africa Recovery*, December 1993–March 1994, p. 9.

major effort to increase indigenous food production. The continent is already deep in financial crisis and heavily dependent on food aid and faces the prospect of net cereal import needs which are expected to more than double to some 20 million tons a year by 2010.

The extreme poverty for the masses is exacerbated by a lop-sided distribution of resources to a few elites, which largely reflects ineffective and corrupt systems of governance. Widespread hunger in Africa often escalates into famine, political violence, and armed conflicts. The recent armed conflicts in both Somalia and Rwanda are illuminating cases. In Somalia, as the grazing land and water wells diminished due to accelerating environmental degradation, disputes over resource use became a major factor in the clan rivalries which eventually led to political violence. In Rwanda, the ruling regime of the Hutu tribe attempted to constrain the use of land by the rival clan, the Tutsi. Ultimately this led to the formation of a rebel army by the Tutsi, which took power in Rwanda through force of arms after hundreds of thousands of civilians had been killed.

East Asia

Trends in growth and distribution   Income inequality and widespread poverty are the twin problems facing the predominat part of the developing world today. One particular region which shows remarkable progress in reducing poverty in both absolute and relative terms is East Asia, including the newly industrialized countries of Taiwan, South Korea, Singapore, and Hong Kong and more recently, the newly industrializing ASEAN economies. According to World Bank estimates (1990),[19] the newly industrializing countries in Southeast Asia – in particular, Malaysia, Indonesia, and Thailand – have made significant economic progress during the 1980s, which has resulted in substantial reduction of poverty as these governments have been able to channel larger public resources into human development. The Bank report, for instance, shows that the ratio of the income share of the top 20 per cent to that of the bottom 20 per cent during the 1980s for the above seven Asian countries averages to 7.27 in comparison to the Latin American countries' average of 18.61. The East Asian ratio comes close to the OECD average of 6.14, which is calculated using a sample of six countries of the United States, Japan, France, German, the United Kingdom, and Italy (Table 11.3). Using various measures of income distribution, other studies (World Bank 1993, Findlay and Wellisz 1993) similarly conclude that unlike in many other developing economies during this period, income distribution in East Asian economies either improved or did not deteriorate at worst.

It is worth pointing out that one of the newly industrializing Asian countries facing problems with income distribution is China. Since 1976, when full-scale economic reform started, the Chinese economy has expanded at dazzling rates of growth, frequently at a double digit rate. Its strategy, centered on urban-based growth poles, especially along selected coastal areas, has led to a widening of the income gap among regions of the country and between cities and farming villages within regions. According to a recent estimate,[20] as disposable income per urban resident has steadily increased in real terms whereas that of farmers has remained unchanged, the ratio of farmer income to that of urban residents has plunged from 58 per cent in 1985 to 39.4 per cent in 1993. Taking more specific examples, in 1992 average per caput income in Guizhou, the poorest province in China, was about one-fifth of that of Shanghai, China's richest city, having fallen from the corresponding figure of 26.6 per cent in 1984. To take an example, at the regional level, in 1993 per caput income in Longchuan County, the poorest region in Guangdong Province, was only 7.6 per cent that in Shenzhen, the province's richest city.

The case of South Korea, as a country in rapid transition to political democracy and economic liberalization, deserves special attention. The distribution of income in Korea drastically improved in the 1960s when government policies emphasized the development of labor-intensive exports. It began to worsen in the mid-1970s when the government resorted to wage suppression and pro-business policies in order to promote exports. After a slight improvement in the early 1980s (Choo and Yoon, 1984), it steadily deteriorated until the reversal in 1990 (Ahn, 1991); the Gini coefficient rose from 0.3472 in 1981 to 0.4318 in 1989. Ahn's estimates deviate somewhat from other studies which claimed improvements in distribution in the late 1980s (Choo, 1993). Ahn claims that other studies underestimate income inequalities in the nor-worker sector, which causes the Gini estimates to appear smaller. The growing inequality in the late 1980s reflected increased wealth concentration among large corporations and uneven developments among sectors and regions. Soaring real estate prices in the context of highly uneven assets distribution further worsened the distribution of income: between 1987 and 1989 land prices rose 93 per cent and landowners, who comprised some 30 per cent of the population, saw their capital gaining 1.7 times the nominal GNP (Lee, 1990).

Although the distribution of income in Korea and Taiwan shows some deterioration for some years, the trend level of inequality in these countries has been much lower compared to developing countries in other regions. More recently, with the instalment of a civilian regime in 1993 there was a policy shift that defused the state's support of big businesses and allowed greater participation of small and medium firms. Income inequality consequently fell markedly. In China, increased efforts have been directed toward the privatization of rural markets and the promotion of small-scale urban and rural industry.

More importantly, it is worth pointing out that the incidence of poverty – defined here as the percent of persons below the poverty line has fallen far more rapidly in East Asia than in other regions. To take an extreme example, the World Bank data shows that the percentage of the poor in Indonesia, which in 1970 recorded 58 per cent as among the highest of all developing economies, fell sharply to a low 17 per cent by 1987.[21] The country is now counted as among the lowest of all developing economies in the poverty measures. There have also been significant reductions in the absolute number of the poor in most of East Asian economies. Nor did the middle-income class appear to have lost grounds in real income over the past two or three decades in these countries.

Causes of distributional change: theoretical considerations

As already mentioned, some developing countries (for instance, East Asian NICs) seem to have adjusted better to changing global environment whereas others (mostly in Sub-Sahel Africa and Latin America) have difficulties in pulling themselves out of economic stagnancy, often, with a deterioration in social and economic conditions. It is argued here that the cross-country variation in income distribution is best explained by the differences in the country's initial pattern of asset distribution as well as its development strategy and policy.

In the case of East Asia, three factors explain the extraordinary combination of rapid growth and low inequality. They are the implementation of land reform, followed by policies to support rural incomes; policy emphasis on manufactured exports that create increased demand for labour and increasingly for skilled labour; and growth in human capital which forms part of a virtuous cycle to generate increased labour demand in turn. The nature and scope of interactions among the three factors will be illustrated below based on the specific experience of Korea. The Korean strategy and experience more or less parallels those of Taiwan and Japan in the earlier stages of development. Singapore and Hong Kong as city states are rather exceptional cases.

The basic development strategy in those larger East Asian countries was based on a two-pronged approach to industrialization. The first prong in the strategy calls for the rapid industrialization at a pace at least exceeding the natural rate of population growth; the second calls for the rise in rural incomes in itself. A labour-absorbing, export-orientated industrial sector coupled with a dynamic agricultural sector is viewed as the key to a growth path leading to sustained growth with equity.

With regard to rural development, although the development strategiy in three cases of Japan, Korean and Taiwan can be characterized as a model of 'industry first and agriculture later', an important lesson to learn is that in none of these countries the importance of agriculture has been overlooked. First of all, the land reform implemented in Korea, Taiwan, and in the Meiji Japan, was the most significant factor contributing to the improvement of the distribution of assets, and consequently of income. Moreover, under a 'tillers to the land' system, land productivity in East Asia rose substantially in spite of the reductions in average farm size (Kim, 1995; Squire, 1981). The East Asian governments also intervened at different times to narrow the urban-rural income gaps through farm price support and rural infrastrure development.[22]

Turning to the question of industrial labour absorption, we begin by noting that the rapid growth in manufactured exports in East Asia leads to the continued demand for labour. Without a sustained growth process, of course, any policies to reduce poverty and to improve the distribution would be virtually impossible in poor countries. The East Asian economies' ability to sustain rapid growth can partly be explained by their industrialization strategy which emphasizes a balanced, simultaneous development of both the export and import-substitution industries in capital and intermediate goods. The priority on capital goods development reflects the strategy to reduce the import dependence. From a longer-run perspective, the balanced growth strategy has resulted in relieving the balance-of-payments constraint, enabling East Asian countries to continue with a sustained pace of industrial development.

Figure 11.4 illustrates the effects of the East Asian model of industrialization. The initial possibilities of producing exportable and importable goods on a per caput basis are shown by the curve $Z_0 Z_0$. For purposes of analysis, the importables are capital and intermediate goods. The line $I–I$ is the international price line whose slope indicates the relative price of exportables to importables. Under the intial protection of the importable industry, the domestic relative price of importables, shown by the line d_0 d_0, is higher than in the case of free trade. The combination of outputs produces in the economy is shown at point P_0 at which the production possibility curve, $Z_0 Z_0$, is tangential to the domestic price line, $d_0 d_0$. The consumption point located along the international price line, I_0, which emanates from production point P_0 is given at C_0 at which the domestic price line is tangential to the highest possible indifference curve (not shown in the diagram). With economic growth over time, the transformation curve shifts outward to $Z_1 Z_1$. The strategy to promote the simultaneous development of export and capital goods industries causes the curve to shift ouward in both goods. If the domestic relative price remains unchanged and equal to the slope of the line $d_1 d_1$ – drawn parallel to $d_0 d_0$, the new production point moves outward to P_1. Consumption takes place at C_1 on the international terms of trade line $I_1 I_1$, where a higher-level indifference curve (not shown) is tangent to the domestic price ratio $d_1 d_1$. The final step is the liberalization of trade. The country will produce at P_2 at which the slope of domestic price ratio is to equal to that of the international price line $I_2 I_2$. The final consumption point moves out to C_2, at which the free trade price line is tangential to the indifference curve. The graph illustrates the possibility of the economy's reaching the higher level of the indifference curve – reflecting the rise in real income – with each step of policy change.

The final factor contributing to the East Asian success has to do with human capital. It is well to note that because of social and family emphasis on education in East Asian culture, the labour force there was, to begin with, relatively well endowed with human capital stock. The rising incomes to the lower classes and increased opportunities for better paying industrial

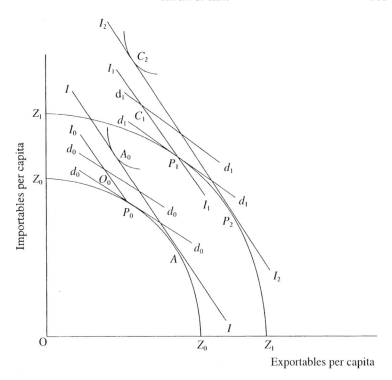

Figure 11.4   Growth and distribution: the East Asian case

jobs meant more and better education and training. As a result, labour productivity improved steadily, which is reflected by increased labour demand. In a nutshell, in addition to the historically determined initiation conditions determined by successful land reforms, the demand side factors which rapidly raised labor demand largely contributed to the increases in employment and real incomes of the workers, thereby contributing to the rapid alleviation of poverty and improved income distribution.

Figure 11.5 shows changes in Korean industrial labour markets over time. The set of the *D* and *S* curves represent the labour demand and supply in the industrial sector over different points in time. Three particular periods are considered; 1960 is the year preceding the installation of Park's regime which initiated the systematic drive toward modern industrialization of the country. The era preceding the start of industrial development can be characterized by a labour surplus economy in which labour redundancy exist, as shown by the flat portion of the labour supply curve *S*.

The industrial labour employment is reflected by quantity OQ_0 at the pre-vailing subsistence real wage rate of OW_0. Korea's industrialization pro-ceeded well, reaching the 'turning point' in the mid-1970s. This is shown by equilibrium position B at which redundant labour disappears. Two forces on the side of labour demand were at work to tighten the labour market; while industrial labour demand continued to expand as industrial goods exports increased, as shown by the shift upward of the curve D_0 to D_1, the the Korean labour force's human capital rapidly accumulated. The combination of the two forces accelerated the expansion of labour demand, shortening the arrival of the turning point. The graph also shows the shift to the right of the labour supply from S_0 to S_1, which reflects the effects of natural growth in the total labour force during the initial stage of surplus labour. The continued advance in industrialization and growing human capital investment has been tightening the labour market, as indi-cated by point C in the early 1990s when the Korean real wage rate caught up with its labour productivity. Note that the new labour supply curve is indicated by S_2, which takes into account the effects of increased rural incomes in the phase after reaching the turning point. The pattern of dynamic evolution depicted in the above Korean illustration applies simi-larly to other East Asian economies in which the success in industrial exports has been based on strong human capital development.

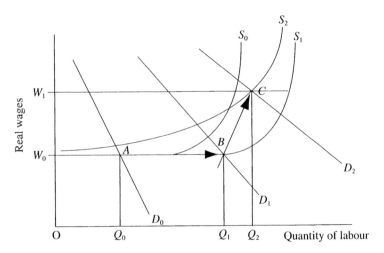

Figure 11.5   Dynamic evolution in industrial labour markets; case of Korea

Political and social consequences of inequality

Asia's newly industrializing nations have a relatively short experience with democratization. The members of society who actively support political democracy in these countries consist mainly of the urban middle class, especially the white-collar groups. In Thailand the civilian government of Chan was able to assert itself in the wake of the bloody military violence in 1992 on the strength of a political coalition essentially supported by Thai's middle-income classes.

More illuminating cases linking political liberalization to equitable growth are those of South Korea and Taiwan. In these countries, rapid industrialization transformed the social structure by gradually broadening the middle classes. This transformation has had broad political consequences because both middle and working classes support democratic systems of government. Taiwan's important steps toward political liberalization were more peaceful in procedure. Taiwan's Lee Tenghui, who became the island's first native president in 1988, appointed Lien Chan as premier, a civilian profession, to replace the military office-turned bureaucrat, Hau Peitsun, a conservative Nationalist leader who was regarded by many as an obstacle to democratization. All Lien's predecessors in the premiership had been mainland Chinese who had fled to Taiwan after losing the Civil War to the Communists in 1949. The appointment defied the objections of the Kuomintang party and reflected the island's new initiative toward political democratization. Lien was expected to pursue democratic reforms. Taiwan's per caput income already exceeded $US 14 000 and the rapid growth of the middle-income class led to the formation of strong political support for democracy. In March 1996, Taiwan had the first direct election of the country's president.

South Korea, the largest and most dynamic economy among East Asian NICs, illuminates the political and social implications of distributional equity. The election of Kim Yong-Sam as a civilian president in 1992 reflects the changed situation in Korea where the middle-income class has emerged as a dominant political force. The middle classes, which steadily grew in numbers during the previous period of rapid industrialization, comprise more than 60 per cent of the Korean population. Kim has responded to this class by following a middle-of-the-road approach; Economic policies have focused on securing continuous flows of income to wider social groups, especially to small businesses and farmers.

This is a case where the success of rapid growth with equity raised the possibility of the inauguration of democracy in a country that had been under authoritarian rule (Muller, 1988). The future of democracy in Korea will depend critically on successfully continuing to avoid excessive income inequality. Bipolarization in income distribution could diminish the middle-of-the-road influence of the middle social classes, allowing the substitution of a repressive regime for political democracy.

In addition to political implications, growing inequality in wealth and privilege engenders social dislocations and disturbances. In China, as the country has become more affluent, disparities in income have also widened, eliminating the sense of security that stemmed from equality in poverty'. The growing regional disparities – particularly serious between the highly developed eastern coastal regions and the backward inland areas – portends potential social and political disturbances. Movements of the population have already been restricted by the government, which will worsen inter-regional income gaps and exacerbate ethnic tensions, since many minorities live in low-income inland regions. In South Korea, during the various periods in the late 1970s and the early 1980s, the situation of economic inequity led to a wave of industrial unrest on the part of workers and other forms of social strife initiated by students, which eventually resulted in the fall of Chun's military regime in 1986 and the subsequent restoration of the civilian regime. The realities as well as the perception by the lower groups of extreme inequities between workers and property-owners prevailed in Korea. The so-called 'prosperity strikes', based on the concept that workers deserve to share the benefits of business prosperity, occurred more frequently during the times when the distribution was more uneven. The Korean case tells us that an equitable development constitutes a functional requirement for the country's political and social stability.

Latin America

Trends in growth and distributions

Post-war development in Latin America started with wide income inequal-ities across the area. Available data circa 1979 (Altimir, 1987) indicate that the Gini indexes were relatively high in Latin American countries compared with other parts of the developing world: for instance, Brazil 0.605; Colombia 0.618; both Mexico and Venezuela 0.500; and Peru 0.568. The import-substitution strategy in Latin American countries failed to generate patterns of sustained growth the fruits of which could be shared equitably.[23] For instance, Mexico and Brazil both had very rapid industrialization without any significant reduction in underemployment and unemployment. The working poor did not necessarily become poorer, but the fruits of growth reached them very slowly, with the consequence that income distribution became more unequal. The political and social instabilities seen today in many Latin American nations have a historical resonance that precedes the revitalization policies adopted in the wake of the debt crisis in the 1980s.

That the earlier import-substitution industrialization strategy in Latin America led to income inequality can be seen from an international comparison shown in Table 11.5. The table compares the income shares of the bottom 60 per cent of the population in selected developing countries. Two East Asian countries – Taiwan and South Korea – exhibit high growth rates with the poorest 60 per cent's income share exceeding 30 per cent. The Asian experiences contrast with those of such Latin American countries as Mexico, Brazil, and Peru, though Costa Rica is a notable exception. The growth rates of the poorest group's income in all three Latin American countries were substantially below the respective national average growth rates during the period in consideration.

The aftermath of the debt crisis in 1982 witnessed Latin America's first extended depression; throughout the remains of the decade income inequality continued to rise. The indebted Latin American countries began to embrace neo-liberal adjustment policies of smaller government, open markets, trade liberalization, privatization and deregulation, which

Table 11.5   Growth in income for the lowest 60 per cent in selected countries

Country	Period of observation	Income share (initial year)	Income share (final year)	Growth rate of income for bottom 60%	Growth rate of national average income
Taiwan	1964–74	0.369	0.385	7.1	6.6
South Korea	1965–76	0.349	0.323	7.9	8.7
Sri Lanka	1963–73	0.274	0.354	4.6	2.0
Costa Rica	1961–71	0.237	0.284	5.1	3.2
India	1954–64	0.310	0.292	1.6	2.3
Philippines	1961–71	0.247	0.248	2.3	2.2
Turkey	1963–73	0.208	0.240	5.1	3.6
Brazil	1960–70	0.248	0.206	1.2	3.1
Mexico	1963–75	0.217	0.197	2.4	3.2
Peru	1961–71	0.179	0.179	2.3	2.3

Source: Chenery (1979) Table 11.5.

resulted in ever larger contingents of the critically poor, low-paid workers, underemployed and unemployed, while middle-income classes saw their living standards and quality of life deteriorating. Throughout the 1980s external debt servicing, reverse resource transfer to abroad, diminution of domestic investment, deterioration of human and physical capital stocks, and inflation became part of the functioning structure of the Latin American economies. The already impoverished situation of more vulnerable groups of society deteriorated further as international donor agencies' adjustment policies called for the contraction of welfare programmes and the rise in the relative prices of basic needs goods. In addition, as the devaluation of the domestic currency, aimed at switching expenditures to tradeable goods, triggered inflation, it began to affect more vulnerable groups such as wage-earners, self-employed workers, and retirees, who had less capacity to negotiate or protect themselves against price increases of imported goods.

During the recent economic recovery (1990–2), some gains in the real incomes of the lower economic classes have been made in a few Latin American countries, but these are the exceptions. According to the ECLAC report (1994, p. 37), the relative inequality of income distribution in the urban areas of Argentina, Honduras, Mexico, Panama and Uruguay declined slightly. On the other hand, the households in the upper strata of these countries also increased their income. The continent's income distribution structures are now more uneven than they were in the late 1970s. This can be seen in Figure 11.6 and Appendix Table 11A.2, which show changes in real income by income strata over the 1980–92 period for Latin American countries. In Mexico the lowest and the lower-middle-income groups made virtually no gains in real income while the richest gained more than 50 per cent over the period. Brazil, Venezuela, and other Latin American countries display similar results: overall average per caput income declined with the burden of the decline falling heavily on the lower income groups.

Table 11.6 presents the comparisons of real per capita income for 1992 calculated as a multiple of the country-defined poverty line income. Real income of the poorest 40 per cent in most Latin American countries declined throughout the 1980s and despite the recovery in the early 1990s still remained below the poverty line in 1992: income of the poorest as a percentage of the poverty line income ranged from 84 per cent in Costa Rica to 28 per cent in Honduras. Moreover, the ratio of income of the richest 10 per cent to that of the lowest 40 per cent was in the range of 10–20 in Latin American countries (Table 11.6). It is worth noting that this figure is substantially above a typical East Asian NIC's.

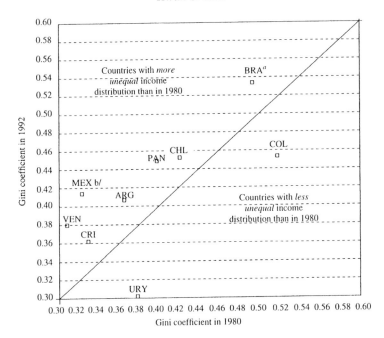

Figure 11.6   Latin America (11 countries, urban areas): changes in income distribution during the 1980s and 1990s

Source: ECLAC, on the basis of special tabulations of data from household surveys in the countries.

Notes:

[a] The data correspond to 1979 and 1990; no information available for 1992.

[b] The data correspond to 1984 and 1992; no information available for 1980.

Key: VEN: Venezuela CRI: Costa Rica MEX: Mexico ARG: Argentina PAN: Panama CHL: Chile BRA: Brazil COL: Colombia URY: Uruguay

For the Latin American region as a whole, between 1980 and 1987 the average real income of wage salary earners fell 15 per cent in the formal private sector and 30 per cent in the public sector while the combined employment of the two sectors rose a bare 3 per cent (PREALC, 1990a). The numbers of the economically active population in the urban informal sector rose 55 per cent while their average real income fell 42 per cent. As a result, the proportion of the population classified as 'poor' rose to 43 per cent by the end of the 1980s (World Bank, 1990, p. 14). Over the decade almost 40 million people were added to the ranks of officially

Table 11.6   *Real per capita income by income strata in 1992*[a]

	(1) Low income	(2) Middle income	(3) High income	Ratio of (3) to (1)
Argentina (Buenos Aires)	1.40	3.79	18.36	3.11
Bolivia	0.52	2.03	9.55	18.37
Brazil[b]	0.56	2.67	15.37	27.45
Chile	0.81	2.63	12.77	15.77
Colombia	0.58	2.31	10.52	18.14
Costa Rica	0.84	2.79	8.55	10.18
Honduras	0.28	1.16	4.96	17.71
Mexico	0.79	2.55	11.43	14.47
Panama	0.64	3.21	11.64	18.19
Paraguay (Asunción)	0.65	2.31	7.23	11.25
Uruguay	1.51	4.22	11.83	7.83
Venezuela	0.71	2.30	8.44	11.89

Source: ECLAC (1994) p. 36.
Notes:
[a] Real income is measured by a multiple of the respective per caput poverty line.
  The low-income stratum consists of the poorest 40 per cent; high-income, the
  richest 10 per cent; and middle income, the remaining in-between groups.
[b] Brazil data correspond to 1990.

defined poverty. In Brazil alone the incidence of poverty rose from 24 to
39 per cent, with the number of Brazilian poor amounting to more than 10
million. In Mexico the incidence of poverty rose from 40 per cent in 1980
to 54 per cent in 1987 (Kim, 1991), and the real minimum wage rate in the
urban sector continued to fall 26.6 per cent over the period from 1988 to
1994 (Lazaroff 1995, p. 49). At present, close to 60 per cent of Mexico's
population of 86 million is under the age of 30. These statistics translate
into a work force that will grow by more than a million people each year.
With the prospect of fewer jobs, wages will be likely to stay flat or possibly be scaled back.[24]

While the urban labour force faces serious difficulties, the situation is
worse in the countryside of many Latin American countries. In Mexico,
for example, imports of US fruits and vegetables since the reductions in
tariffs beginning in the late 1980s have pushed down domestic prices,
causing the failure of almost 40 per cent of Mexico's small agricultural
businesses (Lazaroff, 1995, p. 49). Privatization of communal farms into

competitive businesses has been difficult given the high prices of imported machinery and bank loans.

Causes of immiserization

Unlike the East Asian case, a large number of countries in Africa and Latin America, as noted already, have in recent past experienced a sustained increase in poverty and a deterioration in income distribution. The main cause of growing poverty and inequality is the failure of the economy's maintaining a sustained rate of growth; some of these countries have even shown episodic declines in growth rate. It is all too evident that unless a sustained growth at an adequate pace is achieved in an already highly-unequal economy, reductions in poverty and income inequality would be difficult to achieve. Moreover, provisions of basic education, training, and health care have been largely neglected in many countries in Latin America and Sub-Sahel Africa under a recessionary environment over the past decade or so. The link between education and growth has taken the form of a vicious cycle in the case of Latin America.

To understand the deteriorating trends in economic conditions, it will be useful to contrast with the Asian case in terms of the difference in the country's development strategy. Figure 11.7 shows the production possibility curve Z_0Z, which is similar to that used for East Asia (Figure 11.4). The initial production point, P_0, is on the production possibility curve with the domestic relative price of importables shown by the price line do. Under protection, the domestic price of importable is higher than its international price indicated by the price line I_0. As noted in Figure 11.4, the economy reaches out to the consumption point C_0 on the international price line I_0.

Unlike the East Asian case, the import-substitution-orientated countries are assumed to make no effort to promote export industries, and import substitution is advanced in consumer goods, not in capital goods. As a result, as the economy expands, its transformation curve moves out in the direction of the importable goods sector to a new locus Z_1Z. As the policy is pursued to specialize in goods where increased production takes place, output can be seen to expand along the Rybzinski path, indicated by R *path*. The new equilibrium production point moves up in the north-western direction to P_1, which lies above and to the left of the intial point P_0. More of importables and less of exportable are produced and consumed, as shown by the new consumtion point at C_1. As point C_1 is located to the south-east of C_0, indicating consumer equilibrium at a lower indifference curve. This shows a possibility of immiserizing growth when a lopsided import substitution is advanced under protection over a long period It is well to not that our model is akin to H. Johnson's (1967) example where the immiserizing effects of growth result from accumulation of nationally owned capital in the protected industry.

Moreover, if the import-substitution-orientated industrialization heavily depends on foreign direct investment, as in the case of many African and Latin American countries now, the deterioration in welfare can be accelerated as foreign profits are subtracted to determine national income (Bertrand and Flatters, 1971; and Brecher and Diaz-Alejandro, 1977). Our case demonstrates an additional factor contributing to immiserization, which is attributable to an unbalanced development strategy neglecting a simultaneous indigenous development of export industries and capital and intermediate goods.

The final step involves the shift towards liberalization of trade. In this case, the consumption point moves out from C_1 to C_2 at which the indifference curve is tangential to the international price line I_1. At Point C_2 the consumer is still at lower indifference curve in relation to the initial situation at C_0. The hypothesis postulated here is that production structure remains rigid in the short run in spite of the transition in policy from import substitution towards export expansion. Two reasons can be advanced to explain the difficulties, at least in the short run, in increasing export goods; first, the economy is unlikely to be able to abruptly provide required capital goods and intermidiate components for export industries, and will have to depend more heavily on imports, thereby aggravating the preexisting balance of payments problems. Secondly even if foreign borrowing is feasible, there is the problem of international competitiveness of newly developing export industries in the global market.

Our model demonstrating possibilities for immizerizing growth suggests that unplanned trade liberalization might not be a magic wand for developing countries.

Political and social consequences of inequality

Growing inequality and the impoverishment of large segments of the Latin American population were accompanied by rapidly deteriorating conditions in health care and basic education. In Mexico alone, for instance, as much as 66 per cent of the Mexican population is estimated as currently suffering from malnutrition (Rothman, 1995, p. 41). Taking the continent as a whole, its educational and health care standards today are substantially below the levels that would be expected given the region's current per capita income. During the early 1990s only a little over a half of those

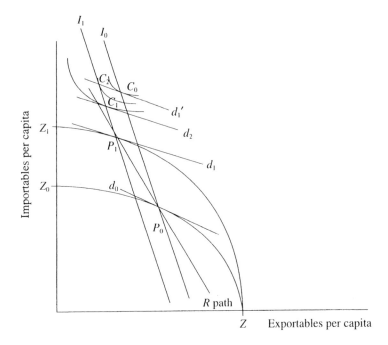

Figure 11.7   Growth and distribution: case of immiserization

entering primary school reached the fourth grade (Inter-American Development, 1994, p. 13). Enrolment rates in secondary school were less than half the eligible age group. When compared to China, which had only one-sixth the average per caput income of Latin America, the burden of disease in the region was also about a third greater. This divergence between the actual situation and the expectations based on the region's average income is attributable to the extreme income disparities prevailing in Latin America.

In a number of Latin American countries, the prolonged impoverishment of the working poor coupled with the detrioration in income distribution has led to labor unrest, drug traffics, and even political violence. In Central America the exacerbation of inequalities has played key roles in social and political violence. Since the mid-1970s large-scale revolts in three out of the five Central American countries have erupted again their governments. In 1979 a popular revolution toppled Nicaragua's Somoza regime. A resurgent guerrilla rebellion continued in Guatemala since 1980 while in El Salvador crippling political violence lasted some twelve years. Booth (1991) contends that government policies for agricultural exports and rapid capital-intensive industrialization in these countries marginalized landless peasants, urban poor, and wage labourers, and in the absence of policies that could have mitigated the exacerbation of poverty, these groups began mobilizing for a rebellion.

In Venezuela, despite a respectable economic growth in 1990 and 1991, the country became more unequal, with an attendant rise in the number of destitute people. The rise in basic goods prices in February of 1989 eventually triggered a riot in the capital city with the record of deaths exceeding 300. The frequent labour strikes that ensued were followed by 1992's twice-aborted military *coups* to overthrow democratically elected President Perez's government. Perez was the continent's leading neo-libral policy-maker.

Brazil in 1985 had a democratically elected civilian government for the first time after twenty years of military regime. Eight years after the new democracy, it faced a new crisis. Brazil's first democratically elected president, Fernand Collor de Mellor, was ousted amidst a scandal involving illegal use of campaign funds. The underlying cause of people's disaffection with the government was the inability of his administration to address the ever-aggravated issue of income distribution and poverty. In Brazil, according to a 1990 census, over 24 per cent of the working population received a minimum wage income. The necessary income to maintain a subsistence living standard was estimated at five times the minimum wage. This implies that some 70 per cent of the working population earned below the effective subsistence income.[25]

In Mexico, which to begin with has one of the most skewed income distribution in Latin America, the income gap between capital and labour had widened throughout the 1980s, accompanied by increased concentration in wealth. During Salinas's presidency, 25 Mexican families controlled some 55 per cent of Mexican assets; half of them are still held by six conglomerates consisting of Grupo Carso, Visa, Vitro, Telmex, Alfa, and Grupo Mexico (Rothman, 1995). Some 37 million Mexicans live in poverty and the Mexican Social Security Institute, the country's largest provider of public health care, covers only a little more than a third of the working population. Economic inequality and deprivation are making Mexican politics more heated than ever. The middle class, which had high expectations of the economic reform, is frustrated with economic conditions. The working masses' unrelenting demands for political participation have been fuelled by the continuous process of economic liberalization. The ruling Institutional Revolutionary Party (PRI), which had never lost national or local elections since 1929, began to lose wide popular support as it lost the governor's elections in Baja California in 1989, Chihuahua in 1990, and Guanajuato in 1991.

Mexico's economic reform, none the less, continues in a top–down fashion. Its political system remains tightly controlled under the absolute power of the presidency of the ruling party, which has created an impetus towards rent-seeking. The extent of rent-seeking has been highlighted most recently by the arrest of Raul Salinas, the brother of the former president, on charges of plotting the murder of rival leader Luis Massieu. Also, the revelations of links between Mexican elites and seven drug cartels and the speculation of drug involvement in three recent assassinations has shed serious doubts on the political system.

A number of clashes, including the recent Chiapas uprising in rural Mexico, have taken place between the existing political structures and the popular forces clamouring for democratization and economic equity. The political imperative of the future Mexican governments will be to gain greater popular support for completing economic and political reforms. Securing popular support will, on the other hand, depend on the ability of the government to implement alternative strategies for more equitable economic growth.

In summary, prospects for stable political democracy in Latin America hinge critically on governments' ability to engineer a sustained growth path with equity. The challenge to create a vibrant, equitable economy looms much larger for the emerging democracies in Latin America than elsewhere. In Latin America growing economic inequality has long solidified the formation and preservation of distinct social classes, planting the seed for social unrest and political instability.

11.2 GROWTH VERSUS EQUITY: SEARCH FOR A NEW LINK

While we have so far analyzed regional variation in the causes and consequences of a country's income distribution, this section focuses on the link between income inequality and its conventionally most important determinant – the country's economic growth. From the historical perspective, the well-known Kuznets' (1955) hypothesis postulates the relationship between distribution and growth: Growing inequality is associated with growth in the earlier stage of the country's industrialization, and after reaching a 'turning point' at which rural labour redundancy in a developing economy disappears, the distribution starts to improve. The hypothesis, encapusulated in his inverted U-curve, assumes the causality from growth to the consequence of distribution, and ignores the possibility of simultaneity in linkage between growth and distribution.

More recently, supply-siders and many neo-liberal economists have been concerned with the impact of distribution on growth, and argued that current inequality should be endured for the sake of future growth and equity. The benefits of economic growth will eventually filter down to the masses. In this context, redistributive policies harming the rich would reduce their incentives for work and investment. Their position has not, however, remained unchallenged as a growing number of economists began to argue the relationship in a reverse direction.

On empirical grounds, a number of anomalies in country experience, which depart from the deterministic directions assumed by Kuznets and the supply siders, have been observed: rising inequality has not been the rule in all newly industrializing nations, any more than falling inequality has been the rule in all industrialized nations. For instance, the recent, cross-sectional results reported in Abelda and Tilly's (1995, p. 7) paper show a negative correlation between income inequality and labour productivity in the OECD countries. During the 1980s countries with relatively faster labour productivity growth, such as Japan, Finland, Germany, the Netherlands, Belgium, and Sweden, were more equal in income distribution (as measured by the ratio of income of the richest 20 per cent of the population to the poorest 20 per cent). On the other hand, countries with slower productivity growth, such as New Zealand, Australia, Switzerland, and the United States, were relatively less equal. Other recent cross-country studies indicate a similar negative relationship between income inequality and per caput income growth (Alesina and Perotti, 1994; Persson and Tabellini 1994).[26] A more comprehensive analysis involving a much larger sample of countries for the period 1960–1985 has been undertaken by Birdsall, Ross, and Sabot (1995). Using the World Bank (1991, Table 30) data in which the ratio of the income shares of the top 20 per cent of population and the bottom 40 per cent is used as the indicator of inequality, the authors find that the inequality variable is negative and significant in determining economic growth rates.

Casual observation on the recent trend in inequality in Europe also casts doubt on the above deterministic models. Over the past decade, income inequality rose during the economic expansion as well as the contraction in the industrialized world. Between 1989 and 1992, the industrial expansion in Sweden, Finland, the United States, the Benelux countries, and England was accompanied by rising unemployment, exacerbating domestic income inequalities. In Ireland, under the neo-liberal export-orientated stragegy, the government, for a long time, benignly neglected the once prominent agricultural sector. With the failure to create sufficient numbers of high value-added jobs, growing occupations shifted to low-paying service industries. Low wages, combined with the already highest unemployment rate in the developed world (Callan and Nolan, 1994, p. 3), have been a recipe for rising poverty. The benefits from growth failed to trickle down to the bottom layers of society.

Admittedly, recent empirical evidence must be judged as rather inconclusive in supporting neither the trade-off or the-rising-tide-lifting-all-boats theory (Michaely *et al.*, 1991, pp. 103–12). Given the paucity of data and the difficulty of disentangling causes and effects, these findings cannot be construed as a generalizable conclusion. None the less, the earlier supplysider's presumption that the country could start with a worsened distribution to have more rapid economic growth later is not simply borne out by the existing data. On the other hand, the positive correlations observed between growth and equity on a global scale comparison do cause us to postulate an alternative hypothesis that rapid economic growth is generally compatible with equitable income distrbution.

If the conventional theory relating distribution to growth is then to be debunked, how do we then explain the relationship between growth and equality? There are two sides of the link that can be examined. On one hand, there is the question of whether inequality leads to rapid growth. and on the other, whether rapid growth is the cause of inequality in a market system. On the basis of the recent empirical data observed in several countries we first hypothesize the following reasons for the negative effects of inequality.

The question of rapid growth as a consequence of inequality can in turn be analysed both from an economic perspective and from the political and social economy perspectives. The economists leaning toward Keynesian economics would look at the role of aggregate demand in a market economy, and deduce the positive effects of increased equity on demand and economic growth.[27] In an earlier simulation exercise, Chinn (1977) showed that income redistribution in favour of poorer classes raises its GDP in Taiwan. Other economists have related increased income equality to increased access to health care, training, and education for the population at large, which in the long term should raise worker productivity and improve the performance of the economy. In particular, income inequality in poorer societies is accompanied by increased incidence of poverty, which directly affects the nutritional level of the workers and therefore their productivity.

From the political and social economy perspective, there are several compelling reasons to believe that inequality hampers a sustained process of growth. First, inequality has its direct and indirect financial costs. Persson and Tabellini (1994) argue that in a society with a widening income gap, policies to improve the distribution most likely result in taxing investment and growth-promoting activities; redistribution becomes economically costly, as a baseline of support needs to be provided for the welfare, health care, education, and training of its populace. Moreover, growing inequality leads to increased expenses of enforcing the law and order in order to protect property rights and the market system. It is worth noting in this context that in an increasingly unequal economy such as the United States the growing numbers of the incarcerated population have been exacting enormous costs for prison upkeeping, which also reflects monumental losses of valuable human resources. The vicious cycle is that as the 'haves' possess more to protect and the 'have-nots' less to lose and less prospects for a better future through work, crime increases.

It is illuminating to contrast this with the economic performance of more equal East Asian economies. While the extreme inequality in Latin America gave rise to intense political pressure to implement expansionary economic policies just to stave off unrest among the marginalized groups, in East Asia, given the less-restrictive constraints on government budget, their governments enjoyed much greater degree of freedom to pursue policies and programmes for economic development.

Second, related to the previous argument is the problem of macroeconomic and political instability that probably follows growing inequality. In highly unequal economies as in Latin American countries, the relatively well-to-do will be faced with the increasing burden of looking after those left behind, and will be likely to exercise their power to avoid burden on taxation. The ruling elite's pursuit of self-interest possibly leads to a situation of fiscal imbalance characterized by chronic budget deficit and inflation. Past experience in many Latin American and African countries reveals how difficult it has been to successfully implement stabilization programmes that could protect savings and investment and induce stable growth. Economic and political instability has been recurrent as these countries could not break out of their cycle of self-defeating policies.

In this context, Sachs (1985) mentions another case in which inequality hampers macroeconomic stability and sustained growth. He points out the self-serving elite in a highly unequal society (as in some Latin American and African countries) would see it to its own interests to preserve an overvalued exchange rate system since it lowers the price of luxury imports which the elite consumes largely. An overvaluation hurts the rural poor and the export sector, exacerbating external imbalance and dampening prospects for sustained growth.[28]

Lastly, there is the problem of a vicious cycle between growing inequality and lower productivity, thereby hampering long-run prospects for sustained growth. In an increasingly unequal economy, particularly in the developing world, the poor find it increasingly difficult to find access for their children even to basic-level education and to basic health care. The consequence on economic development will be damaging, as a larger number of the labour foce becomes unproductive and left out of economic activities, which will further widen the gap between rich and poor. As mentiioned earlier, World Bank studies amply demonstrated the validity of the link between education and growth in the case of East Asian experiences.

Turning to the other side of the link, the question to address now is whether falling inequality is the automatic consequence of growth. By now, there has been plenty of empirical evidence showing that the trickle down mechanism did not work under Reagan and Thatcher. The East Asian experience where growth has been accompanied by low levels of inequality shows that growth itself does not ensure equity without state intervention. The link from growth to distribution cannot be assumed as automatic and inherent in the modern process of economic growth. As pointed out by Fields (1980), inequality is not so much determined by the growth process as by the type of growth. The East Asian experence tells us that there is no need for a trade-off between growth and equity: resources, if properly allocated, can contribute to attainment of both objectives simultaneously. Their governments, to begin with, succeeded in redistributing assests and land, and diligently intervened in markets to help rural development. Also, such policies as investing in human capital (education and public health) and augmenting labour demand, if directed towards the poor, not only reduced income inequality but also stimulated growth. Thus, departing from a vision that regards inequality as an inevitable consequence of the modern growth process, the alternative that sees a virtuous link between growth and equity could significantly alter the future path of actual development of a country. The virtuous cycle between growth and equity can only be established in a mixed economy requiring a judicious, sustained policy intervention to achieve social equilibirum in the political economy.

11.3 CONCLUDING REFLECTIONS

This chapter has argued that economic growth with equity is vital to long-term political and social stability in a democracy, and most importantly, to the very preservation of politically democratic institutions in countries already enjoying a full democracy as well as in countries in transition to it. As Lipset (1969, p. 27) notes, without the continued presence of a viable middle class in society, a genuine, stable democracy would be difficult to preserve. Sustained political democracy thus requires the maintenance of a well-developed and balanced economy, where the majority of the country's population remains in the middle class.

Although systematic cause–effect relationships between types of polity and economy are not easily discernible, history is replete with examples of societies with extreme bipolarization of groups that inevitably led to a rule of one group by another. Such instances of a group's usurping resources to preserve its privileged position have been witnessed in the past movements of Bolshevism, Nazism, or Tojoism. By the same token, economic prosperity shared by wider sectors and social groups in some East Asian experiences released impulses for broader political participation, leading to the path toward political democracy.

Economic equity must be seen as a prerequisite to sustained economic growth. There is telling evidence for the mutually reinforcing relationship that can exist between distributional equity and growth of the economy. Available evidence also tells us that blind pursuit of unfettered market systems is not helping to reduce economic inequalities in society. The search for equitable development calls for bold new visions of development strategy. For the emerging democracies in the developing world, unless better governance is complemented by more comprehensive and radical efforts for increased equality, there simply is no assurance that the tide of democracy will not be reversible. For other industrialized economies, the urgent question that must be addressed is how to attain balanced combinations of societal forces and processes that will sustain a reasonably equitable income distribution in a globally competitive market system.

Notes

1. An earlier version of this chapter was presented at a workshop on trade and development held in Innsbruck, Austria, in May 1996. Without implicating in the final product, the author acknowledges many constructive comments received from the participants in the workshop.

2. For estimates of economic growth rates required for the alleviation of poverty in developing countries, see Kim and Hanson (1982).

3. International Comparison of unemployment rate runs into the conceptual problems of the definition of unemployment. For instance, the World Bank's studies generally show much lower figures because the Bank does not include as 'unemployed' those 'not in the labour force'.

4. This is only in terms of official definition of unemployment, which does not take into account of real wages or 'discouraged' work force.

5. Both the Japanese and US data are the total household money income before taxes and exclusive of capital gains. Comparison of the trends using after-tax income shows similar results.

6. US Department of Commerce, Bureau of the Census.

7. From the perspective of an alternative measure, in 1980 the richest 25 per cent of the American population had 6.3 times as much income as the poorest 25 per cent. By 1992, the richest 25 per cent had eight times as much as the poorest 25 per cent.

8. In 1977, there were 660 000 families, each of which had an annual income of at least $310 000 for a household of four. The average pre-tax income of families in the top 1 per cent swelled to $560 000 annually from $315 000, for a 77 per cent gain in 12 years (in inflation-adjusted dollars).

9. The Congressional Budget Office annual report, 1992. Washington, DC. Also *New York Times*, 5 March 1992.

10. Mizoguich and Takayama (1984) claim that poverty in Japan is a sociological and political problem rather than an economic one. The existence of poverty pockets in the Japanese community is largely due to social segregation of ethnic minority and psychologically handicapped groups.

11. This indicates the proportion of the population whose income falls below a government-defined poverty level. The poverty income for the US household is defined on an annual basis at the level of three times its inflation-adjusted, normal expenditure on food.

12. U.S. Bureau of the Census. Also *New York Times*, 4 September 1992.

13. In 1988, the incidence of poverty was 10.1 per cent for whites; 31.6 per cent for blacks; and 26.8 per cent for Hispanics.

14. The HDI compares life expectancy, literacy rate, and other health-related variables.

15. According to the FBI classification scheme, violent crimes consist of murder, rape, robbery, and aggravated assault; and property crimes, burglary, larceny-theft, and motor vehicle theft.

16. A slight increase in the crime rate in the recent years of the bubble economy may be attributable to the changed economic conditions.

17. See also, United Nations (1993–4, p. 8).

18. Ibid., p. 18.

19. Refer to Appendix Table 11A.1.

20. Ryoshin Minami, *Nikkei Weekly*, 5 June 1995. p. 11.

21. Calculated from World Bank data for various years.

22. During the 1970s, the Korean government used earnings generated from industrial exports to actively promote the development of the agricultural sector.

23. Felix (1983) observed that income distribution in Latin America generally worsened during prosperity, when there were more gains to share, and levelled off or improved during depressions, when rents and profits tended to take relatively greater hits. Cyclical fluctuations in the distribution aside, income inequality in Latin America has risen secularly.

24. Many companies are currently laying off workers, including Dina, the heavy-truck manufacturer, and Pemex, the oil monopoly. Nissan and Ford have been slowing automobile production.

25. The government raised the minimum income by 140 per cent in May 1992 to appease the masses of the population who were improverished, but the wage-hike policy led to financial bankruptcy and accelerated inflation.
26. Interestingly, a negative correlation of growing inequality to growth is found in the context of the domestic economy. A recent study examining growth in income and employment in 85 US cities shows that cities with high levels of urban/suburban inequality have poorer growth rates of jobs and income than cities with milder income disparities (Albelda and Tilly 1995, p. 8).
27. Greater income equality leads to greater demand, since the propensity to spend tends to be greater with low-income families.
28. In contrast, the East Asian economies maintained relatively stable exchange rates over the last two to three decades, which eased the task of containing inflation and of limiting external debt to manageable proportions.

References

Abelda, R. and C. Tilly (1995) *Real World Macro – a Macroeconomic Reader from Dollars and Sense*, 12th edn (Worcester, Mass.: Saltus Press) pp. 6–9.

Agnew, J. (1987) *The United States in the World Economy: a regional geography* (New York: Cambridge University Press).

Ahn, K.S. (1991) 'Trends in the Size Distribution of Income in Korea'. *Collection of Economic Articles* (Seoul: Chung-Ang University Economic Research Institute).

—— and S.D. Kang (1990) 'Trends in and Determinants of the Size Distribution of Income in Korea', *Collection of Economic Articles* (Seoul: Chung-Ang University Economic Research Institute).

Alesina, A. and R. Perotti (1994) 'The Political Economy of Growth: A Critical Survey of the Recent Literature, *World Bank Economic Review*, vol. 8, no. 3, pp. 351–71.

Altimir, O. (1987) 'Income Distribution Statistics in Latin America and Their Reliability', *Review of Income and Wealth*, vol. 33, no. 2, pp. 111–56.

Atkins, A., L. Rainwater and T. Smeeding (1995) *Income Distribution in OECD Countries* (Paris: OECD).

Batra, R. (1993) *The Myth of Free Trade* (New York: Scribner's).

Bertrand, T.J. and F. Flatters (1971) 'Tariffs, Capital Accumulation, and Immiserizing Growth', *Journal of International Economics*, vol. 1, pp. 453–60.

Bigsten, A. (1983) *Income Distribution and Development: Thoery, Evidence & Evidence* (London: Heinemann).

Birdsall, N.D. Ross and R. Sabot (1995) 'Inequality and Growth Reconsidered: Lessons from East Asia', *World Bank Economic Review*, vol. 9, no. 3, pp. 477–508.

Bloom, D.E. and A. Brender (1993) 'Labor and the Emerging World Economy', *Population Bulletin*, vol. 48, no. 2 (October) pp. 2–39.

Bluestone, B. (1990) 'The Great U-Turn Revisited: Economic Restructuring, Jobs, and the Redistribution of Earnings', in J.D. Kasarda (ed.) *Jobs, Earnings, and Employment Growth Policies in the United States* (Boston: Kluwer).

Bluestone, B. and B. Harrison (1982) *Deindustrialization of America* (New York: Basic Books).

Booth, John A. (1991) 'Inequality and Rebellion in Central America', *Latin America Research Review*, vol. 26, no. 1, pp. 33–43.

Brecher, R.A. and C.F. Diaz-Alejandro (1977) 'Tariffs, Foreign Capital, and Immizerizing Growth', *Journal of International Economics*, vol. 7, pp. 317–22.

Callan, T. and B. Nolan (1994) *Poverty and Policy in Ireland* (Dublin: Gill & Macmillan).

Chenery, H. (1979) *Structural Change and Development Policy* (New York: Oxford University Press).

Chinn, D.L. (1977) 'Distributional Equality and Economic Growth: the Case of Taiwan', *Economic Development and Cultural Change* (October) pp. 65–79.

Choo, H.C. (1993) 'Income Distribution and Distributive Equity in Korea', in L.B. Krause and F.K. Park (eds) *Social Issues in Korea: Korean and American Perspectives* (Seoul: Korea Development Institute) pp. 335–60.

—— and D.M. Kim (1978) 'Probable Size Distribution of Income in Korea: Over Time and by Sectors', (Seoul: Korea Development Institute).

—— and J. Yoon (1984) 'Size Distribution of Income in Korea, 1982: Its Estimation and Sources of Change', *Korea Development Review*, vol. 6, pp. 2–18. (in Korean).

Chowdhury, A. and I. Islam (1993) *The Newly Industrialising Economies of East Asia* (London and New York: Routledge).

De Garcia, A. and G. Johnson (1988) *Evangelism and the Poor* (New York: United Nations, UNICEF Publications).

Dovring, F. (1991). *Inequality: the Political Economy of Income Distribution* (New York: Praeger).

ECLAC (Economic Commission for Latin America and the Caribbean) (1994) *Social Panorama of Latin America 1994* (Santiago, Chile).

Federal Bureau of Investigation (1992) *Uniform Crime Report* Washington, DC: US Government Press).

Felix, D. (1983) 'Income Distribution and the Quality of Life in Latin America: Patterns, Trends and Policy implications', *Latin American Research Review*, vol. 18, no. 2, pp. 3–34.

Fields, G.S. (1980) *Poverty, Inequality and Development* (Cambridge University Press).

Findlay, R. and S. Wellisz (1993) *Five Small Open Economies* (Oxford University Press).

Goldin I.,O. Knudsen and D. van der Mensbrugghe (1993) *Trade Liberalization: Global Economic Implications* (Paris and Washington, DC: OECD/World Bank.

Freeman, R.B. (1994) 'Crime and the Job Market', National Bureau of Economic Research Working Paper no. 4910. (Washington, DC).

Glyn, A. and D. Miliband (1994) *Paying for Inequality: The Economic Cost of Social Injustice* (London: the Institute for Public Policy Research).

Harvard School of Public Health (1988) *Hunger in America: The Growing Epidemic*, Report by Physicians, Task Force (Cambridge, Mass.: Harvard University Press).

Inter-American Development Bank (1994) *Annual Report* (Washington, DC).

International Labour Organization (ILO) (1995) *World Employment 1995* (Geneva).

Johnson, H.G. (1967) 'The Possibilities of Income Losses from Increased Efficiency or Factor Accumulation in the Presence of Tariffs', *Economic Journal* (March) pp. 151–4.

Kennedy, K.A., T. Giblin and D. McHugh (1988) *Economic Development of Ireland in the Twentieth Century* (London: Routledge).

Kim, K.S. (1991) 'The Political Economy of Foreign Trade, Industry and Basic Needs in Mexico; Issues and Strategies', in B.W. Poulson *et al.* (eds) *International Economic Integration: Lessons from the 1980s and Prospects for the 1990s* (University of Colorado Economic Institute) pp. 630–45.

—— (1995) 'The Korean Miracle (1962–80) Revisited: Myths and Realities in Strategies and Development', in H. Stein (ed.) *Asian Industrialization and Africa – Studies in Policy Alternatives to Structural Adjustment* (New York: St. Martin's Press) pp. 87–144.

—— and J. Hanson (1982) 'Equitable, Productive Employment Targets for the International Development Strategy', *World Development* vol. 10, no. 5, pp. 417–27.

Koster, M.H. and M.N. Ross (1988) *The Quality of Jobs: Evidence from Distributions of Annual Earnings and Hourly Wages* (Washington, DC: American Enterprise Institute).

Kuznets, S, (1955) 'Economic Growth and Income Inequality', *American Economic Review* vol. 45 (March) pp. 1–28.

Lazaroff, L. (1995) 'So Near to Meltdown', *World Business* (Spring) pp. 48–9.

Lechner, N. (1992) 'El debate sobre Estado y mercado', *Policy Studies Series*, 19 (FLACSO labour report) (Chile: Santiago).

Lee, J.S. (1990) 'Land Speculation in Korea: Causes, Economic Impact and a Proposal for Institutional Reforms', *Korean Economic Review* (Winter).

Lipset, S.M. (1969) *Political Man* (New York: Doubleday).

Michaely, M., D. Papageorgiou and A.M. Chokski (1991) *Liberalizing Foreign Trade: Lessons of Experience in the Developing World*, (Cambridge, Mass.: Blackwell).

Minami, R. (1986) *The Economic Development of Japan – A Quantitative Study* (London: Macmillan).

—— K.S. Kim and H. Yuzawa (1994) 'Long-term Trends in income distribution (in Japan) – Inferences and anlysis', *Keizai Kenkyu*, vol. 44, no. 4, pp. 351–64 (in Japanese).

Mizoguchi, T. (1992) 'Income Distribution in Asia', Discussion Paper, Hitotsubashi University (in Japanese).

—— N. Takayama (1984) *Equity and Poverty under Rapid Economic Growth: Japanese Experience* (Tokyo: Kinokuniya).

Muller, E.N. (1988) 'Democracy, Economic Development, and Income Inequality', *American Sociological Review*, vol. 53 (February) pp. 50–68.

Murphy, K. and F. Welch (1992) 'The Structure of Wages', *Quarterly Journal of Economics*, vol. 107, no. 1 (February) pp. 215–26.

Persson, T. and G. Tabellini (1994) 'Is Inequality Harmful for Growth?' *American Economic Review*, vol. 84, no. 3, pp. 600–21.

PREAL C, (Regional Employment Program for Latin America and the Caribbean) (1990 a) 'Informal Sector', Working paper no. 349 (Santiago, Chile).

—— (1990b) 'Employment and Equity: the Challenge of the 1990s', Working paper no. 354 (Santiago, Chile).

Richardson, D.J. (1995) 'Income Inequality and Trade: How to Think, What to Conclude', *Journal of Economic Perspectives* vol. 9, no. 3, (Summer) pp. 33–55.

Rothman, J. (1995) 'The New Sexenio', *Marketing Management* (June) pp. 41.

Sachs, J. (1985) 'External Debt and Macroeconomic Pefformance in Latin America and East Asia', in W.C. Brainard and G.L. Perry (eds) *Brookings Papers and Economic Activity* Washington, DC: Brookings Institution).

Singer, H.W. (1975) *The Strategy of International Development* (London: Macmillan).

Squire, L. (1981) *Employment Policy in Developing Countries: A Survey of Issues and Evidence* (New York: Oxford University Press).

Stocker, H. (1994) 'Changes in the International Distribution of Income', paper presented to the Kellogg Institute, University of Notre Dame (November).

United Nations (Department of Public Information) *Africa Recovery*, vol. 3/4 (December 1993– March 1994).

United Nations Development Programme (1990) *Humand Development Report* (New York: Oxford University Press).

Wood, Adrian (1994) *North–South Trade, Employment, and Inequality: changing fortunes in a skill-driven world.* (Cambridge: Oxford University Press).

—— (1995) 'How Trade Hurt Unskilled Workers', *Journal of Economic Perspectives* vol. 9, no. 3 (Summer) pp. 57–80.

World Bank (1990) *World Bank Annual Report* (Washington, DC).

—— (1991) *World Development Report 1991* (New York: Oxford University Press)

—— (1992) *World Development Report* (New York: Oxford University Press).

—— (1993) *The East Asian Miracle* (New York: Oxford University Press).

—— (1994) *World Development Report* (New York: Oxford University Press).

Appendix 11A.1

Table 11A.1   Selected economies in the ESCAP region, per capita and household incomes and distribution

| | GNP per capita ($US) | | GDP per capita of lowest 40 per cent of households ($US) 1987 | Year | % share of household income by quintiles[a] | | | | |
	1980	1988			Lowest 20 per cent	Second quintile	Third quintile	Fourth quintile	Highest 20 per cent
Developed economies									
Australia	10 270	12 340	4 270	1985	4.4	11.1	17.5	24.8	42.2
Japan	9 870	21 020	8 630	1979	8.7	13.2	17.5	23.1	37.5
New Zealand	6 910	10 000	3 080	1981	5.1	10.8	16.2	23.2	44.7
Developing economies									
China	290	330	—		—	—	—	—	—
Hong Kong	5 210	9 220	3 270	1980	5.4	10.8	15.2	21.6	47.0
India	220	340	120	1983	8.1	12.3	16.3	22.0	41.4
Indonesia	480	440	160	1987	8.8	12.4	16.0	21.5	41.3
Iran, Islamic Republic of	—	—	—		—	—	—	—	—
Malaysia	1 680	1 940	510	1987	4.6	9.3	13.9	21.2	51.2
Pakistan	290	350	—	1984–5	7.8	11.2	15.0	20.6	45.6
Papua New Guinea	760	810	—		—	—	—	—	—
Philippines	700	630	120	1985	5.5	9.7	14.8	22.0	48.0
Republic of Korea	1 620	3 600	—		—	—	—	—	—
Singapore	4 570	9 070	1 200	1982–3	5.1	9.9	14.6	21.4	48.9
Sri Lanka	260	420	160	1985–6	4.8	8.5	12.1	18.4	56.1
Thailand	670	1 000	320		—	—	—	—	—

227

Table 11A.1 (Continued)

	GNP per capita ($US)		GDP per capita of lowest 40 per cent of households ($US)		% share of household income by quintiles[a]				
	1980	1988	Year	1987	Lowest 20 per cent	Second quintile	Third quintile	Fourth quintile	Highest 20 per cent
Least developed countries									
Afghanistan	—	250[b]		—					—
Bangladesh	140	170	1981–2	70	9.3	13.1	16.8	21.8	39.0
Bhutan	—	180		—	—	—	—	—	—
Lao People's Democratic Republic	—	180		—	—	—	—	—	—
Myanmar	180	260[c]		—	—	—	—	—	—
Nepal	130	180		—	—	—	—	—	—

Notes:
[a] Years vary from 1985–7
[b] 1985
[c] 1987

Sources: World Bank, *World Development Report 1990* (New York, Oxford University Press, 1990), and *World Tables 1987*, 4th edn.

Table 11A.2 Latin America (12 countries, urban areas): percentage variations in real average per capita income of households of different strata, 1980–92

	Argentina (Buenos Aires)	Bolivia	Brazil	Chile	Colombia	Costa Rica	Honduras	Mexico	Panama	Paraguay (Asunción)	Uruguay	Venezuela
Lower stratum (40% poorest)												
% variation (1980–90)	-34	—	-19	—	57	-18	—	-12	-8	—	-15	-37
% variation (1990–2)	32	20	—	19	-12	-7	-4	12	0	-2	22	4
% variation (1980–92)	-13	—	—	—	38	-24	—	-1	-8	—	4	-35
Average per capita income in 1992[b]	1.40	0.52	0.56[c]	0.81	0.58	0.84	0.28	0.79	0.64[d]	0.65	1.51	0.71
Lower middle stratum (deciles 5, 6 and 7)												
% variation (1980–90)	-29	—	-9	—	-8	-12	—	-12	-10	—	-15	-31
% variation (1990–2)	43	10	—	15	-4	-8	-4	16	2	7	22	4
% variation (1980–92)	2	—	—	—	-12	-19	—	2	-8	—	4	-28
Average per capita income in 1992[b]	3.25	1.28	1.65[c]	1.89	1.57	1.99	0.76	1.81	1.86[d]	1.54	3.11	1.66
Upper middle stratum (deciles 8 and 9)												
% variation (1980–90)	-21	—	0	—	-17	-15	—	-2	-4	—	-20	-28
% variation (1990–2)	33	5	—	14	-5	-5	-6	16	2	6	18	7
% variation (1980–92)	5	—	—	—	-21	-19	—	14	-2	—	-6	-23
Average per capita income in 1992[b]	6.23	2.62	4.18[c]	3.76	3.42	3.58	1.63	3.66	3.97[d]	2.89	5.18	3.25

Table 11A.2 (Continued)

	Argentina (Buenos Aires)	Bolivia	Brazil	Chile	Colombia	Costa Rica	Honduras	Mexico	Panama	Paraguay (Asunción)	Uruguay	Venezuela
Upper stratum (richest 10%)												
% variation (1980–90)	–10	—	5	—	7	–8	—	41	34	—	–11	–2
% variation (1990–2)	25	30	—	28	1	5	–9	7	–11	9	1	5
% variation (1980–92)	13	—	—	—	8	–3	—	51	19	—	–10	3
Average per capita income in 1992[b]	18.36	9.55	15.37[c]	12.77	10.52	8.55	4.96	11.43	11.64[d]	7.23	11.83	8.44
All households												
% variation (1980–90)	–22	—	–2	—	26	–13	—	9	8	—	–5	–25
% variation (1990–2)	29	18	—	19	–5	–3	–8	8	–5	5	14	5
% variation (1980–92)	1	—	—	—	20	–16	—	18	3	—	8	–21
Average per capita income in 1992[b]	4.62	2.08	3.16[c]	2.92	2.44	2.49	1.16	2.74	2.72[d]	2.02	3.73	2.30

Source: ECLAC, on the basis of special tabulations of data from household surveys in the countries.

[a] Data correspond to 1994, 1989 and 1982.
[b] As a multiple of the respective per caput poverty lines.
[c] Corresponds to 1990.
[d] Corresponds to 1991

12 Food Aid, North–South Trade, and the Prebisch–Singer Thesis

Kunibert Raffer

12.1 INTRODUCTION

Looking at the numerous contributions of Sir Hans Singer to development economics, two main strands of research can be discerned:

1. his seminal work on the empirical effects of trade on the South, named the Prebisch–Singer thesis after the two economists who rocked the boat of professional complacency exposing a disturbing contradiction between theoretical expectations and practical outcome. After explaining the mechanisms leading to an unequal international distribution of gains between countries (Singer 1950), Sir Hans has played a leading role in the debate on whether a falling trend in Southern net barter terms of trade can be proven by statistical methods, which has engaged economists and statisticians from the 1940s to this very day.
2. his contributions to the issue of food aid.

At first sight these two strands may seem unconnected. Closer scrutiny, however, proves this *prima facie* perception to be wrong. As appropriate for a *Festschrift*, this chapter will elaborate how Sir Hans's interest in food aid connects logically to the Prebisch–Singer Thesis. Seen from this perspective the paper will analyse two current relevant issues: the relation of developmental food aid and emergency food aid within the evolution of total aid, and the role of food aid in the new trade environment resulting from the Final Act of the Uruguay Round. Both are topics to which Sir Hans has very actively contributed. The last section proposes changing our agrarian policies that determine present food aid.

230

12.2 FOOD AID AND THE PREBISCH-SINGER THESIS

Placing food imports, including food aid, within the framework of the Prebisch–Singer thesis makes it necessary to present the relevant points briefly. The unequal distribution of gains between countries (Singer, 1950), or the siphoning off of productivity gains by the North as it was also called by (Prebisch, 1949) are explained by the authors in a perfectly traditional way, mostly by excess demand and excess supply. Briefly put, the periphery (South) has an excess demand for goods needed for development, which can only be obtained in the centre (North). At the same time it can only export relatively few products, which under prevailing market conditions tends to create excess supply. This disequilibrium is exacerbated in the long run because demand for raw materials – and thus for exports by the South – does not grow in line with GSP growth. Discussing the Thesis one must not forget that Southern exports at the end of the 1940s consisted exclusively of raw materials. The present large Southern exporters of manufactures, such as the so-called 'dragons' or 'tigers', did not yet exist. As a historical footnote it might be added that ruling expert opinion considered East Asia a hopeless case at that time. It should also be noted that Sir Hans (Singer, 1986, p. 6) qualified South Korea as having 'in fact followed a policy … on the general lines which Prebisch developed in CEPAL. Many South Korean economists are very conscious of that heritage.' In contrast to often voiced criticism, the unexpected East Asian success did not prove the ideas of Prebisch and Singer wrong.

This inherent developmental disequilibrium between developmental needs and financial means results in falling terms of trade. Factors contributing to falling net barter terms of trade – sometimes wrongly called different 'versions' of the Prebisch–Singer thesis – are:

- *low income elasticity of commodity exports* Northern demand for raw materials increases less than GDP-growth, limiting growth prospects of Southern exports. While this view was hotly attacked initially, it has since been generally accepted, finally, after some 40 years even by the IMF (1987, p. 218) and the IBRD (1987, p. 18). Nowadays this fact is often referred to as the 'delinking of growth and raw material demand'. Strong expansion of raw material exports thus tends to create excess supply.
- *Low elasticities of demand* Lower prices of periphery exports do not stimulate demand sufficiently to make up for lost revenues.

- *necessary imports such as machinery, to promote development, can only be imported from the centre*   In contrast to the centre the periphery's income elasticity of imports is high. Developmental needs result in excess demand.
- *cultural dependence, or the use of resources for luxury consumption* This increases total Southern demand while importing products of little or no use for the country's development. Raúl Prebisch (1976, p. 70) strongly criticized this 'imitation of consumption patterns of the centre' and the attitude 'to ape certain forms of conspicuous consumption' as harmful to capital accumulation and development.
- *oversupply of labour in the periphery*   This keeps wages down, a point elaborated in more detail by Sir W. Arthur Lewis later on.
- *(absence of) market power of factors of production*   Workers (trade unions) and entrepreneurs in the North have sufficient market power to keep Northern prices from falling along with technical progress. The lack of such power in the periphery forces their prices down. This 'para-market' assumption was strongly attacked by critics (cf. Spraos 1983, pp. 23 f.). Considering that orthodox economists had blamed the Great Depression of the 1930s on union power and stickiness of wages this is certainly surprising. International prices kept above their competitive market level increase the costs of imports by (and balance of payments deficits of) the periphery.
- *protection by the centre restricts export outlets*   This increases the pressure of surplus labour in the South, giving additional force to the deteriorating trend. It increases market disequilibria created by the disparity of export possibilities and import needs of the South. Reducing this gap, protectionism by the periphery 'is, up to a certain point, the instrument of correcting the effects of the disparity' between North and South (Prebisch 1959, p. 264), an equilibrating factor.
- *debt pressure*   This was added more recently by Singer (1991a) as an important factor depressing the net barter terms of trade of indebted countries – the need to service debts forcing the periphery to export at any cost.

There exist several ways of closing the persistent gap between needs and financial capabilities, all of them mentioned by Prebisch and Singer: more exports (subsidized or not), import substitution and protection (where appropriate) or inflows of financial resources. Irrespective of how inflows in the form of commercial loans or foreign direct investment are judged, neither commercial lending nor foreign direct investments (practically exclusively in mining and plantations) were realistic options until the

1970s. Given the likely evolution of export incomes aid was the only possible source during the 1940s and 1950s. Sir Hans himself connected the terms of trade controversy to aid:

> which was in fact the natural avenue to which the interest of the United Nations, and my own with it, turned in those years as a result of trade pessimism. Hence the idea of the need for soft financing for development was born and developed at the same time as the work on the terms of trade, with a clear intellectual link between the two. (Singer 1984, p. 296)

Inspired by the success of the Marshall Plan – which has also influenced Sir Hans's thinking – aid was indeed widely seen as the main instrument to fill the gap created by trade imbalances. The Plan's success inspired the attempts to set up a (Special) UN Fund for Economic Development (S)UNFED to administer large-scale soft aid. This idea was successfully prevented by its opponents, most notably the International Bank for Reconstruction and Development (IBRD), which opposed both the involvement of the UN in financial aid and the principle of soft aid (Singer 1989, p. 8). This opposition was, by the way, dropped when the IBRD itself was to get its own soft aid window, the International Development Association, later on.

The European Recovery Programme, as the Marshall Plan was officially called, was to a large extend commodity aid, mostly in the form of food aid: 'food, animal feed, fertilisers accounted for 49 per cent of all procurements in the early phases of the Marshall Plan, declining in the later phases but still representing 30 per cent overall' (Raffer and Singer 1996, p. 60). The Marshall Plan performed a pioneering role in creating a body of operating principles and procedures for subsequent aid to the South. Practices in food aid administration, such as counterpart funds introduced by the Plan have in large measure continued until the present day.

While the option of soft financing for the South by the UN was turned down, a transfer of resources via food aid was quite realistic. The US Agricultural Act of 1949 allowed the use of surplus agricultural produce as food aid. In 1954 the Agricultural Trade Development and Assistance Act (more widely known by its number, PL480) provided the basic legal and institutional framework on which US food aid, although with changes, still rests today. It 'established a relationship between US domestic agricultural interests and foreign aid that has shaped the country's food aid policies and programmes' (Shaw and Clay 1993, p. 215). So, while concessional finance was difficult to get, food aid was easier to obtain. Singer

(1994a, p. 51) explains this very succinctly: 'if you talk about financial aid, you are the taxpayer's enemy, if you talk about food aid, you are the farmer's friend', an important distinction in OECD countries with strong agrarian lobbies.

While food aid may be seen as a substitute for soft financing before the principle of concessional resources was generally accepted by the donor community, it was itself not substituted by soft financing. Food aid has thus a 'precious element of additionality' (Singer 1994b, p. 210), which means that for reasons of agrarian policies it has usually been given in addition to other aid, increasing the North–South flow of resources. This element of additionality shows in the correlation between financial aid and food aid, which 'is positive rather than negative' (Singer 1994b, p. 209).

As the case of the UK illustrates, food aid need not always be additional (Singer 1991b, p. 114). In contrast to most other donors, food and other aid are financed from the same budget in Britain, so that each pound spent on food competes directly with other forms of aid. The absence of major national food surpluses is one further reason for scepticism with regard to food aid and the British attitude to concentrate food aid on emergencies in a rather narrow sense of the word. But this view is not shared by other donors where both administrative structures and agricultural production differ. Thus the present absurd systems of agrarian policies pursued by the USA, the EU or Japan, have not only several negative impacts on the South but at least one small positive side-effect on the world's poor.

Due to historical realities food aid emerged as the prime option to reduce the disequilibrium created by developmental needs and insufficient export revenues. In practice food aid and non-food aid can be perfect substitutes. So-called programme food aid may be an indirect form of financial aid allowing foreign exchange to be freed and used for other purposes than food imports. Due to fungibility food aid may in fact be helpful in financing practically any activity, unfortunately also to finance arms and weaponry (cf. Singer *et al.*, 1987, p. 93).

It should also be mentioned that donors often combine hardly altruistic motivations with food aid. Developing new markets for the USA was named as one of the main goals of PL480 under Title I. Also, 'purchase of strategic and critical materials' and 'procurement of strategic and military equipment' (Shaw and Clay 1993, p. 216) were expressly-stated goals – one but by no means the only example of the desire of donor governments to use aid for military objectives or to disguise military expenditures as aid (cf. Raffer and Singer, 1996). PL480 resources used to buy weapons did in fact turn up as development assistance in OECD aid statistics.

Providing appropriate types of food at concessional terms or as grants does not only reduce the foreign exchange gap created by developmental needs, but can also be specifically targeted to protect the poor. It has the advantage of being able to serve 'a double purpose' (Singer 1994a, p. 65). If sold domestically for local currency or used to finance 'food for work' programmes, it both feeds the hungry by employing them and finances improvements in agricultural production or necessary infrastructure, which finally allows the bringing of local produce to the consumers. In many poor countries infrastructure hinders both the marketing of food and the distribution of food aid, causing high internal transport costs (Singer *et al.*, 1987, p. 146) as well as delayed deliveries. The fact that deficient transport facilities keep supply elasticities of producing farmers relatively inelastic is unfortunately too often disregarded, particularly so by Bretton Woods-type adjustment programmes. To illustrate the deficiency of local infrastructure with the example of Tanzania: 'The facilities for intra-regional transport have been so bad that famine could occur in one area, while no food could be provided from another area with a surplus, even when the distance was below 100 km' (Holm 1994, p. 106).

Naturally, governments can become dependent on programme food aid, which can be at least as bad as dependence on other forms of aid. Some countries have covered such large shares of their budgets from the sale of food aid that the continued delivery of food to be sold domestically becomes a critical condition for securing normal government activities. Bangladesh, where proceeds from selling food aid provided about 25 to 30 per cent of total government revenue (Singer 1994a, p. 65) is a good example. However, food aid is certainly not the only case of 'Dutch disease' in the foreign aid business.

While an outspoken advocate of food aid, Sir Hans has never been uncritical. He has always drawn attention to its problems and shortcomings – which are basically problems of implementation – most recently in a chapter discussing the pros and cons of food aid (Raffer and Singer 1996, pp. 73ff.).

The Marshall Plan's success has been repeatedly quoted by Sir Hans to prove that food aid can be extremely successful if applied judiciously (see, for example, Singer *et al.*, 1987; Singer, 1994a, p. 67). In several of his publications he has pointed out that the biggest recipients of food aid were Western Europe (in the days of the Marshall Plan), India (under PL480 during 1955–70), South Korea, Israel or Greece. As domestic food production has increased quite vigorously in all these countries food aid need not harm or destroy domestic agriculture. In India, for example, food aid at the very least has not prevented the Green Revolution in the Punjab.

On the contrary – he argued – the additional resources provided by food aid and the revenue derived by the Indian government from the sale of food aid have helped to finance the investments in irrigation, transport, extension services, or research, which were the necessary infrastructure for the Green Revolution.

This view is supported by the findings of Shaw and Clay (1993), who assessed impact of food aid on countries in Asia, Latin America, and Africa:

> The experience of the three Asian countries described in this volume, in moving towards self-sufficiency, are consistent with the widespread professional view of practitioners and economists that disincentive effects are avoidable .... (Singer *et al.*, 1987). Nevertheless, as the Bangladesh case illustrates, there are potential problems in making the transition to self-sufficiency in an economy where food aid has an important role in sustaining anti-poverty and food security programmes. Scrutinized more closely, however, the eight studies of recipient countries included in this book suggest collectively that there is little evidence of negative impacts.

There is yet another root of Sir Hans's interest in food aid. His seminal paper on the international distribution of gains from trade (Singer, 1950, p. 481) singled out food imports at commercial prices as one important impediment to development:

> The major proportion of the imports of the underdeveloped countries is in fact made up of manufactured food (especially in overpopulated underdeveloped countries), textile manufactures, and manufactured consumer goods. The prices of the type of food imported by the underdeveloped countries, and particularly the prices of textile manufactures, have risen so heavily in the immediate postwar period that any advantage which the underdeveloped countries might have enjoyed in the postwar period from favourable prices realized on primary commodities and low prices for capital goods has been wiped out.

Research on food aid followed logically from the Prebisch–Singer thesis, as well as Sir Hans's continual interest in distributive justice (Singer, 1984, p. 280). It can provide a nutritional safety net to the poor, or – paraphrasing A. Sen – 'entitle' them to food. As pointed out by the advocates of basic needs, proper nutritional standards allow people to develop their potentials fully and to contribute better towards development.

By combining the issue of North–South trade with food aid Sir Hans has thus overcome one main criticism of traditional development economics made by A. Sen (1983, p. 754), well ahead of many other economists:

Perhaps the most important thematic deficiency of traditional development economics is its concentration on national product, aggregate income and total supply of particular goods rather than on 'entitlements' of people and the 'capabilities' these entitlements generate. Ultimately, the process of development has to be concerned with what people can or cannot do, e.g. whether they can live long, escape avoidable morbidity, be well nourished, be able to read and write and to communicate, take part in literary pursuits, and so forth.

12.3 TOWARDS A NEW PARADIGM

Food aid has always been used both in emergencies and for longer-term developmental purposes. Emergency food aid was originally assumed to be a very small part of food aid, 'it was no more than 10 per cent or so of total food aid up to about ten years ago. But since then emergency food aid has emerged as one of the main uses of food aid' amounting to 'half or more of total food aid' (Singer, 1994a, p. 53). In other words, the increase of food aid by 83.7 per cent in nominal terms between 1983/4 and 1994 (OECD, 1996, p. A37) resulted more or less from higher emergency food aid. Nevertheless, food aid declined as a percentage of total Official Development Assistance (ODA) over these years. Total ODA by the DAC itself fell drastically in 1993, remaining well below the nominal level of 1992 in 1994.

Emergency and distress relief (defined as excluding emergency food aid by the OECD 1996, p. A4), on the other hand, increased dramatically during the same period, amounting in 1994 to slightly more than 12 times the nominal value of 1983–4, increasing from about one per cent to nearly 5.9 per cent of total ODA. The last *Chairman's Report* (OECD, 1996, p. 93) speaks of an 'all-time high' of emergency aid, including aid to refugees and food aid.

The evolution of food aid is embedded in a general tendency of donors to divert ODA to purposes that less (or not at all) orientated towards development. According to the Report 'an increasing number of DAC countries have been reporting expenditures on refugees who have arrived in their own countries' (OECD 1996, p. 95). A year before the OECD (1995, p. 84) saw aid to refugees and disaster relief as 'extreme examples of the way circumstances can thwart intentions', recalling that '[T]he definition of ODA requires that, to be eligible for inclusion, resources should be "for the economic development and welfare of developing countries"'.

The OECD (1995, p. 118) points out that while the definition of ODA has not changed for over 25 years 'changes in interpretation have tended to broaden the scope of the concept'. If donors had not decided to increase the coverage of activities subsumed under ODA, their present performance would be noticeably worse. The concept of development aid has been watered down by donors boosting ODA statistics by including sums with doubtful or no noticeable developmental impact (see Raffer and Singer, 1996, pp. 19f.). Real development aid has declined more sharply than official statistics suggest. Furthermore, 'debt forgiveness' has also risen rapidly. Debt reductions and aid by bilateral donors are frequently used to bail out international financial institutions, such as the IBRD or the IMF. Some reductions covered bilateral loans for failed aid projects. This share of ODA does not finance new and useful projects. To the extent that these debt reductions are simply used to reduce arrears without overcoming the country's debt overhang – which is deplorably often the case – they do not even increase the amount of resources available to the debtor for purposes of development.

While total ODA expressed as GSP percentages has been declining for some time and even nominal ODA fell sharply between 1992 and 1993 without recovering to its 1992 level in 1994, increasing shares of aid are used for purposes which the OECD itself does not consider to be the intended use of ODA. Under present conditions emergency relief has started to crowd out real aid to development, not least because of the way disasters are covered by the media. Funds for purely developmental actions are harder to obtain – the developmental function of aid, reducing the structural disequilibrium shown by Prebisch and Singer – is reduced.

A decade ago Singer *et al.* (1987, p. 86) saw a need to build upon some of the generous responses to calamities to link relief to development by tackling the problems that caused the disaster or by introducing resource-building activities into palliative actions. The fact that grants for purely developmental purposes became harder to obtain, was seen as one reason for bridging the gap between relief and development. Sir Hans (Singer 1994b, p. 207) therefore advocated directing food aid at the 'roots of poverty of which the acute emergency is more a symptom than a cause .... food aid should therefore be directed at creating situations in which emergencies either do not occur or can be coped with without the hectic Geldof-type humanitarian appeal.'

He demanded a wider definition of emergency, including the permanent emergency of underdevelopment, and later on a new aid paradigm, which combines emergency aid and development aid in a closed circle (Raffer and Singer, 1996, p. 195ff.). This paradigm of the relief–development continuum is superior to the conventional paradigm in which disasters are treated as separate interruptions of the development process during which all 'normal' aid would be suspended. By contrast, preventive action must be taken to make emergency less likely to happen, and actual relief action should be combined as much as possible with development work. The next 'normal' development programme after peace has been restored or after the effects of a natural disaster have been overcome should pay special attention to reducing vulnerability to future disasters. Aid, including food aid, should be focused again on reducing the structural disequlibrium of development.

Aid according this new paradigm would, of course, require substantial changes of present ODA policies, which are strongly determined by donors' self-interests, as well as the desire to boost low figures to less embarrassing though still low levels (see Raffer and Singer, 1996). It does require redirecting ODA – or at least substantial shares of it – towards tackling the needs of recipients, particularly of the poor in recipient countries. At a time when further declines in aid are foreseeable – even generous donors such as Sweden are about to cut their financial commitments – it is all the more important that remaining food and non-food aid should concentrate on safeguarding the interests of vulnerable groups, not only on feeding them during acute emergencies but also on enabling them to engage in their countries' economic and social development. Translating Sir Hans's new aid paradigm into practical work provides a useful guideline for doing precisely this. It combines well with other proposals to improve the quality of ODA, such as the UNDP's 20:20 compact or Paul Streeten's (1994, p. 13) demand to help the victims of transition and to cushion the frictions of social and economic changes on those who would otherwise suffer unduly. Like these or other suggested changes to present ODA practice (see Raffer and Singer, 1996, pp. 195ff.) Sir Hans's new paradigm will need strong support against Northern export lobbies and other self-interests of donors. Even after the conclusion of the Uruguay Round food aid might be relatively easier to mobilize due to agrarian interests within OECD countries.

12.4   THE URUGUAY ROUND AND BEYOND

The Final Act of the Uruguay Round brought about substantial changes in the framework of international trade (see Raffer 1995), which are likely to increase the developmental foreign exchange gap described by the Prebisch–Singer thesis. The new rules deprive the South of important policy options available to successful 'tiger' economies. The treaty on Trade Related Investment Measures (TRIMs) enforces the obligation of national treatment, forbidding the use national laws as a bargaining chip when negotiating with transnational enterprises or fostering its own infant industry by demanding the use of domestic inputs in production. No clear definition of a TRIM is provided, but the Agreement's annex explicitly prohibits any requirements of using local inputs, restricting a foreign enterprise's access to foreign exchange in percentages of inflows attributable to it, or any export restrictions.

Agrarian trade was of particular interest to the South affected either as food importers or exporters. Southern exporters have lost substantial amounts due to heavy subsidies by both the EC and the USA destroying so-called 'world market' prices completely. The final result, based on the Blair House agreement, is a far cry from the initial US proposals supported by the South, and critics see potential benefits, particularly with regard to temperate farm products such as cereals and meat, as very limited. Agreed cuts in subsidies remain very limited in scope and subject to a phasing mechanism allowing up to nine years for implementation.

Nevertheless the Agreement of Agriculture is expected to have substantial effects on food aid and food importers. Fewer subsidies of agrarian exports raise food prices for importers that are bound to suffer. In theory higher prices should be good news to Southern food exporters. In practice, though, one may doubt whether the watered-down rules will actually be very helpful to these countries, once they are implemented. They are likely to prove insufficient to establish a level playing field.

Net food importers in the South facing increased import bills at a time of scarce convertible currency will be very adversely affected. Estimates of the likely effects vary. According to UNCTAD (1995, p. 23) annual losses of $300 million to $600 million from higher food prices and the erosion of trade preferences have to be expected for the Least Developed Countries.

Article 16 of the Agreement on Agriculture demands measures in favour of net-importing developing countries and Least Developed Countries as provided for within the Decision on Measures Concerning the Possible Negative Effects of the Reform Programme on Least-Developed and Net Food-Importing Developing Countries. This Decision recognizes 'negative effects in terms of the availability of adequate supplies of basic foodstuffs from external sources on reasonable terms and conditions, including short-term difficulties in financing normal levels of commercial imports of basic foodstuffs.' The main solution indicated is drawing money 'in the context of adjustment programmes', which means increasing the strong dependence of debtor countries on the IMF and the IBRD. Financing more expensive food imports by increased borrowing is not necessarily good advice to a debt-ridden poor country already unable to service debts according to schedule and amassing huge arrears. Sub-Saharan Africa, the region expected to be most severely affected by higher food prices, already had arrears of more than five times the amount of debt service actually paid, according to IBRD-data (see Raffer, forthcoming). New loans for consumptive purposes are certainly not likely to alleviate this problem. In contrast to the wording of the Agreement, the difficulties of most food importers will not be short-term problems – comparable to a phase of illiquidity that can be overcome quickly – but add to the countries' overindebtment.

Furthermore, differential treatment of developing countries regarding export credits and consideration by industrialized countries to improve agricultural productivity and infrastructure by aid were agreed on. But it must be questioned whether donors are really going to reduce their own export outlets in net-importing developing countries by subsidizing competing agricultural production there. The evolution of DAC-aid to Southern agriculture rather confirms scepticism. Analysing the reduced share of agriculture in bilateral ODA, the OECD (1996, p. 93) concludes: 'Depressed food grain prices and surpluses of many agricultural commodities in the late 1980s and early 1990s may also have curbed donors' interest in directing resources to agriculture.'

Article 10.4 of the Agreement on Agriculture, meant to avoid food aid being used to circumvent export subsidy commitments, expresses a clear concern for retaining export markets. The permission to subsidize the destruction of food ('definitive permanent disposal' of livestock) pursuant to para. 9(b) of Annex 2 also indicates a clear interest in managing the market. Southern countries would thus be well advised to use exemptions such as that for the purpose of food security or the provision of foodstuffs at subsidised prices (the latter is considered to be in conformity with para. 4 of Annex 2 by the text) as well as they can. The general problem apart, how such programmes can be implemented with 'no, or at most minimal, trade distorting effects or effects on production' (Annex 2, para. 1), debt-ridden developing countries are unlikely to be able to finance such schemes on a level sufficient to safeguard food security.

Even the very limited reductions in subsidies now agreed on will increase food prices eventually. Sir Hans (Singer, 1994a) expects several effects of higher food prices:

- food aid will become more expensive, and surpluses from which food aid has been given will decline. Thus the willingness to give food aid may be reduced;
- the need for food aid will be increased;
- while there will be winners (such as food exporting Zimbabwe) and losers (net-importers), the latter will tend to be very poor countries. At present food aid is given, as Sir Hans points out, at the expense of Southern exporters both unable to give food aid and to subsidise exports down to the level determined by Northern exporters: 'They are the people who really pay for food aid' (ibid., p. 71). It remains to be seen, however, whether cuts in subsidies will be sufficient to allow Southern exporters to compete.

To protect poor importers Sir Hans (Singer, 1994a) proposed a doubling of the minimum commitment of food aid under the Food Aid Convention, which would bring the contractual minimum to 15 million tons in terms of cereals, the actual level at the time of signing of the Final Act. This demand would guarantee that the quantity of food aid is not reduced. Unfortunately it is unlikely to be accepted by donors, as the determination of the USA to cut food aid substantially highlights (Singer and Shaw, 1995, p. 4).

Higher prices automatically increase the statistical amount of food aid. Subsidized exports presently too hard to qualify as aid jump the hurdle of a 25 per cent grant element, simply because the commercial (reference) price is higher. Sir Hans worried about this fact, demanding 'proper definitions of food aid from that point of view' (ibid., p. 63). One way of avoiding this automaticity transforming exports into aid would be to increase the minimum grant element, agreeing that loans must not be more expensive than before. A minimum grant element of 25 per cent is equivalent to a 'non-grant' or commercial element (CE) of 75 per cent. This condition is satisfied if the new CE is 75 per cent or less of the present value obtained if the transaction had taken place at the 'base price' p_0, defined as the price before Uruguay Round-induced price increases. As base levels (such as of production) are already part and parcel of the Agreement on Agriculture, this proposal would not mean a fundamental change.

It would introduce an element of flexibility into the definition of food aid absent in the present ODA definition by abandoning the long-upheld minimum grant element 25 per cent as the constitutive element for ODA. While this may look like an important change on paper, its practical relevance is far more limited. Most food aid has been provided in the form of grants anyway, recently as much as about 85 per cent (Singer and Shaw,

1995, p. 5). Furthermore, the OECD recommends a grant element of at least 86 per cent for each member's total annual ODA, a target mostly surpassed by DAC members. Aid to Least Developed Countries, likely to have the largest need for food aid had average grant elements of 98.3 (bilateral) and 99.1 (multilateral) (OECD, 1996, p. A47). Although the grant element for ODA loans was only 59.9 on average during the biennium 1993–4, this means that relatively little ODA was actually given with the present minimum grant element.

Sometimes donors even refrain from recording flows qualifying as ODA although they would be technically entitled to do so unless the grant element is perceptibly higher than the minimum. Austria, for instance, a country often criticized for its practice of reporting export credits with a grant element of just above 25 per cent as ODA, decided in 1990 to report only export credits with a grant element of at least 40 per cent as ODA.

Demanding a higher grant element for food aid would thus have few practical effects, if any. On the other hand it would be well in line with Art. 10.4(c) demanding that food aid should be provided 'to the extent possible in grant form'. Increasing the minimum grant element would be one helpful step towards this goal.

Naturally, the effects of the Agreement on Agriculture on food aid depend critically on the evolution of surpluses. If surpluses remain stable or increase while restrictions on export subsidies actually reduce Northern export possibilities, food aid may even rise as the low-cost alternative to outlawed exports.

Singer and Shaw (1995, p. 12) see the Uruguay Round as an opportunity to use surpluses that cannot be exported any longer as food aid. But they also worry whether continued surpluses may tempt major food exporting countries to evade agreed policies, subsidizing exports in breach of the Agreement. At the moment it is still too early to say what will actually happen.

12.5 TOWARDS AN ALTERNATIVE APPROACH

While disincentive effects of food aid on recipient countries have been discussed widely, little has been said about disincentives for policymakers in the North, for whom food aid may provide a humanitarian cloak for their policies. Singer and Shaw draw attention to this link, pointing at 'the continuation of harmful agricultural policies on the grounds that some of the resulting surpluses could be disposed of as food aid' (ibid., p. 11).

From its very start, the US surplus disposal programme, food aid has always been associated with agrarian policies pursued in the North. This historic link often causes major tensions between agrarian interests of donors and developmental needs of recipients as Singer and Shaw (ibid.) point out. Summarizing the effect of our agrarian policies on the South, Sir Hans (Singer, 1991b, p. 120) concluded: 'irrational agricultural policies have outweighed any potential benefit even the food importers (some of whom would be food exporters or self-sufficient but for the CAP or similar US policies). The net effect is certainly harmful to developing countries.'

This assessment as well as the fact that food aid is not a significant causative factor in Northern agricultural policies but determined by them, poses the question whether these policies should not be changed. At present, though, both advocates and critics of food aid accept these policies as a fact of life (Singer, 1991b, p. 120). Instead of attacking the root 'some of the criticism of food aid seems to be misdirected in the sense that what the critics really mean to criticize (rightly) are the agricultural policies, such as the Common Agricultural Policy of the EU, which lead to the surpluses which in turn lead to food aid' (Raffer and Singer, 1996, p. 81).

For a short period at the beginning the Uruguay Round it appeared indeed thinkable that fundamental changes of Northern agrarian policies might be considered, a hope not vindicated by the watered-down outcome. One must therefore realistically assume that proposals for changes will not be welcome in the North. Nevertheless, an alternative scenario of Northern agricultural policies will be sketched very briefly. Naturally, it is both counterfactual and absolutely utopian at the moment. But encouraged by Sir Hans's strong criticism of present agrarian absurdities as well as guided once again (like Sir Hans before) by Jan Tinbergen's dictum that 'The idealists of today often turn out to be the realists of tomorrow' (UNDP, 1994, p. 88) I endeavour to do so all the same.

At present large sums are used every year to subsidize the production of 'butter' and 'meat mountains' or 'milk lakes'. Produced in large quantities food is at the same time of debatable quality. The tragedy of British beef is but one and at present the most prominent illustration. Cases of 'mad cow disease' have been reported in other European countries as well, although – for whatever reason – less frequently. According to the *International Herald Tribune* (2 April 1996, p. 3) the USA faces 'an avalanche of reports of tainted meat and poultry that have caused thousands of cases of illness and hundreds of deaths each year'. Even disregarding the effects of agrarian surpluses on the South, there is sufficient scope for change.

The basic idea I want to sketch is simple: divert payments under the Common Agricultural Policy (or similar schemes in other countries) to finance quality instead of quantity. At the same or even lower costs to the taxpayer products of superior quality could be produced if subsidies were used to support biologically and ecologically sound agricultural products with fewer chemical/poisonous residues. Subsidized production should be reduced to the domestic consumption level plus stocks necessary to guarantee secure supply and possibly food aid. Naturally this would go against powerful vested interests of the agro-commercial complex thriving on the present system and politicians supporting them. It would be a blow against a system which makes it 'economic' to transport potatoes from Northern Germany to Italy to have them washed and bring them back afterwards. It would reduce the many possibilities of making money in a more or less legal way at the cost of consumers, taxpayers and economic efficiency.

Reducing or abolishing the present form of rent-seeking in favour of a system using the same amount or less money to produce better quality should also be seen as an improvement by advocates of the free market. An nth best solution would be upgraded to an $(n-1)$th best solution. Money spent on the production of healthy, good quality meat is certainly preferable to subsidizing present mass production, even to people opposing subsidies as a matter of principle.

This fundamental change would bring considerable advantages to consumers, small peasants, Southern agricultural exporters, and possibly even the budgets of Northern countries:

- consumers would get better quality and less poison at the same if not a lower price;
- negative ecological effects of large-scale farming, especially intensive use of fertilisers, would be diminished;
- positive effects on small peasants and agrarian regions could be achieved;
- no additional costs to the budget, there might even be a potential for savings;
- declining agricultural surpluses in favour of higher quality and therefore *ceteris paribus* fewer exports at heavily subsidised prices; and
- less export dumping of agricultural produce would have positive impacts on Southern countries dependent on agricultural exports and those striving for more food security.

As these measures concern domestic policies of producing countries they could be accommodated within post-Uruguay trade rules. Article 6 of the

Agreement on Agriculture states important exemptions from the calculation of the Current Total Aggregate Measurement of Support. Direct payments under production limiting programmes are exempt if based on fixed areas or yields, fixed number of head of livestock, or if these subsidies are made on not more than 85 per cent of the base level of production. Up to 5 per cent is allowed to Northern countries under *de minimis* as well. Furthermore, Annex 2 contains a host of subsidies for which exemption may be claimed if no price support to producers is provided and under some, not always very precise, conditions (see Raffer, 1995). Payments under environmental programmes and regional assistance programmes, as well as food security programmes and domestic food aid (such as US food stamps) could be used to finance the proposed changes. Domestic food aid would also allow the needy to get their proper shares of better quality food.

Net food importers in the South would have to be supported by food aid, preferably at a level sufficient to improve nutritional standards throughout the South (see Singer and Shaw, 1995, p. 4). This could be done both with remaining, smaller surpluses and food available periodically when stocks have to be re-filled, as well as by triangular transactions. This refers to food aid not physically provided by the countries paying for it but by food exporters in the South. Seen from the point of view of the Prebisch–Singer development gap, triangular food aid is optimal, as it reduces the structural disequilibria of both physical exporters and importers.

References

Holm, M. (1994) 'Food Supply and Economic Sustainability in Urban Areas – A Lesson from Tanzania', in M.A. Mohamed Salih (ed.), *Inducing Food Insecurity, Perspectives on Food Policies in Eastern and Southern Africa* (Uppsala: Nordiska Afrikainstitutet) pp. 104–119.

IBRD (1987) *World Development Report 1987* (New York: Oxford University Press).

IMF (1987) *IMF Survey*, 13 July 1987.

OECD (1995) *Development Co-operation, Efforts and Policies of the Members of the Development Assistance Committee, 1994 Report* (Paris: OECD).

—— (1996) *Development Co-operation, Efforts and Policies of the Members of the Development Assistance Committee, 1995 Report* (Paris: OECD).

Prebisch, R. (1949) 'El desarrollo económico de la América latina y algunos de sus principales problemas', *El Trimestre Económico*, vol. 16, no. 3 (Jul.–Sep.) pp. 447ff. (English version published by UN-ECLA in 1950).

—— (1959) 'Commercial Policies in the Underdeveloped Countries' *American Economic Review, Papers & Proceedings*, vol. 49, pp. 251ff.

—— (1976) 'A Critique of Peripheral Capitalism', *CEPAL Review*, first half of 1976, pp. 9–77.

Raffer, K. (1995), 'The Impact of the Uruguay Round on Developing Countries', in F. Breuss (ed.) *The World Economy after the Uruguay Round* (Schriftenreihe des Forschungsinstituts für Europafragen, Bd. 12) (Vienna: Service Fachverlag) pp. 169–93; (reprinted in *Asian Journal of Economics and Social Studies* vol. 13, no. 3, pp. 187–204).

—— (forthcoming), Debt Management: Problems in Need of More Attention', in D. Gupta and N. Choudhry (eds) *Political Economy of Globalization* (Studies in Globalization and Development, vol. 3) (Boston: Kluwer, forthcoming).

—— and H.W. Singer (1996) *The Foreign Aid Business, Economic Assistance and Development Co-operation* (Cheltenham: E. Elgar).

Sen, A. (1983) 'Development: Which Way Now?', *Economic Journal*, vol. 93, no. 372, pp. 745–62.

Shaw, J. and E. Clay (1993) *World Food Aid, Experiences of Donors and Recipients* (Rome/London/Portsmouth: World Food Programme/Heinemann/ James Curry).

Singer, H.W. (1950) 'The Distribution of Gains between Investing and Borrowing Countries', *American Economic Review, Papers & Proceedings*, pp. 473–85.

—— (1984) 'The Terms of Trade Controversy and the Evolution of Soft Financing: Early Years in the U.N.', in G.M. Meier and D. Seers (eds) *Pioneers in Development*: (Oxford University Press (published for the World Bank) pp. 275–303.

—— (1986) 'Raúl Prebisch and His Advocacy of Import Substitution', *Development & South–South Co-operation*, vol. 2, no. 3 (special issue: *Homage to R. Prebisch*) pp. 1–7.

—— (1989) 'Lessons of Post-War Development Experience 1945–1988', *IDS-Discussion Paper*, no. 260 (IDS, Sussex).

(1991a) 'Terms of Trade – New Wine and New Bottles?', *IDS Sussex*, 5 June 1991 (mimeo).

—— (1991b) 'Food Aid: Development Tool or Development Obstacle?', in H.W. Singer, N. Hatti and R. Tandon (eds) *Aid and External Financing in the 1990s* New World Order Series, vol. 9 (New Delhi: Indus) pp. 109–24.

—— (1994a) 'Problems and Future of Food Aid in the Post-GATT-Era', in *Newsletter, Bruno Kreisky Dialogue Series*, n. 10, pp. 42–75 (bilingual: German and English).

—— (1994b) 'Two Views of Food Aid', in R. Prendergast and F. Stewart (eds), *Market Forces and Development* (Basingstoke: Macmillan) pp. 207–11.

—— and D.J. Shaw (1995) 'A Future Food Aid Regime: Implications of the Final Act of the GATT Uruguay Round', paper presented at the DSA-Conference, Dublin, 7–9 September 1995, forthcoming in H. O'Neill and J. Toye (eds) *A World without Famine?* (Basingstoke: Macmillan).

Singer, H., J. Wood and T. Jennings (1987) *Food Aid, The Challenge and the Opportunity* (Oxford: Clarendon).

Spraos, J. (1983) *Inequalising Trade? A Study of Traditional North/South Specialisation in the Context of Terms of Trade Concepts* (Oxford: Clarendon in co-operation with UNCTAD).

Streeten, P. (1994), *Strategies for Human Development* (Copenhagen: Handelshøskolens Forlag).

UNCTAD (1995) *Analysis of the Modalities to Give Effect to the Decisions on Special Provisions for the Least Developed Countries as Contained in the Final Act of the Uruguay Round*, 21 June 1995 (Geneva: UN (TD/B/WG.83).

UNDP (1994) *Human Development Report 1994* (New York: Oxford University Press).

13 Endogenous Technical Progress and North–South Terms of Trade: Modelling the Ideas of Prebisch and Singer on the Lines of Kalecki–Kaldor

Prabirjit Sarkar

13.1 INTRODUCTION

Is there any secular decline in the terms of trade of the South *vis-à-vis* the North? Seeking an answer to this question has been an important subject matter of research in the field of Development Economics since the publication of two papers by Prebisch (1950) and Singer (1950). Many economists rejected the view of Prebisch and Singer that the terms of trade have a long-term tendency to turn against the South. They raised a number of statistical objections against the data base of the Prebisch–Singer hypothesis. However, Sarkar (1986a) refuted most of the points raised by the critics. There is strong statistical support for the Prebisch–Singer hypothesis (see Thirlwall and Bergarin, 1985; Sarkar, 1986a,b; 1994a; Sarkar and Singer, 1991; 1993).

The next question is: what is the theory behind the trend to deterioration in the terms of trade of the South *vis-à-vis* the North? A number of explanations of the phenomenon of worsening terms of trade can be found in the writings of Prebisch (1950, 1959, 1964) and Singer (1950, 1987). One important explanation offered by both Prebisch (1950, 1964) and Singer (1950, 1987) is the asymmetry in the mechanism of distribution of the fruits of technical progress among the producers and the consumers in the North and the South.

It was pointed out that in the North, factor incomes increased in the process of technical progress and productivity growth. As evidence, Prebisch (1950) cited the case of the USA, where during the 40 years

249

preceding the Second World War, manufacturing production costs declined regularly but the movement of prices did not follow this pattern at all. On the contrary, the prices of Southern exports declined with the improvements in productivity.

In the words of Singer (1950, p. 475):

> technical progress in manufacturing industries showed in a rise in incomes while technical progress in the production of food and raw materials in underdeveloped countries showed in a fall of prices.

The diverse mechanism of distribution of the fruits of technical progress operated as the structures of both commodity markets and labour markets are different in the developed North and the developing South (Singer, 1987, p. 627). As Prebisch (1964) observed, a major proportion of the economically active population of the South is engaged in agriculture and other branches of primary production; besides this, a significant part is engaged in artisan activities and personal services at very low scales of remuneration. 'All these sectors of the population exert constant pressures on the real level of wages in the developing countries and make it extremely difficult for this level to rise in direct proportion to productivity as the latter improves with technical progress' (Prebisch, 1964, p. 15). On the other hand, in the developed countries which make up the North, labour is organized in trade unions and producers in strong monopolistic firms and producers organizations. So the fruits of technical progress and increased productivity are largely absorbed in higher factor incomes rather than in lower prices for the consumers.

Given this diverse mechanism of distribution of the fruits of technical progress, the terms of trade turn against the South in the process of long-term evolution of the world economy through technical progress and productivity growth.

The purpose of the present paper is to examine the theoretical validity of the Prebisch–Singer explanation of the phenomenon of worsening terms of trade. This is done with the aid of a North–South macro model developed on the lines of Kalecki–Kaldor.

13.2   A MACROECONOMIC FRAMEWORK OF THE WORLD ECONOMY

In his Presidential address to the Royal Economic Society (22 July 1976), Kaldor (1976) presented an informal model of the world economy divided into primary and manufacturing sectors. This Kaldorian model comes very close to the so-called 'structuralist' or 'neo-Kaleckian' models.[1] Basically Kaldor (1976) was concerned with the short-term cyclical rather than the long-term trend behaviour of the terms of trade between primary producing and industrialized regions. But his basic framework can be used to deal with the long-term trend behaviour of the terms of trade between the North and the South as done in Sarkar (1994b).

The world economy is divided into two regions, the 'South' and the 'North'. The North–South identification has not been made, however, in terms of the primary sector–manufacture distinction. It is assumed that the goods exported by the South to the North are consumed only by the Northern workers while the goods exported by the North to the South are consumed only by the Southern capitalists. Due to the declining import-ance of raw materials in world trade (South to North and North to South) as noted in Sarkar (1986b), intermediate uses of products are ignored throughout the analysis. Machines used in each region are assumed to be domestically produced.[2]

The South is assumed to face a capacity constraint while the North faces a demand constraint. The market for Southern goods is flex-price; the demand–supply balance is achieved through price adjustment.[3] The market for Northern goods is fix-price; it is characterized by mark-up pricing and output adjustment process.

The price of Northern goods is assumed to be set by applying a fixed mark-up, m_2 to unit labour cost, L_2:

$$P_2 = L_2 (1 + m_2) \tag{13.1}$$

There are two components of unit labour cost, the labour coefficient (per unit labour requirement), l_2 and the money wage rate, W_2. The labour coefficient is fixed by technology. The money wage rate is fixed by wage contracts; at that money wage rate any amount of labour can be hired so that labour supply poses no effective constraint to production. A rise in labour productivity (a fall in l_2) induces the workers to demand more money wages. In the process of technical progress and higher money wages, the product wage, $L_2 = l_2 W_2$ remains unaffected. Given the mark-up, the real wage rate rises in the process of technical progress and labour productivity improvements. But income distribution remains unaffected due to the fixity of mark-up. Following Kalecki (1971), the share of profit in Northern output, θ_2 is given by $m_2/(1 + m_2)$. It can be taken as a measure of the monopoly power of the Northern capitalists.

In the South also, labour supply poses no effective constraint to growth. At a subsistence level wage rate fixed in terms of Southern goods, w_1 any amount of labour can be hired. Given the productivity of labour ($1/l_1$), income distribution is given by the fixity of real wage rate. Following the tradition of Prebisch–Singer, it can be assumed that the real wage rate does not rise in the same proportion (if at all) as the rise in labour productivity. Hence, in the process of technical progress and labour productivity growth, the share of the capitalists in total Southern output ($\theta_1 = 1 - l_1 w_1$) rises.

Following Arrow (1962) and Kaldor (1966), technical progress can be endogenized. Technical progress can be taken as the product of some kind of learning-by-doing process. It can be argued that labour productivity rises with the rise in capital accumulation and output in both the North and the South. Due to the conditions of labour and product markets in the North, income distribution and price of Northern goods remain unaffected. In the South, the share of the capitalists, θ_1, rises in the process of growth and endogenous technical progress.

For simplicity, assume a constant elasticity direct relationship between the share of the Southern capitalists and the level of output:

$$\theta_1 = \bar{\theta}_1 Y_1^{\epsilon_1} \tag{13.2}$$

where $\bar{\theta}_1$ and ϵ_1 are positive constants.

The Southern capitalists save and invest a constant fraction (s_1) of their profit income ($\pi_1 = \theta_1 Y_1$) and spend the rest on the Northern and Southern goods. As the Southern workers do not consume Northern goods, the export demand for Northern goods (X_2) comes from the Southern capitalists. It is inversely related to the North–South terms of trade, P and directly related to the Southern profit income net of savings, $(1 - s_1) \theta_1 Y_1 \equiv C_1$.

Assuming constant elasticities, the Northern export demand function is

$$X_2 = \bar{X}_2 P^{-\mu_1} C_1^{\gamma_1} \tag{13.3}$$

where $\bar{X}_2$, μ_1 and γ_1 are positive constants.

From (13.3), Southern imports measured in terms of Southern goods, $M_1 = PX_2$ can be obtained:

$$M_1 = \bar{X}_2 P^{(1-\mu_1)} C_1^{\gamma_1} \tag{13.4}$$

Given the pattern of income distribution and the saving-investment behaviour of the Southern capitalists, the rate of growth of Southern output ($\hat{Y}_1$) is given by the following equation for a given productivity of capital, q_1:

$$\hat{Y}_1 = s_1 \theta_1 q_1 \tag{13.5}$$

Granted the assumption that the whole of the saving of the Southern capitalists is invested and that the workers do not save, the demand-supply balance for Southern output requires a balance of trade (B_1) equilibrium:

$$B_1 = X_1 - M_1 = 0 \tag{13.6}$$

This equilibrium given by Equation (13.6) is achieved by price adjustment.

Since a balance of trade deficit (surplus) in the South implies a corresponding balance of trade (B_2) surplus (deficit) in the North that is, $B_1 = -PB_2$, the macro balance in the North requires a saving-investment equality:

$$S_2 = I_2 \tag{13.7}$$

In view of surplus capacity, the capital (K)–output (Y) relationship in the North is given by the following equation:

$$Y_2 = u_2 q_2 K_2 \tag{13.8}$$

where u_2, the rate of capacity utilisation < 1 and q_2 is the fixed output–capital ratio.

The pace of capital accumulation in the North (I_2/K_2) is assumed to be a rising function of the rate of profit, r_2:

$$I_2/K_2 = a_2 + b_2 r_2 \tag{13.9}$$

where a_2 and b_2 are positive parameters.

Saving comes only from the capitalists; the whole of profit income in the North ($\theta_2 Y_2$) is assumed to be saved. Hence the share of the Northern capitalists in total output, θ_2 is equal to the saving rate, s_2.

There is a direct relationship between the rate of profit and the rate of capacity utilization:

$$r_2 = \theta_2 Y_2/K_2 = S_2/K_2 \tag{13.10}$$

$$= \theta_2 \, q_2 u_2 \qquad\qquad (13.11)$$

using eq. (13.8).

So in effect the pace of capital accumulation is a rising function of the rate of capacity utilization:

$$I_2/K_2 = a_2 + b_2\theta_2 q_2 u_2 \qquad\qquad (13.9')$$

From the saving–investment equality in the North, the solution for the rate of capacity utilization can be derived (using (13.9), (13.10) and (13.11)):

$$u_2 = a_2/\theta_2 q_2 \,(1 - b_2) \qquad\qquad (13.12)$$

For a meaningful solution of u_2, it is to be assumed that $a_2 > 0$ and $b_2 < 1$.

Putting (13.12) in (13.9'), the rate of growth in the North ($\hat{Y}_2$) can be derived:

$$\hat{Y}_2 = a_2/(1 - b_2) \qquad\qquad (13.13)$$
$$= g_2 > 0 \text{ (as } a_2 > 0 \text{ and } b_2 < 1)$$

This rate of growth is independent of the mark-up and income distribution. For determining the course of the terms of trade, the condition for demand – supply balance for Southern goods, equation (13.6) is to be considered. That is to say, we have to look into the export demand for Southern goods (X_1), given by equation (13.4), and Southern export supply, which is nothing but Southern import demand for Northern goods measured in terms of Southern goods (M_1).

Assuming a constant elasticity function similar to what has been assumed in the case of Southern demand for Northern exports (X_2), given by equation (13.3), the Northern demand for Southern export goods (X_1) is given by the following equation:

$$X_1 = \bar{X}_1 \, P^{\mu_2} W_2^{\gamma_2} \qquad\qquad (13.14)$$

where $\bar{X}_1$ is a positive constant, $W_2 = (1 - \theta_2) \, Y_2$ is the Northern wage income and μ_2 and γ_2 are the given price and income elasticities (both positive).

From (13.2), (13.4) and (13.14), the growth rates for X_1 and M_1 can be estimated (a ^ over a variable indicates its growth rate):

$$\hat{X}_1 = \mu_2\hat{P} + \gamma_2\hat{Y}_2 \qquad\qquad (13.15)$$

$$\hat{M}_1 = (1 - \mu_1)\hat{P} + \gamma_1(1 + \epsilon_1)\hat{Y}_1 \qquad (13.16)$$

Equating the two growth rates given in (13.15) and (13.16) the rate of change in the terms of trade, $\hat{P}$, can be solved:

$$\hat{P} = [(1 + \epsilon_1)\gamma_1\hat{Y}_1 - \gamma_2\hat{Y}_2]/(\mu_1 + \mu_2 - 1) \qquad (13.17)$$

If at least one price elasticity is greater than one, it follows that

$$\mu_1 + \mu_2 - 1 > 0 \qquad (13.18)$$

Given (13.17) and (13.18), the condition for a secular decline in the terms of trade of the South (that is, $P > 0$) is

$$(1 + \epsilon_1)\gamma_1/\gamma_2 > \hat{Y}_2 - \hat{Y}_1 \qquad (13.19)$$

From (13.19), it can be concluded that a secular decline in the terms of trade of the South is inevitable even if the income elasticities of export demand for Northern and Southern goods are equal and the two regions grow at the same rate. In a product cycle scenario,[4] it is likely that the Southern export goods are less income elastic ($\gamma_2 < \gamma_1$). Moreover, in order to catch up with the more developed North, the policy-makers of the South often try to force the pace of growth through a higher saving–investment process (so that $\hat{Y}_1 > \hat{Y}_2$). All these (emphasized in Sarkar, 1996) give a further boost to the process of secular decline that follows from technical progress and the diverse mechanism of distribution of the fruits of technical progress.

To sum up, the ideas of Prebisch–Singer regarding the diverse mechanism of distribution of the fruits of technical progress can be suitably incorporated into a North–South model on Kalecki–Kaldor lines and the phenomenon of secular decline in the terms of trade of the South can be explained.

Notes

1. For different approaches to the Kaldorian model, see Thirlwall (1986) and Molana and Vines (1989).
2. Introduction of machine imports from the North to the South will complicate the model. This has been avoided as our basic objective is to highlight the diverse mechanism of distribution of the fruits of technical progress as an important factor behind the secular decline in the terms of trade.

3.   Exchange rate adjustment is ignored throughout the analysis. The exchange rate is assumed to be fixed and is set equal to unity.
4.   The product cycle literature originates from the work of Vernon (1966). Also see Krugman (1979). A new product is introduced in the North. Initially there is a craze for this product. Its income elasticity is very high. Due to a lack of knowledge of its production technique, the South cannot start its production. The South produces comparatively older goods with a lower income elasticity. By the time the South acquires the knowledge, the North has introduced another new product. This is the product cycle scenario.

References

Arrow, K. (1962) 'The Economic Implications of Learning by Doing', *Review of Economic Studies* (June) pp. 155–73.

Kaldor, N. (1966) *Causes of the Slow Rate of Economic Growth of the United Kingdom* (Cambridge University Press).

—— (1976) 'Inflation and Recession in the World Economy', *Economic Journal* vol. 86 (December) pp. 703–14.

Kalecki, M. (1971) *Selected Essays on the Dynamics of the Capitalist Economy, 1933–1970* (Cambridge University Press).

Krugman, P. (1979) 'A Model of Innovation, Technology Transfer and the World Distribution of Income', *Journal of Political Economy*, vol. 87 (April) pp. 253–66.

Molana, H. and D. Vines (1989) 'North–South Growth and the Terms of Trade: A Model on Kaldorian Lines', *Economic Journal*, vol. 99, pp. 443–53.

Prebisch, R. (1950) *The Economic Development of Latin America and Its Principal Problems* (New York, United Nations ECLA).

—— (1959) 'Commercial Policy in the Underdeveloped Countries', *American Economic Review*, vol. 49 (May).

—— (1964) *Towards a New Trade Policy for Development* (New York: United Nations).

Sarkar, P. (1986a) 'The Singer-Prebisch Hypothesis. A Statistical Evaluation', *Cambridge Journal of Economics*, vol. 10 (December) pp. 355–71.

—— (1986b) 'Patterns of Trade and Movements of Interregional Terms of Trade between the Developing and the Developed Market Economies, 1950–1980', *Economic Bulletin for Asia and the Pacific*, vol. 37, pp. 1–16.

—— (1994a) 'Long-term Behaviour of Terms of Trade of Primary Products *vis-à-vis* Manufactures: A Critical Review of Recent Debate', *Economic and Political Weekly*, vol. 29 (June) pp. 1612–14.

—— (1994b) 'North-South Terms of Trade and Growth: A Macroeconomic Framework on Kaldorian Lines', *World Development*, vol. 22 (November) pp. 1711–15.

—— (1996) 'Growth and Terms of Trade: A North–South Macroeconomic Framework', *Working Paper* 1/96, Centre de Sciences Humaines, Delhi and IEDES-Université Paris Sorbonne forthcoming in *Journal of Macroeconomics*.

—— and H. Singer (1991) 'Manufactured Exports of Developing Countries and Their Terms of Trade Since 1965', *World Development*, vol. 19 (April) pp. 333–40.

—— (1993) 'Manufacture–Manufacture Terms of Trade Deterioration: A Reply', *World Development*, vol. 21 (October) pp. 1617–20.

Singer, H. (1950) 'The Distribution of Gains between Investing and Borrowing Countries', *American Economic Review*, vol. 40 (May) pp. 473–85.

—— (1987) 'Terms of Trade and Economic Development', in J. Eatwell, M. Milgate and P. Newman (eds) *The New Palgrave: A Dictionary of Economics* (London: Macmillan).

Thirlwall, A.P. (1985) 'Trends, Cycles and Asymmetries in the Terms of Trade of Primary Commodities from Developed and Less Developed Countries', *World Development*, vol. 13 (July) pp. 805–17.

—— (1986) 'A General Model of Growth and Development on Kaldorian Lines', *Oxford Economic Papers*, vol. 38, pp. 199–219.

Vernon, R. (1966). 'International Investment and International Trade in the Product Cycle', *Quarterly Journal of Economics*, vol. 80 (May) pp. 190–207.

Part IV
The Distribution of Gains in the Context of Uneven Development

14 Direct Foreign Investment and North–South Trade: Uneven Development or Convergent Growth?[1]

Amitava Krishna Dutt

14.1 INTRODUCTION

A persistent theme in the writings of Hans Singer (1950, 1975) is that direct foreign investment (DFI) from developed economies – collectively referred to here as the North – to less-developed economies – the South – has a detrimental effect on the latter and leads to uneven global development. While Singer's view was shared by many, though by no means all, economists when he first propounded it, and for several years thereafter, it now seems to find few takers. In fact, in recent discussions of the effects of globalization, many scholars and Southern governments earlier critical of transnational corporations (TNCs) have softened or reversed their views,[2] while concerns have instead been raised about jobs disappearing in Northern countries as capital moves to Southern countries with low wages and high productivity (thanks to the transfer of technology by the TNCs) in an increasingly globalized world economy.[3]

Despite Singer's unchanging dismal view of the effects of foreign investment, however, it would be inaccurate to suggest that his views on this issue have not changed over time. Singer (1975) in fact distinguishes between Singer I and Singer II. Singer I of the late 1940s and 1950s focused on different *commodities* and argued that foreign investment in the South does not have beneficial consequences because it goes to primary sectors and not to modern manufactures. The demand for primary goods is income inelastic and the benefits of technological change go to consumers in the form of lower prices rather than to producers in the form of higher incomes. Modern manufactures, on the other hand, are the harbingers of economic development, not just for its immediate product or even for its effects on other industries and immediate social benefits, but for 'its general level of education, skill, way of life, inventiveness, habits, store of technol-

261

ogy, creation of new demand, etc.' Singer II of 1975, after examining the effects of a change in the pattern of foreign investment which increasingly went to the manufacturing sector of less-developed countries, focused instead on differences between *countries*. He argued that

> [t]he investing countries are the seats of multinational corporations, the homes of modern autonomous appropriate technology, and are economically integrated societies ... Being all this, the investing country will tend to be the chief gainer from *any* kind of relationship, whether the trade or investment or transfer of technology involves primary commodities or manufactured goods. (Singer, 1975, p. 59, italics in original)

One interpretation of this view is that because the developed countries are the seats of TNCs which are the main engines of technological change in the world economy, they will be able to ensure – through the development of new products and processes – that even if the South produces manufactured goods, these goods will be relatively inferior to those the developed countries produce in the same sense that primary goods were inferior to manufactured goods at the earlier stage of international development. Thus the superior/inferior manufactured goods distinction is analytically equivalent to the earlier manufactures/agriculture distinction.

While in his transition Singer was reacting to a change in the pattern of DFI from that in primary sectors to that in manufacturing, it has been convincingly argued (see UNCTAD, 1994, ch. 3) that the recent years there has been yet another change in the pattern of DFI. The earlier pattern of 'shallow' integration – in which TNC affiliates were typically stand-alone and only weakly integrated at the production level with Northern counterparts – is becoming increasingly replaced by 'deep' integration in which 'TNCs are turning their geographically dispersed affiliates and fragmented production systems into regionally or globally integrated production and distribution networks' (UNCTAD, 1994, p. 138). The product of TNCs 'is a complex bundle of inputs, produced in a variety of locations, assembled in host or home countries for sale in those countries or anywhere in the world. To identify such a product with a single country becomes, therefore, less and less meaningful' (UNCTAD, 1994, p. 140).

The question naturally arises whether this new pattern of TNC investment implies that DFI now has very different effects. Does the new pattern imply that DFI is good for Southern growth and bad for the North? Or would Singer III now argue that despite the change in the nature of DFI, the consequences for DFI from the South to the North are the same as they were argued to be by Singers I and II?

This chapter attempts to examine this question by analysing the implications of DFI from the North to the South using a simple North–South growth model assuming that DFI can flow into one of two sectors in the South. One sector represents the pattern assumed in Singer I and Singer II, in which the sector produces a good which competes with the Southern good which is an 'inferior' manufactured good. Most models of North–South trade and capital flows in fact assume that DFI flows into the sector which produces the same good as the Southern domestic sector produces. The other sector represents the pattern assumed in the era of 'deep' integration, which we interpret in a simple manner to mean that the sector produces essentially the Northern good: the issue is merely one of the location of TNC production of the integrated Northern good.

The earlier literature on North–South models suggests that the effects of the two types of DFI may well be different. Models such as those of Burgstaller and Saavedra-Rivano (1984) and Blecker (1995), who assume that DFI flows to the South goes to produce the Southern good (so that this represents what we called the traditional pattern of DFI), found that capital flows from the North to the South could result in Southern immiserization or uneven development. On the other hand, Dutt (1995) develops a model in which DFI flows into a Northern good-producing sector in the South (so that DFI is of the newer pattern) and finds that DFI liberalization in the South can reverse the process of uneven international development, and speculates that the new pattern of DFI could have resulted in a new pattern of North–South development more favourable to the South. This paper can be seen as conducting a direct examination of this issue using a model which allows for both traditional and newer types of DFI.

There are several kinds of North–South model, which make different assumptions about the structures of the North and the South. The framework adopted here follows Taylor (1983), who assumes that the Southern economy produces under conditions of competition and fixed real wages, fully employing its stock of capital (so that Southern production is supply constrained), while Northern production is characterized by excess capacity due to the lack of aggregate demand and oligopolistic practices by Northern firms. The treatment of the South seems to have become quite standard, but alternatives regarding the North are available in Findlay (1980), who assumes a Solovian North with full employment of labour and capital, and Molana and Vines (1989), who assume a Kaldorian North with a given real wage.[4] The specification used here stresses differences in the market structures of Northern and Southern goods, and allows for unemployment in both North and the South – although for different reasons; it would probably be the one most in line with Singer's views.

The rest of this chapter is organized as follows: Section 14.2 describes the basic structure of the model; Sections 14.3 and 14.4 examine the behaviour of the model in the short and long runs, respectively. Finally, Section 14.5 concludes.

14.2   STRUCTURE OF THE MODEL

Consider a world economy with two regions, the North and the South. There are two composite goods: one, the Northern good, is produced in the North and in a 'modern' foreign-owned sector in the South, and is used for both consumption and investment; and the other, the Southern good, is produced in the domestically-owned sector of the South and in a more 'traditional' foreign-owned sector, and used only for consumption. Both goods are produced with two inputs – capital (the investment good) and labour – using fixed-coefficients technology. There are two classes in each region: capitalists and workers. Northern capitalists receive profits from production in the North and from the foreign-owned sectors in the South, while Southern capitalists receive profits from production in the domestically-owned Southern sector; there is no investment by Southern capitalists in the North. Workers, who receive labour income, are internationally immobile. These assumptions imply:

$$P_s X_d = r_d P_n K_d + W_d b_d X_d \tag{14.1}$$

$$P_s X_{fs} = r_{fs} P_n K_{fs} + W_{fs} b_{fs} X_{fs} \tag{14.2}$$

$$P_n X_{fn} = r_{fn} P_n K_{fn} + W_{fn} b_{fn} X_{fn} \tag{14.3}$$

$$P_n X_n = r_n P_n K_n + W_n b_n X_n \tag{14.4}$$

where P_i denotes the price of the ith good; X_i the level of production of sector i; r_i the gross rate of profit in sector i; K_i the stock of capital in sector i; W_i the money wage in sector i; bi the labour–output ratio in sector i; and subscript n denotes the Northern good and the Northern production sector, s the Southern good, d the domestic sector in the South, and fn and fs the Northern and Southern good-producing, foreign-owned sectors, respectively, in the South. The exchange rate is fixed between the North and South and set equal to unity.

Northern firms, which operate in an oligopolistic environment, set the price of the Northern good as a mark-up on labour costs, so that the price of the Northern good is given by

$$P_n = (1 + z) W_n b_n \tag{14.5}$$

where z is a constant markup which depends, *à la* Kalecki (1971), on the degree of monopoly in Northern industry. Northern firms maintain excess capacity, and produce to meet the demand for their product. Since Northern firms, which include TNCs, also produce in the South at lower labour costs than in the North, they are assumed to produce at full capacity in the South (we assume that the demand for the Northern good is sufficiently large to warrant this), so that

$$X_{fn} = a_{fn}K_{fn} \tag{14.6}$$

where a_i is the fixed output-capital ratio in sector i while excess capacity is maintained in the North (so that $X_n < a_n K_n$). The reason that TNCs produce in the North at higher costs at all is that Southern production of the Northern good requires TNC investment and technology transfer in the South which, due to imperfect capital and technology mobility due to entry barriers – interpreted broadly to include cultural and political factors – is limited. The market for the Southern good is assumed to be competitive, so that Southern domestic firms and foreign-owned firms producing the Southern good produce with full capacity, implying

$$X_d = a_d K_d \tag{14.7}$$

and

$$X_{fs} = a_{fs}K_{fs} \tag{14.8}$$

and the price of the Southern good is determined to equate full capcity output to demand.

Workers are in unlimited supply in both the North and the South. In the South the real wage for domestic sector workers is fixed, Lewis-like, in real terms (in terms of the Southern good, the only good they consume), while the wages of foreign-sector workers are fixed multiples (which are not necessarily the same) of domestic sector workers, so that

$$V_d = W_d/P_s \tag{14.9}$$

$$W_{fs} = (1 + \mu_s)W_d \tag{14.10}$$

and

$$W_{fn} = (1 + \mu_n)W_d \tag{14.11}$$

where $\mu_i > 0$ are exogenously fixed. Workers in the North receive a fixed money wage, W_n.

Northern and Southern capitalists are assumed to save constant fractions, s_n and s_d, of their income,[5] while workers everywhere are assumed not to save. The Southern good is assumed to be a good for which – at least for some consumer groups – the demand is price and income inelastic. We formalize this by representing consumption behaviour for the Northern workers (which include the unemployed) and foreign-sector workers in the South using a linear expenditure system in which the 'base' level of real consumption of the Southern good is positive, while there is no such base level consumption for the Northern good. After the base level of consumption for the Southern good, C_n (which is given assuming that the Northern labour force is given), is met, we assume that Northern capitalists and workers spend a fixed proportion, α, of their surplus consumption expenditure on the Northern good and the rest on the Southern good. Domestic-sector Southern workers – who are the poorest workers – are assumed to consume only the Southern good. Southern capitalists and foreign-sector workers are assumed to spend a fixed fraction β of their surplus consumption expenditure on the Northern good and the rest on the Southern good, after each foreign-sector worker consumes an amount c_s of the Southern good.[6]

These assumptions imply that the zero excess demand conditions for the Northern and Southern goods are given by

$$
\begin{aligned}
&\alpha[W_n b_n X_n + (1 - s_n)(r_n P_n K_n + r_{fn} P_n K_{fn} + r_{fs} P_n K_{fs} - P_s C_n] \\
&+ \beta[(1 - s_d) r_d P_n K_d + W_{fn} b_{fn} X_{fn} + W_{fs} b_{fs} X_{fs} - P_s c_s \\
&(b_{fn} X_{fn} + b_{fs} X_{fs})] \\
&+ P_n(I_n + I_{fn} + I_{fs} + I_d) - P_n(X_n + X_{fn}) = 0
\end{aligned}
\tag{14.12}
$$

and

$$
\begin{aligned}
&(1 - \alpha)[W_n b_n X_n + (1 - s_n)(r_n P_n K_n + r_{fn} P_{fn} K_{fn} + r_{fs} P_n K_{fs} - P_s C_n] \\
&+ W_d b_d X_d + (1 - \beta)[(1 - s_d) r_d P_n K_d + W_{fn} b_{fn} X_{fn}
\end{aligned}
$$

$$+ W_{fs}b_{fs}X_{fs} - P_s c_s (b_{fn}X_{fn} + b_{fs}X_{fs})] + P_s C_n + P_s c_s$$
$$(b_{fn}X_{fn} + b_{fs}X_{fs}) - P_s(X_d + X_{fs}) = 0, \tag{14.13}$$

where I_i denotes investment in sector i.

We assume that the payments between North and South are balanced, implying

$$P_n(I_{fn} + I_{fs} + I_d) + \beta[(1 - s_d)r_d P_n K_d + W_{fn}b_{fn}X_{fn}$$
$$+ W_{fs}b_{fs}X_{fs} - P_s c_s(b_{fn}X_{fn} + b_{fs}X_{fs})] - P_n X_{fn}$$
$$- (1 - \alpha)[W_n b_n X_n + (1 - s_n)(r_n P_n K_n + r_{fn}P_n K_{fn}$$
$$+ r_{fs}P_n K_{fs}) - P_s C_n] - P_s C_n$$
$$- P_s c_s(b_{fn}X_{fn} + b_{fs}X_{fs}) + r_{fn}P_n K_{fn} + r_{fs}P_n K_{fs}$$
$$- P_n(I_{fn} + I_{fs}) = 0 \tag{14.14}$$

and that this condition is satisfied by the Southern domestic sector investing at the rate determined by the Southern balance of payments. We assume that capital in sector i depreciates at a proportional rate δ_r.

Finally, turning to investment behaviour, we assume that gross investment in the North depends positively on gross profits (as a proxy for profit expectations and as an indicator of the ease of internal financing), negatively on the stock of capital in the North (to account for a fall in the rate of capacity utilization, given the level of output) and negatively on TNC direct net investment in the Northern-good-producing sector in the South (since replacement investment does not represent new investment opportunities, we assume that net investment is relevant here), to capture the fact that TNC investment in the Northern-good-producing sector in the South at least to some extent competes with Northern investment. Northern investment behaviour is represented with a linear function

$$I_n = \gamma_0 + \gamma_1 r_n K_n - \gamma_2 K_n - \gamma_3(I_{fn} - \delta_{fn}K_{fn}) \tag{14.15}$$

where $0 \geq \gamma_3 \geq 1$. We assume that TNC gross investment in each of the sectors in the South is given exogenously at levels determined by the animal spirits of TNCs which are affected by political climate and government policy towards TNCs in the South. Gross investment in the Southern domestic sector will be determined in a manner to be specified later.

Equations (14.1) through (14.15) may be conveniently expressed, after dividing by P_n and with necessary substitutions in terms of the following equations:

$$r_d = \sigma_d a_d p \tag{14.16}$$

where $\sigma_d = 1 - V_d b_d$ is the share of profits in the domestically owned Southern sector and where $p = P_s/P_n$ are the Southern terms of trade.

$$r_{fn} = [1 - (1 + \mu_n)V_d b_{fn} p]a_{fn}, \tag{14.17}$$

$$r_{fs} = \sigma_{fs} a_{fs} P, \tag{14.18}$$

where $\sigma_{fs} = 1 - (1 + \mu_s) V_d b_{fs}$, the share of profits in the foreign-owned Southern-good producing sector in the South,

$$r_n = \sigma_n X_n/K_n \tag{14.19}$$

where $\sigma_n = z/(1 + z)$, the share of profits in the North, and

$$I_d = s_d r_d K_d \tag{14.20}$$

which shows that investment in the Southern domestic sector is equal to Southern domestic savings, which is satisfied because no capital flows into the Southern domestic sector.[7] Using these equations we can rewrite the zero excess demand conditions for the two goods as follows:

$$
\begin{aligned}
&- \{1 - \alpha(1 - s_n\sigma_n) - \sigma_n\gamma_1\}X_n + \{s_d + \beta(1 - s_d)\sigma_d\alpha_d K_d \\
&+ [(\beta - \alpha(1 - s_n))(1 + \mu_n)V_d\beta c_s]b_{fn}a_{fn}K_{fn} \\
&+ [\alpha(1 - s_n)\sigma_{fs} + \beta((1 + \mu_s)V_d c_s)b_{fs}]\alpha_{fs}K_{fs} - \alpha C_n\}p \\
&+ \gamma_0 - \gamma_2 K_n + I_{fn} - \gamma_3(I_{fn} - \delta_{fn}K_{fn}) \\
&- [1 - \alpha(1 - s_n)]a_{fn}K_{fn} = 0
\end{aligned}
\tag{14.21}
$$

and

$$
\begin{aligned}
&(1 - \alpha)(1 - s_n\sigma_n)X_n - \{[s_d + \beta(1 - s_d)]\sigma_d a_d K_d \\
&- [(s_n + \alpha(1 - s_n) - \beta))(1 + \mu_n)V_d + \beta c_s]b_{fn}a_{fn}K_{fn} \\
&+ [(s_n + \alpha(1 - s_n))\sigma_{fs} + \beta((1 + \mu_s)V_d c_s)b_{fs}]a_{fs}K_{fs} \\
&- \alpha C_n\}p + (1 - \alpha)(1 - s_n)a_{fn}K_{fn} = 0.
\end{aligned}
\tag{14.22}
$$

In the next two sections we shall examine the behaviour of this model for the short and long runs.

14.3   THE SHORT RUN

In the short run we assume that the levels of capital stock in each sector, K_i, for $i = n, d, fn$, and fs are given, and that output X_n varies in the North in response to excess demand in the market for the Northern good, and that the price of the Southern good – and hence the terms of trade, p – varies in response to excess demand in the market for the Southern good. In short-run equilibrium we assume that the market for both goods clears.

This implies that in short-run equilibrium (14.21) and (14.22) must be satisfied to solve for u and p for given values of K_i. These two equations can be written as

$$\Sigma \begin{matrix} x_n \\ p \end{matrix} = -\gamma_0 + \gamma_2 K_n - I_{fn} - I_{fs} + \gamma_3 (I_{fn} - \delta_{fn} - K_{fn}) + \qquad (14.23)$$

$$[1 - \alpha(1 - s_n)]a_{fn}K_{fn} - (1 - \alpha)(1 - s_n)a_{fn}K_{fn}$$

where the elements of matrix Σ are given by

$$\Sigma_{11} = -\{1 - \alpha(1 - s_n \sigma_n) - \sigma_n \gamma_1\}$$

$$\Sigma_{12} = \{[s_d + \beta(1 - s_d)]\sigma_d a_d K_d + [(\beta - \alpha(1 - s_n))(1 + \mu_n)V_d$$
$$- \beta c_s]b_{fn}a_{fn}K_{fn} + [\alpha(1 - s_n)\sigma_{fs} + \beta((1 + \mu_s)V_d - c_s)b_{fs}]a_{fs}K_{fs}$$
$$- \alpha C_n\}$$

$$\Sigma_{21} = (1 - \alpha)(1 - s_n \sigma_n)$$

$$\Sigma_{22} = -\{[s_d + \beta(1 - s_d)]\sigma_d a_d K_d - [(s_n + \alpha(1 - s_n) - \beta))(1 + \mu_n)V_d$$
$$+ \beta c_s]b_{fn}a_{fn}K_{fn} + [(s_n + \alpha(1 - s_n))\sigma_{fs}$$
$$+ \beta((1 + \mu_s)V_d - c_s)b_{fs}]a_{fs}K_{fs} - \alpha C_n\}.$$

Let us assume for simplicity that the rate of change in u and p are equal to excess demands in the Northern and Southern goods markets, respectively. Then stability of short-run equilibrium requires that the trace of the matrix,

$$Tr(\Sigma) = -\{\{1 - \alpha(1 - s_n \sigma_n) - \sigma_n \gamma_1\} + \{[s_d + \beta(1 - s_d)]\sigma_d a_d K_d$$
$$- [(s_n + \alpha(1 - s_n) - \beta))(1 + \mu_n)V_d + \beta c_s]b_{fn}a_{fn}K_{fn}$$
$$+ [(s_n + \alpha(1 - s_n))\sigma_{fs} + \beta((1 + \mu_s)V_d - c_s)b_{fs}]$$
$$a_{fs}K_{fs} - \alpha C_n\}\} < 0$$

and that its determinant,

$$|\Sigma| = [1 - \alpha(1 - s_n\sigma_n) - \sigma_n\gamma_1]s_n[\sigma_{fs}a_{fs}K_{fs} - (1 + \mu_n)V_db_{fn}a_{fn}K_{fn}$$
$$+ (s_n\sigma_n - \gamma_1)\{[s_d + \beta(1 - s_d)]\sigma_d a_d K_d - [(\alpha(1 - s_n) - \beta)(1 + \mu_n)V_d$$
$$- \beta c_s]b_{fn}a_{fn}K_{fn} + [\alpha(1 - s_n)\sigma_{fs} + \beta((1 + \mu_s)V_d - c_s)b_{fs}]a_{fs}K_{fs}$$
$$- \alpha C_n\} > 0$$

Sufficient conditions for the stability of short-run equilibrium are:[8]

$$s_n\sigma_n - \gamma_1 > 0 \qquad\qquad (S1)$$

$$\sigma_{fs}a_{fs}K_{fs} - (1 + \mu_n)V_db_{fn}a_{fn}K_{fn} > 0 \qquad\qquad (S2)$$

and

$$\Sigma_{22} < 0, \qquad\qquad (S3)$$

which we assume are satisfied. (S1) implies that the responsiveness of Northern savings to changes in the Northern output exceeds the responsiveness of Northern domestic investment to changes in the same variable, which is a familiar stability condition for macroeconomic models with quantity adjustment. If this condition is not satisfied, a rise in Northern output, through its effect on profit, will increase investment more than saving in the North, implying an excess demand for the Northern good which will lead to a further increase in X_n, resulting in instability. (S2) states that an improvement in the Southern terms of trade will result in an increase in total profits from foreign production in the South, and requires that – given technology and wages in the foreign sectors in the South – capital stock in the Northern-good-producing, foreign-owned sector is not 'too large' compared to the foreign-owned sector producing the Southern good. If the condition is violated, a rise in the Southern terms of trade will have a larger absolute effect on excess demand for the Northern good than its absolute effect on excess demand for the Southern good, violating a standard condition that the own effect of price change must exceed the cross effect. (S3) states that a rise in the Southern terms of trade reduces the demand for the Southern good, and requires that K_{fn} is not 'too large' relative to K_{fs}, consistent with the requirement for condition (S2), and moreover, that C_n not be 'too large' relative to K_d and K_{fs} which, given technological parameters, determines the level of production of the Southern good.

The determination of short-run equilibrium can be shown by using Figure 14.1, in which the *NN* curve shows combinations of u and p at which the Northern goods market clears, so that u becomes stationary, and the SS curve shows combinations of u and p at which the Southern goods market clears, so that p becomes stationary. If we assume that $\Sigma_{12} > 0$, the slope of the NN curve, given by $-\Sigma_{12}/\Sigma_{11}$, will be positive, as shown in Figure 14.1(a). We further assume that

$$\gamma_0 - \gamma_2 K_n + I_{fn} - \gamma_3 (I_{fn} - \delta_{fn} K_{fn}) + I_{fs} > a_{fn} K_{fn} \tag{S4}$$

consistent with our assumption that K_{fn} is not 'too large' and 'small' values of parameters in the Northern investment function. Since this implies that

$$\gamma_0 - \gamma_2 K_n - \gamma_3 (I_{fn} - \delta_{fn} K_{fn}) + I_{fn} + I_{fs} > [1 - \alpha(1 - s_n)] a_{fn} K_{fn}$$

the NN curve will have a negative vertical intercept as shown in Figure 14.1(a). Since $\Sigma_{22} < 0$, the slope of the SS curve, given by $-\Sigma_{22}/\Sigma_{21}$, will also be positive, and the vertical intercept will be positive. Moreover, since

$$|\Sigma| > 0, \ \Sigma_{11}\Sigma_{22} - \Sigma_{12}\Sigma_{21} > 0$$

we have $-\Sigma_{12}/\Sigma_{11} > -\Sigma_{22}/\Sigma_{21}$, so that the NN curve will be steeper than the SS curve. The arrows show the direction of movement of X_n and p when the economy is not on the NN and SS curves, given (S1) and (S3), confirming the stability of the economy. Short-run equilibrium is determined at the point of intersection of the two curves, where both markets clear and given our assumptions equilibrium with positive X_n and p will exist and be unique.[9]

Though, as we have just seen, $\Sigma_{12} > 0$ is sufficient for stability (together with our other assumptions), it is not necessary that it is satisfied for stability. Since the first term in the expression for $|\Sigma|$ is positive, the second term does not have to be positive to make $|\Sigma|$ positive. Also, since given condition (S2), $-\Sigma_{22} > \Sigma_{12}$, it is possible for Σ_{22} to be negative even with $\Sigma_{12} < 0$, so that $\Sigma_{12} < 0$ does not imply the violation of the trace condition as well. The condition $\Sigma_{12} > 0$ states that the effect of a rise in p is to increase the excess demand for the Northern good. It implies that an increase in Southern growth (due to a rise in p which, according to equation (14.16), increases the Southern domestic profit rate r_d, which in turn, according to equation (14.20), increases Southern domestic investment and hence capital accumulation) also implies an increase in Northern output (and Northern investment, as implied by equations (14.15) and

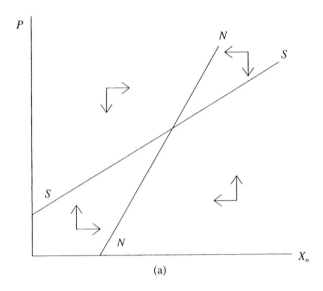

(a)

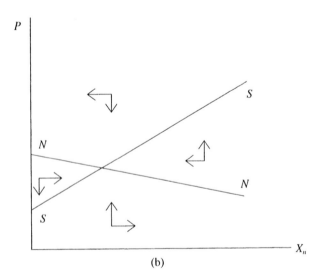

(b)

Figure 14.1

(14.19) since it increases income in the South as well as profit from the ownership of foreign capital in the North, and hence the total demand for the Northern good. However, if K_{fn} is 'too large', Northern profits from foreign capital ownership may not rise with the rise in p (since it squeezes profits in the *fn* sector in the South), and if C_n is 'too large will be a large increase in the money required to pay for the base consumption of the Southern good by Northern workers, leaving less 'surplus' income for spending on the Northern good; thus an increase in p and Southern growth leads to a contraction in excess demand for the Northern good, thereby reducing u.

If we allow $\Sigma_{12} < 0$, the slope of the *NN* curve will become negative, and given (S4), the vertical intercept will become positive, but everything else will remain qualitatively the same. If K_{fn} is not 'too large', the vertical intercept of the *SS* curve will be less than that of the *NN* curve, so that the two curves will intersect in the positive orthant, as shown in Figure 14.1(b). Furthermore, given our assumptions the unique equilibrium will be stable, as confirmed by the arrows in the figure.

To understand how the model works in the short run, and to lay the groundwork for the analysis of the long run in the next section, we next examine the effects of changes in selected parameters of the model. This is most easily done algebraically by adding equations (14.21) and (14.22) to obtain

$$- (s_n - \gamma_1)\sigma_n X_n - s_n[\sigma_{fs}a_{fs}K_{fs} - (1 + \mu_n)V_d b_{fn}a_{fn}K_{fn}]p - a_{fn}s_n K_{fn}$$
$$+ \gamma_0 - \gamma_2 K_n - \gamma_3(I_{fn} - \delta_{fn}K_{fn}) + I_{fn} + I_{fs} = 0 \qquad (14.24)$$

which confirms that total savings by Northern capitalists (from profits from Northern and Southern production) equals total investment by Northern capitalists (in the North and in the foreign-owned sectors in the South), which must be true since there are no capital flows between the sectors owned by Northern capitalists and those owned by Southern capitalists. It may be noted that equations (14.24) and (14.22) can be represented in Figure 14.2 to depict the determination of short-run equilibrium in an alternative way. The *SS* curve is the same as in Figure 14.1, depicting equation (14.22). The *IS* curve represents equation (14.24) and shows combinations of X_n and p implying saving-investment balance for Northern capitalists. Given (S1), (S2) and (S4) it will be a negatively-sloped line with a positive vertical intercept. Short-run equilibrium is determined at the intersection of the two curves.

Now totally differentiating equations (14.24) and (14.22) we obtain

$$- (s_n - \gamma_1)\sigma_n dX_n - s_n[\sigma_{fs}a_{fs}K_{fs} - (1 + \mu_n)V_d b_{fn}a_{fn}K_{fn}]dp = \gamma_2 dK_n$$
$$+ [s_n[1 - (1 + \mu_n)V_d b_{fn}p]a_{fn} - \gamma_3\delta_{fn}]dK_{fn} + s_n\sigma_{fs}a_{fs}dK_{fs} - d\gamma_0$$
$$- (1 - \gamma_3)dI_{fn} - dI_{fs} \qquad (14.25)$$

and

$$\Sigma_{21}\, dX_n + \Sigma_{22}\, dp = [s_d + \beta\,(1 - s_d)]\sigma_d a_d dK_d - [(1 - \alpha\,)(1 - s_n)$$
$$+ [(s_n + \alpha\,(1 - s_n) - \beta\,))(1 + \mu_n)V_d$$
$$+ \beta c_s\,]b_{fn}\,p\,]a_{fn}dK_{fn} + [(s_n + \alpha\,(1 - s_n))\sigma_{fs}$$
$$+ \beta\,((1 + \mu_s)V_d - c_s\,)b_{fs}\,]a_{fs}\,p\,dK_{fs} \qquad (14.26)$$

We can now solve equations (14.25) and (14.26) to examine the effects of changes in K_i, γ_0, I_{fn} and I_{fs} on X_n and p.

Starting with the effect of a change in Northern domestic capital stock, we find

$$dX_n/dK_n = \gamma_2\, \Sigma_{22}/|\Sigma| < 0 \qquad (14.27)$$

and

$$dp\,/\,dK_n = -\gamma_2\{1 - \alpha\,(1 - s_n\sigma_n) - \sigma_n\gamma_1\,\}/|\Sigma| < 0 \qquad (14.28)$$

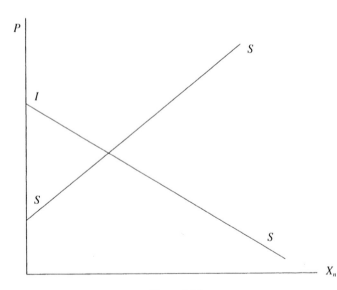

Figure 14.2

A rise in K_n implies that there is a fall in investment demand in the North since capacity utilization falls at a given level of output, which reduces aggregate demand for the Northern good, and hence X_n. The fall in X_n reduces employment and profits in the North, and therefore the demand for the Southern good, thereby reducing the Southern terms of trade. The change in p has further effects on the demand for the Northern good – implying a further expansion when $\Sigma_{12} > 0$ and reducing the expansion when $\Sigma_{12} < 0$. These effects can be verified by noting that the rise in K_n implies a leftward shift in the NN curve in Figure 14.1 since it reduces equilibrium X_n any given p.

The effects of a rise in K_d are shown by

$$dX_n/dK_d = [s_d + \beta(1 - s_d)]\sigma_d a_d s_n [\sigma_{fs} a_{fs} K_{fs}$$

$$- (1 + \mu_n)V_d b_{fn} a_{fn} K_{fn}]\, p/|\Sigma| > 0 \tag{14.29}$$

$$dp/dK_d = -[s_d + \beta(1 - s_d)]\sigma_d a_d (s_n - \gamma_1)\sigma_n p/|\Sigma| < 0. \tag{14.30}$$

This can be verified from Figure 14.2, noting that a rise in K_d moves the SS curve, leaving the IS curve unaffected. The rise in K_d implies a rise in Southern domestic-sector output, which reduces the price of the Southern good due to higher supply, and raises the demand for the Northern good from Southern domestic sector workers and capitalists, as well as by reducing p and increasing surplus income which can be spent on the N good by Northern (and foreign-sector Southern) workers.

The effects of a rise in K_{fn} are seen from

$$dX_n/dK_{fn} = -[q_{fn} s_n /|\Sigma|]\{[1 - (1 + \mu_n)V_d b_{fn} p]\Sigma_{22} + [\sigma_{fs} a_{fs} K_{fs}$$

$$- (1 + \mu_n)V_d b_{fn} a_{fn} K_{fn}][(1 - \alpha)(1 - s_n) +$$

$$[(s_n + \alpha(1 - s_n) - \beta)(1 + \mu_n)V_d + \beta c_s]b_{fn} p]\} < 0 \tag{14.31}$$

and

$$dp/dK_{fn} = \left[a_{fn}/|\Sigma| \right]\{b_{fn} p[(s_n - \gamma_1)\sigma_n [(s_n + \alpha(1 - s_n) - \beta))$$

$$(1 + \mu_n)V_d + \beta c_s] + (1 - \alpha)(1 - s_n \sigma_n)s_n(1 + \mu_n)V_d b_{fn}]$$

$$- (1 - \alpha)[s_n(1 - \sigma_n) + \gamma_1(1 - s_n)]\} \tag{14.32}$$

(where for simplicity we have set $\gamma_3 = 0$), which cannot in general be signed. Equation (14.25) implies that a rise in K_{fn} shifts the IS curve in

Figure 14.2 to the left, given that $r_{fn} > 0$, since it increases savings by Northern capitalists without increasing their investment, *ceteris paribus*. Equation (14.26) implies that a rise in K_{fn} increases the demand for the S good and therefore implies a higher p at any X_n, therefore pushes the SS curve in Figure 14.2 to the right. Thus equilibrium X_n definitely falls, but the effect on p is ambiguous. The rise in K_{fn} increases employment and output in the N-good producing sector in the South, which increases employment and wage income in that sector, as well as profits. All this implies an increase in the demand for the Southern good. However, the rise in K_{fn} also increases Southern production of the N-good, which thereby reduces Northern production of it, which reduces X_n unambiguously. Since this reduces employment and profits in the North, there is also a reduction in the demand for the Southern good. Hence, there is a fall in X_n, and an ambiguous effect on p.

The effects of a rise in K_{fs} are shown by

$$dX_n / dK_{fs} = -\left[a_{fn} p s_n / |\Sigma|\right]\left\{\sigma_{fs}[\alpha C_n - [s_d + \beta (1 - s_d)]\sigma_d a_d K_d \right.$$
$$\left. - \beta\, b_{fn} a_{fn} K_{fn}[(1 + \mu_n)((1 + \mu_s)V_d - c_s)b_{fs} + c_s \sigma_{fs}]\right\} \quad (14.33)$$

and

$$dp / dK_{fs} = \left[a_{fn} p / |\Sigma|\right]\{[(s_n - \gamma_1)][(s_n + \alpha (1 - s_n))\sigma_{fs} + \beta$$
$$((1 + \mu_n)V_d - c_s) b_{fs}] + (1 - \alpha)(1 - s_n \sigma_n)s_n \sigma_{fs}\} < 0 \quad (14.34)$$

As equation (14.25) shows, a rise in K_{fn}, *ceteris paribus*, increases the savings by Northern capitalists without increasing Northern investment, which implies a leftwards shift of the IS curve in Figure 14.2. Equation (14.26) implies that the rise in K_{fn} increases the supply of the S good, resulting in, *ceteris paribus*, an excess supply of the S good, which implies that the SS curve in Figure 14.2 shifts to the left. Thus equilibrium p falls unambiguously, while equilibrium X_n may rise or fall. If C_n is large, so that the effect of a fall in p in raising the demand for the Northern good is large, and β is small, so that the reduction in the Southern demand for the Northern good due to a reduction in p is small, the likelihood of $dX_n/dK_{fn} > 0$ is increased.

Finally, the effects of a rise in autonomous investment (as reflected by a rise in γ_0, I_{fs} and I_{fn}) are similar, since they all shift the IS curve to the right by increasing investment by Northern capitalists (as shown by equation

(14.25)), while leaving the *SS* curve unchanged (as shown by equation (14.26)). The rise in the demand for the *N* good for investment purposes increases X_n, and this expansion in X_n results in a rise in the Northern demand for the *S* good, increasing p.

14.4 THE LONG RUN

In the long run we assume that the short-run equilibrium conditions are always satisfied and that the stock of each kind of capital increases according to net investment:

$$dK/dt = I_i - \delta_i K_i \tag{14.35}$$

The long run dynamics will in general imply changes in the capital stock for each of the four sectors in the model. To render the analysis manageable we assume that apart for exogenous shocks,

$$I_i = \delta_i K_i, \text{ for } i = fn, fs \tag{14.36}$$

This implies that abstracting from exogenous shocks, the stocks of capital in the two foreign-owned sectors in the South are stationary. This assumption implies that we can examine the dynamic behaviour of the world economy in a simple manner by examining the dynamics of K_n and K_d alone.

Substituting into (14.35) from equations (14.15), (14.16), (14.19) and (14.20) we get[10]

$$dK_n/dt = \gamma_0 + \gamma_1 \sigma_n X_n - (\gamma_2 + \delta_n)K_n - \gamma_3(I_{fn} - \delta_{fn}K_{fn}) \tag{14.37}$$

and

$$dK_d/dt = s_d \sigma_d a_d p K_d - \delta_d K_d \tag{14.38}$$

This implies that for given values of the parameters of the model, a long-run equilibrium (without exogenous shocks) for the model is a stationary state in which $dK/dt = 0$. Since this is satisfied for the two foreign-owned sectors in the South by assumption, at a long-run equilibrium we have, from equations (14.37) and (14.38), since net foreign investment in the *fn* sector is zero by equation (14.36),

$$X_n = [-\gamma_0 + (\gamma_2 + \delta_n)K_n]/\gamma_1 \sigma_n \tag{14.39}$$

and

$$p = \delta_d/s_d\sigma_d a_d \tag{14.40}$$

The long-run equilibrium terms of trade are thus given by equation (14.40), while the long-run equilibrium value of X_n depends on the long-run equilibrium value of K_n. The long-run equilibrium values of K_{fn} and K_{fs} are given exogenously by past shocks to I_{fn} and I_{fs}, respectively. For these exogenous values of K_{fn} and K_{fs} we can substitute equations (14.36), (14.39) and (14.40) into equation (14.24) to get

$$K_n = (s_n\gamma_0/\gamma_1)\Lambda - \{s_n[1 - (1 + \mu_n) V_d b_{fn}(\delta_d/s_d\sigma_d a_d)]a_{fn}$$
$$- \delta_{fn}\}\Lambda K_{fn} - [s_n\sigma_{fs}a_{fs}(\delta_d/s_d\sigma_d a_d) - \delta_{fs}]\Lambda K_{fs} \tag{14.41}$$

where $\Lambda = \gamma_1/[\gamma_2 s_n + \delta_n(s_n - \gamma_1)] > 0$, which gives us the long-run equilibrium value of K_n for given values of the parameters of the model, including K_{fn} and K_{fs}. We can also substitute equations (14.36), (14.39) and (14.40) into equation (14.22) to obtain

$$K_d = [\alpha C_n \delta_d/s_d\sigma_d a_d - (1 - \alpha)((1 - s_n\sigma_n)\gamma_0/\gamma_1\sigma_n]\Theta$$
$$+ [(1 - \alpha)((1 - s_n\sigma_n)(\gamma_2 + \delta_n)/\gamma_1\sigma_n]\Theta K_n$$
$$+ [(1 - \alpha)(1 - s_n) + [(s_n + \alpha(1 - s_n) - \beta))(1 + \mu_n)V_d$$
$$+ \beta c_s]b_{fn}(\delta_d/s_d\sigma_d a_d)]\Theta a_{fn}k_{fn}$$
$$- [(s_n + \alpha(1 - s_n))\sigma_{fs} + \beta((1 + \mu_s))V_d$$
$$- c_s)b_{fs}]a_{fs}(\delta_d/s_d\sigma_d a_d)\Theta K_{fs} \tag{14.42}$$

where $\Theta = s_d/\delta_d [s_d + \beta (1 - s_d)] > 0$ and where K_n is given in equation (14.41). The long-run equilibrium value of K_n is thus given by equation (14.41), and substituting this value into equation (14.42) yields the long-run equilibrium value of K_d.

The dynamics of K_n and K_d over time are given by the equations (14.37) and (14.38), where X_n and p have already been shown to depend on K_n and K_d, with $dX_n/dK_n < 0$, $dp/dK_n < 0$, $dX_n/dK_d > 0$ and $dp/dK_d > 0$. We therefore get

$$\partial(dK_n/dt)/\partial K_n = \gamma_1\sigma_n(dX_n/dK_n) - (\gamma_2 + \delta_n) < 0$$
$$\partial(dK_n/dt)/\partial K_d = \gamma_1\sigma_n(dX_n/dK_d) > 0$$
$$\partial(dK_d/dt)/\partial K_n = s_d\sigma_d a_d(dp/dK_n) < 0$$
$$\partial(dK_d/dt)/\partial K_d = s_d\sigma_d a_d(dp/dK_d) < 0$$

when the partials are evaluated at long-run equilibrium. We can depict the long-run dynamics of K_n and K_d using Figure 14.3, where the signs of these partial derivatives imply the slopes of the $dK_n/dt = 0$ and $dK_d/dt = 0$

loci. Starting from a position on the $dK_n/dt = 0$ curve, an increase in K_n reduces Northern output and, as a consequence, Northern profits (see equation (14.27). The reduction in Northern profits, the direct effect of the increase in K_n on investment, and the higher level of investment required for replacement of depreciated capital all imply a reduction in dK_n/dt, making it negative. To increase dK_n/dt to make it return to $dK_n/dt = 0$, we require an increase in K_d, which will increase Northern output and profits through its effect on the demand for the Northern good (see equation (14.29)). Starting from a position on the $dK_d/dt = 0$ curve, an increase in K_n implies a reduction in the Southern terms of trade, which reduces profits, savings and investment by Southern domestic capitalists, implying that dK_d/dt falls and becomes negative. To increase dK_d/dt to return it to $dK_d/dt = 0$, we require a reduction in K_d which will reduce Southern output and increase the Southern terms of trade, thereby raising Southern gross investment, and also reduce the need for investment to replace depreciation, thereby increase Southern domestic capital accumulation. The implication of the dynamics shown in Figure 14.3 is that the long-run equilibrium, L, where the two curves intersect, is locally stable. It is also straightforward to check that the trace and determinant conditions of the

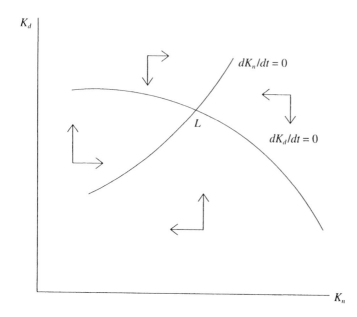

Figure 14.3

(local) stability of long-run equilibrium are satisfied. Thus we are entitled to infer the long-run effects of changes in parameters from an examination of the direction of changes in K_n and K_d implied by equations (14.41) and (14.42).

14.5   EFFECTS OF DIRECT FOREIGN INVESTMENT

We are now in a position to examine the effects of changes in DFI on the nature of global development, in order to examine whether such North–South capital flows imply uneven development or convergent growth. Since our model examines two kinds of DFI, we need to specify which kind of DFI we have in mind. We discuss in turn the effects of the traditional pattern of DFI, into what we have called the *fs* sector, and then the efforts of the newer pattern, into what we have called the *fn* sector. For each kind of investment, we assume that there is an exogenous increase in net DFI which is subsequently followed by a reduction of net investment by the same amount, so that net investment returns to zero. In both cases the rise in investment implies a rise in the level of the stock of capital in the relevant sector, so that to support a higher level of capital stock in the new long-run equilibrium, the level of gross investment (to replace depreciated capital) must be greater in order to maintain a zero level of net investment.

The short run effect of an increase in I_{fs} was found from our analysis of the effects of parametric shifts in the section on the short run: given all stocks of capital, there will be an increase in X_n and a rise in p. This implies an increase in Northern employment and profits, and therefore an increase in accumulation in the Northern domestic sector. It also implies an increase in Southern profits and hence saving and capital accumulation in the Southern domestic sector. Thus an increase in DFI of the traditional kind increases capital accumulation in all regions (except for the modern foreign-owned sector in the South, where the level of capital stock is taken to be fixed exogenously).

This temporary rise in investment in the traditional foreign-owned sector in the South implies an increase in K_{fs} in the long run, after all adjustments in the long run (due to changes in K_n and K_d) are completed, and net investment is restored to its previous level of zero. We can examine the long-run effects on K_n and K_d by using equations (14.41) and (14.42). Equation (14.41) implies that sign of the effects of an increase in K_{fs} on X_n will be given by the sign of $[s_n \sigma_{fs} a_{fs} (\delta_d / s_d \sigma_d a_d) - \delta_{fs}]$ an expression which is equal to $[s_n r_{fs} - \delta_{fs}]$ at long-run equilibrium. This latter expression is simply the difference between the gross saving and gross investment in the *fs* sector.

Although this expression cannot be signed *a priori*, it is reasonable to expect it to expect it to be positive, as can be argued as follows. Equations (14.16) and (14.40) imply that $s_d r_d = \delta_d$. Given better technology in the *fs* sector than in the *d* sector, it is reasonable to expect that $\delta_d > \delta_{fs}$. Moreover, there is a great deal of evidence to suggest that in roughly similar foreign-owned and domestic industries in the South, the rate of profit in the foreign-owned sector exceeds that in the domestically-owned sector, implying that $r_{fs} > r_d$. Finally, assuming that savings rates of Northern and Southern capitalists are roughly similar, we find that $s_n r_{fs} - \delta_{fs} > s_d r_d - \delta_d = 0$, establishing our claim. Of course, if s_d is much larger than s_n, we are not entitled to make this claim. Thus the likely long-run effect of DFI of the traditional type is to reduce the stock of capital in the North.

The effect on Southern domestic capital stock is found from equation (14.42), which suggests that the effect on K_d can be decomposed into two parts. The first can called the *indirect North–South effect*, which is the effect of a change in K_d due to a change in K_n as shown by the second term in the left-hand side of equation (14.42). The second can be called the *direct North–South effect*, which is given by the last term in that equation, which occurs even if there is no change in K_n. In this case, if the rise in K_{fs} reduces K_n, both the direct and indirect North–South effects on K_d are negative, so that there is necessarily a decline in K_d in the long run when there is an increase in I_{fs}. This means, given a_d, that there is also a decline in Southern domestic-sector output in the long run.

The total effect on the South can be measured in a number of different ways. One way is in terms of total capital stock in the South,[11] measured by $K_s = K_d + K_{fn} + K_{fs}$, where we can ignore K_{fn} in this case, which is constant. The total effect on K_s can then be decomposed into three effects: first the *direct DFI effect*, which is the change in K_s due to the change in K_{fs}, and the other two are the two indirect effects mentioned above. If we ignore the indirect North–South effect, assuming that K_n does not change, the total effect (which is the sum of the direct North–South effect and the direct DFI effect, and which can hence be called the total direct effect), is given from equation (14.42) by

$$dK_s/dK_{fs} = 1 - [(s_n + \alpha(1 - s_n))\sigma_{fs} \\ + \beta((1 + \mu_s)V_d c_s)b_{fs}]a_{fs}(\delta_d/s_d \sigma_d a_d)\Theta,$$

from which it follows that

$$\text{sign } dK_s/dK_{fs} = \text{sign } \{\sigma_d a_d[s_d + \beta(1 - s_d)] - [(s_n + \alpha(1 - s_n))\sigma_{fs}$$
$$+ \beta((1 + \mu_s)V_d - c_s)b_{fs}]a_{fs}\}.$$

The sign of the expression on the right hand side depends on the values of a number of parameters, including output–capital ratios and share of profits in the foreign-owned and domestically-owned S-good producing sectors, consumption parameters α and β, saving rates of Northern and Southern capitalists, wage premium in the foreign-owned sector, and labour output ratio in the foreign-owned sector. While this sign is an empirical matter, it is likely that given the technological advantage of the foreign sector, $a_{fs} > a_d$, given protectionist policies in the South regarding consumption goods, $\alpha > \beta$, and given relatively high profit shares in the foreign sector, $\sigma_{fs} > \sigma_d$, so that unless $s_d > s_n$ significantly, the expression is likely to be negative, so that the long-run direct effect on the South of the traditional kind of DFI is a negative one.

The relative development effects on the North and South can also be found from our model if we had values of all the parameters. It could be measured by the difference between K_s and K_n, or by their ratio, which are difficult to sign. What we can say is that even if there is no significant long-run effect on K_n, the long-run effect of an increase in I_{fs} on K_s is negative.

Turning next to the effects of an increase in DFI of the more modern type, given by I_{fn}, the short-run effects were discussed in the section on the short run, where we found that both X_n and p were increased, so that the effects are qualitatively the same as in the case of an increase in I_{fs}. The only difference is that the expansionary effects of a given increase in investment will be less given the fact that in this case there is some associated decrease in I_n caused by an increase in I_{fn}.

In the long run, as in the case of traditional investment, there is an increase in K_{fn}. As before, the long-run implications of this can be examined using equations (14.41) and (14.42). In equation (14.41), the coefficient of the term involving K_{fn} has the same sign as $s_n r_{fn} - \delta_{fn}$, evaluated at long-run equilibrium. Although in this case we cannot make a direct comparison between depreciation rates δ_{fn} and δ_d, and so we cannot definitely infer that at long-run equilibrium $s_n r_{fn} - \delta_{fn} > 0$, this certainly cannot be ruled out. Thus it is possible for K_n to fall as a result of an increase in K_{fn} although it need not.

Thus, as we can see from equation (14.42) the indirect North–South effect in this case can be negative, although it need not. As in the previous case, let us assume that there is no change in K_n. However, equation (14.42) shows that the direct North–South effect in this case is positive since the derivative $dK_d/dK_{fn} > 0$. Therefore, the sum of the direct North–South and DFI effects is necessarily positive, if we measure development in terms of stocks of capital at long-run equilibrium.

14.6 CONCLUSION

This paper has developed a simple model of North–South trade and capital flows to analyse the short-and long-run implications of DFI investment from the North to the South. The model has two goods – a Northern good produced under oligopolistic conditions so that its price is sticky and its market varies due to variations in Northern output, and a Southern good in which competition prevails so that its price varies to clear the market. It has modeled the North as producing a single Northern good, while the South has three sectors, a domestic sector producing a Southern, a foreign-owned sector producing the Southern good, and a foreign-owned good producing the Northern good.

This paper has found that the effects of DFI on global development in the long run depend quite crucially on the nature of this DFI. If we interpret, as argued in this chapter, that the traditional pattern of DFI from the North to the South was to a sector producing a Southern good, and that the more recent pattern involves capital flows to a sector producing a Northern good in a deeply-integrated production system, the effects of DFI depend on whether it is of the traditional or the more modern type. We have found that if DFI has no significant long-run development effects on the North (so that we focus attention on what we have called the direct North–South and DFI effects), the effect on the South of DFI of the traditional kind is most likely to be negative, while that of the modern kind – given our assumptions – will be positive. If we allow for long-run effects on Northern development, then of course the effect on Southern development need not be positive (due to what we have called the indirect North–South effect). The reasons for this asymmetric effect are straightforward: the effects of increases in the capital stock in the foreign-owned Southern-good producing sector in the South worsens the Southern terms of trade, while there is no such necessary effect when there is an increase in the capital stock in the foreign-owned Northern-good-producing sector in the South. If we take all effects into account we would need information about a large number of parameters, and the effects cannot be definitely signed. However, it remains true that one should carefully distinguish between different types of DFI before concluding that the effects of DFI on Southern development are good or bad.

We end with two concluding comments, one empirical and the other on further theoretical issues.

First, it should be stressed that it is not empirically a simple matter to determine exactly which sectors in the South should be classified as Northern good producing sectors, and which should be classified as Southern good producing sectors. Hopefully our analysis has demonstrated the need for such a distinction. Our analysis suggests also that the issue is not one of primary products versus manufactured good, but rather one of the nature of markets of the products produced, whether they are core investment goods, and to some extent their income and price elasticities. What specific kinds of goods are Northern and Southern goods may also change over time, as production technology and consumer preferences change around much of the globe.

Second, although we have argued on the basis of a simple model that there is a theoretical presumption that modern type of DFI may have effects which are different from the effects of the traditional type which Singer I and Singer II were concerned with, and in particular, may have more beneficial effects on the South and hence lead to convergent growth so that the South and the North get closer to each other, the provisional nature of our results should be kept in mind. First, it needs to be stressed that the model of this paper does not imply that the new pattern of DFI will necessarily imply a more beneficial effect for relative Southern development, since except for the case in which there is a negligible effect on Northern development, one needs to have an idea of a large number of parameter estimates to arrive at a definite conclusion about this. Second, the model is based on a number of simplifying assumptions including, for instance, the absence of spillover effects of technology transfer and the constancy of real wages in the South. However, if Singer III is to argue that the new DFI has deleterious effects on Southern development, and lead to uneven development rather than convergent growth, our model can serve as a basis to examine what kinds of mechanisms left out of our analysis negate or even reverse the theoretical presumption of beneficial effects of the newer type of DFI as compared to the traditional type examined by Singers I and II.

Notes

1. Prepared for a conference at the University of Innsbruck, Austria, in May 1996, celebrating Hans Singer's 85th birthday. I am grateful to Professors John-ren Chen and Hans Singer, and to other participants of the Innsbruck conference, for their comments.

2. Compare, for instance, Lall and Streeten (1977) and Lall (1993).
3. See, for instance, the report in *The Economist* (1994) and Schwab and Smadja (1994). See also Wood (1994), although his focus is on the effects of Southern imports on Northern economies, especially on the distribution of income between skilled and unskilled workers in the North.
4. For a comparison of these and other models of North–South trade, see Dutt (1990, ch. 8).
5. We assume that capitalist consumption depends on their gross income, not income net of depreciation. Assuming that consumption is a fraction of income net of depreciation would not change the nature of our results.
6. Unemployed Southern workers are assumed not to consume either the Northern or Southern good, but to consume and produce in an informal sector which is not explicitly considered in the model.
7. This equation can be derived from the zero excess demand conditions and the balance of payments condition.
8. This can be established by noting that (S1) $\Rightarrow 1 - \alpha (1 - s_n\sigma_n) - \sigma_n\gamma_1 > 0$ which, together with (S3) $\Rightarrow Tr(\Sigma) < 0$ and $|\Sigma| > 0$.
9. Note that if $\Sigma_{22} > 0$, given our other assumptions, both slope and vertical intercept of the SS curve will be negative, so that the curve will not lie in the positive orthant at all, which will imply that there will be no short run equilibrium with $X_n > 0$ and $p > 0$.
10. It should be apparent that if we assumed that net investment in the North depended on net profits, among other variables, our analysis would not be qualitatively different. In this case we would have

$$dK_n/dt = \gamma_0 + \gamma_1(r_n - d_n)K_n + \gamma_3(I_{fn} - \delta_{fn}K_{fn}).$$

11. An alternative, which can easily be pursued in our model, would be to consider the level of net output (that is, the sum of output of sectors in the South net of depreciation and profit repatriation).

References

Blecker, R. (1995) 'The New Economic Integration: Structuralist Models of North–South Trade and Investment Liberalization', unpublished (Washington, DC: Department of Economics, The American University).

Burgstaller, A. and N. Saavedra-Rivano (1984) 'Capital Mobility and Growth in a North–South Model', *Journal of Development Economics*, vol. 15, pp. 213–37.

Dutt, A.K. (1990) *Growth, Distribution and Uneven Development* (Cambridge University Press).

—— (1995) 'Transnational Corporations, Direct Foreign Investment, and Growth', in R.E. Rowthorn (ed.) *Transnational Corporations and the Global Economy*.

Economist, The (1994) 'A Survey of the Global Economy', *The Economist*, 1 October, pp. 1–38.

Findlay, R. (1980) 'The Terms of Trade and Equilibrium Growth in the World Economy', *American Economic Review*, vol. 70, pp. 291–9.

Kalecki, M. (1971) *Selected Essays on the Dynamics of the Capitalist Economy* (Cambridge: Cambridge University Press).

Lall, S. (1993) 'Introduction: Transnational Corporations and Economic development', in S. Lall (ed.) *Transnational Corporations and Economic Development* (London: Routledge).

—— and P. Streeten (1977) *Foreign Investment, Transnationals and Developing Countries* (London: Macmillan).

Molana, H. and D. Vines (1989) 'North–South Growth and the Terms of Trade: A Model on Kaldorian Lines', *Economic Journal*, vol. 99, pp. 443–53.

Schwab, K. and C. Smadja (1994) 'The New Rules of the Game in a World of Many Players', *Harvard Business Review* (November).

Singer, H. (1950) 'The Distribution of Gains between Investing and Borrowing Countries', *American Economic Review, Papers and Proceedings*, vol. 2, no. 2 (May).

—— (1975) *The Strategy of International Development* (New York: International Arts and Science Press).

Taylor, L. (1983) *Structuralist Macroeconomics. Applicable Models for the Third World* (New York: Basic Books).

United Nations Conference on Trade and Development (1994) *World Investment Report, 1994. Transnational Corporations, Employment and the Workplace* (New York and Geneva: United Nations).

Wood, A. (1994) *North–South Trade, Employment and Inequality: Changing Fortunes in a Skill-Driven World* (Oxford University Press).

15 The Distribution of Gains between Investing and Borrowing Countries Revisited: The Case of India's Computer Software Sector

V.N. Balasubramanyam and
Ahalya Balasubramanyam

15.1 INTRODUCTION

Hans Singer's thesis concerning the unequal distribution of gains from trade and foreign investment between investing and borrowing countries, first enunciated in 1949 (Singer 1950) has been revisited many times, most importantly by Singer himself some twenty-five years after the first paper was published (Singer, 1972). The first paper identified the nature and the type of trade between the developed and the underdeveloped countries as the principal factor in the unequal distribution of benefits from trade and investment between the two groups of countries. The message of the second paper, which Singer labelled as Singer II, located the source of the unequal distribution of gains from trade and investment, not so much in the nature of commodities traded, but in the nature of the technological endowments and the characteristics of the countries between which trade and investment take place.

It is now another twenty-five years since Singer II was enunciated and the time may be ripe for revisiting both Singer I and Singer II. While Singer I focused on the nature of commodities traded and Singer II focused on the characteristics of the trading countries, we investigate the famous hypothesis concerning the distribution of gains between borrowing and investing countries in the context of trade in services, a much discussed issue during the 1980s and 1990s. Foreign direct investment in services has increased considerably in recent years. Many of the services are in the nature of intermediate inputs and the contribution of services to growth and employment is a much discussed issue. For these reasons, it would be instructive to analyse investment and trade in the context of Singer's thesis.

Our discussion of the thesis is grounded in a case study of India's exports of computer software. This particular case lends itself admirably to a re-examination of Singer's thesis for several reasons. First, it permits a natural extension of the thesis from commodities (Singer I) and countries (Singer II) to services. Second, computer software exhibits several, if not all, of the features of commodities discussed in Singer I. Third, India, the exporting country and the USA and the European Union, the importers of software, exhibit many of the characteristics of the countries identified in Singer II. Finally, the origins and the growth of the software sector in India owe much not only to foreign investment, but also to the brain drain India has experienced in recent years. This feature allows for an extension of Singer's thesis to international factor flows in general.

This chapter is based on information gathered through discussions with a sample of managers of software firms located in Bangalore, Hyderabad and Trivandrum in India. Section 15.2 discusses India's software sector in the context of Singer I. Section 15.3 dwells on the actors involved in the production and trade of software and is designed to explore the relevance of Singer II. The question 'Is there a Singer III centring on services?' forms the subject matter of Section 15.4.

15.2 SINGER I AND INDIA'S COMPUTER SOFTWARE SECTOR

An important facet of Singer I is that the nature and production characteristics of economic activity significantly influences its potential to promote growth. Singer contended that it is manufacturing rather than commodities which provides the stimulus for growth. As Singer put it, manufacturing provides 'the growing points for increased technical knowledge, urban education, and the dynamism and resilience that goes with urban civilisation as well as the direct Marshallian external economies'. Singer argued that as much of foreign investment in the past was in commodities rather than in manufactures destined for export to developed countries, developing countries were deprived of the growth enhancing secondary multiplier and external effects of such investment.

The focus of recent debate has shifted from the commodities versus manufacturing controversy to one of manufacturing versus services. Are services as potent as manufacturing in generating growth? What are the consequences of implanting a high-tech service sector in a developing country for growth and employment? Is it likely that such a sector will turn out to be no more than an export enclave resembling the commodities sector discussed in Singer I?

The computer software sector in India is an ideal case for a discussion of these issues. India's computer software sector has attracted wide attention in the media – The *Financial Times* of London has devoted more than one special issue to it, most leading newspapers in the world, including the *New York Times* and the *Japan Times*, have carried feature articles on the sector and it has featured many times on BBC television and radio. One may wonder why all this fuss, as the share of India in world exports of software at around $750 million amounts to only 1 per cent. The reason for the widespread attention the sector has received is its phenomenal growth at around 47 per cent per annum since 1991. Estimates of the number of people employed in the sector vary widely from 1.4 million to 120 000 people. We guess the lower of the estimates is nearer to the mark in the case of the core of the sector, excluding the so-called table and chair software outfits. Much of the sector, around 60 per cent of the total number of 690 companies which are members of the National Association of Software and Service Companies, is located in the cities of Bombay and Bangalore, the latter is now variously known as the Silicon Plateau of India and the Electronic City.

India's software has attracted world-wide attention not only because of its rapid growth, but also because of the nature of the activity. The software industry is at the leading edge of technological progress, a high-tech industry which is intensive in the use of human capital. The visible presence of the industry in India is seen as proof that high-tech activities such as software can be profitably pursued by developing countries without their economies going through the sequence of agriculture to manufacturing and then on to technologically-intensive services. What Gandhi would have made of Alvin Tofler's colourful description of the co-existence of software with traditional agriculture in India as 'Gandhi with satellites' is anybody's guess, but that software, a part and parcel of the information technology revolution, is a technologically sophisticated activity intensive in the use of human capital cannot be denied. But whether or not software in general and the type of software produced and exported from India in particular generates the sort of growth and development effects noted by Singer is debatable.

Software, much like many of the commodities, is essentially in the nature of an intermediate input. Effectively used, it promotes growth and efficiency in the production of both final goods and services. But it does so in the locale of production of the final goods and services. The gains from its use accrues to the owners of the final goods in whose production it is utilized. This in fact is a distinguishing characteristic of all intermediate services. As T.P. Hill (1977) notes, 'the production of a service cannot generally be distinguished from that of a good by means of the technology used, but by the fact that the producer unit operates directly on goods which already belong to the consumer of the service'. The goods which already belong to the consumer of the which the software producer operates are data and information. In the case of India's software, the information and data belong to the importing countries. Although a domestic market for software exists and exhibits an upward trend, the export market is nearly double the size of the domestic market. The issue then is whether or not software can be effectively used to promote growth and employment in a labour-surplus economy whose manufacturing sector is much too diverse and unsophisticated. We return to this issue later.

Exports of an intermediate services, however, can generate externalities and growth-inducing backward and forward linkages. Software, however, by its very nature utilises very little of other produced inputs. The requirements of a software producing firm are confined to trained labour and hardware, which is in the nature of fixed capital. Much of India's computer hardware requirements are imported, understandably so because of the overwhelming competitive advantage possessed by producers of hardware in the exporting countries.

Admittedly, backward and forward linkages are not the only growth and employment inducing effects a sector can be expected to generate. The very presence of the high-tech sector can promote labour training, create new demands, raise the general standard of education and entrepreneurship. The extent to which a sector generates such growth and development-inducing effects depends on the nature of the output produced by the sector, the general characteristics of the sector and the location of the sector. India's computer software sector covers several types of activities. In this context a classification suggested by Tapasiji Mishra (*Financial Times*, 6 December 1995) is useful:

- *Body shop software produced overseas*   This case refers to temporary movement of Indian engineers to the locale of clients overseas. In the schema of services suggested by Bhagwati (1987), this would represent *mobile provider–immobile user* type of services.

- *Body shop software produced in India*   Indian software engineers produce software or process information and data supplied by clients abroad. This would approximate to the *mobile user–immobile provider* category in Bhagwati's schema. But this type of business is best regarded as belonging to the long distance services, identified by Bhagwati, as it is only the data and information which are mobile and not the users.

- *Building software products for export overseas*:

- *Building software products that take advantage of native expertise* in an application area such as finance and banking.

The last two categories may involve foreign investment by major computer firms such as Motorola and IBM.

At present, the first two categories of software account for the bulk of India's exports, with the second variety, or what the trade refers to as offshore production, gaining in importance. In the case of the first type, India's software experts reside abroad for a few months at a time in the locale of the consumer firm and manufacture software to the specifications of the customer. An example of such trade is the manufacture of software for the requirements of Reebok, the multinational shoe manufacturing firm at the firm's UK headquarters in Lancaster, England. In the case of this variety of software business, whatever little externalities the activity may generate accrues to Reebok. Apart from the employment and earnings accruing to the Indian firm, this sort of activity generates very little dynamic growth-inducing effects for the Indian economy.

The bodyshop software experts are a sort of export enclave of the Singer I variety with the added qualification that they are footloose. Singer argued that economists were slaves to geographers because of their belief that the mere geographical location of an investment would promote the interests of the region in which it was located. India's bodyshop software experts are not even geographically located in India on a permanent basis. They are a peripatetic lot – in one country today, another tomorrow, returning to base only to receive orders on new assignments.

The second variety of bodyshop software – the offshore variety – though located in India, more nearly resembles the export enclaves discussed by Singer and Levin (1950). This sort of bodyshop software ranges from the most elementary sort such as data-entry and data-processing activity to the manufacture of bespoke software for overseas customers. Neither variety forges any sort of backward and forward linkages with the rest of the economy, nor do they generate the wider variety of growth-inducing effects of the sort Singer describes. There are several examples of the elementary data-entry and data-processing type of activity, but the one which exemplifies the export enclave nature of the business is the work relating to the production of yellow pages for British Telecom. In this case, all the out-of-date copies of yellow pages are shipped from England to an Indian firm located in Trivandrum, in the state of Kerala. The Indian firm writes the required software and employs young Indians with first degrees from the local university to enter all the data from the out-of-date yellow pages and update them on the basis of information provided by British Telecom. Admittedly, the opportunity cost of labour, even that of graduates from universities, is close to zero in the state of Kerala, which suffers from a very high rate of unemployment. The data-entry business which rewards the young graduates with a wage much above their opportunity cost and provides a clean environment for work does contribute to the social product of Kerala. But the activity provides little scope for progression to higher rungs of employment in the information technology industry, there is very little learning by doing, and the tasks performed are repetitive with little opportunity for exercising initiative and enterprise. The manager of one such firm in the data entry end of the industry told us that the firm did not provide for further training and the graduates when hired were told that they should not entertain hopes of advancing their careers in the industry. Indeed, one of the applicants for the job was turned down on the grounds that his aspirations and ambition were much too high and the firm could not assist him in fulfilling them.

But what of the more sophisticated end of the offshore software business, which includes turnkey projects for overseas customers and re-engineering of imported software? The software engineers in these occupations are much sought after and in most firms the rate of turnover of labour is as high as 20 to 25 per cent. The salary of an engineer in this segment of the sector at around $400 per month exceeds by a wide margin the wage paid in the manufacturing sector for comparable labour. The firms engaged in this relatively sophisticated end of the software business include both Indian-owned and foreign-owned firms such as Motorola, IBM and Texas instruments, all of which have outposts in Bangalore and Bombay. These firms recruit highly qualified young Indian engineers from the elite Indian education establishments, such as the Indian Institutes of Technology located in Delhi, Bombay, Kanpur, Calcutta and Madras. Substantial salaries paid by the software firms, the opportunity to travel abroad for short spells of work and training the firms provide in addition to on-the-job training are major attractions of the sector to the young graduates whose average age is around 24 years. There are though no obvious linkages between the sector and the rest of the economy, the engineers commune with the clients or more specifically the computers in the clients' firms abroad via the satellite link, flock together in the bars and eating establishments in Bangalore during their leisure hours conversing in the *lingua* of bytes and roms of the trade.

It is also arguable if the sort of young engineers and technicians which the sector attracts are over-qualified for the jobs they do and whether or not the sector utilizes their talents fully. The topmost software firms employ high fliers from elite educational institutions, who would have made excellent researchers and teachers.

The export orientation of the job itself appears to create imperfections in the labour market, resulting in misallocation of labour in the economy. India's exports of software are highly competitive in international markets, the price margin between Indian software and that of the USA may be as much as 60 per cent, which amounts to a huge savings in costs for importers of Indian software.

The cost advantage India enjoys resides in the wage advantage she has over foreign manufacturers of software. On an average, India's software engineers earn around $400 per month where as their counterparts in the USA command a wage of around $4000 per month. It is this cost advantage which accounts for the swift growth of India's exports of software. A wage of $400 per month in purchasing power parity terms in India, however, is a sizeable amount and far exceeds wages in other sectors. The high salary by Indian standards paid by the software firms attracts highly trained young Indian graduates to the sector. Neither the manufacturing sector nor academia can compete with the highly profitable software sector for the services of these young engineers. India has for long invested heavily in the production of engineers and doctors and this supply enables software firms to pick the best brains Indian institutions of higher education can offer. In sum, there is an internal brain drain from the rest of the economy to the software export enclave. The enclave with its link to export markets provides a high private rate of return to those engaged in the sector, but the social rate of return for its investments in education to the country may be pretty low.

Yet another labour market imperfection which appears to have fuelled the growth of the software export enclave in India is sociological rather than economic in nature. This has to do with the positive discrimination policies of the state governments, especially the state government of Karnataka of which the electronic city of Bangalore is the capital. These policies in the realm of education and employment are designed to promote the welfare of the so-called scheduled castes and backward classes. These two categories consists of members of most groups other than the Brahmins. Members of these groups are not only provided with bursaries and various sorts of subsidies for education, but they are also accorded preferential treatment in the recruitment for jobs in the civil service and the academia. The positive discrimination policies of the state places the Brahmins, the privileged caste group of yesteryear, at a substantial disadvantage in their quest for both jobs and admission to institutions of higher learning. The brain drain of 1960s and 1970s, which mostly consisted of Brahmins from the State of Karnataka, was an immediate consequence of such discriminatory policies. In the 1990s, the software sector has provided an internal outlet to the disaffected Brahmins. Software is solely a private sector activity, albeit with considerable government support, and is free of the shackles of the discriminatory policies of the state. The Brahmins, most of whom have to achieve exceptionally high grades at the school level if they are to enter the colleges of engineering at all, find the salaries and the work environment in the software firms most attractive. It is thus that the sector attracts highly qualified engineers, many of whom may be over-qualified for the needs of the software sector.

In sum, the software sector as it has evolved appears to display all the characteristics of an export enclave with the added feature that it harbours a substantial amount of human capital as opposed to unskilled and semi-skilled labour.

15.3   SINGER II AND THE SOFTWARE SECTOR

Singer II shifted the emphasis of the unequal distribution of gains from trade and investment thesis from the characteristics of the different types of commodities to the differing types of countries in the trade and investment relationship. The investing countries are the homes of powerful multinationals in possession of appropriate technologies, while the borrowing countries lack the technological prowess possessed by the investing countries. While the borrowing countries do receive the technology transmitted by the investing countries, this may be inappropriate and incommensurate with their factor endowments. This lack of correspondence between the imported technologies and the factor endowments of the developing countries serve to fortify the enclaves and widen disparities in incomes between those employed in the enclaves and the rest of the society. The inappropriateness of the technology may also destroy rather than create jobs in the developing countries. Singer suggests that the traditional chain which runs from factor endowment to product mix – and then on to technology-factor use should be replaced with the sequence: technology-factor use–unemployment–unequal distribution.

Singer II has been revisited many times and has been the theme of many a debate (Stewart, 1973, Balasubramanyam, 1980). India's software sector, however, suggests some interesting variations on the theme enunciated in Singer II. The actors here are threefold: local Indian entrepreneurs, expatriate Indians and the foreign-owned firms. The locally-owned Indian firms do possess the engineering skills and know-how required to produce software, but they differ from the foreign firms which import their wares in two respects: first, they lack the marketing expertise and in many cases, the finance to start up software firms; second, they are not the manufacturers of the final product. The foreign firms own the information and data which the Indian firms help analyse and process. The Indian expatriates fill one of these deficiencies. Many an Indian software firm has been set up with funds provided by Indian expatriates abroad or by Indians who after a long spell of work abroad have returned home. In some cases, the firms are set up by those who belong to what Bhagwati would refer to as *to and fro* migrants. These are people who manage to reside part of the year in India and part of the year in the USA.

India's software firms are dependent on foreign firms, be they foreign firms in the information technology sector itself, such as Motorola, or manufacturing firms which import software from India, for information concerning markets and products. Such information and in some – though not all – cases finance is also provided by expatriate Indians and the to and fro migrants. There are Indian software firms such as Infosys and Tata Consultancy Services which were established by Indian entrepreneurs. But many other firms have links of one sort or the other with expatriate Indians. The Indian software engineers who are engaged in offshore production of software export the product to their clients abroad mostly via satellite. In other words, they process the data and information of the clients according to the specifications provided by them, from their desks in Bangalore and Bombay. Alternatively, they work for large multinationals located in India who process information for their clients from their software production base in India.

This set-up poses interesting analytical issues. It is often argued that an important characteristic of a service is that it should be produced in the locale of the consumer or the consumer has to move to the locale of the producer. In the case of software, the service is performed from the locale of the producer. The satellite link enables this form of trade in services.

The analytically interesting issue concerns the nature of the service India is exporting. What is India exporting – is it exporting a service with a potential for generating growth-inducing effects, is it exporting a good or is it merely exporting labour, albeit trained labour?

We suggest that the set up, as it exists, serves to promote the export of human capital from India or what amounts to brain drain without emigration. It may be recalled that in Singer II, it is the importation of inappropriate technologies owned by multinationals which results in an unequal distribution of gains from investment. But in the case of India's software, there are no imports of technology. The technology and the human capital are home grown, but they are employed in the export enclaves. Most of the external effects embedded in software accrues to the importers of such software in the overseas markets. In this set up, India experiences an unequal distribution of gains because of two factors: labour market imperfections in India and the absence of a sizeable domestic market for software. As stated earlier, highly trained Indian engineers and technicians find an outlet for their talents in the software sector mostly because of a lack of demand for their expertise in the manufacturing sector. In the past such trained manpower would have resulted in a brain drain from India, but now it is to some extent absorbed by the software sector. But the fruits of such human capital are mostly exported abroad and all of the externalities from the use of software accrues to the importers. In the presence of a sizeable domestic market for software, the outcome could be different.

The software sector would have had two segments – a domestic sector and an export sector. The domestic sector would not only absorb some of the software engineers, but also benefit from the use of software in the production of final gods and services. The services of software engineers would complement the skills of those engaged in the production of final goods and services for the domestic market. Further, with the presence of a domestic market, the allocation of human capital between the software export sector and the domestic manufacturing sector would be much more efficient than it is at present. It would be efficient in the sense that the allocation of skills between the two sectors would be commensurate with their requirements. Admittedly, the relatively high wages paid by the software sector may itself be a factor in the relatively low demand for trained manpower in the domestic sector. This, though, is a feature of export enclaves. It is often alleged that foreign firms in developing countries drain resources from other sectors in the economy because of their ability to pay high wages. In the case of India's software sector both Indian-owned firms and foreign-owned firms orientated to export markets may have drained trained labour from domestic market-orientated activities. Here, it is not so much that the country has imported inappropriate technologies as in Singer II, but it is that the superimposition of a high-tech service sector on an economy with a relatively unsophisticated manufacturing sector may have resulted in a misallocation of trained labour. Further, because of the nature of the service exported, any linkages and externalities embedded in the service accrue to the importers of software.

15.4   IS THERE A SINGER III?

Ever since Singer I was enunciated, a number of studies have attempted to assess the thesis. Singer's postulate concerning the terms of trade between primary products and manufactures has been subjected to a variety of econometric tests. This chapter is not an attempt at evaluating the empirical validity of Singer's hypothesis. It simply asks if Singer I and Singer II, which are grounded in the nature of commodities and the nature of countries engaged in trade and investment, can be extended to trade in services. We have suggested that Singer's thesis may be applicable to certain specific types of services such as software which are traded in exchange for manufactures by developing countries such as India.

The conditions under which the phenomenon is likely to surface, though, may be specific to countries such as India and also somewhat unusual. One such condition is that a technologically advanced sector, for whose output there is as yet no domestic demand, should be established in a relatively poor country. The suggestion here is that developing countries may not gain by their attempts at leap-frogging an ordered sequence of industrialization. The absence of a domestic market is an essential condition for the Singer phenomenon to surface in the context of services such as software – a sector which is intensive in the use of human capital. In the absence of a domestic market, any externalities the sector may generate accrues to the importers of software. The externalities and productivity-enhancing effects are twofold in the case of software. First is the education and training that easily usable software spreads and the second is its impact on the productive efficiency of the manufacturing sector and final service-producing sectors which use software as an input. All of these gains accrue to the importing countries which utilize Indian software in their manufacturing and final services-producing sectors. In the Indian case, there is also an additional feature which may render the establishment of a high-tech service activity socially unprofitable. It is that by standards of developing countries, India produces a disproportionate amount of trained manpower.

Is the scenario sketched in this chapter likely to last for ever? Should India discourage investments in and growth of the software sector? It would be myopic to answer either of these two questions in the affirmative. It is heartening to note that there is an upward trend in the sales of software in the domestic markets in India in recent years. But whether or not its use has enhanced productivity in Indian manufacturing and services is debatable. The effective use of information technology requires substantial investments in education and training. It also requires the presence of a sophisticated end-use sector which can benefit from utilizing the products of the new information technology industry. Furthermore, it requires substantial investments in hardware. At the present time, in a country with a population in excess of 900 million people, there are only 1.2 million personal computers and only eight telephone lines per 1000 population. Effective use of software would require substantial investments not only in imports of hardware, but also in infrastructure and labour training in the use of software. Such training of labour in the effective use of information technology would enhance productive efficiency in the production of both final goods and services and generate productive employment. It should be added that the use of information technology products should not be shunned on the grounds that it would displace labour. Effectively used, information technology could create more jobs than it is likely to displace.

So, is there a Singer III centred on services? The answer has to be a qualified yes. Singer III could arise in the case of specific services such as software in the presence of factors such as the ones outlined in this paper. Singer III may arise in the case of India's software sector not only because of the nature of the product and the characteristics of the actors engaged in the trade, but also because of labour market imperfections which are a consequence of India's education and employment policies. But it is not unavoidable. As argued earlier, investments in education and training and in infrastructure facilities designed to effectively utilize India's comparative advantage in the production of software could enhance both the productive efficiency of the economy and employment opportunities.

References

Bhagwati, J.N. (1987) 'Trade in Services and the Multilateral Trade Negotiations', *World Bank Economic Review*, vol. 1 (September).

Balasubramanyam, V.N. (1980) *The Multinational Enterprise and the Third World* (Thames Essay for the Trade Policy Research Centre, London).

Deardorff, A.V. (1984) 'Comparative Advantage and International Trade and Investments in Services', Discussion Paper no. 137 (Ann Arbor, Michigan: Department of Economics, University of Michigan,).

Hill, T.P. (1977) 'On Goods and Services', *Review of Income and Wealth* (December).

Hindley, B. and A. Smith (1984) 'Comparative Advantage and Trade in Services', *World Economy*, vol. 7, no. 4.

Levin, J. (1960) *The Export Economies: Their Pattern of Development in Historical Perspective* (Harvard University Press).

Singer, H.W. (1950) 'The Distribution of Gains between Investing and Borrowing Countries', *American Economic Review, Papers and Proceedings*, vol. 11, no. 2.

Singer, H.W. (1975) 'The Distribution of Gains Revisited', in Sir Alec Cairncross and M. Puri (eds) *The Strategy of International Development: Essays in the Economics of Backwardness*, (London: Macmillan).

Stewart, F. (1973) 'Trade and Technology', in P. Streeten (ed.) *Trade Strategies for Development* (London: Macmillan).

16 A Prebisch–Singer Growth Model and the Debt Crises[1]

Thomas Ziesemer

16.1 INTRODUCTION

This chapter serves two purposes. Firstly, it tries to capture ideas of Prebisch and Singer on long-run growth. Prebisch (1950, 1959) and Singer (1950, 1958 and 1991) have repeatedly emphasized that developing countries are importers of capital goods. Imported capital goods have to be paid for by exports, either when imported or later, incurring debt in the meantime. If export demand is not unlimited once the small country assumption is dropped, then the customer countries' income, income and price elasticities of export demand matter in the determination of long-run growth rates and the terms of trade.

Secondly, it integrates some aspects of the debt crises as mentioned in the literature that are important when trying to understand the 1982 debt crisis in the Prebisch–Singer model. The introduction of an export demand function allows for an explicit consideration of the effects of a recession when treating the debt crisis as a shock. Moreover, a spread function will be specified in accordance with the empirical literature. The effects of the world income and interest shock on the spread will be discussed.

16.2 A GROWTH MODEL WITH IMPORTED CAPITAL GOODS, LIMITED EXPORT DEMAND AND SPREADS

Production is modelled using a neo-classical production function, where Y is output, K the stock of imported capital goods, L the exogenous labour supply of the country and A the level of technology that is growing at an exogenous rate:

$$Y = F(K, AL) = K^{\beta}(AL)^{1-\beta} \tag{16.1}$$

Capital goods are rented from domestic and foreign households. With p as the relative price of domestic and foreign or exported and imported goods or consumption and investment goods, r as LIBOR, s as spread and w as wage in units of foreign goods, the profits maximized by firms, π, can be written in units of foreign goods as follows:

$$\pi = pF(K, AL) - (r + s)K - wL$$

Maximizing with respect to K and L, given r, s, p and w, yields the first-order conditions (16.1) and:

$$r + s = pf'(k) = pk^{\beta-1}, \quad w = p[f(k) - f'(k)k]A = pk^{\beta}A \tag{16.2}$$

Capital owned by domestic households will be denoted as W, capital owned by foreign households as D, implying $K = W + D$. Capital owned by domestic households changes by savings, $\dot{W}$, which are the difference of income – from capital owned, $(r + s)W$, and wages, wL – and consumption, pcL, where c is the per capita consumption of domestic goods. The budget constraint of the household in units of foreign goods can be written as:

$$\dot{W} = (r + s)W + wL - pcL \tag{16.3}$$

As capital consists of foreign goods, the latter have to be imported. Therefore they have to be paid by exports, either now or later, if debt is incurred. For the sake of simplicity it is assumed that new capital goods are the only imports. If they are paid by debt, $\dot{D}$, the economy has interest costs, $(r + s)D$. The balance of payments equation can be written as follows:

$$\dot{D} = \dot{K} - pX + (r + s)D \quad \text{or} \quad \dot{W} = pX - (r + s)D \tag{16.4}$$

(16.3) is called the savings constraint and (16.4) the balance-of-payments constraint. As domestic goods can be consumed or exported we get:

$$Y - C - X = 0 \tag{16.5}$$

This equation could also be derived from the previous ones and therefore is not independent of them. From the World Bank model we incorporate the export demand function as it was modified by Bardhan and Lewis (1970) and Thirlwall (1983):

$$X = Z^\rho p^\eta = e^{\omega} p^\eta \quad \text{with} \quad \omega = \rho \hat{Z} \tag{16.6}$$

In (16.6), ρ and η are the income and price elasticity of demand. Sachs (1985, pp. 532–5) argues that the decrease of exports relative to the debt service is a central point in the empirical explanation of the debt crisis of 1982, whereas a decrease in the terms of trade is empirically less relevant. As world income or the income of customer countries is a variable in the export demand function (16.6), it is possible to analyse a permanent shock coming from a change in world economic conditions that lead to decreasing exports, a phenomenon that cannot be analysed under a small country assumption. Estimates of the price elasticities of demand yielded values of approximately (–1) in Stern, Francis and Schumacher (1976) and Hentschel (1992) and around (–2.1) for manufactures in Faini *et al.* (1992). If these values would yield inelastic demand functions, a monopolistic central planning optimum would not exist. Therefore a market equilibrium is considered instead of a central optimum.

Households are assumed to maximize a strictly concave utility function $U(c)L$ with properties:

$$U' > 0, \ U'' < 0, \ U'(0) = \infty, \ -U''c/U' \equiv \sigma$$

where σ is constant by assumption. For future points in time this utility function will be discounted by $e^{-\delta t}$ and (16.3) and $W(\tau) \geq 0$ are constraints of the maximization:

$$Max_c \int_t^\infty e^{-\delta\tau} U(c)L \, d\tau \quad \text{s.t} \quad (16.3) \text{ and } W(\tau) \geq 0$$

The last constraint implies that households have limited access to the capital market, in the sense that current wealth always has to be non-negative. This assumption is necessary to ensure the existence of a solution to the maximization problem.

For the problem defined above, the Hamiltonian of the household is:

$$H = U(c)L + \lambda[(r + s)W + wL - pcL] + vW.$$

The necessary conditions for a maximum are the constraints and:

$$H_c = U' - \lambda p \geq 0 \tag{16.7}$$

$$- H_W = -\lambda(r+s) - \nu = \dot{\lambda} - \delta\lambda, \qquad W\nu = 0 \tag{16.8}$$

$$\lim_{t \to \infty} \lambda(t)e^{-\delta t} = 0 \tag{16.9}$$

(16.7) says that marginal utility must be larger than or equal to the relative price multiplied by the shadow price of wealth. (16.8) is the movement of the shadow price of wealth; it is accelerated by a higher discount rate but slowed down by a higher rate of interest. (16.9) is the standard transversality condition, which requires that the growth rate of the shadow price of wealth is lower than the discount rate. This condition is fulfilled because of (16.8) and therefore could be dropped.

In this paper we ignore the case of a corner solution (see Ziesemer 1995a, where it has been discussed in a similar model). The interior solution can be analysed as follows.

Differentiating (16.7) with respect to time and inserting the resulting $\dot{\lambda}$ and λ from (16.7) into (16.8) yields:

$$\dot{c} = c(r + s - \rho - \hat{p})/\sigma \tag{16.10}$$

Higher interest rates provide an incentive for more savings. If this leads to lower consumption, the growth rate of the latter increases. For the rate of time preference the opposite holds. If the terms of trade increase, then domestically-produced goods become more expensive relative to units of imported goods which are used to accumulate savings. Expecting consumer prices to increase causes consumption to shift from the future to the present. Therefore, increasing terms of trade have a negative impact on the growth rate of per capita consumption.

16.3 CONDITIONS FOR BALANCED GROWTH

Before analysing the complete dynamics of the model in the next section, the conditions for balanced growth of output, exports and consumption are derived. These variables are all to grow at a rate which is determined not only by the natural growth rate but also by the growth rate of the world economy or the exporter's customer countries as well as the income and price elasticities of export demand, as emphasized by Prebisch (1950, 1959) and Singer (1950, 1991). It will be made clear that the adjustment towards a steady state, guaranteed in the Solow model by a movement of the interest rate towards its steady-state value, can only be ensured by an adjustment of the spread because the world market interest rate is given exogenously.

To concentrate on balanced growth requirements, in this section the spreads are assumed to be constant. In the next section it is shown that the spreads are indeed constant in the steady state. If the interest rate inclusive of the spread is constant, then (16.2) implies that the terms of trade grow at a rate which is proportional to that of the capital–labour ratio, $k = K/AL$:

$$\hat{p} = (1 - \beta)\hat{k} \tag{16.2'}$$

The steady-state growth rate of the model can now be derived. Equating the growth rates of exports and output, $\hat{X} = \hat{Y}$, and using (16.2') yields (where $n \equiv \hat{A} + \hat{L}$ is called the 'natural growth rate'):

$$\omega + \eta\hat{p} = \omega + \eta(1 - \beta)\hat{k} = \beta\hat{k} + (1 - \beta)n = \beta\hat{k} + n$$

Solving for $\hat{k}$ yields:

$$\hat{k} = (\omega - n)/[\eta(\beta - 1) + \beta] \tag{16.11}$$

The capital–labour ratio in labour-efficiency units is constant, as in the neo-classical standard model, if and only if the export growth rate at constant terms of trade, $\omega = \rho\hat{Z}$, equals the natural growth rate. Another special case that yields this standard result is the small country case of a price elasticity of minus infinity, $\eta = -\infty$ (see Ziesemer 1995b). The growth rate of the terms of trade can be obtained by inserting of the latter result into (16.2'):

$$\hat{p} = (1 - \beta)(\omega - n)/[\eta(\beta - 1) + \beta] \tag{16.12}$$

The terms of trade are only constant if the growth rate of exports $\omega = \rho\hat{Z}$, equals the natural growth rate. If exports grow faster (slower) than efficient labour supply, the terms of trade will increase (fall). Writing the wage equation (16.2) in growth rates, using the results for $\hat{Y}$, $\hat{p}$ and $\hat{k}$ yields the central growth rate of the model:

$$\hat{K} = \hat{p} + \hat{Y} = \hat{w} + \hat{L} = \hat{p} + \hat{X} = \hat{k} + n$$

$$= (\omega - n)/[\eta(\beta - 1) + \beta] + n \equiv g \qquad (16.13)$$

$$= [\omega + n(\eta + 1)(\beta - 1)]/[\eta(\beta - 1) + \beta]$$

If $\omega = \rho \hat{Z}$ is small, then this growth rate can be negative for price inelastic exports, $\eta + 1 > 0$. The ω term in the the growth rate formula capture the 'engine of growth' effect emphasized by Prebisch, Singer and others. The technical progress term in n captures Kravis' (1970) 'handmaiden effect'.[2] If capital goods are imported and export opportunities are limited, then the 'engine of growth' effect is a relevant phenomenon that has to be distinguished from the 'handmaiden effect'. Therefore it is quite natural that it has also been used in the less formal sphere of economic reasoning: 'Economic growth will require increase in imports of capital goods, which must be financed through increased export sales' (Sachs, 1985, p. 548).

Economic historians describe the process of improving the trade balance under price-inelastic export demand as driven by a reduction of imports and therefore investment and growth (see Diaz-Alejandro, 1984, p. 360). Price elasticities have been estimated to be approximately –1. This leads to a maximum of the value of exports, which therefore cannot be increased by terms of trade reductions, leaving the burden of trade balance adjustment to imports. If the world economy is stagnating, then exports can clearly become a retarding factor of growth in this model. With a price elasticity of negative one exports mainly depend on the income of a countries' customers, Z, and the corresponding income elasticity. Terms of trade reductions have an impact on exports only to the extent that export demand is price elastic. As the price elasticities tend to be low the possibility to adjust the trade balance via the export side are rather limited (see also Williamson 1985, comment on Sachs 1985, p. 570).

It remains to be shown that consumption may grow at the same rate as exports, that is that $\hat{p} + \hat{c} + \hat{L} = g$, is possible. Insertion of $\hat{c}$ from (16.10) and $\hat{p}$ from (16.12) into $\hat{p} + \hat{c} + \hat{L} = g$ yields:

$$\hat{p} + \hat{c} + \hat{L} = (1 - \beta)(\omega - n)/[\eta(\beta - 1) + \beta]$$

$$+ (r + s - \rho - \hat{p})/\sigma + \hat{L}$$

$$= g$$

$$= (1 - 1/\sigma)(1 - \beta)(\omega - n)/[\eta(\beta - 1) + \beta]$$

$$+ (r + s - \rho)/\sigma + \hat{L} \qquad (16.14)$$

Except for the spread, this result contains only exogenous variables or parameters. Therefore balanced growth of output, exports and consumption can only take place if the spread obtains a certain value. If there is no spread then balanced growth can only exist if the variables of the above equations randomly generate equal values on the left and the right side. If this is not the case, exports will grow faster (slower) and consumption slower (faster) than output if ρZ is larger (smaller) and/or the interest rate is smaller (larger) than under random equality of both sides.[3]

The last equation determines the value of the spread. To be able to analyse the effects of changes of exogenous variables on the long-run equilibrium value of the spread, some manipulations are necessary. Insertion of g from (16.13) into (16.14) yields:

$$(1 - 1/\sigma)(1 - \beta(\omega - n)/[\eta(\beta - 1) + \beta] + (r + s - \rho)/\sigma + \hat{L}$$
$$= (\omega - n)/[\eta(\beta - 1) + \beta] + n$$

Solving for the spread s yields:

$$s = \sigma[1 - (1 - 1/\sigma)(1 - \beta)](\omega - n)/[\eta(\beta - 1) + \beta]$$
$$+ \sigma\hat{A} - r + \rho \tag{16.14'}$$

This allows an analysis of how the long-run equilibrium value of the spread changes if exogenous variables or parameters change:

$$\partial s/\partial r = -1,$$
$$\partial s/\partial \omega = \sigma[1 - (1 - 1/\sigma)(1 - \beta)]/[\eta(\beta - 1) + \beta] \tag{16.14''}$$
$$= (\sigma\beta + 1 - \beta)/[\eta(\beta - 1) + \beta] > 0$$

An increase of the LIBOR requires an equally large decrease of the spread to keep consumption growth at the balanced growth rate. A decrease in exports requires a decrease of the spread to ensure balanced growth, because a lower steady-state growth rate requires a lower growth rate of consumption which can be obtained from a spread reduction according to (16.10). In other words, these results are due to the fact that higher interest rates and lower export growth would result in growth path at which the rate of growth of consumption is higher than that of output and exports if spreads would not adjust. After a permanent change in world economic conditions, defined as $dr > 0$ and $d\omega < 0$, spreads must decrease to ensure long-run balanced growth:

$$ds = (\partial s / \partial r)dr + (\partial s / \partial \omega)d\omega < 0$$
$$\quad\quad\;\; - \qquad\quad +\qquad\quad\; + \qquad\quad -$$

To analyse whether or not spreads go towards their long-run equilibrium value, they are endogenized below.

16.4   THE DYNAMICS OF THE MODEL AND THE ENDOGENIZATION OF SPREADS

To be able to formulate a long-run equilibrium with constant variables and a tractable form of the dynamics, we define $y \equiv W/pY$ and $z \equiv pcL/pY$. Division of (16.3) and (16.4) by W, substraction of the central growth rate, g, and multiplication of (16.3) and (16.4) by y yields (using $wL/pY = 1 - \beta$ and $z = 1 - pX/pY$ from (16.5)):

$$\dot{y} = (r+s)y + 1 - \beta - z - gy \tag{16.3'}$$

$$\dot{y} = 1 - z - (r+s)D/pY - gy \tag{16.4'}$$

(16.10) will be divided by c on both sides; next, $\hat{p} + \hat{L} - g$ is added to both sides, using the definition of z, multiplying by z and using $\hat{p}$ from (16.12) yields:

$$\dot{z} = z(r + s - \rho)/\sigma + z\hat{p}(1 - 1/\sigma) - (g - \hat{L})z \tag{16.10'}$$

To eliminate the $\hat{p}$ term in (16.10') one can either set $\sigma = 1$ or use the long-run value of $\hat{p}$ from (16.12). In the latter case (16.10') is an approximation that is valid only in the neighbourhood of the steady state. (16.3') and (16.10') can be interpreted as a system of two equations in the two variables y and z at a given spread which still has to be endogenized. In the following it is assumed that the spread is a function of the debt–output ratio, $d \equiv D/pY$, the growth rate ω and the interest rate r:

$$s = s(d, \omega, r) \text{ with } s_d > 0,\, s_{dd} > 0,\, s_r > 0,\, s_\omega < 0 \tag{16.15}$$

In the model consisting of equations (16.3'), (16.4') and (16.10') these are the most straightforward variables of all those that have been discussed in the empirical literature on the explanation of spreads. The debt-output ratio has been found to be significant by Edwards (1984, 1986) for bank credit and bonds with the expected positive sign for both sorts of loans. The debt-export ratio is not included because the strong correlation between exports and GDP in empirical investigations (see, for example, Otani and Villanueva 1990 or Michaely 1977) implies that it suffices to include either the debt-output ratio or the debt–export ratio but not both. The export growth rate did yield a significantly negative coefficient in Feder and Just (1977). The rate of interest was a significantly positive variable in Lee (1991), where the probabilities of reschedulings were explained. It can therefore be considered as a variable that explains country risk and therefore the size of spreads. In McFadden *et al.* (1987) and Demirgüc-Kunt and Detragiache (1994) interest rates are not significant. In both, the choice of variables include the relationship between imports and the domestic product. As imports contain a great share of investment, which is negatively correlated with interest rates, the result of insignificance of interest rates can be attributed to this choice of variables. However, as the ratio of imports and the domestic product is an endogenous variable, and exogenous variables in regressions should be variables which are exogenous in theory, the result of Lee is preferred here. These assumed signs will also be obtained in connection with a second equation besides (16.15) that is necessary to explain s and d, since in (16.15) d is also an endogenous variable.

Equating the values of $\dot{y}$ from (16.3′) and (16.4′) and cancelling terms yields:

$$d = -y + \beta/(r + s) \tag{16.16}$$

Debt and wealth depend negatively on each other and $\beta/(r + s) = K/pY$. (16.15) and (16.16) are two equations to determine s and d. Both functions can be drawn in s–d space (see Figure 16.1). Because of the assumptions made in (16.15) s is a function with a positive and increasing slope. In (16.16) d is a decreasing function of s with an increasing slope. Changes of r, y and ω induce shifts in the curve with the following effects on s and d:

$$s_r(\gtrless)0,\ s_y < 0,\ s_\omega < 0,\ \text{and}\ d_r < 0,\ d_y < 0,\ d_\omega > 0 \tag{16.17}$$

In the following explanation of these results (16.15) will be called the *s*-curve and (16.16) the *d*-curve.

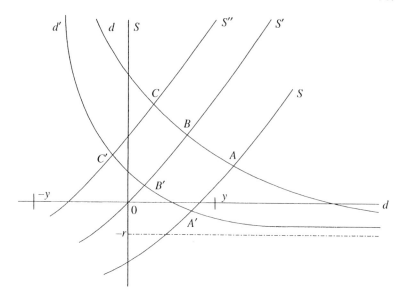

Figure 16.1   The impact of the interest rate, world economic growth and the wealth-GDP ratio on the spread and the debt/GDP ratio

Note: Spreads can be negative (*A′*) or positive (*B′* and *C′*). Debt can be positive (*A′* and *B′*) or negative (*C′*).

According to the assumptions made in (16.15), an increase in the interest rate will shift the *s*-curve upwards, because with higher risk higher spreads are required. The *d*-curve shifts downward or to the left because a higher interest rate implies a lower capital–output ratio and therefore higher debt, given domestic wealth. Therefore *d* will be decreased but the effect on *s* is unclear. In accordance with the results of Lee (1991, 1993) we assume in the following that this effect is positive. This implies that despite all mutual interdependencies, the risk effect of a change of *r* on the spread *s* from (16.15) is stronger than the effect of *r* on credit demand from (16.16).

A higher rate of growth *ω* shifts the *s*-curve to the right and downward because risk is lower under higher exports, and has no direct impact on the *d*-curve. Therefore, *s* falls and *d* increases. An increase in wealth per unit of output, *y*, shifts the *d*-curve to the left because with more wealth less debt is required and has no direct impact on the *s*-curve; *s* and *d* both decrease, because less debt also implies less risk.

This way of modelling also allows for the possibility that a country is in a creditor position. If in (16.15) the interest rate is sufficiently high and world economic growth sufficiently low and the wealth per unit of output is sufficiently high, then the curves may intersect to the left of the vertical axis. In this case the economy is in a creditor position because high interest rates and low export growth provide little incentive to accumulate capital. Moreover, wealth may be high enough to make debt superfluous. It is a major difference between this and the neo-classical standard model that the sign of d also depends on $\omega = \rho\hat{Z}$, the growth rate of the export function.

For purposes of the dynamic analysis the spread function is written as $s(y, \omega, r)$ because of the results summarized in (16.17) and derived from Figure 16.1. This function is inserted into (16.3') and (16.10').

$$\dot{y} = [r + s(y, \omega, r)]\, y + 1 - \beta - z - gy \equiv G_1 \qquad (16.3'')$$

$$\dot{z} = z[r + s(y, \omega, r) - \rho]/\sigma + zp(1 - 1/\sigma) - (g - \hat{L})z \equiv G_2 \qquad (16.10'')$$

To provide a graphical analysis, the partial derivatives of G_1 and G_2 with respect to y and z in the long-run equilibrium are considered ('<<' means 'sufficiently small'):

$$G_{1_y} = s_y y + r + s - g \lessgtr 0 \qquad \begin{array}{l} \text{if } g \geq r + s \\ \text{if } g \ll r + s \end{array}$$

$$G_{1_z} = -1 < 0, \qquad G_{2_y} = zs_y/\sigma < 0, \qquad G_{2_z} = 0.$$

The slopes of the $\dot{y} = 0$ line and the $\dot{z} = 0$ line can be written as follows:

$$\partial z/\partial y \Big|_{\dot{y}=0} = -G_{1_y}/G_{1_z} \gtrless 0 \quad \text{if} \quad G_{1_y} \gtrless 0.$$

$$\partial z/\partial y \Big|_{\dot{z}=0} = -G_{2_y}/G_{2_z} = \infty$$

The $\dot{z} = 0$ line is a vertical line in z–y space. The $\dot{y} = 0$ line is a falling line for $g \geq r + s$ and an increasing line for $g \ll r + s$. In Figure 16.2 arrows indicate the dynamics of the system. Point A in Figure 16.2 is the long-run equilibrium. It is stable only in the saddle-point sense. The initial equilibrium point is denoted as point A also in Figure 16.3.

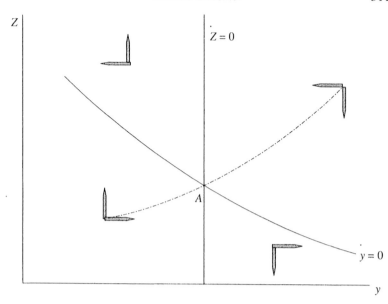

Figure 16.2   Saddle-point stability before the shock: $g \geq r + s$

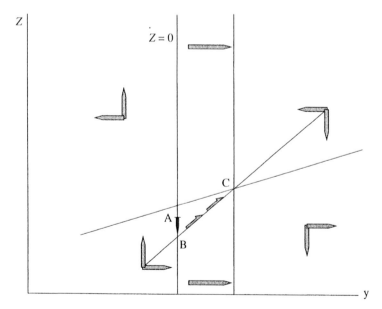

Figure 16.3   The shock and the adjustment when $g \leq r + s$

16.5   THE DEBT CRISIS AS A PERMANENT SHOCK: SHORT-RUN AND LONG-RUN EFFECTS

In the following it is assumed that before a permanent shock that leads to the debt crisis, $g \geq r + s$ is the relevant case (see Figure 16.2) because growth rates were high and real interest rates low. Afterwards $g \ll r + s$ is assumed (see Figure 16.3) because growth rates were low in the 1930s and the 1980s, the lost decade, whereas real interest rates were high. Starting from point A (alternatively, a point on the stable trajectory could be chosen as a starting point), an interest shock, $dr > 0$, and a decrease in the growth of the world economy, $d\hat{Z} < 0$, lead from a decreasing slope of the $\dot{y} = 0$ line to an increasing slope under these assumptions. $\dot{y}$ will become positive because of (3″), so that $G_{1_z} = -1$ implies that the stationary locus for $\dot{y} = 0$ lies at higher values of z after the shock. Also, $\dot{z}$ becomes positive because of (16.10″), implying that the $\dot{z} = 0$ line shifts to the right because of $G_{2_y} < 0$. The new long-run equilibrium point, C, shifts to the upper right of point A. The new stable path can be either below or above point A, depending on which locus is shifted more strongly.

The next step is to discuss short-run effects of the shock defined as effects for a given value of y.

If a jump from point A to the stable trajectory takes place, z can either increase or decrease, depending on whether the stable trajectory is in a higher or a lower position than before the shock. If z falls (increases) exports as a share of GDP, pX/pY, increase (fall), because (16.5) implies:

$$z = 1 - pX/pY \qquad (16.5')$$

If z falls and induces an increase of pX although world economic growth has decreased, $d\hat{Z} < 0$, then the terms of trade must have fallen strongly, to allow for an increase in exports, pX. If z increases and induces a decrease of pX, then this implies that $d\omega < 0$ has not been perfectly compensated by the fall in the terms of trade – for oil exporting and non-oil exporting countries from 1981–3 (see IMF, 1994, p.127) and for a group of selected countries (Sachs, 1985, p. 527) – which is one of two theoretical possiblities. Whether z did go up or down is not very clear from the data (see Ziesemer 1995c, appendix 1). If the new stable saddle path goes through A, z does not change at all for constant values of y and therefore the export ratio pX/pY must be constant in (16.5′). The value of exports falls by the same amount as the GDP does in units of foreign goods.

The increase of the interest rate r and the decrease of the growth rate $\hat{Z}$ or ω increase the spread, $ds > 0$, according to (16.17) and decrease the debt–output ratio, dd < 0, as was shown in the discussion of Figure 16.1. Increasing interest rates, $r + s$, and falling terms of trade, p, require that the marginal product of capital, F_1, increases according to (16.2) and therefore the capital – labour ratio, k, falls. Investment is therefore negative in the model as it was in Chile 1982/83 (see United Nations 1985, 1990). Imports are strongly reduced and the outcome for exports depends on the development and impact of the terms of trade – whether they fall or increase and whether export demand is price elastic or not. Empirically, almost all major debtor countries had decreasing nominal exports since 1982. The only exception here is Mexico (see IMF, various years). Therefore if z and nominal exports fall, the output in labour efficiency units, Y/AL, is falling as well because k falls and because of falling terms of trade. This also holds for GDP measured in units of foreign goods according to (16.5′). Wages measured in domestic units decrease according to (16.2) because the capital – labour ratio is decreasing. Since of $k = W/AL + D/AL$ a fall in k at a constant W/AL implies a falling debt per labour efficiency unit, D/AL, which in turn implies a falling debt, D, because AL is also constant in the short run. Decreasing wages, wL, output, pY, and consumption, pcL, (pcL falls even if consumption as a share of GDP is constant if output falls) are clear signs of a debt crisis of the economy under consideration. In Mexico imports fell by 42 per cent and wages by 32 per cent (Basu 1991, p. 2).

Next we compare the old and the new long-run equilibria and then we consider the transition. The new long-run equilibrium, point C in Figure 16.3, has a higher consumption–GDP ratio, z, and a higher wealth–GDP ratio, y, than the initial equilibrium in point A.

The steady-state growth rate of the model, g, will become lower according to (16.13) after a permanent shock, $d\hat{Z} < 0$ or $d\omega < 0$, implying that output, pY, consumption, pcL, exports, pX, the stock of capital, K, and wages, wL, all grow at a lower rate. The spread, s, decreases according to (16.14″) at a greater rate than the world market interest rate, r, increases, because $d\omega < 0$. Therefore the new equilibrium rate of interest, $r + s$, is lower than the initial one. From (16.17) it follows that at a higher interest rate, r, lower world economic growth, ω, and a higher long-run equilibrium value of the wealth–output ratio, $y = W/pY$, the ratio of debt to output must be lower. A lower $d = D/pY$ and a higher $y = W/pY$ imply a lower ratio of debt to wealth, D/W. From $\beta/(r + s) = K/pY$ in (16.16) it can be seen that the capital coefficient increases because $r + s$ decreases. This also implies that in (16.16) d decreases at a lower rate than y increases. As the capital coefficient increases, the capital–labour ratio, K/AL, also increases and therefore output per labour efficiency unit, Y/AL, also increases. As *AL* is growing, the new output path must be higher than the old one for any point in time.

The last step is to explain how the economy comes from the short-run or 'impact effect' to the higher long-run values of the consumption–output ratio, $z = pcL/pY$, and the wealth–output ratio, $y = W/pY$. As consumption and output decrease, and the growth rates of consumption and wealth both increase through higher interest rates, $r + s$, which appear through the shock, it is plausible that they end up at a higher steady-state value. However, as interest rates, $r + s$, are smaller in the new long-run equilibrium, the spreads must decrease during the adjustment process. This process of spreads jumping upward immediately after the shock but going down to lower than the initial values can be found not only in this model but also in the empirical investigation of Edwards (1986) for Brazil and Mexico.

> For both countries it was slightly negative from October 1980 through mid-1982. It then jumped, reaching peaks of more than 800 basis points for Mexico and 400 basis points for Brazil. In late 1984 and early 1985 the spreads experienced an important decline for both bonds. (Edwards, 1986, p. 582)

For Indonesia, Turkey and the Philippines spreads did decrease again since 1986 (Demirgüc-Kunt and Detragiache 1994, p. 267). Sachs and Huizinga (1987) report similar results:

> In the first round of reschedulings, in 1983, debt was recontracted with an interest spread of about 2 percentage points over LIBOR ... . In the second round of reschedulings, in 1984–85, the spread fell to about 1.2 percentage points. In the recent round the spread has fallen further, to less than 1 percentage point.

Lindert (1989) shows that spreads have been lower on average in the period 1983–6 than in 1977–81.

16.6   SUMMARY, LIMITS OF THE MODEL AND FUTURE RESEARCH

In this chapter some empirical aspects that are important in modelling the Prebisch–Singer ideas on long-run growth and development and the debt crises have been considered. These aspects were integrated into a model to emphasize the role of income and price elasticities of export demand in long-run growth and the role of decreasing exports in understanding the debt crises. The crucial features of the model from the viewpoint of long-run growth are imported capital goods and limited export demand. To understand the debt crisis an empirically plausible specification of the spread function had to be integrated. As the income of the world economy is an explicit variable of the model, a more realistic representation of the forces of long-run growth and the permanent shocks than in the one-good setting with unlimited exports was obtained. The specification of spreads allowed for an analysis of the time path of spreads after a shock that is in close accordance with the empirical literature. The debt crisis as a problem of developing countries caused by a permanent shock with decreasing output, wages and consumption and a level of debt that becomes lower in the short and the long run can also be analysed to some extent in the neoclassical one-good setting. There, however, the trade balance is just one variable. A distinction between imported capital goods and exported domestic goods is not made in that model. The fall of exports and the subsequent development of the terms of trade and the reduction of imports of capital goods become explicit, however, in the model of this chapter.

If – going beyond the narrow framework of this model – debt, D, cannot be reduced because it has been invested in irreversible capital, the analysis may be more complicated.

In the model presented above there is no microeconomic foundation of the spread function based on explicit risk analysis. The specification of the spread function is based on the empirical literature on country risk, leaving microfoundation as a topic for future research that should take export demand functions and imported capital goods explicitly into account.

Notes

1. This chapter is an abbreviated and translated version of ch. 8 of T. Ziesemer (1995c). I would like to thank A.K Dutt, W. Schelkle and P.N. Snowden for their helpful comments. I take full responsibility for the contents.
2. For an extensive interpretation of the growth rate formula in terms of these effects as well as a graphical representation of the impact of income and price elasticities of demand on real wages and the terms of trade the reader is referred to Ziesemer (1995b, Section B) where the same results are obtained in a model without debt.
3. See Ziesemer (1995a) for an extended analysis of this unbalanced growth path case.

References

Bardhan, P.K. and S. Lewis (1970) 'Models of Growth with Imported Inputs', *Economica*, pp. 373–85.

Basu, K. (1991) 'The International Debt Problem, Credit Rationing and Loan Pushing: Theory and Experience', *Princeton Studies in International Finance*, no. 70 (October).

Demirgüc-Kunt, A. and E. Detragiache (1994) 'Interest Rates, Official Lending, and the Debt Crisis: A reassessment', *Journal of Development Economics*, vol. 44, pp. 263–85.

Diaz-Alejandro, C. (1984) 'Latin American debt: I don't think we are it causes Any More', *Brooking: Papers on Economic Activity*, pp. 335–89.

Edwards, S. (1984) 'LDC Foreign Borrowing and Default Risk: An Empirical Investigation, 1976–80', *American Economic Review* (September) pp. 726–34.

—— (1986) 'The Pricing of Bonds and Bank Loans in International Markets', *European Economic Review*, vol. 30, pp. 565–89.

Faini, R.F., Clavijo and A. Senhadji-Semlali (1992) 'The Fallacy of Composotion Argument: Does Demand Matter for LDC Manufactured Exports?', *European Economic Review*, vol. 36, pp. 865–82.

Feder, and R.E. Just (1977) 'A Study of Debt Servicing Capacity Applying Logit Analysis', *Journal of Development Economics*, vol. 4, pp. 25–38.

Hentschel, J. (1992) 'Imports and Growth in Highly Indebted Countries. An Empirical Study', in *et al.* (eds), *Studies in International Economics and Institutions* Berlin: (Springer-Verlag).

IMF (1989, 1991, 1994) *International Financial Statistics Yearbook*.

Kravis, I.B. (1970) 'Trade as a Handmaiden of Growth', *Economic Journal*, pp. 850–72.

Lee, S.H. (1991) 'Ability and Willingness to Service Debt as Explanation for Commercial and Official Rescheduling Cases', *Journal of Banking and Finance*, vol. 15, pp. 5–27.

—— (1993) 'Are the Credit Ratings Assigned by bankers based on the Willingness of LDC Borrowers to Repay?', *Journal of Development Economics*, vol. 40, pp. 349–59.

Lindert, P.H. (1989) 'Response to Debt Crisis: What is Different about the 1980?', in B. Eichengreen and P.H. Lindert (eds) *The International Debt Crisis in Historical Perspective* (Cambridge Mass.: MIT Press) pp. 227–75.

McFadden, D., R. Eckaus, G. Feder, V. Hajivassiliou and S. O'Connell (1985) 'Is There Life after Debt? An Econometric Analysis of the Creditworthiness of Developing Countries', in G.W. Smith and J.T. Cuddington *International Debt and the Developing Countries* (eds) (Washington: The World Bank) pp. 179–209.

Michaely, M. (1977) 'Exports and Growth, An Empirical Investigation', *Journal of Development Economics*, vol. 4, pp. 49–53.

Otani, I. and D. Villanueva (1990) 'Long-term Growth in Developing Countries and its Determinants: An Empirical Analysis', *World Development*, vol. 18, pp. 769–83.

Prebisch, R. (1950) 'The Economic Development of Latin America and its Principal Problems', reprinted in *Economic Bulletin for Latin America*, vol. 7 (1962) pp. 1–22.

—— 'Commercial Policy in the Underdeveloped Countries', *American Economic Review (Papers and Proceedings*, vol. 49, no. 2, pp. 251–73.

Sachs, D. (1985) 'External Debt and Macroeconomic Performance in Latin America and East Asia', *Brookings Papers on Economic Activity*, no. 2, pp. 523–73.

—— and H. Huizinga (1987) 'U.S. Commercial Banks and the Developing-Country Debt Crisis', *Brookings Papers on Economic Activity*, no. 2, pp. 555–606.

Singer, H.W. (1950) 'The distribution of Gains Between Investing and Borrowing Countries', *American Economic Review*, vol. 40, no. 2.

—— (1958) 'Comment on Charles P. Kindleberger, The Terms of Trade and Economic Development', *Review of Economics and Statistics*, vol. 40, pp. 72–90.

—— (1991) 'Terms of Trade: New Wine and New Bottles?', *Development Policy Review*, vol. 9, no. 4 (December).

Stern, R.M., J. Francis and B. Schumacher (eds) (1976) *Price Elasticities in International Trade*. (London: Macmillan).

Thirlwall, A.P. (1983) 'Foreign Trade Elasticities in Centre–Periphery Models of Growth and Development', *Banca Nazionale Del Lavoro Quarterly Review* (September) pp. 249–61.

United Nations (1985) *National Accounts Statistics: Main Aggregates and Detailed Tables, 1982* (New York: United Nations,).

—— (1990) *National Accounts Statistics: Main Aggregates and Detailed Tables, 1988* (New York: United Nations).

Williamson, J. (1988, 1989) *Voluntary approaches to debt relief* (Washington, DC: Institute for International Economics).

Ziesemer, T. (1995a) 'Growth with Imported Inputs, Limited Export Demand and Foreign Debt', *Journal of Macroeconomics* (Winter) pp. 31–53.

—— (1995b) 'Economic Development and Endogenous Terms of Trade Determination: Re-examination and Reinterpretation of the Prebisch–Singer Thesis', *UNCTAD Review*, pp. 17–34.

—— (1995c) 'Ursachen von Verschuldungskrisen: Theorie, Empirie und Politik', *Habilitationsschrift* (September) pp. 314 and ix.

17 Uncertainty in a Model of Small Agriculture in Peru: Some Preliminary Results

Hans Jürgen Jaksch

17.1 INTRODUCTION

There seems to be a growing appreciation that small agriculture is composed of economic units, or, as we also prefer to say in lack of a better terminology, of economic organizations which defy to be subsumed under the heading of conventional microeconomic models, private households or enterprises. Thus, in a voluminous book edited by Hoff *et al.* (1993) the characteristics of these organizations are treated from a theoretical and empirical point of view, apparently exhaustively. On the other hand, there are even textbooks filling this apparent gap in the economic literature (for example, Ellis 1988). However, if one settles down to study the behaviour of this sector of the economy in a certain empirical context, one is overwhelmed by the inability of the literature to explain fully the observed behaviour of the observed facts. To my taste, the first of the mentioned volumes treats too many, and the second one not enough aspects proper to small agriculture. If this is state of the art in the respective field of economics, it has the practical consequence that the economist can give little meaningful advice on what economic policy measures should be undertaken towards this sector of the economy. These could be measures to incorporate this sector further into the existing economic structure, or at least to avoid its further separation from it. The impact of these policy measures could in the extreme be world-wide, since it is small agriculture which in Peru produces the raw material for one of the most important drugs in illegal international drug traffic, cocaine.

Our first positive observation on the theory of the small peasant household or enterprise is that it should not deviate too far from the well-known theoretical models of standard microeconomic theory, at least in its basic conception. This statement must be relativated at once since, in order to capture realistic traits of the economic agents in question, and concepts must be used which are alien to standard microeconomic theory. In our

318

context this will be the concept of uncertainty, of which we regard risk as a special case. standard microeconomic theory can certainly be enriched by adding the concepts of risk and uncertainty, but, we think that its relative importance should be greater in a model of small agriculture.

Let us explain this point of view in an example. In the literature there appears the seemingly exact contraposition of formal and informal agriculture. However, we are convinced that the contraposition is of little help in the context treated here, since the extension and guarantee of property rights, so important in the new institutional microeconomics, is something very relative. This does not only concern the production of coca, but also the landholding of small peasants in southern Peru which is not, or not principally, the coca-producing area of that country (Morales, 1989). Thus, within the peasant villages in this more southern part of Peru, there exists some local enforcement of social customs which apparently is founded in tradition and has little to do with the existing formal law (Gonzales de Olarte, 1994).

We have mentioned the fact that microeconomic model building should be simple and tied to the traditional procedure of economic theory. In addition, it should not be *ad hoc* in the sense that the basis of the model is valid only for the observed circumstance. Too much ad-hockery would, in my opinion, destroy the predictive validity of the model. This validity should certainly be preserved, since we want to use the model for purposes of economic policy, not only as an academic exercise.

In this chapter, we distinguish four areas in which uncertainty governs the behaviour of the small peasant. We first sketch a very simple model for the economic organization in question. This model hardly needs to be explained in formal terms. Since we want to avoid misunderstandings, and in order to point out the areas where uncertainty comes in, we nevertheless present it in some simple mathematics at the end of the next section. Then we outline the four areas where uncertainty determines the actions of the small peasant and characterize its origins more precisely. Finally, we justify our assumptions by referring to the situation of the small peasant in the Andes of Peru.

17.2   A MICROECONOMIC MODEL FOR THE SMALL AGRICULTURAL ORGANIZATION

It is common in economics to model microeconomic and even macroeconomic relations by distinguishing two types of relationships: the first is an idealized description of the set of alternatives from which a decision-maker chooses; the second a principle according to which he or she chooses an element or a subset from this set. Examples are the budget set and the utility function in the theory of the household, the production function and the profit function in the theory of the enterprise, and the Phillips curve (if there exists one) and the preference function of the policy-maker from which he or she chooses an optimal combination of unemployment and inflation rates.

Beginning with the second relationship, we assume that the peasant head of a family which operates the agricultural organization in question, maximizes his utility. Empirically, the decision-maker is mostly a male in the countries to which we refer, and we assume that his utility serves as a proxy for the utility of the entire organization. The arguments of the utility function will be described below, first in a very abstract and then in a more realistic manner.

We do not yet presuppose any properties of this utility function. Especially, we shall try to avoid specifying this function explicitly. Some of the properties of the utility function will follow in the course of our arguments. Even this early we may assure the reader that they are in accordance with standard economic theory.

There are two principal arguments for not considering the maximization of profits instead of the maximization of utility. First, the model of our economic organization is supposed to be only partly market-orientated, and this orientation has probably been even smaller in the past than it is today. Second, in modern microeconomic theory the principle of maximizing a profit function is derived from the assumption that the entrepreneur (for simplicity, we assume a single person) maximizes his utility. Therefore, historically and logically, utility maximization precedes profit maximization.

Let us now turn to the production set which the respective peasant family faces. It consists principally of two types of resources: family labour and land.

Regarding family labour, we assume that the utility function refers to a planning period which we (provisionally) identify with one year. During this year, the labour potential of the family is given, first by the physical and biological composition of the family, and second by habit. Exceeding this potential is impossible, and not working to the limit increases the family utility only if the consumption standard does not decrease. This is possible only if labour productivity increases due to an increase of the available quantities of the other factor(s) of production, or to innovations.

The second factor of production available to the peasant family is land in a given amount and quality. The question of property rights does not arise at the moment. Thus, land is available to the household with certainty during the planning period. However, availability of this land at a later time may at present be uncertain.

Whereas underutilization of labour increases utility if simultaneously all other variables entering the utility function remain unchanged, the utilization of land does not enter the utility function. Thus, it does not make any difference to the household if the respective plot of land is completely utilized or not, provided all other variables remain constant.

Finally, the family produces a single product which it needs for its nourishment. This product, together with leisure, are the only two arguments of the utility function. The family maximizes this utility function under the condition of the given production function.

This problem can easily be solved with the available tools of microeconomic theory. In order to present the starting point of our investigation as clearly as possible, we now turn to a more formal description of our model. All symbols refer to a certain time span, for example a year.

The economic organization maximizes its utility function f with respect to two variables, agricultural output y and leisure x:

$$Max f(0, y, x) \qquad (17.1)$$

$f(0, y, x)$ is strictly monotonically increasing with respect to either of the two variables y and x, and, in this order, lexicographic. The appearance of the symbol zero as a first argument of the utility function f is explained by the fact that in a subsequent generalization of the model we shall consider another consumption good besides the one produced by the economic organization. For the time being, however, we disregard its existence.

(17.1) is maximized under the constraint of a production function g. This function is dependent on two variables, labour l and land a, and at least for the time being we assume that g is differentiable everywhere with respect to the two variables, monotonically strictly increasing with respect to either variable, and strictly concave everywhere:

$$y = g(l, a) \qquad (17.2)$$

Finally, work and leisure time sum to a constant:

$$const. = l + x \qquad (17.3)$$

With regard to (17.2), we do not assume that land is a limitational factor of production with respect to labour. Thus, adding one unit of labour to the amount of labour usually employed on the farm or in the household yields an additional positive amount of output. However, we do not assume that this marginal product is bounded below by a positive number. It can therefore be very small, and for all practical purposes this should be tantamount to a zero marginal product.

The simplicity of the model makes it unnecessary to mobilize the standard mathematical apparatus of the microeconomist in order to derive the consequences of our assumptions. Simple reasoning in plain English should do the trick.

Let us thus assume that the utility of the economic unit is maximized. It then follows from our assumptions that the family labour is fully utilized. For if it were not so, then employing somewhat more labour, and leaving all other variables unchanged, would increase the family's utility since the output increases, and the decreasing leisure does not decrease utility. Thus, in our simple model, the family's labour is fully employed, and the same is true for the available land.

The reader may wonder why we do not assume that leisure has a certain utility of its own, that is, it could be traded off against the availability of the agricultural product produced on the land. To put it more formally, we have not yet explained why we assume a lexicographic utility function, with the first argument the agricultural product and the second one leisure. Since the reasoning for it will draw on the observations of reality, we shall return to it in the final section of this chapter.

Indeed, the simple model which we have shown above does not permit any interesting insights. We therefore generalize it in two steps.

First, let us assume that the peasant household may carry its product to the market and sell it there at a given price. Since the economic organization which we consider here is small in comparison to the total supply and demand at this market, it cannot influence the price by varying the quantity supplied. In addition, for the cash obtained at the market the peasant family could buy a certain amount of another good supplied at this market by an exogenous supplier at a constant price. Again, the economic organization which consists of this peasant family cannot influence the price of this second commodity by a variation of its demand. In addition, we assume that this commodity cannot be produced by the peasant household. Let us analyse the behaviour of our peasant family, especially the manner in which it divides its resources on the consumption of both commodities.

As a mental device, we divide the action of the peasant household into two steps: first, this household produces a certain amount of its agricultural product and sells all of it on the respective market; second, it divides the revenue of this operation into two parts: with the first, it purchases the first commodity, with the second the other commodity, the division of the revenue being such that the organization maximizes its utility (which, of course, is now a function of the quantity of both commodities). Since we assume that transaction costs do not exist, this ficticious subdivision of sales and purchases cannot change the result which we would obtain if we were to assume that the respective organization sells only the quantity it desires to exchange for the other commodity on the market, and with the revenue purchases the desired quantity of the good which is supplied exogenously.

Obviously, a necessary condition for maximizing the organization's utility is that it obtains a maximal revenue from its (ficticious) sales. This, in turn, is the case if both resources are fully employed in the production of the agricultural good. Underemployment of either resource would not increase the organization's utility. Given this maximal revenue, we proceed in a second step to derive its division on the two commodities. This is completely analogous to the procedure in standard microeconomic theory, and we therefore do not analyse this problem further. Of course, a few assumptions about the formal properties of the family's utility function are necessary in order to make this derivation conclusive: similarly, this analysis must take into account the first step where the maximal revenue of the household is determined. Otherwise, a result could be that the family repurchases more than the amount of its product which it has originally supplied on the market. However, this is impossible if it does not have other cash resources than the (ficticious) sale of its agricultural product.

We again turn to a more formal presentation of our microeconomic model.

In addition to the commodity produced by the economic organization in question, we now consider another consumption good z which the organization can only purchase on the market, and which enters the utility function in addition to y. We therefore obtain:

$$Max \ f \ (z, y, x) \tag{17.4}$$

For any given amount of z, f has the properties assumed above for f in the case of $z = 0$, and we assume that f is first maximized with respect to the two consumption goods, that is the variables z and y, and only when these quantities are given, with respect to x. For any given x, we assume f to possess the usual properties of a microeconomic utility function.

As we have argued above, z and y can be traded in a market at a given positive price, which we call p and q respectively. Let $x = x'$ be the minimal amount of leisure which the household needs for its survival. We then obtain from (17.3):

$$l' = \text{const.} - x'$$

Inserting this into the production function (17.3) leads to:

$$y = g(l', a) \tag{17.5}$$

which is monotonically strictly increasing if we augment a. Maximization of (17.4) thus implies the maximization of (17.5) with respect to a. Let us assume that we obtain this maximum for $a = a'$, and that the respective output of the product of the economic organization is $y = y'$.

The (ficticious) sale of this quantity in the market would yield the revenue qy'. The economic organization now maximizes $f(z, y, x')$: since x' is given, this utility function is maximized with respect to z and y only.

Because f is assumed to have the respective properties, this yields the necessary optimizing conditions well known from the standard microeconomic analysis of the private household:

$$p/q = -[\delta f(z, y, x')/\delta y]/[\delta f(z, y, x')/\delta z]$$

From this equation and the budget constraint

$$gy + pz = qy'$$

we deduce the quantities y'', z' which the economic organization finally consumes.

The inclusion of a commodity which is produced outside of the small family farm generalizes the simple model which we have outlined in the first step, and which is valid for an economic organization of that type if it is isolated from the outside world. However, the (unique) output of the agricultural commodity is not the only asset which the small family farm can sell on an external market.

As a second generalization, we assume that the economic organization in question also may supply labour on this market, either 'in the city', or to some other economic organization which is not necessarily a peasant household-enterprise. The wage rate is paid in money and given, that is, it cannot be varied by the family by varying its labour supply. All other assumptions which we have made above remain valid in this model.

As has been derived above, it can again be proved that, in order to maximize the utility function, the household is fully employed, either producing its agricultural product, or working outside of the economic organization. Of course, family members may also work part-time in one and part-time in the other activity.

If this is accepted, there remains the question of how the labour supply is divided into labour at home and labour outside the organization. Here, the aim must be to maximize total revenue, again assuming ficticiously that all of the agricultural product is sold at the given price in the market. This maximal revenue then is used to (ficticiously) repurchase part or all of the product sold before, and, if the total maximal revenue permits this, even purchase some additional quantity of this product, while the remainder of the revenue is used to purchase the product supplied from the outside of our economic organization.

In order to determine the maximal revenue, we may proceed in the following way: assume that for a given input of land (here, total land that is available to the family) the product is a strictly monotonically increasing, concave and differentiable function of the input of labour. (This is a property of agricultural production functions which is usually assumed in microeconomic theory.) Then, the value marginal product (that is, the derivative multiplied by the product price) decreases along this function, and we assume that it does so continuously). If total revenue is maximized, then either this value marginal product equals the wage rate, yielding uniquely the division of labour of the family on both the internal and external use; or, this value marginal product exceeds the wage rate for all points of the function, all labour is used on the family farm, and if the wage rate exceeds the value marginal product for all points of the function, all labour is sold on the external market, and none remains for use on the family farm. Let us finally introduce the assumption that labour can also be sold outside of the family farm into our formal model.

First, we now must subdivide the amount of labour which is available to the family farm into three components: leisure (x), the amount of labour used for production within the farm (l), and the amount of labour sold in the free market m. Instead of (17.3), we obtain the more general equation

$$\text{const.} = x + l + m \qquad (17.6)$$

If both l and m have been determined, we may proceed as described above in order to compute the values of y'' and z', that is, the respective amounts of both commodities, the one produced at home and the one bought in the market, which the organization consumes.

A necessary condition for maximizing the utility function is that the economic organization maximizes its revenue from its real and ficticious sales in the market. These sales now consist of two commodities: the produce of the family farm, already considered above, and the amount of labour sold at the given price of w outside of this economic organization. It therefore maximizes

$$gy + wm = qf(l, a') + wm$$

under the condition of (17.6), where $x = x'$, a given constant.

Solving (17.6) for m and inserting into this equation shows that this is equivalent to the maximization of

$$qf(l, a') - wl$$

with respect to l. A necessary condition for an interior maximum is

$$q(\delta f(l, a')/\delta l) = w$$

the equation which we have discussed in the text. If no interior maximum exists, we must choose the derivative either as small or as large as possible.

It is true that this simple model may overstate the facility of members of the economic organization to migrate. To a certain extent, the introduction of uncertainty may capture the inhibitions that farmers face when they consider leaving their homesteads. If this does not reflect these inhibitions adequately, a certain fixed cost of migration must be taken into account.

We think that this simple model contains all necessary ingredients for a model reflecting the complex reality of small farms in Peru. However, if we let our model stand as it is, we doubt that new insights into the behaviour of the small economic organization can be gained, because, in our opinion, a very important aspect of its economic activity is missing: the uncertainty of the results of its actions. Provisionally, we shall distinguish uncertainty at both places where our economic organization is active, namely in producing the agricultural product and in selling labour on the outside labour market. This will be explained in more detail in the following section. It will be convenient to remember the simple basic model of the economic organization, which assumes that this organization is not connected to the outside economy, and which is described by (17.1) to (17.3) above, and its extension in two steps, where in the first step we assume that the organization can trade its product in the outside market, and in the second we consider the possibility of even selling its labour to an outside demand.

17.3   UNCERTAINTY AS A NATURAL AND AS AN INSTITUTIONAL PHENOMENON

Contemplating the variables that are open to be realistically defined as uncertain, we begin with the set of assumptions concerning the production activities of the peasant family. First, all human activity, and especially agricultural production, is open to uncertainty regarding the production result. This is partly due to the fact that natural conditions, such as sunshine and rainfall, influence the amount of the product harvested after several months or even a year after beginning the production process. In this case, the output is a variable which may exceed, but may also run short of, the expected quantity. This type of uncertainty, well known in the economic literature, already yields a number of problems and questions which we think show that even the first step of our simple theoretical model, the one described by (17.1) to (17.3), can be used to explain some of the observed phenomena.

The first question may be the one of how to introduce the uncertainty about the outcome of the agricultural production process into this model. The first and perhaps formally most simple procedure, so well known from standard econometric modelling, is to introduce an additive stochastic variable into the production function and to assume some properties of a probability distribution from which this stochastic variable is drawn. Thus, if this variable is stochastically independent of all other variables appearing in the model, then it still seems to be reasonable to assume the validity of (17.1) to (17.3). This means that the economic organization would still maximize its utility by fully using its resources in order to produce the agricultural good in question. If, however, we compare the utility of the organization derived from any two different harvest periods, this utility in general will vary since the output will vary because the hazards of the weather and other natural factors have been taken into account.

As a first consequence, it follows that the organization probably would do well to develop certain storage facilities for the agricultural product, for it may well be that a bad harvest means starvation, even if its formal consequence is euphemistically described as a situation of 'smaller utility'. On the other hand, storage of the output will be connected with certain losses and other costs connected with maintaining the storage facilities, which could probably be minimized if this economic unit has access to fiat money, as it is assumed in the extension of our basic theoretical model. Even this observation does not end the story. Assume that the access to fiat money is twofold, to a national currency which loses its value over time relatively fast, but in unpredictable steps, and to a foreign currency the purchasing power of which is much more stable over time (but which perhaps can even be obtained only by sales of one's product or labour which are legally questionable). It may thus be not only a rational choice to gain access to this currency, but it may even be mandatory in order to survive the hazards of agricultural production in a certain environment.

From these considerations it follows that the introduction of uncertainty into the production function of the economic organization already permits us to pose a number of very realistic questions even if we start with a simple and abstract model, and if we do consider a type of uncertainty quite well known in the economic literature.

However, connected with the production function may exist some other type of uncertainty, which is, contrary to the one previously described, man-made: the uncertainty about the title of the land which is used as a factor of production. Only if this title is established beyond doubt, and if the credibility of the government or other institution or person issuing this title is firmly and objectively enforced, is there no uncertainty as to the results of the production activities of the peasant family.

If this is not so, the peasant family must count with payments in money or kind in order to maintain its land as a factor of production, facing eviction or other type of violence if it does not comply with the demands of the powerful. This type of uncertainty, which certainly has to do with the institutional arrangements of production, must also appear in our model.

In the following section, we will describe some of the complicated rules that a peasant in the Peruvian Andes faces if he and his family works on a lot of land from which they derive their means of existence. If we introduce uncertainty about the property rights into our simple theoretical model above, we have to consider a sequence of harvest periods over time and the uncertainty of working on the determined lot in the future periods. This uncertainty affects possible investments in the land (not yet considered in the theoretical model), and storage activities, which may have to do with the uncertainties about agricultural output and thus relate to the uncertainties connected with the production activity.

We now turn to the second factor of production which appears in our model, labour. Of course, there are the general hazards connected with labour input, even when working on one's own farm, that are especially connected with the worker's health. However, we do not think that it is very important to introduce uncertainty of this kind into our model, since health problems of this sort can probably be taken into account by the peasant at the beginning of the production period if these problems recur regularly, and epidemic deceases affecting the whole family probably cannot be foreseen by the head of the family anyhow.

There remains the uncertainty connected with employment outside of the family farm, for example the uncertainty of finding employment when a member of the family migrates into the city. It is probably a well-taken point of view that employment in the city is rationed (Harris and Todaro 1970). This means that at the going wage rate in the city, there is unemployment on the urban labour market. The reasons for the immobility of the wage rate downward may simply be the fact that the wage rate is not only a market price, but that labour income is bounded below since the worker must be able to sustain himself from his total earnings. Following Harris and Todaro more closely, as Behrman and Hanson (1979) do, it may also be that labour union practices limit the wage rate from below and thus ration the demand for labour. In any case, finding even a part-time and not at all well-paid employment in the city is an uncertain event, and this must be taken into account by a worker who decides to migrate.

The question now arises as to how to model this type of uncertainty within the above model. It is true that the migrating worker does not necessarily find employment outside of his family organization with certainty. As a first approximation, we may assume that the labour supply function on the outside labour market is stochastic, and the simplest way of how to include a stochastic variable into this model would be to add one to the labour supply function of the economic organization on this outside market. In addition, it would be necessary to stipulate further that this variable can only assume non-positive values that can be interpreted as enforced leisure due to unsuccessful search for an outside employment. However, in addition to Harris and Todaro 1970, we must assume that characteristics other than the expected value of the probability distribution(s) in question are important for a rational decision of the peasant to look for paid employment outside of the family farm. It may well be that his search for employment leads to personal desaster. If the prospective migrant perceives correctly that the risk of starving in one situation is greater than in another one, the worker will be less inclined to look for outside employment in the first of these cases, even if the expected value of employment is (somewhat) smaller in the second than in the first.

In addition, we must consider the uncertainty that the worker incurs if he or she migrates in order to work in another agricultural activity which is not protected by the law. Here the uncertainty in obtaining a certain wage is connected with the economic success or failure of this activity, and probably depends on the threat of being in discord with one of the connected parties, be they legal or illegal. The work in this case is not necessarily agricultural work, but may also consist of some simple industrial activity or transportation.

To repeat, we see two broad areas where uncertainty must be introduced into our model: the basic agricultural production of the economic organization in question, and its sale of labour outside of its proper place of living and work. Both of these areas, in turn, are again divided into two subareas each. In the first case, it is natural hazard as well as social organization which may threaten the returns of peasant family's activity and hence the utility derived from this product. In the second case, the sale of one's person labour outside of the family's original habitat leads to uncertain returns, either because the demand for this labour is rationed by natural or institutional bounds, or because the institutional setting under which this sale takes place is not certain and established without powerful opposition.

We treat all of these four points, and their respective appearance in Peru, in the following section.

17.4   SOME EMPIRICAL OBSERVATIONS ON SMALL AGRICULTURE IN PERU

Economics as a science of the world around us is not a purely formal or logical exercise. Even if we regard our study as a predominantly methodological or theoretical one, the assumptions underlying the model presented above can be justified by facts which are described already in the existing literature.

For Peru, the most informative descriptions of the existing situation of small agriculture, with some theoretical explanations, are Gonzales de Olarte, 1994, and Gonzales de Olarte *et al.*, 1987. Without necessarily following the theory of these authors, we accept their description of the general economic situation of small peasantry in Peru and refer the reader in detail to this literature and the sources used by these authors. The general economic situation of Peru, however, is probably most clearly presented in the report of the World Bank 1994. Unfortunately, this report does not explicitly treat a very important aspect of the Peruvian situation, namely the illegal production of coca for the export of cocaine. This has a profound impact on the overall economic situation of this country.

Though small agriculture has played an important role in Peruvian history, its participation in the overall economic activity has declined in recent decades. This is due to the smaller population growth in this sector of the economy in comparison to the rest of the country, caused also by migration from the countryside. Presently, small agriculture should comprise about two-thirds (my own estimate) of the population active in agriculture, or about 20 per cent of the Peruvian population.

Small agriculture in our sense mostly settles at heights of 2000–4000 metres in the Andes – 77 per cent of the agricultural establishments in this range could be called small agriculture. In the southern Peruvian provinces of Junin, Cuzco, Puno and Ayacucho, 55 per cent of the agricultural establishments qualify as small agriculture.

These economic organizations are run on the average by a family of five. A minimal plot size of 0.36 hectares is mentioned in the quoted literature and a maximal one of 7.5 hectares, the most frequent size being about 1 hectare or 2 hectares. Contribution of this type of small agriculture to Peruvian GNP is is reported to be about 4 per cent.

The fact that the economic organizations which we consider here have a principal asset, namely land, in strongly varying sizes means that we can distinguish 'rich' from 'medium' and 'poor' peasant families. It is true that this means that our sample is inhomogeneous in important aspects. However, according to Gonzales de Olarte (1994) the behaviour of these peasant families varies with their wealth (as measured by the size of the land that they work on). Let us see if we can explain some of these variations with the aid of the theoretical model described in the previous sections.

One of these differences among the small farms is the main crop produced by them. (We refer the reader to Gonzales de Olarte 1994 for a closer description of the different crops that must be considered here, as well as the kinds and numbers of lifestock to be considered in this context.) However, one observation due to Gonzales de Olarte (and other authors) should be mentioned right away: the wealthier a peasant family is, the more likely it is that this family will take risks with respect to the output which it produces.

This fact can easily be explained if we consider the theory outlined above. Let us assume that the farm output can be produced in two alternative ways that, for the sake of simplicity, vary only with respect to the distribution of the random variable which we again assume to be additive in the production function. Assume even that these distributions have the same expected value, but have a different variance. Then a greater variance may mean a more pronounced danger of starvation, and it is reasonable that the economic organization chooses to produce with the first production function.

This consequence remains true if the latter production function is disturbed by an additive random variable which possessess a greater expected value than the first one, at least if there do not exist adequate storage possibilities for the economic organization, or cash reserves to overcome deficiencies of the agricultural output. The wealthier an organization is, say with respect to its landholding, the more likely it will be that facilities of this kind will be available, and we therefore can assume that the organization chooses a more risky crop if it is wealthier.

An alternative model to the one used above would be one derived from game theory, where the poorest organization, but not necessarily a richer one, would choose a minimax strategy when facing the natural hazards of agricultural production. Then the organization would realize the output which it can secure for itself in the long run, regardless of the natural hazards in question. This approach would consider all other outputs or production processes open to the economic organization, and it may well be that an optimal strategy in this sense consists in changing crops. However, the economic organization would secure for itself the minimum of the maximal possible outputs applying a mixed strategy in the sense of game theory. This means that the average output in the long run is the organization's target, and not the output in each production period which we have considered in our model.

Turning now to the other aspect of landholding which is connected via property rights to uncertainty, we must mention the official, that is legal aspects of landholding which, however, do not exhaust the set of rules which the organization must follow. In addition, it must obey a set of rules valid in the community to which this organization belongs, and enforced by sanctions from within this community.

Discussing these prescriptions would lead us too far into the singularities of how to model the uncertainty stemming from these property rights. We therefore mention only one facet of the official rights: The land allocated to the economic organization is under certain conditions not to be sold – that is, the proprietor cannot transfer the property rights of 'his' land at will.

Again we do not go into the details of this rule, which of course (at least outwardly) is meant to protect the proprietor against undue risks. However, in this case uncertainty is diminished by limiting the property rights, not by enforcing them. This probably also diminishes the utility of the economic organization, since it may be impossible to use the land as a collateral if credit is needed, and we have pointed out that credit or money may be the most economical way of bridging years of bad harvests and therefore a small supply of food to the farming family.

Reality therefore provides us with a very complex picture with respect to the output of the economic organization which we consider here, and the same is true with respect to the labour input. Whereas it is natural that the use of other kinds of inputs, as tools and, to some extent, pesticides and herbicides, becomes more important as the wealth of the peasant family increases, we shall not stress this point too much but at once concentrate on the other important input of our economic organization, labour.

Again, the picture is very complicated if we consider it in all detail (Gonzales de Olarte 1994). We shall simplify it according to our needs and hope not to leave out any important fact.

First, the family is the basic unit supplying labour on the land. Apart from migration, this labour is something like a fixed factor for the decision-maker, the family head, since the family has to be fed regardless of whether its members are employed or go idle. There is a seasonal cycle of employment, so some months of the year must be bridged with the repair of the house and the tools which are used to till the soil.

An important aspect of the family farm is that work is interchanged in kind among the families of the community, and it is usual to help out other families in times of high demand for labour. This is done reciprocally, so if one family helps out another one, the second family is bound to help out the first one in a similar situation. Rich farmers also employ labour paid in money wages, often recruited from (poorer) relatives, and hire out some of their land in some kind of sharecropping. However, all of these arrangements do not disturb the picture so much that we cannot uphold the basic theoretical construction of a family farm which we have presented in the section 17.2 above.

Even though in the farms there seem to be periods in the year when no urgent work in the fields presses the family, leisure is apparently not a value cherished for its own sake, at least outside the customary time necessary to eat and sleep. It may be that historically leisure above this minimal physical standard was never available, and we have therefore refrained from giving leisure a utility of its own. The lexicographic property of the utility function mentioned in the second section above is derived from this observation.

Let us now turn to the sales of labour outside of the farm. Here, we do not consider the fact that labour may be sold to some of the ('rich') farms themselves.

The fact that agricultural production underlies seasonal fluctuations makes it natural that idle farm labour looks for employment outside of the farms. This is empirically established, with some interesting additional empirical detail (Gonzales de Olarte 1994). Leaving out for the time being the wealthiest peasants, the poorer a family is, the more it tends to migrate in order to look for outside work. This is true with respect to the average number of days worked outside by a family member. In addition, the poorer a farmer family is, the further it seems to migrate in order to look for a job outside of the farm. Members of poorer families move as far as the capital of Peru, Lima, whereas members of richer families tend to move to the nearest provincial capital, for example Cuzco. The poorer people tend to be harder pressed to look for remunerative employment than the richer ones, at the same time, the richer ones seem to be more reluctant to move from the land which provides most of its livelihood. An exception to this rule apparently are the (very) rich people among this sample, since they also migrate, feeling apparently secure to return to their possessions after having earned an income outside of the farm. Relating this to the descriptions above of the hazards of finding a remunerative employment in the city, and sticking to the poor to medium families, we may say that the willingness to incur risk in looking for urban employment increases with increasing poverty of the peasant family.

In this context, we should also consider the movement to other activities such as as coca production for the export of coca paste or cocaine. However, we shall leave this important aspect out for the moment, since here small agriculture is concerned which does not necessarily conincide with the areas mentioned above. Geographically, a more northern part of Peru is concerned than the four provinces mentioned above, and we do not have adequate information about it at the moment.

Let us finally try to incorporate the uncertainty which is related to the difficulty of finding urban employment to the theoretical model of the two previous sections above. The basic idea again is that the poorer a family is, the less it can afford uncertainty about the outcome of a certain economic activity, for a negative result means starvation or near starvation. Now let us suppose that such a family is exposed to the random fluctuations of the agricultural output of its family farm, and that it is impossible to reduce these fluctuations by shifting the production to other techniques or even another agricultural product. If this family decides to look for employment outside of the economic organization, it may face the risk of being employed only part-time, but even this part-time employment may suffice for survival. A wealthier family, however, may face damage, but not starvation, on its land if the vicissitudes of the weather diminish its agricultural crop, and therefore may be less likely to migrate.

The argument can even be extended to cover the observation that the very wealthy families again show a higher propensity to migrate. Thus, migration may be risky and only the poor migrate because they have little to loose. A very tentative and not yet proved hypothesis could be that the expected salary (and living conditions) in the city may be so high as to not only provide a stimulus for seeking a better means of survival (to the poor), but also a relatively high standard of living (in the understanding of the members of the very wealthy peasant family) if the search for employment is successful.

This last result is very preliminary and must be proved by more theoretical and empirical work. However, we feel certain that the inclusion of uncertainty a simple theoretical model as the one which we have presented above should yield better insights into the behaviour of small agriculture than deterministic models can.

References

Behrman, J. and J.A. Hanson (1979) 'The Use of Econometric Models in Developing Countries', in: National Bureau of Economic Research', *Short-term Macroeconomic Policy in Latin America*. (Proceedings of a Conference held in Isla Contadora, Panama, 31 October – 2 November 1975) (New York: NBER) pp. 1–38.

Ellis, F. (1988) *Peasant Economics, Farm households and agrarian development* (Cambridge: Cambridge University Press).

Gonzales de Olarte, E. (1994) 'En las fronteras del mercado', *Economía política del campesinado en el Perú* (Lima: Instituto de Estudios Peruanos).

——, R. Hopkins, B. Kervyn, J. Alvarado and R. Barrantes (1987) *La lenta modernización de la economía campesina. Diversidad, cambio técnico y crédito en la agricultura andina* (Lima: Instituto de Estudios Peruanos).

Harris, J.R. and M.P. Todaro (1970) 'Migration, Unemployment and Development: A Two-Sector Analysis', *American Economic Review*, vol. 60, pp. 126–42.

Hoff, Karla *et al.* (eds) (1993) *The Economics of Rural Organization: Theory, Practice and Policy* (Oxford University Press).

Morales, E. (1989) *Cocaine – White Gold Rush in Peru* (Tucson: University of Arizona Press).

World Bank (1994) 'Peru At the Crossroads: Building a Modern State' (Mimeo, 31 March 1994).

18 The Interest Cost of a Buffer Stock is Not a Social Cost[1]

John Spraos

18.1 INTRODUCTION

The stockpiling of a buffer stock scheme following a good harvest involves no resource cost. It is a gift of the gods and the incomes generated by buying the stock are matched by the producers' transitory saving or reduced dissaving (relatively to the position without a buffer stock) so that there is no increased consumption to crowd-out anything else, even temporarily. If producers are credit-rationed, the buffer stock does generate increased consumption in the good harvest period but the producers gain from better intertemporal distribution of their consumption exceeds the interest cost of the buffer stock. The policy implications are explored.

If the proposition of my title is true, as I believe it is, it is likely to have interesting implications. This is my justification for focusing on buffer stocks despite the fact that international commodity agreements, which have sponsored most buffer stock schemes, are unfashionable right now. Only one survives with active market intervention capability – in rubber. (See Gilbert, 1996, for a recent survey, which he has called an 'obituary notice'.)

The proposition of my title is entirely true for buffer stocks which compensate for supply shifts due to natural causes (weather, pests, diseases). I will confine myself to these. I will try to establish the validity of the proposition and will then consider its implications for policy and for the assessment of buffer stock schemes.

My methodological innovation is that I integrate an extra dimension in buffer stock analysis – the producers in their capacity as consumers – and this takes me into general equilibrium or macroeconomic territory. But do not fear – there will be no maths beyond the most trivial.

18.2   ASSUMPTIONS

I will assume that the buffer stock scheme is subject to two rules: it must break even over the cycle and it must liquidate fully in a lean production period the stocks it accumulates in a fat period.

For expositional convenience, imagine a two-sector world: a coffee sector and the Rest. *R*-goods are demanded by everybody but coffee-producers do not use coffee. (Weaker assumptions, such as constant or proportionate to output consumption of coffee by coffee-producers, would have served equally well.) The coffee crop is uniquely fixed each period by the weather and is price-invariant (vertical supply schedule). It is also perfectly predictable.

To exclude extraneous influences, adopt the usual *ceteris paribus* convention: nothing changes unless caused directly or indirectly by the coffee supply shift or by the operation of the buffer stock. The demand function for coffee is among the things that do not change over time (though not the quantity demanded, which responds to price).

The demand function is also known to everybody. Together with the assumption of coffee crop predictability, this means that next period's as well as this period's price, with or without a buffer stock, can be exactly calculated. (Uncertainty is hugely important but it does not concern me here.)

As I want to focus on the interest cost of the buffer stock, I assume, without loss of generality, that there are no other costs of carrying or managing the stock.

18.3   THREE CRITICAL POINTS

To establish the proposition of my title, I have to substantiate three basic points.

First, the extra output of coffee in a fat period is a gift of the gods, albeit a temporary one. To accumulate stocks of it is not an investment involving the withdrawal of resources from alternative uses at which they produce a yield commensurate (in a Pareto-efficient economy) with the rate of interest. There is, then, no opportunity cost to correspond to the interest paid on financing the stock accumulation. (I enunciated this blindingly obvious proposition some years ago (Spraos, 1989) but then tried to show that this led to a market failure in futures markets for commodities. This was partly, at least, wrong.)

The second point that needs to be made is more complicated and it is in making it that I go beyond the partial equilibrium framework to which the analysis of buffer stock schemes has been typically confined. The issue to be faced is this: buffer stock purchases of coffee generate income and if this gives rise to an increase in total consumption in the fat period, god-gifted though the stock may be, the additional consumption involves the withdrawal of resources from other uses and thus an opportunity cost – the loss of yield in these other uses. So, to prove the contention of my title, I have to show that the income from buffer stock purchases is all saved.

This, however, cannot be shown unfailingly. So, as my third point, I have to show that, to the extent that some or all of the buffer stock-generated extra income is consumed in the fat period, it yields a consumer surplus to producers at least equal to the interest incurred by the buffer stock.

18.4   INTER-TEMPORAL OPTIMALITY FOR PRODUCERS' CONSUMPTION AND ITS CONSEQUENCES

The key to most of what follows is a very simple optimality condition which says that, subject to the budget constraint (non-increasing debt over the relevant time horizon) consumption spending in successive periods must be equalized (when prices are unchanged) regardless of income fluctuations.

A digression on credit rationing

I do not need to spell out the optimality condition. It is congenial to common sense and the underlying maximization routine is familiar. But as I also want to pay attention to an important exception – in some cases so important that it may be the rule rather than the exception – let me say this. At the point at which the condition is satisfied, the undiscounted marginal utilities of consumption in this period and the next are equal, while at the same time the market rate of interest just cancels out the rate at which next period's consumption is discounted.

This cancelling out is critical but it will not hold for credit-rationed individuals. For the way you get your private discount rate down to the market rate of interest is by adjusting your saving/dissaving flow. (This is 'permanent' saving, as distinct from 'transitory' saving that is needed to equalize consumption intertemporally in the face of fluctuating income.) But, if you are credit-rationed, you cannot dissave because you cannot borrow. (If you have assets to run down, you are not credit-rationed.) You would be happy to borrow at the market rate of interest against next period's income (presumed to be higher) but you cannot do it. The rate at which you discount next period's consumption stays higher than the market rate of interest. Or, to say the same thing in another way, if your inter-period income difference could be narrowed (as it could be by a buffer stock operation if you were a primary producer) by shifting one dollar's worth of consumption from the next period to this, your total utility over the cycle would be enhanced by the rate of interest on that dollar and more.

Forgive me for having gone on at such length about this but, in the context of primary producers, credit rationing must be given fair prominence.

Consumption equalization and transitory saving

For the moment, however, I set aside the problems of credit rationing and assume that consumption equalization is achieved. As for borrowing, it happens that it has no place in the next subsection, so I will introduce it as and when I need it.

I begin by spelling out the equalisation condition:

> coffee-producers' spending on R-goods in fat period = ditto in lean period
>
> (18.1)

To identify the implications of this for the transitory saving of producers, I note the following relations which are either identities or follow directly from the assumptions:

> coffee-producers' spending on R-goods in fat period = fat period revenue from coffee sales – producers' transitory saving
>
> (18.2)
>
> fat period revenue from coffee sales = fat period spending on coffee by consumers + buffer stock spending
>
> (18.3)
>
> coffee-producers' spending on R-goods in lean period = revenue from coffee sales + dissaving + interest on transitory saving
>
> (18.4)
>
> producers' revenue from lean period coffee sales = lean period spending on coffee by consumers – buffer stock sales
>
> (18.5)

buffer stock sales = buffer stock spending + interest on latter

$$(18.6)$$

interest cost = buffer stock spending $\times$ rate of interest (r)

$$(18.7)$$

interest on producers transitory saving = transitory saving $\times r$

$$(18.8)$$

By using (18.2) and (18.3) to substitute in the left-hand side of (18.1), while using (18.4) – (18.8) to do the same in the right-hand side, we obtain

$(2 + r)$ (buffer stock spending – producers' transitory saving) = consumers' spending on coffee in lean period – ditto in fat.

$$(18.9)$$

Equation (18.9) is fundamental. I will consider its implication first under the assumption that the demand for coffee is unity-elastic throughout the relevant range and will turn later to the more typical case of inelastic demand.

A special case: unity-elastic demand

I do not need to tell you that unity-elastic demand means that consumers' spending is the same regardless of fat or lean periods and regardless of buffer stock presence or absence. In the absence of the buffer stock it means also that aggregate coffee-producers' earnings are the same across periods. It does not mean that every producer's earnings are the same. I will, however, resort to the device of the 'representative' producer: his earnings stay constant and so he does not need to borrow to equalize consumption. For the other producers I will assume that the pluses and minuses in their responses (relatively to the representative producer) cancel out. This is a drastic simplification but I have reason to think that, to the extent that it fails, it creates no problems that I do not tackle later (albeit under inelastic demand) when I allow for borrowing and credit rationing.

One more simplification: a producer who is credit-rationed will equalize consumption when his income is constant because he has no choice. But suppose his total income over the cycle is left the same but a higher share accrues in the first period (which is something the buffer stock can bring about). He will then gain by inequalizing his consumption, spending more in the first period of each production cycle. I will exclude this, but only to save expositional aggravation, because the issues raised are, again, no different from those I will confront shortly.

Having thus made the ground a little more author-friendly, I can build on it an edifice which is small but possessed of very clean lines under the unity elasticity specification.

Clearly, the right-hand side of (18.9) is zero, since expenditure is the same at all points on the coffee demand schedule. In that case, what the buffer stock spends in the fat period is matched exactly by the transitory saving of producers, no more, no less. You cannot get much cleaner lines than that.

Although this result does not generalise, it offers such an important insight that I will linger on it.

First, a point that is peripheral to my theme but seems worth making. We know that, under unity-elastic demand, the consumers' spending on coffee is the same across periods and regimes and therefore their spending on R-goods is the same too. And we know that coffee producers' spending is also the same right across the inter-temporal income gap created by the buffer stock being bridged by transitory saving and the interest thereon. Nevertheless, as you would expect, it is not the case that there are no welfare gains resulting from the buffer stock. Coffee-consumers, despite spending the same in each period under both regimes, gain from the inter-temporal evening-out of the volume of coffee which they consume. If I was in the business of drawing diagrams, which I am not, I would have come up with a triangle of consumers' surplus.

You could argue that, under my assumptions, consumers do not need a buffer stock to get their triangle. They could do it by carrying transitory stocks themselves, financed by borrowing (unless some of them are credit-rationed too). I would have no quarrel with that or with professional stock-carriers achieving the same thing in response to intertemporal arbitrage opportunities in futures markets. The case for a public provision through a buffer stock must appeal to considerations which I have ruled out here. But at present I am not concerned with the issue of public versus private provision. As I want, however, to focus on buffer stocks, please grant me, for the sake of argument, that the buffer stock has an exclusive licence to carry stocks.

Note that in the diagram that I am not drawing there would be no triangle representing a gain for producers because their supply (= marginal cost) schedule is assumed to be vertical. (There would be a producers' gain from redistribution if coffee-consumers spent more but, under unity-elastic demand, they do not.)

These observations about welfare triangles are not news. But what about a welfare triangle for producers in their capacity as consumers? This takes us to the territory I am exploring. The answer is that there is no triangle to be had on this side either. The reason is that, with unity-elastic demand, coffee-sales proceeds are stable pre-buffer stock and are destabilized by the buffer stock operation. The best that the producers' response can do, through transitory saving, is to restore their spending pattern to the *status quo ante*. (This does not generalise to inelastic demand wherein the buffer stock can partially stabilize the income of coffee-producers.) However, whether in my territory or not, I am not interested here in welfare triangles. I have other fish to fry.

Second, then, what answer do we get to the crucial question: does any social cost correspond to the interest cost incurred by the buffer stock? I have already observed that for a negative answer it is not enough that the buffer stock be god-gifted. Additionally, the buffer stock purchases must not generate extra consumption. We now know that they do not. The producers save what the buffer stock spends in the fat period. Said another way, the buffer stock spending creates matching saving, as in the widow's cruse parable, famously catapulted by Keynes on to a biblically untutored economics profession.

In effect, then, the buffer stock borrows from the producers and the interest which it pays accrues to the producers. (The assumption is that producers deposit their saving in a bank or other financial intermediary. An alternative scenario, in which savings are kept under the mattress, has very different and very interesting implications but is not explored here.) A consolidated account of producers and the buffer stock would show zero net borrowing/lending and no interest disbursed or received. Exactly the same picture would emerge, in every detail, if there was no buffer stock but the producers kept off the market, in the fat period, a volume equal to what the buffer stock would have purchased had it existed, and then disposed of it in the lean period.

Nobody bears the interest cost of the buffer stock because there is no cost to bear: the stock is god-gifted and the income created by its acquisition does not give rise to consumption claims on resources.

The more typical case: inelastic demand

As we move to the more typical case of inelastic demand, some of the simplicity goes but much of the ground to be covered will not be different in essentials.

Now the increase in the coffee-producers' fat period revenue resulting from the change of regime is larger than the buffer stock spending. Nevertheless, as before, only the consumption implications of the revenue generated by the buffer stock spending are relevant for the purpose in hand. Revenue earnings in excess of that are redistributive and so of no interest here because they generate no claims on output. (The redistribution originates from the consumers' extra spending on coffee which results, inevitably under inelastic demand, from the price rise engineered by the buffer stock's purchases. As coffee consumers spend more on coffee at the higher price, they spend less on R-goods. If now the coffee producers, whose income benefits from the redistribution, are credit-rationed, they will spend more on R-goods to a matching extent. No net change here. If, on the other hand, the coffee producers were not credit-rationed, their revenue from redistribution would not induce them to spend more on R-goods consumption because they would already be achieving intertemporal equalisation of R-consumption through borrowing. They will merely substitute payment out of income for borrowing. So, is there a net change in this case? No, not in this case either, because the credit flow no longer taken up by the coffee-producers will find its way back to some coffee-consumers in their other capacities and will crowd-in commensurate spending on R-goods. With our attention, then, remaining exclusively focused on the consumption implications of buffer stock spending, let us look once more at equation (18.9). Demand now being inelastic, the right-hand side is positive, from which it follows that:

$$\text{producers' transitory saving} < \text{buffer stock spending} \qquad (18.10)$$

In the light of this, I invite you to think of buffer stock spending in two parts. One part is matched by coffee-producers' saving and all that was said before holds. This part evidently does not generate extra consumption of R-goods.

The remaining part of the buffer stock spending does not generate extra consumption either, if it all accrues to non-credit-rationed producers. They were already equalizing consumption inter-temporally by borrowing. They now pay out of income and the credit which they release is absorbed (ultimately) by the buffer stock. Thus, reduced dissaving by coffee-producers (compared to pre-buffer stock) matches the remaining part of the buffer stock' spending. There is conceptually no difference from the part that is matched by transitory saving.

When, however, some of the remaining part accrues to credit-rationed coffee-producers (as would be expected to happen), it will generate additional R-goods consumption. A part of the buffer stock spending will then involve a social opportunity cost to match the interest cost of the associated borrowing.

Do we then have an exception to the principle enunciated in my title? We do not, I am happy to say. The gain to credit-rationed coffee-producers from improving their intertemporal allocation of R-goods consumption is larger than the interest cost attributable to the buffer stock spending which has served to ease the credit constraint. This follows from what I said when I introduced the subject of credit rationing. In a weaker form – at least equal to the interest cost, not larger – it can be instantly deduced from the fact that, pre-buffer stock, the coffee-producers concerned would have happily incurred the interest cost if they had not been thwarted by credit rationing. Thus, the interest cost of the buffer stock even when, as in this instance, it reflects a genuine opportunity cost, is fully offset by a surplus accruing to coffee-producers in their capacity as consumers.

One point still needs tidying up, although it does not raise anything new.

The set of equations (18.2) – (18.8) does not incorporate borrowing. As I explained earlier, I chose to introduce borrowing *ad hoc*, when relevant, and have done so already. But note that without borrowing the consumption equalization condition may not be attainable. In the case previously considered it was attainable, post-buffer stock, because the fat period coffee-producers' revenue was larger than the lean period's (which is impossible, under inelastic demand, without a buffer stock, but is rendered possible by the buffer stock operations) and so, transitory saving could bridge the gap. But if, despite the buffer stock, coffee-producers' revenue is less in the fat period than in the lean, transitory saving will widen the intertemporal consumption gap, not narrow it. There will, therefore, be no transitory coffee-producers' saving to serve as a counterpart to the buffer stock spending, not even partially.

Does the buffer stock spending mean more consumption in those circumstances? Yes, if it accrues to credit-rationed producers. No, if it accrues to non-credit-rationed producers, because it would not then affect consumption (relatively to pre-buffer stock), it will only affect the financing of it – from income instead of through borrowing. We have encountered both alternatives before and what was said about them remains applicable.

So, I think I can say that the claim of my title is also borne out, unequivocally, in the context of inelastic demand. The story is a little more complicated than under a unity-elastic demand but, when producers are not credit-rationed, the principle is the same: it is the turn-round in transitory savings between pre-buffer stock and post-buffer stock that matches the buffer stock spending and, of course, it is material to know what happens to the transitory dissaving of the pre-buffer stock situation. It just happens that in the case of unity-elastic demand there is no dissaving pre-buffer stock to take into account. (The pre-buffer stock coffee-producers' revenue is equal between the two periods, so their consumption could be equalized without recourse to dissaving.)

Note, in passing, that there is another insight yielded by the case of unity-elastic demand which is echoed in the inelastic demand case. In the latter, non-credit-rationed coffee-producers gain nothing, in their capacity as consumers, from the buffer stock (since, through borrowing, they were able to equalize their consumption intertemporally pre-buffer stock) if the consumers' total spending on coffee over the fat and lean periods combined is the same with and without the buffer stock. However, unlike the case of unity-elastic demand, total coffee spending over the cycle can be more or less with the buffer stock than without. In that event, there will be a gain or loss, respectively, for producers – but only of the redistributive kind. (It has been shown by Newbery and Stiglitz [1981] and could have been inferred earlier from Turnovsky [1976] that over-the-cycle spending is lower with a buffer stock when the demand schedule is inelastic and isoelastic. But, as can be inferred from Massell [1967], it is higher with the buffer stock when the demand schedule is linear.)

Back on the main track, to round-off the summary of the inelastic demand case. When coffee-producers are credit rationed, the buffer stock clearly generates net consumption claims on the economy in the fat period and so diverts resources from other uses but the beneficiaries of the diversion – the coffee-producers – gain a utility surplus in excess of the interest cost incurred by the buffer stock. So in this case too, though for a very different reason, the interest cost of the buffer stock is not a net social cost for the economy.

18.5 IMPLICATIONS FOR POLICY AND EVALUATION

A policy of subsidization of the buffer stock's interest cost appears to fit the circumstances which have been identified, but not straightforwardly, because it suboptimizes the intertemporal allocation of coffee consumption.

Optimality in the coffee consumption area requires that

lean period price = fat period price × (1 + rate of interest).

This allows correctly for consumers' discounting of future consumption. On the other hand, with subsidization, the buffer stock break even rule is satisfied when:

lean period price = fat period price × [1 + rate of interest × (1 – rate of subsidy)].

This relation, which represents a difference between the sell and buy price of the buffer stock to which it is constrained to adhere, conflicts with the consumers' optimality condition: it leads the buffer stock into carrying more stock for consumption in the lean period than is consistent with the consumers' discounting of future consumption.

Thus a pro rata subsidy on interest costs would cause a departure from a first-best position and is not be recommended if there was no suboptimality elsewhere that needed to be offset. And there would be none in the vicinity of the problem at hand if coffee-producers were not credit constrained.

But if, as is typical, many coffee-producers are credit-rationed, the intertemporal allocation of their consumption is suboptimally constrained and would be further eased if the buffer stock intervention was larger than in the absence of a subsidy. An interest subsidy would then attain a welfare improvement, with the resulting loss of coffee-consumers' surplus being balanced, up to a point, by larger gains of the producers' consumer's surplus. This is a classical second-best optimum, with a deviation from the optimality rule being engineered in one area to relieve, in part, a deviation in another area. (A distributional weight higher for producers than for consumers would extend the subsidy further.)

A first-best position could be attained, in principle, by attacking directly the distortion created by credit rationing through subsidizing/guaranteeing credit to producers. But to insist on that or nothing, would make the best the enemy of the good, especially, since the policy aimed at the first-best position cannot be well targeted and is liable to be abused.

You could argue that for policy purposes the god-gifting of the stock is excess baggage, since the subsidization of the buffer stock interest can rest directly on the credit-rationing of coffee-producers. In a qualitative sense, I would assent to that. But in a quantitative sense it is not correct. Without the stock as a free gift, the net gain from each unit of additional coffee producers' consumption in the fat period, made possible by the easing of the credit constraint, would be equal to a bit of the conventional welfare triangle. With god-gifting, the whole of the rate of interest is also a net gain. It follows that the optimal stock and the optimal subsidy are also bigger.

Nevertheless, it is arguable that my analysis makes a more useful contribution in the area of evaluation of buffer stock schemes. The typical failure to integrate into buffer stock thinking the producers in their capacity as consumers can be very misleading. Consider how misleading in the context of a buffer stock scheme which is facing a unity-elastic demand for coffee and is otherwise in line with my assumptions: consumers gain a (probably small) welfare triangle; coffee-producers in their capacity as producers (no other capacity being considered) lose an amount equal to the interest cost of the scheme; the buffer stock operation breaks even. Conclusion: the economy as a whole (probably) loses. I have established clearly that this is wrong. It fails to take into account that, in their capacity as consumers, it is optimal for coffee-producers to equalize their consumption intertemporally through saving transitorily in the fat period an amount equal to what the buffer stock spends, the interest paid by the buffer stock accruing, as a result, to the producers and thus not constituting a net cost of the scheme. The complications that arise when demand is inelastic affect the details but not the moral of this simple case.

If, to ask for the consumption side of coffee-producers to be fully integrated in cost–benefit evaluations of buffer stocks, is a counsel of perfection, a short cut would be to treat as zero the interest cost of the buffer stock in cases where the stock can be approximately viewed as god-gifted and to make lesser adjustments in other cases, as appropriate.

This could make a practical difference, and not just in the quantitative assessment of buffer stock experience (which it is bound to do) but also in qualitative terms, tipping the balance from negative to positive. The reason for thinking this is that the interest cost is not a small part of total buffer stock costs (in the Australian scheme for wool, the interest cost constituted nearly three-quarters of the total – see Don *et al.*, 1992) and quantitative assessments close to the positive negative borderline are not unknown in the literature (Burger and Smit, 1989).

Note

1. This paper was written for a *viva voce* delivery.

References

Burger K. and H.P. Smit (1989) 'Long-Term and Short-Term Analysis of the Natural Rubber Market', *Weltwirtschaftliches Archiv*, vol. 125, pp. 718–47.

Don H., B.H. Gunasekera and B.S. Fisher (1992) 'Australia's Recent Experience with the Collapse of its Wool Buffer Stock Scheme: Some Key Lessons', *World Economy*, vol. 15, pp. 251–69.

Gilbert C.L. (1996) 'International Commodity Agreements: An Obituary Notice', *World Development*, vol. 24, pp. 1–19.

Massell B.F. (1969) 'Price Stabilization and Welfare', *Quarterly Journal of Economics*, vol. 83, pp. 284–98.

Newbery D.M.G. and J. Stiglitz (1981) *The Theory of Commodity Price Stabilization* (Clarendon Press).

Spraos J. (1989) 'Kaldor on Commodities', *Cambridge Journal of Economics*, vol. 13, pp. 201–22. Reprinted in T. Lawson, J.G. Palma and J. Sander (eds) *Kaldor's Political Economy* (Academic Press, 1989).

Turnovsky S.J. (1976) 'The Distribution of Welfare Gains from Price Stabilisation: The Case of Multiplicative Disturbances', *International Economic Review*, vol. 17, pp. 133–48.

19 Supra-National Compensation Schemes for Temporary Export Losses: A Critique

John Toye[1]

19.1 THE RATIONALE OF COMPENSATION SCHEMES FOR TEMPORARY LOSS OF EXPORT REVENUES

One important theme of discussions of international economic policy over the last fifty years has been the problem of the volatility of world prices of primary products. As Hans Singer has reminded us recently, Keynes in 1942 went so far as to describe this problem as 'one of the greatest evils in international trade' (Singer, 1996, p. 1). Much debate and a number of practical policy experiments have flowed from Keynes's perception. One popular policy approach to countering volatility was the devising of international commodity agreements (ICAs) aimed at keeping the prices of commodities within a pre-agreed range. This approach reached its zenith with the agreement at UNCTAD IV in Nairobi in 1976 on an Integrated Programme on Commodities. The IPC is now generally regarded as a failure, and the debate that continues is about why it failed. Some identify the unwillingness of the developed countries to fund the IPC Common Fund adequately as the main cause. Others attribute this failure to the fatal ambiguity of the stabilization objectives of the ICAs themselves, along with underlying conflicts of interests between producers, and between producers and consumers, which quickly reasserted themselves.

Whatever the real causes were, however, experience seems now to have proved that the creation and maintenance of ICAs is extremely difficult. In addition, even if a commodity's price can be stabilized by this means, there are different problems of volatility that do not necessarily vanish, or may actually be aggravated thereby. It is a commonplace that 'stabilisation of money prices will not stabilise but will instead destabilise money income if the main source of instability is unpredictable fluctuation in production, and stabilisation of money prices or incomes will not stabilise purchasing power or real income if the general price level is changing' (Johnson, 1967, p. 141). It was considerations of these kinds that had already in the 1960s encouraged interest in another type of policy intervention. This aimed at countering the *effects* of the volatility of commodity prices, rather than trying to limit the volatility itself. The objective of stabilization in this type of intervention was to be export *earnings* from commodities, not commodity *prices*. The latter would be allowed to fluctuate according to market demand and supply, but when this led to unusual reductions in export earnings, appropriate compensation would be supplied by supra-national agencies.

Two supra-national agencies, the European Community/Union (EC/EU) and the International Monetary Fund (IMF), operate schemes whose purpose is to compensate the governments of developing countries for temporary losses of export revenues. In circumstances of European anxieties about security of commodity supplies, the EU/EC introduced its STABEX scheme in 1975 as a component of the Lomé I Agreement, and it survives today in an altered form as part of Lomé IV. (In this paper we neglect SYSMIN, another stabilisation scheme of the EC/EU designed specifically for minerals export revenues, on which see Raffer and Singer, 1996). The IMF had already set up a Compensatory Finance Facility in 1963, which lasted until 1988 when it became the Compensatory and Contingency Financing Facility and changed in substance much more than in name. The origins of these and similar schemes go back to discussions in the United Nations in 1953 about a mutual insurance scheme for third world countries affected by export instability (Seemann and Stolt, 1992, p. 14). A World Bank study of supplementary financing in 1965 planned a Bank export compensation scheme, but this proved abortive (Hewitt, 1993, pp. 80–1).

What is the rationale for such schemes? The conventional justification is a developmental one. It is that, in developing countries, it is the government's responsibility to undertake medium and long-term programmes of expenditures for development, on physical infrastructure and human capital formation, to create an enabling environment for the growth of economic activity. In the absence of such government intervention, various types of market failure would lead to less than optimal investment in these areas, and thus to slower economic growth than is desirable or necessary. However, the temporary loss of export revenues will cause a loss of indirect and direct tax revenue that would have been raised from the production of the missing exports and from the incomes of their producers. This will in turn disrupt the implementation of the planned public spending programmes, if a balanced budget is maintained. Since such disruption is undesirable, compensation should be paid to governments when export receipts are unusually low in order to maintain the spending programmes that will hasten growth in the future.

Moreover, if compensation is given in full for the lost export revenues, it would be more than enough to replace the government's lost tax revenues. After the government had deducted its lost tax revenues, it would be able to pass on the remainder of the compensation to those who would have produced the missing exports. This could be done as a price subsidy to the product or in the form of income support for the producer, or as quick-yielding, production-enhancing investments in the affected sector. Any or all of these measures would, through their multiplier effects, counteract any incipient depression in the rest of the economy.

The simple developmental rationale given above for these quasi-automatic compensation schemes immediately prompts a rather fundamental question. It is whether short-run instability of export revenues really is a developmental problem. Is there evidence that countries whose export revenues are unstable have slow rates of economic growth? Despite the general presumption made on *a priori* grounds that this must be so, 30 years of investigation of this point in the economic literature has been markedly inconclusive, with distinguished authors appearing on either side of the debate. The usual problems of measurement have been come to the fore – the reliance, in the absence of suitably long time-series, on cross-section studies; disputes about the appropriate composition of the cross-section sample; the fact that exports appear both as the independent variable and as a component of the dependent variable GDP; and whether statistical association also implies causality. Without embarking on a review of this extensive literature here, it is enough to note that the high instability/slow growth thesis has not been decisively rejected, and indeed continues to be maintained in recent contributions (for example, Love, 1992). One link of the causal chain has also been recently re-affirmed, that between unstable tax revenues and unstable government expenditures (by Bleaney, Gemmell and Greenaway, 1995). Thus it would be wrong to conclude categorically that the instability of export revenues is a pseudo-problem. It remains necessary to keep an open mind on this. There is also some evidence that volatility of the *terms of trade* has an unfavourable effect on growth (Singer and Lutz, 1994).

The STABEX and CFF schemes each define the problem in their own ways. The primary objective of STABEX was to channel resources to commodity producers in countries whose earnings from a particular commodity had declined temporarily. Putting extra resources in the hands of governments whose revenues had declined because of an export shortfall was only a secondary objective, while, oddly, it was stated that there was no intention to remedy balance of payments problems. Since additional foreign resource inflows would obviously alleviate such problems, this denial must be related to the diplomacy of the demarcation of roles between the EC/EU and the IMF. For its part, the IMF concentrated on the need to forestall short-run balance of payments difficulties, and less on the need to maintain the momentum of government investments for development, although the former could be expected to be helpful to the latter. Short-run balance of payments difficulties were seen as likely to arise from 'events specific to each country, such as floods, political events and changes affecting the markets for particular products' (Goreux, 1977, pp. 613–14). Thus the CFF's scope was always broader than that of STABEX, and in particular envisaged the use of compensation payments to tide over adjustment to declines in the market for individual commodities.

Three questions may be asked about these rationales for compensating temporary export losses. The first is why, when temporary falls occur in a country's export revenues, is intervention by a supra-national agency necessary? If the short-term instability of these revenues causes slow growth, why cannot the national government itself stabilise them, by adding part of them to reserves in unusually good years and releasing them from reserves in particularly bad years? One answer might be that supra-national intervention through compensation schemes is adding to the country's total resources, either by making outright grants or by lending at below market interest rates, whereas national intervention would merely stabilize existing flows. This is so, but it does not imply that the extra resources should by transferred by an export loss compensation scheme. The choice of that instrument for the transfer needs some additional justification.

Another answer might be that the national government is not capable of itself managing the task of export revenue stabilisation, for various reasons. It may not be able to calculate accurately the trend rate around which to try to stabilise; it may not be able to confine all exports to official channels; or it may be tempted to divert reserves accumulated in good years for other purposes. There may be merit in the argument that, for these sorts of reasons, stabilisation of export revenues is something that national governments ought not to attempt to do. (However, this does not necessarily mean that supra-national agencies should attempt it.) But in fact many developing countries' governments equipped themselves with institutions like Marketing Boards and Central Banks that allow them to break the one-to-one link between the net earnings from trade and changes in the size of the domestic stock of money. The actual context in which supra-national compensation schemes operate is still, in most cases, far different from that of the pure currency board model which is assumed in the rationale for supra-national intervention (Walters and Hanke, 1992, pp. 558–61). Thus it is pertinent to raise the issue of the possible interactions between supra-national compensation schemes and the workings of Marketing Boards and Central Banks. In particular, do their workings have the effect of discouraging exports, for the loss of which the supra-national scheme then provides compensation?

The second question concerns the distribution of the compensation payments between the government and others. Assuming that they exceed the government's own loss of tax revenue, is there – or should there be – an obligation on the government to pass through the residual, and what mechanisms exist for doing so? Bear in mind that others can consist of public corporations which the government can regulate well or badly, as well as the private sector. Within the private sector, how are appropriate recipients to be identified, given that loss of export revenues can arise from failure of internal supply as well as failure of external demand? How will such payments affect the normal functions of price signals, and will the supply response be distorted by them, for example by retaining land and labour in the production of commodities which have poor long-run prospects?

The third question is about the effectiveness of supra-national compensation schemes in reducing instability. There is nothing intrinsically stabilizing about the injection of a compensatory payment as such. Its effectiveness in reducing instability depends entirely on the timing of its receipt in relation to the time profile of the receipt of export revenues. If it arrives when these are still falling, it will be stabilizing, but if it arrives when these have already recovered, it will be destabilizing. Schemes which, like both the EC/EU's in its original form and the IMF's, require repayment of the compensatory finance ('repurchases' in the Fund's terminology) may be additionally destabilizing if the repurchases fall due when export revenues are once again unusually low. For effective stabilization, the timeliness is all.

It is the contention of this chapter that, accepting for the sake of argument the high instability/slow growth thesis, the success of supra-national compensation schemes depends on the precise ways in which they solve the three problems of

1. their interaction with national government agencies that influence trade;
2. the distribution of payments between government and others; and
3. the timing of the receipts and repayments.

There are important trade-offs between timeliness, on the one hand, and controlling national government trade policies and its use of compensation payments, on the other.

19.2   QUASI-AUTOMATICITY

In this connection, it is important to note that schemes of compensation for unusually low export revenues were originally designed to be quasi-automatic. Quasi-automatic means that their outcomes are the result of the application of pre-specified rules to particular cases. They thus lack the possibility of the compensating authority exercising discretion in relation to the circumstances of individual applications. Quasi-automaticity simplifies the decision-making process and thereby shortens response times and improves the timeliness of compensation. Being rule-bound in this way does not, evidently, preclude some change in the rules from time to time. But at any one time 'the donor allocates transfers through a largely arithmetic rather than judgmental mechanism' (Hewitt, 1982, p. 23). As we shall see, the rules of both schemes under consideration here have changed their rules quite dramatically at the end of the 1980s, and in a direction that greatly increased conditionality. We shall explore the reasons for this change and its consequences.

The rules of a scheme normally include the following elements. The financial regime for the scheme has to be established. Compensation may be given (as under STABEX) only for the export earnings shortfalls of certain commodities, and, when this is so, these eligible commodities first have to be identified and listed. Rules then have to define what is meant by 'unusually low' export revenues by specifying an appropriate comparison, for example, compared with the average of the previous x years. A set of rules must determine how the amount of compensation is to be related to the size of the shortfall of actual revenue from the defined 'normal' revenue, the date at which compensation will be paid, and whether it should be paid as a grant or a loan. Finally, since payments are quasi-automatic and not fully automatic and (as we have argued above) various issues about control are present, the nature of any conditions on payments must be spelled out in advance. Such conditions may include restrictions both on government policies and on the use of the compensation payments. We set out in Table 19.1 a brief guide to the differences in the rules of the revised versions of both schemes, i.e. the rules currently operated by the EC/EU's STABEX scheme, in the Lomé IV version, and the IMF's post-1988 CCFF.

Table 19.1   A comparison between STABEX (Lomé IV) and the CCFF

	STABEX (Lomé IV)	CCFF
Total finance available	2485 mio for 1975–89, no individual country quotas	No overall limit but individual drawings limited to 100 per cent of country's IMF quota
Thresholds	Commodity must account for 5 per cent of country's total export earnings (one per cent LLDCs), 4 per cent in the case of sisal.	None, but drawings cannot be in excess of net shortfall in total export earnings.
Coverage Commodity	49 products specified in Convention	All merchandise and service exports to all destinations; tourism, remittance of workers and cereal imports are included.
Country	Members of the ACP group	All IMF members
Shortfall period	Calendar year	Any period of 12 consecutive months
Deadline for request	3 months after end of calendar year	6 months after shortfall year ends
Reference value	Trend value calculated in nominal terms as average of export earnings over previous 6 years, then a deduction of highest and lowest years.	Trend value of total export earnings calculated in nominal terms as 5-year geometric mean centred on shortfall year
Use of transfers	Must be, in the first place, used to promote economic and social development, in the affected sector	Not to be used for development purposes nor for forward transactions
Terms	Grants to all ACP-states	Interest rates equal to those on credit tranche purchases for all members
Repayment	Not an obligation any longer	On fixed quarterly schedule 3 to 5 years after borrowing; early repayment may be required if balance

Table 19.1   (Continued)

	STABEX (Lomé IV)	CCFF
		of-payments perform-ance is better than expected.
Decision-making delay	Average 'no problems arising' of 2.5 to 4 months	Decision may be issued one month after request with drawing following immediately.
Conditions	Automatic transfer if the EEC is satisfied that shortfall did not arise from restrictive or discriminatory practices by ACP-state; ACP must inform Commission of use of transfers.	There must be a balance-of-payments need. Shortfall must be temporary and largely attributable to circumstances beyond the control of the member. Members must pledge to co-operate with the Fund in seeking appropriate solutions; if drawings are over 50 per cent of a member's quota the Fund must be satisfied that past co-operation has been adequate.

Source: Seeman and Stolt (1992) pp. 62–4.

19.3   THE EC/EU STABEX SCHEME

The EC/EU STABEX scheme dates from 1975 and the period of negotiations for a New International Economic Order. It was designed to provide an instrument of EC/EU-ACP development co-operation that was immune from the arbitrary behaviour that characterized some other aid donors' practices, and capable of providing a secure and predictable financial basis for medium term development planning. Unlike the IMF's CCF, it was a scheme of compensation for the loss of export earnings only from certain commodities. The value of transfers was determined on a product-by-product basis. Losses were calculated by comparison of the year in question with the average export earnings over the preceding four years (Lomé I–III), or over four of the preceding six years, having excluded the years of both highest and the lowest earnings (Lomé IV). Unlike the CCF, there is no room in the calculation for projections of future export earnings.

As well as being restricted to only certain commodities, the STABEX scheme is restricted by focusing only on ACP exports of those commodities to the EC/EU or other ACP states – but with certain exceptions. The system now applies to earnings from exports by each ACP state to the Community of each eligible product, and to exports of eligible products from ACP states to other ACP states. But, if for the average of the two years preceding the application year, at least 70 per cent of an ACP state's (or 60 per cent if the ACP state is an LLDC) export earnings from products covered by the system do not come from exports to the Community, the system is applied to its exports of eligible products regardless of the destination. This is set out in Article 189 of the Lomé IV Convention. The position for Lomé I–III was similar. Exceptions notwithstanding, STABEX contrasts with the CFF in providing only partial compensation for a shortfall in export revenues. This has the interesting implication that it is possible for compensation to be paid when the revenue shortfall from the eligible commodities is less than the revenue increase from non-eligible commodities and total export revenues have thereby increased (Hewitt, 1996, p. 233).

STABEX certainly had a quasi-automatic character under the first three Lomé Agreements. Claims were submitted to the EC/EU by the ACP state, and checked for accuracy of calculation and the fulfilment of various other conditions of the scheme, and then payments were made. In this respect STABEX transfers were similar to IMF CFF drawing rights until the late 1980s. Indeed, they were at times referred to by the EC/EU itself as 'transfer rights', reflecting its juridical and contractual approach to development co-operation, although now the Commission insists on the use of the term 'eligible transfers' (Raffer and Singer, 1996, pp. 88, 90). The conditions of payment did not include any that refer to human rights abuses, or to the type of political or economic regime prevailing in the ACP state concerned. Nor was the absence of such conditions an aberration or oversight in the design of the scheme. It was one its principal features, if not the principal feature. Motivated by the highest aspirations of the time, it intended to give donor and recipient an exact equality of status in the aid relationship. If a recipient should not criticise a donor's human rights record or choice of economic and political model, neither should a donor criticize a recipient's. Much credit was taken by the EC/EU in the 1970s for this enlightened instrument of aid, which had finally removed aid from the machinations of high politics.

Would that it were so easy to separate aid from entanglements in high politics! To decide to give a state compensation for lost export earnings in all conceivable political circumstances is itself a political decision which has political consequences. For example, in Ethiopia, STABEX transfers provided 124 million ECU to the Mengistu government, the excellence of whose record on human rights has been much questioned (Toye, 1996, p. 17). The principle of contractuality in aid is not enough. The content of the contract is what matters, and the STABEX contract of Lomé I to III contained inadequate safeguards. The only way for the EC/EU to have avoided giving large sums of forex to governments like that of Mengistu would have been to take exceptional action to cut off this aid on political grounds, which was the very thing it had said it would never do. This is the Catch-22 of the attempt to give politically neutral aid.

Giving aid without regard to the economic model adopted by the recipient also causes problems. A particular problem arises when, as with STABEX, the amount of aid varies inversely with specific types of export receipts. There are types of economic model which discourage exporting by imposing high implicit rates of taxation on exports. Maintaining a seriously over-valued exchange rate in order to secure artificially cheap imports drives a substantial wedge between the world price of any export and the price received in domestic currency by its producer. There is no visible taxation of the exporter, but the disincentive effect is equivalent. The response of the exporter is twofold, either to produce less, or, more likely with a tree crops such as coffee and cocoa, to smuggle supplies out of the country. In either case, receipts for exports leaving by official channels will fall. If we assume that this fall is gradual year by year, compensation will always be due, even though the normal base level for the calculation of compensation is also falling.

Unlike the CFF, STABEX never had the stabilization of export receipts of eligible commodities as its paramount objective. In view of the scheme's name, and the declared objective of 'remedying the harmful effects of the instability of export earnings' in Article 186 of Lomé IV, this is a somewhat ironical situation. It arose because STABEX, like other development co-operation instruments, was negotiated jointly between the EC/EU and the ACP countries, and the latter took a different view of its purposes from the former, leading to compromises and a blurring of objectives. The ACP states saw STABEX as just another form of programme aid, and one with the advantages of quick disbursement and highly concessional terms. The EC/EU by contrast saw the compensation payments as a means of addressing short-run production problems of the commodity in respect of which the payment was made. However, there was no legal mechanism within the original scheme whereby the EC/EU could make its view of the matter prevail. As a result, under Lomé I–III, STABEX receipts came to be used as general balance of payments support, and the EC/EU had difficulty obtaining *ex-post* reports on the uses of the funds – to which it attached importance, despite the fungibility of forex and budgetary resources.

To the extent that ACP countries had problems with this original form of STABEX, they centred mainly on three issues, all of which were related to its quantity. One was on the commodity coverage of the scheme: as noted, it did not apply to all exports and specifically excluded products, such as beef and sugar, whose European producers the EC/EU was protecting. In response to this, the number of eligible products has been expanded from 29 to 49 between Lomé I and Lomé IV. For the eligible commodities, compensation was often further restricted to loss of earnings on exports to the EC/EU and other ACP states. The generosity of the formula for calculating compensation was also questioned, because of additional 'small print' restrictions on eligibility because of a product dependence threshold and a procedure known as *abattement*. Finally, and unlike the CFF, the size of the STABEX budget was pre-determined. As a result, in some years it was not possible to settle all claims for transfers in full. Large falls in the world price of coffee, cocoa, oil crops, cotton and tea in 1980, 1981, 1987 and 1988 caused the STABEX budget to be insufficient to meet in full all the demands for transfers. Even after some extra resources were found and added in, only between 50 and 60 per cent of transfer entitlements were actually paid out in those years.

STABEX had been framed on the basis of the assumption the loss of export earnings was due to a temporary interruption of supply, and that its cause was truly external to the recipient country, and outside its own area of policy control. For that reason, the transfers were originally made reimbursable, except in the case of the least developed ACP states, on the expectation that particularly bad years for export earnings were likely to be followed by better years again. However, an evaluation of the early operations of the scheme found that 'in the majority of cases, the [commodity] sector's revenue problem was one of *long-term decline in the volume of production* (and exports) rather than one arising purely as a result of short-term fluctuations' (Hewitt, 1982, p. 28, original italics).

It had been appreciated from the beginning of the STABEX scheme that loss of export earnings can be a consequence of government policies as well as of global changes that are outside the government's control. Transfers were not permitted in such cases. But at the start, the nature of such policies had been conceived of quite narrowly. They were thought of as deliberate and overt acts, such as the imposition of bans on exports to the EC/EU or other ACP states. But in the 1980s, the EC/EU had to broaden its understanding of government policies that caused loss of export earnings. It came to appreciate that trade and foreign exchange regimes maintained by governments in many of the ACP states embodied substantial disincentives to the production for export (or at least for the export through official channels) of eligible commodities.

In response to these changed understandings, the EC/EU negotiated changes to STABEX, at Lomé III but most substantially at Lomé IV. Initially, as explained above, the uses to which the STABEX transfers were put could be decided by the recipient country alone. The relevant conventions did not permit the imposition of any conditionality by the EC/EU. Thus, whatever the stated purposes of the scheme, and whatever the process by which the transfers were acquired, from an economic point of view they were equivalent in the hands of the recipient to programme aid or general balance of payments support. Since Lomé IV, the EC/EU has insisted that the STABEX transfer should no longer be able to be used simply as general balance of payments support. STABEX transfers now require a new form of agreement called a Framework of Mutual Obligations, or FMO, one for each separate year of application. In the FMO, the recipient has to make, and the EC/EU has to approve, a substantial analysis of the causes of the export earnings shortfall. Also, the recipient has to specify, and the EC/EU has to agree, the precise uses of the transfer, which are restricted to the sector of origin (normally agriculture, either for product improvement or diversification *within* the sector). The detailed definitions and rules, to which the FMO must conform, are set out in the 25-page document entitled *Principles, Guidelines and Rules for the Use of STABEX Transfers under Lomé IV* (CEC, 1991).

In making this change, the EC/EU explicitly confronted the trade-off between timeliness of intervention and effectiveness, defined by them as ensuring the use of transfers to assist the sector that suffered the loss of exports. In 1990 a Commission briefing document on STABEX stated that one of its acknowledged virtues was its speed. 'By virtue of the fact that it is triggered automatically and acts fast, the system is well thought of by the ACP countries, particularly those with economies dependent on a small number of agricultural products covered by STABEX' (CEC, 1990). But the officially approved Lomé IV guidelines on STABEX strongly discounted the virtue of speed.

With the aim of using resources more efficiently than in the past, we must try to prevent STABEX from becoming a stop-gap relief or being used indiscriminately as a budgetary resource. In doubtful cases, therefore, faced with the choice between speedy action, on the one hand, and effectiveness and viability, on the other, the balance must come down in favour of the latter. In view of the problems and delays of all kinds that are to be encountered on each side, one or two months, or even four, are neither here nor there, and certainly less important than the damage that could be caused by hasty, ill-considered action. The new provisions on the use of transfers constitute a turning point in the development of the system. (CEC, 1991)

Thus the authors of the new 1991 principles and guidelines recognised that the FMO procedures would add significant delays. But they then argued strongly that where there was a choice between speed and the FMO process, the latter was to take precedence. This order of priority has indeed become the cause of serious delays in the disbursement to beneficiaries of Lomé IV STABEX transfers.

Although stabilization is not the paramount objective of STABEX, the speed of disbursement is nevertheless an important element in the effectiveness of the scheme. As the early evaluation noted, 'we can expect to find ... that the STABEX contribution is more valuable, the faster the transfer is made' (Hewitt, 1982, p. 24). The new FMO procedure introduced an extra stage in the transfer process, one that in the Ethiopian case has varied between four months and one year. The time taken is related to the number of conditions that are to be negotiated. Some of these could with advantage be dispensed with. The 'substantial analysis of the causes of the shortfall' in export earnings that triggered the transfer tends to become more of a list of possible factors than a substantial analysis. In any case, elaborate precautions to target the transfers by means of the FMO to particular uses could be largely an exercise in window-dressing, since money is fungible.

Further potential sources of delay in the new system arise because now STABEX transfers have to be spent via two different mechanisms, EDF contracts and a facility requiring pro forma invoices and letters of credit. The former is available only to public sector enterprises, and is financially more advantageous, with better payment terms and waiver of import duty. EDF procurement is restricted by rules of origin, which incidentally have the effect of raising the price of the import, but which also is a very lengthy process from tender design to final delivery. The net effect of production of the FMO, the sector specificity of the beneficiaries and the procedural requirements of the EDF and letter of credit mechanisms is to make disbursement to the beneficiaries exceedingly slow. In 1993, no STABEX payments were made at all, and in 1994 the European Court of Auditors reported that 450 of the 790 million ECU authorised under Lomé IV was still blocked in the European bank accounts of the recipient ACP states (Hewitt, 1996, p. 230).

The additional delays introduced into STABEX in Lomé IV are very likely to have the effect that the compensation becomes pro-cyclical, rather than counter-cyclical as is necessary to reduce instability. It is clear that this situation is not sustainable. Methods to short-circuit some of the existing procedural requirements will have to be found urgently to un-block the flow of STABEX disbursement. While adequate audit safe-guards have to be maintained, the more active and elaborate management approach of STABEX will have to be relaxed, and, indeed, has already begun to be relaxed. More STABEX money should flow through national forex auctions, and the documentation requirements for audit should become less onerous, especially that of providing a customs declaration certificate.

A key feature of STABEX transfers under Lomé I to III was that, once the transfers were received by the central bank of the recipient country, it constituted an amount in local currency that was equivalent, using the official (over-valued) exchange rate, and this amount was distributed directly to local beneficiaries. This method of proceeding has two clear implications. The first is that, since the beneficiaries were allocated the domestic currency with which to purchase their foreign exchange, to them the forex was a free good. They therefore had no incentive, apart from whatever difficulties might be involved in securing future allocations, to economise on their demand for forex or to use wisely the amount that they were allocated. The second implication is that no counterpart funds were constituted, and that therefore the secondary benefit to the government budget was lost.

Lomé IV changed this situation in various ways. First, a list of particu-lar objectives was identified for each separate STABEX operation. Second, these new extra purposes aimed at neutralizing some of the gov-ernment policies that had led to the erosion of export earnings in the past. Third, detailed arrangements made for the generation and use of the coun-terpart funds (CF) arising from the STABEX transfers to finance the activ-ities associated with each objective. However, this new logic itself did not last long. It made no sense for the EC/EU and every other donor to try to insist that the CF generated from its own aid be used only to finance very specific government expenditures. By this time, many ACP countries had adopted structural adjustment programmes. Many had devalued their currencies to realistic levels and had constituted foreign exchange auctions through which aid could be channelled. Given the increasing importance of CF, they would in future have to be applied coherently within the framework of structural adjustment policies, as budgetary support to economic and social sector programme and project expenditures, expenditures on programmes designed to strengthen the reform process and expenditures to meet the local costs of externally funded projects. The targeting of the CF is a dubious practice to the extent that it succeeds in inducing the government to make expenditures additional to those that it would have made anyway.

Moreover, the mechanism through which the EC/EU (like other donors) would have to exert its influence over the use of its CF changed accordingly. In future, any influence can be exercised only through participation in World Bank Public Expenditure and Public Investment Reviews. The EC/EU is ill-prepared to do this. In the run-up to Lomé IV, it adopted the position that IMF/World Bank structural adjustment programmes were deficient in two major respects. First, the design of these programmes was over-generalized and ideological in origin. The EC/EU advocated instead 'fitting in with [each country's] political and economic models' and 'respecting the direction [each country] has taken in development options and strategies' (CEC, 1992, p. 17). Second, the design of adjustment programmes had unduly neglected the social dimensions of adjustment, thus placing additional burdens on the most vulnerable section of society – the poor, the unemployed, women and children. Whatever the truth of these criticisms in the 1980s, the situation had markedly changed by the time that Lomé IV became operative. Policy changes within the Bank left the EC/EU without a distinctive agenda on adjustment. More to the point, it lacked the technical macroeconomic skills within its Delegations to make significant contributions to designing programmes that did fit the economic circumstances of individual countries. Finally, in countries where the national government genuinely 'owned' its programme, the EC/EU found it hard to insist on its right to a place at the programme negotiating table.

A popular view about the EC/EU's development Cooperation assistance is that the policies are excellent, but the implementation of them is poor. But, if the above account of STABEX is anywhere near correct, the reverse is true. It is the high-level policies which have been based on confusion and contradiction. STABEX was not initially well designed for the political and economic conditions in which it had to operate. It was limited by the blurring of its objectives, its limited product coverage and budget and the absence of any effective element of conditionality in its rules.

However, the re-design of STABEX under Lomé IV to make it 'more effective' has done the opposite, by adding to disbursement delays and using the FMO procedure to try to gain inappropriate forms of control over the use of transfers. Faced with the realities of structural adjustment, Lomé IV's reliance on out of date criticisms of IFI practice and unrealistic views of how easily the EC/EU could contribute to the policy dialogue, seems a recipe for impotence.

The popular view, in our opinion, makes a false distinction between policy and execution. A good policy is not one that sounds good or seems enlightened, it is one which has systematically related its objectives to the details of implementation in the circumstances that are likely to prevail. The STABEX instrument has not in important respects satisfied this criterion of good policy, and it is hardly surprising that when put into effect it has been quickly ensnared in bureaucratic tangles and delays of its own making. In contrast, the implementation of STABEX has often been a relatively successful rearguard action to limit the damage that would otherwise be wrought by confused policy parameters.

19.4   THE IMF COMPENSATORY FINANCING FACILITY

The IMF's Compensatory Financing Facility (CFF) was set up in February 1963 to be a more or less automatic fund for largely non-conditional assistance to IMF member countries experiencing temporary export shortfalls for reasons beyond their control. Originally confined to shortfalls of merchandise exports, its coverage was widened in 1979 to include earnings from workers' remittances and tourism, and in 1981 to include temporary increases in cereal import requirements arising from climatically induced harvest failures.

The CFF has mainly been used by developing country Fund members, but their calls on it were slight until the mid-1970s. However, between 1976 and 1985 annual CFF drawings averaged SDR 1.3 billion, nearly a quarter of the total credit extended by the Fund (Kumar, 1989, p. 773). During this period, the conditions for making CFF drawings were not onerous. As indicated in Table 19.1, all that was required was the member country's assurance that it would co-operate with the Fund and the Fund's agreement that the causes of the shortfall were largely outside the control of the drawing country, and that there was a balance of payments 'need'.

While this light conditionality persisted, the CFF was able to perform a modest stabilizing role. Kumar has compared indices of export revenue instability without and with CFF purchases, and also with purchases and repurchases for 1975–85. Of the 79 countries that made drawings in this decade, instability increased for 16 (purchases only) and for 14 (taking purchases minus repurchases into account). For the remainder, their use of the CFF was mildly stabilising, varying between 2 and 24 per cent. Over the whole sample there was a mean reduction of instability of just over 5 per cent (ibid., pp. 783–4).

When interpreting these numbers it should be borne in mind that the measured reduction in instability depends to some extent on the size of the CFF drawing relative to the size of the export shortfall. There was not always a one-to-one relationship, either because purchasers bumped up against quota limits or because the inclusion of forecasts for two future years in the calculation allowed 'over-compensation' if the forecasts proved unduly pessimistic. Nevertheless, the major influence in generating a generally stabilising result must be the timeliness of the drawings. In fact, the mean time lag between the end of the shortfall year and the CFF drawing was slightly less than four months (ibid., p. 782). This speedy response must in turn have been made possible by the lightness of the conditionality involved in processing requests.

But towards the end of the 1975–85 period the balance of payments difficulties of many developing country Fund members were interpreted by the Fund as being too severe to be dealt with any longer as the outcome of temporary export shortfalls. The Fund increasingly insisted that requests for the use of the CFF had to be dealt with in conjunction with Fund-supported adjustment programmes. Demand for the CFF peaked in 1983 at 2.6 billion SDR (Hewitt, 1996, p. 227). Thus in the 1980s the CFF was converted into a modest source of supplementary finance mainly confined to member countries that had already agreed a stand-by credit or other high conditionality programme with the Fund. In effect, the progressive narrowing of access to the CFF in this way has turned it into another high conditionality facility.

In 1988 a contingency facility was added for those countries whose stand-by or other programmes ran into difficulties because of unforeseen deterioration in either their export or import prices, or in international interest rates. These changes have been recognised by re-naming the CFF as the Compensatory and Contingency Financing Facility or CCFF (Killick, 1995, pp. 14–17). However, the terms of this new facility are not attractive to governments, and it has been little used. It has been suggested that 'the time normally required for renegotiation rules it out as a source of first-line liquidity' (Green, 1995, p. 122). The Fund's main useful innovation to deal with worsening external circumstances has been to relax its credit maxima for a programme when external conditions worsen. But it also calls on countries to build up their foreign exchange reserves in antic-ipation of external crises, and to impose more restrictive domestic credit policies if external flows are unexpectedly favourable. While this is sens-ible in principle, it has been criticized as 'an inefficient attempt at fine-tuning', so that 'the combination of high conditionality, negotiation lags and symmetry make the Compensatory and Contingency Facilities virtu-ally inaccessible as first-line liquidity sources' (ibid.).

In parallel with this transformation of the CFF, the IMF has deepened its conditionality markedly. Between 1968 and 1977 the average pro-gramme contained six performance conditions. But by the period 1984–7 the average number exceeded nine (Killick, 1995, p. 35). The traditional focus of IMF conditionality has been, and remains, the restriction of domestic credit creation, the reduction of budget deficits and exchange rate devaluation. But in the 1980s other forms of conditionality that relate to economic structures have been given increased emphasis by the Fund. Among these is trade liberalization. In 1989 the Fund rephrased the main objective of its stand-by programmes as a sustainable balance of payments 'in the context of an open trade and payments system'. Some countries which are unwilling to liberalize trade have been refused programmes, while in some programmes trade liberalization has been made a perform-ance criterion (ibid., p. 23). Another new point of emphasis has been on the need to move agricultural producer prices closer to market-clearing levels. These trade and agriculture issues did not provide the main example of the Fund's new structural conditionality, however. Both came a long way second to a variety of fiscal reform conditions (ibid., p. 26).

Thus the Fund has, on the one hand, moved away from its more or less automatic scheme of compensation for loss of export earnings, which had experienced modest success in its stabilization objective. On the other hand it has extended the reach of its conditionality to include trade liberal-ization and more market-related agricultural producer prices. Taken together, these developments of the 1980s can be interpreted as indicating that the Fund has reached two conclusions about the value of schemes of automatic compensation for loss of export earnings. The first is that it is not necessary or helpful to try to make a close link either between the size of the export shortfall and the amount of extra credit made available, or between the use of the extra credit and reforms in the specific commodity sector responsible for the shortfall in earnings. The second conclusion to be attributed to the Fund is that observed shortfalls of export earnings may be caused in part by government trade and agricultural pricing policies, and so may not be temporary falls below a constant or rising trend, but part of a persistent downward trend which is not wholly beyond the control of the recipient government. Not only will the automatic provision of compensatory finance fail to address this problem, it will actually reduce the urgency of reforms to the trade and agricultural pricing regimes.

The question remains whether the current high conditionality policies of the Fund have effectively addressed the problems of a self-inflicted decline in the trend of exports either. It is certainly possible to show that Fund-supported programmes which include supply-side conditions have been more successful than those with only demand management conditions (Khan and Knight, 1985). It is also possible to point to individual countries, such as Ghana, the Gambia, Morocco and Costa Rica, which both benefited from a reduction in export instability under the old CFF and achieved improved economic performance under high-conditionality Fund–Bank programmes in the 1980s. But, against that, countries like Bangladesh and Malawi have turned mixed economic performances under high conditionality, having benefited much from the old CFF, and others like Côte d'Ivoire and Jamaica that did badly under high conditionality after having derived little benefit from the old CFF (Killick, 1995, pp. 94–101). Country case studies thus show a variety of experiences, positive and negative.

The Fund has attempted a broader evaluation of the results of its high-conditionality ESAF programmes, based on the 19 countries which had drawn on this facility between its inception in 1987 and 1992. It concluded that 'the experience under ESAF arrangements has in general been favourable' (Schadler *et al.*, 1993, p. 39). But the methodology used was that of before and after comparisons, rather than comparison of actuals with a plausible counterfactual scenario. Moreover, no use was made of an index of implementation to measure the intensity of effort in meeting the policy conditions of the ESAF loans. There is thus no way in which the 'after' outcomes can be linked consequentially to the meeting of the ESAF policy conditions. These and other critical points have been well made by Killick (1995, pp. 76–81).

What is of interest in the study in the present context is its demonstration of an improvement in export volumes from around 2 per cent in the pre-SAF/ESAF period to around 7 per cent when the programmes were in place. Again, however, there is no clear linking of this improvement back to the changes in trade and exchange rate systems, the abolition of price controls and the reform of Marketing Boards, all of which were subjects of policy conditionality. But, whatever the causes, the growth of export volumes in least developed countries marks an important departure from the stagnation or decline of volumes in the previous decade. Despite this, however, their return to external viability remains problematic. This is because the terms of trade for all but 4 of the 19 countries declined, the decline for the most severely affected (Uganda) being 21.3 per cent.

19.5   CONCLUSIONS

Both STABEX and the IMF's CFF addressed themselves to declines in export revenues of developing countries that were temporary in nature, and caused by short-run interruptions in domestic supplies. The former provided transfers in the expectation, usually disappointed, that they would be used to solve the problem that had caused the supply interruption. The latter was conceived as an insurance scheme that would assist the balance of payments at times of special need. What the creators of neither had anticipated was that supply problems would be chronic, that export volumes of key commodities in eligible countries would decline continuously and that government policies would themselves contribute to this decline.

By the late 1980s, all of these things had become apparent, and both schemes were modified to increase their degree of conditionality. The attempt to achieve this for STABEX with Lomé IV was misconceived in various ways, including the targeting of fungible resources on particular sectors, and, after the agreement to pool CF with other donors, being unable to exert much influence over the content of conditionality. The IMF compensation facility ceased after 1988 to have an existence independent of high-conditionality programmes and so has to be judged in the much broader context of SAF/ESAF evaluations. There is some evidence of countries with ESAF programmes experiencing growth of their export volumes, but it is not clear that this is attributable to the implementation of policy conditions. At the same time, the balance-of-payments benefits of this growth has been significantly reduced by a simultaneous decline in their terms of trade.

Hans Singer (1991, p. 48) has suggested that the recent growth of export volumes is indeed the result of successful policy conditionality, and the cause of the decline in commodity producing countries' terms of trade. He concludes that the design of policy conditionality does therefore involve a fallacy of composition, because it assumes that increased commodity exports will necessarily make each individual country that complies with the conditions that promote such exports better off, whereas in fact it may not become so, because many other countries are doing the same and in aggregate the additional supplies are forcing down the world price of the commodity.

The fallacy of compensation thesis raises an essentially empirical question. It is whether the recent volume increases in commodity exports are indeed largely produced by countries undergoing structural adjustment and complying with policy conditions designed to promote commodity exports. There may be some commodities where the decline in the world price is the result mainly of extra supplies originating in countries without IMF–World Bank adjustment programmes, but rather, because of their general economic success, able to produce with the advantage of a low cost-structure and superior quality control. Since some commodities (like beverage crops) have experienced more precipitous price declines than others, it would make sense to concentrate on researching these, as a priority.

My own hypothesis would be that, for beverage crops, a significant source of the additional supply has been new entrants who have no need of IFI adjustment loans, rather than the traditional producers who do. Taking cocoa as an example, it is clear that in the period 1982/3 to 1991/2 the production of cocoa beans grew rapidly in Malaysia and Indonesia, which were not acting under IFI conditionality, and that the large increased production from Côte d'Ivoire, although the latter did have some IFI loans, was not the result of loan conditionality, but of a planned expansion programme started in 1971. Meanwhile the output of traditional producers such as Brazil and Cameroon stagnated, although Ghana's output did jump by 100 000 tons, or about 7 per cent of world output, in 1987/88, as a result of IFI policy advice (Kofi, 1994, p. 30). Further commodity-by-commodity analyses along these lines are needed to assess the fallacy of composition argument.

Be that as it may, the operation of STABEX and the CFF was designed for a global context in which international commodity agreements succeeded in maintaining long-term average prices, and not merely in stabilizing them around a falling trend. When commodity prices took a downward trend, as they did in the period after 1975, ICAs were often used to try to arrest the trend, rather than to stabilize the price around the trend. This was one major factor causing their collapse. No international commodity agreements are operating in the mid-1990s, a fact that must be attributed to the difficulty of getting agreement on the precise slope of the declining trend around which to stabilize. At any rate, the downward trend of commodity prices has continued and the IMF itself has concluded that for policy purposes such declines should be regarded as permanent. This may be regarded as a belated official acknowledgement of the validity of the original Singer–Prebisch thesis. But it did invalidate the long-run price assumption on which compensation schemes for temporary export revenue losses rested. In the 1990s, the problem of export revenue volatility is a relatively minor one for many poor countries, when placed alongside the Singer–Prebisch problem of secular decline in their terms of trade.

For Keynes, it was the 'wide and rapid fluctuations in the world prices of primary products' that was the evil, not any long-term trends, either up or down. The evil arose because such volatility aggravated the trade cycle. A sudden price rise induces a wave of new investment, made on an over-optimistic forecast of long-run price, which in turn leads to excess supply and a price crash which impoverishes all producers. Keynes objected to the waste of resources caused by boom and slump, and wanted to find ways to curb the real losses inflicted by speculative behaviour. There is no lack of evidence that such behaviour does occur in primary commodity markets, especially in tree crops and in the mining industry. It remains true that 'if people knew more about the future they could plan better and use resources to better advantage' (Pincus, 1967, p. 285). The real problem is where is the true knowledge of the future going to come from? Who can say authoritatively which component of a price change is trend, and which is volatility? Private sector forecasters cannot do it: if they could, they would make more money by acting on their forecasts than by selling them to others. Governments can act as if they knew, but cannot make their view stick once it loses credibility with the private sector. As Keynes himself said in another context, our views of the future are conventional, bolstered by polite and pretty techniques. The problem of radical uncertainty still lies at the heart of all attempts to limit commodity price volatility.

Let us return now to the three questions raised in the opening section. Is there a legitimate role for supra-national agencies in stabilizing export revenues in the short term? Twenty years of experience with STABEX suggests that, if there is a supra-national function to be performed, the EU/EC has failed to identify it and perform it. Under Lomé IV STABEX became 'merely an elaborate mechanism for providing project aid', having been 'emasculated as regards its ... counter-cyclical functions' (Hewitt, 1996, pp. 234–5). The CFF, by contrast, did succeed for a while in playing a genuine if modest stabilising function. But it ran foul of the institutions set up by governments ostensibly for their own stabilisation efforts, but in fact used in ways that over-taxed export commodities and caused a long-term contraction in their supply. Both schemes lacked adequate conditionality.

How should compensation payments be distributed between the government and others? This problem was never resolved in practice by either scheme. In the early years of STABEX, the reporting of its uses was unsatisfactory in many recipient ACP states (Seemann and Stolt, 1992,

p. 40), but much of the transfers were treated as programme aid. Under Lomé IV, the transfers became project aid, whose use was restricted to the sector where the (increasingly frequent) 'temporary' shortfalls occurred. Money is fungible, so the impact of the transfer depends on whether or not the government would have undertaken the projects that it officially financed without the transfer. Since the counterfactual information is lacking, statements about impact (including the suggestion that the current form of STABEX is perpetuating primary product dependence) are unreliable. The CFF allowed the proceeds of the drawing to remain in the hands of the government, although curiously they were 'not to be used for development'. Neither scheme stipulated that the government had to pass on anything over and above its own shortfall in tax revenues.

The CFF at least can show a mildly positive performance in relation to the third question: are supra-national compensation schemes effective in reducing export instability? This never seems to have been empirically demonstrated for STABEX during its pre-Lomé IV existence, and is most unlikely to be the case under Lomé IV. It is the characteristic of quasi-automaticity which, while it lasted, gave both schemes their stabilizing potential. But ultimately quasi-automaticity could not be reconciled with the need for more appropriate conditionality.

Note

1. I am grateful to Adrian Hewitt for supplying relevant material, and to Alfred Maizels, Kunibert Raffer and other participants at the Innsbruck Conference for helpful comments on the original version. In part, this paper is based on my contribution to an evaluation study of development co-operation between the EU and Ethiopia carried out by an IDS team under the direction of Simon Maxwell in 1995/96.

References

Bleaney, M., N. Gemmell, and D. Greenaway (1995) 'Tax Revenue Instability with Particular Reference to Sub-Saharan Africa', *Journal of Development Studies*, vol. 31, no. 6 (August).

CEC (1990) *The Export Earnings Stabilisation System (STABEX)*, DE 63 (January).

—— (1991) *Principles, Guidelines and Rules for the Use of STABEX Transfers under Lomé* (Brussels, February).

—— (1992) *The Role of the Commission in Supporting Structural Adjustment in ACP States* (Luxembourg: Directorate-General for Development).

Goreux, L.M. (1977) 'Compensatory Financing: The Cyclical Pattern of Export Shortfalls', *IMF Staff Papers*, vol. 24, no. 3 (November).

Green, R.H. (1995) 'The IMF in Sub-Saharan African Structural Adjustment: No Lenders of First Resort', in G.K. Helleiner *et al.* (eds) *Poverty, Prosperity and the World Economy. Essays in Memory of Sidney Dell*, London: Macmillan.

Hewitt, A.P. (1982) *Synthesis Report on the Overall Impact of STABEX Operations, 1975–79, based on Ten ACP Case Studies* (London: Overseas Development Institute).

—— (1993) 'Commodity markey instability and compensatory financing', in A.P. Hewitt and M. Nissanke (eds) *Economic Crisis in Developing Countries* (London: Pinter).

—— (1996) 'A Singular Attempt to Combine Aid and Compensatory Finance: The Mixed Success of STABEX 1975–95', in O. Stokke (1996) *Foreign Aid Towards the Year 2000: Experiences and Challenges* (London: Frank Cass).

Johnson, H.G. (1967) *Economic Policies Towards Less Developed Countries* (London: Allen & Unwin).

Khan, M. and M.D. Knight (1985) *Fund Supported Adjustment Programs and Economic Growth*, Washington DC: International Monetary Fund, Occasional Paper no. 41).

Killick, T. (1995) *IMF Programmes in Developing Countries. Design and Impact* (London: Routledge, for the Overseas Development Institute).

Kofi, T.A. (1994) *Structural Adjustment in Africa. A performance Review of World Bank Policies under Uncertainty in Commodity Price Trends: The Case of Ghana* (Helsinki: UNU World Institute of Development Economics).

Kumar, M.S. (1989) 'The Stabilising Role of the Compensatory Financing Facility: Empirical Evidence and Welfare Implications', *IMF Staff Papers*, vol. 36, no. 4 (December).

Love, J. (1992) 'Export Instability and the Domestic Economy: Questions of Causality', *Journal of Development Studies*, vol. 28, no. 4 (July).

Pincus, J. (1967) *Trade, Aid and Development. The Rich and Poor Nations* (New York: McGraw–Hill).

Raffer, K. and H.W. Singer (1996) *The Foreign Aid Business Economic Assistance and Development* (Cheltenham: Edward Elgar).

Schadler, S., F. Rozwadowski, S. Tiwari and D.O. Robinson (1993) *Economic Adjustment in Low-Income Countries. Experience under the Enhanced Structural Adjustment Facility* (Washington DC: International Monetary Fund, Occasional Paper no. 106).

Seemann, T. and U. Stolt (1992) *Analysing the Effectiveness of STABEX: The Case of the Gambia* (Department of Economics at the University of Lund).

Singer, H.W. (1991) 'Alternative Approaches to Adjustment and Stabilization', in H.W. Singer (ed.) *Structural Adjustment and Agriculture* (FAO, Rome, Training Materials for Agricultural Planning, no. 25).

—— (1996) 'Commodity stabilisation: the rounded whole policy', mimeo, (Brighton: Institute of Development Studies).

—— and M. Lutz (1994) 'Trend and Volatility in the Terms of Trade: Consequences for Growth', in D. Sapsford and W. Morgan (eds) *The Economics of Primary Commodities: Models, Analysis and Policy* (Aldershot: Edward Elgar).

Toye, J. (1994) 'The Appraisal and Evaluation of Structural Adjustment Lending: Some Questions of Method', in R. Prendegast and F. Stewart (eds) *Market Forces and World Development* (Basingstoke: Macmillan).

—— (1996) 'Sectoral Report: Programme Aid', in *An Evaluation of Development Cooperation between the European Union and Ethiopia, 1976–1994* (Brighton: Institute of Development Studies).

Walters, A. and S.H. Hanke (1992) 'Currency Boards', in P. Newman, M. Milgate and J. Eatwell *The New Palgrave Dictionary of Money and Finance*, vol. 1 (London: Macmillan).

Part V
The Role of the International Agencies

20 The World Bank, 'Global Keynesianism' and the Distribution of the Gains from Growth

Paul Mosley

'I would like to see the Board of the Bank composed of imaginative expansionists, and the Board of the Fund of cautious bankers.' (J.M. Keynes, 1945/1991, p. 194)

'Why did the World Bank move away from project lending to policy lending which included conditionality? In my interpretation there was a certain personal element involved. When Robert McNamara took charge of the World Bank he discovered to his dismay that he had become a poor man compared to his previous situation. As US Secretary of Defense he had handled large multi-billion dollar budgets. The World Bank was a relatively small affair under the project basis because what we had not realised at Bretton Woods but which had become clear after 10 or 15 years of World Bank operation [is that] under the project basis you cannot push out a lot of money. Mr McNamara was groping for something to give the World Bank and himself a bigger role to play in the world.' (H.W. Singer, 1994, p. 46)

20.1 INTRODUCTION

Sir Hans Singer, whom this volume celebrates, was a pupil of John Maynard Keynes at Cambridge, and in 1945, attended the Bretton Woods negotiations at which Keynes and others designed the institutions which now seek to regulate and stimulate the international economy: the World Bank, the IMF and the GATT. Sir Hans has provided, ever since that time, frequent creative suggestions concerning the way in which all of those institutions, separately and in relation to the UN system, should set about the task of global economic governance, with a particular flurry of activity around 1994/5 when the Bretton Woods institutions celebrated their half-century. By this time, of course. the Bretton Woods institutions had departed from their original Articles of Agreement and implicated the World Bank progressively more deeply in policy-based programme lending alongside its original project lending functions. This paper attempts, a little belatedly, to take up some of the concerns aroused by that flurry of activity, with particular reference to the World Bank, which Keynes, as we saw above, saw as having the principal stimulative and entrepreneurial role. The concerns have been expressed by Sir Hans in the following way:

> The shift to programme lending and policy conditionality tied in with three other developments. First, the withering away of the development functions of the UN ... created a gap into which it was tempting and easy for the World Bank to move together with the IMF. Second, the debt crisis of the 1980s made the developing countries pliant in accepting conditionality pressures from the Bretton Woods institutions ... Third, in the process of replacing the UN as a focus of development policy guidance and in line with trends in the major industrial countries. the World Bank developed, again together with the IMF, a new 'Washington Consensus' emphasising government failures, market orientation. liberalisation, privatisation, etc. ... Now the purpose of this is, I am using the language of the IMF and World Bank now, to cut down today but in doing so lay the foundations for subsequent sustainable growth. Now the fact is that if you cut down today it is just as likely that if you cut investment today that does not lay the foundations for subsequent growth, that does exactly the opposite. The IMF are quite fond of illustrating their policy with the French proverb *reculer pour mieux sauter*. The trouble is that what we have today is that in all too many cases the developing countries stand on the edge of an abyss and therefore by stepping back they don't gain manoeuvring space for moving forward but they fall into the abyss. (Singer, 1995, p. 469, and 1994, p. 55)

The concern expressed by Sir Hans is, of course, one which has to be confronted not only by the World Bank but by every aid donor, since Bank and donors share the objective of stimulating development in poor countries. The specific question which is addressed in this paper is whether developing countries are likely to move further away from the abyss if Bank and donors relax their posture and increase the volume of project aid (or unconditional programme aid) which they supply. The answers to this question which emerge from the literature on 'North–South models', and their implications for the future strategy of the Bank and other aid donors, are reviewed. The story in brief is that the answer depends on the way in which any aid increase is financed, and on how effective the increase can be made in terms of induced developmental expenditure within poor countries. This story is used to support the case for a Bank which is something like an expanded version of its present International Development Association (IDA); more focused on poorer countries, softer in its financial terms, but possibly to Sir Hans' chagrin, tougher in its conditionality.

20.2 NORTH–SOUTH MODELS, 'GLOBAL KEYNESIANISM' AND THE FINANCING OF AID FLOWS

It has always been a standard right-wing objection to the Keynesian approach of fighting macroeconomic slumps, through deficit financing that it is hard to adopt effectively in an open economy, for such financing, if conducted unilaterally, sucks in imports which put a brake on the deficit-financing economy's ability to sustain expansion. This critique has been applied not only to deficit financing in industrialized countries of the type practised by France in 1981, but also to the new generation of 'structuralist' arguments which advocate a deficit-financed big push in developing countries to strengthen the supply side of the economy (see for example Stiglitz, 1993, pp. 39–49). It has been extended by Stewart (1983, chs 4 and 5) to suggest that the globalization of trade and financial markets imparts a deflationary bias: if one government reflates alone, the international financial markets will undermine it; if one country deflates on its own, the international financial markets will reinforce it. Such a deflationary bias became patent as early as the 1970s, but of course reached its climax during the global recession of the 1980s.

It was the merit of the Brandt Commission (1980), one of the first practical contributions to fighting that recession, to articulate at the same time an important counter-argument to the standard critique of Keynesian aggregate demand expansion by government, namely that if such expansion can be globally or even regionally co-ordinated, it need not be self-defeating. This proposition has subsequently been formalized by the literature known as 'North–South models'. In such models, international aid from North to South plays a crucial role in stimulating both the depressed economies of the South, directly, and the depressed economies of the North, through extra demand in the South induced by the aid. In the primitive model of the Appendix to this paper, the level of income in both the South and the North depends on the level of aid flows A_{12} and the aid effectiveness coefficient I_2; providing that the latter is positive, an increase in the former, by whomever provided, will both help developing countries step back from the abyss and stimulate the exports of industrialized countries. In this sense, there are 'mutual interests' not just in development, but in aid; aid acts, in case of need, as a counterpart to the deflationary bias imposed by the globalization of trade and finance.

This noble vision needs to be qualified in two ways. Firstly, if the primitive model is modified by paying proper attention to the way in which aid is financed, it turns out to matter a great deal whether any increase in international aid flows is financed by borrowing from the banks, or by a balanced-budget expansion in which the increased aid flow is paid for by higher taxes or by cuts in domestic public expenditure; for a deficit-financed expansion of aid will push up the level of world interest rates, and thence both raise the debt service payments due from Southern countries and depress the level of demand in the North to an extent dictated, in the model of the Appendix, by the size of the coefficient d_1. This downward pressure on Northern demand will then pass through to the prices of Southern commodity exports and to their terms of trade via the mechanism made famous by Sir Hans Singer (1950). By contrast, if the increased aid flow is financed from tax payments or expenditure reductions, no such deflationary backlash materializes. It is to the credit of Rob Vos (1993) to have pointed out this asymmetry by means of a structuralist model in which the South, unlike the North, is characterized by labour surplus, flexible prices of commodities and labour, and rationed credit markets. The significance of the asymmetry depends, of course, on the slope of the IS and LM curves, and in particular on the size of the coefficient d_1 by which Northern output responds to the level of world interest rates. The sensitivity of output in North and South to the mode of financing emerging from Vos's simulations is portrayed in Figure 20.1. But already, it appears, 'global Keynesianism', to be sure of its effect, logically needs to take the form of balanced-budget expansion rather than the unbalanced-budget variety if it is to avoid neutralizing its own intended effects.

The second caveat is that if aid, of any sort, is to stimulate the global economy it needs to be effective in the specific sense of raising Southern output; in the notation of the model, the coefficient I_2 needs to be positive. That it is, and that therefore more aid is what the South needs, has been assumed by a large literature ranging from the Brandt Commission Report, previously cited, to Cassen (1986), United Nations (1988) and most recently Helleiner (1995). Sadly, however, there is very little econometric

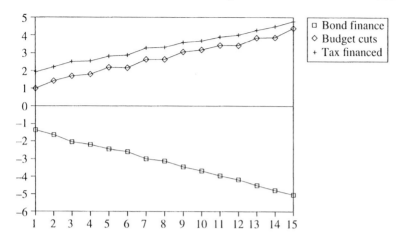

(a) Impact on real income North, Q_N (% deviation from baseline)

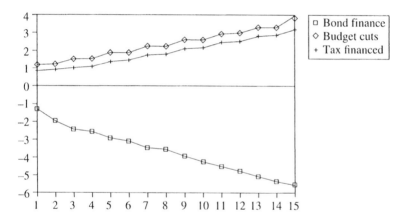

(b) Impact on real income North, Q_s (% deviation from baseline)

Figure 20.1   Impact of an increase in North–South transfers

Source: Vos (1993).

evidence to support this contention at a global level. Table 20.1 collates
the findings of a range of econometric investigations by different authors,
the general message of which is that the net impact of aid (the partial
regression coefficient l_2) is neutral overall, probably positive in most
Asian countries and almost certainly negative in most African countries.
There are however signs, not yet robust ones, of an improvement even in

Africa in recent years. Such an improvement, if it has indeed occurred, is in a way to be expected, both because of the partial success of policy dialogue (for example, greater exchange-rate competitiveness) and because the elimination of the domestically-financed development budget in Africa countries has virtually wiped out the scope for 'fungibility', or switching, of aid (Mosley and Hudson, 1996).

It remains the case that the measured ability of aid flows to trigger sustained growth in developing countries has been poor, and particularly poor in the poorest countries. This does not, as such, destroy the Brandt Commission's case for stimulating the global economy through aid flows – for even if 100 per cent of such flows leaks into consumption in the recipient economy, a good proportion of that increased consumption will manifest itself as increased exports by donor countries – possibly more, cynics would say, than if it had been 'productively' used. This is the international analogue to Keynes' argument for stimulating the economy by setting unemployed men to dig holes in the ground, if no other possible public projects existed. However, the Brandt Commission's vision is not a licence to waste aid money – any more than Keynes' metaphor is an argument for using the entire public-works budget to dig up buried bottles. If

Table 20.1   Evidence on the effectiveness of aid[a]

	1960–70	1970–80	1980–90	1970–90	1990–94
Africa	−0.01	−0.09	−0.09		0.18[b*]
	(0.27)	(0.63)	(0.41)		(5.23)
Asia	0.09	0.46[c]	0.67[c]		
	(1.31)	(2.03)	(2.49)		
Latin America	0.02	1.01	1.97		
	(0.06)	(1.19)	(1.51)		
All LDCs	−0.04[c]	−0.03	0.04[†]	0.00[††]	
	(2.12)	(0.07)	(0.87)	(0.03)	

Sources: Mosley, Hudson and Horrell (1987) Table 3 for all regressions except:
[*] Africa 1990–94 from Mosley and Hudson (1996), Appendix 6
[†] All LDCs 1980–90: from Reichel (1995), Table 3 (2SLS estimation)
[††] All LDCs 1970–90: from Boone (1994).
Notes:
[a] partial regression coefficients with growth of GDP (% p.a.) as dependent variable.
[b] indicates significance at the 1 per cent level.
[c] indicates significance of a coefficient at the 5 per cent level.

the local multiplier for the $100 billion currently transferred as aid is insignificantly different from zero in the aggregate – which at least until recently appears to have been the situation in much of the Third World – then, at the very least, the gains from aid have been needlessly biased away from the South. That, of course, is what both the Marxists and the Bauer – Friedman right have been arguing all along – except that they would substitute the word 'inevitably' for the word 'needlessly'.

I have argued elsewhere (Mosley, 1987, 1996) that the word 'needlessly' is right, and spelled out a reform programme which might bring about an improvement in aid effectiveness and a reduction in poverty at the same time. The essentials of this are greater emphasis on the removal of imperfections in foodcrop markets and capital markets affecting smallholders and the informal sector; the jettisoning of the unworkable parts of the structural adjustment programme, including much privatization and trade reform; directed credit to export-competitive sectors; and performance-contingent protection. Where, and only where, elements of this package have been shown to work in particular countries, it would be right to back them up with tougher conditionality, including 'down payments' of reform currently requested as *ex ante* conditions. Much of this programme, indeed, has already been implemented, not only in South-east Asia, but also in some African political economies, including Mauritius and, increasingly, Uganda. It is therefore reasonable to describe it as a plausible manifesto rather than a wish-list. However, it remains quite a long way away from the intentions of the major donors, with the exception of the Japanese. This brings us back, inevitably, to the World Bank: both the lead violinist and, at least in terms of intentions, the conductor of the aid-donor orchestra.

20.3 IMPLICATIONS FOR THE WORLD BANK

As recently exposed by the First Deputy Managing Director of the IMF (Fischer, 1993, p. 1) none of the Bretton Woods institutions retains its original functions. The IMF was set up to police an adjustable-peg exchange rate system which disappeared in 1973, the GATT has disappeared altogether, and the World Bank, in part as a result of Mr McNamara's 'groping ... for a bigger role' has developed new functions (equity finance, policy-based lending, and conventional aid through IDA) which complement, and in many ways overshadow, the (non-aid-financed) 'projects for the purposes of reconstruction and development' provided for at Bretton Woods.

The implication of the foregoing argument is that these processes should go further. For it is the IBRD part of the World Bank (the original hard-loan component) which least obviously, at the end of the twentieth century, extends the range of the international financial system: it makes medium-term loans for infrastructure and other purposes to middle-income countries, but then so do private banks, which do not inflict on the clients the transactions costs, in terms of compliance with conditionality, or in some cases the interest rates which the Bank inflicts. Furthermore, it is the IBRD part of the Bank which is most liable to inflict an increase in the real cost of lending on the international financial system, not only because it is bond-financed – such that any major increase in transfers runs the risk of pushing the supplier of loans up the supply curve (the Vos argument), but also because the Bank is increasingly exposed to the risk of a major default which might dent its international credit rating. It already has $2.8 billion of loans in non-accrual status (*Annual Report 1994*, Notes B and E to Financial Statements, pp. 189 and 205), and the fact that the grace periods on many loans recently provided to eastern European and FSU countries are now coming to an end makes this figure likely to increase over the next five years. None of these arguments applies to IDA, which provides concessional credits to low-income countries which, for the most part, are unable to access commercial credit markets, so that additionality and progressivity are guaranteed. In many ways the erosion of IBRD which we are advocating is being brought about by the market; formerly enthusiastic middle-income customers of the Bank, from Malaysia to Thailand to Chile to Mauritius, now realize that it is financially cheaper, as well as less administrative and politically costly, to borrow from the markets rather than from the Bank. This erosion should not be resisted it is the measure of the Bank's success in these countries. But if IBRD is to retreat, that makes it the more important that what remains – in particular IDA – should act, in Keynes' words, as an 'imaginative expansionist', counteracting rather than reinforcing the deflationary pressures of the IMF. As Sir Hans has noted (page 377 above) the Bank has sometimes been tempted to go the reinforcement route, there by exacerbating the risks of a cumulative collapse of the supply side. Luckily, however, the Bank is a pluralistic institution which speaks with numerous voices, many of them – especially on the project side – both expansionist and imaginative.

We have argued that IDA ('the Bank as a fund'), and associated cofinancing from bilateral and multilateral donors, is the major instrument through which the retreat from the abyss in the poorest countries will have to be financed in the twenty-first century. As most of Table 20.1 illustrates, the track record of this instrument, especially in Africa, is far from happy. But if aid has failed, aid must succeed; for when it is already financing the entire government development budget in most of low-income Africa and there is no private sector to speak of, there is by definition no other instrument which can do the job in the short term. There are signs of hope all over the horizon, from the World Bank's poverty initiatives, to the beginnings of green revolution and demographic transition in the poorest countries, to successful institutional transfers between Asia and Africa, to the hesitant and unconfirmed signs of a return to growth and aid-effectiveness in much of Africa in the middle 1990s. Once these seeds have taken root, the prospects for a mutually supportive growth process that is even-handed between North and South – the vision that has animated idealists from the Bretton Woods founding fathers to Brandt to Sir Hans Singer – will brighten beyond measure.

References

Boone, P. (1994) 'The impact of foreign aid on savings and growth', unpublished paper, London School of Economics.

Brandt Commission (1980) *North – South: a Programme for Survival* (London: Pan).

Cassen, R. *et al.* (1986) *Does Aid Work?* (Oxford University Press).

Clark, W. (1984) *Cataclysm: the North-South Conflict of 1987* (London: Pan).

Fischer, S. (1993) 'The IMF and World Bank at fifty', paper prepared for conference on The Future of the International Monetary System and its Institutions, International Centre for Monetary and Banking Studies, Geneva, 2–4 September.

Helleiner, Gerald (1995) 'Africa in the globalised economy; looking ahead', unpublished paper presented at conference on 'Sub-saharan Africa: Looking ahead', Copenhagen, 1–2 November.

Kingman, P. (1993) 'Towards a counter-counterrevolution is development theory', *World Bank Economic Review Supplement*, 15–39.

Keynes, J.M. (1945, 1991) *The Collected Writings of John Maynard Keynes*, vol. xxvi, *Activities 194–46: Shaping the Post-war World: Bretton Woods and Reparations* (London: Macmillan).

Krugman, P. and A.J. Venables (1995) 'Globalisation and the inequality of nations' *Quarterly Journal of Economics*, vol. 110 (November) 857–879.

Mosley, P. (1987) *Overseas Aid: its Defence and Reform* (Brighton: Wheatsheaf).

Mosley, P. (1996) 'The failure of aid and adjustment policies in Sub-saharan Africa: Counter-examples and Policy Proposals', *Journal of Africa Economies*, vol. 5, pp. 406–43.

——, J. Hudson and S. Horrel (1987) 'Aid, the public sector and the market in less developed countries', *Economic Journal*, vol. 97, pp. 616–42.

—— and J. Hudson (1996) *A Study of Aid Effectiveness in 29 ACP Countries*, unpublished report, IDC, University of Reading.

Moutos, T. and D. Vines (1989) 'The simple macroeconomics of North–South interaction, *American Economic Review Papers and Proceedings*, vol. 79.

Reichel, R. (1995) 'Development aid, savings and growth in the 1980s: a cross-section approach', *Savings and Development*, vol. 19 (September) pp. 279–97.

Singer, H.W. (1950) 'The division of gains between investing and borrowing countries' *American Economic Review Papers and Proceedings*, vol. 40 (May).

—— (1974) 'The distribution of gains from trade and investment – revisited' *Journal of Development Studies*, vol. 11 (July).

—— (1983) 'North-South multipliers', *World Development*, vol. 11, pp. 451–4.

—— (1994) 'An assessment of the World Bank' in Friedrich Ebert Foundation', *50 Years of Bretton Woods System: the Role of the IMF, World Bank and GATT in the World Economy* (October).

—— (1995) 'Historical background to the Bretton Woods system and its relation to the United Nations system', in B. Etemad, J. Batou and T. David (eds) *Towards and International Economic and Social History: Essays in Honour of Paul Bairoch* (Geneva: Editions Passe Present).

Stewart, M. (1983) *Controlling the Economic Future: Policy Dilemmas in a Shrinking World* (Brighton: Wheatsheaf).

Stiglitz, J. (1993) 'Comment', pp. 39–49 in Krugman, op.cit.

Taylor, L. (1981) 'North-South trade and Southern growth: bleak prospects from the structuralist point of view', *Journal of International Economics*, vol. 11, pp. 589–606.

United Nations (1988) *Financing Africa's Recovery: Report and Recommendations of the Advisory Group on Financial Flows for Africa* (New York: Department of Public Affairs).

Vos, R. (1993) 'Aid flows and the international transfer problems in a structuralist North–South model', *Economic Journal*, vol. 103, pp. 494–509.

—— (1994) *Debt and Adjustment in the World Economy: Structural Asymmetries in North – South Interactions* (London and The Hague: Macmillan and Institute of Social Studies).

Appendix: An Ultra-Simple North–South Model

Notation

Y = income
I = investment
C = consumption
G = government expenditure
T = tax revenue
X = exports
M = imports
M_0 = money stock
r = world rate of interest
e = average exchange rate prevailing between North and South
A = aid flows from North to South

P = private capital flows from North to South
Q = index of political conditions in South

Subscript 1 denotes North, subscript 2 denotes South. Capital letters denote variables, lower-case letters (except in the case of e and r!) denote fixed parameters.

The North

$$Y_1 = C_1 + I_1 + G_1 + X_1 - M_1 \tag{20.1}$$

$$C_1 = a_1 + b(Y_1 - T_1) \tag{20.2}$$

$$I_1 = c_1 - d_1(r) \tag{20.3}$$

$$r = zM_0 = z_1(G_1 - T_1) + z_2(G_2 - T_2) \tag{20.4}$$

$$G_1 \text{ is autonomous} \tag{20.5}$$

$$X_1 = f_1 e + g_2 Y_2 + u_1 = M_2 \tag{20.6}$$

$$M_1 = h_1 Y_1 - j_1 e + u_2 = X_2 \tag{20.7}$$

The South

$$Y_2 = C_2 + I_2 + G_2 + X_2 - M_2 \tag{20.8}$$

$$C_2 = a_2 + b_2 Y_2 \tag{20.9}$$

$$I_2 = c_2 - d_2(r) \tag{20.10}$$

$$G_2 \text{ is autonomous} \tag{20.11}$$

$$e = e(X_1 - M_1) \tag{20.12}$$

Implication 1

Northern exports and income (X_1, Y_1), rise as Southern income rises and vice versa.

International capital flows

Concessional:

$$A_{12} = kY_1 \tag{20.13}$$

In other words, aid flows from North to South are a fixed percentage of Northern income. In a more sophisticated model, they would reflect also the business cycle and the political complexion of Northern governments.

Non-concessional:

$$P_{12} = n(r) + pQ \tag{20.14}$$

Note that in the presence of capital flows from North to South, the Southern investment equation (20.10) will need to be written as

$$I_2 = c_2 - d_2(r) + l_2 A_{12} + s_2 P_{12} \tag{20.10'}$$

Implication 2

The level of income in the South and in the North depend on the size of aid and private capital flows (A_{12}, P_{12}) and the aid-effectiveness coefficients l_2, s_2.

Implication 3

The level of interest rates will rise, Northern investment and income fall, and Southern terms of trade fall if budget deficits rise for *any* reason, in particular a sudden increase in aid flows financed by expansion of the budget deficit.

21 An Economic and Social Security Council at the United Nations[1]

Frances Stewart and Sam Daws

21.1 INTRODUCTION

Hans Singer has contributed more than perhaps any other individual to the development of the United Nations as we know it today and to proposals for its reform. His most recent proposals for reform, 'Revitalising the United Nations: Five Proposals', argued for improved global economic management, including the creation of an Economic Security Council. In this paper we develop further the case for such a Council. (Singer, 1995b).

There are a large number of *world* problems that cannot be solved by national action because they involve more than one and sometimes many nations. These problems have been growing in number and magnitude with the globalization of the world economy. Yet the global level economic and social institutions that we have today were designed 50 years ago, as a result of the meetings in San Francisco leading to the design of the United Nations institutions and the deliberations at Bretton Woods which were responsible for the creation of the International Monetary Fund and the World Bank. There have been some changes since then, in particular the development of UN specialized agencies and recently the creation of the World Trade Organization. While the institutions themselves have developed in function and scope over the last 50 years, the basic structure remains as it was in 1945. This structure is not adequate to deal with today's problems.

In 1945 there was already a major gap in the world institutional structure: there were no institutions responsible for world economic governance, nor for protecting the poor at a world level. But then this gap was less apparent than it is today – partly because it was expected that the institutions that were created might develop to fulfil this role, especially the International Financial Institutions (IFIs) and the Economic and Social Council of the UN (ECOSOC); partly because the need for such functions to be fulfilled was, perhaps, less apparent.

The gap is more glaring today for a number of reasons. First, the globalization of markets that has occurred in recent decades has created new needs for global economic policies. Secondly, increasing global environmental problems and rising consciousness of their importance has pointed to the urgent need for action at a world level. Thirdly, the issue of world poverty and the moral, political and legal imperatives for action to eradicate it, is in the forefront of the world agenda, not hidden in the policies and practices of colonial states, as it was in 1945. Since 1945 institutional progress on these issues has been mixed. On the negative side, the world institutions created in 1944–5 have not made a major contribution to world economic governance. Their role has been less than what might have been expected and indeed less than was envisaged by Keynes, one of the chief architects of the post-Second World War institutions; consequently, *ad-hoc* solutions have been adopted which are unsatisfactory from many points of view. More positively, however, there has been some progress in relation to poverty and social needs – for example, in the work of UNICEF, of UNDP, in IDA, and in the recognition of Social and Economic Human Rights – but while poverty eradication has been recognized as a key objective, the achievements in this area have been nowhere near proportionate to the size of the problem.

There is an urgent need for a new institutional approach to world economic and social governance. Yet the fiftieth anniversary of the United Nations is slipping by with regress rather than progress on world institutional developments, largely for political and financial reasons. The decision-makers of 1944 and 1945 showed unusual imagination and boldness in designing a new monetary system and institutional structure that was intended to prevent a recurrence of the devastating economic and social situation and the consequential political repercussions that followed the First World War. Although it is clearly more difficult to motivate people to take such bold measures in less cataclysmic times, the need is no less today.

It is our view that the creation of an Economic and Social Security Council at the United Nations would provide a structure to deal with issues of world economic governance and world action towards poverty and social needs in a systematic and politically realistic way. This chapter is intended to explain why such a council is needed and what its functions and structure should be.

The chapter is organized as follows: Section 21.2 considers why neither national governments nor the market can by themselves solve the problems of world economic and social governance and identifies the functions needed of world institutions, particularly taking into account the developments over the past 50 years that have increased the need for world institutions. Section 21.3 reviews the existing international institutions, pointing to their inadequacies and some of the consequences stemming from this. Section 21.4 develops the case for an Economic and Social Security Council (ESSC) and presents an overview of how it might be structured and function. It also briefly reviews some similar proposals. Section 21.5 considers functions, composition and procedures in more detail. The final section comes to some conclusions.

21.2 THE NEED FOR WORLD ECONOMIC AND SOCIAL GOVERNANCE

Global institutions are needed to promote action to maximize world welfare in situations where neither governments nor markets are likely to act in a way that will do so. The basic problem with national action is that governments can be expected mainly to act in a way that will contribute directly to their own objectives, taking little account of the international repercussions of that action. This is rational from the perspective of maximizing national welfare in the short term, but each nation will suffer when other nations behave in the same way given the large interactions between countries. Global institutions are needed to ensure that the international implications of national action are taken into account and countries (and markets) are constrained to act in a way that will promote global welfare.

There are three types of reason why such global action may be needed, which parallel the reasons for government action within a nation. The first is that neither governments nor markets take into account the full global consequences of their actions where externalities are involved, that is, where some of the consequences of national actions impinge outside national borders. The second is that some activities cannot be controlled domestically even if governments want to do so. The third is that there are some objectives which are agreed at a world level, but which are not shared by particular governments, or, sometimes, particular governments share but cannot achieve the agreed objectives because of limitations in their resources or power.

Collective action because of externalities

In principle, international institutions should provide the collective action that is necessary to promote world welfare, which neither governments acting on their own, nor the market would provide. Because of free-rider problems and deficiencies in information, only collective action will bring about the desired results in some situations where international externalities are significant.

The arenas where relevant externalities arise at a world level are:

1. *Environmental issues*, where national action has international effects – such as damage to the ozone level; excessive carbon dioxide emissions; sea pollution, and so on. In these areas, world environmental regulation is essential. In many of these cases, there exist world public goods which have to be protected at a world level;

2. *Economic externalities*, where national economic activity has world repercussions. For example, interest rate policy in one country can affect capital flows elsewhere; budgetary policy can affect world levels of activity; tariffs not only affect the domestic market but also the markets of others. In the 1930s, the competitive tariff escalation came to be known as 'beggar-my-neighbour' policies because of these international externalities.

Phenomena that cannot be controlled nationally

There are some activities that cross borders and are impossible to control without international co-operation. These include activities that governments dislike and wish to control, such as international criminal rings, drug production and trading; some types of arms production and trading. They also include more desirable activities, such as international movements of labour and capital, whose movement governments may wish to regulate or tax.

World objectives, especially in relation to economic and social rights

There is formal agreement, embodied in the International Covenants on Human Rights, that people the world over have certain rights of both a negative (freedom from …) and positive (freedom to …) kind. The first category involve political liberties; the second the right of access to social and economic goods.[2] At a less formal level, there is world-wide acceptance that abysmal poverty should be eliminated wherever it occurs; that certain abuses of human beings, such as those to be observed in so-called complex political emergencies such as have recently occurred in Rwanda or Bosnia, are not to be tolerated. Yet, as is only too obvious, national action cannot be relied on to secure these rights and objectives, either because the governments in question lack the resources or power (financial, administrative or political) or because they lack the will.

International action then becomes imperative; and international institutions are needed to carry out or supervise the action necessary.

Changes in the last half-century

These have increased the need for global action of all three types. The actuality of the UN and Bretton Woods institutions never lived up to their original conception (Singer, 1995b); a much greater degree of global economic management had been envisaged, especially by Keynes, with more powerful instruments to enforce it (for example, the bancor). Moreover, the 50 years since the present world institutions were established have seen some dramatic changes, both political and economic, many of which have increased the need for collective action at a world level, and hence the imperative of institutional reform. They have also changed political realities and thus made the old structure of decision-making obsolete.

The end of colonialism and the growth in the number of nations

An early and radical political change was the dismantling of colonialism and the creation of independent states. Fifty-one countries made up the United Nations in 1945. By 1995, 185 countries were members. Most of the countries which acquired independence over these years had very low incomes and appalling social indicators. With political independence came the desire to acquire economic independence and to catch up economically and socially with the industrialized countries.

The end of communism

The second dramatic political change concerns the revolutions of 1989 and the dismantling of the old Soviet sphere of influence. This too has had major implications for the functioning of world institutions. It also increased the number of countries seeking assistance from world financial institutions – in this case in their transition to a market economy. Like the ex-colonial countries, these countries are greatly affected by the IFIs but do not have any power over them. The change has also meant, in the short term at least, that the UN Security Council has been rejuvenated, released from the paralysis of the Cold War.

Changing economic power

In 1945 the countries which came to be named the 'Third World' were fairly uniform in some respects: poverty was a dominant characteristic of their economies, they had limited industrial sectors, low savings and very poor health and education, life expectancy and literacy. But since then developments have diverged markedly. Some countries grew at a spectacular pace – notably those in East Asia. Others jogged along slowly for some time, but recently have accelerated impressively – South-East Asia and China. Others did fairly well until the 1980s and then collapsed under the weight of deteriorating commodity prices (Africa) and the debt crisis (Latin America). Among the industrialized countries too, performance differed with recovery in Europe, and growth rates substantially above those of North America, and Japan achieving very high growth rates for about thirty years after 1950.

The net effect of economic developments since 1945 has been a massive change in the world distribution of output. The dominance of the USA and Europe has been greatly reduced as the economic status of Japan and latterly developing countries have increased (Table). The changes in political status and economic development since 1945 have not been properly reflected in the structure of decision-making in world institutions. 'Democratic' institutions such as the General Assembly have expanded their membership and voting rights as new countries joined the United Nations. But the structure of those institutions whose membership and/or voting rights is intended to reflect countries' political or economic power in the world, such as the Security Council and the IFIs, has not changed in accordance with these new realities (to be discussed further below).

Globalization

'Globalization' describes the growing importance of international links that have resulted from the rapid expansion of global markets which has taken place over the past few decades at an accelerating pace. Inevitably, globalization has enlarged the magnitude of externalities between nations, thereby increasing the need for world institutions to deal with them. Globalization has expanded opportunities for some countries, but not others, leading to uneven development and reinforcing the need for international redistributive processes to assist those countries and people who have suffered rather than gained.

Globalization occurred as a response to changes in technology, regulations and economic structure. Trade expansion resulted from improvements and cost reductions in transport and communications, the progressive removal of trade restrictions, increasing convertibility of currencies and changes in economic structure which increased the potential for international specialization. The growth of international capital movements was also the joint product of technology change and deregulation of capital markets, with the removal of controls in many countries. The massive investments necessary for some new technologies, such as in electronics and aircraft, have meant that in these areas the world economy is dominated by very few multinational enterprises. Consequently, global markets in trade, capital, technology and manpower are expanding; each is becoming increasingly significant when expressed as a proportion of domestic resources (that is, resources produced and used in the same country).

Globalization of the world economy means that international repercussions of domestic activity are becoming more and more important; it also means that national action alone cannot regulate or tax many cross-border transactions. Hence the need for global institutions to regulate such activity has increased along with globalization. Major elements in globalization are:

● *The growth in world trade* International trade has grown faster than production for many decades. In aggregate world trade grew more than one-and-a-half times as fast as output, annually, in 1950–94. Over this period, output oncreased fivefold while the value of world trade multiplied fourteen times. The proportion of world output accounted for by exports almost doubled between 1965 and 1993, rising from 11 per cent to 21 per cent. This means that countries are increasingly dependent on world markets – that is, on events outside their own country – for the dynamism of their own economy.

But the growth of world trade has been uneven, leading to increasing disparities among developing countries. Eight countries had export growth of over 10 per cent p-a, 1980–93, and another 24 had growth of between 5 and 10 per cent. But over the same period, 21 developing countries experienced annual falls in exports. The rapid export growth countries were more concentrated among middle-income countries (over two-thirds of the countries with over 5 per cent annual growth), while the falls were more concentrated among low-income countries (14 of the 21 countries; data from World Bank, 1995).

Low-income countries suffered especially from the almost unprecedented fall in commodity prices which occurred over this period. Between 1980 and 1994, a weighted index of 33 commodities (excluding energy) fell by 50 per cent (United Nations, 1995). Within manufactures, also, the terms of trade for products produced by developing countries worsened (although not as sharply as primary products). The gainers were producers of high technology products.[3]

● *The growth in international financial markets*   These expanded first on the basis of the recycled earnings of the oil-producing countries in the 1970s. Large surpluses (and deficits) in the world have continued to fuel the markets, while deregulation and technological change have led to the effective internationalization of many of the world's financial markets. Computerized dealings are estimated to transmit more than $US 300bn across national borders each day (UNDP, 1992). Between 1979 and 1989, the share of cross-border equities in total turnover more than doubled from 6 per cent to 14 per cent. Unregulated financial flows can cause severe problems for both developed and developing countries. For example, the major source of problems for many Latin American countries in the 1980s was the excessive bank lending of the 1970s. While this seems to have been cured, at least temporarily, by the Brady initiative and debt rescheduling, a new problem has arisen with the resumption of capital flows, especially those focused on portfolio investment. Money that can enter a country fast can also go out as fast, creating havoc with the domestic economy. Mexico's experience in December 1994 provided a clear example and warning for countries with similar dependence on capital inflows. Speculation on financial markets may lead to sharp exchange rate fluctuations, unjustified depreciation or appreciation, and can cost governments $ billions in one day, effectively transferring resources from governments to those (the upper one per cent of the world's income-earners) who participate in financial markets.[4]

Distribution of capital flows among countries is a further problem leading to a need for corrective action at a global level. In general capital markets favour middle-income countries. Low-income countries, which accounted for nearly three-quarters of developing country population, received 15 per cent of gross disbursements in 1970 and less than 9 per cent in the 1980s.

● *Transnational corporations*   These have acquired increasing significance. By the early 1980s, trade between the 350 largest TNCs amounted to an estimated 40 per cent of global trade (Charles, Oman, quoted in Ghai, 1993). Global sales of foreign affiliates in host countries are estimated to have grown by 15 per cent per annum in 1985–90 (United Nations, 1990, quoted in Ghai, 1993) much faster than the growth of output. TNCs dominate international technology flows: for the USA four out of five of technology receipts are intra-firm, with over 90 per cent for Germany. Even in more arms-length forms of technology transfer the source of technology supply largely consists of the 'same multinationals which dominate direct foreign investment' (Lall, 1987).

The rising importance of transnational companies requires some international authority to regulate and tax them – since they are far larger than the national economies of many third world countries, and these countries cannot control their activities, nor indeed can much larger countries.[5] Again the distribution of investment presents a problem. Developing countries as a whole receive only a small proportion of the total financial flows associated with TNCs. The share of developing countries in global foreign direct investment fell from 31 per cent in 1968 to 25 per cent (1980–84) to 17 per cent (1988–9; data from UNDP, 1992). FDI is concentrated in a few mainly middle – income developing countries: three-quarters went to ten countries in the 1980s: Brazil, Singapore and Mexico received over a third of the flows; China, with 10 per cent of the total, is the only low-income country among the 'top ten' recipients.

Globalization and poverty

Although globalization has been associated with economic growth among developing countries as a whole this growth has been uneven and *poverty has not been eliminated*. Estimates for 1989 suggest that over one billion people fell below the poverty line; in Sub-Saharan Africa 52 per cent (165 m.), in South Asia over 550 million or 49 per cent of the population and in Latin America 104 million or 25 per cent of the population were poor (estimates of Chen *et al.*, 1994). In some countries, poverty rates as high as 70 per cent of the population or more have been noted. High infant and maternal mortality rates and malnutrition, low levels of education especially among females, poor access to water and sanitation are other symptoms of deprivation in many poor countries.

Globalization has left a vacuum in governance

National governments cannot regulate, monitor or tax many international activities adequately; nor do they redistribute resources on a significant scale to the world's poor. If globalization continues at an accelerating pace, which seems likely as a result of further deregulation and technological changes, the hole in world governance, like that in the ozone layer, will get dangerously large.

New objectives

As is to be expected over a 50-year period, particularly one that saw such major political and economic changes, the objectives widely adhered to by the world community have also changed.[6]

The main economic objectives behind the post-Second World War institutions were high levels of employment and the establishment of a prosperous world economy based on the promotion of free movement of goods, services and capital.[7] In the event, in the first 20 years after the system was initiated, the developed countries experienced full employment and their dominant economic problem then appeared to be inflation rather than unemployment. Subsequently, when unemployment reappeared in the industrial countries and underemployment emerged as a growing problem in developing countries, the IFIs seem to have lost sight of the employment objective, placing emphasis on inflation control, sometimes at the expense of employment and output. This was partly due to the resurgence of monetarist philosophy.

Since 1945, other important economic and social objectives have gained prominence in response to political developments and developments in views about priorities. These include:

• *Development of third world countries* (and now *promotion of successful transition*)   This emerged naturally after developing countries acquired political independence. The World Bank took this objective on as its major remit at an early stage.

• *Elimination of poverty*   At first, it was believed this would be the automatic outcome of development, but as the failure of 'trickle down' became apparent, 'Basic Needs' was accepted as an objective by the World Bank, soon to be displaced, however, by stabilization and adjustment. In the 1990s, poverty reduction has again emerged as an important world objective.

• *The fulfilment of economic and social rights*   (as noted above) In principle, this objective is closely related to both the development and the poverty elimination objectives. In practice, they have been separated, with Economic and Social Rights dealt with within the UN, in the Committee on Economic, Social and Cultural Rights, while the poverty objective has been regarded as the remit of the World Bank.

• *Problems of the unregulated market system for the environment*   This occurs at many levels (ranging from soil erosion in particular villages to the world greenhouse effect) and has given growing weight to environmental considerations and the objective of *sustainable development*.

● *High levels of employment*   Finally, because the employment objective so clearly enunciated at Bretton Woods was subsequently neglected, it has become necessary to reintroduce high levels of employment as an objective, both in developed and developing countries.[8]

The objectives listed above are broadly accepted by the international community, in rhetoric if not action. There are other objectives arising from our analysis of globalization on which agreement at an international level is not yet in evidence, but which would require international action if and when agreement on them were reached. These entail the need to monitor and regulate international markets, including:

● capital markets, where unregulated transactions can be destabilizing, and where the proposed Tobin tax on transactions is gaining increasing support;
● commodity markets, where fluctuating prices and adverse terms of trade continue to present severe problems, especially for the poorest countries;
● TNCs, whose income is often inadequately taxed;
● technology markets (encompassing TNCs) where unjustifiably high prices are often charged and technology transfer and dissemination restricted.

Why we need global economic and social institutions

To summarise: global institutions are needed so that national economic and environmental externalities can be incorporated into decision-making; to help regulate international transactions; and to contribute to world social and economic justice, especially the elimination of poverty. The need for world institutions to fulfil these functions has grown significantly over the past 50 years, partly because globalization has increased the problems caused by unregulated transactions and the magnitude of externalities between nations and partly because global markets have not eliminated poverty, but have been associated with divergent performance across the world, with some parts growing rapidly and others regressing. The market cannot be relied on to eliminate these divergencies; rather it tends to promote them. Hence the need for international action to secure redistribution between and within nations. Finally, growing consciousness of the environment has created a new need for international regulation.

21.3   DEFICIENCIES IN EXISTING INTERNATIONAL
INSTITUTIONS

The Charter of the United Nations provides that:

'the United Nations shall promote
a.   higher standards of living, full employment, and conditions of social progress and development;
b.   solutions of international economic, social, health and related problems; and international cultural ad educational cooperation; and
c.   universal respect for, and observance of, human rights and fundamental freedoms for all without distinction as to race, sex, language or religion' (Article 55).

In principle, then, the Charter requires the United Nations to fulfil the functions of world economic and social governance discussed earlier in this Chapter. In practice, there exists a large range of international institutions – some would say too many – in the UN family with economic and social functions. Yet none of them adequately fulfils the global functions that we have identified above. Existing institutions which might appear to have global functions of the sort desired are: ECOSOC, (reporting to the General Assembly) at the heart of the UN, with both economic and social functions; the Commission on Human Rights and the Committee on Economic, Social and Cultural Rights (both of which report to ECOSOC), particularly in their role in the definition and implementation of the International Covenant on Economic, Social and Cultural Rights; the two International Financial Institutions – the IMF and World Bank – which were instituted as specialized agencies of the United Nations, in principle subject to the overall co-ordination of the UN General Assembly and ECOSOC and which were assigned some central economic functions.[9]

In the original conception at Bretton Woods the UN was to be responsible for macroeconomic policy coordination, development planning and aid; the IMF would provide the international liquidity necessary to achieve support stable exchange rates, world growth and full employment; and the World Bank (called the International Bank for Reconstruction and Development) would provide financing for projects in Europe during reconstruction and in developing countries (Singer, 1995a)

In practice, this is not how responsibilities worked out. The UN (in the form of its key organs – Security Council, General Assembly, ECOSOC) has actually had minimal international economic functions: it has not carried out any of the suggested tasks – neither macroeconomic coordination nor development planning, while the aid it has been responsible for has been on a small scale relative to that of other multilateral and bilateral flows. Development planning (or policy-making) functions have been assumed by the World Bank as well as a major part of international aid. No international institution has taken systematic responsibility for macroeconomic coordination.

The UN Charter gave the *Security Council* primary responsibility for the maintenance of international peace and security, and uniquely in the UN system it can take decisions under Chapter VII of the UN Charter which are binding on all UN Member States of the UN. Its membership consists of five permanent members (China, France, Russian Federation, UK and USA) and 10 members elected from all UN members, for a period of two years, to ensure the participation of members from all the major geographical regions of the world. There have been calls for the Security Council to expand its interpretation of 'a threat to international peace and security' to include economic and social factors, and to a small degree recent interventions to provide humanitarian assistance and a recognition of the role of peace-keeping in post-conflict peace-building are steps in this direction. However, while there is considerable latitude, in theory, for the Security Council to interpret its remit to embrace the social and economic dimensions, in practice the traditional division of labour has been preferred with economic and social issues left to the General Assembly and ECOSOC. Moreover, the exclusion of Japan and Germany and the veto power make the Security Council, as at present constituted, an unsuitable body for global economic and social decision-making.

ECOSOC

Responsibility for discharging the major economic and social functions in the Charter was given mainly to ECOSOC, acting under the authority of the General Assembly. ECOSOC was authorised to undertake studies and report on international economic, social, cultural, educational, health and related matters, to make recommendations on any matter to the General Assembly and to prepare draft conventions for the Assembly. ECOSOC was also authorised to coordinate the activities of the specialized agencies in the economic and social arena.

ECOSOC has 54 members, a considerable enlargement from its original membership of 18. Each year one-third of the membership is subject to election for a three-year period. Although there is no formal distinction between permanent and non-permanent members, as in the Security Council, four of the five permanent members of the Security Council –

France, the UK, the USA and the USSR/Russian Federation – have been *de facto* permanent members.[10] The other members consist of representatives of all the major regions of the world, thirty five from developing regions, thirteen from developed and six from Eastern Europe.

Each member of the Council has a vote and decisions are made by a majority of those voting. Consequently, developing countries, with the majority of membership, can dominate decision-making.

ECOSOC discharges most of its work through commissions and committees. There are 10 functional commissions including the Commission on Human Rights, five regional economic commissions, four standing committees, including the Committee for Development Planning and the Committee for Economic, Social and Cultural Rights.

It is widely agreed that ECOSOC has been ineffective. According to one observer, in practice 'its contribution has been very limited indeed (Quinn in Alston, 1992).[11] Another comments that 'The Council has proved superfluous to the UN system for substantive purposes (O'Donovan, 1992). ECOSOC has not provided a locus of world economic and social decision-making. Various reasons have been suggested for this:

- the membership is too large for the body to be effective;
- it is overloaded with work. In spite of efforts to streamline its agenda and working methods, the Council has some 150 bodies reporting to it;
- its agenda overlaps with that of the General Assembly;
- it does not have sufficient power to be able to ensure co-ordination, especially *vis-à-vis* the UN specialized agencies. The powers of recommendation that ECOSOC *does* possess are often not used to the full; instead, like the General Assembly, it often adopts decisions and resolutions which 'mostly represent consensus-seeking compromises of great generality.[12]
- a further key, political problem is that world economic and social decision-making must receive the assent of the major economic powers. Without this resolutions will inevitably be inoperational. Given the democratic structure of representation and voting in ECOSOC and the General Assembly, these will never be accepted as the locus of world economic decision-making by the economically powerful nations.

The Commission on Human Rights

In principle the Commission on Human Rights might have made a contribution to the social and economic aspects of world governance by helping to implement the International Covenant on Economic Social and Cultural Rights and the Declaration on the Right to Development. However, in practice the Commission has mainly confined its attention to Civil Development and Political Rights, where it has investigated a large number of cases, with only partial success. Its achievements in the field of economic and social rights have been insignificant. According to Alston, 'The Commission's lengthy debates have done very little to promote the core normative content of economic rights let alone the human rights dimensions of debt, world trade and development cooperation' (Alston, 1992, p. 191). With respect to extreme poverty, the Commission's role was confined to drawing the attention of the General Assembly and all United Nations bodies to the issue, urging ECOSOC to give it 'the necessary attention' and requesting the Sub-Commission to study it.

The Committee on Economic, Social and Cultural Rights

This is an independent expert body, established by ECOSOC in 1978,[13] to monitor developments related to the implementation by States of the International Covenant on Economic, Social and Cultural Rights. Since then the Committee has clarified the norms contained in the Covenant, expanded the information base and set in place a system of monitoring country performance. Potentially, this committee provides an important venue for monitoring individual country performance with respect to these positive rights. But it has no effective power of enforcement if States are not fulfilling their obligations under the Covenant. By intention it focuses on *national* behaviour and does not have a remit to address international social or economic issues. Its system of monitoring could, in principle, provide the basis for international action with respect to economic and social rights within particular countries.

The Committee for Development Planning

This too is an international committee of experts which meets annually with the remit of evaluating the programmes of UN organs and specialised agencies relating to economic planning and reviewing, on a biennial basis, progress in implementing the International Development Strategy. It has no powers, but can make recommendations to ECOSOC. Hence its effectiveness is limited by the use ECOSOC makes of its reports.

The IMF and World Bank

In principle, the IMF and World Bank, as specialized agencies of the UN, are subject to the overall coordination of the UN General Assembly and ECOSOC. As Singer notes, 'In practice it would be difficult to think of any example where the Bretton Woods Institutions have been in any way influenced by UN resolutions' (Singer, 1995a).

The IFIs have their own decision-making structures, with Boards of Directors, where voting power is proportionate to financial contributions to the institutions. This means that the USA and Western Europe dominate the decisions of these institutions.

The system of weighted voting in the IMF[14] is based on each member being assigned a quota in the form of 'Special Drawing Rights' (SDRs) reflecting a county's economic position and strength. The assessment of the quota is determined by economic data such as GNP, currency reserves, foreign trade potential etc. Each member is given a basic stock of 250 votes plus one vote for each part of its quota equivalent to 100 000 SDRs. The regulations governing voting in the Fund are dispersed over the entire Agreement, and are very complex. Generally, decisions require a simple majority of votes cast. Certain important decisions (such as the determination of charges for the use of the Fund's facilities) call for a majority of 70 per cent of the total voting power. Amendments to the Fund's Articles of Agreement or decisions such as changes in quotas, the use of IMF gold, the allocation and cancellation of SDRs or modifications to the principles of their valuation require a majority of 85 per cent. Since the USA holds almost 18.5 per cent of the total voting power, this gives it the power of veto over any decision which requires this majority.

To be a member of the World Bank, a country must first be a member of the IMF, then it must buy a share or shares of the capital stock of the Bank, each share being valued at $US 100 000. Less than 10 per cent of this money must actually be physically paid to the Bank, the remainder is 'callable' if the Bank needs to fulfil contractual obligations. The distribution of such capital shares provides the basis for the apportionment of voting rights within the organs of the Bank. In a similar formula to that used by the IMF, each member has 250 votes plus one further vote per share of stock held. The result is that seven industrialized states, namely the USA, the UK, Germany, France, Japan, Italy and Canada control just under 50 per cent of the votes. Industrialized countries as a whole hold a majority of votes in the World Bank.

This difference in decision-making is a key element in explaining:

1. why in practice the IFIs have acquired so much more power than the UN[15] in economic matters;
2. how they have interpreted their mandate; and
3. why they have not performed their role satisfactorily from a world perspective.

Both the IMF and the World Bank are powerful economic actors on the world stage, much more so than the UN. In some ways they have acquired more power than was originally envisaged, especially through policy-conditionality. As a result of the active use of such conditionality, both the IMF and the World Bank have been enormously influential in determining the economic policy of borrowing countries, that is, much of the Third World, although their power has rarely extended to the non-borrowing industrial countries. It is clear that the World Bank has come to be a much more significant world player than originally envisaged. It has acquired responsibility for a large proportion of total aid flows, it dominates thought about development through its voluminous publications, and it has extended its policy-conditions way beyond broad policy directions, such as enhancing the role of the market and encouraging openness of trade regimes, to detailed meso and even micro policies. However, it has not used its power to enforce improvements in social policies.

But while both institutions frequently dominate economic policy-making of their clients, which collectively account for most of the countries of the world, albeit not the most important countries economically, they have not fulfilled the role needed of *global* economic institutions. They have dealt with countries, one-by-one, and have not taken a global perspective. The IMF is, perhaps, particularly culpable in this regard, as at Bretton Woods it was intended that it should be responsible for ensuring adequate world liquidity to support world full employment and economic growth. But the Bancor, recommended by Keynes, intended for this purpose, was not agreed at Bretton Woods. In the 1970s, tentative steps were taken in the direction of ensuring adequate world liquidity through the issue of Special Drawing Rights, but the experiment was not repeated, even during the world depression of the early 1980s.

Thus although both the IMF and the World Bank are in some sense *world* institutions – that is, their operations cover the world – in essence institutions they are not *global*. They do not take into account interactions of one country on another, even when they are giving advice to a series of countries. They do not co-ordinate world economic policy. They rarely propose global solutions to global problems. For example, neither institution proposed a global solution to the debt problem of the 1980s, although clearly this was essential, and eventually one was introduced by the US Secretary to the Treasury. On the environment, an issue taken up enthusiastically by the World Bank, the approach adopted has been to insert environmental safeguards into particular projects, not to consider global (or even national) regulation.

The issue of poverty reduction is in principle accepted as an important consideration by both institutions. Yet the Bank and Fund's programmes have done very little to reduce poverty, sometimes indeed themselves contributing to worsening poverty, while specific programmes to reduce poverty have been so small-scale as to be almost negligible in relation to the size of the problem (see Stewart, 1995). Again the need for international action is not recognized.

Thus neither institution fulfils the functions needed of a world or global economic and social institution as identified above.

Consequences of the deficiencies in existing institutions

Despite the plethora of institutions, none takes the pivotal role needed in global economic and social issues. The consequences of this lacuna are that some issues are left without any form of international governance; for others *ad-hoc* solutions are arrived at.

World economic reviews, appraisal of coordination needed and recommendations for policy changes are conducted by *ad-hoc* groupings of the most powerful industrialized countries – for example the G7, consisting of the USA, Germany, France, Japan, the UK, Italy and Canada, or the G5 (the same group excluding Italy and Canada) and occasionally the G3 (the USA, Germany and Japan.) *Developing countries are completely excluded from these discussions and decisions.* The macroeconomic co-ordination achieved by these groupings has been very unsystematic and rather ineffective.[16]

More democratic and effective forms of international regulation have been achieved in specific areas, where international discussions are initiated involving all the main parties affected and subsequently international agreements are reached. Some environmental issues have been dealt with in this way: for example, on fossil fuels and carbon dioxide; on aerosols; on the law of the sea[for the further examples/details you wanted for this section I have been phoning Andrew Hurrell all week – no reply so I left a message on his answering machine at home for him to get back to us].

A third approach has been to convene world meetings on particular subjects: for example, women in Beijing in 1995; population in Cairo in 1994; the environment in Rio in 1992. These are genuinely participatory, allowing not only most countries but also many NGOs to make a contribution. They draw attention to issues but they lack effective follow-up mechanisms to implement agreed *Programmes of Action.*

The fourth solution is a non-solution: it is neglect. This was what happened to the debt situation for much of the 1980s, until eventually the USA saw how costly failure was and helped to bring about a solution. But in many other areas neglect continues: there are no effective policies against violations of social and economic rights; multinational companies are able legitimately to avoid taxation; short term capital flows are unregulated; commodity prices fluctuate and deteriorate without any international intervention; many environmental abuses continue unsupervised.

Ad hoc solutions are often better than nothing, but they do have serious defects:

- in general response is late because the problem has to get bad before it is noticed, then it takes time to convene specific meetings and to devise solutions;
- issues are not looked at as a whole, but one-by-one – women on one occasion, children on another, for example:
- the membership of the particular groupings can be arbitrary, and is often undemocratic, dominated by a few powerful nations;
- there are, as just noted, major gaps including the lack of any systematic policies towards world income distribution and the enforcement of human rights.

21.4 THE CASE FOR A WORLD ECONOMIC AND SOCIAL SECURITY COUNCIL

It is clear that there is a large gap in world institutions that urgently needs filling. There is neither economic nor social governance at a world level. As a consequence, world depressions (or inflation) can emerge through the unco-ordinated action of national governments; world income distribution is the outcome of myriad unrelated actions, resulting in huge differences in income levels among nations and people; there is no world enforcement of internationally agreed social and economic rights; and the unregulated power of TNC and international capital is growing, sometimes leading to instability of national economies.

We believe that the creation of a World Economic and Social Security Council (ESSC) is needed to fill this gap. The ESSC would replace the present Economic and Social Council and would have the mandate of ensuring that key economic and social functions required at an international level are carried out. We do not envisage elaborate new structures. The ESSC would not itself execute decisions, but would request other institutions – for example, the IFIs, the WTO, as well as national governments – to take the action that it identified as necessary. However, where no suitable institution existed it would be able to create one. The ESSC would need a small permanent secretariat to guide its work, and three advisory panels of experts, one focusing on the Council's economic, one on its social and one on its environmental functions.

Its membership would be small, and contain both semi-permanent and elected members, with the proviso that the constitution would contain provisions for reviewing the semi-permanent membership every 20 years. Semi-permanent membership would be awarded to the 11 countries with the greatest economic power, based on average GNP over the previous five years. Decision-making would not require unanimity, like the present Security Council, but would be on the basis of a two-thirds majority such that decisions could not be made without the consent of each of the major groupings in the world, but no single country would be able to veto decisions.

The ESSC would have the broad directions of its mandate laid down. But it could add to its functions over time, as it felt appropriate. This would allow it to react creatively to new, and unenvisaged issues that might require international action.

The ESSC would be convened twice a year to review progress in the world economy as a whole, and on social and economic rights and poverty reduction; to receive reports on actions taken in response to requests it had made previously; and to identify and consider any major new problems. Special meetings could be convened in between these meetings, if a particular crisis arose. It would be expected that the meetings would be attended by ministers of finance, prime ministers/presidents attending if particularly important decisions were to be taken.

We spell out the proposed functions, structure and operational rules proposed in greater detail below. Here we wish to explain why we believe this sort of Council could succeed where existing structures have failed.

1. The first reason is that the Council would reflect the reality of economic and political power in the world, through its permanent membership and voting structure. A major problem with ECOSOC is that developing

countries have a majority, so the developed countries refuse to give it any power. A 'democratic' structure which fails to give any additional voice in decision-making to the economically powerful countries will not be in a position to take effective action, as the story of ECOSOC shows. The result has been that decisions are taken in bodies where developing countries are excluded completely (for example, G3, G5, G7), or where they can always be overruled (IMF, World Bank). The proposed ESSC would incorporate developing countries and countries in transition. They would be in a position to raise issues they wished to be considered, and, collectively, to veto action they did not like.

2. The ESSC would be small (membership around 20) so as to make it a much more manageable body than ECOSOC.

3. It is intended that the political standing of those participating would be high so those present would be in a position to commit their governments.

4. The ESSC would not itself execute any of its decisions, but would request other (normally already existing) bodies to do so. Hence the functions of existing institutions would not be duplicated and a large bureaucracy would not be needed. For International Institutions, including the IFIs and other specialized agencies the directions of the ESSC would be mandatory, overruling their own Boards of Directors. National governments would be recommended to take action, although the ESSC might at some stage devise penalties if national governments systematically rejected requests.

History of proposals for an Economic Security Council

The idea of creating a high level Council at the UN to oversee major international economic developments is not new. Over the past 10 years or so, there have been a series of proposals for the creation of a high level Council at the UN with economic (and sometimes social) functions, similar to that proposed here (these are described by Arnold, 1995). It is worth reviewing these briefly to indicate the wide support the idea has from most independent observers of the UN system:

- in his report to the UN's Joint Inspection Unit, Bertrand (1985) recommended the establishment of an Economic Security Council to act as a UN forum to deal with economic problems;
- WIDER proposed a World Economic Council with similar functions;
- the Nordic United Nations Project (1991) recommended a high level International Development Council to give effective guidance

and cohesion to the executive organs of the UN's operational activities;

- the UNDP's *Human Development Report 1994* proposed an Economic Security Council which would be a 'decision-making forum at the highest level to review the threats to global economic security and agree on the necessary action' (p10).
- The Report of the Commission on Global Governance (1995) also supported the establishment of an Economic Security Council.
- The Report of the Independent Working Group on the Future of the United Nations (1995) recommended the establishment of two Councils: an Economic Council and a Social Council. The Economic Council 'should, in consultation with the Social Council, the Security Council and the General Assembly, be empowered to formulate guidelines to integrate the work of all UN agencies and international institutions, programs and offices engaged in economic issues (p. 29). The Social Council 'should be empowered to supervise and integrate the work of all UN activities related to Social Development (p. 36).
- Ul Haq *et al.* propose the establishment of a Development Security Council 'to provide a decision-making forum at the highest level to ensure global human security ... to review critical social and economic threats to people all over the globe and to reach political agreement on specific policy responses' (1995, p. 10).

All of these recommendations have been justified by similar reasoning to that put forward earlier in this chapter. Essentially each arises from the same conclusion – that there is an absence of economic and social governance at a world level and that severe adverse consequences flow from this.

21.5   FUNCTIONS, COMPOSITION AND PROCEDURES OF THE ESSC

The main functions proposed are:

1. to review the functioning of the world economy and identify major problems from the point of view of ensuring sustained economic growth and high levels of employment; to take action on any problems, including requesting action from governments, the IFIs, specialized agencies of the UN; instituting further studies; convening international meetings, and so on.

2. to review progress in the promotion of social goals and poverty reduction; to take action at both international and national levels as with economic problems; and
3. to review world environmental problems and identify appropriate action;

The composition and procedures of the UN ESSC

Five main issues need to be addressed. On each, considerable negotiation would be needed in order to settle on a formula that would be acceptable internationally. Here we make some suggestions as a starting point for discussions.

1. *Optimum overall size of the council*

The optimum size for any entity depends on the size most likely to maximise its efficiency and effectiveness. A Council of just one or two members, for example, would be very efficient, but clearly not effective as it would lack the legitimacy conferred by a more representative membership. However, a Council with too many members would be in danger of being both inefficient and ineffective. The experience of other UN bodies, including that of ECOSOC, suggests that a membership of around 20 may be the best solution. Within this number the geographical distribution of UN membership can be represented adequately, yet the Council would still be small enough to allow the genuine exchange of views, complex negotiations and executive decision-making, in contrast to the bland, consensus-orientated decisions that so often characterize larger UN bodies such as ECOSOC and the General Assembly.

2. *Categories of membership*

The Council would have two types of membership: semi-permanent and non-permanent (say 11 semi-permanent; 10 non-permanent). Semi-permanent members would be drawn from leading industrialized and developing nations based on economic strength. The countries represented in this category would be reviewed every 20 years, to allow for major changes in economic status, but it would be expected that most would retain their membership of this category. Non-permanent members would be elected for a period of three years, nominated by their regional electoral group and approved by the UN General Assembly. Retiring members would be eligible for re-election after a three-year interval.

3.   *Criteria for membership and method of election*

There are no criteria for selection of permanent members of the Security Council, who were chosen in 1945 for political reasons and have not been reviewed since. This has led to some serious anomalies. It would be preferable to have a explicit criteria or criterion for selection of semi-permanent members of the ESSC, which would then provide a basis for the review of membership every 20 years. One possibility would be simply to select the 11 countries with the largest total GNP over a five-year period immediately proceeding the date the ESSC is established, and thereafter at twenty-year intervals, to be semi-permanent members. Non-permanent members would be elected on the basis of equitable geographic distribution, the number of states from each region reflecting the number of countries each region contains. Alternatively the same formula for numbers per region could be adopted for non-permanent members as that used for non-permanent members of the Security Council.[17] There is little difference between the two, as shown in Table 21.1. Flexibility could be introduced into the formula for the distribution of elected members, so that if the semi-permanent membership happened to omit a major geographical region of the world because of the economic criteria on which that category is based, additional weight could be given to that region in the selection of elected members.

On this basis, the present the list of semi-permanent members would be:

Table 21.1   Proposed representation of ESSC

Regional groups	No. of semi-permanent members	No. of non-permanent members[a]
Western Europe and other	4	1 (2)
Eastern Europe	1	1
Asia	2	3 (2)
Africa	0	3
America (N., S., Caribbean)	4	2
Developed countries	8 (inc. Russia)	2 (3) (inc. E. Europe)
Developing countries	3	8 (7)

[a]Unbracketed figures are in proportion to the membership of the UN in each region; bracketed numbers are the same distribution as the current non-permanent members of the Security Council.

The US; Japan; Germany; France: Italy; the UK: China; Canada; Brazil; the Russia Federation; Mexico.

4. *Voting procedure*

Each member would have one vote. A voting procedure is needed that is more flexible than the unanimity rule of the Security Council, where the vote of just one country is enough to veto action; but is more stringent than purely majority voting so that major groupings in the world cannot be outvoted when they act together. We propose that a majority of two-thirds would be required for both procedural and non-procedural issues. This means that neither developed nor developing countries can pass resolutions without at least some support from members from the other category.

5. *Relationship to other UN bodies and to other intergovernmental and non-governmental entities*

The procedure for participation of non-members, consultation with other interested parties, and the receipt of communications from non-governmental entities would be modelled on the Provisional Rule of Procedure of the UN Security Council.

Advisory committees

Three Advisory Committees of experts should be established – to deal with the social, environmental and economic functions of the ESSC. The Economic Committee could replace (or consist of a transformation of) the present Committee for Development Planning. The Committee for Social Development could replace the current Social Commission. These committees would help identify outstanding issues in each area, recommending an agenda for the ESSC.

Place of the ESSC in the UN system as a whole

The ESSC would be a new Principal UN Organ, replacing ECOSOC. The Commissions and specialized agencies of the UN now reporting to ECOSOC would report to the ESSC. The World Bank and the IMF would also report to the ESSC. The reform would provide an opportunity to review the work of the functional commissions, standing committees, expert and *ad hoc* committees, with the aim of reducing their number and streamlining their functions. In particular it is recommended that the abolition of the following Committees and Commissions should be considered:

The Committee on New and Renewable Sources of Energy and Energy for Development, the Commission on Science and Technology for Development, the Committee on Natural Resources, the Committee on Development Planning, and the Ad Hoc Group of Experts on Public Administration and Finance. Many of the functions of these bodies are already duplicated elsewhere in the UN system, those that are not would be subsumed by the three new ESSC Advisory Committees.

21.6   CONCLUSIONS

There are evidently a number of important economic, social and environmental issues for which global action is needed. Yet despite their large number, the present set of international institutions do not fulfill the functions needed at a world level. The most powerful economic institutions (the IMF and the World Bank) basically operate on a country-by-country, not a global basis. Moreover, the industrialized countries alone determine the agenda of the IFIs. Various organs of the UN (the General Assembly and ECOSOC) have global social and economic functions but, in practice, do not use them productively. The ineffectiveness of these institutions is partly due to their large size, and partly to their 'democratic' structure which means that the economically powerful countries can be overruled by developing countries in these arenas.

The current vacuum in decision-making has led to various *ad-hoc* solutions which are unsatisfactory because they are unsystematic and often exclusionary (that is, developing countries are left out of decisions which affect them), while some issues are completely neglected.

The creation of a new Principal organ of the UN has been proposed in this paper – an Economic and Social Security Council – which would overcome many of the weaknesses in the current system. The membership and voting structure of this Council would be such that the strongest economic powers would gain most representation and power, yet weaker countries in all regions of the world would be represented and have some power.

The ESSC would replace ECOSOC, which is generally agreed to have been ineffective. The ESSC would not itself have any administrative duties, but would operate by requesting action from existing institutions, including the IFIs, UN agencies and national governments. Consequently the changes proposed would not represent a further burgeoning of the UN. Indeed, the replacement of ECOSOC and the abolition of some of the bodies reporting to it would lead to a slimming down of the UN as a whole, with an increase in its effectiveness.

The virtues of a Council of this kind would be similar – in the economic and social arenas – to those of the Security Council in security matters – that is, it would provide a flexible venue where urgent global issues could be considered at a very high level. It would not, of course, compel world leaders to take action that they disliked. But it would ensure systematic discussion of major issues, leading to action in those areas where sufficient consensus existed.

Ad hoc solutions to particular problems can sometimes be more effective than action at a world level. But these can also be partial and unrepresentative. The new ESSC would not prevent *ad-hoc* initiatives, but would ensure that they were reviewed at a world level.

International institutions cannot create consensus where none exists; but they can encourage and facilitate more 'one world' and less nationalistic and piecemeal approaches to global developments. This is a contribution that we believe an ESSC would make. This chapter is, we hope, written in much the same the spirit that we have learnt from Hans Singer's life and writings – optimistic, taking a global perspective, yet not entirely unrealistic.

Notes

1. This paper was initially prepared for Christian Aid. We are grateful for their support.
2. Positive human rights were recognised in the International Covenant on Economic, Social and Cultural Rights, which came into force in 1976; and the Declaration on the Right to Development (1986); negative Rights in The Covenant on Civil and Political Rights, also 1976. Both positive and negative rights were embodied in the Universal Declaration proclaimed by the General Assembly in 1948.
3. UNDp 1992 estimates that nominal prices of manufactures produced by industrialised countries rose by 35 per cent over the 1980s while those produced by developing countries rose by 12 per cent.
4. On 'Black Wednesday'· in 1992 the British government lost around $US 3bn.
5. A recent study by Ernst and Young of 210 TNCs found that 49 per cent were being investigated over transfer pricing in the UK and 83 per cent had been involved in a transfer pricing disputeat some time. In 1994–5 the Inland revenue collected £6.1 billion from companies and individuals for non-compliance, equivalent to 3.5p on Income Tax (*Financial Times*, 23 November 1995).
6. 'World' objectives are not, in general, agreed and enunciated. Hence there is inevitably some subjectivity in identifying them. The objectives above are deduced from declarations, Covenants and so on, from the UN and from prominent political leaders.
7. See the Articles of Agreement of the International Monetary Fund.

8. It is significant that the World Bank's 1995 *World Development Report* is devoted to employment, while the ILO published its first *World Employment Report* in 1995.

9. The authorised history of the World Bank in its first quarter of a century states: 'the Bank and Fund became specialised agencies of the United Nations. But they became rather "special" specialised agencies' (Mason and Asher, 1973, p. 58).

10. The other permanent member of the Security Council, China, was a member for all years except 1961 to 1971.

11. All recent evaluations agree on this. See for example, Childers and Urquhart, 1994; the Nordic UN Project (Arnold, 1995); and the report of the Independent Working Group.

12. The Nordic UN Project, The United Nations in Development, 1991, p. 37, cited in Arnold, 1995, p. 26.

13. Originally it was named the *Sessional Working Group on the Implementation of the International Covenant on Economic, Social and Cultural Rights*, but in 1985 after modifications to its composition, organization and administrative arrangements it was renamed the *Committee on Economic, Social and Cultural Rights*.

14. The information on the voting procedure of the IMF and World Bank sections has been taken from Wolfrum (ed.) 1995, pp. 656–57 and 726–7.

15. Since the IFIs are, in principle, part of the UN, one ought to say 'the rest of the UN' but the huge gulf between the IFIs and the rest of the UN means that they have come to be regarded as quite distinct entities.

16. 'Moreover, this body [G7] is considered no more effective than the UN General Assembly or ECOSOC. It has not even proved effective, in co-ordinating policies among the seven member countries' (Singer, 1995b)

17. Formula contained in General Assembly Resolution 1991 (XXVIII) of 17 December 1963.

References

Alston, P. (ed.) (1992) *The United Nations and Human Rights: A Critical Appraisal* (Oxford: Clarendon).

Arnold, T. (1995) 'Reforming the UN: its Economic Role', Institute of Economic Affairs, *Discussion Paper*, 57.

Bertrand, M. (1985) *Some Reflections on the Reform of the United Nations*, JIU/REP/859 (Geneva).

Chen, S., G. Datt and M. Ravallion (1994) 'Is Poverty Increasing in the Developing World?', *Review of Income and Wealth*, vol. 40, no. 4, pp. 359–75.

Childers, E. and B. Urquhardt (1994) 'Renewing the United Nations System', *Development Dialogue*, no. 1.

Lall, S. (1987) 'Technology Transfer, Foreign Investment and Indigenous Capabilities', processed, Oxford, Institute of Economics.

Mason, E. and R. Asher (1973) *The World Bank since Bretton Woods* (Washington, DC: The Brookings Institution).

O'Donovan, D. (1992) 'The Economic and Social Council', in P. Alston (ed.) *The United Nations and Human Rights: A Critical Appraisal* (Oxford: Clarendon).

Ghai, D. (1993) 'Structural Adjustment, Global Integration and Social Democracy', in D. Prendergast and F. Stewart (eds) *Market Forces and World Development* (London: Macmillan).

Quinn, J. (1992) 'The General Assembly into the 1990s', in P. Alston (ed.) *The United Nations and Human Rights: A Critical Appraisal* (Oxford: Clarendon).

Ravallion, M. (1993) 'Growth and Poverty: Evidence for Developing Countries in the 1980s', *Economic Letters*, vol. 48, pp. 411–17.

Singer, H.W. (1995a) 'Historical Background to the Bretton Woods System and its Relation to the UN System', in B. Etemad, J. Batou and T. David (eds) *Pour une histoire économique et sociale internationale. Mélanges offerts a Paul Bairoch* (Geneva: Editions Passe Present).

—— (1995b) 'Revitalising the United Nations: Five Proposals', *IDS Bulletin*, vol. 26, pp. 35–40.

Stewart, F. (1995) *Adjustment and Poverty: Options and Choices* (London: Routledge).

The Nordic UN Project (1991) *The United Nations in Development* (Stockholm).

The Report of the Commission on Global Governance (1995) *Our Global Neighbourhood* (Oxford University Press).

The Report of the Independent Working Group on the Future of the United Nations (1995) *The United Nations in its Second Half Century* (New York: Ford Foundation).

Ul Haq, M., R. Jolly, P. Streeten and K. Haq (1995) *The UN and Bretton Woods Institutions* (London: Macmillan).

United Nations (1992) *World Investment Report: Transnational Corporations as Engines of Growth* (New York: United Nations).

—— (1995) *World Economic and Social Survey 1995* (New York: United Nations).

UNDP (1992) *Human Development Report 1992* (New York: United Nations).

United Nations General Assembly (1995) *Restructuring and Revitalization of the United Nations in the Economic and Social Fields*, Report of the Secretary General, A/50/697, 27.

World Bank (1995) *World Development Report* (Washington, DC: World Bank).

Wolfrum, R. (ed.) (1995) *United Nations, Law, Policies and Practice* (Amsterdam: Martinus Nijhoff).

World Bank (1994) *World Development Report 1994* (Washington, DC: World Bank).

22 The IMF as International Lender of Last Resort? A Reappraisal After the 'Tequila Effect'

Nicholas Snowden

22.1 INTRODUCTION

The devaluation of the Mexican peso on 20 December 1994 marked the first crisis of confidence affecting international investors to follow the revival of portfolio flows to the 'emerging markets' in the first half of the 1990s. In its initial response the IMF agreed to lend $7.8 billion, the largest individual loan in its history, to support the country's stabilization programme. Having indicated that it would seek an additional $10 billion of commitments from the central banks of other 'emerging market' LDCs, the Fund was later to announce its willingness to supply this sum as well after the governments approached were to prove unforthcoming. With the capital account nature of the crisis demanding a departure from normal practice in the immediate disbursement of the initial $7.8 billion open disagreement arose between the permanent members of the Fund's Executive Board. The requirement to act decisively in a 'last resort' capacity (the $17.8 billion commitment represented $3\frac{1}{2}$ times as much as any previous loan to an individual member) clearly conflicted with the normal application of Fund conditionality. Objective criteria for lending appeared to be undermined by political pressure for action from the Fund's principal member.[1]

Support for the loan from the US administration contrasted sharply with its insistence at the time of the Fund's establishment that the organization should not finance capital outflows (Solomon, 1977, pp. 12–13). Although the Articles of Agreement continue to permit the imposition of controls on capital movements the contemporary integration of global financial markets in increasingly taken to imply that the provisions are a 'relic from the original Bretton Woods par value regime' (Guitian, 1995, p. 816). Crises involving large-scale capital movements may therefore be expected

418

to become a common trigger for Fund intervention in the emerging market context.

If the Mexican example suggests a requirement for prompt and relatively large-scale financial injections to address capital market crises, other recent developments reveal the IMF to be increasingly subject to contrasting pressures elsewhere. In the transitional economies generally, and especially in Russia, which was promised the second-largest ever Fund loan of $10.2 billion in February 1996, the Fund has become involved in the process of microeconomic (supply side) reforms and institution-building policies. Together with the extensive reform policies being financed by the ESAF facilities for the poorest members, Fund programmes are clearly acquiring a longer-term character. In the case of the ESAF arrangements, for example, a medium-term time frame of three years is envisaged. The observed tendency for one programme to be followed by another effectively extends further the time period of Fund involvement and is seen by some observers as potentially undermining monetary character of the institution (Duisenberg and Szasz, 1991).

The diverse requirements which these examples illustrate, and the controversies associated with them, suggest that a reconsideration of the future role of the IMF on the basis of 'first principles' may be a useful. The present chapter attempts to develop such a perspective in order to distinguish from among the many proposals for Fund reforms those which would be consistent with a coherent view of the organization's role in a rapidly changing global environment. When carefully interpreted, and in the light of recent assessments concerning their role in the domestic context, it is argued that a useful framework is offered by the early interpretation of the IMF as an embryonic world central bank.

Since the parallel often arises in somewhat informal remarks in the contemporary literature, an attempt is first made to identify the key elements in the analogy. It is noted that discussion in this context has often been in connection with a systemic issue, the adequacy of global liquidity, which international developments have done much to undermine as a policy concern. Before turning to the issues raised by more pertinent aspects of the parallel, however, a perspective is initially adopted in the form of evidence that global conditions indeed have an important effect on the overall demand for IMF support. Taken together with subsequent evidence, a general conclusion is that the need for Fund involvement to 'catalyse' other financial inflows is probably at least as important an issue as that of the adequacy or otherwise of its own resources. The more detailed policy discussion which follows is motivated in part by this view applied to the context of private capital transfers.

Recognizing an important distinction in the Fund's operating context the rationale for the medium-term commitment of its resources to externally indebted countries is reconsidered, together with the question this commitment raises concerning the 'seniority' of IMF claims over those of other creditors. Even in the case of official creditors, where a degree of *de facto* seniority for the Fund appears traditionally to be accepted in Paris Club negotiations, contemporary discussions of official bilateral and multilateral debt reduction strategies imply that creditor fiscal considerations may undermine this recognition. Developments since the beginning of 1995, however, suggest that it is especially the position with respect to private creditors which needs to be clarified and the framework adopted here indicates how this might be attempted. .

22.2   THE CENTRAL BANK PARALLEL

The literature has traditionally distinguished two key functions for a central bank corresponding to macroeconomic and microeconomic perspectives (for example, Goodhart, 1988, pp. 5–8). Control over the growth rate of the national money supply provided the macroeconomic rationale whereas concern with the soundness of individual banks justified the microeconomic, or industry level, focus on prudential regulation. A link between the two levels was provided by a public goods consideration. If, in the course, for example, of a policy of monetary restraint certain banks were to experience difficulties, the threat of a generalized 'run' could oblige the central bank to provide large-scale liquidity relief thereby undermining the initial macro objectives.

The macroeconomic parallel

In the early application of these ideas to the international role of the IMF, it was the macroeconomic function which commanded attention. The original Keynes Plan would have introduced 'bancor' accounts at an International Clearing Union. Since all countries would have been members, current account surpluses would automatically have matched the (bancor overdraft financed) deficits of other members without the Union ever being at risk of illiquidity (Keynes, 1969). Since the Union would have the power to issue its own liabilities (bancor accounts) it could control the growth of international liquidity in a manner directly analogous to that of a national central bank administering the monetary base. Although in the event the 'par value' system was to be based on the US$ a further proposal (based on Keynes' earlier scheme) to reform the IMF along the lines of an international central bank was to become influential (Triffin, 1960).

Under the par value regime, with national currencies readily identifiable, the case for an international central bank requires clarification. Certain historical episodes at the national level had shown that commercial banks issuing (differentiated) cheques could be prevented from over-issue by the emergence of a clearing house system (Goodhart, 1988, ch. 3). 'Excess' cheque issues would be accepted on demand by the clearing house (a dominant commercial bank) which would then present them to the issuing bank for redemption from currency reserves. In the par value system, national central banks were essentially in the position of the cheque issuing banks in this example: over-issue of national currency (relative to demand at fixed exchange rates) would lead to leakage from the bank's foreign currency reserves.

While the growth of liquidity at the national level was thus automatically controlled, this was not the case for international reserves and certain weaknesses observed in the clearing house system suggest a basis for the Triffin proposal in that context. Domestically, individual commercial banks could maintain a demand for their issues by making them relatively attractive and, moreover, there was nothing in the clearing house mechanism to prevent participating banks in the aggregate from increasing their issues too quickly (Goodhart, op. cit., p. 30). These considerations were of direct relevance to an international dollar exchange standard in which excess dollar issues were acceptable as reserves to other central banks. Further, their accumulation was likely to lead to monetary expansion (and inflationary consequences) in the recipient economies. Even if the growth of dollars was not excessive relative to the growth in demand for international reserves, this incremental demand could only be met by US payments deficits. As dollar liabilities grew relative to US gold reserves, a crisis of confidence in the currency could not be excluded. Once again, therefore, Triffin's concern was macroeconomic with his proposal intended to produce a controlled and sustainable growth of world liquidity.

A related strand of the domestic banking literature concerning the notion of competing monies may be used to assess how far such liquidity control arguments for an international central bank have been undermined by the adoption of floating exchange rates. An unregulated money supply, consistent with a finite domestic price level, could be envisaged if perfectly competitive institutions were to issue 'brand named' monetary claims with varying exchange rates in terms of real goods (Klein, 1974). Despite the temptation for these suppliers to increase their 'output' thereby financing the purchase of real goods and assets at the expense of current holders, the analysis shows how a stable equilibrium may be established. Irrespective of the merits of this market alternative to central bank control of the domestic money supply the model certainly suggests that the issue of differentiated national monies which trade at floating exchange rates is, in principle, a substitute for such an institution internationally.

Klein's framework, however, raises an important issue concerning the holding of reserves in the absence of the centralised control of liquidity. A finite price level for commodities in terms of any one of the competing monies could only be assured if, either, holders were able to anticipate with certainty all future issues of that money, or if consumers and producers made the same calculations of the benefits to the producer of future deception. In these circumstances, the issuer would invest in reputational capital such that the return on the investment, the resulting marginal reduction in funding costs, would equal the incremental cost of its acquisition.

Under floating or freely adjustable international exchange rates the proposition that holders could predict with certainty all the future issues of a particular national currency (or even the objectives behind these issues) is clearly extreme. The argument thus serves to emphasize the central role of reputation in determining exchange rate behaviour and, as Klein suggests, holdings of reserves of a reliable currency are an obvious choice for reputational investment. Reputation and confidence issues, however, are more directly implied by the second component of the central bank analogy.

Prudential regulation and the last resort function

Historically, the supervisory function associated with central banks appears to have preceded concern with liquidity management (Goodhart, 1988, p. 7). With commercial bank balance sheets characterised by liquid liabilities (deposits) and relatively illiquid assets (loans) central banks were required to bear the ultimate responsibility of providing last resort liquidity to the system should the need arise. While this implied insurance is necessary to guarantee the smooth functioning of the payments mechanism, it naturally introduces potential moral hazard difficulties when deposit costs become insensitive to the loan risks chosen by bank managements. The supervisory function of central banks was therefore closely connected with their last-resort loan obligations.

In contemporary circumstances, the need to maintain confidence in the financial system has led to the emergence of deposit guarantee schemes as a superior alternative to last resort lending. The two measures are only fully equivalent if the last resort commitment is independent of the quality of the collateral which the bank receiving assistance can offer (White, 1989). Nevertheless, although the insurance scheme may be funded by premia levied on participating institutions the last resort function of the central bank would remain essential if a systemic crisis were to threaten to exhaust the resources available to the scheme (McCarthy, 1980). Although equity considerations (the protection of small savers) have been invoked to justify state backed deposit insurance (ibid), the externalities based arguments are of more interest in the international context.

Diamond and Dybvig (1983) offer a theoretical justification for deposit insurance to control the risk of 'runs' on the commercial banking system. If the function of banks is to transform illiquid loans into liquid financial assets for wealth-holders' portfolios, it is shown that runs are a possible outcome if a positive rate of return is payable when deposits are withdrawn. If a critical fraction of depositors withdraw before the underlying (assumed productive) loans mature, the banks will have insufficient funds to meet their obligations and it thus becomes rational for all depositors to withdraw as soon as suspicions of bank difficulties arise. On this view, the justification for deposit insurance is that it stabilizes an inherently unstable but otherwise desirable structure of 'insurance' contracts in which depositors may have confidence in the liquidity of their funds should the need arise.

If such an externalities case for last resort lending can be constructed in the domestic case, what parallel arguments may be advanced to justify IMF lending to sovereign states? Although the decline in capital inflows to other emerging markets following Mexico's recent difficulties (the 'tequila effect') offers some parallels, the differences are equally evident. While recognized as an alternative (albeit inferior) solution in the domestic banking environment (Ibid.), a possible response to a sudden deterioration in international funding conditions facing a country borrower is the suspension of convertibility. Moreover, the parties affected by the suspension, rather than comprising a mass of small depositors, would be participants in the international capital markets where risks are explicitly priced. By contrast, the earlier justification for Fund support during the debt crisis of the 1980s was based on the need to avoid contractionary consequences in the international banking system. It was in part because this potential need for official intervention was thought to have been eliminated that a number of observers welcomed the move to capital market intermediation in the 1990s.

To construct a more robust case for Fund financial intervention, an alternative argument for last-resort lending facilities in the banking context may be noted. Goodhart argues that modern bank runs have not involved a flight to cash but simply a rush to transfer deposits to institutions viewed as relatively safe: problems at individual banks have not produced a generalized crisis (Goodhart, 1988, p. 96). Nevertheless, the collapse of a bank can still produce economic costs in view of the illiquid nature of loan portfolios. If loans are recalled in an attempt to finance deposit withdrawal real economic effects may be anticipated and, moreover, transactions cost considerations may render immediate replacement with a loan from another bank difficult to achieve.

Transferring this argument to the international dimension, it appears that the case for Fund support need not rest on financial contagion effects between countries. The basic difficulty is that an external crisis is likely to produce real domestic economic disruption. While a suspension of capital account convertibility may be a relatively low (economic) cost option internationally, it is likely that more harmful interventions in trade may follow. Policies concerned with the liberalisation of external payments would tend to be disadvantaged with long-term trade and investment implications. On this interpretation, the justification for Fund lending is that avoidance of inefficient policies is an external benefit which would be absent in the calculations of potential private foreign creditors. The Fund's own justification for the recent Mexican loan was in these terms and was consistent with the sentiments expressed in the first of its Articles of Agreement.

This justification for stabilization lending immediately invites the criticism that the Fund is being 'blackmailed' into supporting policies which are in any case in the interests of a country to adopt (for example, Vaubel, 1983). Nevertheless, policies chosen as a result of short-term exigency can lead to the emergence of interests which oppose their later reform. Similarly, trade-orientated policies are intended to foster sectors of the economy which, after subsequent development, would help to ensure their continuation. The case for Fund support is therefore to sustain policies which may take some time to develop a committed domestic constituency.

If this constitutes the public goods case for IMF financial support, it is clear that the nature of that support must differ from the assistance provided by central banks in the domestic environment. In cases where a run affected commercial bank is found to be insolvent (rather than simply to be illiquid after panic deposit withdrawals triggered elsewhere), a deposit insurance scheme would have to absorb the negative net worth as the institution was dismembered or taken over by another bank (White, 1989). Since these drastic solutions are unavailable in the case of sovereign states, the option of very short term financial involvement appears to be closed. At least until other external fund suppliers emerge the last resort lender must be repaid from the improving cash flow of stabilization and adjustment policies: a medium-term financial commitment is thus likely to be required.

Reflecting the earlier discussion, the policy issues raised by this commitment will be considered from an aggregative viewpoint prior to focusing on the relationship between Fund finance and other (particularly private) sources. A motivation for the initial macroeconomic perspective is once again suggested by the domestic parallel with Fund involvement at the country level: bank runs in general tend to arise when overall economic conditions have turned adverse (Goodhart, 1988, p. 101).

22.3   SYSTEMIC ASPECTS OF FUND FINANCE

The earlier argument that floating exchange rates had undermined the central banking rationale for the Fund to control the growth of international liquidity also noted that a purpose remained for country holdings of international reserves. Their role in sustaining confidence in the domestic currency was emphasised and a connection may be seen with the case currently being made for a new issue by the Fund of SDRs. The Fund's argument for a new allocation of around $54 billion is that it could save the poorer developing countries around $1.5 billion in interest costs annually if their receipts were used to finance the holding of foreign exchange reserves (*Financial Times*, 22 March 1996). Moreover, an equity argument for a new issue has been noted in that thirty seven new members of the Fund have joined since the last allocation in 1981 (IMF, 1995).

In response to the continuing concern of some governments that such an allocation could be inflationary at the global level it has been pointed out that poorer states are in need of more reserves to hold rather than to spend, and that the more developed countries have ready access to international capital markets: reserve holdings at the aggregate level are thus demand determined. If, however, a part of reserve demand is justified by the need to maintain confidence in the national currency a possibly more serious query arises in that augmented reserve holdings made possible by the issue of SDRs need do little in themselves to improve this confidence. If a directed allocation of SDRs were to prove possible constitutionally, therefore, their release to countries conditioned on policy reforms (rather than by formula alone) could be justified in principle although the proposal would certainly be unpopular in practice.

If a further SDR allocation could serve to augment the resources available for support of country programmes it would help to address a criticism of the Fund which has a systemic element independent of the international reserve management issue. The finding that a little over half of IMF programmes fail, in the sense that the initial targets are not met, has been attributed in part to the inadequacy of the financial resources supplied in support by the Fund (Killick and Malik, 1992). Certainly, the rather unsuccessful econometric attempts to relate IMF financing to economic characteristics at the country level afford considerable scope for non-economic factors to determine the overall level of programme funding (for example, Bird, 1992). Nevertheless, some aggregative evidence on the funding adequacy issue may be offered.

The regression equation reported in the appendix to this chapter tests the simple hypothesis that (the logarithm of) the ratio of developing country 'purchases' (loans) from the Fund to their 'repurchases' (repayments of principal) will be negatively related to the percentage change in industrial country GDP. The justification is partly that an increase in industrial country economic activity will tend to improve developing country terms of trade in view of supply constraints in the latter. Volume improvements in trade (and financing) may also occur, leading to a reduced demand for IMF resources net of what the formulation implicitly assumes to be the effective one for one refinancing of past facilities. To ensure data stationarity the first differenced relationship is reported with the formulation including the current and one period lagged value of the industrial country GDP variable. All data are taken from the IMF *International Financial Statistics Yearbook 1994*.

It is perhaps surprising that approaching half of the change in the finance/refinance ratio can be 'explained' by the industrial country activity measure. The comparison of predicted and actual values reproduced in Figure 22.1 appears to confirm a pattern of dependence over the years 1966–93. Whatever the validity of such a crude 'reduced form' relationship, some interest attaches to the suggested substantial shortfall of IMF net financing (relative to that 'predicted' by industrial country activity) over the years 1985–8. The finding coincides with the critical observation widely drawn from international financial flow data that the Fund contributed to the lingering international debt problem by extracting resources from the developing world at this time (e.g. Helleiner, 1992). Although the chart suggests that exogenous conditions might have merited an expansion of IMF net lending, at least during 1984–6, it did not occur. From 1988–9, there is some indication of a correction.

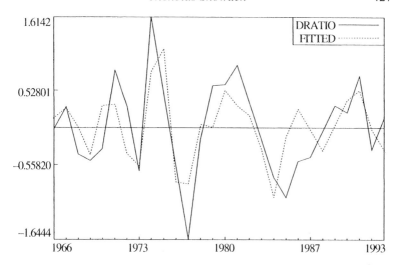

Figure 22.1   Plot of actual and fitted values

Although evidence of the relationship between IMF financing and that of other suppliers will be presented below, a further observation arises at this stage. The pattern observed implies that external conditions play some aggregate role in determining the commitment of Fund resources, although the adequacy of this sensitivity is unclear at the country level. Especially in view of the relative dormancy of financing under the Fund's Compensatory and Contingency Financing and Buffer Stock Financing Facilities it is clear that the Fund does not explicitly distinguish external from internal causes of financial difficulties: adjustment (through the conditionality provisions of the programmes actually in use) effectively always accompanies financing.

If the validity of the Fund's basic policy prescriptions is accepted, the discussion has emphasised the issue of the adequacy of the financial support offered. While the Fund's own allocations are relevant, however, the enhanced magnitudes of international capital flows witnessed in the present decade raise the question of the relationship between IMF involvement and the supply of other forms of finance. International capital market integration is providing a further link between economic conditions in the developed and developing countries and it is important that Fund policies evolve in a manner which provides a stabilizing influence on these relationships. Recent proposals from outside of the Fund, as well as current thinking within it, may not contribute to this objective.

22.4   LAST RESORT LENDING, IMF SENIORITY AND PRIVATE CAPITAL

Following the Mexican crisis, international policy discussions have leaned strongly towards the need for financial support (under Fund auspices) in the event of 'capital account' crises. Current discussions of GAB enlargement reflect the magnitudes of the envisaged potential needs whereas a proposal for a new IMF facility to assist countries to finance substantially increased international reserve holdings as a counter to speculative attacks has been put forward independently (Kenen, 1993). The Fund's preference for developing countries to move towards removing capital account restrictions appears to add urgency to the construction of such financial defences. If the intensity of current discussions on these matters indicates an international awareness that capital account liberalization can involve negative as well as positive externalities, however, a return to the central banking analogy suggests that alternative approaches may have more satisfactory results both at the country level and in the aggregate.

Referring to the earlier discussion of the IMF's 'last resort' lending role and the necessary commitment of its loans for more than the very short period involved in the domestic case, one justification for the Fund's traditional insistence on its 'senior creditor' position is suggested. Whereas the objective behind domestic last-resort loans is to maintain the liquidity of bank deposits, the employment of Fund (or GAB member) resources to underwrite the liquidation of the claims of official or professional private investors is not easily justified. The original intention that the IMF should not finance capital outflows was consistent with this position although recent developments show the extent to which it has been undermined.

The figures in Table 22.1 refer to two groups of countries for which external obligations are a distinguishing characteristic. Severely indebted lower (middle)-income countries (SILICS and SIMICS) are as defined by the World Bank and the 'cash flow' rate of return for various external creditor classifications in relation to their own claims are displayed. The creditor rate of return is defined as the negative of the net transfer from each group with the latter being new commitments minus both principal and interest payments (Bulow *et al.*, 1992). In the case of the IMF, the nearest comparable calculation deducts repurchases (loan repayments) and charges (mainly interest) from purchases (loans) and expresses the result as a fraction of Fund credit outstanding to each country group.

Since the figures in Table 22.1 are on an annual cash flow rate of return basis from the creditor perspective, a negative sign implies a net new lending commitment whereas a positive sum is the receipt of debt service

Table 22.1   Cash flow calculations by creditor grouping
(annual % of outstanding claims)

SILICS	1990	1991	1992	1993	1994	1995
Multilateral Official	–5.1	–2.8	–3.6	–2.8	–3.1	–2.1
Bilateral Official	–0.14	0.5	–0.68	0.02	0.43	0.24
Private Guaranteed	3.6	2.8	10.7	0.19	5.0	4.5
Private Non-Guaranteed	6.5	7.0	4.2	5.3	7.3	9.2
IMF	7.5	2.8	3.5	6.4	–4.2	19.8

SIMICS	1990	1991	1992	1993	1994	1995
Multilateral Official	0.05	3.9	6.4	2.6	5.3	1.1
Bilateral Official	0.57	0.19	1.1	1.4	2.9	–2.6
Private Guaranteed	3.6	4.5	5.8	1.9	2.4	2.7
Private Non-Guaranteed	–2.9	–6.0	–30.5	–25.8	–14.9	–2.9
IMF	7.8	8.9	18.5	15.4	–1.5	–42.1

Source: World Debt Tables (vol. 1, Analysis and Summary Tables) 1996.

with new commitments deducted. A pattern of interaction between the creditor groups is evident in both debtor categories.

In the case of the SILICS (concentrated in Sub-Saharan Africa) new commitments by the multilateral institutions (excluding the Fund) have been somewhat more than offset (summing cash totals over the years 1990–5) by the net outflows to private guaranteed[2] and non-guaranteed creditors. Seniority for the Fund also appears to have been observed with the institution continuing to recoup its earlier commitments; a development dating from 1987 and which has been subject to critical comment elsewhere (Oxfam, 1996). From the viewpoint adopted here, however, it is not clear that net repayments to the Fund are inappropriate provided that the loans are replaced by longer term commitments from other sources. The figures reflect, for instance, the commitment of concessional World Bank (IDA) funding which, together with ODA flows, imply gains in terms of reduced future debt service payments. Perhaps of more concern would be the continuing burden of (partially) servicing previously contracted private debts. For example, the net new commitment of the Fund shown for 1994, when added to that of the multilateral official sector for that year, is substantially offset by the continuing private sector outflows.

A similar query is raised in the case of the SIMICS (typically in Latin America) where a remarkable recovery of non-guaranteed private investment during the 1990s has permitted the other creditor groups to extract significant funds on a continuing basis. A striking feature in this case, nevertheless, arises with the slowdown in inflows and the temporary collapse of capital market confidence associated with the Mexican crisis in 1994–5. The last resort role of the Fund is especially clear in 1995, when some support from the bilateral official sector also becomes evident. With Mexico dominating the most recent figures, the Fund commitment coincides with a sign change in the net flows on private finance (summing the guaranteed and non-guaranteed components). A recent authoritative summary was as follows: 'Faced with the stark choice of disorderly default or a bail-out, the international community opted for the latter' (Kenneth Clarke).

As the report containing this quotation makes clear, however, the decision may cause foreign bond investors to regard some large borrowers as being judged too important by the 'international community' to be permitted to default (*Financial Times*, 23 April 1996). The present direction of policy discussion involving the expansion of the General Arrangements to Borrow (GAB) to finance large-scale interventions appears likely to reinforce this assessment. For reasons unassociated with domestic policy, therefore, bonds issued by small country borrowers would come to be judged relatively risky implying unfavourable adjustments in required yields. An alternative strategy for the relationship between the Fund and private capital suppliers is clearly worthy of consideration if such a predictable distortion in international capital markets could be avoided.

22.5   LOAN INSURANCE? THE FUND AND THE MARKETS

Whereas political unease over the Mexican rescue suggests that blanket 'deposit (loan) insurance' funded by the GAB is unlikely, the domestic analogy also emphasizes that without prior supervision of country borrowing policies such guarantees would be inappropriate. An alternative strategy has long been recognized in which the IMF (or a specialist institution such as the World Bank affiliated International Centre for Settlement of Investment Disputes) would take on a function similar to Chapter 11 proceedings under the US Bankruptcy Code (Cohen, 1989). Following the Mexican crisis, the idea has received further attention with the role of the IMF being emphasized (Eichengreen and Portes, 1995). In this proposal, the suspension of loan service payments would be approved by the Fund

under the authority of its Article VIII(2)(b) which concerns the legal unen-
forceability of foreign exchange contracts deemed to be contrary to the
exchange control regulations of the Fund member. The standstill would
then be followed by Chapter 11-type negotiations in which foreign creditor claims would be brought in line with the debtor's repayment capacity.
An important further role of the Fund would be to monitor and approve
the subsequent policies of the country.

By avoiding *ex post* loan insurance, proposals of this type would be
consistent with an important distinction between the position of the IMF
and that of a central bank in relation to its domestic commercial counterparts. Extensive deposit insurance requires supervision of the behaviour of
bank management to avoid the moral hazard incentives offered by the
resulting risk insensitive cost of deposit funds. Similarly, deposit insurance schemes are typically limited in terms of the value of individual bank
accounts guaranteed. Large depositors are thought able to judge risks
being taken with their funds and the *caveat emptor* principle is held to
apply. While the latter should apply *a fortiori* to international bond
investors, the Fund is unable to regulate the behaviour of a sovereign
borrower outside of the stabilization context.

Although this emphasizes that the Fund should not generally become
involved in the support of private lenders during sovereign loan crises, it
also raises the question as to whether it could enhance the efficiency of
international capital allocation in the non-crisis context when information is still likely to be incomplete. If compulsory supervision is impossible in this context, incentives would seem to exist for countries to submit
voluntarily to Fund monitoring of their macroeconomic policies. Since
debt crises have typically followed difficulties in this area, a Fund *impri-
matur* would offer assurance to potential investors helping thereby to
raise the volume and to improve the terms on which finance would be
forthcoming.

The proposal for more vigorously expressed policy surveillance under
Article IV consultations prompted by the Mexican crisis, and agreed at
the Halifax meeting of the G7 countries in July 1995, could be of value in
this connection. Publication of the proceedings could serve as a form of
'credit rating' exercise with the Fund focusing on macroeconomic policy
and the wisdom of the current reliance on external resources. Despite hesi-
tancy within the Fund membership some support for the voluntary public
disclosure of the records of Article IV consultations has been expressed
(Henning, 1996). If markets cannot be informed directly through publication, perhaps a powerful signal could be provided alternatively by
Fund support for loan guarantees of country bond issues. Although the

guarantees would probably be offered through a separate agency, confidential Fund advice would help to determine the terms (if any) of the guarantees to be offered in each case (Cline, 1995). Cooperation with the World Bank would also appear appropriate in view of the Bank's reported interest in expanding its loan guarantee activity (Henning, 1996).

In addition to the benefits to the country of the improved terms and availability of external finance which a guarantee scheme could be expected to generate, the ability of the Fund to withdraw its own resources after a shorter time-period might also be implied. If the analogy with domestic banking suggests that support for loan guarantees would be a natural activity for the IMF, however, the same frame of reference also indicates that some fundamental issues concerning coverage would need to be addressed. In the case of deposit insurance, pressures to extend coverage from only a certain class or magnitude of individual deposits to the total deposit base have been experienced (McCarthy, 1980). Although small savers are seen as being more in need of protection than wholesale depositors (and there has often been concern with the financial exposure of the insurer) disadvantages of partial coverage have increasingly been recognized (Ibid). Uninsured deposits are likely to become much more sensitive to adverse news or rumour concerning banks paradoxically increasing the likelihood of at least a partial run on the institution. Effectively, in the event of eventual bank insolvency, the insurer will exercize a senior claim over available resources increasing the risks confronting uninsured creditors.

A close approximation to these hazards could be anticipated if international loan guarantees were to cover a substantial part of outstanding indebtedness and would have consequences for the Fund's view of the liberalization of capital accounts. To minimize losses for the insurer (itself, the Bank or a separate agency) a potential conflict would arise if capital flight were to jeopardise the continued servicing of the insured debt. To make *ex-ante* deposit insurance operational, the Fund would need to be ready to sanction the suspension of capital account convertibility for non-insured funds at the earliest sign of trouble. Insurer intervention prior to insolvency has been proposed for similar reasons in the domestic case (White, 1989).

The objective behind loan guarantees and the publication of the results of Fund-country consultations would be to enhance the supply and assurance of external finance for countries following sustainable macroeconomic policies. It is suggested here, however, that this objective may require the Fund to adopt a more sceptical view of capital account convertibility than its apparent present enthusiasm indicates.

22.6 CONCLUSIONS

A parallel continues to be drawn in the literature between the role of the IMF and that of a domestic central bank. Early writers envisaged an almost direct correspondence with foreign exchange reserves being denominated only in terms of the liabilities of the international institution which, in controlling their growth, would determine the evolution of global liquidity. Although floating exchange rates have gone far to render this aspect of the analogy irrelevant, it has been suggested that much nevertheless remains.

The international 'lender of last resort' aspect of the Fund linked to its policy conditionality echoes somewhat the need for a central bank to exercise prudential regulation alongside its parallel domestic commitment to the commercial banks. If this commitment is needed to avoid the occasional enforced liquidation of an illiquid loan portfolio, Fund lending should seek to avoid damagingly abrupt domestic adjustments in the face of foreign exchange shortages: turning domestic into tradeable resources at short notice certainly suggests a similar fundamental difficulty which the institution is attempting to address.

Careful use of an analogy, however, requires that key differences be noted. In this case, the need for Fund financial support to be committed for more than the short time frame of domestic central bank activity was emphasized. At the aggregate level, evidence was supplied to support the view that the IMF sought to reverse its earlier commitments in the late 1980s rather too quickly in view of global economic conditions. More narrowly, the extended nature of Fund involvement raised the question of the institution's status with respect to other (especially private) external suppliers of finance.

The emergence of very substantial private inflows to the developing countries in the present decade, while offering a new source of development finance, has raised the potential for external crises of considerable magnitude. In these circumstances, one interpretation of the Fund's role would be to avoid the emergence of an extreme transfer problem if capital market sentiment were to turn against a country as in the recent Mexican case. Unfortunately, discussion in the aftermath of that crisis has tended to emphasise the need for a financial 'war chest' in order to support a growing commitment (within the Fund and elsewhere) to liberalized capital accounts.

It has been argued here that this orientation is probably mistaken. Drawing on the domestic banking literature, it is suggested that the suspension of convertibility should, on occasion, be explicitly supported by the Fund. In addition to easing the external crisis from the country view-point, this option is necessary if the Fund's senior creditor status is to be protected. The present discussion of large-scale (GAB-originated) financing threatens to invert this established precedence thereby distorting the risk sharing benefits that securitized international financial markets were supposed to offer. Having recognized that difficulties are likely to arise on occasion as a result of adverse changes in financial market sentiment, it was also suggested that the Fund should try directly to stabilise that sentiment by measures including taking part in the international guarantee of certain loan issues. As in the domestic case of deposit guarantees, supervision of the recipient of the guaranteed funds is required and the surveillance role of the Fund would need to be accepted by countries as a *quid pro quo* for the financial benefits that this institutional support would imply. In its enthusiasm for capital market deregulation, it would seem appropriate that the Fund be reminded that its function, like that of a domestic central bank, is to allow those markets to deliver their benefits while addressing the potentially damaging externalities which may attend their liberalization.

Notes

1.   Whereas the Executive Board normally reaches decisions by consensus six abstentions, including those of the UK and Germany, were recorded when formal approval for the Mexican facility was sought.
2.   Private loans ultimately guaranteed by the government of the debtor country.

References

Bird, G. (1992) 'The Bretton Woods Institutions and Developing Countries: Analysing the Past and Anticipating the Future' in his *International Aspects of Economic Development* (London: Academic Press, 1992).

Bulow, J., K. Rogoff and A.S. Bevilaqua (1992) 'Official Creditor seniority and Burden-Sharing in the Former Soviet Bloc', *Brookings Papers on Economic Activity*, vol. 1. pp. 195–234).

Cline, W.R. (1995) *International Debt Reexamined* (Washington, DC: Institute for International Economics)

Cohen, B. (1989) *Developing Country Debt: A Middle Way* (Essays in International Finance no. 173, International Finance Section, Dept of Economics, Princeton University).

Diamond, D.W. and P.H. Dybvig (1983) 'Bank Runs, Deposit Insurance and Liquidity', *Journal of Political Economy* (vol. 91, pp. 401–19).

Duisenberg, W.F. and A Szasz (1991) 'The Monetary Character of the IMF', in *International Financial Policy: Essays in Honour of Jacques Polak* (Washington, DC: IMF).

Eichengreen, B. and R. Portes (1995) 'Crisis? What Crisis? Orderly Workouts for Sovereign Debtors' (London: Centre for Economic Policy Research).

Financial Times, The, 'IMF sees Savings for Poorest in SDR Allocations', 22 March 1996, p. 7.

——, 'G-10 Finance Chiefs Warn on Bail-Outs in Mexico-Style Crises', 23 April 1996, p. 22.

Goodhart, C.A.E. (1988) *The Evolution of Central Banks* (Cambridge, Mass: MIT Press).

Guitian, M. (1995) 'Conditionality: Past, Present and Future', *IMF Staff Papers* vol. 42, pp. 792–835).

Helleiner, G. (1992) 'The IMF, the World Bank and Africa's Adjustment and Internal Debt Problems: An Unofficial View', *World Development,* vol. 20, no. 6, pp. 779–92. pp. 779–92.

Henning, C.R. (1996) 'Political Economy of the Bretton Woods Institutions: Adapting to Financial Change', *World Economy,* vol. 19, pp. 173–93.

IMF (1995) 'SDRs: International Reserve Asset also Serves as Unit of Account', *IMF Survey* (September) p. 21.

Kenen, P.B. (1993) 'Reforming the International Monetary System: An Agenda for Developing Countries', in J.J. Teunissen (ed.) *The Pursuit of Reform: Global finance and the developing countries* (Netherlands Ministry of Foreign Affairs).

Keynes, J.M. (1969) 'Proposals for an International Clearing Union', reprinted in *The International Monetary Fund, 1945–65, vol. III: Documents* (Washington, DC: International Monetary Fund), pp. 19–36.

Killick, T. and M. Malik (1992) What Can We Know About the Effects of IMF programmes? *The World Economy,* vol. 15, pp.

Klein, B. (1974) 'The Competitive Supply of Money', *Journal of Money and Credit and Banking* (Vol. 6, pp. 421–53)

Mc Carthy, I.S. (1980) 'Deposit Insurance: Theory and Practice', *IMF Staff Papers,* vol. 27, pp. 578–600.

Oxfam (1996) *Multilateral Debt: The Human Cost* (Oxford: Oxfam).

Solomon, R. (1977) *The International Monetary System* (New York: Harper & Row)

Triffin, R. (1960) *Gold and the Dollar Crisis* (New Haven: Yale University Press).

Vaubel, R. (1983) 'The Moral Hazard of IMF Lending', *World Economy,* vol. 6, pp. 291–304.

White, L.J. (1989) 'The Reform of Federal Deposit Insurance', *Journal of Economic Perspectives,* vol. 3, pp. 11–29.

Appendix

Table 22A.1   Ordinary least squares estimation

Dependent variable is DRATIO
28 observations used for estimation from 1966 to 1993

Regressor	Coefficient	Standard error	T-Ratio (Prob)
CON	−0.054896	−0.093748	−0.58557 [0.563]
DGDPW	−0.19594	0.049694	−3.9430 [0.001]
DGDPW(-1)	−0.19844	0.049467	−4.0116 [0.000]

R-Squared	0.52267	F-statistic F(2, 25)	13.6874 [0.000]
R-Bar-Squared	0.48448	S.E. of Regression	0.49307
Residual Sum of Squares	6.0780	Mean of Dependent Variable	−0.0013284
S.D. of Dependent Variable	0.68673	Maximum of Log-likelihood	−18.3448
DW-statistic	1.9126		

Diagnostic tests

Test statistics	LM version	F version
A: Serial Correlation	Chi-Sq (1) = 0.013296 [0.908]	F(1, 24) = 0.011402 [0.916]
B: Functional Form	Chi-Sq (1) = 0.012391 [0.911]	F(1, 24) = 0.010625 [0.919]
C: Normality	Chi-Sq (2) = 1.0441 [0.593]	Not applicable
D: Heteroscedasticity	Chi-Sq (1) = 0.19653 [0.658]	F(1, 26) = 0.18378 [0.672]

A: Lagrange multiplier test of residual serial correlation
B: Ramsey's RESET test using the square of the fitted values
C: Based on a test of skewness and kurtosis of residuals
D: Based on the regression of squared residuals on squared fitted values

23 The World Food Programme: Linking Relief and Development[1]

D.J. Shaw

'Emergencies require immediate action. Food security must be a priority. But beyond the urgent demands of the moment, we must look to the longer term. Food for humanitarian assistance must over time become food for development. And this must be followed by self-sustaining food production in time of peace. Understanding this continuum and making it work is one of the most challenging physical and intellectual projects of our time. You who are working on food for development are peacemakers for the future.' (Boutros Boutros-Ghali, Secretary-General of the United Nations, *Address to WFP Staff*, April 1993

23.1 INTRODUCTION

Perhaps of all the many issues and concerns that Hans Singer has addressed in his long and illustrious career, his greatest international contribution and recognition has related to the subject of food aid (Singer, 1986; Clay and Shaw, 1987). The epistemic community has long recognized that no other person has made such a dominant impact in the international debate on food aid (Hopkins, 1992). He also played a strategic role in the establishment of the World Food Programme (WFP), the food aid organization of the United Nation system.

In many ways, food aid has acted as the resource that has bound Singer's deep and abiding interest in issues such as unemployment, human capital formation and social welfare, trade, redistribution with growth, soft lending and strong international institutions for the benefit of developing countries, stimulated by the early influence of Schumpeter, Keynes, Beveridge and Archbishop Temple, and his early work in the depressed areas of the United Kingdom. (Singer 1992; Oakenshott, Owen and Singer 1937; Singer, 1940; Singer 1943; Singer, 1986).[2]

WFP was established in 1961 as a joint undertaking of the United Nations and the Food and Agriculture Organization of the United Nations (FAO) on a three-year experimental basis with a target of $100 million of resources. Since then, it has grown to become the largest source of grant aid for poor people in developing countries in the United Nations system, and the primary source of international food aid for both development and disaster relief. In 1994, WFP reached an estimated 57 million of the poorest people in the developing world with over three million tons of food at an operating cost of $1.4 billion. Over 32 million were the victims of natural and man-made disasters in 41 countries. In addition, 24.5 million received WFP aid through 225 development projects in 83 countries.

With its dual role in relief and development, WFP is in the forefront of the United Nations attack on hunger and poverty. In accordance with its mandate, WFP assistance takes three forms: support for economic and social development programmes and projects; meeting emergency food needs and providing associated transport and logistics support; and generally promoting world food security. In these ways, WFP is well placed to play a major role in linking relief and development. WFP gives special attention to supporting disaster prevention, preparedness and mitigation projects, and post-disaster rehabilitation and reconstruction activities, as part of development programmes. Conversely, its emergency assistance is used, to the extent possible, to serve both relief and development purposes. In both cases, the overall aim is to build self-reliant households and communities (WFP 1994b).

WFP performs a number of vital tasks in emergencies. It provides emergency relief food from its own regular resources. It also administers the International Emergency Food Reserve (IEFR), the international standby facility. Increasingly, WFP has been called upon to help coordinate the food aid operations of large-scale international relief efforts. In so doing, WFP makes its unique transport and logistics services available to the international community. With the co-operation of donor countries, WFP has helped to improve port, storage and inland transportation systems during relief operations the benefits of which have remained after the emergencies have passed. Services have been provided to donors for the purchase, transportation and monitoring of food commodities for their own bilateral aid programmes. And a WFP International Food Aid Information System (INTERFAIS) has been developed that provides a database for decision-making on food aid operations throughout the world. WFP has the largest global food aid operational network with staff in 85 country offices serving 90 developing countries. They can assist in the assessment of needs, requisition food and organize its distribution from borrowed in-country stocks, or WFP can divert ships carrying its food aid consignments to ports close to where emergencies have occurred.

This chapter gives an indication of the role that Singer has played in the food aid debate and his contribution to the establishment of WFP. It describes briefly the antecedents and origins of WFP; the changing focus of its work as disasters and emergencies have increased; and it unique role in linking relief and development assistance; and identifies some major concerns for the future.

23.2   ANTECEDENTS AND ORIGINS

WFP has its origins in various attempts to set up some form of multilateral world food security arrangement and to rationalize food production and trade for the benefit of both producers and consumers, in developed and developing countries. These attempts have focused attention on two basic concerns: first, to reconcile the interests of producers and consumers by protecting them from uncontrolled fluctuations in world agricultural prices; and secondly, to use agricultural output in excess of market requirements to assist developing countries, without creating disincentive to agricultural production and trade.

The pre-history and birth of WFP are a tale of three cities: closely tied up with United States agricultural and foreign policy and the interests of the World Bank in Washington DC, and with work conducted in the United Nations in New York and the Food and Agriculture Organization of the United Nations (FAO) in Rome (Singer *et al.*, 1987; Singer, 1993).

United States food aid originated in relief assistance provided to victims of natural disasters, famines and civil disturbances at the beginning of the nineteenth century. Large-scale food aid was provided to Europe after the First World War, and again after the Second World War under the Marshall Plan when approaching one-third of a total aid package of $13.5 billion consisted of food, feed and fertilizer. But it was the Agricultural Trade Development and Assistance Act of 1954 – which became widely known by its number, Public Law (PL) 480 – that was to institutionalize and provide the legal framework for US food aid basically in the form that still endures. PL 480 marked a recognition that world food shortages and US surplus agricultural production could no longer be considered to be isolated and temporary occurrences. It established a relationship between US domestic agricultural interests and foreign relations and aid that has shaped the country's food aid policies and programmes to this day (Wallerstein, 1980; Shaw and Clay, 1993).

By the late 1950s, both the Republican administration of President Eisenhower and the Democratic presidential campaign of John F. Kennedy had begun to consider favourably the general idea of a multilateral food aid programme. During the latter, it was proposed to hold an international conference on food and agriculture (similar to the one convened at Hot Springs, Virginia by Franklin D. Roosevelt) 'to deal on a constructive multilateral basis with the food needs of the world', and 'pending such a conference and creation of "a world food agency", negotiate long-term agreements for donor countries to supply food commodities for food-for-work schemes' (Kennedy, 1960), clearly the embryo of WFP.

The strong support of the subsequent Kennedy administration for a multilateral approach to the use surplus agricultural commodities as a supplement to bilateral arrangements led the United States to propose the setting up of a three-year experimental UN programme with a fund of $100 million of which it was prepared to provide 40 per cent. The primary aim would be to meet emergency needs. At the same time, pilot projects would be conducted in other fields, such as school lunch and labour-intensive programmes in order to develop diversified experience.[3]

Meanwhile, at the United Nations in New York, negotiations had been going on during the 1950s concerning a proposal to establish a soft aid UN Special Fund for Economic Development (SUNFED). Singer played an active part in this initiative by preparing reports on SUNFED and working with the various rapporteurs, committees, groups and bodies concerned with the Special Fund.[4] He described his emerging interest in food aid at that time as follows:

> It was also in casting around for possible financing for SUNFED that I became very interested in 1954 in the establishment, under Public Law 480, of the U.S. food aid program and in the possibility of an international food aid program which had begun to emerge in Rome. (There was also a direct link with the local counterpart funds arising from P.L. 480 and the financing of IDA). This interest led me to my involvement in laying the ground for the U.N./FAO World Food Programme, and it has remained an active interest. (Singer, p. 301)

In 1960, when acting as an adviser to Dag Hammarskjöld, the then UN Secretary-General, Singer drafted a proposal that the World Bank should be responsible for targeting food aid toward the reconstruction and development projects that it was supporting. Hammarskjöld contacted the then President of the World Bank, Eugene Black, proposing that the Bank establish a separate management division to undertake multilateral food aid. This proposal was declined. However, the SUNFED proposal was assumed by the Bank in the form of its soft financing window, the International Development Association (IDA). The proposal that Singer and others had also worked on to establish a United Nations expanded technical assistance programme did succeed, and the United Nations Development Programme (UNDP) was eventually created. At the same time, Singer and other members of the epistemic community began to push for an expanded programme of food assistance in the form of an independent multilateral food aid agency in the United Nations system (Hopkins, 1992, p. 242; and personal communication with Hans Singer, 26 January 1996).

From its inception, FAO had persistently advocated the establishment of some form of world food security arrangement and the constructive use of surplus agricultural commodities. A World Food Board was proposed in 1946 and an International Commodity Clearing House in 1949 (Lamartine-Yates, 1955). Several studies were conducted in the 1950s concerning such issues as the disposal of agricultural surpluses (Blau, 1954) and the establishment of principles and guidelines (FAO, 1954), the constructive use of agricultural surpluses to finance development in developing countries (Ezekiel, 1955), and functioning of a world food reserve (Blau, 1956). A number of resolutions were passed by the FAO Council and Conference, ECOSOC and the UN General Assembly on these and related subjects, which led to nothing or called for further studies.

A resolution was adopted by the UN General Assembly in October 1960 on the 'Provision of Food Surpluses to Food-Deficient People through the United Nations System' (UN, 1960). The resolution invited FAO, in consultation with governments of member states, the UN Secretary-General, specialized agencies and other international bodies

to establish without delay procedures by which, with the assistance of the United Nations system, the largest practicable quantities of surplus food may be made available on mutually agreeable terms as a transitional measure against hunger, such procedures to be compatible with desirable agricultural development as a contribution to economic development in the less developed countries and without prejudice to bilateral arrangements for this purpose and compatible with the principles of the Food and Agriculture Organization.

FAO was also invited to

> undertake a study of the feasibility and acceptability of additional
> arrangements, including multilateral arrangements under the auspices
> of the Food and Agriculture Organization, having as their objective the
> mobilization of available surplus foodstuffs and their distribution in
> areas of greatest need, particularly in the economically less developed
> countries.

The UN Secretary-General was requested to report on

> the role which the United Nations and the appropriate specialized agen-
> cies could play in order to facilitate the best possible use of food sur-
> pluses for the economic development of the less developed countries.

It was stressed that measures should be taken against the dumping of
agricultural surpluses on the international markets and to protect
food – exporting developing countries which would 'best be assured by
multilateral trading practices'.

23.3   EXPANDED PROGRAMME OF SURPLUS FOOD UTILIZATION

The FAO Director-General appointed a small group of 'high level, independent experts' to assist him in preparing his report, of which Singer was
appointed chairman.[5] The group met at the height of the Keynesian consensus, with emphasis on full employment, active government demand management and a welfare state (Singer, personal note). Of the five members of
the group, three were direct students of Keynes, one was an economic
development thinkers in his own right, but fully in the Keynesian tradition,
and the fifth an agricultural expert in the New Deal tradition.

   The group's report had a strong Keynesian flavour, dealing with the creation of additional demand through food aid, treating food as a subsistence
fund, emphasizing the potential of food aid for adding to investment and
mopping up rural unemployment, and analysing multiplier effects of food
aid. The whole emphasis, as might have been expected from such a
Keynesian group in such a Keynesian period, was to deal with the surplus
problem by expanding demand rather than by curtailing production. The
expert group was very much aware of earlier proposals to set up a World
Food Board and an International Commodity Clearing House, the

Marshall Plan after the Second World War and the earlier work of FAO. And all its recommendations were in accordance with the FAO *Principles of Surplus Disposal*.

Singer had a special position in the group. Not only was he chairman but he represented the interests of the United Nations in general and of the Secretary-General in particular. He also brought to the group the unique and profound experience he had gained in working on the proposals for SUNFED and an expanded programme for technical assistance, and an interest in a multilateral form of PL480. Given such a like-minded group, and the wealth of documentation and experience available, it is hardly surprising that its report was handed to the Director-General 19 days after the commencement of its work at FAO in Rome. A number of its recommendations were well in advance of the time but their value were subsequently recognized.

Certain basic considerations influenced the group's report (FAO, 1962). Information available at the time indicated that over half the population of the world was either undernourished or malnourished. In the light of that fact, and making allowances for the existence of unused food stocks, the world food problem was seen basically as one of deficiencies, not surpluses. Underdevelopment was recovnized as the basic cause. Poverty for many beside plenty for few used to be a general phenomenon, nationally and internationally. However, for about one-third of the world's population in the developed countries it was a memory, fading rapidly or gradually as development took place; for the other two-thirds it was still a grim reality. Developing countries within the world economy were akin to under-privileged, low-income people within a national economy. The group observed that with the growth of wealth within the developed countries, inequalities of income had diminished. Equality of opportunity, full employment and a minimum of subsistence were an accepted part of their social philosophy. Nothing similar obtained within the international community. The basic aim should be 'to apply the principles of social progress accepted within the rich countries to the world as a whole. Only if this is done can we talk of an international community'.

The group (in an understandable spirit of optimism, which would be considered outrageous today) considered that the resources to implement such a programme were available. In its opinion, a transfer of two-thirds to three-quarters of one per cent of the gross national product of the developed countries over five years, and probably less for another decade, would provide sufficient means for helping people in the developing countries to help themselves. (Under the Marshall Plan, the United States had transferred about 3 per cent of its GNP for four years running – 1948–52).

The group observed that this would represent a much smaller international redistribution of income than the national redistribution of income achieved by progressive taxation within most of the developed countries, when they were less rich that they were in 1961 adding 'To think that the developed world cannot spare three quarters of one cent from each dollar of its income for an international program of economic aid is to show failure of imagination and failure of will'.

Food aid from the food surpluses that existed was seen to be an important part (estimated to be one-sixth to one-quarter) of the resources needed for economic development in the developing countries. Far from being a waste, it could be a blessing – if matched by other resources and used as an essential part of a coherent aid programme – shades again of the Marshall Plan and, to use the Keynesian concept, of turning the stone of surpluses into bread for development.[6]

A central part of the expert group's case was that food products form an important part of capital in its original sense of a 'subsistence fund'. Additionally employed workers have to be fed during the construction period before the fruits of investment can supply their needs, or enable them to buy their subsistence. Without such a fund, additional investment would be impossible and inflation rampant. Food surpluses used for economic development would enable hungry people to produce either their own food or other products to buy food. Freedom from hunger could ultimately be achieved only through freedom from poverty.

The group estimated that about $12 500 million of agricultural commodities would become available over a five-year period (1961–5) for use outside normal market channels either bilaterally or through the United Nations system.[7] It analysed the needs and possibilities of using these resources in the framework of national programmes for accelerated economic and social development in developing countries, and recommended that about two-thirds should be used in economic development programmes and one-third for social development.

Food aid for economic development

It was estimated that $1550–$1650 million of surplus food a year could become available for economic development programmes over a five year period. The general principles of international aid for promoting economic development were enunciated.[8] The aim would be to provide each developing country with a positive incentive for maximum national effort to increase its rate of growth. Ideally, aid should be allocated where it would have the maximum catalytic effect of mobilizing additional national effort, or prevent a fall in national effort. The primary criterion was, therefore, to maximize additional effort, not to maximize income per dollar of aid. International aid should strengthen the national effort and drastically shorten the time to reach the desired goal to the point where a satisfactory growth rate could be achieved on a self-sustaining basis.

It was noted that capacity to absorb capital, including food aid, was a limiting factor and was more limited at a low level of development, where a high proportion of technical assistance must precede a large capital flow, echoing Singer's theory of pre-investment (Singer, 1964) and the work done on an expanded programme of technical assistance that preceded the establishment of UNDP. Absorptive capacity could be stepped up appreciably but there were limits to the pace and extent at which it could be expanded. Technical absorptive capacity should determine the amount of aid, while the capacity to repay should be largely determine the method of financing it.

Distinction was made between foreign capital inflow and international aid, the latter referring to those parts of capital inflow that normal market incentives do not provide. Within international aid, distinction was made between: (i) long-term loans; (ii) grants and soft loans, and (iii) grants or sales of surplus products for local currency payments or on some other soft loan basis. Surplus food was considered as a most important part of capital aid and economic development was regarded as the most important and largest part of a productive use of surplus food. In reality, however, the group recognized that the whole of imported surplus food products would not be used for additional investment. A good economic development policy would see to it that a major part was used for raising investment but a part would merely bolster consumption. The latter part would satisfy demand for consumption due to the multiplier effects of investment and would be a valuable antidote to inflation. A withdrawal of surplus food would lead to a reduction in both consumption and investment. The group assumed that two-thirds of surplus food would be offered as investment aid and one-third for increased consumption.

The group considered that it was only possible to estimate what part surplus products can form of total investment, and of total aid, within the framework of a country's development programme, anticipating by more than three decades the programme approach that was to be adopted by WFP (WFP, 1994a). The various projects comprising a development programme are interrelated and reinforce each other. A programme, not a project, approach determined the criteria of productive use of aid capital, including food aid (Singer, 1965). Foreign aid capital increased the range of the programme as a whole. Since this might require a reshuffle and changes in several projects, a single aid input cannot with any exactness be said to have been given to one specific project only, and should be considered as a contribution to the whole programme.

The incorporation of food surpluses in economic development programmes, where they can be seen in conjunction with other resources, was considered the most desirable way of programming their use. Where developing countries did not have full development programmes, however, it was possible to go ahead with projects that would have high priority in any programme. Previous economic policy and development programmes may not have fully taken into account additional availabilities of surplus food. A widening of the development programme would then be appropriate by adding 'food-intensive' and 'labour-intensive' projects that required a minimum of other matching resources, a low import content, and a short gestation period. Construction of rural roads and soil conservation works, such as terracing and bunding, were illustrations of such projects. The degree of inflation from such projects might thus be minimized while additional employment would yield both human and economic gains. In many developing countries, especially in Africa, which were in transition from a subsistence to a money economy, the availability of additional surplus foods might facilitate a division of labour and accelerate the process of monetization.

The group observed that economic growth increased the demand for agricultural products. For technological, psychological and institutional reasons, it was hardly ever possible to speed up domestic agricultural production to the same extent. In the interval, additional food should be supplied if economic growth was not to be stifled. Specific country studies would indicate the proportion of additional foodstuffs required for that purpose. On the basis of several country studies that had been undertaken, the group estimated that from one-sixth to one-fifth of total aid should, on average, consist of food products. Surplus food could also serve to prevent development programmes from being cut down or dislocated when, for example, external buying power was suddenly reduced as a result of an unforeseen sharp decline in the world market price of a country's main export product or as a result of a sharp increase in international food prices.[9] While these measures might conflict with the principle of additionality, the group felt that they might be so important to economic development in some developing countries that they might be considered to fall within the provisions of the FAO *Principles of Surplus Disposal.*[10]

National food reserves

The group proposed that a small part (about 8 per cent or $200 million a year) of the total surplus food that was estimated to become available over a five-year period should be allocated for the establishment of national food reserves in developing countries to the extent that they could equip themselves with appropriate facilities and institutional arrangements. Surplus storable foods could be made available for the initial stocks of food reserve agencies as one-time contributions, although this did not preclude later contributions to offset prolonged periods of sub-normal production caused by such factors as drought. Developed countries not supplying surplus food could provide other outlays (for example, storage facilities) necessary for establishing national food reserves.

An international emergency food reserve

In addition, the group proposed the establishment of an international emergency food reserve to provide relief grants to the victims of famines and other physical disasters (no reference was made to man-made disasters). These grants would be provided from national food reserves. Since they would be on a scale larger than could be offset by normal types of acquisition, additional surplus food could be used to rebuild the stocks depleted by emergencies. The group estimated that about $150 million a year would be required for this purpose.[11]

Food aid for social development

In addition to the provision of surplus food for supporting economic development, the group proposed that such resources be made available to promote social development. Two criteria were suggested for planning such programmes: (a) moving gradually toward a situation in which the developing countries themselves would be able to take over these functions; and (b) avoiding action that would depress prices to domestic producers or lessen incentives for maximum food production in the recipient countries.

Four types of social development programmes were identified. The channeling of surpluses into such uses was regarded as not detrimental to local agricultural production since it represented additional consumption and the effects on added and improved nutrition could be striking.

First, *land reform programmes* during which there might be a decrease in agricultural production or an increase in consumption by farm families so that deliveries to the urban markets, the 'food capital' of industrialization, would be reduced. In both cases, food surpluses could be provided to offset the shortfall. The group estimated that about $50–100 million would be required a year for this purpose.

Secondly, *school feeding programmes* should be supported at a cost of about $500 million a year as part of the process of human capital formation which had come to be recognized as basically necessity, and as productive, as physical capital formation. As the report put it, 'Feeding the young is investment; feeding the old is relief'. The better feeding of school children, and of young people in higher educational institutions, was seen as a move in the direction of equality of opportunity, which was regarded as a basic concept in fostering self-help toward economic development. It was estimated that around $7000 million per year ($2500 million for foodstuffs and $4500 million for transport and distribution) was required to feed all children between the ages of 5 and 14 in the developing countries with a single meal a day of 60 grams of wheat, or its equivalent, and 25 grams of dried skim milk. Half that amount would be required if the programme were restricted to those actually in school. It was considered that the availability of meals would encourage school attendance and improve food habits.

While there were sufficient cereals surpluses, there was a serious lack of supplemental protein foods, particularly dried milk. Three possible solutions were proposed: supporting livestock development programmes in developing countries with feed grains; providing more protein supplements in surplus-producing countries; and making cash grants available from developed countries with no food surpluses. In addition, young people from developed countries were encouraged to make a personal contribution to the implementation of school feeding programmes, anticipating the advent of the Peace Corps programme of the United States and the Volunteer Service Programme of the United Nations.

Thirdly, it was proposed that the possibility of extending aid to the poorer students at the *secondary and higher levels of education and in training programmes* should be explored. This was regarded as a very important foundation group in economic development. A major obstacle in implementing development programmes in developing countries was a shortage of trained personnel. The expert group considered that aid in overcoming this shortage was a long-term matter but was one of the most fruitful investments that could be made. Where inability to finance their subsistence while in education and training was a limiting factor, provision of some resources for institutional feeding might be considered, at least on a modest scale. The cost of providing two simple, but nourishing, meals to half the students and trainees in higher education and vocational training centres was estimated to be $1500 million a year. The group suggested that $100 to $200 million a year be devoted to such 'food scholarships' over a five-year period.

Lastly, it was proposed that $200 million be provided per year over a five-year period in *relief and welfare programmes* for the old, handicapped and destitute.

International machinery

Having suggested what to do, the expert group then proposed how to do it. In a spirit of pragmatism, the group recognized that a major part of international aid would continue to be administered bilaterally but proposed that it should be 'bilateral aid within a multilateral framework'.[12] While there was no dogmatic reason to assume that either bilateral or multilateral operations were preferable or more effective in themselves, the group felt that a 'multilateral framework for bilateral action is better than bilateral action without such a multilateral framework'. A consultative, multilateral framework would assure that bilateral and international aid activities would provide a coherent and consistent country development programmes. Existing institutions should be used rather than creating new ones, but some additional functions and changes in the division of labour among them was envisaged. For incorporating the use of surplus food into development programmes, and advising on the general economic requirements of the developing countries, the group envisaged that FAO would work closely with the United Nations, particularly perhaps with its Regional Economic Commissions.

To ensure that surplus food was combined with additional financial aid in packages of assistance, the FAO and United Nations would work closely with such financial agencies as the International Bank for Reconstruction and Development (IBRD) and the newly established soft-lending facility of the World Bank, the International Development Association (IDA). Much of the technical and training work involved, as well as pilot projects and necessary surveys, could lead to action by the United Nations Special Fund and the Expanded Programme of Technical Assistance of the United Nations, later to become the United Nations Development Programme (UNDP). It was assumed that coordination between the FAO, the United Nations, the UN financial agencies and the other UN specialized agencies concerned would be secured through the normal administrative machinery of the Administrative Committee on Coordination (the highest administrative body of the UN system, which consists of the heads of the UN agencies under the chairmanship of the Secretary-General), with ECOSOC serving as the organ for coordinating governmental policy.

Country programming

The group highlighted the vital function of country programming. While emphasizing the diverse circumstances of developing countries, it underlined that the additional use of food surpluses could only be programmed on a country-by-country basis. The suggestion of general schemes such as a 'world food reserve' or a' world food bank' would not amount to much more than a different name or label for what was called an 'additional food surplus utilization programme'. The essential step would still be the translation of the programme into concrete action, which could only be done at the country level. Several basic principles were proposed. Country programming should be approached entirely with the interest of the recipient developing country in mind: it should be demand and not supply driven. All potential recipients of additional food surpluses should be treated on a basis of equality so that each country had the same opportunity to participate. Uniform and high standards should be applied in assuring that additional surplus food was only used for constructive and important objectives, which international organizations could ensure.

The individual country programme, drawn up with the help of the international organizations, should normally include a financial assessment specifying the types of additional financial assistance, other than surplus food, as well as technical assistance, which would enhance the value of the programme This would apply both to action by international lending agencies and to technical assistance and pre-investment assistance of all kinds. An approximate idea of the amounts of aid available should be provided. Surplus-giving countries should, therefore, indicate their willingness to earmark surplus food as aid. Since it was not known what part of total requirements would be handled multilaterally, which would result from the preference of individual countries, part of the total earmarkings should be made available on a flexible basis for multilateral transactions.

The chief limiting factor to a surplus food utilization programme was seen to be not so much the availability of supplies but rather in the capacity of developing countries to absorb those supplies into their economies at a high level of effectiveness. A related limiting factor was for the developing countries to provide the necessary correlated domestic effort. It was also noted that the willingness of developed countries to place their surpluses at the disposal of developing countries could not be indefinitely counted upon. The utilization of surplus food would not be entirely costless to donating countries since it would involve them in supplementary action. Planning and programming machinery in the developing countries, the international organizations, and among the donor countries should be developed to take better, and more immediate, advantage of the availability of surpluses to further economic and social development.

The proposals of the expert group were fully taken into account in the reports of the Director-General of FAO and the Secretary-General of the United Nations to ECOSOC. Joint proposals were made by the UN and FAO regarding procedures and arrangements for the multilateral utilization of surplus food, including the establishment of a 'Surplus Utilization Fund' to be administered by a joint 'UN/FAO Surplus Utilization Division', later to be called the World Food Programme and the WFP Secretariat respectively.[13] The political climate was so opportune that within less than a year after the expert group had submitted its report, WFP was established by parallel resolutions passed by the FAO Conference and the United Nations General Assembly at the end of 1961.[14]

23.4   WFP MANDATE

From its inception, WFP has operated under certain basic tenets (Shaw, 1970). The broad developmental scope of WFP was expressed in the title of the original proposal for its creation, 'Development through Food'. The activities of WFP were to be people-centred, based on the strong conviction that sustained development could best be achieved if beneficiaries of WFP assistance had a personal or collective stake in the implementation of the development projects supported by the Programme. WFP was born in the halcyon days of the United Nations. The first United Nations Development Decade of the 1960s had just been launched.[15] A newly accepted principle of international solidarity had expressed itself in greater willingness to give assistance to developing countries, led by the United States that made the original proposal to establish WFP as a three-year experimental programme (1963–5). All contributions to WFP's resources were to be made on a voluntary basis as a supplement to bilateral food aid, and in addition to other forms of aid.

Priority was given to benefiting poor and food insecure people in rural area in the most needy, food-deficit countries with the aim of promoting food and agricultural development and nutritional self-reliance. Emphasis was placed on supporting development projects with specific objectives and target groups, rather than providing general programme aid. Preference was given to direct distribution of food commodities to specified beneficiaries; sales were to be highly restricted and kept under constant review. A multifaceted concept of 'additionality' was made a keystone of WFP's policies and programmes. The provision of food aid was to increase the levels of consumption, investment, employment and income beyond what would have been possible without such assistance. An underlying concern was to provide food aid in ways that actively promoted development in poor developing countries, rather than merely to dispose of agricultural surpluses, and to avoid disruption or discouragement of agricultural production or trade.

The earlier experience of providing United States food aid under the Public Law 480 had an important influence on the size and form of WFP. By the time WFP became operational in 1963, some 98 million tons of food aid (in grain equivalent) had been shipped under the PL 480 programme the bulk of which was in the form of programme aid for balance of payments and budget support in the recipient countries, mainly to further US political and commercial interests. This programme had attracted considerable criticism and controversy (Schultz, 1960). WFP was deliberately kept small so as not to complete with the large bilateral food aid programmes. It was also restricted to project as opposed to programme support to test out approaches in various types of pilot activities and because it was felt that it would be easier to monitor and evaluate results and observe any disincentive effects on agricultural production and trade. A modest $100 million experimental programme (the same size as the expanded programme of technical assistance that had been proposed earlier) was therefore proposed for a three year period at a time when the USA alone was delivering around $1.5 billion of food aid a year.

The advantages of the multilateral channeling of food aid were appreciated at the outset. Food aid was to be provided with no political or commercial strings. Contributions could be made by many countries, developed and developing, that complemented each other, leading to international burden-sharing, facilitating resource management and making food deliveries cost-effective and timely. A close rein was to be kept on programme and administrative overheads, which at less than 6 per cent of total annual expenditure, was one of the lowest of any development agency.

Finally, WFP was expected to stand at the other end of the aid spectrum, away from neo-colonialism and paternalism. Even by the standards of the United Nations system of the time, WFP was to be non-interventionist. Developing countries were to be sovereign in the matter of receiving aid for the implementation of their own development plans and programmes. They were also to be responsible for the utilization of the aid they received in accordance with agreed purposes once it had arrived at the port or frontier station. The roles of WFP staff were restricted to providing supervision, advisory assistance and training.

The original resolutions establishing WFP identified three types and fields of assistance for the Programme:

1. establishing adequate and orderly procedures on a world basis for meeting emergency food needs and emergencies inherent in chronic malnutrition, which could include the establishment of food reserves;
2. assisting pre-school and school feeding programmes; and
3. supporting economic and social development projects, particularly when related to labour-intensive works programmes and rural welfare.

Initial restricted emergency assistance

There was one issue, however, that was to cause debate from WFP's inception. While, uniquely in the United Nations system, WFP could respond to both emergencies as well as support development projects, where should the emphasis lie, or to put it in terms often discussed, what should be the 'balance' between WFP resources for emergency operations and development projects? Initially, only 25 per cent of the commodities pledged to WFP were earmarked for emergencies, including the establishment of national food reserves. Those commodities were not held in store by WFP but were to be on call in donor countries.

It soon became evident that emergency relief was a complex issue, conceptually as well as in practice. Emergency food aid operations were defined for WFP's purposes as arising out of 'critical food shortages or famine resulting from sudden or unexpected occurrences' (WFP, 1964). In the light of experience, that definition was found to be too general and was amended to 'urgent situations in which there is clear evidence that an event has occurred which causes human suffering or loss of livestock and which the government concerned has not the means to remedy; and it is a demonstrably abnormal event which produces dislocation in the life of a community on an exceptional scale' (WFP, 1970). Even that expanded definition was to cause problems. A distinction was made between food aid needs arising from such situations and assistance required to meet the nutritional needs of vulnerable groups and chronic or structural food deficits associated with balance of payments problems. WFP did not use its emergency assistance in the latter case, for which other arrangements and forms of assistance were available, such as those provided by the IMF.

Three problems faced WFP in responding to emergencies. The first was the size of resources allocated for that purpose. The second was its inability to provide assistance quickly. The third were basic operational problems, such as the sustained supply of staple and acceptable foodstuffs, the size and suitability of containers and packaging, and the provision of adequate storage. It was considered that situations of chronic malnutrition *per se* should not necessarily be identified as emergencies, though they should be carefully watched in order that early preventive action may be taken in the event that they developed into situations that qualified for WFP's emergency aid. WFP's policy was to use its development assistance to support projects that attacked the root causes of chronic malnutrition.

It was evident that the original allocation of WFP resources for meeting emergencies was inadequate. The governing body was regularly requested to increase WFP's annual emergency resources until an alternative and additional source became available with the creation of an International Emergency Food Reserve (IEFR) in 1975. It was also evident that resources were insufficient to contribute to food reserves, except on a very limited scale. Contributions were also made to price stabilization schemes to provide an incentive to producers without pricing poor consumers out of the market but again these were modest and have remained only a small part of WFP's portfolio.

As commodities pledged to WFP were held in donor countries around the world, and as WFP did not have its own transportation and distribution facilities but had to purchase them with limited cash resources, it was found that it could not function as an immediate, short-term source of relief. WFP's limited cash resources has remained a major problem affecting all operations. A formula was agreed upon at inception whereby the resources pledged to WFP could be made in the form of appropriate commodities, acceptable services (including transport and other services) and cash, aiming at the cash and services components amounting, *in the aggregate*, to at least one third of total contributions. Contributions could be made by intergovernmental bodies, other public sources and non-governmental organizations (NGOs) but, in reality, have been provided mainly by governments on a voluntary basis.

During the first decade of WFP's operations, 105 countries pledged resources. The bulk of contributions were made by a small number of developed countries but many developing countries contributed small, but symbolically significant, resources. The original target of one-third of total resources in cash and services was predicated on operational needs related only to supporting development projects. No allowance was made for the higher transport and insurance costs of emergency operations, or of the need to purchase food close to where disasters occurred. Some donors also tied their contributions to their own domestically produced commodities and services and designated them to specific emergency operations of their choosing, thus reducing their value and flexibility, and increasing the uncertainty of their availability, as they tended to be residual to commercial transactions and, therefore, subject to substantial variation.

A key problem was that the cash and services component was fixed at one third of total contributions 'in the aggregate' on the understanding that in the spirit of international solidarity and burden-sharing prevailing at the time of WFP's inception, countries with food commodities to offer would supply food, while those without would provide cash and services to move the food and to administer food aid operations. This did not happen and WFP has faced a problem of insufficient cash resources, which has intensified as its involvement in emergency operations has grown.

Evaluating WFP's experience with emergency operations at the end of the three-year experimental period in 1965, the Executive Director wrote: 'The conclusion is reluctantly reached that it is important to make clear to countries suffering disasters the inevitable limitations to which the supply of World Food Programme emergency food is subjected' (WFP, 1965). It took several months to deliver food commodities from donor countries. Even more time was often required to synchronize the arrival of different food consignments from different sources.

WFP development aid

Emphasis was, therefore, placed on providing food aid for development projects. Two main areas of development assistance emerged: agricultural and rural development; and the development of human resources (see Table 23.1). The former, which over the years has taken up the major part of WFP's development resources, included a range of development projects that increased agricultural production, improved rural infrastructure, and supported agricultural settlement schemes, with small amounts allocated for the establishment of food reserves. The main functions of WFP development aid were to stimulate increased employment and income in food-for-work programmes in which food formed part of the wage; provide an incentive for community development programmes; and tide people over the period of settlement on new lands or during the transformation of traditional farming systems until food self-reliance could be achieved.

The development of human resources through improvements in nutrition, health, education and training has also remained a major concern of WFP, in keeping with the recommendations contained in the expert group

Table 23.1 WFP development commitments by type of activity, 1963–94 ($USm.)

| Year | Total Value | Agricultural and rural development | | | | | | | | | | Human resource development | | | | | | Other | |
| | | Agricultural production | | Rural infra-structure | | Settlement | | Food reserves | | Subtotal | | MCH and primary school | | Secondary and other educational training | | Subtotal | | Industry and mining | |
		Value	(%)	Value	(%)	Value	(%)	Value	(%)	Value	(%)	Value	(%)	Value	(%)	Value	(%)	Value	(%)
1963–74	1429	528	37	225	16	150	10	39	3	942	66	335	23	136	10	471	33	16	1
1975	393	133	34	41	10	46	12	—	—	220	56	169	43	4	1	173	44	—	—
1976	642	341	53	98	15	40	7	6	2	479	75	136	21	27	4	163	25	1	0
1977	367	125	34	35	9	56	15	—	—	222	60	125	34	20	6	145	40	—	—
1978	392	162	41	30	8	36	9	4	1	228	58	139	36	25	6	164	42	—	—
1979	492	217	44	62	13	44	9	6	1	327	67	149	30	16	3	165	33	—	—
1980	479	120	25	58	12	65	13	14	3	249	52	216	45	14	3	230	48	—	—
1981	543	202	37	105	19	128	24	10	2	449	83	75	14	19	3	94	17	—	—
1982	613	326	53	61	10	70	11	—	—	467	76	139	23	7	1	146	24	—	—
1983	696	343	49	63	9	66	10	5	0	472	68	208	30	15	2	223	32	—	—
1984	925	431	47	80	9	39	4	15	2	555	60	332	36	25	3	357	39	14	2
1985	642	345	54	102	16	37	6	49	8	499	78	107	16	37	6	144	22	—	—
1986	629	348	55	33	5	80	13	—	—	510	81	83	13	37	6	120	19	—	—
1987	621	211	34	70	11	17	3	—	—	298	48	307	49	16	3	323	52	—	—
1988	779	314	40	70	9	49	6	—	—	433	56	294	38	52	7	346	44	—	—
1989	575	326	57	21	4	39	7	1	0	388	67	162	28	26	5	188	33	—	—

Table 23.1 WFP development commitments by type of activity, 1963–94 ($USm.)

| Year | Total | Agricultural and rural development | | | | | | | | | | Human resource development | | | | | | Other | |
| | | Agricultural production | | Rural infra-structure | | Settlement | | Food reserves | | Subtotal | | MCH and primary school | | Secondary and other educational training | | Subtotal | | Industry and mining | |
		Value	(%)	Value	(%)	Value	(%)	Value	(%)	Value	(%)	Value	(%)	Value	(%)	Value	(%)	Value	(%)
1990	480	141	29	51	11	18	4	—	—	210	44	260	54	10	2	270	56	—	—
1991	448	189	42	92	21	5	1	6	1	292	65	134	30	22	5	156	35	—	—
1992	421	104	25	82	19	4	1	—	—	190	45	230	55	1	0	231	55	—	—
1993	253	82	32	22	9	1	—	—	—	105	42	132	52	16	6	148	58	—	—
1994	254	67	26	27	11	19	8	3	1	116	46	73	29	65	25	138	54	—	—

Source: WFP.

report that led to WFP's establishment. The main support has been given to the most vulnerable groups of women and pre-school children through mother and child health (MCH) programmes and primary school children through school feeding programmes, with smaller amounts allocated to secondary and higher educational institutions and training programmes. The proportion of WFP development assistance going to support human capital formation has increased in recent years as an adjunct to the rapid increase in emergency situations and as poor developing countries have found it increasingly difficult to provide the domestic resources required for agricultural and rural development projects.

During the three decades from the commencement of its operations, WFP development assistance grew substantially to become the large source of grant aid in the United Nations system for poor people throughout the developing world. Over that time WFP invested about $13 billion, involving more than 40 million tons of food, in over 1600 development projects to combat hunger and promote economic and social development. Many millions of poor people, in nearly every developing country, benefited directly, many millions more benefited indirectly from the development projects supported. A number of countries that were recipients of WFP development food aid in the past no longer need this form of assistance. In other countries, the need for food aid has substantially declined. There remain, however, many developing countries where the need remains substantial. Over time, the focus has shifted to Africa in view of its special and multiple problems as well as to Asia where the majority of the world's poor and food insecure remain.

Increasing involvement in emergencies

While emphasis was initially placed on food aid for development, however, it was recognized that a multilateral organization administering food aid could not stand aside while countries were stricken by disasters. The humanitarian impulse of food aid was too strong. WFP aid was most effective towards the end of an emergency period when assistance provided from other sources tended to diminish but when disaster victims still needed food aid while they undertook reconstruction and rehabilitation work.

To some extent, the problem of quick delivery in emergencies was overcome through borrowing food from locally available stocks either provided by WFP for approved development projects, or of the government or other aid agencies, on a replenishment basis. Paradoxically, WFP's ability to use this devise became more widespread as its assistance for development projects expanded throughout the developing world, giving an early indication of the benefits to be gained from WFP supporting both development and relief operations. More timely response was possible in the case of slow maturing emergency situations, such as those caused by drought, especially after the introduction of the Global Information and Early Warning System on Food and Agriculture (GIEWS) by FAO in 1975, which gave advance notice of an impending disaster. Even then, however, response to early warning was not always speedy and delays were experienced.

Three types of emergencies were identified: (1) sudden natural calamities, such as earthquakes, floods, volcanic eruptions, and similar unforeseen disasters; (2) slower maturing emergencies arising from food scarcity conditions caused by drought, crop failures and pests and diseases; and (3) man-made disasters caused by war and civil unrest, resulting in refugees and displaced people.

Emergency operations have grown dramatically from a small, but important, component of WFP's activities to become a major part of WFP's work (Table 23.2). Total commitments for emergency assistance (at current prices) increased from an annual average of $15 million during the first ten years of WFP operations (1963–74) to almost $900 million in 1992. If resources committed for protracted refugee and displaced person projects (PROs), which began in 1989 (see below), are included (Table 23.3), total emergency relief assistance committed in 1992 reached $1.4 billion. While WFP development assistance tripled in the 1970s, its emergency aid increased tenfold. This imbalance continued in the next two decades to such an extent that while two-thirds of WFP assistance went for development projects and one third for emergency relief (including PROs) five years ago, the reverse is now the case (see Figure 23.1).

Major changes have taken place in the proportions of WFP aid going to the three types of emergencies over the past 30 years (Table 23.2). At the end of the first decade (1963–74), almost half went to emergencies caused by drought and crop failures, about one third to those afflicted by sudden natural disasters, and less than a fifth to refugees and displaced people. At the end of the second decade in 1984, over half WFP emergency commitments went to man-made disasters, over 40 per cent to emergencies caused by drought, and only 6 per cent to sudden natural disasters. By the beginning of the 1990s, the bulk of WFP emergency assistance was directed to saving the lives of refugees and displaced people caught up in civil wars and ethnic and religious conflict.

A special sub-set of WFP development assistance was established for refugees and displaced people in protracted situations lasting for more

Table 23.2 WFP commitments for emergency operations[a] by type, 1963–94 (US$m.)

Year	Total commitments[b]		Sudden natural disasters			Drought/crop failures			Man-made disasters		
	No.	Value	No.	Value	Share in total (%)	No.	Value	Share in total (%)	No.	Value	Share in total (%)
1963–74	190	151.0	66	48.1	32	71	73.9	49	53	29.0	19
1975	29	58.1	14	25.6	44	8	12.2	21	7	20.3	35
1976	26	47.7	9	8.6	18	6	14.5	30	11	24.6	52
1977	37	85.5	8	26.2	31	21	43.2	50	8	16.1	19
1978	57	90.7	19	37.0	41	14	22.4	25	24	31.3	34
1979	67	122.5	14	11.7	10	14	41.1	33	39	69.7	57
1980	62	191.5	7	10.1	5	23	61.8	32	32	119.6	62
1981	53	178.2	8	7.1	4	16	39.3	22	29	131.8	74
1982	68	193.2	15	21.5	11	20	39.2	20	33	132.5	64
1983	68	200.3	5	6.2	3	29	86.1	43	34	108.0	54
1984	63	233.7	4	17.6	8	35	96.4	41	24	119.7	51
1985	55	230.4	5	9.4	4	21	71.6	31	29	149.4	65
1986	50	182.6	6	3.3	2	8	35.2	19	36	144.1	79
1987	79	271.3	6	8.0	3	16	76.9	28	57	186.3	69
1988	65	254.0	6	27.5	11	16	50.1	20	43	176.4	69
1989	46	93.1	2	1.1	1	9	19.7	21	35	72.3	78
1990	32	131.6	5	4.2	3	10	29.8	23	17	97.6	74
1991	44	390.8	5	6.7	2	13	141.2	36	26	242.9	62
1992	55	896.8	6	7.2	1	14	517.1	58	35	372.5	41

Table 23.2 WFP commitments for emergency operations[a] by type, 1963–94 (US$m.)

Year	Total commitments[b]		Sudden natural disasters			Drought/crop failures			Man-made disasters		
	No.	*Value*	*No.*	*Value*	*Share in total (%)*	*No.*	*Value*	*Share in total (%)*	*No.*	*Value*	*Share in total (%)*
1993	54	737.5	4	5.3	1	5	31.0	4	45	701.2	95
1994	45	857.9	1	0.7	0	9	177.2	21	35	680.0	79

Source: WFP

[a] As from 1989, excludes commitments for protracted refugee and displaced person operations.
[b] Expansions of emergency operations are counted separately.

Table 23.3   WFP commitments*ᵃ* for protracted refugee and displaced person projects by region, 1989–94 ($USm.)

Year	Total	Latin America and the Caribbean		North Africa and Middle East		Sub-Saharan Africa		South and East Asia	
		Value	Share in total (%)	Value	Share in total (%)	Value	Share in total (%)	Value	Share in total (%)
1989	266.4	2.5	1	20.1	8	121.0	45	122.8	46
1990	335.6	3.7	1	18.0	5	189.8	57	124.1	37
1991	557.7	2.7	0	20.0	4	425.0	76	110.0	20
1992	510.2	0.7	0	98.1	19	323.9	64	87.5	17
1993	482.1	1.5	0	82.3	17	328.3	68	70.0	15
1994	256.2	1.7	1	72.1	28	138.0	54	44.4	17

Source: WFP.
ᵃ Including budget revisions.

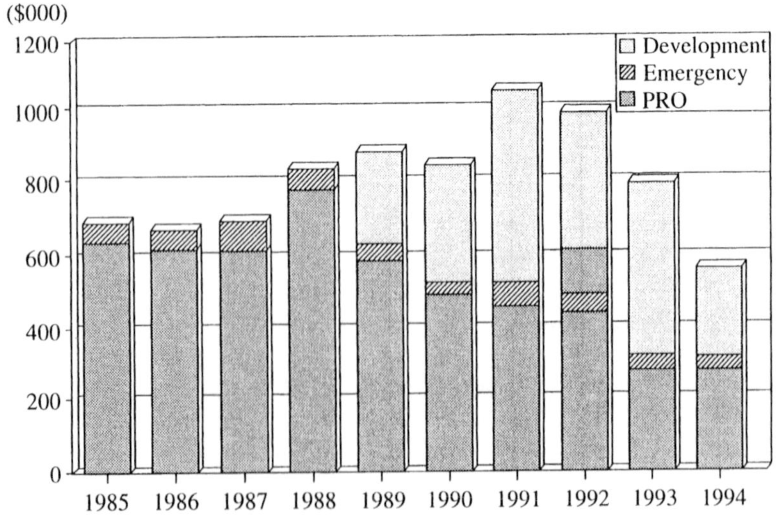

Figure 23.1   WFP commitments for development projects, emergency and protracted refugee and displaced person operations, 1985–94

Source: WFP.

than one year (Table 23.3). This facility has added considerably to WFP's overall emergency relief assistance. It reached over $557 million in 1991 as man-made disasters not only increased in number and scale, but also in duration. It has subsequently declined as some of the war situations have been resolved and victims have returned home, increasing the demand for food aid for reconstruction and rehabilitation programmes.

The regional distribution of WFP emergency relief has shown marked changes over the past three decades, reflecting significant shifts in the need for food aid that have taken place. Those changes have mainly affected three regions, sub-Saharan Africa, South and East Asia and, more recently, the former Yugoslavia and the newly independent states of the former Soviet Union. In the early years of WFP operations, most of WFP emergency aid went to meet disasters in Asia, especially those resulting from drought that affected large numbers of people in South Asia (Bangladesh, India and Pakistan).

Subsequently, sub-Saharan Africa has received most of WFP's emergency aid. Natural disasters have continued to occur in Asia but, over time, the countries of that region have taken steps to increase their capacity to address emergencies, and mitigate their effects, without appealing for international assistance. The countries of sub-Saharan Africa have been less able to cope. Large-scale, complex and prolonged catastrophes have occurred in which wars and drought have simultaneously occurred, resulting in the largest share of WFP assistance for PROs going to that region. The most recent development has been the provision of emergency relief for countries of the former Yugoslavia and Soviet Union. In 1993, over half of WFP's emergency aid was committed for those countries, mainly for the victims of man-made disasters caused by war, ethnic cleansing and the disintegration of the old political order.

Five milestones may be singled out in the inexorable increase in WFP's involvement in emergency operations (Shaw, 1996).

First, the African food crises of the 1970s, and 1980s, and the call for coordinated action, propelled WFP's involvement in emergency operations not only in terms of the amount of emergency aid it delivered but also its role in the co-ordination of the food aid operations in large-scale international relief efforts. WFP experience led to the development of unique expertise in transport and logistics operations. In addition WFP's international food aid information service (INTERFAIS) was developed, which now provides a database for food aid operations worldwide.

Secondly, special measures were taken to meet the internal transport, storage and handling (ITSH) costs of its food aid in the least-developed countries. Lack of adequate transport and storage facilities was identified as one of the major constraints which, combined with their cost, greatly inhibited least-developed countries from absorbing the larger amounts of food aid that they required. They also slowed the utilization, and caused wastage, of the food aid they received. In 1973, it was agreed to defray up to 50 per cent of the ITSH costs in least-developed countries, later further extended to countries recognized by the UN General Assembly 'as if' least-developed countries by virtue of their urgent need for external aid.

It was later agreed that all ITSH costs for emergency operations and PROs should be subsidized by WFP. In 1976, assistance was approved for the improvement and/or construction of storage facilities in those countries, and to provide WFP cash resources to improve warehouse management. These undertakings placed a heavy drain on WFP's limited cash resources, particularly after the steep increase in world oil prices in the 1970s. It was agreed, therefore, to allow the sale of limited amounts of grain in the eligible countries to offset ITSH costs. This, too, created difficulties as ITSH costs rose and larger volumes of grain were supplied for sale.

Thirdly, the World Food Conference of 1974 widened further WFP's responsibility for emergency operations (UN, 1975a). The Conference recognized the need to increase WFP's resources. Governments were recommended to earmark stocks or funds for meeting international emergency requirement, as envisaged in a International Undertaking on World Food Security (IUWFS) that was proposed at the Conference. It was recommended that part of those stocks should be placed at the disposal of WFP. The governing body of WFP was reconstituted into the Committee on Food Aid Policies and Programmes (CFA) to provide a form for intergovernmental consultation on all food aid, including emergency assistance from all sources. The CFA has given more attention to emergency food aid issues than to any other single subject. The establishment of a Global Information and Early Warning System by FAO was recommended, which has subsequently helped to improve the response to impending emergencies. WFP field staff are among the principal sources of information for this system.

Fourthly, on the recommendation of the World Food Conference, the UN General Assembly passed a resolution in 1975 establishing an International Emergency Food Reserve (IEFR) (UN, 1975b). The resolution urged all countries to subscribe to the proposed IUWFS, and build up and maintain world foodgrain reserves to be held nationally and regionally, and located strategically, large enough to cover foreseeable major production shortfalls. It was proposed that the wheat and rice components of the reserve should be 30 million tons. Pending the establishment of this world foodgrain reserve, developed countries and developing countries in a position to do so were urged to earmark stocks and/or funds to be placed at the disposal of WFP as an emergency reserve to strengthen the capacity of the Programme to respond to crisis situations in developing countries. The aim was a target of not less that 500 000 tons.

Modalities of IEFR operations were approved by the CFA in 1976 and revised and enlarged in 1978 (WFP, 1978). This facility was seen as a continuing reserve with yearly replenishments determined by the CFA. The Reserve was originally regarded as a multilateral standby arrangement to provide WFP with an initial, quick-response capability. It did not entail WFP holding physical stocks in strategic locations. Donors were required to announce their contributions to the IEFR one year in advance and to take measures to ensure that food for emergencies was shipped in the most expeditious manner. They were also required to assume responsibility for meeting transport and related costs. Developing countries could make interest-free loans of commodities to the Reserve, which would be used by WFP in the initial stages of an emergency, especially where such arrangements could speed up food deliveries. Part of the contributions to the IEFR were to be made in commodities such as rice and white sorghum to take account of the food habits of emergency victims.

To strengthen the speed of IEFR operations, an Immediate Response Account (IRA) was set up in 1991 as an integral part of the Reserve. The IRA has an annual target of $30 million in cash for the purchase of food close to where emergencies occur.

Finally, and more than any other factor, the escalation of man-made disasters and the resultant revised working arrangement between WFP and the United Nations High Commissioner for Refugees (UNHCR) have greatly increased WFP's involvement in emergency operation. In 1970, there were 2.5 million refugees in the world. A decade later, there were 11 million. In 1993, the number was 18.2 million. In addition, there are an estimated 24 million people, displaced from their homes in their own country, who have often the same need for protection and assistance as refugees (UNHCR, 1993).

Civil wars and internal conflicts have become the principal causes of violence, destruction and the displacement of people as conflicts within, rather than between, nations have increased and as rivalry among the major military powers have subsided. During 1989–90, there were 33 armed conflicts in the world, only one of which occurred between states. National, religious and ethnic fundamentalism, disintegration of the old political order, and the process of 'ethnic cleansing' have resulted in a rapid and large increase in the number of people in distress, presenting a major problem to host governments and the international community. The scale and complexity of the problem, and the lack of sufficient resources, is threatening to undermine the established system of taking care of these people. In the wars of the past decade, far more civilians, especially women and children, have been killed and disabled than soldiers.

Most of the conflicts have occurred in poor countries or in newly created states following the collapse of the previous political order. Few have the resources, administration or logistics to cope without substantial external assistance. Several disasters have been exacerbated by the lethal combination of was and drought. The international community has given generously to come to the aid of the afflicted. Steps have been taken to strengthen coordination within the United Nations system to respond to their needs as the scale, complexity and duration of the problem have increased, large numbers of people have become involved, and the cost of providing assistance has escalated.

As the food aid organization of the United Nations system, WFP has automatically assumed a major role in providing life-saving food. In 1994, WFP provided food relief to 16.5 million displaced people and 8.5 million refugees in 41 countries. Its unique expertise in transport and logistics has been an added factor in WFP's involvement. A third contribution has been in what might be termed 'persuasive diplomacy', obtaining access to ports, establishing access corridors to people in zones of conflict, and helping to keep the fragile peace in war situations through the provision of food.

Within the already acute difficulties of people in man-made disasters are the special problems of those caught up in protracted situations often lasting many years. A WFP study revealed several shortcomings in the ways in which protracted refugee and displaced person operations (PROs) were funded and conducted (WFP, 1989). It was noted that not only had the proportion of WFP emergency assistance going to man-made emergencies increased dramatically since 1979, but that PROs (defined as lasting more than one year) had also increased. An ever-increasing share of WFP's emergency aid had therefore been allocated to PROs, leaving less to meet other types of emergencies. In addition, PROs had special characteristics that set them apart from other types of emergencies, which called for special treatment.

Solutions to three particular problems had to be found: how to provide an assured and continuous food supply that was not only adequate for good health but also sufficiently varied and flexible enough to meet changing needs; how to meet basic non-food needs; and how to cater for developmental as well as survival needs in terms of nutrition, health, education and training, and, where possible, provide employment and income-earning opportunities. To achieve these objectives, WFP's governing body agreed in 1989 that PROs should no longer be funded from WFP's emergency resources but from a special sub-set of its development aid. Donors were invited to contribute resources over and above their normal pledges to WFP for PROs to be supplemented by up to $30 million a year from WFP's regular resources.

Another step has been to establish close working arrangements between WFP and UNHCR. Over the years, these two organizations have established perhaps the closest partnership within the UN system. A memorandum of understanding (MOU) was signed between them in 1985. More recently, their joint working arrangements have been thoroughly reviewed and revised to contend with the explosion of the refugee problem, and a new MOU came into force in January 1994. These new working relationships carry far-reaching implications for WFP.

The Programme is now committed to respond to refugee situation, including PROs, on a priority basis. To the extent that WFP's development resources do not expand, an increasing share of those resources will go to refugees (see Figure 23.1). Paradoxically, WFP assistance to other types of emergency operations might also suffer with a declining development project portfolio. The amount of borrowing from WFP stocks for development projects in developing countries would become more limited. In addition, a reduction of WFP-assisted development projects for disaster prevention, preparedness and mitigation could lead to an increase in the demand for emergency aid.

A broader view must recognize that armed conflict is not the only force that is affecting normal development of nations and their people, particularly their children (UNICEF 1995). A silent 'economic emergency' continues, often accompanied by misplaced adjustment programmes, which is resulting in the economic and social marginalization of the poorest people in the poorest countries (Cornia *et al.*, 1987). In the past ten years, such factors as falling commodity prices, rising military expenditure, poor returns on investment, the debt crisis, and structural adjustment programmes have drastically reduced the real incomes of some 800 million people in some 40 developing countries. In Latin America, the reduction has been as much as 20 per cent: in sub-Saharan Africa, often much more. At the same time, cuts in essential social expenditure have resulted in a reduction of programmes in nutrition, health, education and training, especially for the poor. An underclass is being created, underfed, undereducated and unskilled passed by in the economic and social progress that has been achieved.

Mutual benefits can be forthcoming from associating food aid with adjustment programmes (Shaw and Singer 1988; Sukin 1988).[16] The adjustment process can be strengthened, and ameliorated for the poor, while food aid provided within the adjustment framework focused on poverty alleviation can be more effective. This is not to imply that food aid can be used like some 'magic dust' to work wonders and overcome the mistakes and errors of badly designed adjustment programmes. But food aid does have special characteristics that are particularly appropriate for addressing the macroeconomic difficulties of poor countries, and the microeconomic concerns of poor households and communities in those countries. To take an extreme example, if malnutrition among pre-school children increases as a result of adjustment measures and leads to irreversible loss of physical and mental capacity, this can in no sense be described as 'laying the foundation for viable future economic growth', the purported basis for adjustment programmes. It is at this point that food aid could be usefully deployed to counterbalance the tendency for adjustment programmes to be unduly austere and contractionary, rather than supportive and expansionary, in the economy.

Four major roles for food aid have been identified in structural and sector adjustment programmes (WFP, 1987). First, general financial support may be given by providing: foreign exchange savings through supplying food aid in place of commercial imports; and budgetary support through the creation of funds from food aid sales. Both can be used in programmes that benefit poor, food insecure people. Secondly, food aid can be used to support reform in a particular sector of an economy, as in the case of cereal market restructuring and pricing policy reform that provides incentive for poor producers to increase food production without pricing poor consumers out of the market. Thirdly, food aid can also be invested in specific types of development projects that increase employment and income, and provide training, for the poor. And fourthly, food aid can support compensatory employment and nutrition measures for those who lose their jobs or cannot afford price increases of basic food commodities as a result of the adjustment process.

23.5   LINKING RELIEF AND DEVELOPMENT

The division of external assistance into 'development' and 'emergency' aid, each with its separate agenda, terms, legislation, financing, and operating agencies (even separate units within the same aid agency), has dichotomized what in the real experience of developing countries is not separate, the inter-relationship between disasters and the development process. Attempts are now being made to remove this artificial dichotomy.

UN General Assembly resolution 46/182 of 1991 (UN, 1991) emphasized the inter-dependence between humanitarian assistance and development, and the need for a 'continuum of action' from early warning and prevention of, and preparedness for, disasters to the all-important transition from relief to reconstruction, rehabilitation and development, not as a linear, but as a circular, process in which relief assistance supports and protects development and development mitigates the effects of disasters (Hay, 1986; Singer, 1996). One of the goals of development is to provide a protective shield in case disaster strikes. Development measures are also called for after the devastation of natural and man-made emergencies. And normal development activities are hardly feasible unless they are built on a firm foundation of successful rehabilitation and reconstruction work (Maxwell and Buchanan-Smith, 1994).

There is a close, and growing, link between poverty and vulnerability to recurring emergencies, particularly those caused by drought. If, for example, the food security of the most vulnerable people could be improved at the household and community level through development projects that provide employment, income and assets, the continued need for emergency assistance could be considerably reduced. The major focus should be on supporting national disaster mitigation and rehabilitation programmes through labour-intensive works programmes that would provide simultaneously: (a) immediate employment and income, thereby alleviating poverty and strengthening self-help capacity; and (b) construction and improvement of the infrastructure needed to increase agricultural production, stimulate rural development, and strengthen measures against future droughts and other disasters. Together with these labour-intensive works programmes, targeted food, nutrition and health interventions could improve the well-being of the poor and help them withstand future food shortages (von Braun, 1991; Shaw, 1995; WFP, 1992a). Much of this is not new. It builds on the experience of countries in Asia, particularly of China (WFP, 1994c) and India (Shaw and Clay 1993).

From its inception, WFP has been supporting employment-creation projects for poverty alleviation and food security in food deficit countries in areas such as water management, environmental protection, transport infrastructure, market restructuring, price stabilization and food reserves. Of special importance, WFP has been the largest source of assistance in the UN system for projects involving and benefiting poor women in developing countries. Women have been a key target group not only because they (and their children) have often been the worst affected by disasters but because they play a pivot role in the process of survival, recuperation, rehabilitation and the return to household food security (Quisumbing *et al.*, 1995; WFP, 1992b).

WFP-assisted development projects have also been designed to expand rapidly when emergencies occur to provide additional food and employment when household food production or incomes collapse. Quick-action projects have been approved for reconstruction and rehabilitation activities after disasters, subsequently followed by full-fledged development projects. Advance shipments have been made to approved projects following early warning of an impending disaster to allow the expansion of project activities to accommodate disaster victims, rather than provide emergency assistance. And employment has been provided in the agricultural off-season, and in times of emergency, to strengthen local infrastructure and sustain economic activity, thereby preventing people from migrating from their homes in search of food and employment, keeping the household unit intact and speeding the recovery process after emergencies have struck.

WFP emergency operations and PROs may also be adapted, if circumstances allow, to facilitate development initiatives. WFP has collaborated with other agencies so that emergency food aid can be combined with financial and technical assistance to provide disaster victims with employment in food-for-work programmes, building on the experience of countries in Asia. In urban areas, where purchasing power exists, it might not be appropriate to distribute free food during emergencies. Food might be sold through the market, thereby meeting food needs, restraining the rise of food prices, encouraging the continued functioning, or revitalization, of local markets, and generating funds for humanitarian and reconstruction purposes. Another dimension of emergencies relates to returnees and the demobilization of soldiers when disasters and conflict end. Food aid can help tide people over the period of resettlement and readjustment, and help engage them in reconstruction and rehabilitation work.

Experience has shown that to be fully effective, WFP food aid must be coordinated with financial and technical assistance provided by other agencies. WFP has been a strong supporter of the need to improve and strengthen coordination within and outside the UN system, in accordance with its mandate. More needs to be done, however, and more systematically, to ensure that a higher proportion of WFP assistance is provided through co-funded projects, in association with other UN and bilateral agencies, and in closer collaboration with NGOs. WFP country directors now have the delegated authority to provide resources to NGOs up to $200 000, or 5 per cent of the total WFP food commitment to a development project, to enable them to implement their own projects, provided they have similar objectives and target groups as WFP. WFP country directors also have authority to purchase up to $50 000 of food locally in advance for an emergency operation approved by WFP, which can also be used by NGOs.

There are significant differences between emergencies arising from war and civil conflict and those caused by drought and sudden natural disasters. In the former, peace-making and peace-keeping operations linked to humanitarian relief are required to ensure that food aid and other essential needs reach the afflicted population. Prevention and preparedness measures may be difficult and complex, and rehabilitation leading to development more protracted. Paradoxically, refugees and displaced people might be better off that the poor, indigenous population that hosts them as only they may be entitled to external assistance. In both man-made and drought-induced emergencies, a broad area development approach to the relief-development continuum should be adopted that takes into account the needs of the entire population – refugees, displaced, returnees and indigenous, and the totality of national and local resources and aid available, in comprehensive and integrated programmes.

In response to the call by the donor community to improve coordination among UN agencies in emergency situations, the UN Secretary-General created a Department of Humanitarian Affairs (DHA) in April 1992. Close cooperation has been established between the DHA, the UN Security Council, the UN Department of Political Affairs, UN peace-keeping operations and NGOs in order to reach people in distress who might be isolated in inaccessible areas with relief aid and protect their lives and those of relief workers and their supplies, in accordance with the Secretary-General's *Agenda for Peace* (Boutros-Ghali, 1992).

The DHA provides leadership in the United Nations system's response to emergencies, including: the promotion of efforts to address their root causes and to facilitate the transition from relief to development; the formulation of an overall policy framework for action; the setting up of coordination arrangements at the country level and assigning responsibility among the UN agencies concerned; and the consolidation of inter-UN agency appeals for assistance. A Central Emergency Revolving Find (CERF) of $50 million, managed by DHA, came into operation in May 1992. DHA chairs meetings of a UN Inter-Agency Standing Committee, established as an important instrument for UN system-wide co-ordination in emergencies. WFP has established close working arrangements with DHA.

However, the linkage between providing humanitarian assistance and peace-keeping and peace-making operations remains dangerously confused. The role of the UN in providing humanitarian relief to those caught up in war zones is clear and accepted. But how far should the UN go in containing or mitigating the fighting? Should the UN cross the Mogadishu line between peace-keeping and peace-making, transcend sovereignty, cut out the political process and 'leave it to the military', even though there may be serious political differences and a selective application of UN mandates, resolutions and sanctions? There are as yet no clearly established rules, guidelines and modalities. In conflict situations, various attempts have been made to make food aid part of the solution, and not part of the problem. In some cases, there has been a deliberate attempt to separate humanitarian relief from peace-keeping operations. In others, humanitarian aid has been provided under military escort. And in still other situations, military action has gone first, clearing areas of conflict before relief assistance has been supplied. There is no easy solution and much will depend on the nature of the conflict in each situation.

23.6   ISSUES AND CONCERNS: AN AGENDA FOR FUTURE ACTION

WFP's experience has highlighted the need for action on certain key issues and concerns.

A new food aid regime

Conclusion of the GATT Uruguay Round, the signing and ratification of the Final Act (GATT Secretariat, 1994), and the setting up of the World Trade Organization provide a major opportunity for establishing a new food aid regime within a liberalizing global economy (Shaw and Singer, 1995). A large part of so-called 'trade' does not take place as straight market transactions at free international prices. It is conducted through a labyrinth of various forms of bilateral agreements that provide discounts from the 'commercial' international price (itself reduced by overhanging surpluses and domestic production subsidies) in many direct and indirect ways. This 'grey area' food aid, which is perhaps quadruple the level of statistically recorded food aid (12.9 million tons in 1994) does not reach the poor and food insecure but is provided for short-run political and commercial (market protection and penetration) purposes.

If this hidden food aid is now forced out into the open and brought within the disciplines of food aid as defined in the Final Act, a major step would have been taken in dealing with the world hunger problem and, by extension, with the eradication of poverty.

A broadened definition of emergency assistance

Much could be gained if the definition of emergency assistance was expanded from an immediate, short-term response to provide relief to encompass pre-disaster and post-disaster action and aid in the continuum between relief and development.[17] Conceptually, disasters would no longer be seen in isolation but in their full setting, and their effects on development would be taken into account. Resources and assistance would be provided for disaster prevention, preparedness and mitigation measures and would not dry up when required for rehabilitation and reconstruction after disasters have occurred, thereby helping the development process. And the planning, design and implementation of assistance programmes for relief and development would be executed by integrated government and aid administrations within common legislative and execution procedures and financial provisions.

A truly multilateral and fully subscribed IEFR

Current multilateral arrangements for responding rapidly to emergencies would be largely adequate if donors respected the provisions that they approved. These include the IEFR and its IRA, and the special provisions from PROs. While the IEFR has improved and increased WFP's ability to respond to emergencies, it has not lived up fully to its original expectations as a multilateral facility for initial quick-reaction to disasters whenever and wherever they occurred. Contributions to the IEFR have often not been announced in advance. A high proportion of contributions have been tied and designated by donors to specific emergencies and food commodities *after* emergencies have occurred, eroding the multilateral nature of the facility and making it difficult to respond rapidly and flexibly to all emergencies. Contributions to the Reserve have fluctuated considerably in response to demand. And cash contributions have fallen short of requirement.

As a result, WFP usually has access to only about 100 000 tons of food at the beginning of each calendar year to programme for emergencies. Additional resources may be mobilized through special appeals but this can increase the lead time for delivery of emergency food aid by several months. Only 10 per cent of IEFR contributions were made in advance in 1994. Consequently, a timely and adequate response to all, and especially the less publicized, emergencies has proved to be difficult. WFP's response was therefore often inadequate in the initial phases of major emergencies owing to the lack of cash resources to purchase and deliver the food required (WFP, 1995).

Improved early warning and response arrangements

Experience has repeatedly shown that accurate, timely and commonly available information of an impending disaster, coupled with sound and speedy response, are key factors in mitigating their effects. Significant improvements have been made in addressing emergencies since FAO's GIEWS became operational. The almost textbook precision of the international response to the major drought in southern Africa in the early 1990s, when an estimated 18 million people face the spectre of famine and starvation, showed the value of improved telecommunication systems. Planning and scheduling of food aid shipments were facilitated, port and inland transport congestion avoided, costs reduced, and timely delivery ensured.

There are now good prospects for major improvements in early warning and tracking systems through the application of remote sensing and satellite imagery linked to a worldwide computerized information superhighway. Such systems should have common, multilateral ownership. They would produce common information that would have the confidence of all concerned, and would produce a common response. However, for the full benefits of these systems to be realized, they will need to be backed up by response systems with adequate resources in order to react quickly and effectively to the onset of emergencies.

The United Nations organizations have developed a valuable network of early warning systems from sudden, natural emergencies and slow, maturing disasters related the crop failure and impending famine caused by drought and other factors. No such systems have been developed for man-made emergencies. A major problem has been the principle of state sovereignty, which has been conventionally respected by the UN system in conformity with Article 2.7 of Chapter 1 of the United Nations Charter. But this Article also states that 'this principle shall not prejudice the application of enforcement measures under Chapter VII of the UN Charter on 'Action with respect to Threats to the Peace, Breaches of the Peace, and Acts of Aggression' (UN, 1945). This provision has assumed particular significance not only as man-made emergencies have increased in incidence, scale and duration but as many of them have occurred within, not between, countries. This has had practical consequences. WFP's General Regulations were amended in 1992 to allow it to provide humanitarian relief assistance at the request of the UN Secretary-General instead of waiting for a request from a national government, which might never come (WFP, 1993).

In his *Agenda for Peace*, the UN Secretary-General points to the need for an early warning system with political indicators to assess whether a threat to peace exists and to analyse what action might be taken by the United Nations to alleviate it (Boutros-Ghali 1992, pp. 15–16). Recommendations for preventive action would be made by the Secretary-General to the Security Council and other UN agencies as appropriate. He further recommends that ECOSOC provide reports to the Security Council on those economic and social developments that may, unless mitigated, threaten peace and security. He also recognized that regional arrangements and organizations have an important role in early warning and response. The returns from national and donor investment in these early warning and response systems would be considerable. Human and economic suffering and damage could be avoided or mitigated, and the enormous cost and diversion of resources in protracted relief and peace-keeping operation saved. An international programme combining financial aid and technology and skills transfer should therefore be given the highest priority.

Co-ordinated action in a multilateral framework

As the report of the expert group pointed out, there is good reason to re-commend that a multilateral framework should be used for co-ordinated action. There is no dogmatic reason to assume that multilateral, bilateral or NGO operations are preferable. Each has its comparative advantage that should be used to maximum benefit in each specific situation. But no single donor or aid agency has the resources, competence or capacity to address the problems of developing countries alone. A multilateral frame-work of action would help to fuse the many and diverse contributions that could be made, take the politics out of aid, and focus on the developmental needs of developing countries through their own development plans and programmes.

Steps are now being taken to improve coordination within the UN system, although serious problems remain, especially to coordinate action at the country level where it matters most. However, increasing concern is being expressed about future international aid. First, there is a general expectation that aid will decline in real terms. Secondly, an increasing pro-portion of that aid will go to address the symptoms, and not the causes, of development problems in Third World countries, mainly in the form of relief. Thirdly, it is expected that an increasing proportion of aid will be provided bilaterally rather than multilaterally through the UN system, in an uncoordinated way, and directed mainly for political and commercial objectives. Fourthly, of the aid this is provided multilaterally, the major portion will go through the Bretton Woods institutions (the International

Monetary Fund and the World Bank), mainly for macroeconomic adjustment and reform measures, with the remainder going to the rest of the UN system for human resource development and damage limitation. Fifthly, assistance that is now going to countries of the former Yugoslavia and Soviet Union will be at the expense of that going to the developing countries, particularly in Sub-Saharan Africa, which will result in the marginalization of that region. And lastly, increasing conditionality will be applied to assistance by donors instead of accepting the principle of contractuality, which would apply conditions as much to the giver as to the receiver of aid.

Addressing emergencies is assuming greater urgency in aid agencies, attracting more and more staff time and attention. As most agencies have had their staff levels frozen or reduced, this must inevitably result in decreased attention to development. Even if resources for development were to remain unaffected, therefore, the impact of those resources may be reduced as less staff time is available to ensure that they are used in the most effective and creative ways to get at the root causes of chronic vulnerability. The resources of national governments are similarly likely to be diverted by increasing pressures to meet immediate relief needs. This shift in attention and resources from development to short-term relief, and from chronic to transitory vulnerability to disasters, is occurring despite much recent work which pointed to the complex interrelationships between the different causes of disasters and vulnerability to them. (see, for example, Dreze and Sen, 1989). Thus, at the very time when more is being understood, it appears likely that fewer resources, manpower and attention will be made available to help fight the problem.

Vulnerability to disasters is not a static phenomenon (Crawshaw and Shaw, 1995). There have been important recent shifts in terms of who are the most vulnerable; the causes of vulnerability; regional variations; and the ability or otherwise to cope. Yet the international community has not shown itself to be well able to adjust to these shifts. Too little attention has been paid to the dynamics of vulnerability, and to address causes, not symptoms. New approaches are needed to address the changing incidence of vulnerability as national and international situations evolve. New indicators of vulnerability are also required. Mapping populations and areas that are particularly vulnerable would be a useful first step in targeting assistance (Shaw and Hutchinson, 1993). Generals have been accused of fighting the next war with the tactics of the last. As a generalization, that sentiment seems to be true of development and relief agencies. The challenge is to change this perspective in the future.

Policy framework: understanding emergencies

In conclusion, while there has been much operational experience gained in addressing disasters, there remains the need for a clear policy framework based on a sound understanding of the causes of different types of emergencies, how they affect different people and, if external assistance, including food aid, is required, the best ways in which to provide it.

It is important to disaggregate the effects of disasters both to better understand their full effects and to design and implement intervention programmes that address their impact, especially on poor people. The poor are not a homogeneous group. There are significant differences among them, and in the solutions to their problems. Compare, for example, small farmers on resource-rich, and poor, land; pastoralists; landless workers; the poor in urban areas; and women who are single heads of households. Distinction should also be made between the poor and the poorest – those who have the least assets, are more prone to mortality, illness and low physical performance, often associated with chronic malnutrition and related diseases – who may not be able to respond quickly to assistance and improved conditions.

Targeting is a key concern in the design and implementation of intervention programmes. It is a strategic factor in ensuring access and outreach to the poor. Four considerations have an especially important effect on the effectiveness or otherwise of targeting: criteria for selection; administrative feasibility and costs; participation by the poor themselves; and the type, form, method and level of resource transfer.

Emergency relief is a highly emotive subject. Provoked by the media, the basic instinct is to dispatch food and other essentials with the greatest possible speed to people in distress without a precise understanding of what caused the problem and what constitutes the best response. Or, in solving the immediate problem, are more problems created for the process of rehabilitation and subsequent development?

A study of the major famines of the past has revealed that starvation and death occurred not so much because of the unavailability of food but because poor people lost access ('entitlement') to it either because they could no longer produce the food they needed or because they no longer had the income to buy it (Sen, 1981). To ensure food security, it was realized that not only should there be increased food production in developing countries, and stability of supplies, but that poor people should have access to the food they need either by producing it themselves or by having employment to provide the money to buy it.

At the same time, it was noted that food security could either be chronic or transitory (World Bank, 1986). Chronic food insecurity involves a continuously inadequate diet caused by a persistent inability to acquire food by whatever means. Transitory food insecurity is a temporary decline in a household's access to enough food arising from instability of food production, prices or income. Policies and programmes for reducing chronic and transitory food insecurity differ. For the former, they include increasing food supply (through production, imports or improving market integration), subsidizing consumer prices and targeted income transfers. For the latter, they may include stabilizing supplies and prices and assisting vulnerable groups directly through aid programmes. In any country, the food insecure comprise different groups. Cost-effective programmes to improve their food security should be tailored to the needs and circumstances of each of them.

Notes

1. The author was associated with the World Food Programme for over 30 years, first as a Consultant, then as a Senior Evaluation Officer, and subsequently as Senior Economist and Head of the Policy Unit in the Office of the Executive Director, Economic Adviser, and, finally, as Chief of the Policy Affairs Service. He has collaborated with Hans Singer in several publications on food aid.
2. Hans Singer did his early professional work by immersing himself in the problems of the depressed areas of Britain that experienced high and protracted unemployment in the inter-war years. He carried this profound experience into his subsequent work on development economics and policy and on developing countries at the United Nations and, subsequently, at the Institute of Development Studies, University of Sussex (Rostow, 1990).
3. The full text of the United States proposal, made by George McGovern, the first Director of the Food for Peace Programme, Executive Office of the President in the Kennedy Administration is given in FAO 1962, Appendix 4, pp. 121–2, and is reproduced in FAO, 1985, Appendix 4, pp. 315–16.
4. An autobiographical account of Singer's involvement in these initiatives is given in Singer (1984) 'The Terms of Trade Controversy and the Evolution of Soft Financing: Early Years in the U.N.', in G.M. Meier and D. Seers (eds) *Pioneers in Development* (New York: Published for the World Bank by Oxford University Press) pp. 275–311.
5. The expert group consisted of Dr M.R. Benedict, Professor of Agricultural Economics, University of California at Berkeley; Dr. J. Figuer, ex-President of the Republic of Costa Rica; Dr V.K.R.V. Rao, ex-Vice-Chancellor, University of New Delhi, Director of the New Delhi Institute of Economic Growth, and former Ph.D. student with Singer at Cambridge University in England; Dr P.N. Rosenstein-Rodan, Professor of Economics, Massachusetts Institute of Technology; and Dr H.W. Singer who was designated as Principal Officer, Office of the Under-Secretary for Economic and Social Affairs, United Nations, New York and appointed chairman of the group.

6. Keynes in his *Proposal for an International Clearing Union* (April 1943), which became the basic document for the establishment of the Bretton Woods system, stated that we need to recycle surpluses from strong to weak areas and, thus, offset the contractionist pressures which might otherwise overwhelm in social disorder the hopes for a better post-war world. As he further stated, we need to repeat in the international field the same miracle, already performed in the domestic field, of using finance as a tool 'for turning stone into bread'. Singer suggested that 'This Keynesian vision also governs the objectives of turning the stone of financial and food surpluses in the industrial world, and of under-employed resources and malnourished children in the Third World into the bread of human investment in healthier and more productive children' (Singer and Longhurst, 1986, p. 33).

7. US food aid shipments to all countries (not only developing countries) in 1959/60 amounted to about $1500 million (at Commodity Credit Corporation costs), excluding ocean transportation.

8. Rosenstein-Rodan undoubtedly had a strong influence here. He noted that the general principles of an international aid policy were first studied at the UN Economic Commission for Latin America (ECLA) preparatory conference for *Quintandinha* in the summer of 1954. These principles were used in the doctrine of aid policy in his 1961 paper (Rosenstein-Rodan, 1961) and later used and applied in the *Alliance for Progress*, the United States aid programme for Latin America. He had also developed the theory of the 'big push', that is, that there is a minimum level of resources that must be devoted to a development programme if it is to have any chance of success, which was used in the report of the MIT Center for International Studies on the objectives of US economic assistance programmes for the US Senate in 1957 (MIT, 1957; Rosenstein-Rodan, 1984).

9. The IMF introduced a *Compensatory Financing Facility* in 1963 and a *Compensatory and Contingency Financing Facility* in 1988 to help developing countries overcome these problems. These facilities have been relatively little used mainly owing to the strict conditionalities applied to them.

10. Paragraph 5 of the FAO *Principles of Surplus Disposal* states: 'In weighing the advantages to countries benefiting from special disposal measures against the possible harm done to other countries, account must be taken of the relationship of possible sacrifices to the economic capacity of the country concerned, and in particular of the effects of such sacrifices on their rate of development' (FAO, 1954).

11. Writing over 20 years later, Singer recognized that the expert group's report did not deal with a number of important areas. He noted that: the report had little to say about emergencies and did not foreshaddow the creation of the IEFR; that while referring to the nutritional needs of school children and students, it made little reference to the critical importance of adequate nutrition at the preschool stage and for expectant and nursing mothers; and that it did not deal with triangular transactions as an important modality for providing food aid (Singer, 1983).

12. Drawing on the MIT (1957) study on the objectives of US economic assistance programmes (FAO, 1962, p. 104).

13. Singer recalls that when presenting the expert group's report to the Director-General of FAO (B.R. Sen) and the Secretary-General of the United Nations

(U Thant), he was doubtful of the title 'Expanded Program of Surplus Food Utilization' and raised the question as to whether it should be something more 'developmental and humanitarian'. He cannot recall how and when the term 'World Food Programme' first came to be applied to the administrative unit in place of a 'Surplus Food Utilization Unit'. He was largely responsible for maintaining the United Nations' interest in launching WFP as a joint UN/FAO undertaking. He records that the expert group felt very much aware of the vision of the first Director-General of FAO, John Boyd-Orr, in proposing the creation of a World Food Board and adds 'Although, like much of Keynes's vision at Bretton Woods, this proved to be Utopian, I can say we felt that in a modest way we were following in the footsteps of both Boyd-Orr and of Keynes'. Singer also recognizes the debt the expert group had to the earlier work of FAO on the use of food surpluses, particularly the pilot study conducted by Ezekiel in India in 1955 (Ezekiel, 1955). (Singer, 'Multilateral Food Aid in Context'. Personal Note, Institute of Development Studies, 30 August 1991.

14. WFP was established as a three-year experimental programme by parallel resolutions of the FAO Conference and the United Nations General Assembly adopted on 24 November 1961 and 19 December 1961 respectively. WFP was established on a continuing basis, 'for as long as multilateral food aid is found feasible and desirable', by parallel resolutions adopted by of the two bodies on 6 December and 20 December 1965 respectively.

15. In his first address to the United Nations General Assembly on 15 September 1961, President John F. Kennedy proposed that the decade of the 1960s be designated as the 'United Nations Decade of Development' under which 'the United Nations existing efforts in promoting economic growth can be expanded and coordinated' (United Nations 1961 'Official Records of the General Assembly', 16th Session. Plenary Meetings, vol. 1 (New York: United Nations, pp. 53–9). Singer was given responsibility in the UN Secretariat for drafting the *Proposals for Action* for the Decade, which included references to the roles of WFP both for development and in emergencies. (United Nations 1962 *The United Nations Development Decade: Proposals for Action*. New York: United Nations, pp. 91–92, and Personal Communication, 26 January 1996).

16. Singer has been a persistent critic of adjustment programmes as advocated by the IMF and the World Bank for being unnecessarily contractionist and harmful to the poor, and a strong advocate of the benefits that food aid can bring to the adjustment process (see, for example, Singer 1991).

17. Singer has advocated this should be done (see Singer, 1994).

References

Blau, G. (1954) *Disposal of Agricultural Surpluses* (Rome: FAO).
—— (1956) *Functions of a World Food Reserve: Scope and Limitations* (Rome: FAO).
Boutros-Ghali, B. (1992) *An Agenda for Peace* (New York: United Nations).
Braun, J. von (1991) *A Policy Agenda for Famine Prevention in Africa*, Food Policy Report (Washington, DC: International Food Policy Research Institute).

Clay, E. and J. Shaw (eds) (1987) *Poverty, Development and Food*, Essays in Honour of H.W. Singer on this 75th Birthday. (London: Macmillan). See 'Introduction' by E. Clay and J. Shaw, pp. 1–5.

Cornia, A., R. Jolly and F. Stewart (eds) (1987) *Adjustment with a Human Face. Protecting the Vulnerable and Promoting Growth. A Study by UNICEF* (Oxford: Clarendon Press).

Crawshaw, B. and J. Shaw (1995) 'Changing vulnerability to food security and the international response. the experience of the World Food Programme', in T.E. Downing (ed.) *Climate Change and World Food Security* (Berlin: Springer) pp. 207–26.

Dreze, J. and A. Sen (1989) *Hunger and Public Action* (Oxford: Clarendon Press).

Ezekiel, M. (1955) *Uses of Agricultural Surpluses to Finance Economic Development in Under-developed Countries: A Pilot Study in India* (Rome: FAO).

FAO (1954) *Disposal of Agricultural Surpluses. Principles Recommended by the FAO* (Rome: FAO). Subsequently revised and expanded in four versions as *Principles of Surplus Disposal and Consultative Obligations of Member States* (3rd edn, 1992).

—— (1962) *Expanded Program of Surplus Food Utilization*. Report by the Expert Group to the Director-General of FAO. Published in FAO, *Development through Food. A Strategy for Surplus Utilization*, Freedom from Hunger Campaign Basic Study no. 2, revd edn (Rome: FAO) pp. 69–1120; republished in FAO (1985) *Food Aid for Development*, Economic and Social Development Paper, no. 34 (Rome: FAO) pp. 278–314.

Gatt Secretariat (1994) *The Results of the Uruguay Round of Multilateral Trade Negotiations. The Legal Texts* (Geneva: General Agreement on Tariffs and Trade Secretariat).

Hay, R.H. (1986) 'Food Aid and Relief-Development Strategies', *WFP Occasional Papers*, no. 8 (Rome: WFP), reproduced in *Disasters*, vol. 10, no. 4 (1986) pp. 273–87.

Hopkins, R.F. (1992) 'Reform in the International Food Aid Regime: The Role of Consensual Knowledge', *International Organization*, vol. 46, no. 1, pp. 225–64.

Kennedy, J.F. (1960) 'Press Release, 31 October'. Meyer Feldman Papers, Box 9, File Food for Peace Program (10/60–1/3/61) (Boston: John F. Kennedy Library).

Lamartine-Yates, P. (1955) *So Bold An Aim* (Rome: FAO).

Maxwell, S. and M. Buchanan-Smith (eds) (1994) 'Linking Relief and Development' *IDS Bulletin*, vol. 25, no. 4 (Brighton: Institute of Development Studies). MIT (Massachusetts Institute of Technology) Center for International Studies (1957) *The Objectives of United States Economic Assistance Programs*, For the Special Committee to Study the Foreign Aid Program (Washington, DC: United States Senate).

Oakenshott, W.F., A.D.K. Owen and H.W. Singer (1937) *Men Without Work: Report to the Pilgrim Trust* (Cambridge University Press).

Quisumbing, A., L. Brown, H. Feldstein, L. Haddad and C. Pena (1995) *Women: The Key to Food Security* (Washington, DC: International Food Policy Research Institute Food Policy Report).

Rosenstein-Rodan, P.N. (1961) 'International Aid for Underdeveloped Countries', *Review of Economics and Statistics*, vol. 43, no. 2 (May).

—— (1984) 'Natura Facit Saltum: Analysis of the Disequilibrium Growth Process', in G.M Meier and D. Seers (eds) *Pioneers in Development* (New York: Published for the World Bank by Oxford University Press), pp. 205–26.

Rostow, W.W. (1990) 'H.W. Singer', in *Theorists of Economic Growth from David Hume to the Present* (New York and Oxford: Oxford University Press) pp. 411–14.

Schultz, T.W. (1960) 'Value of U.S. Farm Surpluses to Underdeveloped Countries', *Journal of Farm Economics*, vol. 42, no. 5 (December) pp. 1019–30.

Sen, A. (1981) *Poverty and Famines: An Essay on Entitlement and Deprivation* (Oxford: Clarendon Press).

Shaw, D.J. (1970) 'The Mechanism and Distribution of Food Aid: Multilateral Food Aid for Economic and Social Development', *Journal of World Trade Law*, vol. 4, no. 2 (March/April) pp. 207–37.

—— (1986) 'Poverty, Development and Food: Basic Needs Revisited. Report of the Seminar in honour of H.W. Singer on his 75th Birthday' *IDS Discussion Paper*, no. 217 (Brighton: Institute of Development Studies, June).

—— (1995) 'Future Directions for Development and Relief with Food Aid', in J. von Braun (ed.) *Employment for Poverty Reduction and Food Security* (Washington DC: International Food Policy Research Institute) pp. 252–74.

—— (1996) 'The World Food Programme and Emergency Relief', *Advanced Development Management Program Series* no. 20 (Tokyo: Sophia University).

—— and Glay, E. (eds) (1993) *World Food Aid: Experiences of Recipients and Donors* (Rome, London and Portsmouth, New Hampshire, USA: World Food Programme in association with James Currey and Heinemann): Ch. 3. 'India: Towards Cereal Self-Sufficiency and the Transformation of Food Aid' (pp. 56–75); ch. 17. 'United States of America: Changing Priorities in Promoting Development, Humanitarian Relief and Agricultural Trade' (pp. 215–38).

—— and Hutchinson, B. (eds) (1993) 'Disaster Mitigation'. Special Issue of the *Arid Lands Newsletter*, vol. 34 (Fall/Winter) (Tucson: University of Arizona).

—— and Singer, H. (eds) (1988) 'Food Policy, Food Aid and Economic Adjustment', *Food Policy* (Special Issue), vol. 13, no. 1. See 'Introduction' by J. Shaw and H. Singer, pp. 2–9.

—— and Singer, H.W. (1995) 'A Future Food Aid Regime: Implications of the Final Act of the GATT Uruguay Round', IDS *Discussion Paper*, no. 352 (Brighton: Institute of Development Studies). See different versions under the title 'A Future Food Aid Regime: Implications of the Final Act of the Uruguay Round', in *Food Policy*, vol. 21, no. 4 (August 1966); and in H. O'Neill and J. Toye (eds) (1996) *A World Without Hunger?* (London: Macmillan for the Development Studies Association).

Singer, H.W. (1940) *Unemployment and the Unemployed* (London: King & Son).

—— (1943) *Can We Afford Beveridge?* (London: Fabian Society Research Pamphlet).

—— (1964) 'An Example of the New Pragmatism: Toward a Theory of Preinvestment', in H.W. Singer *International Development: Growth and Change* (New York: McGraw-Hill Series in International Development) pp. 18–25.

—— (1965) 'External Aid: For Plans or Projects', *Economic Journal*, vol. 75, pp. 539–45.

—— (with the collaboration of S.J. Maxwell) (1983) 'Development through Food: Twenty Years' Experience', in *Report of the World Food Programme/*

Government of the Netherlands Seminar on Food Aid (The Hague, 3–5 October 1983) pp. 31–46.

—— (1984) 'The Terms of Trade Controversy and the Evolution of Soft Financing: Early Years in the U.N.', in G.M. Meier and D. Seers (eds) *Pioneers in Development* (New York: Published for the World Bank by Oxford University Press, pp. 275–311).

—— (1986) 'Some Reflections on Past Interests and Activities', in D.J. Shaw (1986).

—— (1991) 'Food Aid and Structural Adjustment in Sub-Saharan Africa', in E. Clay and O. Stokke (eds) *Food Aid Reconsidered: Assessing the Impact on Third World Countries* (London: Frank Cass) pp. 180–90.

—— (1992) 'The Influence of Schumpeter and Keynes: On the Development of a Development Economist'; revised version of a paper originally presented at a Conference on *Zur deutschsprachigen wirtschaftswissenschaftlichen Emigration nach* 1933 (University of Hohenheim).

—— (1993) 'Statement on the Occasion of the World Food Programme's 30th Anniversary' (Rome: WFP).

—— (1994) 'Two Views of Food Aid', in R. Prendergast and F. Stewart (eds) *Market Forces and World Development* (London: Macmillan for the Development Studies Association).

—— (1996) 'Linking Relief and Development', *Advanced Development Management Program Series*, no. 19 (Tokyo: Sophia University).

—— and R. Longhurst (1986) 'The Role of Food Aid in Promoting the Welfare of Children in Developing Countries', in J.P. Greaves and D.J. Shaw (eds) *Food Aid and the Well-Being of Children in the Developing World* (New York: United Nations Children's Fund and World Food Programme) pp. 27–66.

—— J. Wood and T. Jennings (1987) *Food Aid. The Challenge and the Opportunity* (Oxford: Clarendon Press).

Sukin, H.E. (1988) 'US Food Aid for Countries Implementing Structural Adjustment', *Food Policy*, vol. 13, no. 1, pp. 98–103.

UN (1945) *Charter of the United Nations* (New York: United Nations).

—— (1960) *Provision of Food Surpluses to Food-Deficient Peoples through the United Nations System*, United Nations General Assembly Resolution 1496 (XV) adopted at the 908th Plenary Meeting, 27 October (New York: United Nations).

—— (1975a) *Report of the World Food Conference, Rome 5–16 November 1974*, Doc. E/CONF. 65/20. (New York; United Nations). See particularly Resolution XVIII, 'An Improved Food Aid Policy', pp. 15–16.

—— (1975b) *Development and International Economic Cooperation*, Resolution 3362 (S-VII) adopted by the UN General Assembly during its Seventh Special Session, 1–16 September. UN General Assembly Official Records, Supplement no. 1, Doc. A/10301 (New York: United Nations).

—— (1991) *Strengthening of the Coordination of Humanitarian Emergency Assistance of the United Nations*, United Nations General Assembly resolution 46/182, adopted on 19 December 1991 (New York: United Nations).

UNHCR (1993) *The State of the World's Refugees. The Challenge of Protection* (London: Penguin).

UNICEF (1995) *The State of the World's Children* (Oxford: Oxford University Press for the United Nations Children's Fund).

Wallerstein, M.B. (1980) *Food for War-Food for Peace: United States Food Aid in a Global Context* (Cambridge, Mass.: MIT Press).

WFP (1964) *Synopsis of World Food Programme Policies*, Doc. FP1/1 (Rome: WFP).

—— (1965) *Report on the World Food Programme by the Executive Director* (Rome: WFP).

—— (1970) *Food Aid and Related Issues during the Second Development Decade.* Report of the Intergovernmental Committee of the World Food Programme in response to Resolution 2462 (XXIII) of the United Nations General Assembly. Doc. WFP/IGC: 17/5/Rev. 1 (Rome: WFP) p. 15.

—— (1978) 'Modalities of Operation of the International Emergency Food Reserve', in *Report of the Sixth Session of the United Nations/FAO Committee on Food Aid Policies and Programmes*, Doc. WFP/CFA 6/21, Annex IV (Rome: WFP).

—— (1987) *Roles of Food Aid in Structural and Sector Adjustment*, Doc. WFP/CFA:23/5 Add/1. (Rome: WFP).

—— (1989) *Review of Protracted Emergency Operations for Refugees and Displaced Persons*, Doc. WFP/CFA:27/P/7 (Rome: WFP).

—— (1992a) *Disaster Mitigation and Rehabilitation in Africa*, Doc. CFA:34/P/7-B (Rome: WFP).

—— (1992b) *Food Aid Working for Women. The World Food Programme and Women in Development* (Rome: WFP).

—— (1993) *Basic Documents for the World Food Programme. General Regulations, Part D. Procedures. Eligibility for Assistance*, 5th edn, September (Rome: WFP).

—— (1994a) *The World Food Programme and the Programme Approach*, Doc. CFA:38/P/6 (Rome: WFP).

—— (1994b) *WFP Mission Statement*, Doc. CFA:38/P/5 (Rome: WFP).

—— (1994c) *China's National Experience with food Aid Policies and Programmes*, Doc. CFA:38/P/4. (Rome: WFP).

—— (1995) *Annual Report of the Executive Director 1994: Linking Relief and Development*, Doc. CFA:39/4 (Rome: WFP).

World Bank (1986) *Poverty and Hunger. Issues and Options for Food Security in Developing Countries* (Washington, DC: World Bank Policy Study).

24 Employment and Development

Samir Radwan

24.1 INTRODUCTION

'Employment is a very vital element in economic development ... Employment, just as education and health, is not only an instrument for economic growth, but it is important in itself because it constitutes part of the very purpose of development.' (Hans Singer, 1969)

The history of economic thought on employment and development over the last half a century cannot be complete without reference to the contribution of Hans Singer. Between his early writings on the post-Recession crisis of unemployment in England, and recent reflections on employment within the context of globalization, there has been a continuous quest to set up the terms of the debate.

Other chapters in this volume address the contribution by Hans Singer in the areas of trade and aid, an outstanding contribution by any standards. In this chapter, I shall focus on his thinking on the relationship between employment and development by reflecting on three moments in time: the work done for the Pilgrim Trust in 1938 where he documented the conditions of 'men without work'; his contribution to the ILO's World Employment Programme, and in particular the Kenya Report which gave birth to the term 'informal sector'; and his critique of the recent neo-liberal writings on employment in a globalising economy. My contention is that there is a clear thread that runs through all these contributions: that is the concern for the human aspect of employment. Hans Singer managed to change the terms of debate in those three crucial periods.

In 1938, The Pilgrim Trust enquiry published an influential report (*Men Without Work*) on the problems faced by the unemployed in the UK. One of the key researchers of this enquiry was Hans Singer. An outstanding feature of the enquiry was the emphasis given to understanding the human aspect of the problem of unemployment.

While the Report [*Men Without Work*] has the objectivity appropriate to a piece of scientific research, it should never be forgotten that the enquiry was concerned with the actual experiences, too often the sufferings of human beings and that the formal array of figures in the statistical tables which have been compiled relate to living men and women, not to abstractions.[2]

Throughout his long and illustrious career, Hans Singer continued to brilliantly expound the need to give economics a human face (and never a face lift!) and to always ground theorising in concrete situations and problems. We at the ILO owe a great deal to Hans Singer for his close involvement with the World Employment Programme and for ensuring that the human factor in economic development is never forgotten. It was thus a great honour and pleasure to have been invited to present a paper at the conference in celebration of Hans Singer's 85th birthday.

The global crisis of employment

Over 60 years since the Great Depression of the 1930s, the world is once again confronted by a severe crisis of unemployment not only in the industrialized but also in the developing and transitional countries. In the industrialized countries the post-war era of full employment has come to an end and there has since the early 1970s been a steady rise in the level of unemployment. In large parts of the developing world, apart from East and South-east Asia, the growth of modern sector employment has declined significantly while low productivity informal sector activities continue to expand. In east and central Europe, the collapse of centrally planned economic systems has given rise to unprecedented mass unemployment.

It thus comes as no surprise that the concern with employment has assumed worldwide proportions, featuring strongly in recent meetings of the G-7, the OECD, the European Union and at the 1995 Copenhagen World Summit on Social Development. This concern has in part been fuelled by the heightened competitive environment resulting from the growing integration of the world economy – or globalization. These are truly revolutionary times in which we live in. Rapid technological progress and the nearly universal adoption of market-based policies for development have resulted in an unprecedented growth in international trade, flows of foreign direct investments (FDI) and globalised production systems. This process of globalization has evoked both positive and negative reactions. On the one hand, they are seen to offer the prospect of gains from freer trade and improved allocation of resources. On the other, they pose new problems for national policy autonomy and the economic and social adjustments that are entailed (Lee, 1995).

While present forecasts suggest that globalization will have a significant positive impact on growth and employment (Greenaway and Milner, 1995), there are very real concerns about its possible negative effects. In the words of Michel Hansenne, the Director General of the ILO:

> An important question that has to be asked is whether the economic forces of the international market will suffice on their own to guarantee social progress for everyone, everywhere. The liberalization of international trade and capital movements certainly offers reasonable possibilities of worldwide growth, employment creation and poverty alleviation. But there is no guarantee that greater social justice will automatically result from it. On the contrary, it will impose a heavy burden of adjustment on all countries, and on all social groups within countries, and there is a serious risk that entire nations and social groups will become increasingly marginalized as a result. The social dimensions of globalization need to be given much greater weight by the international community, and to be fully taken into account in the establishment of rules, mechanisms and policies for the management of the global economy. (ILO, 1994, p. 91; see also Bowles and Gintis, 1995, p. 560)

Despite impressive achievements, many of the problems of world poverty and deprivation remain unresolved and are unlikely to improve without political commitment to social development. Indeed, the numbers of the poor could rise still further as the world labour force grows from 2.5 billion to a projected 3.7 billion in 30 years time.[3] At present, it is estimated that 120 million or so people are unemployed worldwide (ILO, 1986). In many countries, workers continue to lack representation and work in unhealthy, dangerous and demeaning conditions. President Franklin Roosevelt once stated that, 'economic policy cannot be a goal in itself; it can only provide the means to achieve social objectives' (Valticos, 1994). As the twentieth century draws to a close, we are more than ever faced with the challenge of seeking effective and sustainable human development strategies which are both equitable and growth enhancing. In our search for practical and socially-orientated employment policies for the future, we can make no better a start than to revisit the writings of one of the foremost thinkers and advocates of economic development with a human face.

24.2 THE GREAT DEPRESSION AND INTELLECTUAL INFLUENCE OF KEYNES

Between the two World Wars, the industrialized countries plunged into an economic crisis of unprecedented dimensions. Unemployment rose to record levels and was stubbornly persistent. The prevailing tradition in economic thinking was unprepared to deal with this seemingly insurmountable crisis. Neo-classical economic theories assumed that full employment was an economy's normal operating level and that departures from it would be minor and transitory. Indeed, within the idealized world of traditional equilibrium economics, there can never be involuntary unemployment. In the Great Depression of the 1930s, this theoretical image of a self regulating economy appeared to be far out of touch with existing realities (Barber, 1967).

As governments groped desperately for solutions to the crisis of unemployment, a new model for macroeconomic management that went beyond conventional and traditionally accepted concepts was to emerge. That was the Keynesian model of aggregate demand management expounded in *The General Theory of Employment, Interest and Money*. Many of the lessons of this pathbreaking work are reflected in Hans Singer's contribution to the Pilgrim Trust Unemployment Enquiry which led to the publication of *Men Without Work* (1938), *Unemployment and the Unemployed* (1940) and a series of related papers and articles. Singer's experience from working in the depressed areas of Britain, was later to provide an important link to what were at that time viewed to be similar problems in the developing countries.

> Clearly this work on depressed areas and unemployment was a forerunner to the work on developing countries. I had already been forced to think about 'vicious circles' and 'poverty traps'. During the Kenya ILO Employment Mission, in particular 1971–72, I often thought back to my work in the 1930s (in the Brazilian Northeast) Here certainly the experiences of earlier work in the United Kingdom came vividly to mind. (Singer, 1985, pp. 276, 278)

In a collection of essays in honour of his 65th birthday, Hans Singer reflected on the question, 'what did I learn from Keynes that I applied directly in later life?'[4] In his answer to this question, he notes six key lessons. While all six points reveal much about Singer's approach to economic analysis and practical policy making, it is particularly instructive to reiterate four of these.

First, the concept that the real resources of a country are its human resources and that the purpose of economic analysis and policy must be to prevent the waste and dissipation of human resources through unemployment. Second, that we are in control of our own destiny, that by social and economic planning we can achieve socially agreed objectives, such as full employment and a more even distribution of wealth. Third, that the creation of productive employment is the best means of reducing poverty and that fuller employment and economic growth go together. Fourth, that the purpose of theory must be to help resolve the problems of the day.

Like Keynes, Singer has always held that economics is not a universal truth applicable to all countries to all countries and all conditions but a framework of thinking to mould to different circumstances (Clay and Shaw, 1987, p. 1). This search for alternatives to orthodox economic thought was particularly important to the founding of development economics. As noted by Singer,

> There was also a more intellectual link. As my fellow 'pioneer' Albert Hirschman has pointed out, in some sense Keynes was the real creator of development economics insofar as he broke with 'mono-economics' – the view that economics consists of a body of universal truth applicable in all countries and in all conditions. (Singer, 1985, p. 277)

This view is also clearly expounded by Singer in one of his early works, *Unemployment and the Unemployed* (1940):

> there is no 'Unemployment' which can be accounted for by a single cause, and which can be cured by a single policy, but there are only 'Unemployments', that is to say, many different kinds of unemployment with very different causes, with very different effects, and with very different cures.[5]

The rejection of theoretical and abstract simplifications, no matter how refined, in favour of inductive methods based on actual observation and practical experience is characteristic of much of Singer's work. His ability to cut to the heart of the matter and to marshall his considerable powers of systematic enquiry to critically examine the soundness of orthodox economic ideas still remains to be surpassed.

On many of the pressing economic problems of the day, Hans Singer has been highly influential in leading our thinking into new directions and in setting the agenda for international development policy. The following section examines some of the key contributions that Hans Singer has made to development economics, especially in understanding the employment problems of developing countries.

24.3   EMPLOYMENT AND DEVELOPMENT

Employment and linear-stages of development – challenging the orthodoxy

During the 1950s and 1960s, one of the major doctrines of the development literature was that successful economic development could be realized only through the twin forces of substantial capital accumulation and rapid industrial growth. This combined with the view of development as comprising a series of successive stages of economic growth, through which all countries must pass, gave rise to an economic theory of development primarily based on finding the right quantity and mixture of savings, investment and foreign aid. Rostow's stages of growth model and the Harrod–Domar capital – output growth model provided a logic and simplicity that were too irresistible to refute and became the basis for development planning.

Both these models, however, assumed the existence of a set of conditions, similar to those in the industrialised countries, which were either not present or irrelevant to the developing world. Following numerous failures and growing disenchantment with a strictly economic theory of development, a radically different approach which sought to combine economic and institutional factors into a social systems model of international development and underdevelopment began to emerge (Todaro, 1994). Hans Singer was foremost in highlighting the failings of directly applying economic concepts from the industrialised countries to the developing countries without due consideration of the actual conditions which exist in these countries.

> When the colonial era came to an end and the world turned to the problems of the two-thirds of mankind living in the poorer countries, we perhaps inevitably applied the same intellectual process to the developing countries (Keynesian model), identifying their problem as economic growth, only to discover that the real problem lay elsewhere, and prominently in the field of human resources, including those of employment and unemployment. (Emmerij and Ghai, 1976, p. 134)

Together with economic pioneers, Lewis, Myrdal, Prebisch and Rosenstein-Rodan, Singer began to depart from the flexibility and substitutability assumed by neo-classical economics and introduced elements of structural analysis. The structural approach sought to create a more realistic framework for analysing development problems by identifying rigidities, lags, shortages and other characteristics of developing country economies (Meier, 1985, p. 20). Singer was thus among the first to appreciate the failures of apparently satisfactory rates of capital accumulation and growth rates of output to provide adequate employment opportunities and to relieve massive low end poverty in developing countries (Bruton, 1976, p. 71). Many of the criticisms which he raised of the prevailing mechanistic view of development are now widely accepted and continue to be subjects of great importance.

First, Singer questioned the notion that the essence of economic development should be identified solely with the growth of GNP. He noted that the concept was notoriously difficult to measure and excluded large subsistence sectors which were highly important to developing countries. Apart from the technical difficulties of calculating GNP, Singer was also highly critical of the implicit suggestion that economic development is a uni-directional, linear affair. In his essay on Keynesian Models of Economic Development, he noted

> This is what I might call a 'unistic' theory of development, where it is assumed that there is one single indicator, the GNP, which gives a satisfactory index of something which we call 'development'. There is one single direction – it either goes up or it goes down or it stays the same. Now my suggestion is ... that development is not a unidirectional unistic affair. Rather development is multidimensional and certainly dualistic. (Singer, 1969, p. 35)

Today, such criticisms of GNP as a development indicator may appear common place. It should however be remembered that during the time when Singer wrote this comment, this would have amounted to virtual economic heresy. The emergence of development indicators which go beyond the calculation of national income owes much to the Singer's penetrating analysis.

Second, it was noted that the concept of GNP said very little about employment. Singer stressed that while the modern sector should grow, it was necessary to recognize that the impact on the traditional sector may be favourable or unfavourable. In doing this he raises the question of whether growth in the modern sector together with growing unemployment, growing distress and growing destruction of traditional industries can be said to be development. In his answer, he stresses the importance of recognising employment as a fundamental component of economic development:

> I would suggest that it is misleading to pick out GNP, which is largely oriented towards the modern sector, and includes the market transactions, while employment as such is not included in the GNP. Employment is a very vital element in economic development. It is employment which keeps people linked to the growth of their country, makes them participate in its development, keeps them training for future jobs and presumably has value in itself. Employment, just as education and health, is not only an instrument for economic growth, but it is important in itself because it constitutes part of the very purpose of development. (Singer, 1969, pp. 35–6)

Third, in line with the argument for employment promotion, Singer also called for a better understanding of demographic factors, in particular the need to invest in human resources. He noted that while attention was being paid to physical capital formation and the optimization of capital output ratios, very little was being done to ensure long-term development by investing in the education and welfare of children.[6] For Singer, the conditions in which the children of a country live and are brought up and prepared for subsequent life are much more important as long-term strategic factors in the development process than physical capital investment. These were all factors which were not considered in the prevailing development model of that time. On this point, it is worth noting that recent research on the 'economic miracle' of the East Asian NICs highlighted the critical factor of education and human capital development.

In his involvement with the ILO World Employment Programme, Hans Singer, provided much of the empirical evidence to substantiate his argument that the conventional development approach based on the Harrod-Domar model, with its heavy emphasis on the modern sector and on GNP growth, were inappropriate to the situation of many developing countries. One of the many important lessons that we can draw from Singer's critical review of the Harrod–Domar model is that we should not allow the formal accuracy of an economic model to blind us from the reality of situation on the ground. As stated by Singer, 'There are rarely any one single formula or approach which can be applicable to all situations' (Singer, 1969, p. 42). This approach to economic analysis is in part grounded in the view that different 'rules of the game' apply to developing countries and that non-orthodox policies are required (Singer, 1985, p. 277).

Employment problems in developing countries: the Kenya mission

In 1971, Hans Singer led what was to become a highly influential ILO World Employment Programme Mission to Kenya. This mission was taken at a time when Arthur Lewis's two sector model of structural change was the received view of how developing economies can transform their domestic economic structures from a heavy emphasis on traditional subsistence agriculture to a modern urbanized industrialized economy (Lewis, 1955). This model made three key assumptions: the existence of rural surplus labour and full employment in urban areas; a competitive modern sector labour market guaranteeing the continued existence of constant real urban wages up to the point where the supply of rural surplus labour is exhausted; and that the rate of labour transfer and employment creation is proportional to the rate of modern sector capital accumulation (Torado, 1994, pp. 76–7; Jolly *et al.*, 1973, p. 12).

The mission to Kenya, however, uncovered substantial evidence which contradicted the expectations of the structural change model. In particular, it was observed that unlike the historical development of Western Europe – the pace of modern sector growth was taking place at a much slower rate than that of urbanization. Indeed, it was found that the modern sector had not fulfilled the hopes placed in it as the engine of economic growth and the duration of the transition was totally underestimated (Emmerij and Ghai, 1976, p. 57). Contrary to the assumption of constant real urban wages, it was found that urban wages were rising even where substantial open unemployment existed, creating dualism and inequalities in the economic structure (Singer and Jolly, 1973). This, together with deteriorating rural incomes, attracted jobseekers far in excess of the quantity justified by the number of job vacancies in the modern sector. The result of this mismatch being the rapid growth of the urban informal sector – a term which was coined by the mission.

The urban informal sector has ever since been a topic of much research. The new paradigm of the informal sector as essentially the sector of the 'working poor' has also had significant policy implications and impact.

In particular, it questioned the earlier concept of activities outside the informal sector as being no more than 'disguised unemployment', a drag on the economy, a marginalised underclass, a disgrace to 'modernisation', a source of illegality or even criminality, environmental pollution in the slum areas, etc., with the policy conclusion that the urban informal sector had to be kept under tight control, regulated, modernised, reduced and if possible suppressed ... By contrast the new insight initiated by the World Employment Programme was that the informal sector – while it might contain an 'underclass' element with all the above bad characteristics – was essentially something quite different: a way of survival for those whom the formal economy could not provide employment, a substitute for a missing social security system, a safety net, a link with earlier and indigenous traditional and craft technologies, a necessary labour reservoir or 'labour sponge' pending the growth of the modern sector. (Singer, 1992, pp. 53–4)

The many recommendations that were contained in the Kenya Mission report (ILO, 1972) were to set an urban development agenda which continues to be relevant to this day. It was stressed that a major shift in government policies towards active encouragement and support are required. A fundamental re-orientation was called for in health standards, housing standards, licensing policy, access of the sector to loans and technology, policies relating to industrial estates and rural industrialization, government contract policy and specifications, technological research decisions on products appropriate to the local economy and the development of subcontracting by larger-scale enterprises (Singer and Jolly, 1973, p. 108).

Given that gains from economic growth in the Kenya[7] had not reached a large proportion of the population, Hans Singer pushed strongly the idea of redistribution from growth. This called for a reorientation of government expenditure towards the poorer regions and poorer elements of the population, as well as the adoption of an overall economic policy which would shift employment and earning opportunities in the direction of these poorer groups (Singer and Jolly, 1973 p. 113). While the economic conditions in many African countries today have worsened to such a degree that the notion of redistribution appears utopian, the recommendations formulated by Singer have an important message that should not be ignored. This is essentially that economic growth is a necessary and not a sufficient condition for development, and that there is great deal of harm in assuming a necessary contradiction between growth and equity (Ansari and Singer, 1977, p. 77). It also highlights, Singer's long standing contention that mainstream economics does not pay enough attention to distributive efficiency or justice.

While mainstream economics concentrated on the problem of allocative efficiency (where comparative advantage ruled supreme), my interest was from the beginning more in the direction of distributive justice or rather distributive efficiency as I saw it as a follower of Alfred Marshall, R.H. Tawney, and William Beveridge. (Singer, 1985, p. 280)

It was also noted by Singer during the Kenya mission that not only had the modern sector employment failed to expand in absolute terms, it had also failed to increase in proportion to the actual increase in production. According to Singer, this phenomenon was due to the introduction of new labour-saving capital-intensive technologies which were wholly inappropriate to the local factor endowments enjoyed by developing countries (Singer, 1969, p. 137). Essentially, he concluded that developing countries were caught in a 'technology trap'. This argument was based on the observation that when the Western countries began to industrialise, they were able to develop on the basis of an evolving technology.

At the beginning the prevailing technology was labour-intensive but gradually, as crude labour became relatively less abundant in those countries and higher skills and capital become more abundant, the technology changed in the same direction of requiring less labour and more capital and higher skills. The developing countries of today have no choice but to use the capital intensive technology developed in, by and for the richer industrialized countries and imported for them. (Ibid.)

Based on a re-analysis of his classic work on *The Distribution of Gains*, in which he stressed the importance of factor use as opposed to factor endowment, (Singer, 1971, p. 62), Singer saw a great need for developing labour-intensive technologies which would permit a rise in productivity without detriment to employment. The concept of an appropriate technology mix for development has had wide appeal and continues to be an area of much interest. However, it is no easy matter to devise superior labour-intensive technologies or to introduce them once devised. Moreover, recent experience of the East Asian NICs have demonstrated that it is feasible for countries to use borrowed technology as a means to accelerate economic growth and achieve high rates of employment. Perhaps, the issue for the future is not so much the control of technological development but the ability of being able to generate innovations and adapt new technology to local conditions.

Now, over 20 years since the Kenya Mission first identified the urban informal sector as a major area of policy concern, we face a substantially changed environment which requires new insights on the future of employment. The 1980s has often been referred to as the 'lost development decade' of mounting debts, rigorous adjustment, international economic recession and stagnation of the modern sector. These global factors combined with continued population growth and rural–urban migration has for many countries, especially in Africa, resulted in an unprecedented growth of the informal economy. Perhaps, one of the most significant development which we are witnessing in this closing decade of the twentieth century is that of globalization. We are thus faced with the enormous task of dealing with new issues even before we have resolved old ones.

24.4 EMPLOYMENT IN A GLOBAL ECONOMY

Among Hans Singer's most important contributions to development economics is his effectiveness in leading our thinking into new directions. His presentation at December 1949 meeting of the American Economic Association of the paper, *The Distribution of Gains Between Investing and Borrowing Countries* (1949–50), opened an area that has proved, over the past decades, to be of primary importance in both research and policy. Like many of his other findings, the notion that primary producers faced worsening terms of trade went against the conventional wisdom of that time. Again, like many other occasions, his views have profoundly influenced development economics, policy and practice.[8]

Essentially, Singer saw that as primary producers, developing countries were locked into a uneven trading relationship where technical progress in the production of food and raw materials did not lead to an increase but to a fall in prices. On the other hand, producers of manufacturing goods were locked into a virtuous circle where technical progress resulted in a concomitant rise in incomes.[9] Within this framework, less emphasis was placed on the traditional neoclassical competitive market paradigm and more on bargaining power, financial power, and control of marketing, processing and distribution.

> It seemed to me that to think of the distribution of gains in terms of only the amount of labour saved by specialization was to neglect an essential element. The assumption of equal exchange in impartial 'fair' markets seemed in conflict with the facts of unequal market and technological power. The dice were loaded against one of the trade partners. (Singer, 1985, pp. 280–1)

This line of thinking was to give rise to new models of development based on concepts of dependency and dualism. However, while Singer was wary of the inherent biases in the international economic structure, he maintained the view that a major solution to the unemployment problem in developing countries still remained in international trade (Singer, 1969, p. 141). The problem was that international institutional frameworks were required to ensure that trade did play the role of the 'engine of growth' conceptually attributed to it.

In recent years, dependency and dualistic development theories have been subsumed by concerns for the new phenomena of globalization. The globalization of the world economy is seen in many quarters as a major step towards fostering further growth and economic prosperity. However, while there is a general consensus that potential benefits of globalization will far outweigh the costs, the problem of the marginalization of the least developed countries, and growing international inequality is an emerging area of concern. On these issues, Hans Singer has been a strong critic of market-orientated policies which ignore the social dimension. In particular, he has advocated for policies which can correct or shift the market process to a more egalitarian direction (Singer, 1989). In this respect, in his recent review of the research of the World Employment Programme, he stressed that in some ways the process of 'flexibilization' of labour markets is at the expense not only of living standards and employment security but also of human capital formation in terms of skills, chances of on-the-job training, learning from experience, and so on (Singer, 1992, p. 31). These are all vital prerequisites for development.

From an even broader political and social perspective the danger is of a creation of an insecure and impoverished underclass, undermining the political and social stability essential for the successful implementation of any adjustment programme and the resumption of growth. Solving supply side problems need not involve 'structural adjustments' that increase inequality – the social democratic economies of northern Europe have shown that success can be based on interventions for long-term productivity in the form of active labour market policies, human resource development, wage equalization and high levels of trade union membership (Bowles and Gintis, 1995, p. 560).

On the issue of global production and the implications for employment, Singer notes that there are a host of questions that have yet to be answered. Given the present alarmist views on the job-destroying effects of imports from, and the relocation of production to developing countries, the following are an important list of research areas that could shed some light on the present debate:

1. What is the organisation of labour markets which attracts multinationals and other foreign investors?

2. Do they prefer the low wages provided by completely unorganised labour markets (perhaps with much female and youth employment and subcontracting even down to the self-employed and informal sector) or do they prefer the industrial peace and stability in employment and skill development which contracts with responsible unions bring?

3. What is the relative importance as determinants of location by foreign investors, on the one hand, of wage levels and labour market organisation? (Singer, 1992, p. 19).

Singer once noted that:

> Until we know something of these effects, we can scarcely hope to deal with them successfully, and the object of this enquiry has been, first to find out something about them, and secondly to consider in the light of that knowledge the efficacy of the various efforts (both statutory and, in particular, voluntary) which are being made to deal with them. (Ibid., p. 1)

This, in my view is the position which we are at in terms of the relationship between the future of employment and globalization. Much empirical research will be required as a basis for answering the above and other questions which are of great importance for the prospects of developing countries. At the ILO, we have for some time been working on these and other issues of critical importance to the future of employment policies in the global economy. Despite the significant growth in world trade and flows of foreign direct investment, there is continued anxiety over the issue of job creation. Part of the cause for this concern is that the gains from expanding world trade and output have so far been unevenly distributed. Amongst the developing countries, the East and South-East Asian economies have accounted for the major share of the gains, while Sub-Saharan Africa continues to be increasingly marginalized. Globalization is also posing serious distributional problems within countries, with major economic reforms for international competitiveness resulting in high social costs. In the least developed countries, integration into the global economy will be difficult to achieve without well-developed market institutions constrained by the absence of a stable system of property rights, a highly unequal distribution of assets and severe market distortions.

Globalization sets limits on the effectiveness of traditional instruments for influencing the level and quality of employment. The challenge of restoring full employment and a sustainable distribution of gains will be formidable. Given the increasingly integrated nature of the world economy, solutions will need to found through co-operative international action.

This will require a commitment by all countries to the objective of restoring full employment. In the recent *ILO World Employment Report 1995*, a number of directions were put forth for cooperative international action. This noted that three key factors had made the 'Golden Age' of 1950–73 possible: the high priority given to the objective of full employment in the international economic system; the social consensus in the industrialized countries over the distribution of national income that made non-inflationary growth feasible; and stable monetary and trading arrangements in the global economic system. In order to move back towards this path of growth and employment there will need to be a reform of the international monetary system to dampen the destabilizing effects of speculative financial flows on exchange and interest rates and greater coordination of macroeconomic policies. At the same time, a stable institutional framework for promoting freer international trade and flows of foreign direct investment will improve allocation and efficiency. Similarly, international action is required to assist the least developed countries in overcoming their marginalization. This will help reduce international inequality and in turn sustain the process of globalization.

24.5 CONCLUSION

While global competition challenges many conventional redistributive policies, we should not accept that it necessarily means that egalitarian policies are inconsistent with new economic realities. Ultimately, the chief impediments to egalitarianism in the globally integrated economy may not actually be a dearth of economically viable programmes, but rather a surfeit of political obstacles (Bowles and Gintis, p. 581). What we do know is that unemployment does not only mean a present problem, as Singer once described it is a 'non-stop show', that is, unemployment creates unemployment, which in turn creates unemployment, which in turn creates unemployment, and so on (Singer, 1940). In closing, I would like to leave the last word with Hans Singer.

In the nineteenth century it was the widespread fashion to believe that in economic and social life there was an 'invisible hand' at work making things work out in a pretty good way, even in the absence of any special policy or other intervention to that end ... we have abandoned this belief nowadays as being too much in conflict with the observed facts ... Can we sleep, quietly trusting to the 'invisible hand' in unemployment policy? (Ibid.)

Notes

1. Director, Development and Technical Cooperation Department, ILO, Geneva. Mr. Hoe Lim provided considerable research of the literature for which I am most grateful. All views are the author's, and do not necessarily reflect those of the ILO.
2. Preface to Pilgrim Trust (1938) *Men Without Work* (London: Cambridge University Press) p. vii.
3. In 1995 there were an estimated 2.5 billion men and women of working age in the world's labour force, almost twice as many as in 1965. Estimates project a further worldwide increase of 1.2 billion by 2025. This expansion, moreover, has been geographically skewed. Since 1965 growth in the labour supply has varied substantially across regions: from 40 per cent in the world's high-income economies to 93 per cent in South Asia and 176 per cent in the Middle East and North Africa. 99 per cent of the projected growth in the labour force from now to 2025 will occur in what are today's low and middle income countries (Source: ILO Labour Statistics).
4. H.W. Singer (1976) 'Early Years (1910–1938)', in A Cairncross and M. Puri (eds) (1976) *Employment, Income Distribution and Development of Strategy: Problems of the Developing Countries* (London and Basingstoke: Macmillan) p. 7.
5. H.W. Singer (1940) *Unemployment and the unemployed* (London: P.S. King & Son) p. 59.
6. Unlike Keynes, Singer had a greater interest in long run economics.
7. The Kenyan economy had been expanding regularly at the high rate of 7 to 8 per cent per annum in terms of aggregate production ever since independence.
8. Singer's terms of trade thesis and the resulting policy recommendation of import-substitution has been subject to controversy among economists (see B. Balassa (1985) comment to Singer's article on *The Terms of Trade Controversy and the Evolution of Soft Financing: Early Years in The UN*). However, Singer, maintained that with the exclusion of oil the terms of trade thesis is borne out by observed trends.
9. Ibid., p. 48.

References

Ansari, J. and H.W. Singer (1977) *Rich and Poor countries* (Baltimore and Londons Johns Hopkins University Press).

Barber, W.J. (1967) *A History of Economic Thought* (Harmondsworth: Penguin).

Bowles, S. and H. Gintis (1995) 'Productivity-enhancing egalitarian policies', *International Labour Review*, vol. 134, no. 4–5, pp. 559–85.

Bruton, H. (1976) 'Employment, productivity and Income Distribution', in A. Cairncross and M. Puri (eds) (1976) *Employment, Income Distribution and Development Strategy: Problems of the developing countries – essays in honour of H.W. Singer* (London and Basingstoke: Macmillan).

Cairncross, A. and M. Puri (eds) (1975) *The Strategy of International Development: Essays in the Economics of Backwardness by H.W. Singer* (London and Basingstoke: Macmillan).

—— and —— (eds) (1976) *Employment, Income Distribution and Development Strategy: Problems of the developing countries – essays in honour of H.W. Singer* (London and Basingstoke: Macmillan).

Clay, E. and J. Shaw (eds) (1987) *Poverty, Development and Food: Essays in honour of H.W. Singer on his 75th birthday* (London and Basingstoke: Macmillan).

Emmerij, L. and D. Ghai (1976) 'Employment problems in developing countries: Lessons from the World Employment Programme', in A. Cairncross and M. Puri (eds) (1976) *Employment, Income Distribution and Development Strategy: Problems of the developing countries – essays in honour of H.W. Singer* (London and Basingstoke: Macmillan).

Greenaway, D. and C. Milner (1995) 'The World Trade System and the Uruguay Rounb: Global Employment Implications', *International Labour Review*, vol. 134, no. 4–5, pp. 497–517.

ILO (1986) *Economically Active Population Estimates and Projections: 1950–2025* (Geneva).

—— (1972) *Employment, Incomes and Equality: A strategy for increasing productive employment in Kenya* (Geneva).

—— (1994a) *Visions of the Future of Social Justice: Essays on the Occasion of the ILO's 75th Anniversary* (Geneva).

—— (1994b), *Defending Values, Promoting Change, Social Justice in a Global Economy: An ILO agenda* (Geneva).

Jolly, R. *et al.* (1973) *Third World Employment: Problems and Strategy* (Harmondsworth: Penguin).

Lee, E. (1995) 'Overview of the Special Issue on Employment Policy in the Global Economy', *International Labour Review*, vol. 34, no. 4–5, pp. 441–50.

Prendergaast, R. and H.W. Singer (eds) (1991) *Development Perspectives for the 1990s* (London: Macmillan).

Lewis, A.W. (1955) *The Theory of Economic Growth* (London: Allen & Unwin).

Meier, G. and D. Seers (eds) (1985) *Pioneers in Development* (London: published for the World Bank by Oxford University Press)

Signer, H.W. (1940) *Unemployment and the Unemployed* (London: P.S. King & Son).

—— *et al.* (1938) *Men Without Work: A Report to the Pilgrim Trust* (London: Cambridge University Press).

—— and W.A. Jöhr (1955), *The Role of the Economist as Official Adviser*, (London: George Allen & Unwin).

—— (1964) *International Development: Growth and Change* (New York, Toronto and London: McGraw-Hill Book Co.).

—— (1969) 'Keynesian Models of Economic Development and their limitations: An Analysis in the light of Gunnar Myrdal's "Asian Drama"', *UN Asian*

Institute for Economic Development and Planning, Occasional Papers (December).

—— and S. Sciavo-Campo (1970) *Perspectives in Economic Development* (Boston: Houghton Mifflin).

—— (1971) 'The Distribution of Gains Revisited', paper presented at the Inter PAS Conference at the Institute of Development Studies, 1971.

—— and R. Jolly (1973) 'Unemployment in an African setting: Lessons of the Employment Strategy Mission to Kenya', *International Labour Review*, vol. 107, no. 2 (February).

—— (1976) 'Early Years (1910–1938)', in A. Cairncross and M. Puri (eds) *The Strategy of International Development: Essays in the Economics of Backwardness by H.W. Singer* (London and Basingstoke: Macmillan).

—— (1977) *Technologies for Basic Needs* (Geneva: ILO).

—— (1985) 'The Terms of Trade Controversy and the Evolution & Soft Financing: Early Years in the UN', in Meier and Seers (eds), *Pioneers in Development* (London: Oxford University Press).

—— (1989) 'The World Bank: Human Face or Facelift? Some Comments in the Light of the World Bank's Annual Report', *World Development*, vol. 17, no. 8, pp. 1313–16.

—— (1992) *Research of the World Employment Programme: Future priorities and selective assessment* (Geneva: ILO).

—— and S. Roy (1993) *Economic Progress and Prospects in the Third World: Lessons of Development Experience since 1945* (Aldershot: Edward Elgar).

Todaro, M. (1994) *Economic Development* (5th ed) (New York: Longman).

Valticos, N. (1994). The ILO is 75-years-old: The objectives, structure and methods of the ILO in Facing the Future' in ILO (1994), *Visions of the Future of Social Justice: Essays on the Occasion of the ILO's 75th Anniversary* (Geneva).

25 Reaching the Poor: Prospects and Constraints[1]

Sartaj Aziz

As early as May 1950, in his famous essay 'Distribution of Gains Between Investing and Borrowing Countries' Hans Singer pointed out that 'the import of capital into underdeveloped countries for the purpose of making them into providers of food and raw material for the industrialized countries may have been not only ineffective in giving them the normal benefits of investment and trade but may have been positively harmful'.

In the next four and a half decades, Professor Singer pursued his sacred mission with relentless zeal and extraordinary devotion. The most outstanding quality that I have found very heart warming in my long association with Hans, has been his compassion for the poor. Whether he was exploring the theories of international trade or the intricacies of food aid policies, his main concern was their impact on the poor people. That is why I have chosen to speak today on prospects and constraints of reaching the poor.

In a way it is reassuring that after nearly two decades of dilly-dallying, poverty has moved, once again, to the top of global agenda. Four major international summit level meetings on Environment in June 1992, Population in September 1994, Social Development in March 1995 and Women and Development in September 1995, have all recognized that without a drastic reduction in poverty, environmental degradation cannot be reversed, population growth will be difficult to check, broad-based social and human development will not be possible and the living conditions of women and children in most developing countries will remain miserable.

Poverty as the root cause of hunger was identified more than two decades ago, particularly at the 1974 World Food Conference, leading to the first major international effort to deal with objectives of reducing poverty and increasing food production in an integrated manner. The Conference

recognized the vital importance of mobilizing the people through their organizations for rural development, and particularly of involving small farmers and landless labourers in the planning and operation of

503

programmes aimed at improving their living standards and those of their families and at bringing about a more equitable distribution of income.

In the 1980s, the concept of entitlements was added to the debate on poverty, to demonstrate that unless the poor possess some land to grow their own crops or can market their labour at reasonable prices, they will remain poor and hungry.

It has now been finally discovered that the critical threshold is to find ways and means of elevating the poor from the category of mere 'beneficiaries' to that of participants in joint endeavors to improve peoples' productivity and well-being. And that threshold cannot be crossed until the poor are empowered to deal with their own destinies. The actual experience in designing projects and policies for the benefit of the poor proves convincingly that the privileged classes in a society normally pre-empt the bulk of these benefits allowing only a trickle to filter through.

The concept of empowerment is an important component of the broader concept of sustainable development because social sustainability is not possible without developing a country's human capital. If the bulk of a country's population is poor and cannot get the knowledge and skills to become useful members of the society, then the most precious part of that country's resources – namely namely its human resources, will remain under-utilized. This in turn will affect the utilization of its more limited natural resources and thus retard development process as a whole.

Meaningful human development is not possible without observing the principle of equality of opportunity, particularly in the following areas:

1. adequate access to education and health facilities by the poor communities;
2. access to knowledge, skills and extension services;
3. access to credit and other agricultural inputs on reasonable terms;
4. assured access to land and its legal tenure.

There is no single formula or model under which these objectives can be achieved. It depends primarily on the focus of political power and whether it is positive, neutral or negative towards the poor. In countries where the political leadership is genuinely interested in helping the poor, there is vast scope for rapid changes in institutions and attitudes in favour of the poor. But where the power structure is controlled by the feudal elites or other vested interests, which will not offer more than crumbs to the poor, the task will be much more difficult. It will then require a different approach for organizing the poor in order to win or snatch their entitlements.

25.1 CONSTRAINTS AND OBSTACLES

To most outside observers the objective of reaching the poor, appears so desirable and so harmless that we often overlook many constraints that stand in the way.

Social inequality is often a major cause of economic inequality. In countries in which social inequalities, arising from land ownership, religious or ethnic differences predominate, they constitute the most serious obstacles in reaching the poor.

The second set of constraints arise from political factors. In most emerging multi-party democracies, the ruling party has a strong temptation to use all the resources of its command and the full force of its administrative authority for its political survival and for the party's re-election. In such a situation, there is considerable discrimination against political opponents and the criteria adopted for building rural infrastructure like roads or electricity, location of schools and health facilities and provision of credit, are guided by political considerations. Whenever there is a change of government, the new ruling party shifts its patronage to its own supporters. A sustainable programme of rural development requires a more mature political system in which policies and programmes which empower the poor can be formulated, without discrimination.

Then there are local rivalries based on feudal, ethnic or sectarian difference. These often over-ride any concerns about poverty or hunger. There are very few successful examples of movements or programmes for organizing the poor that can cut across these rivalries.

The fourth set of constraints rise from bureaucratic attitudes and inefficiencies. Poor communities are in any case suspicious and apprehensive about those in authority because in the past they have often been victims of their repression and exploitation. They are, therefore, reluctant to interact with them or to respond to their initiatives. An effective process of rural development requires a government that is accountable to its people.

A STRATEGY FOR REACHING THE POOR

Most of us assembled here have seen at first hand, different faces of poverty; we are all committed to the elimination of poverty; many of us have been actively involved in activities that benefit the poor. But there is a valuable opportunity to launch a more determined attack on the problem.

A strategy for reaching the poor must fit into a broader strategy for poverty alleviation. A key prerequisite for poverty alleviation is access to productive resources. In addition to land reforms, where possible, new assets must be created and placed at the disposal of the poor through land reclamation or irrigation, provision of agricultural machinery or tubewells or development of livestock and fisheries. Many pilot projects undertaken by financing institutions have demonstrated how this important objective of providing productive resources to the poor can be achieved. It is important to scale-up such activities by increasing domestic and international resources available for such programmes.

The second part of his strategy should focus on improving the skills and knowledge of the poor. Because of the number of poor people involved (at least 1000 million in 1995), this will be more difficult and time consuming task. But if the targets of 'education for all' and 'health for all' can be achieved by the year 2005 or even 2010, a good start will have been made in launching a determined attack on the problems of poverty.

The third component of the strategy is organizational and institutional. Without a proper organization, the poor, in their individual capacity and with their limited resources, cannot achieve the minimum necessary access to land, water, credit or technology or their due share in development funds or subsidies. The key element in the process of empowerment is organizing the poor. The civil society consisting of non-government or community organizations has a key role in organizing the poor, mainly because governments including local governments, cannot free themselves from the inherent political constraints and are, therefore, often a part of the problem.

Over the past three decades, a very large number of civil society organizations have gained valuable experience in organizing the poor and promoting social change in the rural society. But most of them are small and localized with a limited capacity to undertake pilot projects. The time has come to 'scale them up' not just for the expanded delivery of inputs or services, but to initiate or accelerate the process of meaningful development.

Countries in which the overall environment for grass root organizations is positive or at least neutral, these organizations, given adequate international support can make rapid progress in organizing the poor for improving their lives. Even in countries in which the environment is negative and hostile, community organizations can play an important role in creating awareness, undertaking pilot projects and delivering some benefits and services to the poor.

Note

1.   The views expressed in this chapter are purely personal.

26 The Role of the International Agencies: An Assessment[1]

Jon Wilmshurst

In commenting, and sometimes criticising, the six substantial papers presented in this session I must acknowledge the debt we owe to Hans Singer in addressing the key issues. Central strands in his wide interests have been an internationalist approach, preoccupation with human development and employment, concern for the poor and advocacy of international aid. All are relevant to this session.

The papers are so varied that a coherent commentary is virtually impossible. Three elementary points – perhaps a statement of the obvious – can be suggested in considering the role of the international agencies.

1. They have two main roles which are quite separate. The first is to provide the framework for global economic and social relationships, an orderly system which is conducive to world development. The second is international aid, the transfer of resources from rich to poor countries. These two roles should not be confused.

2. The agencies should complement the activities of the private sector, in some cases correcting for market failure. But they should not compete with, or crowd out, private activities. Dirigisme should be avoided.

3. They must always recognise the primacy of national governments. International agencies cannot influence activities within countries irrespective of government policies. In relation to international aid, for example, the agencies must consider whether national policies in aid recipients are supportive, counter-productive or, in extreme cases, so bad that the prospects for effective aid outcomes become minimal.

This leads us to some equally elementary comments on the specifications for effective international agencies. Each agency needs to have a clearly defined role without duplicating significantly the role of some other agency. Analytical work is a partial exception to this – there is certainly room for more than one approach to international economic and social issues – but overlaps of a major kind in executive functions are unlikely to be productive.

The agencies should also be highly conscious of the three Es – the need for economy, efficiency and effectiveness. There is widespread perception of inward-looking bureaucracies, more concerned with their own well-being than adding value in their specified roles. This is one of the motivations for the current review of the UN system commissioned by the G7 countries. So cost-effectiveness in pursuing its agreed mission should be a basic tenet for each agency.

A third principle is that the agencies must recognize in their international aid activities that each aid-recipient country is unique. Although there are some fundamentals in economic and social development – such as, for example, that a country cannot run a balance of payments deficit forever – there are no universal solutions to development problems. The policy and investment mix required is specific to each country and there is no place for dogma.

Most of the ideas in the six papers measure up to these background criteria well. Abandoning attempts to maintain coherence, my principal reactions to the papers are as follows:

- Any non-concessional investments by the World Bank group run the risk of crowding-out the private sector, so both IFC and IBRD activities need to be assessed for additionality and value-added (Mosley).
- Stewart and Daws have identified a gap in the international regulatory structure, but the proposed UN Economic and Social Security Council would face two real-world problems: how to define its functions in a way which found universal acceptance and, subject to that, how to stop individual countries from withdrawing when they perceived that the actions of the Council infringed their national interests.
- The discussion of the IMF role by Snowden is timely and touches on an issue raised above, whether it is sensible to combine central banking functions with those of an aid agency.
- The arguments for giving more attention to longer-term development in food aid, as well as to emergency needs, are well-directed by Shaw but two tests should be applied: is food aid more effective than financial aid for such purposes and are we sure that provision is not supply-driven?
- The global employment issues addressed by Radwan are complex and the agenda is wide, but more priority should be given to an issue that has been relatively hidden in recent debate. This is the large number of unemployed and illiterate people of working age in low income coun-

tries where the seemingly unsurmountable problem is that there are not enough resources to equip them for higher productivity work. How do we stop this particular problem from escalating?

● Empowerment of the poor, as suggested by Sartaj Aziz, must be right and is consistent with democratic objectives. Despite the well-publicized cases of autocratic governments which promote effective development, there are numerous cases of the reverse effect and no evidence overall that democracy impedes development. The need to give priority to the rights of women is also relevant to this.

Note

1. The views expressed in this chapter are those of the author and do not necessarily reflect the views of the Overseas Development Administration.

Part VI

Hans Singer: Student and Scholar

27 Joseph A. Schumpeter: The Man and the Economist

Wolfgang F. Stolper

27.1 HOW WE EXPERIENCED SCHUMPETER IN BONN

Lieber Hans,

We both go back a long way, and of all the celebrants present I have probably known you the longest, your wife excepted. Our friendship goes back to 1931 when I came to Bonn, and we two are, I believe, the last survivors of Schumpeter's Bonn seminar, a seminar of whose members many were to lead distinguished lives. Günther Harkort retired as Secretary of State for Economic Affairs, and we both met him also in our professional capacity, you as an international civil servant, I – who essentially remained an academic throughout my life – on loan first to the Nigerian, then to the American Government. There was August Lösch, whose *Räumliche Ordnung* became a famous and influential book, and whose memory we both joined to honor in Heidenheim. There was Herbert Zassenhaus who, like you became a distinguished international civil servant. There was also Martin Wiebel who retired as the Rome correspondent of the *Frankfurter Zeitung*. There was Sudhir Sen who, attracted by Schumpeter, chose to study in Bonn rather than the then for an Indian more usual London School of Economics. He later became a member of Gandhi's inner circle and a director of the Damodar Valley Authority and he ended his active life like you at the United Nations. There was Hiroshi Furuutchi, then a lowly Third Secretary of the Japanese Embassy assigned to study in Bonn with Schumpeter, and whose last position, I have been told, was Japanese Ambassador to Pakistan. There was Theo Wessels, then assistant to Beckerath, who after the War became Rector of the University of Cologne. And there was, of course, a steady stream of foreign visitors, mainly from England and Japan.

As you may gather, Bonn was a lively and intellectually stimulating place. Although Schumpeter was undoubtedly the main attraction, it would be quite misleading to omit the names of Spiethoff, Herbert

513

v. Beckerath and 'Papa' Rössle who contributed their share to the intellectual and social atmosphere. Spiethoff's seminar was superb. And Schumpeter was a brilliant sparkling lecturer, so much so that he seems to have become somewhat suspect to the more staid Swedes. The social atmosphere played a major role in our lives, especially during carnival time which in the Rhineland is indeed taken very seriously. We were, after all, very young in 1931.

The usual picture of German universities with distant professors insisting on their dignity and originality, lording it over assistants and students, not caring and making personal contact difficult, certainly did not fit Bonn.

It was Spiethoff who had brought Schumpeter back into academic life, fighting very nasty rumors with an insistence on facts, a fight in which also my father was actively involved. These rumors kept resurfacing when Schumpeter – at the suggestion of the Prussian Ministry of Education and not at his own initiative – was considered for a 'Berlin chair. I have found the Berlin faculty protocols, and it is a very sad file. Only Emil Lederer defended Schumpeter's honor and importance as an economist. The rest of the faculty insisted that he was a man of questionable character who had nothing of value contributed to economics. Worst of all, all accusations against Schumpeter were in the form of innuendos and made in a manner which made it impossible for Schumpeter to defend himself.

Thus there had been in 1919 a cabinet inquiry about the so-called Kola affair which completely exonerated Schumpeter. Yet the Cabinet decided to keep the result secret, for reasons that were never stated. A bank director, never named, appeared in the middle of the night at the editorial office of the newspaper which had published the false accusations against Schumpeter, requesting that they *not* be corrected. Otto Bauer refused to give the name or names of the persons who had spread the rumours.

Yet it can be proved beyond the shadow of a doubt that it was not Schumpeter who sabotaged the socialization of the Alpine Montan Gesellschaft. In fact, he had not the power to do what he was accused of not doing. The Biedermann Bank was liquidated in 1926, two years after Schumpeter had resigned as its President. Later parliamentary hearings about the Biedermann Bank led to a report of about 95 printed pages in which Schumpeter is named twice in a minor role, but his testimony had never been sought and he knew nothing of this report which appeared after he had left for Bonn. The requests for a copy of the internal report by Schumpeter or my father were not even answered. The judicial inquiry in connection with the Braun–Stammfels affair, which dealt with Schumpeter's investment activities, completely exonerated him and 13 others.

In short, Schumpeter emerges from the documentary evidence completely innocent of wrongdoing, but perhaps also as innocent of worldly wisdom. He lost his fortune not by speculation but by innocently giving a guarantee for a loan to Braun–Stammfels. He was the victim of 'Brotneid' and 'Beamtentratsch', as the secret hearings stated, of professional jealousy and gossip. The left accused him of anti-semitism, while the right accused him of being a friend of the Jews and a member of the Austrian school of economics whose cradle had stood in Galicia! He certainly made it easy for his detractors by his completely unbourgeois behavior. He did not, after all, have to keep a race horse or wear silk shirts during the miserable days of 1919.

In any case, the Schumpeter we knew in Bonn was in fact a broken man, living for his work and his students. But we did not know this at the time, and indeed some of his more flamboyant mannerisms continued through his Harvard period. He always had time for us, he participated in all our social activities, and I remember one of his interventions during a public oral exam, when the examinee could not answer one of Spiethoff's questions. Before Spiethoff could make any discouraging remark, Schumpeter chimed in: 'Aber lieber Freund, muss man das wirklich wissen?' ('But my dear friend, does one really have to know this?')

Born in 1883 in the Austro-Hungarian monarchy, he had a meteoric rise, made a private fortune in Cairo and landed in Graz thanks to the intervention of the law professors in Graz and of Böhm-Bawerk with whom he had had a scholarly controversy. No: Böhm-Bawerk was *not* jealous of his brilliant student, any more than Schumpeter was jealous of Keynes. It happens that I wrote to Hans Singer about this question, and Hans confirmed that whatever coolness there was in the personal relations between these two great men was due to cultural differences rather than professional jealousy.

These cultural differences include the First World War which Schumpeter deplored from the beginning. Schumpeter was a thoroughgoing Anglophile and Slavophile, as well as a convinced patriot of the Double Monarchy. He loved the Double Monarchy because it was *not* a nation state. He wanted to convert it into a Triple Monarchy with the Czechs becoming an equal partner. He disliked the Hungarians because they wanted out of the Monarchy and because of their Magyarisation policy which suppressed the Slav and other minorities and which had no counterpart in a Germanisation policy of the Austrian part. He referred to this as the *österreichische Staatsidee*, and its sensibleness is now daily before our eyes in the Balkan troubles. The greatest troubles are not in the former Austrian but in the former Hungarian lands, and of course in Serbia.

Keynes was luckier. Where Keynes' world gradually tired and diminished, the British Empire being gradually devolved with grace and wisdom, as Schumpeter put it, Schumpeter's world collapsed in a catastrophe amid the nationalist ideas which he hated. With it disappeared what he called that civilized conservativism to which he might give his loyalty, which would never appear again. To some extent he did bear this stroke of fate. But then his mother to whom he was greatly attached, died and within a short few months so did his second wife who was the great love of his life, as well as the newborn son. Keynes' private life, however unorthodox developed in stable, tolerant surroundings and it never became an issue during his life time. The bases of Schumpeter's life simply disappeared.

To me, Schumpeter is a tragic figure. He continued to work in a world in which he was increasingly a stranger. He helped where he could, quietly and unostentatiously. He was not anti-Semitic or anti-anything else. I found letters from Cläre Tisch, possibly his most interesting student, whom he kept morally and intellectually alive by discussing her scholarly ideas and to whom he sent affidavit after affidavit. But Cläre Tisch decided to sacrifice herself to take care of Jewish orphans and finally wrote not to send any more affidavits; her future address would be unknown. It was Auschwitz. Once Keynes had changed his attitude towards saving, he refused to sign anti-Keynesian letters, referring to Keynes as an intelligent and responsible man. But, in our modern idiom, he refused to be politically correct.

It has become fashionable to debunk the reputations of great men. It may be good to remind biographers of the biblical injunction: let him who is without sin cast the first stone.

27.2   MAJOR CONTRIBUTIONS

I turn now to Schumpeter the economist. Schumpeter left his monumental and unfinished *History of Economic Analysis*, which in the opinion of so different scholars as Jakob Viner and Jürg Niehans is not likely to be surpassed in the foreseeable future. Schumpeter was not only immensely erudite. As Ragnar Frisch wrote to Schumpeter: 'I have never met a person with your ability ... and eagerness to understand the other fellow's point of view and to do him justice.' I have used this letter as the motto of my Schumpeter book. Schumpeter left an important economic-sociological-historical study entitled *The Crisis of the Tax State*. He also left an unfinished money book. I will not talk about those.

But he also left us many important articles ands four major works in which he developed his 'vision' and his theoretical analyses.

It is, of course, true that the development of non-linear dynamics (about which, I assure you, I know preciously little) and of the computer has allowed not only simulation where precise mathematical formulations are impossible, as well as analyzing enormous numbers of facts which simply could not be done before, facts, for that matter, which were not available before. I will come back to this aspect of modern developments along Schumpeterian lines.

Wesen und Hauptinhalt appeared in 1908 when Schumpeter was 25-years old. Its originality has in my (and also in Shionoya's) opinion been much underestimated because so much of it has become common place since. Later theoretical developments have made it so much out-of-date as to make a simple revision impossible, as Schumpeter himself stressed in a letter to Redvers Opie.

In *Wesen* Schumpeter dismissed the need for any psychological explanations for stationary equilibrium economics, with which Wieser in an otherwise glowing review definitely disagreed. Schumpeter also dismissed the need for the assumption of an economic man. As Smithies pointed out, there was not an ounce of utilitarian blood in Schumpeter's veins. Any kind of motivation would do in stationary situations. Motivations did become important in an evolutionary situation.

Schumpeter originally, that is, in 1912, rejected biological analogies. But since then, biology has changed dramatically. There are now biological analogies. Schumpeter pointed to mutations as analogues to innovations and even confessed to a liking for *évolution créative*. My colleague Theodore Bergstrom has been modeling the rationality of altruistic behaviour, and Paul Samuelson among others has been writing about group vs. individual maximizing behavior, neither of which can be handled satisfactorily by the assumption of an economic man.

The central point of *Wesen* is that the explanatory value of equilibrium economics is limited to adaptive processes.

The *Wesen* was followed less than four years later by the *Theory of Economic Development* which established Schumpeter's international reputation and led to Schumpeter's appointment in 1913 as the first (and only) Austrian exchange professor at Columbia University which conferred an honorary degree on the 30-year-old visitor.

The second and much revised edition appeared in 1926. Later German editions were reprints of this edition but with additional forewords. The English translation by Redvers Opie which appeared in 1934 was further shortened and revised. Schumpeter collaborated actively with Opie both on the shortening and on the translation itself. Like all good translations it is really a rewriting.

The reception *The Theory* in France and the Anglo-Saxon world was very friendly. It was less so closer to home. After all, many economists before Schumpeter had given the entrepreneur a crucial role, and some reviewers essentially said: brilliant. But what else is new?

But this showed a thorough non-understanding. A first chapter stressed that the circular flow contained nothing which could explain evolution. Yet evolution: interest, profits were clearly economic phenomena. The point of the book is essentially that there are all the time opportunities for doing new things, that new things got done when someone had the energy and creative will to do them, and that this amounted, in our language, to a discontinuous change in production functions which came from *inside* the economic system. Schumpeter's evolutionary theory explained why and how economic equilibria were destroyed, why the economic system was pushed away from equilibrium, something the analysis of adaptive processes did not even try do.

In this process there is nothing automatic. It takes a *real* person to affect the change who becomes an entrepreneur when he does so and only for as long as he does so. His motivation has more in common with that of the artist than the homo oecomicus. *Any* change is an innovation including the development of the industrial system itself.

The entrepreneur is not a factor of production, and entrepreneurs are not a class. They exist everywhere at all times. What makes them a capitalist phenomenon is how they get hold of the resources required to execute their ideas. In a feudal or in a socialist system, there is a direct command over resources. The capitalistic entrepreneur on the other hand does not in principle own resources, he has to buy them, as a rule with borrowed money which, as a matter of fact 'though not of logical necessity' is created for the purpose.

Evolutionary processes take place in historic time. Nothing is instantaneous nor can anything once done be undone. The movement away from equilibrium comes to an end when the innovations begin to pour their products on the market, starting a process of adjustment, originally called an *Einordnungsprozess* which later became more dramatically a process of creative destruction and which at present is deplored as downsizing, an unpleasant neologism. Referring to market imperfections is a most inadequate explanation because these imperfections are an *inevitable* consequence of evolution.

There is one point which I want to mention specially: the zero rate of interest in equilibrium. Schumpeter does not for a moment deny that time preference may produce a positive rate for consumption loans, but he considers this trivial, self-evident, uninteresting. He is talking about productive interest which is linked to and indeed paid out of profits, which are in turn the result of innovations.

Unlike in Böhm-Bawerk's or Wicksell's theory there is no *real* rate of interest because there is also no real capital as distinct from capital goods. Wicksell admits a zero rate in a state of capital saturation. No such state is conceivable for Schumpeter, because, as already stated, there is always something to be done. For Schumpeter, capital is a sum of money used for productive purposes, and the demand for this capital dries up temporarily and cyclically.

Schumpeter really is after combining historic uniqueness with theoretical penetration. *Business Cycles* was his grand attempt to work this out in detail. Its major theoretical innovation was a four-phase cycle and a three-cycle scheme. It was not well received, partly because his approach was not understood, partly because it appeared at a bad time in which statistical techniques changed drastically. At a time when statistical analysis spent much effort on measuring the length of cycles – and Schumpeter also did this – his insistence that what was needed was detailed historical study was perhaps felt to be unpleasantly reactionary. Remember also that Tinbergen's study of American and British Business Cycles which dethroned the importance of turning points was yet in the future.

It is therefore useful to mention a letter to his friend Wesley Mitchell who had asked Schumpeter for his dating of events, particularly of the long waves. Schumpeter obliged but then wrote in detail why he considered such dating at best only a very rough affair.

There were at any one moment different influences present. There were truly unique and extra-economic events, like the San Francisco earthquake (or this year's record snowfall). There were the internal reactions of an economy, Wicksell's rocking horse analogy. But there were also the systemic changes in production functions which Schumpeter thought were central to understanding of how an evolutionary economy worked and which he thought he could explain. His three-cycle scheme was intended to come to grips with the multiplicity of wave-like movements, (though he stressed that there was nothing sacred about the number 3) and only detailed historical analysis could establish the importance of each factor. So Schumpeter was prepared to state that the economy rose, even if the statistics showed a decline, if he could establish that the decline was due to unique events. Before thus is condemned as arbitrary let me remind you that this is done routinely for seasonally adjusted series.

Capitalism, Socialism and Democracy is considered by some a pot boiler, by others, for example McCraw of the Harvard Business School, arguably the best analysis of the real capitalist economy and its inherent tendencies of change.

Its most controversial point is probably the supposed prediction of the coming of socialism. But Schumpeter explicitly did not predict anything but he discussed the results of presently visible tendencies if continued unchecked. Also, Schumpeter's definition of socialism is quite different from that of Mises or Hayek, and he considered England's going off the Gold Standard in September 1991 a more important portent of things to come than anything that happened in Soviet Russia. Russian events were for him understandable by Tsarism, not Marxism, retrogressive events delaying the coming of socialism. The collapse of the Soviet Union confirms, it does not contradict his analysis.

How far we have moved away from the world of nineteenth-century capitalism is shown by the difficulties of establishing a common European currency. All that it is desired to establish is what was taken for granted before 1914, to re-establish what the Gold Standard achieved. Of course, gold is a barbaric relic, and quite unnecessary. Restrictions on national economic behavior are necessary. To talk of giving up sovereignty is, to put it mildly, peculiar. Nobody thought of having given up anything before 1914. There is a vast overestimation of how much freedom of action any individual country really can have. Of course, times have changed; that is precisely the point.

27.3 SOME FURTHER DEVELOPMENTS

I should like to end this part of my tribute to Hans by just mentioning the work of eight scholars who have made significant contributions along Schumpeterian lines.

Ragnar Frisch in his famous contribution to the Cassel *Festschrift* explicitly introduced a mechanical analogy to model some aspects of Schumpeter's analysis of the effects of innovation. He did so after Schumpeter had refused to accept an earlier version. His was the only attempt which appeared during Schumpeter's life time and it is discussed in *Business Cycles*.

Nelson and Winter modelled the behaviour of individual firms without profit maximizing assumptions, their analysis proceeding by simulation and occasionally by sufficiently simplifying assumptions to allow an analytic solution.

Richard Goodwin worked out more general and purely mathematical models to generate fluctuations which bear a family resemblance to observed time series. He referred to his results as Schumpeter's 'vision confirmed'.

Brian Arthur established empirically the 'path dependency' of results, which basically shows that a decision maker changes his surroundings for better or for worse by whatever decision he has made.

Douglas North has recently received the Nobel Prize for his work showing how history shapes the development of institutions. He has singled out Schumpeter as the only economist to have even tried to analyse the pressures that lead to changes in economies.

Scherer, decades ago, published a path-breaking analysis of some 20 000 patents which showed, among other things, that about 10 per cent of all patented innovations received about 90 per cent of the profits. Building on Scherer's findings and assuming that real historic time had to elapse for innovations to penetrate the economy, Nordhaus produced a simple model to explain the actual fluctuations of patents. I found most intriguing that the list of innovations which got the profits and had the most effect had a strikingly Schumpeterian sound: telephone, computer and the like, This suggests that the most basic phenomena may not be the business cycles but the long waves which themselves work in an irregular fashion – which Spiethoff had already observed!

All these scholars, with the exception of North, start explicitly with a Schumpeterian inspiration.

History matters. Theory matters. Evolution, not equilibrium, is the central phenomenon. The future is in principle not foreseeable. Theoretical explanations are rational but not deterministic. Extrapolation of the past to the future may work for a time but may then suddenly become misleading. These are perhaps the most important messages of Schumpeter's work.

27.4   A PERSONAL TRIBUTE

This has been a scholarly symposium with scholarly papers, as befits such an occasion. But it is also a birthday party. So I ask your indulgence for a few more minutes. Good fortune has brought me to Europe and allowed me to join the many well-wishers whose life you, lieber Hans, have touched.

It has already been mentioned that you were one of only four persons to whom the English Cambridge awarded a PhD between the two Great Wars. I never read your thesis, though I did read Alec Cairncross's thesis in mimeographed form. I believe that I even quoted it in my doctoral thesis which Harvard in the American Cambridge awarded me.

When I taught the Honors Seminar in Theory in Swarthmore College, I used Wicksell's Lectures as a text and supplemented it by assigning important articles. Among those was Hans Singer's article on British rents in *Econometrica* which was a condensation of the thesis. This article, the result of detailed historical research, is an inter-penetration of historical, statistical and theoretical analysis which is the characteristic of modern theory at its best. Schumpeter had reason to regret that you left theory. There were other articles which I assigned in my location theory.

I also remember a lecture in Ann Arbor which met with a huge success. For you talked with authority and 'not as one of the scribes'.

But I want to tell of two incidents which this assembly of friends might possibly be interested in. You probably have forgotten the first which illustrates on a trivial level your far from trivial enthusiasm and commitment.

Spiethoff had bought a calculator, a big, noisy mechanical contraption which just could do the four basic operations. We were all enthusiastic about this modern marvel, none more so than you. I recall vividly how you demonstrated to us how simple it had now become to multiply 2×2!

But there was also a far from trivial matter. The Nazis had come to power, a catastrophe for us personally, for Germany and for the world. There were vicious attacks on you which we, you and your fellow students, met head on. We did actually succeed in having the attacker thrown out of the student SS for dishonourable behavior. The story bears retelling, although I have told it already elsewhere.

The bulletin board had an announcement telling us that we could buy the *Festschrift* for Spiethoff which Schumpeter had organized at a discount. One of the contributors was Professor Kurt Singer (no relation), at that time in Tokyo. Someone had written vicious anti-Semitic remarks directed at Hans. Hans, being an honorable man, wrote beside the remarks: 'Will whoever wrote this at least sign his name, or else he is not only a swine, but also a coward' or words to this effect.

When nothing happened we, Hans' fellow students, decided to take matters into our own hands. With the help of the assistants who showed us the hour exams, we identified the writer. I then went to Cologne on the back of a big BMW motorcycle belonging to a fellow student to consult a graphologist, who gave us his written expertise that the handwriting on the announcement indeed belonged to the identified writer.

We then called a meeting of the *Fachschaft*. Although an elected President, I was no longer allowed to attend. So August Lösch had to carry on the fight. Before leaving for the meeting, Lösch gave me some money with instructions where to send it in case he had to run.

The student was then accused of having written the remarks which he denied. He was then confronted with the expertise, and censured by the *Fachschaft*. This came to the ears of the Student SS which in turn called a meeting and expelled the student for dishonourable behaviour – which, of course, was not of having written the remarks but of having denied of having done so.

There was an aftermath involving only me. The head of the Student SS and I ran into each other on the street and he asked me to join him for a glass of beer which I accepted after having made sure that he knew who I was. He then thanked me profusely for having helped the SS to rid itself of such a dishonorable character! He also mentioned that there were only 10 000 Nazis in Bonn, and that the population could club them to death if it so chose.

I do want to tell that story for a reason. Although we did not understand how power worked or to what depth pure evil could descend – had we known we might have been less impetuous – we *did* know how to behave honourably. There may be many things in your life, lieber Hans, as there surely are in mine, which you regret. I am certain that there are none of which you need be ashamed.

Lieber Hans, you are an extraordinarily intelligent person. But there are many just as intelligent. You are also an extraordinarily compassionate person, and I must confess that I for one do not have your capacity for compassion. But you are something much rarer still: You are one of the very few people I would call truly good, *ein wahrer Mensch*.

Lieber Hans, this has been a wonderful occasion to renew face-to face a friendship which has been kept alive for more than six decades by letter and occasional meetings. You have enriched the life of many people, I am grateful that mine is among them.

28 Modern Relevance of Keynesianism in the Study of Development

Hans W. Singer[1]

INTRODUCTION

In the concluding lines of his pioneering work, *The General Theory of Employment Interest and Money*, Keynes speaks of 'defunct economists' setting the agenda for the 'madmen in authority' who believe that they 'hear voices in the air'. In 1936 when he published the *General Theory*, the 'madmen in authority' he had in mind were Hitler and Mussolini (and perhaps Stalin). Now Keynes himself is a defunct economist – he died almost exactly 50 years ago. Today's 'madmen in authority' are followers of the neo-classical counter-revolution, preaching the blessings of market orientation and the horrors of government intervention, strongly represented in the IMF, World Bank, and some powerful governments dominating the G7, all following the ideology of the 'Washington Consensus'. The question arises whether the agenda set by Keynes is still valid and relevant today and whether the 'madmen in authority' unwillingly or unknowingly are still guided by it.

In one sense the answer to that question is all too obvious – so much so that it is almost obscene to ask it. In the industrial countries effective demand and investment are clearly below the 'warranted' full employment level, that is labour supply plus the rate of productivity growth. Unemployment in Europe alone on the official count amounts to 18 million people (equivalent with their family members to the population of the UK or France or Italy). Beyond that – just as the Keynesians explained – there is a vastly larger number of people suffering from disguised unemployment: that is, not working at the full level of their productive capacity or working short-time, or not offering themselves in the labour market because of the absence of jobs. The present catchword for what the Keynesians called open plus disguised unemployment is social exclusion. As I am writing these lines the European Union is embarking on its Inter-Governmental Conference (IGC) in which the unemployment issue has

524

emerged paramount on the agenda. Seemingly conquered in the Golden Age of the Keynesian Consensus in the 25 years 1945–70, unemployment re-emerged around 1971 or 1973 (with the breakdown of the Bretton Woods system and the OPEC quadrupling of oil prices respectively) and has by now been a problem of 25 years standing. After 25 years it should be clear, just as Keynes told us 60 years ago, that there is no self-correcting tendency, in the absence of purposeful macroeconomics governance, for economies to correct themselves and return to a full employment equilibrium.

However, my subject is the relevance of Keynesianism in the study of development, meaning the development of the poorer or Third World countries rather than the industrial countries. Here the relevance of Keynes and Keynesianism is even more glaringly obvious – in this case referring more to the later Keynes who was the guiding spirit in establishing the new international economic order at Bretton Woods in 1944 rather than the Keynes who wrote the *General Theory* in 1936. I need only mention one single dominant fact to establish this. It is estimated that at present there is something like a $500 billion per year resource outflow from the developing countries, offsetting many times over the reverse flow of aid. This $500 billion outflow is made up of four major items:

1. **Terms of trade losses**: compared with, say, 30 years ago, the terms of trade of the primary commodities and simple low-tech manufactures on which most developing countries still depend have sharply deteriorated in relation to their imports of high-tech manufactures. This factor alone amounts to a tax of 20–25 per cent on the export earnings of developing countries.

2. **Debt servicing**: these debts have their origin in the early 1970s arising from the way in which the big financial surpluses of the OPEC countries were dealt with and recycled by the commercial banking system. This amounts to another 20–25 per cent tax on export earnings. The debt pressure and terms of trade losses are mutually interrelated (in a way which Keynes had already described 15 years earlier than the *General Theory* in connection with the reparations imposed on Germany after the First World War).

3. **Repatriation of profits and transfer pricing**: this source of outflows by foreign investors and especially multinational corporations operating in developing countries is volatile and in any case difficult to estimate, but it may well be of a similar order of magnitude to terms of trade losses and debt servicing.

4. **Capital flight from developing countries**: also volatile and difficult to control or even to trace, this is facilitated by the globalisation of financial services and currency transactions. Assets held in developed countries are subject to less risk of inflation, devaluation, and political instability.

What is the point of listing here these four major drains which together deprive the developing countries of half or more of their potential export earnings? The point is that under the arrangements which Keynes proposed in his preparatory memoranda for Bretton Woods and which were partially implemented during the Golden Age of the Keynesian Consensus in the 1950s and 1960s these catastrophic drains would not have occurred. Terms of trade losses would have been avoided or reduced by stabilization of primary commodity prices through international buffer stocks and international commodity agreements. Keynes was a fervent supporter of such stabilization. He even proposed initially a world currency based on a bundle of 30 primary commodities, thus automatically stabilizing their average price (without ruling out fluctuations of individual commodities against this average). This would also have contributed to global macro-economic stability: in slack times when commodity prices were low international buffer stocks would have been accumulated, thus injecting additional liquidity into the world economy, and vice versa in case of inflationary demand pressures and high commodity prices. In the system proposed by Keynes there was in addition to the IMF and World Bank an essential third pillar: an International Trade Organization with commodity price stabilization as its major function. In fact the ITO was duly negotiated and established in Havana in 1947 but never came into existence, failing to obtain ratification by the US Congress. The newly-established WTO does not have any of the commodity functions envisaged for the ITO.

Similarly, debt servicing would not have arisen, or would be much less under the Keynesian Consensus. Keynes had proposed an international tax on balance of payments surplus countries (for 'exporting unemployment') and liquidity support for balance of payments deficit countries from an 'International Clearing Union' – his original term for the IMF, but visualized as much larger and operating with less conditionality (to save deficit countries from having to deflate).

The transfer of profits out of developing countries and repatriation of investment by multinational corporations would also have been prevented if Keynes's original ideas had been followed. He advocated control of capital movements and strict regulation of foreign investment (as practiced by South Korea during their successful rise to the status of an industrial power). In his own words: he wanted 'homespun economies'. He was deeply suspicious of financial markets and the 'casino economies' which dominated them. 'The proper job of finance is to see that nothing is done on purely financial grounds.'

As far as capital flight is concerned, this also would have been eliminated or reduced by controls on globalization and capital movements. In any case, if the economies of developing countries had been put on the expansionary path of full employment growth suggested by Keynesianism (as expressed by the Harrod–Domar formula to which we turn later), the incentive for capital flight would have been much less.

So much for the question of relevance of Keynesianism to our current development problems. We now turn to two specific contributions of Keynesianism to our understanding of development policy: the concept of disguised unemployment and the Harrod–Domar model of sustained growth.

DISGUISED UNEMPLOYMENT

The concept of disguised unemployment is associated more directly less with Keynes himself than with one of his closest disciples and followers, Joan Robinson.[2] Keynes himself had thought of the labour supply only in two broad categories: one part fully employed and another part fully unemployed. The purpose of his macroeconomic proposals was to increase the first part and reduce the second part. Joan Robinson pointed out that there is in fact a more complicated spectrum in the labour market. Apart from those fully employed and fully unemployed, there are those who are employed at low productivity, partly employed with reduced working hours, self-employed because of the absence of an employer willing to take them on, and so on. A reduction in effective demand for labour may show as much or more in these intermediate categories of disguised unemployment as in the official unemployment figures.

Joan Robinson's concepts, like those of Keynes, were initially applied to the UK and industrial countries in general, as indicated by her favourite identification of disguised unemployment with 'selling matches in the Strand'. This is certainly of direct relevance at the present time. Quite recently, John Eatwell of Cambridge University has undertaken a detailed study of disguised unemployment in the G7 countries.[3] According to his results, relating to 1990, disguised unemployment – mainly in the form of low-productivity employment in the services, construction, and agriculture sectors – was larger than open published unemployment. According to his figures, in 1990 average open unemployment in the G7 countries (simple average of the 7 countries) was 6.7 per cent. But true unemployment including disguised unemployment was 14.9 per cent. In other words disguised unemployment was 8.2 per cent compared with open unemployment of 6.7 per cent. Between 1973 and 1992 the percentage of part-time employment increased from 16 per cent to 23 per cent in the UK, and from 14 per cent to 21 per cent in Japan, from 16 per cent to 18 per cent in the USA, from 10 per cent to 16 per cent in Germany and from 6 per cent to 13 per cent in France.

However, it soon became apparent that the most important application of the concept of disguised unemployment is in developing countries. Here full and open unemployment is not usually practicable – except by support through the kinship system – because there is no social insurance and a fully unemployed person could simply not survive. Moreover, in the agricultural sector, which provides the main reservoir of labour in developing countries, work is in any case shared among all the household members and in the same way in slack seasons unemployment is shared among the household members. Furthermore the available data show that labour productivity in agriculture and also in services is much lower than in manufacturing. It was thus a small step from there for the early development economists to draw the conclusion that the low-productivity agricultural sector constituted a labour reserve and the transfer out of this sector into higher productivity sectors, particularly manufacturing, was the royal road to development. In fact, a rudimentary model of this kind had already been sketched by Adam Smith in *The Wealth of Nations*. The economist most strongly associated with this strategy of using the disguised agricultural employment as an opportunity for economic growth through transfer was Arthur Lewis, with his emphasis on 'unlimited supplies of labour.'[4] Joan Robinson herself in 1937 was also well aware of this application to developing countries, for in addition to mentioning 'selling matches in the Strand' she also mentions 'cutting brushwood in the jungles'.

The strategy of using disguised unemployment in agriculture as a means of growth by transfer to higher-productivity industry has been criticized as leading to lopsided development through neglect of agriculture, notably by T.W. Schultz.[5] This criticism may be legitimate in relation to the emphasis on industrialization and the 'urban bias' inherent in treating agriculture mainly as a reservoir for feeding the labour demands of industrialization. But it is not legitimate when applied to the concept of disguised unemployment as such. It is quite open to policy-makers to decide to deal with the problem by reducing the degree of disguised unemployment in agriculture itself, by raising the productivity and output of farming. Which is the better strategy – or rather the best combination of the two strategies – is a matter of analyzing which combination yields the highest net benefits in terms of economic growth. In support of Arthur Lewis, it can be stated that a reduction of the proportion of population in agriculture and an increase in the share of industrial production in GDP has been an invariable feature of economic growth. In support of T.W. Schultz, the example of the Green Revolution in India and Pakistan, or the high agricultural productivity in Korea and Taiwan, can be quoted as demonstrating the potential of a more agriculture-led growth. Another element in favour of the Schultz position was introduced by the Harris – Todaro model. This pointed out that because of the different levels of earnings in agriculture and formal industrial employment the volume of transfer from rural to urban areas would be excessive and hence a significant proportion of the transfer would amount to a transfer from low-productivity employment in agriculture to urban unemployment, or at best to equally low-productivity employment in the urban informal sector. But the balance was tilted back again towards the Lewis position when the ILO Employment Mission to Kenya pointed out that the developmental productivity of employment in the urban informal sector was larger than had previously been assumed.[6]

THE HARROD–DOMAR FORMULA

Like disguised unemployment, this other influential contribution of Keynesianism to development studies was due less to Keynes himself than to one of his close disciples, in this case Roy Harrod. Keynes himself, until he later (1942) became involved in the preparation of the post-war international economic order, was interested in the practical problems of reducing unemployment in the UK, and not what would happen once full employment had been achieved and how it could be sustained: 'In the long run we are all dead.' When Keynes exceptionally and outside his main work gave some attention to long-term problems, as in his essay on 'The economics of our grandchildren', he did this not in terms of a dynamic model of continued growth of GNP. On the contrary, he thought of the long-run equilibrium as one of reaching a plateau of reasonable satisfaction of basic needs when further accumulation and growth would be pointless and the fruits of further technical progress would be taken in the form of increased leisure, development of non-economic artistic and cultural activities and improved quality of life. In this respect Keynes was the forerunner of development economists like Dudley Seers, Paul Streeten, and others, who also questioned the objective of growth of GNP as the beginning and end of economic development.

Harrod's model (later supplemented by Evsey Domar) does not belong to this school of thought. It explores the preconditions for self-sustaining dynamic economic growth over time, implicitly accepting this as equivalent to development. It directly derives from Keynes in so far as like Keynes it uses the concept of the multiplier and puts capital accumulation or physical investment at the centre of the analysis as the element most suitable for manipulation in order to produce, the warranted growth rate which leads to full employment. The basis of Harrod–Domar is so simple as to amount almost to a tautology. The rate of growth is determined by the share of investment in output (in equilibrium equal to the share of saving) divided by the capital–output ratio. If the rate of investment is 12 per cent and the capital–output ratio is 3 (that is, three units of capital are needed to produce one unit of output in all subsequent years) the rate of growth will be 4 per cent. If the rate of population increase is 1 per cent per annum, then the rate of per caput income growth will be 3 per cent. Simple, but all the same illuminating and also controversial.

The formula is illuminating because capital accumulation or physical investment is clearly an important element in economic growth, just as disguised unemployment identified structural transformation from agriculture and industrialization as important elements in development. A high and steady rate of investment has been an outstanding feature of the high-performing East Asian economies. A recent authoritative study of these economies finds that 'these countries top the international league tables not just with respect to the long-term growth of their GDP but also to their national savings and investment rates.'[7] More questionable was the limitation of the concept of investment to physical capital. Development economists have come to place more and more emphasis on the importance of human capital (which Keynes, concentrating on short-term problems and the UK, took more or less for granted, as he did the capacity to supply higher rates of capital investment). In the formal sense this is not a valid criticism of the Harrod–Domar formula itself, which remains tautologically true. An increase in human capital – say better education, higher skills, or better health – will improve the capital–output ratio and by lowering it increase the rate of sustainable growth. Mathematically it makes no difference whether human capital is taken care of by adding it to investment in the enumerator or by lowering the capital–output ratio in the denominator.

However, while it may make no difference mathematically, it is true to say that by expressing everything in relation to physical capital accumulation the formula may lead to a neglect of other factors important for growth. The role of technical innovation for instance, as emphasized by Schumpeter, is not easily accommodated in the Harrod–Domar formula. Does it find expression in additional capital formation – this seems to be at odds with Schumpeter's emphasis on 'creative destruction' – or in improving the capital–output ratio? Also, in the Harrod–Domar formula the rate of investment and the capital–output ratio are presented as two separate and presumably independent factors. Keynes himself, in line with neoclassical growth theory, seemed to believe that continued capital accumulation would be associated with a falling marginal efficiency of investment. Subsequent development economists, like Kaldor, have presented development models where growth feeds upon itself with constant or increasing returns, that is, an incremental capital–output ratio (ICOR) equal to or lower than the average capital–output ratio, the foundation of the 'new growth theory'. Myrdal's cumulative causation may also lead to similar results, but in a downward as well as an upward direction. With these new insights the Harrod–Domar model may be seen to be in the nature of a razor's edge (as Harrod himself had already made clear) where a steady rate of growth is achieved almost by rare accident and the normal case would be either inflation or stagnation or in fact a combination of both in the form of stagflation. Deviation from the warranted rate of growth would be self-amplifying.

The Harrod–Domar formula does not distinguish to what extent the crucial rate of investment, and the crucial increase in the rate of investment needed for full-employment growth, are to be achieved by public or private investment. But Keynesians, while advocating a mixed economy, tended to stress the catalytic role of public investment and the complementary relation between the two. Reliance on private investment might also involve the acceptance of income inequalities and of a high rate of profits (a major source of savings and investment). Many Keynesians, and Keynes himself in his later life, wanted greater equality in the form of a welfare state moving towards a *Pareto optimum*; hence they were leaning towards *public* investment and strategic *public* investment planning, project appraisal and cost–benefit analysis. This had an influence on the early development economists who were much concerned with techniques of development planning. The early Indian Five-Year Plans and the Mahalanobis model on which these plans were based served as a centre-piece of analysis and debate.

The emphasis on physical capital accumulation also provided an intellectual basis for aid to developing countries. Aid was supposed to go into capital formation rather than consumption. Moreover, aid was supposed to be a transfer from capital-abundant donor countries with low marginal returns to capital (that is, a high capital–output ratio) to poorer countries with little capital and hence a favourable capital–output ratio. The success of the Marshall Plan – the most formidable aid project of the time – also seemed to support the emphasis on capital investment. However, this last point could also be questioned: it was pointed out that the success of the Marshall Plan might be due to the ready availability of human capital in the recipient countries and also to the fact that rehabilitation and reconstruction is easier and has a lower capital–output ratio than building up capital from scratch. Also it could be pointed out that the development institutions were in place, which leads us to the criticism of the Harrod–Domar formula that it does not explicitly include institutional factors in the growth formula. Political stability, solid financial institutions, social harmony, the rule of law, and soon are clearly factors in economic growth, but do not explicitly figure in the Harrod–Domar formula, although Harrod and Domar would have readily accepted them as important determinants of bouth the rates of investment and the Incremental Capital–Output Ratio.

CONCLUSION

Thus in answer to the question raised by our title, we may point to disguised unemployment and the Harrod–Domar formula as two examples of Keynesianism which have had a deep and lasting effect on development thinking and development policy. Neglect of employment effects (including disguised unemployment), maintenance of effective demand on a full-employment sustainable growth path and of the promotion of capital accumulation (both physical and human) has had harmful effects in the stabilization and structural adjustment programmes imposed on developing countries. There are new signs that this is being recognised and that the pendulum is swinging back from the excesses of the neo-liberal counter-revolution and towards an updated Keynesian Consensus.

The neo-classical counter-revolution, proclaimed as supplying an alternative (and superior) development paradigm to that derived from the original Keynesian revolution, is not really an alternative but a supplement. Once full employment has been achieved and sustained much of the neo-classical teaching about the importance of the market as a welfare-maximizing allocative force becomes valid and relevant. But the Keynesian principle of full-employment effective demand comes first. It is the dog which should be wagging the neo-classical tail. Today, under the

Washington Consensus, the tail is wagging the dog, with unhappy results for development economics – and, perhaps more important, for the developing countries.

Notes

1. I am grateful to Adrian Wood for comment on an earlier draft.
2. J.V. Robinson, 'Disguised Unemployment', in *Essays in the Theory of Employment* (London: Macmillan, 1937).
3. John Eatwell. *Disguised Unemployment: the G7 Experience*, UNCTAD Discussion Paper no. 106, November 1995.
4. W.A. Lewis: 'Economic Development with Unlimited Supplies of Labour', *The Manchester School*, May 1954.
5. T.W. Schultz, *Transforming Traditional Agriculture* (New Haven, Conn.: Yale University Press, 1964). Ironically Arthur Lewis and T.W. Schultz received a *joint* Nobel Prize in Economics.
6. ILO, *Employment, Incomes and Equality – a strategy for increasing productive employment in Kenya* (Geneva: International Labour Office, 1972).
7. Ajit Singh. 'The Causes of Fast Economic Growth in East Asia', in *UNCTAD Review* (1995) p. 118.

Professor Sir Hans W. Singer: Academic Education and Honours, Career and Publications

Compiled by D.J. Shaw

ACADEMIC EDUCATION, HONOURS AND CAREER

Academic education and honours

Diploma in Political Economy, Bonn University, Germany, 1931; PhD in Economics, Cambridge University, England, 1936; Honorary Fellow, Institute of Social Studies, The Hague, The Netherlands, 1975; hon. doctorate *Universidad Nacional del Litoral*, Santa Fe, Argentina, 1989; hon. DLitt, University of Sussex, England, 1990; hon. DLitt, Glasgow University, Scotland, 1994; hon. doctorate *Universidade Técnica de Lisboa*, Portugal, 1994.

Other honours

Frances Wood Memorial Prize, Royal Statistical Society, England, 1939, for work on unemployment statistics; President, Society for International Development (SID), New York Chapter, and President, SID, UK Chapter; President, UK Development Studies Association, 1988–90; knighted (Knight Bachelor), 1994 for services to economic issues; Alan Shawn Feinstein World Hunger Award for Research and Education, Brown University, United States, 1994/95.

Early career, 1936–47

Researcher, UK Pilgrim Trust Unemployment Enquiry 1936–8; Assistant Lecturer, University of Manchester, England, 1938–44; Economist, UK Ministry of Town and Country Planning, London, 1945–6; Lecturer, Glasgow University, Scotland, 1946–7.

Career with United Nations 1947–69

Ending as full Director (D2), posts included: directorships of the Economic Division of UNIDO (United Nations Industrial Development Organization); and

UNRISD (United Nations Research Institute for Social Development). Chief of UN Development Section; Special Adviser to the UN Under-Secretary for Economic and Social Affairs. Director of Policies and Programming Division of United Nations Economic Commission for Africa, in Addis Ababa, Ethiopia); Chairman of Preparatory Secretariat Group, and Secretary of Governmental Committee, for the establishment of UN Special Fund for Economic Development. Secretary of UN Committee on Commodity Trade. Secretary of the UN Committee of Development Planning, etc. Senior UN Interregional Adviser on Development Planning. UN Adviser for the development of North-Eastern Brazil and the northern region of Thailand. Head, UN Technical Assistance Programming Mission to Kenya. Leader of many UN missions to developing countries and Economic Adviser to the governments of many developing countries. Chairman of Group of Experts on the establishment of UN World Food Programme. In charge of UN Secretariat work on: the Report of the UN Secretary-General on Proposals for Action of the First United Nations Development Decade of the 1960s; the establishment of the African Development Bank; the World Food Programme; the UN Special Fund, and on drafting the UN World Plan of Action for the Application of Science and Technology to Development. Member of: the Preparatory Committee for the Stockholm Conference on the Relationship between Environment and Development; the UN Expert Panel on Science and Technology; and the UN Committee on Social Planning. Consultant to the ILO on the establishment and operation of the World Employment Programme, specifically its Asian branch (ARTEP).

Conjointly Professor, Graduate Faculty, New School for Social Research, New York, 1947–69. Visiting Professor, Williams College, Williamstown, Massachusetts, USA, 1965.

Institute of development studies, university of Sussex, England, 1969 to present

Professorial Fellow and Emeritus Professor. Fellow of Institute since 1969. Many consultancies to developing countries and for international organisation (see 'Reports' in Section B of List of Publications). On editorial boards of various journals.

LIST OF PUBLICATIONS

Section A: books and pamphlets

This list of publications adds to that produced in Sir Alec Cairncross and M. Puri (eds) *Employment Income Distribution and Development Strategy – Problems of Developing Countries: Essays in Honour of H.W. Singer* (Macmillan, 1976) pp. 245–53. The late Joyce Stacey, former secretary to Hans Singer, assisted in compiling the lists of the earlier works. Caroline Pybus and Dawn Widgery of the Institute of Development Studies (IDS). University of Sussex, UK, assisted in producing the lists of the more recent works. Appreciation is given to IDS for supporting this work.

This list includes contributions by Hans Singer to books edited by him or written or edited or produced by others. Publications for the United Nations, other international bodies and governments are listed separately in Section B.

1. *Materials for the Study of Urban Ground Rent*, Cambridge University dissertation, approved for PhD degree in Economics, 1936. Short printed abstract available. Results summarized by Colin Clark in *National Income and Outlay* (Macmillan, 1937) and in his *Conditions of Economic Progress* (Macmillan, 1940).

2. (With W.F. Oakeshott and A.D.K. Owen) *Men Without Work: A Report to the Pilgrim Trust* (Cambridge University Press, 1937).

3. 'The Regional Distribution of Unemployment', in *Pilgrim Trust Unemployment Enquiry Interim Report*, with Preface by Dr William Temple, then Archbishop of York, 1937.

4. 'Changes in the Distribution of the Industrial Population', in *Pilgrim Trust Unemployment Enquiry Interim Report*, with Preface by Dr William Temple, then Archbishop of York, 1937.

5. 'Transference and the Age Structure of the Depressed Areas', in *Pilgrim Trust Unemployment Enquiry Interim Report*, with Preface by Dr William Temple, then Archbishop of York, 1937.

6. 'Unemployment and Health', in *Pilgrim Trust Unemployment Enquiry Interim Report*, with Preface by Dr William Temple, then Archbishop of York, 1937.

7. *Unemployment and the Unemployed* (London: King and Son 1940).

8. *Standardised Accountancy* (Cambridge University Press, for the National Institute for Economic and Social Research, 1943).

9. *Can We Afford 'Beveridge'?* Fabian Society Research Pamphlet (London, 1943).

10. *How Widespread are National Savings?* Circulated as a pamphlet by the National Savings Committee (London, 1946).

11. 'Some Accounting and Economic Aspects', in *The Working Party Reports* (London: Association of Certified and Corporate Accountants, 1948).

12. (With C.E.V. Leser) *Industrial Productivity in England and Scotland* Published as Reprint IV by the Department of Social and Economic Research, University of Glasgow, Scotland, 1950. Also read as a paper to the Royal Statistical Society, London, and printed in the *Journal of the Royal Statistical Society*.

13. *Economic Development of Under-Developed Countries* (Rio de Janeiro: Vargas Foundation, 1950). Based on a series of lectures delivered in Rio de Janeiro, Brazil (in Portuguese).

14. *Economic Development Projects as Part of National Development Programmes* Reprinted as part of the official proceedings of the Development Institute, Lahore, Pakistan, 1951.

15. *O Nord–Este: Estudo Sôbre O Desenvolvimento Economico Do Nordeste* (Economic Development of the Brazilian North-East), Comissao de Desenvolvimento Economico de Pernambuco, Recife, 1952. (Also published in English as a UN Technical Assistance, Report, 1953.)

16. 'The Economics of Technical Development', *Yearbook of Education* (London, 1954).
17. (With W.A. Jöhr) *The Role of the Economist as Official Adviser* (London: Allen & Unwin, 1955).
18. (Part contributor) *Economics of Under-Development* (Oxford University Press, 1958).
19. 'Development Plans in Asia', in Robert J. Barr (ed.) *American Trade with Asia and the Far East* (Milwaukee, Wis.: Marquette University Press, 1959).
20. 'The Dilemmas of Under-Developed Countries', in William D. Grampp and E.T. Weiler (eds), *Economic Policy Readings in Political Economy*, The Irwin Series in Economics (Homewood, Ill.: Irwin Inc., 1961).
21. 'Tendencías Recientes del Pensamiento Económico Sobre los Países Sub-desarrollados' ('Recent Tendencies in Economic Thinking about Underdeveloped Countries') in *Revista de Economia Latinoamericana*, 1961.
22. *International Development, Growth and Change*, McGraw-Hill Series in International Development New York: McGraw-Hill, 1964.
23. (co-edited with Nicolas de Kun and Abbas Ordoobadi) *International Development, 1966* New York: Oceania Publications, 1967).
24. *Disarmament, International Development Economics* (contributor), Stanford Law Society, 1967.
25. 'The Concept and the Role of Capital. Social Development: Key Growth Sector' (ch. 1) and 'Strategies of Capital Accumulation. A Balanced View of Balanced Growth' (ch. 3) in Shanti S. Tangri and H. Peter Gray (eds) *Capital Accumulation and Economic Development* (London: D.C. Heath & Co., 1967).
26. (With S. Schiavo-Campo) *Perspectives in Economic Development* (Boston: Houghton Mifflin, 1970).
27. *Britain's Role in the Second Development Decade*, pamphlet prepared for the UK Standing Conference on the Second UN Development Decade (member of the committee which prepared this report) (London, 1971).
28. 'Overseas Trade and Investment Patterns can Reinforce Exploitation' in Martin Wolfe (ed.) *The Economic Causes of Imperialism*, Major Issues in History Series (London: John Wiley and Sons, 1972).
29. (with Javed Ansari) *New Forms of International Co-operation for Technical Assistance* (London: Allen & Unwin, 1973).
30. 'La Empresa International Como Exportadora de Tecnologia (Spanish translation of 'The Foreign Company as an Exporter of Technology') in Miguel S. Wionczek (ed.) *Comercio de Technología y Sub-Desarrollo Económico* (Mexico: Coordinación de Ciencias, 1973).
31. 'International Policies and their Effect on Employment', in Karl Wohlmuth (ed.) *Employment Creation in Developing Societies. The Situation of Labor in Dependent Economies* (New York: Praeger, 1973).
32. 'International Policies and their Effect on Employment', in Willy Sellekaerts (ed.) *Economic Development and Planning. Essays in Honour of Jan Tinbergen* (London: Macmillan, 1974).
33. 'Why Do We Need New Approaches?', in David Wirmark (ed.) *The Rich and the Poor – New Approaches Towards a Global Development Strategy* (1975). International Colloquium organized by the Friedrich Naumann Stiftung and the Swedish Liberal Party, 24–9 Nov. 1974.

34. *The Strategy of International Development. Essays in the Economics of Backwardness* by H.W. Singer, Sir Alec Cairncross and Mohinder Puri (eds) (London: Macmillan, 1975).

35. 'Early Years (1910–1938)', in Sir Alec Cairncross and Mohinder Puri (eds) *Employment, Income Distribution and Development Strategy. Problems of Developing Countries. Essays in Honour of H.W. Singer* (London: Macmillan, 1976).

36. 'Income Distribution and Population Growth', in Hamish Richards (ed.) *Population, Factor Movements and Economic Development. Studies presented to Brinley Thomas* (Cardiff: University of Wales Press, 1976).

37. 'Wirtschaftswachstum oder Bekämpfung der Armut? Dreissing Jahre Wandel im Entwicklungsdenken der Vereinten Nationen' (Economic Growth or Fighting Poverty? Thirty Years of Change in the Development Thinking of the United Nations) in Jens Naumann (ed.) *Auf dem Weg zu sozialen Weltwirtschaft* (Berlin: R. Sperber, 1978).

38. (With Javed Ansari) *Rich and Poor Countries* (London: Allen & Unwin and Baltimore: Johns Hopkins University Press, 1977). 2nd edn, 1978; 3rd edn, 1982, 4th edn 1988. Also published in Spanish as *Países Ricos Y Pobres* (Madrid: Edicones Piramides, S.A., 1982) and in Portuguese as *Países Ricos – Países Pobres*, trans. J.R.B. Azevedo Rio de Janeiro, São Paulo: Livros Tecnicos e Cientificos Editora, 1979).

39. 'Environmental Factors in Project Analysis: A Conceptual Note', in Harry I. Greenfield *et al.* (eds) *Theory for Economic Efficiency: Essays in Honor of Abba P. Lerner* (Cambridge, Mass.: MIT Press, 1979).

40. 'Poverty, Income Distribution and Levels of Living. Thirty Years of Changing Thought on Development Problems', in *Reflections on Economic Development and Social Change. Essays in Honour of Professor V.K.R.V. Rao* (Delhi: Allied Publishers Private Ltd, for the Institute of Economic Growth, 1979). Also published in Spanish by Fondo de Cultura Economics, Mexico (1981).

41. 'The Role of Human Capital in Development' (Lecture delivered at Bristol University, UK, January 198) in Roger M. Garrett (ed.) *North–South Debate – Educational Implications of the Brandt Report* NFER–Nelson, Oct. 1981. Also published in *Pakistan Journal of Applied Economics*, vol. 2, no. 1 (1983).

42. 'North–South and South–South: The North and ECDC (Economic Co-operation Among Developing Countries)' in Breda Pavlic, Raul R. Uranga, Boris Cizelj and Marjan Svetlicic (eds) *The Challenges of South–South Cooperation* (Colorado: Westview Press, 1983).

43. 'Reflections on Our Response to the Poorest of the Third World', in Anthony Jennings (ed.) *Our Response to the Poorest of the Third World* (Oxford: Pergamon Press, 1984).

44. 'Appropriate Technology for a Basic Human Needs Strategy', in P.K. Ghosh (ed.) *Third World Development: A Basic Needs Approach*, International Development Resource Books, no. 13 (London: Greenwood Press, 1984).

45. 'The Terms of Trade Controversy and the Evolution of Soft Financing: Early Years in the UN', in Gerald M. Meier and Dudley Seers (eds) *Pioneers in Development. A World Bank Publication*, published for the World Bank by Oxford University Press (New York and Oxford, 1984). Also *IDS Discussion*

Paper, no. 181 (Nov. 1982). Published in Spanish as 'La controversia de la relación de intercambio y la evolucion del financiamiento en condiciones concesionarias: los primeros anos en la ONU', in Gerald M. Meier and Dudley Seers (eds) *Pioneros del Desarrollo*, published for the World Bank by Editorial Tecnos, Madrid (1986).

46. (With Javed A. Ansari and Robert H. Ballance) *The International Economy and Industrial Development: Trade and Investment in the Third World* (Brighton: Harvester, 1982). Translated into Turkish as *Uluslararasi Ekonomi ve Sinai Kalkinma: Ucuncu Dunyara Dis Ticaret ve Yatirim* (Istanbul: Caglayan Kitabevi, 1985).

47. 'Further Thoughts on North–South Negotiations: A Review of Bhagwati and Ruggie', in Jagdish N. Bhagwati and John Gerard Ruggie (eds) *Power, Passions and Purpose. Prospects for North–South Negotiations*, (Cambridge, Mass.: MIT Press, 1984). Also in *World Development*, vol. 13, no. 2 (1985).

48. 'Aid', 'Dual Economy', 'Underdevelopment'. Contributions to Adam Kuper and Jessica Kuper (eds) *The Social Science Encyclopedia* (London: Routledge & Kegan Paul, 1985).

49. 'Relevance of Keynes for Developing Countries', in Harrold L. Wattel (ed.) *The Policy Consequences of John Maynard Keynes* (New York: M.E. Sharpe, 1985).

50. 'The Ethics of Aid', in M. Wright (ed.) *Rights and Obligations in North–South Relations: Ethical Dimensions of Global Problems* (London: Macmillan, 1986).

51. (With Parvin Alizadeh) 'Import Substitution Revisited, in a Darkening External Environment' in *Im Spannungsfeld von Wirtschaft, Technik und Politik, Festschrift für Bruno Fritsch* Munich: (Gunter Olzog Verlag, 1986). Reproduced in *RAZVOJ/Development–International*, vol. 1, no. 2 (Jul.–Dec. 1986, with amended reprints later.) Also in Sidney Dell (ed.) *Policies for Development. Essays in honour of Gamani Corea* (London: Macmillan, 1988).

52. 'Collective Self-Reliance in the Service of Africa's Employment and Basic Needs', in *The Challenge of Employment and Basic Needs in Africa. Essays in honour of Shyam B.L. Nigam and to mark the tenth anniversary of JASPA* (Jobs and Skills Programme for Africa) (Nairobi: Oxford University Press, 1986).

53. 'What Keynes and Keynesianism Can Teach US About Less Developed Countries', in A.P. Thirlwall (ed.) *Keynes and Economic Development*, The Seventh Keynes Seminar held at the University of Kent at Canterbury, 1985 (London: Macmillan, 1987). Also in Ali M. El-Agraa (ed.) *Protection, Cooperation, Integration and Development: Essays in Honour of Professor Hiroshi Kitamura* (London: Macmillan, 1987).

54. (With John Wood and Tony Jennings) *Food Aid. The Challenge and the Opportunity* (Oxford: Clarendon, 1987).

55. (With Neelamber Hatti and Rameshwar Tandon (eds) *Economic Theory and New World Order*, New World Order Series: vol. 1 (New Delhi: Ashish Publishing House, 1987). Includes: 'The New International Economic Order: An Overview' and 'The Second Brandt Report: A Common Crisis'.

56. (With Neelamber Hatti and Rameshwar Tandon (eds), *International Commodity Policy*, New World Order Series, vol. 2 (New Delhi: Ashish Publishing House, 1987).

57. 'Terms of Trade and Economic Development', in J. Eatwell, M. Milgate, P. Newman (eds) *The New Palgrave: A Dictionary of Economics*, vol. 4 (London: Macmillan, 1987).

58. (With Neelamber Hatti and Rameshwar Tandon (eds)) *Technology Transfer by Multinationals* New World Order Series, vol. 3 (New Delhi: Ashish Publishing House, 1988).

59. (With Neelambar Hatti and Rameshwar Tandon (eds)) *New Protectionism and Restructuring*, 2 vols, New World Order Series, vol. 4 (New Delhi: Ashish Publishing House, 1988).

60. (With Neelamber Hatti and Rameshwar Tandon (eds)) *Resource Transfer and Debt Trap*, 2 vols, New World Order Series, vol. 5 (New Delhi: Ashish Publishing House, 1988).

61. (With Neelambar Hatti and Rameshwar Tandon (eds)) *Challenges of South-South Co-operation*, 2 vols New World Order Series, vol. 6 (New Delhi: Ashish Publishing House, 1988).

62. (With Soumitra Sharma (eds)) *Economic Development and World Debt*, vol. 1 (London: Macmillan, 1989).

63. (With Soumitra Sharma (eds)) *Growth and External Debt Management*, vol. 2 (London: Macmillan, 1989).

64. 'Aid Not Trade? The Evolution of Soft Financing in the Early Years in the United Nations', in Johan Kaufmann (ed.) *Effective Negotiation: Case Studies in Conference Diplomacy* (The Hague: Martinus Nijhoff, 1989).

65. 'Lessons of Post-War Development Experience, 1945–1988, in W.L.M. Adriaansen and J.G. Waardenburg (eds) *A Dual World Economy* (The Netherlands: Wolters-Noordhoff, 1989).

66. 'The Vision of Keynes: The Bretton Woods Institutions', in Erik Jensen and Thomas Fisher (eds) *The United Kingdom – The United Nations* (London: Macmillan, 1990).

67. (With James Pickett (eds)) *Towards Economic Recovery in Sub-Saharan Africa* (London: Routledge, 1990).

68. (With Neelambar Hatti and Rameshwar Tandon (eds)) *North–South Trade in Manufactures*, New World Order Series, vol. 7 (New Delhi: Indus Publishing Co., 1990).

69. (With Neelambar Hatti and Rameshwar Tandon (eds)) *Trade Liberalization in the 1990s*, New World Order Series, vol. 8 (New Delhi: Indus Publishing Co. 1990).

70. 'Food Aid', in C.K. Eicher and J.M. Staatz (eds) *Agricultural Development in the Third World*, 2nd edn, Johns Hopkins Studies in Development (Baltimore: Johns Hopkins University Press, 1990).

71. (With Neelambar Hatti and Rameshwar Tandon (eds)) *Aid and External Financing in the 1990s* (New World Order Series, vol. 9 (New Delhi: Indus Publishing Co., 1991).

72. (With Neelambar Hatti and Rameshwar Tandon (eds)) *Joint Ventures and Collaborations*, New World Order Series, vol. 10 (New Delhi: Indus Publishing Co. 1991).

73. (With Neelambar Hatti and Rameshwar Tandon (eds)) *Foreign Direct Investments*, New World Order Series, vol. 11 (New Delhi: Indus Publishing Co., 1991).

74. (With Neelambar Hatti and Rameshwar Tandon (eds)) *Adjustment and Liberalization in the Third World*, New World Order Series, vol. 12 (New Delhi: Indus Publishing Co., 1991).

75. 'Food Aid and Structural Adjustment Lending in Sub-Saharan Africa', in Edward Clay and Olav Stokke (eds) *Food Aid Reconsidered – Assessing the Impact on Third World Countries*, EADI Book Series 11 (London: Frank Cass, 1991).

76. 'Foreword' to *Participatory Development: Learning from South Asia* by Ponna Wignaraja, Akmal Hussain, Harsh Sethi, Ganeshan Wignaraja, (Karachi: United Nations University Press, Tokyo/Oxford University Press, 1991).

77. (With R. Prendergast (eds)) *Development Perspectives for the 1990s* (London: Macmillan, for the Development Studies Association, 1991).

78. 'Agriculture-Based Industrialization in Sub-Saharan Africa', in *African Development Perspectives Yearbook 1990/91: Industrialization based on Agricultural Development* (Hamburg: Lit, 1992).

79. 'Impact of Trade Policy Reform in the Shadow of the Debt Crisis', in R. Adhikari, C. Kirkpatrick and J. Weiss (eds) *Industrial and Trade Policy Reform in Developing Countries* (Manchester University Press, 1992).

80. 'Lessons of Post-War Development Experience: 1945–88' in Soumitra Sharma (ed.) *Development Policy* (London: Macmillan, 1992).

81. (With Luisa Montuschi (eds)) *Los Problemas del Desarrollo en Améric Latina – Homenaje a Raúl Prebisch* (The Development Problems of Latin America – a Homage to Raúl Prebisch) (Argentina: Fondo de Cultura Económica/Serie de Economia, 1992).

82. Autobiographical article in Philip Arestis and Malcolm Sawyer (eds) *A Biographical Dictionary of Dissenting Economists* (Aldershot, UK: Edward Elgar, 1992).

83. (With Anthony Carty (eds)) *Conflict and Change in the 1990s, Ethics, Laws and Institutions* (London: Macmillan, for the Development Studies Association, 1993). This includes H.W. Singer's Presidential Address on 'Adam Smith: Forebear of Development Studies'.

84. (With Sumit Roy) *Economic Progress and Prospects in the Third World: Lessons of Development Experience Since 1945* Aldershot, UK: Edward Elgar, and Vermont, USA: Brookfield, 1993).

85. (With J. Edström), 'The Impact of Trends in Terms of Trade on GNP Growth', in Machiko Nissanke and Adrian Hewitt (eds) *Economic Crisis in Developing Countries. New Perspectives on Commodities, Trade and Finance. A Collection of Essays in Honour of Alfred Maizels* (London: Pinter, 1993).

86. 'Jan Tinbergen – Champion of World Security and Equity', in A. Jolink and E. Barendrecht-Tinbergen (eds) *Gedeelde Herinneringen*, (Shared Memories). *Essays in honour of Jan Tinbergen for his 90th birthday*, published by A. Jolink, University of Rotterdam, Rotterdam, 1993.

87. 'The Bretton Woods Institutions and the UN', in *Briefing Notes in Economics*, no. 8, The American International University in London, 1994.

88. 'Structural Adjustment Programmes: Evaluating Success', in Jan Willem Gunning, Henk Kox, Wouter Tims and Ynto de Wit (eds) *Trade, Aid and Development. Essays in Honour of Hans Linnemann* (London: Macmillan, 1994.

89. 'Two Views of Food Aid', in Renee Prendergast and Frances Stewart (eds) *Market Forces and World Development* Macmillan, for the Development Studies Association, (London: 1994).

90. 'Prospects for Development', in S. Mansoob Murshed and Kunibert Raffer (eds) *Trade, Transfers and Development: Problems and Prospects for the Twenty First Century* (Cheltenham: Edward Elgar, 1994).

91. 'From Project Lending to Programme Lending: Shifting World Bank Priorities', in John D. MacArthur and John Weiss (eds) *Agriculture, Projects and Development: Papers in Honour of David Edwards* (Aldershot, UK: Avebury, 1994).

92. (With Matthias Lutz) 'Trend and Volatility in the Terms of Trade: Consequences for Growth', in David Sapsford and Wyn Morgan (eds) *The Economics of Primary Commodities – Models, Analysis and Policy*, (Cheltenham: Edward Elgar, 1994).

93. 'An Assessment of the World Bank', in *50 Years of Bretton Woods System: The Role of the IMF, World Bank and GATT in the World Economy*, Friedrich–Ebert Foundation and Richmond College, (Oct. 1994).

94. 'An Historical Perspective', in Mahbub ul-Haq, Richard Jolly, Paul Streeten and Khadija Haq (eds) *The UN and the Bretton Woods Institutions – New Challenges for the Twenty-First Century* (London: Macmillan, 1995).

95. 'Rethinking Bretton Woods from an Historical Perspective', in *Promoting Development: Effective Global Institutions for the Twenty-First Century* (Washington DC: Pluto Press and Center of Concern, 1995).

96. 'Historical Background to the Bretton Woods System and its Relation to the United Nations System', in Bouda Etemad, Jean Batou, Thomas David (eds) *Towards an International Economic and Social History – Essays in Honour of Paul Bairoch* (Geneva: Editions Passé Présent, 1995).

97. (With K. Raffer) *The Foreign Aid Business. Economic Assistance and Development Co-operation* (Cheltenham: Edward Elgar, 1996).

98. (Co-editor with Marjan Svetlicic) *The World Economy: Challenges of Globalization and Regionalization* (Basingstoke: Macmillan and New York: St Martin's Press, 1996).

Section B: Reports for the United Nations, other international bodies and governments

This list does not include the many internal reports that Hans Singer produced when a member of the Secretariats of UN agencies.

1. *Relative Prices of Exports and Imports of Under-developed Countries* (New York: United Nations Department of Economic Affairs Lake Success, Dec. 1949).

2. 'Education and Economic Development', in Proceedings of the United Nations Educational, Scientific, and Cultural Organization (UNESCO)

Economic Commission for Africa (ECA) Conference on *Development of Education in Africa*, Addis Ababa, Ethiopia, May 1961.

3. 'Some Significant Trends in Economic Work of the United Nations', paper presented to New York University, *Annual Review of the United Nations Affairs* (1961).

4. *Development Through Food: A Strategy of Surplus Utilization*, Food and Agriculture Organization of the United Nations (FAO) pamphlet, 1961. (Chairman of the Expert Group which prepared this report.) Reproduced in FAO, *Development Through Food*, Freedom from Hunger Campaign Basic Study, no. 2 (1962) and in FAO *Food Aid for Development*, Economic and Social Development Paper no. 34 (1985).

5. *The United Nations Development Decade – Proposals for Action*. Report of the Secretary-General (New York: United Nations, 1962).

6. 'The Project of an African Development Bank'. Submitted to the Conference of Heads of States, Addis Ababa, Ethiopia, 1963, and published in *Revue de Science Financière* (Paris, 1963).

7. 'Problems of Industrialization of Under-Developed Countries', in Jean Meynaud (ed.) *Social Change and Economic Development* (Paris: UNESCO, 1963).

8. 'Some Neglected Aspects of the Role of Children and Youth in Developing Countries'. Statement and working paper presented at the United Nations Children's Fund (UNICEF) Round Table Conference, Bellagio, Lake Como, Italy, 1964, and reprinted in Herman D. Stein (ed.) *Planning for the Needs of Children in Developing Countries: Report of a Round Table Conference* (New York: UNICEF, 1964).

9. 'Co-ordination of Technical Assistance and Development Planning: Determination of Priorities'. Paper presented at the UN Technical Assistance Board Seminar on *National Co-ordination of Technical Assistance*, Addis Ababa, Ethiopia, Jan. 1964.

10. 'Effects of Patents on the Economy of Under-Developed Countries'. Contribution to a UN study on *The Role of Patents in the Transfer of Technology to Developing Countries* (UN E/3861/Rev. 1) (New York: UN, 1964).

11. 'Development Decade – A General Review'. Statement for the Annual Conference of Non-Governmental Organizations, 26–7 May 1964.

12. 'The Potential Importance of Industrial Estates for African Countries'. Paper prepared for the UN Economic Commission for Africa, seminar on *Industrial Estates*, Addis Ababa, Jun. 1964.

13. 'Methods of Planning for the Needs of Children' Prepared for the UNICEF Conference on *Planning for Children and Youth in Asia*, Bangkok, Thailand, 1966.

14. *Social Policy and Planning in the National Development: Report of the Meeting of Experts on Social Policy and Planning* (Rapporteur of Committee) for UN Social Commission and Economic and Social Council, Stockholm, Sep. 1969.

15. *A Regional Development Plan for the Northern Region of Thailand*. A report prepared for the UN and the Government of Thailand, 1969.

16. *Social Defence Policies in Relation to Development Planning*. Report of Meeting of Experts (Chairman of Committee) for UN Social and Economic Council, Rome, Italy, 1969.

17. 'The Sussex Manifesto: Science and Technology to Developing Countries during the Second Development Decade' (Chairman of group and co-author of report) in *Science and Technology for Development* (UN publication E. 70.I.23) 1970, Also IDS Reprint 101 (1970).

18. *World Plan of Action for the Application of Science and Technology to Development* (UN Sales No. E. 71.II.A.18) (New York: UN, 1971).

19. 'International Aid to Development' in *Les Carnets de l'Enfance/Assignment Children*, UNICEF, no. 14, New York, Ap–Jun. 1971.

20. *Science and Technology to Developing Countries during the Second Development Decade*, (New York: UN, 1971).

21. 'Forms and Causes of Extreme Underdevelopment' for Expert Group meeting on *Industrialization in Countries at Early Stages of Development with Special Reference to Small-Scale Industry*, United Nations Industrial Development Organization (UNIDO), Vienna, 6–10 Dec. 1971.

22. *The Great Experiment: Science and Technology in the Second UN Development Decade*. Popular version of the *World Plan of Action* (UN No. 71.I.19) (New York: UN Centre for Economic and Social Information 1971).

23. *Environment and Development (Founex Report)*. UN Preparatory Committee for the Stockholm Conference on the Environment (Member of Committee) (Paris and The Hague: Mouton, 1972).

24. (With Richard Jolly) *Employment, Incomes and Equality: A Strategy for Increasing Productive Employment in Kenya* Report of United Nations Development Programme (UNDP) International Labour Office (ILO) Employment Mission to Kenya (Geneva: ILO, Nov. 1972).

25. *Children in the Strategy of Development*, Executive Briefing Paper no. 6. Prepared for the UN Centre for Economic and Social Information and UNICEF, New York 1972. Also in French, *La Place de 'L'Enfance dans la Stratégie due Développment*, (Document d'Information, no. 6, établi pour l'information économique et sociale de Nations Unies et pour le Fonds des Nations Unies pour l'enfance), UN, New York, 1973. Also published in Spanish as *Los Ni/nos en la Estrategia para el Desarrollo'*, (Documento Informativo para Ejecutivos, no. 6, preparado para el Centro de Información Económica y Social de las Naciones Unidas y el Fondo de las Naciones Unidas para la Infancia) (New York: United Nations, 1973).

26. *The Quest for an Employment Strategy in Developing Counties and its Relationship to the Work on Human Resources Indicators*. Paper for UNESCO Committee on Social Planning, Paris, Nov./Dec. 1972.

27. *Distribution of Costs and Benefits of Regional Groupings among Developing Countries* (Geneva: UN Conference for Trade and Development (UNCTAD), 1972).

28. *Effect of Taxation on Income Distribution in Developing Countries: Addendum – Studies in Tax Reform Planning* (UN ESA/ECOSOC/L1/ Misc.2/Add.3) (New York: UN 1973).

29. (With Richard Jolly and Dudley Seers) 'The Pilot Missions under the World Employment Programme'. Prepared for the ILO World Employment Programme Meeting on *Evaluation of Comprehensive Employment Missions* (ILO E.0078.1:11) (Geneva: ILO, Mar. 1973).

30. 'Population Growth and Income Distribution'. UN document prepared for the International Symposium on Population and Development, Cairo, Egypt, June 1973, preparatory to *World Population Conference*, 1974.

31. *Science and Technology in the Second UN Development Decade: International Development Strategy* (Consultant), (UN E/CA/10) New York, 31 Jul. 1973.

32. 'Introduction' and 'The European Economic Community and Developing Countries', in *Report of the International Symposium on Growth and World Equilibrium*, Elsinore, Denmark, 6–8 Aug. 1973.

33. (With Stuart D. Reynolds) 'Aspects of the Distribution of Income and Wealth in Kenya' Prepared for UNESCO Conference on *Human Resources Indicators*. Issued as UNESCO Document (SHC/WS/3–4) (Paris, 1 Nov. 1973). Revised version subsequently issued as *IDS Discussion Paper*, no. 41, (Feb. 1974).

34. (With Brian Johnson and Bruce Mackay) 'New Forms of International Co-operation for Technical Innovation' A paper presented at a UN Institute for Training and Research (UNITAR) Weekend Seminar, IDS, 30 Jun.–2 Jul. 1972, published in Harold Caustin, *The Search for New Methods of Technical Co-operation*, UNITAR Conference Report no. 4 (New York: UNITAR, 1974).

35. 'Income Distribution and Population Growth', in *The Population Debate: Dimensions and Perspectives*, vol. 1, papers of the World Population Conference, Bucharest, 1974, New York: UN, 1975).

36. *Employment and Youth*, Commonwealth Youth Programme Occasional Papers (London: Commonwealth Secretariat, 1975).

37. 'Use of Locally Available Resources in Health and Socio-Economic Developments', in *Paediatric Education in Rural Health*, papers presented at Reunion Meeting of Past Fellows of the UNICEF/World Health Organization (WHO) Course for Senior Teachers of Child Health, New Delhi, Oct. 1975.

38. (With Stuart D. Reynolds) 'Aspects of the Distribution of Income and Wealth in Kenya', in *The Use of Socio-Economic Indicators in Development Planning* (Paris: UNESCO, 1976).

39. 'Policies for Urban Informal Sector in Brazil' (joint Consultant and Contributor). Memorandum prepared for *Mesa Redonda sobre Politicas de Emprego paro o Sector Informal Urbano*, Brasilia, 2–6 Feb. 1976 (Geneva: ILO, 1976).

40. *Technologies for Basic Needs* (Geneva: ILO, 1977).

41. (with Biplab Dasgupta and Brian Johnson) *Environment and Development: A Conceptual Overview*. Report submitted to the United Nations Environment Programme (UNEP), Nairobi, Kenya Jan. 1978.

42. *A Survey of Studies of Food Aid*. Document (WFP/CFA: 5/5–C) prepared for the World Food Programme (WFP), Rome, Mar. 1978.

43. 'A Summary Survey of Studies of Food Aid' in Harmut Schneider, *Food Aid for Development*. Report on the Organisation for Economic Co-operation and Development (OECD) Development Centre Expert Meeting on Scope and Conditions for Improved Use of Food Aid for Development, held in Paris, 30–31 Mar. 1978 (Paris: OECD, 1978).

44. (With Juliette Stephenson) *The Expansion of Processing in Developing Countries and International Policy Requirements* Commonwealth Economic Paper no. 10 (London: Commonwealth Secretariat, Oct. 1978).

45. *International Co-operation for the Generation and Diffusion of Appropriate Technology and Appropriate Products for Industrialization* (Consultant). Paper prepared for UNCTAD, Geneva, Feb. 1979.

46. 'The Basic Needs Approach to Development Planning'; 'New Trends in Development Strategies'; 'The New International Economic Order: An Overview'; 'Poverty, Income Distribution and Levels of Living: Twenty-Five Years of Changes in Thinking about Development'; 'The Common Fund Debate', in *Seanza Lectures 1978* Seoul: The Bank of Korea, Sep. 1979).

47. 'Introduction' and 'Poverty Implications of the Lima Target', in *Industry and Development*, Special Issue no. 3, for the Third General Conference of UNIDO, no. E.79.II.B.2.) (New York: UN, 1979).

48. 'A Note on Brandt: Points of Broader Significance for the UNDP'. A report prepared for and circulated by UNDP, New York (Mar. 1980).

49. (with Nancy O. Baster) *Young Human Resources in Korea's Social Development: Issues and Strategies* (Seoul: Korean Development Institute, March 1980).

50. (with P. Mishalani) *Commodity Development Activities: Potential for DC LDC Negotiations*. Report submitted to UNCTAD, Geneva (Apr. 1980).

51. *Research Suggestions for the Proposed UNCTAD Research and Training Centre* (Consultant). Document prepared for UNCTAD, Geneva (Jun. 1980)

52. *International Agricultural Adjustment: Revised Guidelines*. Report submitted to FAO, Rome (Jul. 1980).

53. *Beyond the Brandt Report: Some Problems of Trade and Trade Promotion*. Extracts from lecture at UNCTAD/General Agreement on Tariffs and Trade (GATT), Geneva (13 Aug. 1980).

54. *Basic Needs in an Economy under Pressure: Findings and Recommendations of the ILO/JASPA Basic Needs Mission to Zambia* (Contributor and Member of Mission), (Geneva: ILO, 1 Sep. 1980) (JASPA: Jobs and Skills Programme for Africa)

55. *Poverty, Malnutrition and Food in Zambia*, Country Case Study for World Development Programme, Report IV (Geneva: ILO, 1981).

56. *Innovatory Uses of Food Aid: A Task for the Eighties?* Paper to WFP, Rome (Mar. 1981).

57. *The Brandt Report – A Basis for a Second Korean Miracle?* (Seoul: Korean International Economic Institute, April 1981).

58. 'The Basic Needs Approach to Development Planning', (in Indonesian: 'Pendekatan Kebutuhan Dasar dalam Perencanaan') in Thee Kian Wie (ed.) *Pembangunan Ekonomi dan Pemerataan: Berberapa Pendekatan Alternatif* (Djakarta, 1981).

59. (With others) *Report on the First Policy Seminar on Children* (Manila, Philippines: UNICEF, 1982).

60. (With E.J. Clay) *Food Aid and Development: The Impact and Effectiveness of Bilateral PL 480. Title I – Type Assistance.* AID Program Evaluation Discussion Paper, no. 15 (Washington, DC US Agency for International Development, Dec. 1982).

61. (With Stephany Griffith-Jones) 'Multilateral Aid to Developing Countries' in *Study on the International Financial and Trading System*, Background Paper no. 9 London: Commonwealth Secretariat, Apr. 1983). Also in

Towards a New Bretton Woods. Challenges for the World Financial and Trading System. Selected background papers prepared for a Commonwealth Study Group, vol. 1 (London: Commonwealth Secretariat, Nov. 1983).

62 (With E.J. Clay) *Pricing Policies for Food Aid*, Technical Paper no. 8, for Commonwealth Consultative Meeting on *Food Pricing and Marketing Policy*, London, 3–6 May 1983 (Food Production and Rural Development Division, Commonwealth Secretariat in collaboration with Guelph University, Ontario, Canada).

63. (With Simon Maxwell) 'Development Through Food: Twenty Years' Experience', in *Report of the World Food Programme Government of the Netherlands Seminar on Food Aid*. Contribution to 20th Anniversary of WFP Seminar held in The Hague, The Netherlands, 3–5 Oct. 1983.

64. (With others) 'The Impact of World Recession on Children', ch. 4 in *The State of the World's Children, 1984* (New York: UNICEF, 1984).

65. (With R.H. Green) 'Sub-Saharan Africa in Depression: The Impact on the Welfare of Children', in Richard Jolly and Giovanni Andrea Cornia (eds). *The Impact of World Recession on Children*, a study prepared for UNICEF, (Oxford and New York: Pergamon, 1984). Published in French as 'L'Afrique Subsaharienne en crise: l'impact de la récession sur le bien être des enfants' in *L'Impact de la Récession Mondiale sue les Enfants* (UNICEF: 1984). And in Spanish as 'Effectos de la recesion en el Africa subsahariana sobre el bien-estar de la infancia' in *Effectos de la Recession Mundail Sobre la Infancia* (Siglo XXI de Espana Editores for UNICEF, 1984).

66. 'Industrialization: Where Do We Stand? Where Are We Going?', *Industry and Development*, no. 12 (New York: UNIDO, 1984). Published in French as 'L'Industrialisation: où en sommes-nous, où allons-nous?', *Industrie et développement*, no. 12 (UNIDO, 1984). Also published in *Korean Development Policy Studies* (1984), and in *METU Studies in Development*, vol. 11, nos. 1–2 (Ankara, Turkey: METU – Middle East Technical University, 1984).

67. (With others) 'Economists Comment on UNCTAD's Role'. Contribution to Symposium on Future Role of UNCTAD, in *UNCTAD Bulletin*, no. 205 (Sep. 1984).

68. (With E.J. Clay) 'Food Aid and Development: Issues and Evidence'. A survey of the literature since 1977 on the role and impact of food aid in developing countries, *World Food Programme Occasional Papers*, no. 3 (Rome, Sep. 1985).

69. 'Foreword' to Thomas G. Weiss, *Multilateral Development Diplomacy in UNCTAD* (London: Macmillan, 1986).

70. (With Richard Longhurst) 'The Role of Food Aid in Promoting the Welfare of Children in Developing Countries', in J.P. Greaves and D.J. Shaw (eds) *Food Aid and the Well-Being of Children in the Developing World*, UNICEF/WFP Workshop held at UNICEF Headquarters, New York, 25–6 Nov. 1985 (New York: UNICEF and WFP, 1986).

71. *The African Food Crisis and the Role of Food Aid in Coping with It*. Address to the World Food Day Symposium, Tokyo, 16 Oct. 1987. Published by the Japan FAO Association, Tokyo (in Japanese and English).

72. 'A Development Economist's View'. Contribution to WHO Round Table on 'How Should Information on Health Care be Generated and Used?' in *World Health Forum*, vol. 8 (1987).

73. 'How to Foster Diversification, Not Dependence' (with Adrian Hewitt) in *Africa Recovery*, vol. 4, nos. 3–4 (Oct.–Dec. 1990). Published by the Communications and Project Management Division of the UN Department of Public Information, New York.

74. 'Foreword' to Guy Standing and Victor Tokman (eds) *Towards Social Adjustment: Labour Market Issues in Structural Adjustment* (Geneva: ILO, 1991).

75. *Structural Adjustment and Agriculture: Report of an In-Service Training Seminar for FAO Staff*. Training Materials for Agricultural Planning no. 25 (Rome: FAO, 1991).

76. 'UNCTAD in a Changing World', *UNCTAD Bulletin*, no. 12 (Nov.–Dec. 1991).

77. *Research of the World Employment Programme: Future Priorities and Selective Assessment* (Geneva: ILO, 1992).

78. 'Commentarios sobre "Raúl Prebisch, 1901–1971: La Búsqueda Constante"', (Commentary on 'Rauúl Prebisch 1901–1971: the Constant Quest') in Enrique V. Iglesias (ed.) *El legado de Raúl Prebisch* (Washington, DC: Banco Interamericano de Desarrollo, 1993).

79. (With Stephany Griffith-Jones) *New Patterns of Macro-Economic Governance*, UNDP Human Development Report, Office Occasional Paper no. 10 (New York, 1994).

80. (With Stephany Griffith-Jones, Alicia Puyana and Christopher Stevens) *Assessment of the IDB Lending Programme 1979–92*, A study commissioned by the Inter-American Development Bank, *IDS Research Report* no. 25 (1994).

81. 'Half a Century of Economic and Social Development Policies of the UN and Bretton Woods Institutions'. Iqbal Memorial Lecture, Eleventh Annual General Meeting of the Pakistan Society of Development Economists, Islamabad, Pakistan, Apr. 1995.

82. 'Is a Genuine Partnership possible in a Western Hemisphere Free Trade Area?' in *Trade Liberalization in the Western Hemisphere* (Washington, DC: Inter-American Development Bank (IDB) and Economic Commission for Latin America and the Caribbean (ECLAC), 1995).

Section C: Articles

A number of articles have been published in more than one journal, and in languages other than English. Articles have also been reprinted in various volumes. Book reviews and letters to newspapers are not included. Those articles that appear in books edited by Hans Singer or edited by others are included in Section A.

1. 'Can Overcrowding Automatically Disappear?' *Review of Economic Studies* (1935).

2. 'The "Courbe des Populations" – A Parallel to Pareto's Law', *Economic Journal* (1936).

3. 'Income and Rent', *Review of Economic Studies* (1936).

4. (With A.P. Lerner) 'Some Notes on Duopoly and Spatial Competition', *Journal of Political Economy*, vol. 45, no. 2 (Apr. 1937). Reprinted in The

International Library of Critical Writings in Economics, Melvin L. Greenhut and George Norman (eds) *The Economics of Location*, vol. 1, Cheltenham: Edward Elgar, 1995.)

5. 'Notes on Spatial Discrimination', *Review of Economic Studies* (1937).
6. 'The Law of Diminishing Elasticity of Demand', *Economic Journal* (1938).
7. 'Prices and the Trade Cycle', *The Manchester School* (1938).
8. 'Price Dispersion in Periods of Change', *Economic Journal* (1938).
9. 'The Process of Unemployment and the Depressed Areas, 1935–38', *Review of Economic Studies* (1938).
10. 'The Process of Unemployment and Regional Labour Markets', *Review of Economic Studies* (1938).
11. 'The Inflexibility of the Price System', *Manchester Statistical Society* (1939).
12. 'The Coal Question Reconsidered', *Review of Economic Studies* (1941).
13. 'Some Disguised Blessings of the War', *The Manchester School*, vol. 12, no. 2 (1941).
14. 'The German War Economy' – a series of articles in consecutive issues of *Economic Journal* (Jun.–Sep. 1941 to Jun.–Sep. 1944).
15. 'Urban Land Values in England and Wales, 1845–1913', *Econometrica* (1942).
16. 'German War Finance', *Banker* (1942).
17. 'Beveridge Plan Economics', special issue of *Westminster Newsletter* (1943).
18. 'The German War Economy', *Manchester Statistical Society* (1943); also in *Review of Economic Studies* (1943).
19. 'The National Income', *Discovery* (1944).
20. 'An Economist's View of Accountants', *Accountancy* (Aug. 1944).
21. 'Wage Policy in Full Employment', *Economic Journal* (Dec. 1947); see also 'Wage Policy in Full Employment – A Rejoinder', *Economic Journal*. (Sep. 1948).
22. 'Economic Progress in Under-Developed Countries', *Social Research* (1949).
23. 'Gains and Losses from Trade and Investment in Under-Developed Countries'. Paper delivered to the American Economic Association meeting in 1949, and reprinted in the Proceedings, *American Economic Review*, supplement (1950). Also published in Spanish as 'Comercio poco Desarrollados, *El Trimestre Económico* (Mexico, Apr.– Jun. 1950).
24. 'International Approaches to Modernization Programmes'. Paper presented at Round Table of 1949 Annual Conference of Milbank Memorial Fund, 1949, published in *Milbank Memorial Fund Quarterly* (Apr. 1950).
25. 'Capital Requirements for the Economic Development of the Middle East', *Middle Eastern Affairs* (Feb. 1952).
26. 'India's Five-Year Plan – A Modest Proposal', *Far Eastern Survey* (Jun. 1952).
27. 'Mechanics of Economic Development', *Indian Economic Review* (Aug. 1952 and Feb. 1953).
28. 'The Brazilian "Salte" Plan – A Historical Case Study of Government Borrowing for Economic Development', *Journal of Economic Development and Cultural Change* (Feb. 1953); reprinted in Spanish in *El Trimestre Económico* (Mexico, Apr.–Jun. 1953).
29. 'Obstacles to Economic Development', *Social Research* (Spring 1953).

30. 'The Theory of Federal Finance – A Comment', *Economic Journal* (Sep. 1953).
31. 'Problems of Industrialization of Under-Developed Countries'. Paper presented to the *Conference on Economic Progress of the International Economic Association*, Sta Margherita Ligure, Italy (Sep. 1953).
32. 'Working Models of Economic Development, Economic and Financial', *Ekonomi Dan Keuangan Indonesia*, no. 4 (Apr. 1954).
33. 'Population and Economic Development'. Paper presented to the *World Population Conference*, Rome, Italy (1954).
34. 'Terms of Trade – Barter vs. Factoral – and Gains, from Trade', *Contribuicoes a Analise do Desenvolvimento Economico* (Rio de Janeiro, 1957).
35. 'Comment' on C.P. Kindleberger's 'The Terms of Trade and Economic Development', *Review of Economics and Statistics*, vol. 40 no. 1, p. 2, supplement (Feb. 1958).
36. 'Distributed Dividends, Earnings Cover and the Price of Shares', *Bankers Magazine*, no. 1370 (May 1958).
37. 'Deficit Financing of Public Capital Formation with Special Reference to the Inflationary Process in Under-Developed Countries'. Paper presented to the Jamaica Study Conference on Economic Development, Jun. 1957. Published in *Social and Economic Studies*, vol. 7, no. 3 (Sep. 1958).
38. 'A Footnote to Professor Kuznets' Quantitative Aspects of the Economic Growth of Nations', *Economic Development and Cultural Change*, vol. 7 no. 1 (Oct. 1958).
39. 'The Concept of Balanced Growth: Theory and Practice'. Paper presented to the Conference on Economic Development on the occasion of the 75th anniversary of the University of Texas. Published in *Proceedings of the Conference*, Texas University Press, 1959. Reprints also in a special supplement to the *Texas Quarterly* (Aug. 1958) and *Malayan Economic Review* (Oct. 1958).
40. 'Differential Population Growth as a Factor in International Economic Development', *Economic Journal*, vol. 69 (Dec. 1959).
41. 'Stabilization and Development of Primary Producing Countries', (Introductory Statement and Epilogue, Symposium II), *Kyklos*, vol. 12, no. 3 (1959).
42. 'Stability and Progress in the World Economy', *Kyklos*, vol. 12, fasc. 2 (1959).
43. 'Problems of Small-Scale Industry'. Paper presented to the International Economic Association, Regional Conference on *Economic Development in Africa South of the Sahara*, Addis Ababa, Ethiopia, Jul. 1961.
44. 'Use and Abuse of Local Counterpart Funds', *International Development Review*, vol. 12 no. 3 (Oct. 1961).
45. 'Demographic Factors in Economic Development in Tropical Africa South of the Sahara'. Paper presented to the *Social Science Research Council Conference*, Chicago, Nov. 1961.
46. 'Trends in Economic Thought on Under-Development', *Social Research* (1961).
47. 'Basic Problems before the Geneva Conference on Trade and Development'. Paper presented to New York University and published in the *Annual Review of United Nations Affairs, 1963–196* (New York University Press, 1964).
48. 'International Aid for Economic Development – Problems and Tendencies'. Paper prepared for the Calcutta Meeting of the Society for International

Development (SID), Nov. 1963. Subsequently published in *Revue de Science Financière* (Paris, 1964).

49. 'Social Development: Key Growth Sector', *International Development Review*, SID (Mar. 1965).

50. 'Comments' on *Capital Movements, The Volume of Trade and the Terms of Trade* by H.M.A. Onitiri. Presented at the International Economic Association Round Table Conference on Capital Movements and Economic Development, Washington, DC, 21–31 Jul. 1965.

51. 'External Aid: For Plans of Projects', *Economic Journal*, vol. 75 (Sep. 1965).

52. 'Problems of Social Planning and Social Development', *Journal of Development Administration* (Khartoum, Sudan, 1965).

53. (With Caroline Miles) 'Research Activities of the United Nations', *American Economic Association, Annual Meeting* (1965).

54. 'Overcoming Obstacles to Development: Midway in the Development Decade'. Statement at Overseas Studies Committee Conference, Cambridge University, 1965.

55. 'The Notion of Human Investment', *Review of Social Economy*, vol. 24, no. 1 Mar. 1966). See also 'El Concepto de Inversion Humana'. Published by Universidad del Valle.

56. 'Comments' on *The World Poverty Gap* by William S. Vickrat. Presented at the Columbia University Priorities Conference, September 1966, and reprinted in *New University Thought*, special issue 66/67, vol. 5, nos 1 and 2 (Detroit, USA, 1967).

57. 'Pre-Conditions for Regional Economic Integration', *International Development Review*, (Sep. 1967).

58. 'Over-All Development Planning and Policies', *African Institute for Economic Development and Planning* (Dakar, Senegal, 20 Oct. 1967).

59. 'International Aid. Targets, Commitments and Realities', *Inter Economics*, no. 2, Monthly Review of International Trade and Development (Feb. 1968).

60. *Some Practical Issues of International Economics*, IDS Communications no. 6 (Mar. 1968) originally written for IDS Founding Conference 1966.

61. 'Sir John Hicks on Growth and Anti-Growth', *Oxford Economic Papers*, vol. 20, no. 1, (Mar. 1968).

62. 'Kritische Bemerkungen zur Festlegung der Ein-Prozent Klausel' ('Critical Remarks on the Determination of the 1 per cent Aid Target') *Wirtschaftsdienst* (Jul. 1968).

63. 'Debate on the Next Development Decade', FAO *Ceres*, vol. 1, no. 4 (Jul.–Aug. 1968).

64. (with A.C. Doss) 'Technical Assistance to Kenya: Some Thoughts on Flows and Programming', *East African Economic Review* (Jun. 1969); also in *IDS Communcations* no. 55 (1969).

65. 'Dualism Revisited: A New Approach to the Problems of the Dual Society in Developing Countries', *Journal of Development Studies*, vol. 7, no. 1 (Oct. 1969); also in *IDS Communications*, no. 41 (1969).

66. 'Keynesian Models of Economic Development and their Limitations: An Analysis in the Light of Gunnar Myrdal's Asian Drama', UN Asian Institute for Economic Development and Planning, *Occasional Papers* (Dec. 1969); also in *IDS Communications*, no. 54 (1969).

67. 'That One Percent Target', *IDS Bulletin*, vol. 2, no. 2 (Dec. 1969).

68. 'Science and Technology', *Venture*, special issue on development, January 1970.

69. 'Some Problems of International Aid', *Journal of World Trade Law*, vol. 4, no. 2, March/April 1970.

70. 'Social Implications of Aid Programs. A Contribution to Technical Assistance and Development', *Proceedings of the Truman International Conference on Technical Assistance and Development* (May 1970). Also published by The Hebrew University of Jerusalem, Israel (1971).

71. 'A World Employment Programme', *Rural Life* (3rd qu, 1970).

72. 'The Foreign Company as an Exporter of Technology', *IDS Bulletin*, vol. 3, no. 1 (Oct. 1970).

73. 'Primary Products, Exports and Growth: The Case of Thailand', *Journal of Developing Areas* (Apr. 1971).

74. 'A New Approach to the Problems of the Dual Society in Developing Countries', *UN International Social Development Review*, no. 3 (1971).

75. 'Development Revisited' (questions Eugene Black's 'contract approach' to development), *International Development Review*, vol. 13, no. 3, (1971).

76. 'Rural Unemployment as a Background to Rural/Urban Migration in Africa'. Paper for Conference on *Urban Unemployment in Africa*, IDS, Sussex, September 1971).

77. 'Unemployment in Developing Countries', *Pax et Libertas*, vol. 36, no. 4 (Oct.–Dec. 1971).

78. 'The Technology Gap and the Developing Countries', *International Journal of Environmental Studies*, vol. 3 (1972).

79. 'The Riderless Horse' (article on employment and growth), *The Internationalist*, no. 7 (Nov. 1972).

80. (With Richard Jolly) 'Unemployment in an African Setting: Lessons of the Employment Mission to Kenya', *International Labour Review*, vol. 107, no. 2 (Feb. 1973).

81. 'The Development Outlook for Poor Countries: Technology is the Key', *Challenge* (New York, May/June 1973).

82. 'The Outlook for the Poor World', *New Internationalist*, no. 5 (Jul. 1973).

83. 'The Commodity Boom and Developing Countries', *New Society*, vol. 25, no. 569 (30 Aug. 1973).

84. (With Richard Blackburn, Frank Ellis, Peter Hadji-Ristic, Angus Hone, Percy Selwyn, Nick Stamp, Richard Stanton and J. Ann Zammit) 'Trade Liberalization, Employment and Income Distribution: A First Approach' *IDS Discussion Paper*, no. 31 (Oct. 1973).

85. 'Rural Employment as a Background to Rural-Urban Migration in Africa'. Paper presented at Conference on *Urban Employment in Africa*, IDS (Sep. 1971); published in special issue of *Manpower and Unemployment Research in Africa – A Newsletter*, vol. 6, no. 2 (Center for Developing-Area Studies, McGill University, Montreal, Quebec, Nov. 1973).

86. 'Der Schlüssel heisst Technologie: Entwicklungsaussichten der Dritten Welt' (German translation of 'The Development Outlook for Poor Countries: Technology is the Key'), *Evangelische Kommentare*, no. 11 (Stuttgart, Nov. 1973).

87. (With David Kaplan), 'Cost-Benefit Analysis and the Allocation of Resources to Crime Prevention' *IDS mimeograph* (1973).

88. 'La Empresa Internacional como Exportadora de Technologia' (Spanish translation of 'The Foreign Company as an Exporter of Technology), *Comercio de Technologia y Subdesarrollo Económico* (Mexico: Coordinación de Ciencias, 1973).

89. 'Transfer of Technology in LDCs', *Inter Economics*, no. 1 (Hamburg: Verlag Weltarchiv, Jan. 1974).

90. 'Wenn die Rohstoffe teurer werden: Die Auswirkungen auf die Länder der Dritten Welt' (German translation of 'The Commodity Boom and Developing Countries'), *Evangelische Kommentare*, no. 3 (Stuttgart, Mar. 1974).

91. 'A Mirror and a Chimera', *New Society*, vol. 27, no. 597 (14 Mar. 1974).

92. 'Transfer of Technology and its Impact on Development'. Paper presented at *Conference on Investment in Developing Countries*, organized by Danish Industrialization Fund for Developing Countries, Hornbaek, Denmark, April 1974.

93. 'Global Oil Crisis will be Life or Death for the "NOPEC" Countries', *Third World*, vol. 3, no. 7 (Apr. May 1974).

94. (With Richard Jolly and Dudley Seers), 'The Pilot Employment Missions and Lessons of the Kenya Mission' *IDS Communication*, no. 111 (Jun. 1974).

95. (With Mohinder Puri), 'Aid and Donor Countries' GNP *Inter Economics*, no. 7 (Hamburg: Verlag Weltarchiv, July 1974).

96. 'O Fracasso das Receitas do Desenvolvimento', *Novas, Utopias* (São Paulo, Brazil, 8 Sep. 1974).

97. 'Auf dem Weg in eine Welt des Hungers – Krisenhafte Entwicklungen in der Nahrungsmittelversorgung' (German translation of 'The World Food Crisis – Part of an Interlocking Series of World Problems'), *Evangelisch Kommentare*, no. 10 (Stuttgart, Oct. 1974).

98. 'A Note on the Implications of the Oil Price Increases for British Aid Policy', *IDS Bulletin* (Special Oil and Development Issues) vol. 6, no. 2, (Oct. 1974).

99. (With S.B.L. Nigam) 'Labour Turnover and Employment, Some Evidence from Kenya', *International Labour Review*, vol. 110, no. 6 (Dec. 1974).

100. 'La Strategia per lo Sviluppo Technologico e il Piano Mondiale di Azione delle N.U.' (Italian translation of 'The Strategy for Development Technology and the Least-Developed Regions of the United Nations), *Scienza & Tecnica 7 – Annuario della EST (Enciclopedia della Scienza e della Tecnica)* (Milan: Mondadori, 1974).

101. 'Resources and Employment', *The Economic Times Annual, 1974* (New Delhi: Economic Times of India 1974).

102. 'Postcript' to UN World Food Conference, Rome, Nov. 1974, *People*, vol. 2, no. 1 (1975).

103. 'Trade Expansion, Employment and Income Distribution', *IDS Bulletin* (Special International Research Issue) vol. 6, no. 4 (Mar. 1975).

104. 'Für Exporte braucht man zwei – Mehr Nahrungsmittel durch Ausweitung des Handels', (You need two for exporting – more food through expanded trade) *Evangelische Kommentare*, no. 4 (Stuttgart, Apr. 1975).

105. (With George Blazyca) 'Statistics on Particular Problem Areas – Poverty, Inequality and Income Distribution', *IDS Communication 114: Statistical*

Policy in Less Developed Countries. Based on discussions at Conference on *Statistical Policy in Less Developed Countries*, IDS, Sussex, May 1975.

106. (With R.H. Green) 'Towards a Rational and Equitable New International Economic Order: A Case for Negotiated Structural Changes', *World Development*, vol. 3, no. 6 (Jun. 1975).

107. 'The Distribution of Gains from Trade and Investment – Revisited', *Journal of Development Studies*, vol. 11, no. 4 (Jul. 1975).

108. 'Im Interesse beider Seiten. Vorstoss für eine neue Rohstoffpolitik' ('In the Mutual Interest: Initiative towards a new Raw Materials Policy') *Evangelische Kommentare*, no. 7 (Jul. 1975).

109. (With R.H. Green and R.H. Stanton) 'Developed Country Initiatives for Forthcoming International Economic Conferences, 1975/76'. Report of Conference at the IDS, Sussex, 25–26 Jul. 1975.

110. (With Lyn Reynolds) 'Technological Backwardness and Productivity Growth', *Economic Journal*, vol. 85, no. 340 (Dec. 1975).

111. (With Paul J. Isenman) 'Food Aid: Disincentive Effects and their Policy Implications', *IDS Communication*, no. 116 (December 1975). Also published as *A.I.D. Discussion Paper*, no. 31 (1975) by Agency for International Development, Washington, DC; and in *Economic Development and Cultural Change*, vol. 25 no. 2 (Jan. 1977). Reprinted in Vernon W. Ruttan (ed.) *Why Food Aid?* (Baltimore and London: Johns Hopkins Press, 1993).

112. 'Five Wasted Years', *SID Focus: Technical Cooperation*, IDR/1976/1.

113. 'Beyond Commodity Policy: Structural Changes and Financial Compensation', *IDS Bulletin* (Special UNCTAD IV Issue, Nairobi, May 1976), vol. 7, no. 4 (1976).

114. 'Uber die Rohstoffpolitik hinaus' ('Beyond Commodity Policy'), Ein Vorschlag im Vorfeld der UNCTAD IV, *Evangelische Kommentare*, no. 5 (May 1976).

115. 'An Elusive Concept' (Article on Financial Transfers), FAO *Ceres*, (Special Issue on Development), vol. 9, no. 4 (Jul.–Aug. 1976).

116. 'Die Zukunft des Entwicklungsprogramms der Vereinten Nationen' ('The Future of the UNDP'), *Vereinte Nationen*, 5/76 (Bonn Oct. 1976).

117. 'Hilfe oder Umverteilung. Enttauschende Ergebnisse der UNCTAD IV' ('Aid or Redistribution. Disappointing Results from UNCTAD IV'), *Evangelische Kommentare*, vol. 9, no. 10 (Oct. 1976).

118. (With Paul J. Isenman) 'Food Aid: Its Potential Disincentives to Agriculture', *Development Digest*, vol. 15, no. 2 (Apr. 1977) pp. 15–24.

119. 'Transformation Assistance from Developed Countries to Developing Countries. An Aid to Trade Expansion', *Korean Economic Journal*, vol. 16, no. 2 (Jun. 1977). Also published in *IDS Discussion Paper*, no. 110 (May 1977).

120. 'New Trends in Development Strategies', in *Report on the Ninth Course: Household Statistics (1 March – 24 June 1977)* Munich Centre for Advanced Training in Applied Statistics for Developing Countries (1977)

121. 'Reflections of Sociological Aspects of Economic Growth Based on the Work of Bert Hoselitz', *Economic Development and Cultural Change*, vol. 25, supplement 977 (in honour of Bert Hoselitz) (1977).

122. 'Appropriate Technology for a Basic Human Needs Strategy', *International Development Review*, vol. 19, no. 2 (1977).

123. 'Nothing is Simple' (Article on Terms of Trade), FAO *Ceres* (Special Issue on Agriculture and Development), vol. 10, no. 6 (Nov.–Dec. 1977).

124. 'Poverty, Income Distribution and Levels of Living: Twenty-Five Years of Changes in Thinking about Development', *Seoul National University Economic Review*, vol. 11, no. 1 (Dec. 1977). Special issue in commemoration of the 30th Anniversary of Seoul National University.

125. 'Reflections on the Lima (25 per cent) Target'. Paper presented at the Institute of Social Studies 25th Anniversary Conference, 16–20 Dec. 1977, The Hague, The Netherlands.

126. (With Walter Eigel) 'Technologie. Die Notwendigkeit technologischer Alternativen für die Dritte Welt' ('Technology – the Need for Technological Alternatives for the Third World'), *Internationale Entwicklung*, 1978/IV (Vienna: OFSE, 1978).

127. 'The Common Fund Debate. Where Do We Stand Now?', *Round Table* (The Commonwealth Journal of International Affairs) no. 271 (Jul. 1978). Also published in *Asian Journal* (Journal of the Research Institute of Asian Economies, Seoul, Korea) no. 26 (Sep. 1978).

128. 'The New International Economic Order: An Overview' (Revised version of a lecture presented to the 12th Seanza Central Banking Course, The Bank of Korea, Seoul, Sep. 1978) *Journal of Modern African Studies*, vol. 16, no. 4 (1978).

129. 'Development Prospects of NICs in a Changing World', *KIEI Seminar Series*, no. 17 (Seoul: Korea International Economic Institute, Sep. 1978).

130. 'The Crisis of Transition: A Brief Rejoinder' (to John Friedmann's 'The Crisis of Transition: A Critique of Strategies of Crisis Management'), *Development and Change*, vol. 10, no. 1 (Jan. 1979).

131. (With S.J. Maxwell) 'Food Aid to Developing Countries: A Survey', *World Development*, vol. 7, no. 3 (Mar. 1979).

132. 'The Role of Newly Industrialising (Middle-Income) Countries in the World Economy'. Paper presented to the International Symposium on *New Directions of Asia's Development Strategies'*, Institute of Developing Economies, Tokyo, 13–16 Mar. 1979.

133. 'Transfer of Technology – A One-Way Street', *Internationale Entwicklung*, 1979/III (Vienna: OFSE, 1979).

134. (With Paul Isenman), 'The Price-Disincentive Effect of Food Aid Revisited: A Reply', *Economic Development and Cultural Changes*, vol. 27, no. 3 (Apr. 1979).

135. 'The Basic Needs Approach to Development Planning'. Paper prepared for the seminar on *Setting and Implementing of Statistical Priorities* held at the Munich Centre for Advanced Training, 6–25 Aug. 1979.

136. 'A Generation Later: Kurt Mandelbaum's *The Industrialisation of Backward Areas* Revisited', *Development and Change* (A special issue entitled 'Plus &c change … Essays in honour of Kurt Martin'), vol. 10, no. 4 (Oct. 1979).

137. 'Has the Korean Model a Future in a Changing World', *KIEI Seminar Series*, no. 30 (Seoul: Korea International Economic Institute, Nov. 1979).

138. 'The Care for Social Welfare Policy in Korea', *Asian Economies*, no. 32 (Seoul: Research Institute of Asian Economies, Mar. 1980).
139. 'Put the People First – World Development Report 1980', *The Economist* (Aug. 1980).
140. 'The Brandt Report: A "Northwestern" Point of View', *Third World Quarterly*, vol. 2, no. 4 (Oct. 1980).
141. (With Javed Ansari) 'Trade Access and Employment in Developing Countries: A Survey', *Canadian Journal of Development Studies*, vol. 2, no. 2 (1980).
142. 'Comments on Graham Bird's Strategy for World Economic Development', *Journal of International Studies*, Millennium vol. 9, no. 3 (Winter 1980–1).
143. 'Overview of Discussion and Conclusions', *Critical Issues in Development in the 80s* (Liaison Bulletin, OECD, 1981).
144. 'The British Government and the Brandt Report', *IDS Bulletin*, vol. 12, no. 2 (May 1981).
145. 'International Food Problems', *Times North–South Supplement* (2 Oct. 1981).
146. 'Policies and Programs for Young Human Resource Development in Korea, 1982–86'. Published in *Child Development Policies in Korea: An Approach to Young Human Resource Development in the 1980s* (Seoul: Korea Development Institute, 1981).
147. 'The New International Economic Order', *Economics* (the quarterly journal of the Economics Association) vol. 17, p 4, no. 76 (Winter 1981).
148. (With R.A. Mahmood) 'Is There A Poverty Trap for Developing Countries? Polarisation: Reality or Myth?', *World Development*, vol. 10, no. 1 (1982).
149. 'The Political Economy of Foreign Aid', *Lloyds Bank Review* (Jan. 1982).
150. 'North–South and South–South: The North and Intra-Third World Co-operation', *Development and Peace*, vol. 3 (Spring 1982). Published by the Hungarian Peace Council and the World Peace Council, Budapest.
151. *Brandt: Mutual and Conflicting Interests in Relations with the Third World.* Third Biennial Adam Weiler Memorial Lecture, Sussex University, England, 1982. Published as *IDS Discussion Paper*, no. 185 (Jan. 1983).
152. (With Edward Clay (eds)), 'Food as Aid, Food for Thought' *IDS Bulletin*, vol. 14, no. 2 (Apr. 1983).
153. 'The Role of Human Capital in Development', *Pakistan Journal of Applied Economics*, vol. 2, no. 1 (Summer 1983).
154. 'The Ethics of Aid', *Asian Journal of Economics*, vol. 2, no. 3 (1983). Also published in *IDS Discussion Paper*, no. 195 (Oct. 1984).
155. 'North–South Multipliers', *World Development*, vol. 11, no. 5 (1983).
156. 'Il Secondo Rapporto Brandt. Una sola strategia per una crisicommune' ('The Second Brandt Report: a single strategy for a common crisis'), *Cooperazione* (Journal of the Italian Ministry of Foreign Affairs – Department for Development Co-operation), vol. 8, no. 34, (Oct. 1983).
157. (With R.H. Green) 'Sub-Saharan Africa in Depression: The Impact on the Welfare of Children', *World Development*, vol. 12, no. 3 (Mar. 1984).
158. 'Relevance of Keynes for Developing Countries', *Estudos de Economia*, vol. 4, no. 4 (Jul.–Sept. 1984).

159. 'The Second Brandt Report: "A Common Crisis"', *The Nonaligned World*, vol. 2, no. 3 (Jul.–Sep. 1984).

160. 'Ideas and Policy: The Sources of UNCTAD', *IDS Bulletin*, vol. 15, no. 3 (Jul. 1984). Special issue entitled 'UNCTAD: The First Twenty Years'.

161. 'Success Stories of the 1970s: Some Correlations', *World Development*, vol. 12, no. 9 (1984).

162. 'The Concept of Development and the Ethics of Aid' (with Albert Lauterbach), *Vienna Institute for Development*, Occasional Paper 84/4 (1984).

163. 'Modelos de Industrializacao' ('Models of Industrialization'), *Revista Critica de Ciencias Sociais*, no. 14 (Nov. 1984).

164. (With John Wood) 'Aid: Time to Rationalize' *Compass News Features* (16 Nov. 1984).

165. 'Industrializacion: Donde Estamos? Adonde Vamos?' ('Industrialization: Where are we? Where are we going?'), *Industria y Desarrollo*, no. 12 (1985).

166. 'The African Food Crisis and the Role of the African Development Bank', *Proceedings of a Symposium held in Tunis, Tunisia on 10 May 1984* (Abidjan, Côte d'Ivoire: African Development Bank, 1985).

167. 'Una Via Complementare Al Dialogo Con Il Nord' ('Complementary Route to the North–South Dialogue'), (translated into Italian by Sergio Minucci), *Politica Internazionale* (1985). (This volume was prepared for the 2nd National Conference on Development Co-operation organised in Rome by the Development Co-operation Department of the Italian Ministry of Foreign Affairs, 11–14 Jun. 1985.)

168. 'Some Problems of Emergency Food Aid for Sub-Saharan Africa', in 'Sub-Saharan Africa: Getting the Facts Straight', *IDS Bulletin*, vol. 16, no. 3 (Jul. 1985).

169. 'Der Beitrag zu Wirtschaftlicher Zusammenarbeit und Entwicklung' (40 years of the United Nations: Contribution to Economic Co-operation and Development), *Vereinte Nationen* (Oct. 1985).

170. 'Hans Singer at 75: IDS at 20', *IDS Annual Report* (1985).

171. (With S. Bhadwan Dahiya) 'The Roots of Industrialisation Strategy in India: 1949–56', *Asian Journal of Economics and Social Studies*, vol. 5, no. 2 (Apr. 1986).

172. 'Some Reflections on Past Interests and Activities', *IDS Discussion Paper*, no. 217 (Jun. 1986).

173. 'South–South Trade Revisited in a Darkening External Environment', *Development and South-South Cooperation*, vol. 2, no. 2 (Jun. 1986). Published by the Research Centre for Co-operation with Developing Countires, Ljubljana, Yugoslavia.

174. (With Paul Streeten) 'Yuvarlack Masa: Kalkinma Iktisadi: Yasiyor Mu?' ('Future Development: Where Do We Go?'), *Iktisat Dergisi* (1986).

175. 'Famines and Food Mountains', *Compass*, Special Issue on 'Perspective 87: Famines and Food Mountains', Compass News Features (17 Dec. 1986).

176. 'Raúl Prebisch and His Advocacy of Import Substitution', *Development and South–South Cooperation*, vol. 2, no. 3 (Dec. 1986).

177. (With Parvin Alizadeh) 'Import Substitution Revisited in a Darkening External Environment', *Asian Journal of Economics and Social Studies*,

vol. 5, no. 3 (1986). Also published as 'Strategija Supstitucike Izvoza u Sve Tezim Uvjetima' ('Import Substitution Revisited in a Darkening External Environment') *Razvoj Development*, vol. IV, no. 1 (Jan.–Mar. 1987). With a Summary in English.

178. 'Food Aid: Development Tool or Obstacle to Development?', *Development Policy Review*, vol. 5, no. 4 (Dec. 1987). Also in *Irish Studies in International Affairs*, vol. 2, no. 3 (1987).

179. 'The World Development Report 1987 on the Blessings of "Outwards Orientation": A Necessary Correction', *Journal of Development Studies*, vol. 24, no. 2 (Jan. 1988).

180. (With S. Bhagwan Dahiya) 'Objectives, Strategies and Techniques: Forty Years of Changing Thought on Development Planning', *Indian Journal of Economics*, vol. 68, pt 3, no. 270 (Jan. 1988).

181. (Guest editor with John Shaw) 'Food Policy, Food Aid and Economic Adjustment', Special Issue of *Food Policy*, vol. 13, no. 1 (Feb. 1988). See 'Introduction' (with John Shaw).

182. 'New Voices in Defence of Aid', *Development Policy Review*, vol. 6, no. 1 (Mar. 1988).

183. (With Patricia Gray) 'Trade Policy and Growth of Developing Countries: Some New Data', *World Development*, vol. 16, no. 3 (1988).

184. 'Development Crisis of the North', *Mainstream* (New Delhi: 30 Apr. 1988). Paper presented at the Conference on *Poverty, Development and Collective Survival: Public and Private Responsibilities*, 19th World Conference of SID, New Delhi, 25–8 Mar. 1988.

185. 'Development Crisis in the North', *Development*, 2/3 (1988).

186. 'Industrial Development in Africa: What are the Options?', *Razvoj Development-International* vol. 3, nos. 1–2 (1988).

187. 'Industrialization and World Trade: Ten Years after the Brandt Report', *Vienna Institute for Development and Co-operation Report Series*, no. 2 (1988), on *The World Ten Years After the 'Brandt Report'*.

188. (With P. Sarkar) 'Debt Pressure and the Transfer Burden of the Third World Countries, 1980–86', *Asian Journal of Economics and Social Studies*, vol. 7, no. 4 (1988).

189. 'When Pursuit of Surplus Ends', *India International Centre Quarterly* (Spring 1989).

190. 'The Relationship between Debt Pressures, Adjustment Policies and Deterioration of Terms of Trade for Developing Countries (with Special Reference to Latin America), *Institute of Social Studies Working Papers* (The Hague, The Netherlands, Jul. 1989).

191. 'El Desarrollo en la Posguerra. Lecciones de la Experiencia de 1945 a 1988' ('Post-war Development: Lessons of Experience 1945–1988'), *Comercio Exterior* (Banco Nacional de Comercio Exterior, SNC) Mexico (10 Jul. 1989).

192. 'The African Food Crisis and the Role of Food Aid', *Food Policy*, vol. 14, no. 3 (Aug. 1989).

193. 'Industrialisation and World Trade: Ten Years After the Brandt Report', *IDS Discussion Paper*, no. 264 (Aug. 1989).

194. 'A More Human Way Forward', *Southern African Economist* (Oct./Nov. 1989).

195. (With Prabirjit Sarkar) 'Manufactured Exports and Terms of Trade Movements of Less Developed Countries in Recent Years (1980–87)', *IDS Discussion Paper*, no. 270 (Nov. 1989).

196. 'Lessons of Post War Development Experience: 1945–1988', *IDS Discussion Paper*, no. 260 (Nov. 1989).

197. 'Pomoc un Hrani i Dugovi' ('Food Aid and Debt', in Croatian), *Privredni Razvoj in Medunarodni Dugovi* (World Development and International Debt), published for Yugoslav Academy by the Economic Faculty, Zagreb University, (1989).

198. 'The World Bank: Human Face or Facelift? Some Comments in the Light of the World Bank's Annual Report', *World Development*, vol. 17, no. 8 (1989).

199. 'Responses of James Ingram's Paper: Sustain Refugees' Human Dignity', *Journal of Refugee Studies*, vol. 2, no. 3 (1989).

200. 'Lessons of Post-War Experience', *African Development Review* (Journal of the African Development Bank), vol. 1, no. 2 (Dec. 1989).

201. 'The Debt Issue – A Historical Perspective', *Oeconomic* (Rotterdam: Erasmus University, 1989).

202. '"Reading between the Lines". Comment on World Bank Annual Report 1989', *Development Policy Review*, vol. 8, no. 2 (Jun. 1990).

203. 'The 1980s: A Lost Decade – Development in Reverse?', *Global Economic Policy*, vol. 2, no. 2 (Fall 1990).

204. 'Third World Debt Burden Unchanged', FAO *Ceres*, vol. 22, no. 2 (Nov.–Dec. 1990).

205. (with Prabirjit Sarkar) 'Manufactured Exports of Developing Countries and Their Terms of Trade Since 1965', *World Development*, vol. 19, no. 4 (1991).

206. 'Beyond the Debt Crisis', *Journal für Entwicklungspolitik*, VII JG–3/1991.

207. 'Die aktuellen GATT-Verhandlungen im Lichte der Verschuldung der Dritten Welt und der Welthandelspolitik' (The current GATT negotiations in the light of Third World debts and global trade policies) in *GATT und die Dritte Welt*, Renner Institut (13, 28 June 1991).

208. 'Terms of Trade: New Wine and New Bottles?', *Development Policy Review*, vol. 9, no. 4 (Dec. 1991).

209. (With Prabirjit Sarkar) 'Debt Crisis, Commodity Prices, Transfer Burden and Debt Relief', *IDS Discussion Paper*, no. 297 (Feb. 1992).

210. 'United Nations: Changes in Store', *Spur* (Newspaper of the World Development Movement) (May/Jun. 1992).

211. (With Jerker Edström) 'The Influence of Trends in Barter Terms of Trade and of Their Volatility on GNP Growth' *IDS Discussion Paper*, no. 312 (Nov. 1992).

212. 'Beyond the Debt Crisis', *Development* (1992).

213. 'The Influence of Schumpeter and Keynes on the Development of a Development Economist', *Discussion Paper*, no. 68 (1992) Institut für Volkswirtschaftslehre, Universität Hohenheim.

214. (With David Sapsford and Prabirjit Sarkar) 'The Prebisch–Singer Terms of Trade Controversy Revisited', *Journal of International Development*, vol. 4, no. 3 (1992).

215. (With Jerker Edström) 'The Influence of Trends in Barter Terms of Trade and of their Volatility on GNP Growth' *IDS Discussion Paper*, no. 312 (1992).

216. 'International Governance – Intentions and Realities', *Development and International Cooperation*, vol. 9, no. 16, Ljubljana: Centre for International Co-operation and Development, Jun. 1992).

217. 'Food Aid – A Historical Perspective', *World Food Programme Journal*, 30th Anniversary Edition, no. 25 (Jul.–Sep. 1993). Reprinted as 'New Orientations in Food Aid' in *Culture and Agriculture: Orientation Texts on the 1995 theme*, Paris: UNESCO, 1995).

218. (With Prabirjit Sarkar), 'Manufacture–Manufacture Terms of Trade Deterioration: A Reply' *World Development*, vol. 21, no. 10 (1993).

219. 'The Bretton Woods System: Historical Perspectives', *Third World Economics*, no. 71 (Aug. 1993).

220. 'Alternative Approaches to Adjustment and Stabilization', *Third World Economics*, no. 72 (Sep. 1993).

221. 'Is a Genuine Partnership Possible in Western Hemisphere Free Trade Area? Some General Comments', *Development and International Cooperation*, vol. 9, no. 17 (Ljubljana: December 1993). Centre for International Cooperation and Development (Ljubljana: December 1993).

222. 'Développement: "Nous Souffrons d'un Fétichisme Financier"'. (Development: we suffer from financial fetishism). Interview by Jean-Marc Fontaine in *Alternatives Economiques*, no. 114 (Paris/Dijon, Feb. 1994).

223. 'La Création de la CNUCED et L'Evolution de la Pensée Contemporaine sur le Développement' ('The Creation of UNCTAD and the evolution of current development thinking'), *Revue Tiers-Monde*, vol. 35, no. 139 (Jul.–Sep. 1994).

224. 'Ein Dollar, eine Stimme – Weltbank und Weltwährungsfonds als Teil des UN-Systems' ('One dollar, one vote – the World Bank and IMF as part of the UN system'), *Der Überblick*, 3/94 (Sep. 1994). Also published as 'Bretton Woods and the UN System', *Ecumenical Review*, vol. 47, no. 3 (Jul. 1995).

225. 'The "Golden Age" of the Tinbergen Consensus on Planning – Tinbergen's Contribution to the United Nations', *Internationale Samenwerking*, (Magazine of the Development Cooperation Information Department of the Dutch Ministry of Foreign Affairs) (Nov. 1994).

226. 'Tinbergen and International Policy Making' in Piet Erhal and Thijs Ruyter van Steveninck (eds) *Out of the darkness light!* Proceedings of the Memorial Symposium for Jan Tinbergen, 17 Dec, 1994, Erasmus University, Rotterdam.

227. 'Aid Conditionality', *IDS Discussion Paper*, no. 346 (Dec. 1994). Also published in ADMP Series Bulletins, no. 14, Advanced Development Management Programme, Sophia University Tokyo, 1995. Also published in Japanese: *Ritsumeikan Economic Review* (Dec. 1995).

228. 'Was Heist Schon Erfolgreich?' (What Does Successful Mean?), *Südwind*, Das Entwicklungspolitische Magazin Osterreichs no. 7–8/94 – Die Zeitschrift des Osterreichischen Informationsdienstes für Entwicklungspolitik, A-1090 Wien, Berggasse 7, 16 Jahrgan, Verlagspostamt 1090, Wien (1994).

229. (With Matthias Lutz). 'The Link Between Increased Trade Openness and the Terms of Trade: An Empirical Investigation', *World Development*, vol. 22, no. 11 (1994).

230. *Probleme und Zukunft der Ernährungshilfe in der Post-GATT-Ära* ('Problems and Future of Food Aid in the Post-GATT'), Bruno Kreisky Dialogue Series 10 (Vienna, 1995).

231. 'Austin Robinson and Keynes: Two Forecasts', *Cambridge Journal of Economics*, vol. 19 (1995).

232. 'Bretton Woods and the UN System', *the ecumenical review*, vol. 47, no. 3 (Jul. 1995).

233. (With Richard Jolly) 'Fifty Years On: The UN and Economic and Social Development: An Overview' and 'Revitalizing the United Nations: Five Proposals' in *Fifty Years On: The UN and Economic and Social Development* (co-edited with Richard Jolly), IDS Bulletin, vol. 26, no. 4 (Oct. 1995). Also in *A Felicitation Volume of Reminiscences and Writings from Authors World Wide in honour of Prof. C Suriyakumaran*, 'By a Distinguished Group of Authors Worldwide', in association with KVG de Silva & Sons, Colombo (1995).

234. 'Propuesta para Una Moneda de Reserva Basada en Materias Primas', (Proposal for a Reserve Currency based on primary commodities) *Pensamiento Iberoamerican: Revista de Economica Politica*, vol. 27 (1995). Special Issue on 'El Sistema Financiero Globalización e Inestabilidad'.

235. 'Are the Structural Adjustment Programmes Successful?', *Pakistan Journal of Applied Economics*, vol. 11, nos. 1 and 2 (1995).

236. 'A Future Food Aid Regime: Implications of the Final Act of the GATT Uruguay Round' (with John Shaw), *IDS Discussion Paper*, no. 352 (Sep. 1995). Different versions of this paper published in *Food Policy*, Special Issues on 'The Uruguay Round Agreement on Trade and Developing Countries', vol. 21, no. 4 (Aug. 1996); and in H. O'Neill and J. Toye (eds) *A World Without Famine?* (Basingstoke: Macmillan, for the Development Studies Association, forthcoming).

237. 'The Future of Food Trade and Food Aid in a Liberalizing Global Economy', in Ellen Messer and Peter Uvin (eds) *The Hunger Report: 1995*, published by Gordon and Breach Publishers, Australia, Canada, China, France, Germany, India, Japan, Luxembourg, Malaysia, The Netherlands, Russia, Singapore, Switzerland, Thailand, United Kingdom, on behalf of Alan Shawn Feinstein World Hunger Program, Brown University, RI, USA (1996).

238. *Linking Relief and Development*, ADMP Series Bulletin, no. 19 (Tokyo: Advanced Development Management Programme, Sophia University, 1996).

239. 'Heinz Arndt: Historian of Ideas', *Journal of Asian Economics*, vol. 7, no. 1 (1996).

240. 'A Global View of Food Security' for International Symposium on *Food Security and Innovations: Successes and Lessons Learned*, Mar. 1996, University of Hohenheim.

241. 'Kurt Martin/Mandelbaum: An appreciation', *DSA forum*, no. 51 (Apr. 1996).

242. 'Beyond Bretton Woods – a New Framework for International Co-operation' in *Politik und Gesellschaft*, 2/1996 (Bonn: Friedrich-Ebert-Stiftung).

243. 'Modern Relevance of Keynesianism in the study of development', in *Curso de Mestrado em 'Desenvolvimento e Cooperacao Internacional'* no 21 (Instituto Superior de Economia e Gestao 1995–6).

244. 'The United Nations and Bretton Woods Institutions' *Occasional Papers*, no. 13, Current Issues in Social Sciences and Humanities (The London Office of Hosei University, 1996).

Index